dBASE III PLUS™:
The Complete Reference

dBASE III PLUS™: The Complete Reference

Joseph-David Carrabis

Osborne **McGraw-Hill**
Berkeley, California

Osborne **McGraw-Hill**
2600 Tenth Street
Berkeley, California 94710
U.S.A.

For information on translations and book distributors outside of the U.S.A., please write to Osborne **McGraw-Hill** at the above address.

A complete list of trademarks appears on page 731.

dBASE III PLUS™: The Complete Reference

0 DODO 9 9 8 7 6 5 4 3 2 1 0

ISBN 0-07-881012-4

This is my fourth book and I'm becoming aware that no man is an island.

As a student of mathematics, I am obsessed with catastrophe theory. The editors can tell you that every conceivable discontinuity occurred while preparing this book. There are more people to acknowledge than I'd care to admit, but...

First and foremost, Scott Darling of Centronics Corporation in Hudson, New Hampshire. The figures in this book couldn't have been created without Scott's help in acquiring a Centronics PS220 printer for the duration of the project. My old beast was dying and Centronics offered the PS220 to help me complete this book. Many thanks to Scott and Centronics.

Second, Wendy Greenberg of the American Programmers Guild in Danbury, Connecticut (12 Mill Plain Road, 06811, [203] 794-0396). The printer needed some fancy software to capture all the III PLUS screens accurately. Wendy and the APG offered INSET as the solution, and it was the right one.

Third comes Steve Siminoff of White Mountain Computers in Nashua, New Hampshire. I've used a lot of computers and do things with them that make designers cringe, and I'm not the easiest customer to get along with. Steve showed more than nominal patience in getting me a system I liked.

Fourth, my beloved wife, Susan. She shows me nothing but patience and understanding when my back is against the wall and deadlines are passing me by. Many thanks for dragging me away from the computers.

I saved this one for last, but the acknowledgment isn't least. Thank You for letting me know the ten years of Ezekiel are at an end.

ACKNOWLEDGMENTS

This book is dedicated to my sister, Bernadette, who keeps on losing copies of the books I give her. Now, dear sister, every copy will be yours.

CONTENTS

The two big questions to consider when buying a book are whether the book suits your needs and whether it can be easily understood. This introduction will let you know the book in a nutshell, including why I wrote it and how I think you should use it.

My goal in this book is to make a comprehensive listing of dBASE III PLUS functions and commands, including the LAN functions and commands. My job is to be thorough. That isn't always easy with a program like dBASE III PLUS—there is an incredible amount the program can do, and an incredible amount you can do once you learn to program in dBASE III PLUS. The book provides detailed examples of the commands and functions as they are used in working dBASE III PLUS code. This should give you a better understanding of how each command or function is used as well as the advantages and disadvantages of its use. I'll cover the variety of ways you can use each command and function and how to make the most of what dBASE III PLUS can do.

Question: Is this really a complete reference? Nothing is ever complete. This comes as close to complete as you'd like a reference to be and still be able to carry it under one arm.

So, who is the book for? It is for you, if

1. You want a thorough explanation of each dBASE III PLUS feature

2. You want an information source that explains how each dBASE III PLUS command and function behaves in various situations

3. You don't have time to experiment

4. You're using dBASE III PLUS and need to get up to speed quickly

5. You have your own applications in mind and can't get them elsewhere

6. And, in particular, if you want examples of how commands and functions are used in working code, something not greatly developed in either the Ashton-Tate documentation or existing dBASE III PLUS books

Your best bet is to use this book as an information source, a quick reference to dBASE III PLUS commands and functions. Ideally, you'll use this book as a guide to proper dBASE III PLUS coding. You can go to the dBASE III PLUS documentation if you want a definition of a command or function, but you'll find that information here as well. This book is also a source of each command or function in working code. You'll be able to take the code blocks in this book and apply them to your applications with little or no modification. That should save you a great deal of work. At the same time, using the code blocks will force you to learn more about what dBASE III PLUS is as you make modifications to suit your own purposes.

The first part of this book explains how III PLUS uses different file types, what each file is for, and how they work together. The second part deals with dBASE III PLUS commands. The command chapters are organized by purpose. You can probably find the information you need simply by analyzing what you're doing and then looking for applicable terms. For instance, if you want to change some data in a database, you are going to EDIT the data. The commands that are relevant to editing data are in the "Data Editing Commands" chapter. Selecting one particular record from the entire database involves LOCATING that one record. Commands relevant to locating a single record are grouped in the "Data Location Commands" chapter and include LOCATE, FIND, SEEK, CONTINUE, GOTO, n, and their variations.

The last section of this book deals with the functions. Like the commands part of the book, the functions chapters are organized by purpose. All functions that deal with manipulating alphanumerics are found in the "String Functions" chapter. All functions that manipulate dates and time are found in the "Date Functions" chapter. To use this book most effectively, you must know what you're trying to do with your application, so you can choose the correct commands and functions without having to experiment.

If you want to get up to speed as quickly as possible, you can order a disk containing all the codes in this book. I've laid out the disk in subdirectories that correspond to the chapters and sections in this book. You can acquire the disk by using the order form at the back of the book. Messages can be left for me on CompuServe at #76137,1300, and on the Source at #BEM 948.

—Joseph-David Carrabis

What You Need to Know About dBase III PLUS

Chapter 1 describes the hardware and software you need to run dBASE III PLUS and what you should do if something goes wrong during installation.

What You Need to Use dBASE III PLUS

Ashton-Tate has gone out of its way to make dBASE III PLUS accessible to as many PC and PC-clone users as possible. That means you don't need the most up-to-date, high-powered computer to use dBASE III PLUS. The minimum requirements are a 256K PC or PC clone with two disk drives and a monitor, and PC-DOS 2.0 or higher or MS-DOS 2.1 or higher. You can run dBASE III PLUS on a machine with DOS 3.0 or higher, but you must have a minimum of 384K memory.

To get as much from dBASE III PLUS as possible, you will need an 80-column printer and extra memory. You don't need 100 megabytes of memory or a 200-gigabyte CD ROM, but a hard disk will make your applications run faster, and increased board memory will allow you greater freedom in using dBASE III PLUS. You can use printers with carriages wider than 80 columns.

dBASE knows if you have a printer accessible or not. It will use any monitor that a PC can handle (color or monochrome) and will use as much memory and as many drives as are available to the system.

dBASE almost installs itself. All you have to do is answer a few simple questions. Primarily this involves telling III PLUS the serial number of your disk and entering a company name, if you have one.

Occasionally something will go wrong during installation. dBASE will alert you if it detects a problem. Some problems will arise if you try to install III PLUS on the directory or subdirectory of a hard disk that also has dBASE III or III VAR (the Developer's Release). The best thing to do in such a case is to "uninstall" the earlier version of dBASE III. (This doesn't apply if dBASE II is on the disk.) The best source of information on installing dBASE to a hard or floppy disk system is the "Getting Started" booklet that is included in the documentation.

If something goes wrong before installation is complete (before you return to the DOS prompt), you can either shut off the machine or reboot the system by holding down the CTRL, ALT, and DEL keys simultaneously. Version 1 users, note: This doesn't fuddle the install count because reducing the install count is the last thing SUPERLoK does during installation. SUPERLoK is the copy-protection method used by Ashton-Tate on the dBASE III PLUS System Disk #1. However, stopping the installation procedure before SUPERLoK is finished chews up available hard disk space. Version 1.1 users don't have to worry about SUPERLoK.

If you're using a hard disk system and something goes wrong, first make sure that dBASE will run on your computer. A list of hard disk compatibles can be found in the "Getting Started" booklet in the dBASE III PLUS package. All Kaypro 16 and PC computers can be added to that list (in fact, they were used during the writing of this book). Version 1 users: Should SUPERLoK stop before completing installation, run the DOS CHKDSK utility. This cleans up your disk and reclaims any space taken up by parts of incomplete files. You do this by getting back to the hard disk DOS prompt and typing

CHKDSK /F [RETURN]

This assumes that the DOS CHKDSK.COM utility is available to your hard disk. The CHKDSK.COM file is on your PC/MS-DOS master disk if it is not already on the hard disk.

DOS asks you if you want to reclaim lost clusters. Answer by typing

Y [RETURN]

CHKDSK then converts lost chains into files. These files are gathered and written as FILEnnnn.CHK files, which can be ERASEd or DELETEd to free disk space. You can DELETE these files by typing

DEL FILE*.CHK [RETURN]

The result is free space on your hard disk. This procedure doesn't disturb any valid files.

You won't have any of these problems on a floppy disk system. Yes, there are a few advantages to floppy systems. A typical CHKDSK listing is shown in Figure 1-1.

If something goes wrong and installation stops, simply try installing dBASE again. There are several reasons for installation to

---

```
C:\>chkdsk

10584064 bytes total disk space
  307200 bytes in 6 hidden files
   49152 bytes in 11 directories
 4943872 bytes in 302 user files
   36864 bytes in bad sectors
 5246976 bytes available on disk

  524288 bytes total memory
  298896 bytes free

C:\>
```

Figure 1-1.   The DOS CHKDSK utility cleans up hard and floppy disks by finding unclosed files

stop, and not all of them are serious. If you can't install III PLUS on your system, try running dBASE from the master disk.

If you cannot run dBASE from the master disk, take your package back to your dealer. Ask to try dBASE on one of the dealer's computers (preferably the same make and model as the one you had trouble with). If dBASE won't install on that machine, try installing another dBASE package on the same machine. If that fails, dBASE will not run on the make and model of computer you're using. If the second package does work, the problem was in the original dBASE package. Take the new package home and try again.

If your original package runs on the dealer's machine, chances are your floppy disk drive needs to be either cleaned or aligned. Take it to your dealer and have it tuned up. Misaligned heads can cost you data and other files and are common with portable computers.

If all else fails, contact Ashton-Tate directly. Ashton-Tate customer support can be reached at (213) 329-0086 between 8:00 A.M. and 4:00 P.M. Pacific Standard Time every business day. If the problem is not pressing, you can leave messages for Ashton-Tate on The Source or CompuServe. If you subscribe to The Source, you can reach customer support by typing

ASHTON [RETURN]

at the —> prompt. You can reach customer support on CompuServe by typing

GO ASHTON [RETURN]

at any menu prompt.

dBASE III PLUS
File Types

dBASE III PLUS, like dBASE II and earlier versions of dBASE III, uses file extensions to tell you what type of file it uses in a given situation. The extension is the part of a filename that comes after the period (.). Almost every filename the computer uses has the form

FILENAME.EXT

Users can decide what the first part of the name will be. You can call your files ACCOUNTS, RECEIVAB, or INCOME; most programs allow you to give the file a first name so you'll be better able to find the file when you want to use it again.

The last part of the filename is usually assigned by the program you're using. Framework II, for example, assigns database, word processing, and spreadsheet files the extension "FW2". It assigns "TCM" to telecommunications files.

The dBASE programs are like most other programs in that they decide what last name to give each file. (In truth, you are given the option of deciding a file's last name; that option will be discussed in more detail in Chapter 3.

People familiar with dBASE II and the different versions of dBASE III are familiar with the following dBASE file types:

```
DBF -- DataBase File
DBT -- DataBase Text file (Memo field file, dBASE III only)
FRM -- report FoRM file
FMT -- ForMaT file
LBL -- LaBeL file
MEM -- MEMory variable file
NDX -- iNDeX file
PRG -- PRoGram file (also used for procedure files)
TXT -- output TeXT file
```

To that list dBASE III PLUS adds the following file types:

```
CAT -- CATalog file
QRY -- QueRY file
SCR -- SCReen file
VUE -- ViEw file (often spelled "VUE" in some areas)
```

As mentioned earlier, dBASE III PLUS doesn't force you to use the default file extensions. The easiest way around using the defaults is to give a particular file the extension you want. You must call the file by this extension in future work sessions, however. For example, you can

CREATE TEMP.CAT

This tells III PLUS to make a new database, normally a .DBF file, and call it "TEMP.CAT". This means you will be using a DBF file with a .CAT extension. The .CAT extension is normally used to signify CATALOG files.

This ability is useful when designing SAY, GET, PRG, FMT, and like files. All such files are standard ASCII files that contain various III PLUS commands. All these files serve different purposes, however. The SAY file paints a screen, a GET file transfers information from the user to the system and vice versa, a PRG file holds III PLUS commands that work with the system, and an FMT file performs the same functions as GET and SAY files when the FMT file is made memory-resident with a SET FORMAT TO filename command and used with either an APPEND or INSERT. You may want to use all these files for a given application.

Say you wanted to create a book library system that used LIBRARY.PRG, LIBRARY.FMT, LIBRARY.DBF, LIBRARY.N1, LIBRARY.N2, LIBRARY.GET, LIBRARY.SAY, LIBRARY.TMP, and LIBRARY.FRM files. You would actually be using three program files (PRG, SAY, and GET), two database files (DBF and TMP), and two index files (N1 and N2). Using nondefault extensions allows you more freedom in grouping files according to their original purpose — which is, in this example, working with a book library.

This chapter is broken into sections that cover different file types. Each section provides an explanation of the file type, how that file type is used in a dBASE III PLUS work session, how to create the file type, and, finally, any restrictions on the file type's use.

Filename.CAT — the CATALOG File

The CATALOG file is really nothing more than a database file with a specific purpose and special extension. You could create a file that does the exact same thing as this file. (See Figure 2-1 for the CAT file structure). In fact, so many users did so that Ashton-Tate decided it would be a good idea to include the file as part of the system.

What exactly is a CATALOG file? A CATALOG file is a kind of file filter. III PLUS uses it to mask files unrelated to a given application.

Assume you have a particular application in mind. You want to develop a system that will work with a group of files you use to keep track of your article and book writing. You have several different database and index files on disk, but now you're only interested in the MAGAZINE, BOOK, INCOME, and EXPENSE databases. Also, you're only interested in the MAGAZINE and MAUDS, BOOK and BAUDS, RFROM and RFOR, and PTO and PFOR index files.

Remember that you have several different database and index files on your disk. You want a way to work with a select group of them. In fact, you don't want to know the other DBF and NDX files exist when you're working on your magazine and book files.

You start by telling III PLUS

SET CATALOG TO WRITE

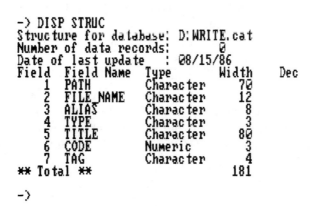

```
-> DISP STRUC
Structure for database: D:WRITE.cat
Number of data records:        0
Date of last update   : 08/15/86
Field  Field Name   Type       Width     Dec
    1  PATH         Character      70
    2  FILE_NAME    Character      12
    3  ALIAS        Character       8
    4  TYPE         Character       3
    5  TITLE        Character      80
    6  CODE         Numeric         3
    7  TAG          Character       4
** Total **                       181

->
```

Figure 2-1. The CATALOG file gives information about files associated with a specific database

```
-> DIR *.CAT


4947968 bytes remaining on drive.
-> SET CATA TO WRITE
Enter title for file WRITE.cat: :ALL DBFS FROM WFAL
-> USE MAGAZINE INDE A:MAGAZINE,A:MAUDS
Enter title for file MAGAZINE.dbf: :ALL MAGAZINE ENTRIES
-> USE BOOK INDE A:BOOK,A:BAUDS
Enter title for file BOOK.dbf: :ALL BOOK ENTRIES
-> USE INCOME INDE A:RFROM,A:RFOR
Enter title for file INCOME.dbf: :WRITING INCOME
-> USE EXPENSES INDE A:PTO,A:PFOR
Enter title for file EXPENSES.dbf: :WRITING EXPENSES
-> DIR *.CAT
WRITE.CAT            CATALOG.CAT

    697 bytes in     2 files.
4939776 bytes remaining on drive.

->
```

Figure 2-2.   III PLUS creates a new catalog when you use the SET
               CATALOG TO filename command

as shown in Figure 2-2.

This tells III PLUS to create a new CAT file called WRITE.CAT. Next, you tell III PLUS what files you want to work with, as shown in Figure 2-2. From this point on, whenever you want to use just this group of files, all you need to do is type the SET CATALOG TO WRITE command.

The CATALOG file acts as a file filter to the III PLUS system in that it displays only DBF, DBT, NDX and related files it knows about. For instance, say you SET CATALOG TO WRITE. Now you want to USE a DBF file, but you are not sure which database is part of the system. You ask III PLUS for a list of databases in the WRITE application by typing

USE ?

III PLUS responds by listing all databases entered into the WRITE.CAT file, as shown in Figure 2-3.

But you also wanted two NDX files to work with the MAGA-ZINE database file. III PLUS remembers this. After you've selected

Select a DATABASE from the list.

```
ALL MAGAZINE ENTRIES
```

Figure 2-3. The WRITE.CAT file lists databases available to the WRITE application

the MAGAZINE.DBF file, III PLUS shows you the associated NDX files (see Figure 2-4).

How does III PLUS keep all this information in the CAT file? To know that, you have to understand the structure of the CAT file, shown in Figure 2-1.

A CATALOG file shows file associations through the CODE field. This field acts as a pointer to the database file in the association. In Figure 2-5, MAGAZINE.DBF is the first DBF file that is listed in WRITE.CAT; it has a code of 1. The two NDX files associated with the MAGAZINE database, MAGAZINE.NDX and MAUDS.NDX, are located in different WRITE.CAT file records, but their code numbers are both 1, the same code number as MAGAZINE.DBF.

The BOOK.DBF file has Code 2, meaning it is the second DBF file listed in the WRITE.CAT file. The BOOK.NDX and BAUDS.NDX files, associated with the BOOK.DBF file, also have code values of 2. This applies also to the INCOME.DBF file and the RFROM.NDX file. It doesn't matter if you USE a database and don't summon its associated files until much later. The CAT file will associate files by code. This association of files also applies to FMT, FRM, and other

```
NAME
```

Position selection bar - ↑↓. Select - ←┘. Leave menu - ↔.
Select index file(s) to be used with the chosen file.

Figure 2-4. Once a database has been selected, III PLUS reads the CATALOG file to find any associated files, such as NDX files

```
-) DISP ALL TRIM(PATH),TRIM(FILE_NAME),TRIM(ALIAS),TRIM(TYPE),CODE,TRIM(TAG)
Record#  TRIM(PATH)
TRIM(FILE_NAME) TRIM(ALIAS) TRIM(TYPE) CODE TRIM(TAG)
       1   D:MAGAZINE.dbf
MAGAZINE.dbf     MAGAZINE     dbf          1
       2   A:MAGAZINE.ndx
MAGAZINE.ndx     MAGAZINE     ndx          1
       3   A:MAUDS.ndx
MAUDS.ndx        MAUDS        ndx          1
       4   D:BOOK.dbf
BOOK.dbf         BOOK         dbf          2
       5   A:BOOK.ndx
BOOK.ndx         BOOK         ndx          2
       6   A:BAUDS.ndx
BAUDS.ndx        BAUDS        ndx          2
       7   D:INCOME.dbf
INCOME.dbf       INCOME       dbf          3
       8   A:RFROM.ndx
RFROM.ndx        RFROM        ndx          3
Press any key to continue...
```

Figure 2-5. The CAT file structure shows file associations through the use of the CODE field

files. Note, then, that CAT files work by first knowing about DBF files and then associating other files to those DBF files (except in the case of UUE files, covered later in the text).

As a final note, changing disks or directories can have disastrous effects on CAT files. As shown in Figure 2-6, changing disks causes III PLUS to erase information in the CAT file. This problem can be avoided by either shutting off the CAT file or closing it. You can shut the CAT file off with the command

SET CATALOG OFF

You can close the CAT file completely with the command

SET CATALOG TO

without using any filename.

The first method keeps the CAT file active but doesn't alter it based on work activity. Note that the CAT file, when used through the SET CATALOG TO command, occupies work area 10. This can be seen in Figure 2-7, where the DISP STAT command shows work area 10 containing the WRITE.CAT file.

```
-> SET CATA TO WRITE
A:MAGAZINE.ndx does not exist.  Deleted from catalog
A:MAUDS.ndx does not exist.  Deleted from catalog
A:BOOK.ndx does not exist.  Deleted from catalog
A:BAUDS.ndx does not exist.  Deleted from catalog
A:RFROM.ndx does not exist.  Deleted from catalog
A:RFOR.ndx does not exist.  Deleted from catalog
A:PTO.ndx does not exist.  Deleted from catalog
A:PFOR.ndx does not exist.  Deleted from catalog
->
```

Figure 2-6.   Changing disks or directories when using CAT files can change the information listed in the open file

```
-> DISP STAT

Currently Selected Database:
Select area: 1, Database in Use: D:EXPENSES.dbf   Alias: EXPENSES

Select area: 10, Database in Use: D:WRITE.cat   Alias: CATALOG.

File search path:
Default disk drive: D:
Print destination: LPT1:
Margin =      0
Current work area =    1   Delimiters are ':' and ':'

Press any key to continue...

*** INTERRUPTED ***
->
```

Figure 2-7. The SET CATALOG TO filename places the CAT file in
work area 10

Filename.DBF — the DATABASE File

The DBF file is the most easily recognized file of any of the dBASE
files. This is the file that gives the dBASEs their character, and it is
from this file that the dBASEs attain their power.

The III PLUS DBF file is identical to dBASE III DBF files; both
use MEMO fields. It is not similar to dBASE II DBF files, and modifications must be made to either file before a dBASE II DBF can be
used in III PLUS and vice versa.

Basically, the III PLUS DBF file can be likened to a spreadsheet,
the entire database file being the spreadsheet. Each database record
becomes a column of data, and each field becomes a row of values.
This is shown in Figure 2-8.

A DBF file is created with the CREATE command, as in

CREATE filename

Figure 2-9 shows a typical DBF file-creation screen. (Note here
that SET MENUs is ON.)

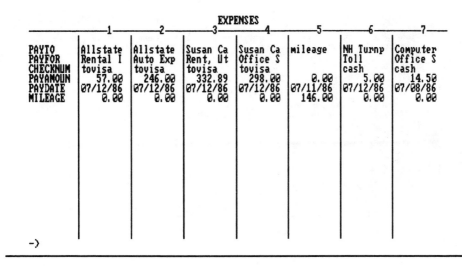

Figure 2-8. This figure shows how a database can be likened to a spreadsheet with records as columns and fields as rows

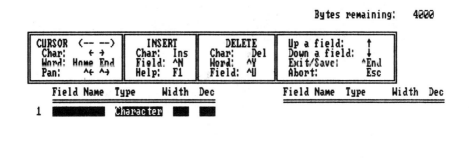

Figure 2-9. A typical III PLUS DBF file-creation screen

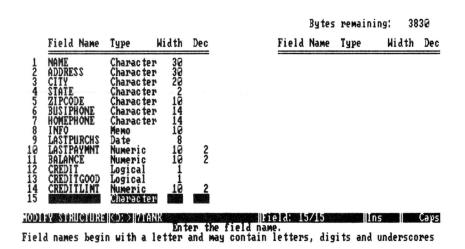

Bytes remaining: 3830

	Field Name	Type	Width	Dec
1	NAME	Character	30	
2	ADDRESS	Character	30	
3	CITY	Character	20	
4	STATE	Character	2	
5	ZIPCODE	Character	10	
6	BUSIPHONE	Character	14	
7	HOMEPHONE	Character	14	
8	INFO	Memo	10	
9	LASTPURCHS	Date	8	
10	LASTPAYMNT	Numeric	10	2
11	BALANCE	Numeric	10	2
12	CREDIT	Logical	1	
13	CREDITGOOD	Logical	1	
14	CREDITLIMT	Numeric	10	2
15		Character		

MODIFY STRUCTURE <C:> 7TANK ‖Field: 15/15 ‖Ins ‖ Caps

Enter the field name.
Field names begin with a letter and may contain letters, digits and underscores

Figure 2-10.   This figure is similar to Figure 2-9, except that fields have already been defined

In Figure 2-9, III PLUS has been told to CREATE TANK. III PLUS realizes this means that the user wants to make a new database with the name "TANK". Figure 2-10 shows some of the data fields filled in for the new database.

The DBF file-creation screen gives you a great deal of information regarding the file you're creating. The upper-right corner tells you the number of bytes left in the record. Each DBF record can contain 4000 bytes of information. Across the top of the screen we see two sets of identical columns, each containing

Field Name   Type   Width   Dec

It is these columns that tell III PLUS the particulars of each field. The particulars are defined as

Field Name   This is where you tell III PLUS the actual name of the field, such as ADDRESS, CITY, FIRSTNAME, PO—NUMBER, DATE—IN, and so on. Note that the field name can be any combination of letters and numbers but can only be ten characters long. You can use fewer than ten characters in the field names if you wish. There is an advantage to using all ten characters in a field name, however. Primarily, you can be more descriptive as to what each field represents. For example, DO and DI can be used as field names for date-out and date-in fields, but "DATE—OUT" and "DATE—IN" are much more descriptive of what goes into each field.

There can be no spaces in the field name; the first character *must* be a letter. The common way to show spaces in a field name is to use the underscore (—) character (as in "PO—NUMBER" and "DATE—IN").

Type   This column tells III PLUS what type of data to allow into the field.

The most general data type is CHARACTER, as it allows any character as input. If you aren't sure what type of data is likely to go into a field, use the CHARACTER data type. On the other hand, if you want to be sure that only certain types of data get into a given field, you should specify the data type in this area. Remember that an address such as "32 Foxmoor Circle" is character data. The type is specified by a one-letter entry (C for CHARACTER, M for MEMO, D for DATE, L for LOGICAL, and N for NUMERIC).

Width   This column tells III PLUS how wide the field is going to be. You may want to place an individual's entire name in a NAME field, so you'd make that field 40 characters wide. You may want to place an individual's first name in one field, FIRSTNAME, and the last name in a LASTNAME field. That being the case, you'd tell III PLUS to make the FIRSTNAME and LASTNAME fields 20 characters each.

Note that there are exceptions to this. Telling III PLUS that a field type is LOGICAL automatically creates a one-character-wide field. Telling III PLUS a field type is MEMO automatically creates a ten-character-wide field.

Dec   This column is ancillary to the Width column already described. The only time III PLUS lets you enter data to this column is when you've specified a field type of NUMERIC. This column lets you tell III PLUS how many decimal places to use in your numeric fields. For example, specifying a NUMERIC field 10 characters wide with two decimal places would show ninety-nine as 99.00. Ninety-nine with a three-character width and no decimal places is 99. At four characters and one decimal place, it is 99.0. NUMERIC fields can take a maximum of 19 characters.

The STATUS line at the bottom of the screen tells you that you're in CREATE mode, that you are CREATEing a file called TANK on drive C, and that you're in FIELD 1 of 1 total. The next line prompts you for a field name. The last line on the screen tells you what kind of information is allowed. Compare Figure 2-9 with Figure 2-10. In Figure 2-10, several fields have been entered, and you are being prompted for a field type. (Note that these screens are shown with SET STATUS ON.)

The last thing to know about DBF files has to do with the design phase. Figure 2-11 shows another menu that pops up during DBF MODIFYcation or CREATEion. This menu allows you quick movement among the DBF fields, as well as the ability to SAVE the file or ABANDON it.

Bottom		Top		Field #		Save		Abandon	9:51:44 am

Enter field number: 1   tes remaining: 3399

	Field Name	Type	Width	Dec		Field Name	Type	Width	Dec
1	CLIENT_ID	Character	10		16	RESULT	Memo	10	
2	CLNAME	Character	30		17	FOLLOWUP	Logical	1	
3	CLADDRESS1	Character	30		18	NEXTCONTCT	Date	8	
4	CLADDRESS2	Character	30		19	BILLING	Character	1	
5	CLCITY	Character	20		20	LASTPURCHS	Date	8	
6	CLSTATE	Character	2		21	PURCHSAMNT	Numeric	10	2
7	CLZIPCODE	Character	10		22	BALANCE	Numeric	10	2
8	BUSIPHONE	Character	14		23	CREDITCARD	Character	4	
9	HOMEPHONE	Character	14		24	CCNUMBER	Character	25	
10	INCOME	Numeric	12	2	25	EXPDATE	Date	8	
11	LEAD	Character	20		26	STORECREDT	Logical	1	
12	REFERENCE	Character	254		27	CREDITLIMT	Numeric	10	2
13	BANK_REF	Memo	10		28	CREDITGOOD	Logical	1	
14	SALES	Character	20		29	CLHISTORY	Memo	10	
15	CONTACT	Date	8		30	PURCHSHIST	Memo	10	

MODIFY STRUCTURE ||C: > ||CHAPTER9 ||Field: 1/30 || Caps
Position selection bar with ↔. Select with ↵.

Figure 2-11.   The menu shown here is available with either CREATEing or MODIFYing a DBF file by pressing the CTRL-HOME key combination

Also note that if SET SAFETY is ON, III PLUS warns you if another DBF file exists with the same name. You can either use the name or stop the operation and opt for another DBF filename.

Each database file can contain any combination of CHARACTER, NUMBER, LOGICAL, MEMO, and DATE data types. The limitations to the DBF file are its size. Both number of records and number of fields allowed in each record have an upper limit. The maximum number of records allowed in any one database is one billion records. The maximum number of fields per record is 128. The maximum size for any database file is two billion bytes.

Even with all this tempting available space, however, you never want to create a database with 128 fields per record. You especially never want to create a database that holds more than 1M of data. Either extreme will slow down your system and severely limit what can be done in any one work session. A good size for a III PLUS database is under 1M, around 500K. If you have a database that will go significantly over 500K, find some logical way to break it up into smaller files.

Also, no III PLUS database record should be more than 30 fields long. A good size for a database record is around 20 fields. Again, if you have a database designed for more than 30 fields, break it into smaller files and use either the SET RELATION TO or JOIN command to juggle the necessary information.

Filename.DBT—the DATABASE MEMO (Text) Field File

The DBT file is an ancillary file to the DBF file. It is used to hold large amounts of text data. You can tell which DBTs belong to which DBF's because the two files share the same first name. Figure 2-12 shows DBF and associated DBT files with the same name.

This field came about because the dBASEs only allow 254 characters in a CHARACTER field. This is a healthy dollop of information, but sometimes 254 characters isn't enough. There will be times, such as when you're dealing with client and patient information, that you'll want to enter extensive amounts of text data. Several 254-character CHARACTER fields would put a severe limit on a DBF

```
D:\>C:

C:\>CD DB3

C:\DB3>D *.DB*


        10 File(s)    4898816 bytes free
  Directory of  C:\DB3
  Volume in drive C has no label
CONFIG    DB       384   13-08-86   13:46
HELP      DBS    66560   13-11-85   15:01
PASSWORD  DBF      266    9-07-86    9:12
PASSWORD  DBT     1155    1-07-86   13:34
PROMPTS   DBF      354   14-08-86    8:00
SAVETANK  DBT     1024    2-07-86   22:39
TANK      DBF      862   15-08-86   15:21
TANK      DBT      512   16-07-86   22:04
TEMP      DBF       98    2-07-86   22:56
TEMP      DBT      513    2-07-86   22:56

C:\DB3>
C:\DB3>
```

Figure 2-12.   This DOS DIR listing shows DBFs and their associated DBTs with the same filename

record that has an upper limit of 4000 characters for all data in the record. The solution, of course, is to create another file that can hold all the text, without limits.

To that end, Ashton-Tate designed the MEMO field. This field appears in the DBF file (see Figure 2-10) as TYPE MEMO and WIDTH 10. In truth, the MEMO field in the DBF file is nothing more than a pointer to another file. This other file has the DBT extension.

The MEMO field and DBT file have some interesting properties. First, note that the MEMO field appears filled in the data-input screen shown in Figure 2-13. You enter data to the MEMO field by first placing the cursor in that field. Next, type

[CTRL-PGDN]

Figure 2-13. A fairly sophisticated data-entry screen

You will then find yourself in the actual MEMO DBT file. Figure 2-14 shows a sample MEMO FIELD with its own word processor.

Note that you will be placed in the dBASE III PLUS Text Editor unless you specify a different word processor in the CONFIG.DB file with the WP command. Text is typed in at this point. You exit from the DBT file by typing

[CTRL PGUP]

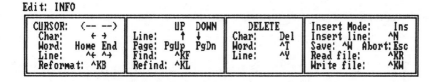

Figure 2-14. A dBASE III PLUS database MEMO field is actually a separate DBT file with its own word processor, such as is shown here

The exception to this is if you're using a word processor other than the dBASE III PLUS Text Editor. In that case, you'd exit from your word processor as you normally do.

No matter which word processor you use to enter data into a MEMO field, III PLUS will create a DBT file.

It is worth knowing that III PLUS isn't the most efficient beast when creating a DBT file. No matter how much information you enter into a MEMO field, III PLUS lops off 512 bytes for every 512 or fewer bytes of data. In other words, if you type in 79 characters of information, III PLUS stores it in 512 bytes. If you type in 500 bytes, it stores it in 512 bytes. If you type in 513 bytes, III PLUS stores that in 1024 bytes. (You entered one more byte than 512, the minimum file size, so III PLUS allocates an extra 512 bytes to hold it.)

Furthermore, you can only use the III PLUS Text Editor for 5000 or fewer bytes of information. You can enter over 5000 bytes, but III PLUS will only store the first 5000 bytes in the DBT file.

If you use another word processor to edit your MEMO fields, you can create and save files as large as your word processor will allow. Using an external word processor also allows you to print your DBT MEMO fields. You can DISPLAY and LIST the MEMO fields no matter what word processor you use.

DBT files behave strangely when their DBF files are PACKed and ZAPped. PACKing, the removing of DELETEd records, doesn't remove the space taken up by DELETEd MEMO fields in the DBT files. The data in the DELETEd MEMO field is gone, but the space the MEMO fields used on disk is not freed for other uses. ZAPping, the permanent removal of all records in a DBF file, collapses the associated DBT file.

Filename.FMT—the FORMAT File

The III PLUS FMT file is primarily used for adding and modifying data to a given database. In actuality, any full-screen editing operation can make use of the FMT file, and most often the FMT file is considered a part of custom entry forms. This section describes the basics of the FMT file and its place among the other dBASE III PLUS file types.

The FMT file is actually a command or program file that becomes memory-resident and contains two types of commands, @...SAY and @...GET. Consider the database designed in Figure 2-10. You want to design a screen form that will transfer data from that database to the user and vice versa. First, you must create a screen you'd like to use, such as the screen shown in Figure 2-13.

You create that screen using the MODI SCREEN command. The MODI SCREEN command sets the III PLUS screen generator into motion. The screen generator is a subprogram built into the III PLUS system. It takes information about how you want the screen laid out and generates the necessary SAY and GET commands.

Using the MODI SCREEN command results in the creation of two or three files. The two files that are always generated are the SCR and FMT files. The FMT file is shown as the following listing:

```
a   2,  3    SAY  "NAME"
a   2, 11    GET  TANK->NAME
a   4,  3    SAY  "ADDRESS"
a   4, 11    GET  TANK->ADDRESS
a   5,  3    SAY  "CITY"
a   5, 11    GET  TANK->CITY
a   5, 42    SAY  "STATE"
a   5, 48    GET  TANK->STATE
a   5, 53    SAY  "ZIPCODE"
a   5, 61    GET  TANK->ZIPCODE
a   7,  3    SAY  "BUSIPHONE"
a   7, 15    GET  TANK->BUSIPHONE
a   7, 42    SAY  "HOMEPHONE"
a   7, 53    GET  TANK->HOMEPHONE
a   9,  3    SAY  "INFO"
a   9, 15    GET  TANK->INFO
a  11,  3    SAY  "LASTPURCHS"
a  11, 15    GET  TANK->LASTPURCHS
a  11, 25    SAY  "LASTPAYMNT"
a  11, 37    GET  TANK->LASTPAYMNT
a  13, 25    SAY  "BALANCE"
a  13, 37    GET  TANK->BALANCE
a  15,  5    SAY  "CREDIT"
a  15, 17    GET  TANK->CREDIT    PICTURE "Y"
a  16,  5    SAY  "CREDITGOOD"
a  16, 17    GET  TANK->CREDITGOOD    PICTURE "Y"
a  17,  5    SAY  "CREDITLIMT"
a  17, 17    GET  TANK->CREDITLIMT
a   0,  1    TO 18, 78    DOUBLE
```

The SCR file is a screen-image file that is unprintable in this book. The third file is the TXT file.

This screen TXT file is not to be confused with the TXT output file. The screen TXT file for Figure 2-13 is shown as the following listing:

```
Field definitions for Screen : TANK.scr

Page  Row  Col  Data Base    Field        Type     Width Dec
   1    2   11  TANK         NAME         Character    30
   1    4   11  TANK         ADDRESS      Character    30
   1    5   11  TANK         CITY         Character    20
   1    5   48  TANK         STATE        Character     2
   1    5   61  TANK         ZIPCODE      Character    10
   1    7   15  TANK         BUSIPHONE    Character    14
   1    7   53  TANK         HOMEPHONE    Character    14
   1    9   15  TANK         INFO         Memo         10
   1   11   15  TANK         LASTPURCHS   Date          8
   1   11   37  TANK         LASTPAYMNT   Numeric      10
   2
   1   13   37  TANK         BALANCE      Numeric      10
   2
   1   15   17  TANK         CREDIT       Logical       1
   PICTURE Y
   1   16   17  TANK         CREDITGOOD   Logical       1
   PICTURE Y
   1   17   17  TANK         CREDITLIMT   Numeric      10
   2


Content of page :  1


    NAME      XXXXXXXXXXXXXXXXXXXXXXXXXXXXXX

    ADDRESS  XXXXXXXXXXXXXXXXXXXXXXXXXXXXXX
    CITY      XXXXXXXXXXXXXXXXXXXX          STATE XX
ZIPCODEXXXXXXXXXX

    BUSIPHONE   XXXXXXXXXXXXX               HOMEPHONE
XXXXXXXXXXXXX

    INFO        XXXX

    LASTPURCHS  XXXXXXX  LASTPAYMNT  XXXXXXXXX

                        BALANCE     XXXXXXXXX

       CREDIT       X
       CREDITGOOD   X
       CREDITLIMT   XXXXXXXXX
```

This file includes information about the screen image used to create the FMT file with the MODI SCREEN command and is primarily used for documentation purposes.

The important thing to remember for this part of the book is that the FMT file generated is an ASCII file, just like any III PLUS PRG file. This means you can edit the FMT file just as you would edit any PRG file. You could just as easily create an FMT file using the MODI COMM and MODI FILE commands. Of course, that assumes you can visualize the screen and then translate your mental picture into x and y screen coordinates.

The distinct advantage to using the FMT file is that you can use it with the SET FORMAT TO filename command. The SET FOR-MAT TO filename command tells III PLUS to take the file named in the command and place it in memory. From that time on, whenever III PLUS gets an APPEND, INSERT, EDIT, or other full-screen editing command, it automatically clears the screen and puts up the screen depicted in the FMT file. This feature also works for multi-screen FMT files.

There are two ways to use the FMT file in a dBASE III PLUS work session. The first way, described earlier, is to use the SET FORMAT TO filename command somewhere early in your work session or PRG file, as shown in the following listing.

```
** AN EXAMPLE OF THE "SET FORMAT TO" COMMAND
*
CLOSE ALL
CLEAR
*
** DATABASES IN THE UNIVERSE CATALOG ALL SHARE A COMMON
**STRUCTURE
*
SET CATA TO UNIVERSE
USE ?
*
** THE TANK.FMT FILE CAN BE USED FOR ALL UNIVERSE
**DATABASES
*
SET FORMAT TO TANK
APPEND
```

The other option is to use the FMT file as if it were a PRG file and DO it, as shown in this listing:

```
** AN EXAMPLE OF THE FMT FILE USED AS A PRG FILE
*
CLOSE ALL
CLEAR
*
** DATABASES IN THE UNIVERSE CATALOG ALL SHARE A COMMON
**STRUCTURE
*
```

```
SET CATA TO UNIVERSE
USE ?
*
DO WHIL .T.
   DO TANK.FMT
   APPEND
*
   IF LEN(TRIM(field1)) = 0
      EXIT
   ENDI
*
ENDD
```

Filename.FRM — the REPORT FORM File

It is not enough to manage and manipulate data in the DBF file. Usually, your data is only as good as your method for retrieving and reporting that same data back to you. This is where the FRM file comes in.

The FRM file is generated and used by the dBASE III PLUS REPORT command. The FRM file tells III PLUS what FoRM you'd like the finished REPORT to take, either on the screen or printed out. Consider a listing of all expenses incurred during a life as a writer. Uncle Sam would like to see that information recorded on a Schedule C IRS form. Actually, you (the writer) would like to know that information every quarter for purposes of filing a Schedule SE.

Consider the database you designed in Figure 2-10. You've entered all the relevant data. Now you need a way of getting that data back out of the system, preferably in an ordered way. What you can do is CREATE a REPORT FORM.

Before you actually design the FRM file, you have to let III PLUS know what database to work with. You specify a database, knowing that the FRM file is more concerned with the DBF structure than the DBF itself. The FRM file and the REPORT command aren't finicky about what DBF file they work with, but they are finicky about what fields are used in the FRM.

You can use the TANK database shown in Figure 2-10 to generate a REPORT FORM that can be used for any database with the fields shown in that figure, provided the fields in the other databases are of the same type (N, M, C, D, or L).

Remember that the field types and names make up the database structure, and it is the structure the FRM file works with, not the actual database.

There are two ways to create or modify an FRM file. You can use either the command

MODI REPORT filename

or the command

CREATE REPORT filename

These commands allow you to create new FRM files or edit existing FRM files.

The actual FRM file generator is a subprogram in the III PLUS system. It is menu-driven and prompts you for all the information it needs. For example, say you want a listing of the NAME, BALANCE, and LASTPAYMNT in each record, broken down by CITY. You start by telling III PLUS you want to USE the TANK database with the command

USE TANK

Next, you tell III PLUS you're going to design a new FRM file with

CREA REPO CITYTANK

The FRM filename, CITYTANK, is selected merely because the TANK.DBF file is listed by the CITY field. III PLUS starts the FRM design process with the screen shown in Figure 2-15.

You use this screen to tell III PLUS what format to use for the FRM file. You can enter a page title, set margins, set lines per page, set line spacing, specify whether to EJECT a sheet of paper before or after printing the FRM, and specify whether or not to create a PLAIN report. You make choices by moving the cursor to the desired function and pressing RETURN to open the function for editing (as listed in the cursor menu and prompt lines at the bottom of the screen). The difference between PLAIN and regular reports can be seen in Figures 2-16 and 2-17. Figure 2-16 is a regular report. Figure 2-17 is a PLAIN report. The PLAIN and EJECT options are also available directly from the REPORT command.

Figure 2-18 shows the next phase of FRM file design and is

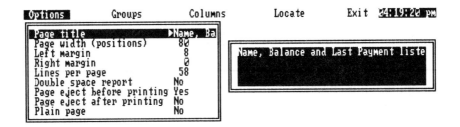

Options▓   Groups   Columns   Locate   Exit ▓4:19:20▓ PM

```
┌─────────────────────────────────┐
│Page title            ►Name, Ba │
│Page width (positions)      8▓  │
│Left margin                  8  │
│Right margin                 0  │
│Lines per page              58  │
│Double space report         No  │
│Page eject before printing Yes  │
│Page eject after printing   No  │
│Plain page                  No  │
└─────────────────────────────────┘
```

```
┌────────────────────────────────────┐
│Name, Balance and Last Payment liste│
│                                    │
│████████████████████████████████████│
│████████████████████████████████████│
└────────────────────────────────────┘
```

```
┌──────────────────────┬──────────────────────┬─────────────────────────┬──────────────────────┐
│CURSOR   <── ──>      │Delete char:   Del    │Insert column: ^N        │Insert:     Ins       │
│ Char:      ←  →      │Delete word:   ^T     │Report format: F1        │Zoom in:  ^PgDn       │
│ Word:   Home End     │Delete column: ^U     │Abandon:      Esc        │Zoom out: ^PgUp       │
└──────────────────────┴──────────────────────┴─────────────────────────┴──────────────────────┘
```

CREATE REPORT▓▓▓ ⟨D:⟩CITYTANK.FRM▓▓▓▓▓▓ Opt: 1/9 ▓▓▓▓▓▓▓▓▓▓ Caps
Enter report title. Exit - Ctrl-End.
Enter up to four lines of text to be displayed at the top of each report page.

Figure 2-15. The introductory screen for designing a REPORT FoRM file is shown here

```
-> USE TANK INDE CITYTANK
-> REPO FORM CITYTANK
         Page No.     1
         07/16/86
                  Name, Balance and Last Payment listed by City

         Name                        Balance Last Payment


         ** For -> Hartswell
         Sue Schnieder                350.00      57.80
         Don Teirney                    0.00      75.00
         ** Subtotal **
                                      350.00     132.80

         ** For -> Manchester
         John Bajagaloop              225.00      25.00
         Murray Elliot                600.00     340.00
         ** Subtotal **
                                      825.00     365.00

         *** Total ***
                                     1175.00     497.80

-)
```

Figure 2-16. A regular report

```
-> REPO FORM CITYTANK PLAIN
                        Name, Balance and Last Payment listed by City

        Name                                    Balance Last Payment


        ** For -> Hartswell
         Sue Schnieder                           350.00         57.80
         Don Teirney                               0.00         75.00
        ** Subtotal **
                                                 350.00        132.80

        ** For -> Manchester
         John Bajagaloop                         225.00         25.00
         Murray Elliot                           600.00        340.00
        ** Subtotal **
                                                 825.00        365.00

        *** Total ***
                                                1175.00        497.80

    ->
```

Figure 2-17.   A PLAIN report

```
Options          Groups          Columns          Locate          Exit  04:31:10 pm
                ┌──────────────────────────────────────────┐
                │ Group on expression      City            │
                │ Group heading            For ->          │
                │ Summary report only      No              │
                │ Page eject after group   No              │
                │ Sub-group on expression  LASTPAYMNT      │
                │ Sub-group heading         Last Payment   │
                └──────────────────────────────────────────┘




┌─────────────────────┬────────────────────┬──────────────────────┬─────────────────────┐
│ CURSOR  <-- -->     │ Delete char:   Del │ Insert column:   ^N  │ Insert:      Ins    │
│ Char:    ←   →      │ Delete word:   ^T  │ Report format:   F1  │ Zoom in:    ^PgDn   │
│ Word:   Home End    │ Delete column: ^U  │ Abandon:        Esc  │ Zoom out:   ^PgUp   │
└─────────────────────┴────────────────────┴──────────────────────┴─────────────────────┘
CREATE REPORT    |<D:>|CITYTANK.FRM          |Opt: 1/6       |          | Caps
         Position selection bar - ↑↓.  Select - ←┘.  Leave menu - ←→.
Enter a field or expression on which to break for the first level of subtotals.
```

Figure 2-18.   Once style defaults are set, the FRM file needs to know how
                to order (or group) the information

primarily used when you wish to have the database information grouped along certain lines. You decided earlier to have the REPORT give listings broken down by CITY; therefore, you want to group on the CITY expression (the CITY field in the TANK.DBF file).

The heading can be anything you wish. A summary report is one that only shows group totals, not individual records in each group. The difference between a summary report and a regular report can be seen in Figures 2-16 and 2-19. Figure 2-19 shows a summary report. You tell III PLUS to generate a summary report on the Groups menu of the REPORT FORM generator (see Figure 2-20). "Page eject after group" tells III PLUS to throw a page after each group during printed output.

You may wish to break your groupings down further. This is accomplished with the "Sub-group on expression" and "Sub-group heading" functions of the Groups menu. A subgrouped REPORT can be seen in Figure 2-21.

After you've defined the FRM groups, you can tell III PLUS

```
-> REPO FORM CITYTANK
        Page No.     1
        07/16/86
                        Name, Balance and Last Payment listed by City

        Name                                    Balance Last Payment


        ** For -> Hartswell
        ** Subtotal **
                                                350.00        132.80

        ** For -> Manchester
        ** Subtotal **
                                                825.00        365.00
        *** Total ***
                                                1175.00       497.80

 ->
```

Figure 2-19.   Another form of the finished REPORT, this time using the Summary option

dBASE III PLUS: The Complete Reference

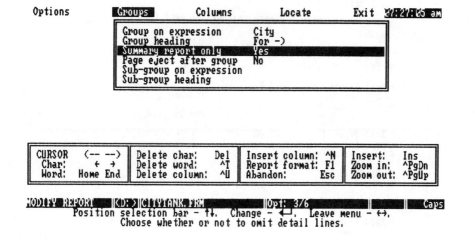

Options   Groups   Columns   Locate   Exit

Group on expression	City
Group heading	For ->
Summary report only	Yes
Page eject after group	No
Sub-group on expression	
Sub-group heading	

CURSOR	<-- -->	Delete char:	Del	Insert column:	^N	Insert:	Ins
Char:	← →	Delete word:	^T	Report format:	F1	Zoom in:	^PgDn
Word:	Home End	Delete column:	^U	Abandon:	Esc	Zoom out:	^PgUp

MODIFY REPORT   (D:)CITYTANK.FRM   Opt: 3/6   Caps
Position selection bar - ↑↓. Change - ↵. Leave menu - ↔.
Choose whether or not to omit detail lines.

Figure 2-20. The Groups menu of the REPORT FORM design screen allows you to specify summary reports

what information to list on the report. An example of this sort of report formation is shown in Figure 2-22. Each column allows you to enter the column contents (the database field to list in the column), a heading for the column, the column width, the number or decimal places for a numeric expression, and whether or not to total the column. Only numeric expressions can be totalled in a column. Note that you can use the IIF( ) function to customize any column field in your FRM.

Another option on the REPORT FORM design screen is to Locate column expressions (see Figure 2-23). This option allows you to move quickly to column expressions for editing. You can also use this menu option to insert new or delete existing column expressions. To insert new columns via the Locate menu, first place the cursor on the column expression that will follow the new column, tap RETURN, and then type CTRL-N. III PLUS automatically moves the columns over and places you on the Columns menu at a blank, inserted column.

You can delete existing columns by placing the cursor on the offending column expression and pressing first RETURN, then CTRL-U, to delete the entry.

Name, Balance and Last Payment listed by City

Name   Balance

** For -> Hartswell

* Last Payment -   57.80
  Sue Schnieder   350.00
* Subsubtotal *
                                         350.00

* Last Payment -   75.00
  Don Teirney   0.00
* Subsubtotal *
                                           0.00

** Subtotal **
                                         350.00

** For -> Manchester

* Last Payment -   25.00
  John Bajagaloop

Figure 2-21. This report is produced with the Sub-group option that allows you to break the report down beyond the master grouping

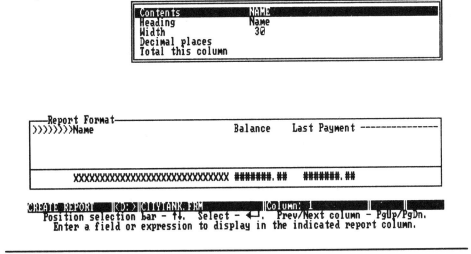

Figure 2-22. The FRM file is made up of columns of data grouped as specified

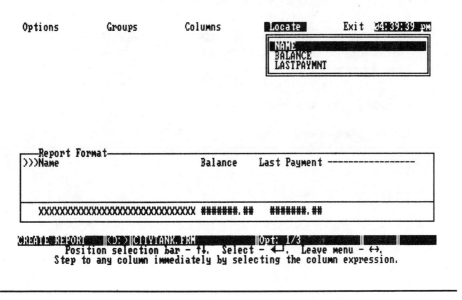

Figure 2-23. The Locate option on the FRM design screen allows you to move quickly from column to column

The last step to FRM file design is saving the file to disk. Once the REPORT FORM is designed to your liking, you save it to disk by moving the cursor to the Exit menu option, placing the cursor on the Save option, and typing RETURN.

Filename.LBL — the LABEL File

The LBL file is similar to the FRM file in that both files are designed to take information from the database and format it for specific output. In the LBL file, the output format is a printed label, although you can send the output to the screen for editing purposes or to a disk file for use with the DOS PRINT command. This option allows you to print labels when not inside the dBASE III PLUS system.

There are many similarities between the REPORT FORM design system and the LABEL design system. The first step in designing a LABEL is to choose a database or structure. Like the REPORT FORM, III PLUS's LABELs are not actually concerned with the DBF file. They are more concerned with the fields in the DBF file. The LABEL generator uses the fields, not the actual database, to generate the labels.

Once a database has been selected, you start the LABEL design process by typing either

CREATE LABEL filename

or

MODI LABEL filename

Either command allows you to create new or edit existing LABEL forms.

The first screen you see on the LABEL design system is shown in Figure 2-24. This figure also shows one of the III PLUS label default

```
 Options                    Contents                 Exit  03:02:27 am
┌────────────────────────────────────────────────────────────┐
│ Predefined size:        3 1/2 x 15/16 by 1                   │
│                                                              │
│ Label width:            35                                   │
│ Label height:            5                                   │
│ Left margin:             0                                   │
│ Lines between labels:    1                                   │
│ Spaces between labels:   0                                   │
│ Labels across page:      1                                   │
└────────────────────────────────────────────────────────────┘
```

```
MODIFY LABEL      <C:> TANK.LBL                 Opt: 1/7                    Caps
          Position selection bar - ↑↓.  Select - ↵.  Leave menu - ↔.
          Select a standard label size: (Width x Height by Number across).
```

Figure 2-24.   This is the opening screen on the CREATE and MODIFY LABELS command LABEL generator

sizes. III PLUS knows five different label sizes, and you can flip through them by placing the cursor on the "Predefined size:" line and pressing RETURN. Note that III PLUS not only knows the different sizes, but the different print specifications for the different size labels. Figure 2-24 shows one-up 3 1/2 × 15/16 labels. Note that the "Lines between labels" and "Labels across page" are both 1, and that "Spaces between labels" is 0. You can override any of these defaults and even create a new label definition simply by placing the cursor on the desired default, pressing RETURN, and typing in the new information.

The second step in LABEL design is telling III PLUS what information to place on the LABEL form. That is done by moving the cursor to the Contents menu option, then moving it to the label line you want to place information on, and typing RETURN. You can also press the F10 key to display available fields in the database (see Figure 2-25). Note that in Figure 2-25 the text specifies the use of two database fields on one line. dBASE III PLUS will warn you if you try

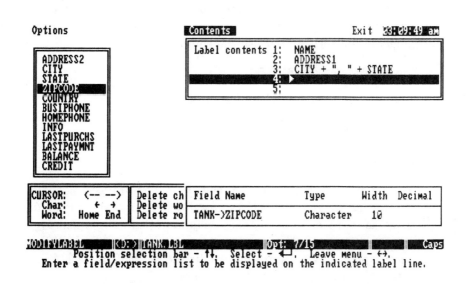

Figure 2-25. The second part of LABEL design is filling in the contents of the LABEL form

to enter an improper expression on a line, such as

CITY, STATE

III PLUS will not let you leave the line until you edit the entry to create a proper expression. You can place two or more fields on the same line provided you know what the fields are and how III PLUS will allow you to put them together.

In this case, you know that both the CITY and STATE fields are CHARACTER fields (the box at the bottom of Figure 2-25 tells you what field type you're working with). You can place both fields on the same line provided you use III PLUS's rules for placing character strings side by side. You do this by typing (for example)

CITY + ", " + STATE

The last step in LABEL design is to save the LABEL file to disk. Note that, as with all the other form generators, you can always press the ESC key and then type **Y** to exit without saving the new form or saving changes made to an existing file.

Once the LABEL is saved to disk, you can begin outputting labels to the screen, to the printer, or to a disk file.

Of course, it would be nice to see if you've laid out the labels properly before you print them. One way to check this is to send the labels to the screen. You use the command

LABEL FORM filename SAMPLE

This command tells III PLUS to send a filled label form to the screen. Figure 2-26 shows this SAMPLE output. You can send a SAMPLE LABEL to the printer with

LABEL FORM filename SAMPLE TO PRINT

The purpose of this is to give you the opportunity to position your printer labels with III PLUS's idea of where they should be. You can print as many samples as necessary to get the alignment right. To admit defeat, you simply press ESC. Note that the SAMPLE option doesn't print any data; it merely fills the defined LABEL form with asterisks (*) for purposes of alignment.

Once you're satisfied with the SAMPLEs, you save the file and get the actual labels with data from the selected database (see Figure 2-27).

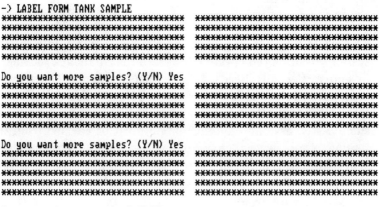

Figure 2-26.   Printing SAMPLE LABELS can save you a lot of time and money when your printer and III PLUS disagree on the size and shape of labels

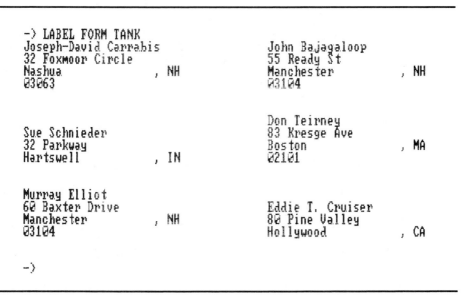

Figure 2-27.   As a further check of the accuracy of your labels, you can send them to the screen before sending them to the printer

The MEM file is an important part of programming in the III PLUS system. Assume you create a program that manages your accounts or inventory. Perhaps there is information that is not related to any database but is relevant to the program you've created. Assume further that this information changes many times during a typical work session. Lastly, assume the information must be carried from this work session, where several changes have been made, to the next work session with those changes intact. This type of information usually takes the form of memory variables. III PLUS allows you to carry memory variables from one work session to the next with the MEM file.

A MEM file is nothing more than a file containing declared memory variables and their values. Figure 2-28 shows how using a MEM file can reload SAVEd memory variables into dBASE III PLUS. This saves the user or programmer the time of having to rede-

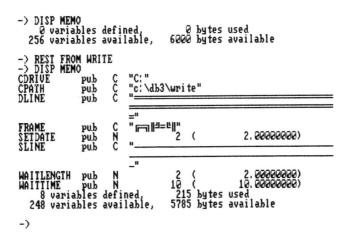

Figure 2-28. The MEM file is used to store memory variables from one work session or part of an application and recall them in another work session or part of an application

fine the variables during each work session. It also provides a historical tracing of variables, carrying information from one work session to the next.

There are certain restrictions to the use of MEM files, however. For example, if you RESTORE the memory variables in one MEM file, and then RESTORE the memory variables from another MEM file, the second file's information clears memory before loading in its contingent of variables. This means you'd lose all the information RESTOREd from the first MEM file. An example of this is shown in Figure 2-29. The variables restored from the WRITE.MEM file are erased before the LIBRARY.MEM variables are RESTOREd. Further, variables with the same name in the two files (such as

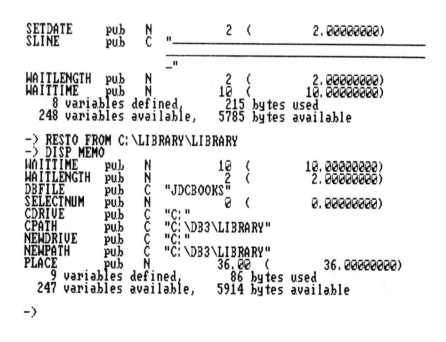

```
SETDATE      pub  N            2 (          2.00000000)
SLINE        pub  C   "_____

                      _____

                      _"
WAITLENGTH   pub  N            2 (          2.00000000)
WAITTIME     pub  N           10 (         10.00000000)
        8 variables defined,      215 bytes used
      248 variables available,   5785 bytes available

-> RESTO FROM C:\LIBRARY\LIBRARY
-> DISP MEMO
WAITTIME     pub  N           10 (         10.00000000)
WAITLENGTH   pub  N            2 (          2.00000000)
DBFILE       pub  C   "JDCBOOKS"
SELECTNUM    pub  N            0 (          0.00000000)
CDRIVE       pub  C   "C:"
CPATH        pub  C   "C:\DB3\LIBRARY"
NEWDRIVE     pub  C   "C:"
NEWPATH      pub  C   "C:\DB3\LIBRARY"
PLACE        pub  N        36.00 (         36.00000000)
        9 variables defined,       86 bytes used
      247 variables available,   5914 bytes available

->
```

Figure 2-29.   MEM files can be used to both clear and load memory. Here, variables RESTOREd from WRITE.MEM are written over when variables are RESTOREd from LIBRARY.MEM

CPATH and CDRIVE) are given new definitions. This can be disastrous when several different MEM files share similarly named variables, but the variable definitions are vastly different.

This problem is partially solved by using the ADDITIVE qualifier when RESTOREing a MEM file, as is done in Figure 2-30. The ADDITIVE qualifier tells III PLUS to leave existing variables in memory but to write over existing variables if similarly named variables are being loaded. Note that in Figure 2-30, where the ADDITIVE qualifier is used in the RESTORE command, the SETDATE variable is kept in memory, whereas it isn't kept in Figure 2-29. Also note that the CDRIVE and CPATH variables have the LIBRARY .MEM values, not the WRITE.MEM values.

The last thing to note about MEM files is that they'll store *all* active memory variables when the MEM file is activated. During a

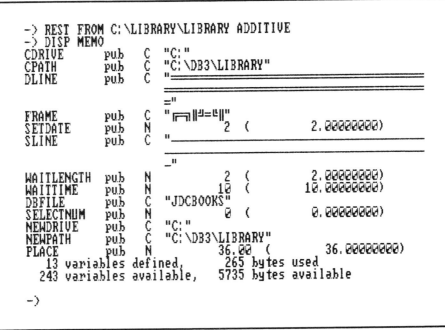

Figure 2-30. MEM files can also be used to load additional variables into memory without clearing existing memory variables. This is done by using the RESTORE FROM filename ADDITIVE command

normal work session, several variables are declared and used. A standard accounting system for a 35-employee firm engaged in a service industry, for example, can use as many as 200 memory variables in a work session. Good programmers know that memory space is at a premium and RELEASE memory variables as soon as they're done with them. Sometimes this is not advisable. There are times, such as in engineering applications, that several memory variables must be kept active.

You might not need to store all those active variables to a MEM file, however. Unless the variables are RELEASEd, they will be stored. How much memory can be used to store these MEM files on disk? That depends on the precision and number of variables you wish to store. The LIBRARY.MEM file shown in the figures in this section takes up 368 bytes on disk. The WRITE.MEM file requires 241 bytes and the TANK.MEM file only 121. A file with several tens of variables, each variable with a high degree of precision, can take up several thousand bytes of disk space. The solution to this is to RELEASE the variables you do not wish to save (see Figure 2-31).

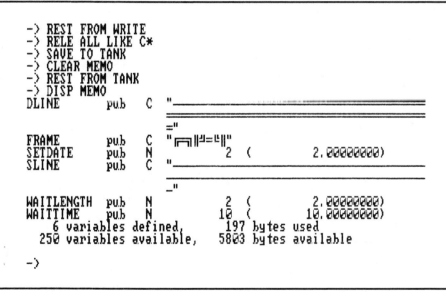

Figure 2-31. MEM files provide a quick way to clear memory space, using the RELEASE, SAVE TO, and RESTORE FROM command combination

Memory variables are RESTOREd FROM the WRITE.MEM file with the command

REST FROM WRITE

Suppose you follow the example in Figure 2-31. You don't wish to keep all those variables in the TANK.MEM file, so you

RELEASE ALL C*

which erases all variables that fit the C* form (CPATH and CDRIVE) from memory. You want to SAVE the remaining memory variables to the TANK.MEM disk file, so you

SAVE TO TANK

The rest of Figure 2-31 shows that the TANK.MEM file only contains the variables you're interested in.

Filename.NDX—the INDEX File

The most important file, for data organization purposes, is the NDX file. This is the file created whenever you INDEX your database on any field or combination of fields. To understand how the NDX file works, you have to learn something about primary and secondary keys in a database.

A database's primary key is the record numbers III PLUS assigns to each record in the database. The record number is called the *primary key* because III PLUS uses it to find a given record. Whenever you want to find information in a database, you probably will use a SEEK, LOCATE, or FIND command. Rarely, you will use the GOTO command.

The reason for this is that the GOTO command has the form

GOTO record number

and few users know the exact record number they're interested in. You may know that you're interested in all clients in Boston, Massachusetts, but not the individual record numbers for each of the clients who meets that criterion. If you did have that information, you could GOTO each of the records.

You need a way to convert the way III PLUS finds records — through the primary key, which is the record number — into a way you can find records. You do this is by creating a *secondary key* to the database. Using the TANK.DBF as an example, you know that you've defined the records to hold information on NAME, ADDRESS, CITY, STATE, ZIPCODE, and so on. This information takes the form of the fields in the record.

You know that you're interested in everyone in the database who meets the following criterion:

CITY = "Boston" .AND. STATE = "MA"

That criterion can be used as a secondary key when you use the LOCATE command.

LOCATE FOR CITY = "Boston" .AND. STATE = "MA"

III PLUS will dutifully look at each record, starting at the first record in the database. As soon as it finds a record that matches CITY = "Boston", it looks at that record's STATE field to see if STATE = "MA". If those two criteria are met, III PLUS stops at that record. To find the next record that meets your criteria, you use the command

CONTINUE

III PLUS starts at the record immediately following the one it stopped at and begins looking for the next record that meets the search conditions.

If you think this can be a painfully slow process on a large database, you're right. You need a way to speed up your secondary-key search process.

How about organizing your database along field lines? You can create a list of the CITY entries and put a record number beside each CITY entry. All you have to do then is extract all the "Boston" entries and look at the corresponding record numbers. If you really want to be slick, you could create a list of CITY and STATE entries. That way, you'd only have to look for the "Boston" "MA" entries and look at their corresponding records. That would speed up your process considerably.

That is exactly what a secondary key, in the guise of an NDX file, does. You create an NDX file by selecting which field or fields you want as your secondary key. To use the search key listed here, you'd

INDEX ON CITY+STATE TO filename

III PLUS allows you to INDEX on any combination of fields, provided the fields can be made into the same data type. For instance, you can't INDEX ON a CHARACTER and a DATE field together, but you can

INDEX ON character field + DTOC(date field) TO filename

The reason you can get away with that is that you've used the DTOC( ) function to change the DATE field into a CHARACTER field during the INDEXing.

So much for creating an NDX file. How do you use one?

The NDX file allows you to FIND and SEEK information in a database quickly. To retrieve the first record of Boston, Massachusetts, clients you could

```
USE TANK
INDEX ON CITY+STATE TO TANK
FIND "Boston MA"
```

This bit of code assumes TANK has not been INDEXed yet and produces a screen such as the one shown in Figure 2-31. III PLUS is telling you how many records it has INDEXed and how much of the DBF file has been successfully INDEXed. Once the DBF file is INDEXed, you can FIND things in it, provided those things are in the index field (as shown in Figure 2-32). Figure 2-33 shows how an NDX file can add multi-level order to a file. Note that the CITY + STATE INDEX give higher priority to CITY than to STATE.

The other method for retrieving information from an INDEXed DBF file assumes the NDX file already exists. You can

```
USE TANK INDE TANK
FIND "Boston MA"
```

```
-> USE TANK
-> INDE ON NAME TO NAME
   100% indexed          240 Records indexed
-> INDE ON CITY+STATE TO CITYSTAT
   100% indexed          240 Records indexed
->
```

Figure 2-32. INDEXing the TANK.DBF file with SET TALK ON produces information on the size of the database and the amount of data INDEXed

```
-> INDE ON CITY+STATE TO CITYSTAT
   100% indexed          240 Records indexed
-> GOTO TOP
-> DISP NEXT 15 CONTACT,CITY,STATE
Record#  CONTACT                  CITY            STATE
    53   Marshall Bonfire         Arlington       TX
    60   Marshall Bonfire         Arlington       TX
    73   Marshall Bonfire         Arlington       TX
   209   Marian Thompson          Atlanta         GA
    13   Judy Francesco           Auburn          MA
    98   C. A. Stevens            Aurora          CO
   203   Will Fastie              Baltimore       MD
   107   Janet Elliot Danforth    Bangor          ME
   122   K. Neill Foster          Beaverlodge     AL
   123   K. Neill Foster          Beaverlodge     AL
   227   Stuart David Schiff      Binghamton      NY
   230   Stuart David Schiff      Binghamton      NY
   231   Stuart David Schiff      Binghamton      NY
   140   George Gendron           Boston          MA
   141   George Gendron           Boston          MA
-> FIND "Marshall Bonfire"
No find
->
```

Figure 2-33. TANK.DBF is INDEXed on CITY and STATE to TANK.NDX, but asking for something not in the index field causes III PLUS to tell you that your item of interest can't be found

or

```
USE TANK
SET INDE TO TANK
FIND "Boston MA"
```

There are several ways to use NDX files with the SEEK, FIND, SET INDEX TO, SET ORDER TO, USE database INDEX, and INDEX ON field(s) TO filename commands.

At this point it is important to know the limits on the NDX file. Most important, you cannot INDEX ON a field that is more than 100 characters long. That automatically rules out INDEXing on MEMO fields. You can INDEX on a combination of fields, such as CITY + STATE + ZIPCODE + NAME. Realize that doing so might create an index field longer than 100 characters, which will cause III PLUS to present an error message.

One way around this problem is to use the TRIM commands to remove dead spaces in the key field. For example, INDEXing on a 30-character NAME field will produce index fields 30 characters wide, even though you may never enter a name 30 characters long. The name of the author of this text, Joseph-David Carrabis, is 21 characters long. In a 30-character NAME field, that name wastes nine spaces. If you TRIM the name, it will go into the NDX file as only 21 characters long. Thus, you can use the TRIM command on several fields that, unTRIMmed, might be well over 100 characters long. The TRIM function is discussed in Chapter 21.

Filename.PRG — the PROGRAM and PROCEDURE Files

Once you've gotten past the use of the dBASE III PLUS prompt and are comfortable with how III PLUS works, you'll probably want to start writing some programs. The programs (or, as Ashton-Tate prefers to call them, command files) are the files that have the .PRG extension. III PLUS PRG files come in three basic types.

The first type of PRG file is one you're familiar with. It is the FMT file. You'll remember from earlier in this chapter that the FMT file is really nothing more than a collection of SAY and GET commands. The main differences between the FMT files and other PRG files are that the FMT files only have SAY and GET commands and that the FMT files become memory-resident when the SET FORMAT TO filename command is used.

The second type of PRG file is the standard PRG file. Any program listing in this book can be considered a standard PRG file.

The third type of PRG file is actually the III PLUS PROCEDURE file. There is a fundamental difference between the III PLUS PRG files and the III PLUS PROCEDURE files, though.

A PROCEDURE file is a collection of subroutines that are called from a main program with the SET PROCEDURE TO filename command. This command causes III PLUS to find the PROCEDURE file on disk and then loads that file into memory. In that sense, the PROCEDURE file is similar to the FMT file. Once called, the file loads into memory and stays there during the work session. The only way to rid memory of the PROCEDURE file is to use either

SET PROCEDURE TO

with no filename, which tells III PLUS not to use any PROCEDURE files, or to call another PROCEDURE file into memory with

SET PROCEDURE TO another file

The latter method, of course, still keeps some PROCEDURE file in memory.

There is no functional limit to the size of the PRG file in any form except that of the PROCEDURE file. The file can be as long as needs required, provided no more than 32 separate procedures are included in the file. Should you wish to use a PROCEDURE file that you suspect won't fit in memory, recognize that III PLUS will take as much of the file into memory as will fit. Once the file is accessed a few times, DOS will recognize which parts of the file should take priority in the PROCEDURE buffer.

Before you read over the list of caveats associated with PRG files, you should note that keeping the names of PROCEDURE files straight can be confusing. For example, suppose a user has two systems that call in PROCEDURE files: a professional writing system and a personal library system. The writing system has 62 files associated with it and the library system has more than 100 files associated with it. That means there are many filenames to handle. To keep system-wide names as similar as possible in such a setup, that user could use the *.PRC* extension on *PRoCedure* files. This simple technique would allow the user to have a directory listing in which the files share similar first names, but the separate extensions on the names tell you all you need to know about their use.

Remember that you must use the extension when calling a PROCEDURE file without the .PRG extension. For example, if there is a PROCEDURE file called ADVERT.PRG, you could call it into memory with

SET PROCEDURE TO ADVERT

If you have the exact same file named ADVERT.PRC, however, you would have to use

SET PROCEDURE TO ADVERT.PRC

There is nothing else different about the two files or their use.

As stated earlier in this section, there are few caveats concerning these files. There is no limit to their functional size, but there is a limit to their input size when using the dBASE III PLUS Text Editor. The III PLUS Text Editor has a 5000-character limit on the size of a file being edited.

You can, however, use any ASCII text editor to create program files as large as you'd like. The DOS EDLIN.COM editor, for example, is a serviceable editor with the advantage of listing output by line number.

Filename.QRY — the QUERY File

The QUERY file is one of the new items in dBASE III PLUS's repertory. The best way to describe the QRY file is to consider how you tell III PLUS to find specific information.

III PLUS, like all the other dBASEs, considers information in only one way — logically. The information either IS or IS NOT what you're interested in. That is the computer's point of view. In truth, you may be interested in things that are close to but not quite what you're looking for. Unfortunately, III PLUS can't give you best guesses, and that limits you as to how you look for information.

How do you separate the IS from the IS NOT?

Consider a DBF file of more than 1000 entries. You want to find the three records that meet certain conditions. Do you really want to list all 1000 records and scan them yourself?

No, you do not. Fortunately, III PLUS and the other dBASEs allow you to tell them how to scan for the information. The scanning method involves the use of a database *filter*.

LIST THE NAMES OF CLIENTS WITH OVERDUE ACCOUNTS

is a filter. The specific filter, depending on how you've set up your database and program, could be

BALANCE > 0 .AND. DATE( ) - LASTPAYMNT > 30

or, if you're more economical in your designs,

OVERDUE

This assumes OVERDUE is a LOGICAL field. Therefore, the OVERDUE field need only be TRUE to act as a filter.

You may need to assess overdue accounts frequently. If that is the case, you don't want to type in your filter each time you want to ask (QUERY) the database who meets the condition. That is where the QRY file comes in.

The QRY file actually provides a method of making a permanent type of filter. The filter doesn't have to remain permanent during a work session; it need only be called when particular conditions are to be met. The QRY file's permanency comes from the fact that the filter conditions can be saved to disk and summoned whenever necessary.

There are two basic ways to establish these logical filters in III PLUS. The first and most obvious way is to use the command

SET FILTER TO expression

This can be used in programs, from the III PLUS prompt, and so on.

The other way is to CREATE a QRY file, which is an unprintable file (see Figure 2-34) that tells III PLUS what to use as a filter.

Those who develop a system to work either as a complex PRG environment or as a preset prompting system (one that uses the interactive III PLUS environment but has some system defaults designed in) can make a great deal of use of the QRY file. Usually these systems rely heavily on the user's predictability. The developer can, with a high degree of accuracy, anticipate what the end user will need in screens, prompts, and filters. The QRY file allows the devel-

```
-> DIR *.QRY
C1@CQRY.QRY        NAMES.QRY

    143 bytes in     2 files.
4710400 bytes remaining on drive.

-> TYPE NAMES.QRY
♦4$

-> DISP STAT

Currently Selected Database:
Select area:   1. Database in Use: C:\LIBRARY\JDCBOOKS.dbf   Alias: JDCBOOKS
Filter: LEFT(TRIM(TITLE),LEN("T"))="T" .AND..NOT.LEFT(TRIM(AUTHOR),LEN("A"))="A"
 .AND.(CATEGORY= "Science Fiction" .OR.CATEGORY= "Fantasy")

File search path:
Default disk drive: D:
Print destination:  PRN:
Margin =         0
Current work area =    1   Delimiters are ':' and ':'

Press any key to continue...
```

Figure 2-34. The QUERY designed in this section and saved to disk as
NAMES.QRY shows the filter as it would look if you typed
in the correct dBASE III PLUS command

oper to create the necessary filter files before installing the system.
These QRY (filter) files can then be called either through the
ASSIST mode, as in Figure 2-35, or through the use of the command

SET FILTER TO FILE ?

when a CAT file is being used.

The next thing to consider is how QRY files are created. You can
do this through the ASSIST module or through the command

CREATE QUERY filename

or the command

MODIFY QUERY filename

as shown in Figure 2-36. These two figures show how III PLUS
creates a QRY file from the dBASE prompt. Figure 2-36 assumes a
DBF file is in USE. III PLUS prompts you for the name of a DBF
file to USE if one is not declared. Note that III PLUS also wants to

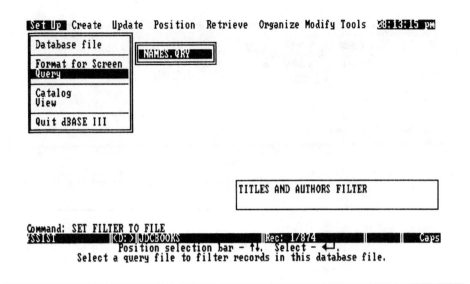

Figure 2-35. Any QRY file can be accessed through the ASSIST module, provided the correct drives have been set

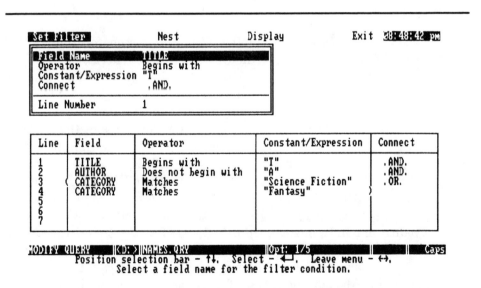

Figure 2-36. The QRY file can be created through the CREATE QUERY and MODIFY QUERY commands, as shown here

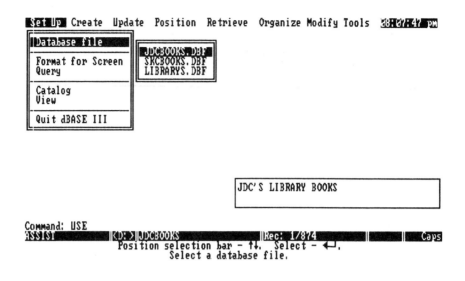

Database file
Format for Screen
Query
Catalog
View
Quit dBASE III

JDCBOOKS.DBF
SKCBOOKS.DBF
LIBRARYS.DBF

JDC'S LIBRARY BOOKS

Command: USE
ASSIST   KD: > JDCBOOKS   Rec: 1/874   Caps
Position selection bar - ↑↓. Select - ↵.
Select a database file.

Figure 2-37. The ASSIST module needs to know what DBF file to use before it allows you to CREATE a QRY file

know if the DBF file is INDEXed. The reason for this is that INDEXed DBF files allow the QRY command generator to use FOR and WHILE qualifiers in creating the filter. (More information on the FOR and WHILE qualifiers can be found in Chapter 9 in the sections on the FIND and SEEK commands.)

Assuming you start to create a QRY file through the ASSIST module, you would first have to declare a DBF file, as in Figure 2-37. Figure 2-37 shows the Set Up part of the ASSIST module being used to select a database. Once that is done, you tell III PLUS that you want to CREATE a new query file, as shown in Figure 2-38. III PLUS prompts you for a QRY filename. Note that III PLUS is typing your commands, in standard dBASE III PLUS form, on the bottom of the screen.

Note also that, regardless of whether you started to build your QRY file though the ASSIST module or through the CREATE QUERY or MODIFY QUERY command, you would begin to design the QRY file at this screen.

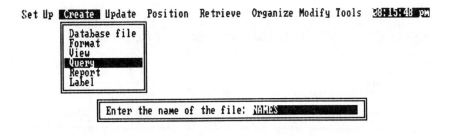

Command: CREATE QUERY

Enter new value. Finish with ↵.
Specify a file name.

Figure 2-38. Once III PLUS knows which DBF file to USE, you can go to the ASSIST CREATE menu options and begin CREATEing a QRY file

Remember that the QRY file is designed to offer a specialized way of generating filters. With that in mind, you begin designing your QRY file by using the Set Filter menu option. The first thing to do is select the database fields you're interested in for this QRY file (see Figure 2-39). You do this by moving the cursor to the FIELD NAMES prompt under Set Filter and pressing RETURN. III PLUS shows you a list of the available fields on the right side of the screen. Another box opens up in the middle of the screen that gives you information about the particular database field the cursor is on. Figure 2-39 shows the TITLE field under the cursor, and the middle box tells you that the TITLE field is a CHARACTER type and is 60 characters wide. Beneath the middle box is the QRY box. That box is where the QRY is built and displayed.

At this point, it is useful to remember that the QRY file is a filter to the DBF file. Further, the QRY file is a series of filters in one file. That is, you don't need to create several QRY files to put limits

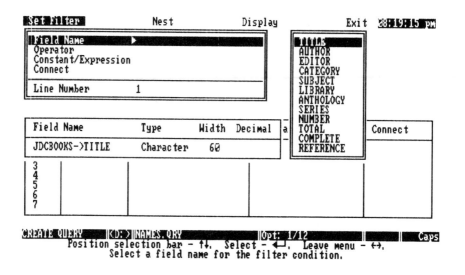

Figure 2-39.   III PLUS tells the QRY designer everything necessary for
creating the QRY file, such as database field names, their
TYPE and their width

on several database fields. Now, thinking of the QRY file as a series
of filters in one file and realizing that each filter is a limit on a particular database field and that the limiting method must be LOGI-
CAL to dBASE III PLUS, recognize that you must use some kind of
LOGICAL operator to tell dBASE III PLUS what the filter (QRY) is.

The QUERY design screen uses the OPERATOR prompt on the
Set Filter menu option to place the LOGICAL operators in the QRY
file. These operators can be seen in Figure 2-40. Note that these
operators can work on CHARACTER, NUMERIC, DATE, and LOGI-
CAL fields, but that each field type will produce different results
with each operator.

For example, NUMERIC matches must be exact. But, if SET
EXACT OFF is used before the QRY file is accessed, CHARACTER
matches won't necessarily be EXACT matches. III PLUS will only
find the first occurrence of matching first characters. The COMES
AFTER operator will return NUMERIC greater-than values,

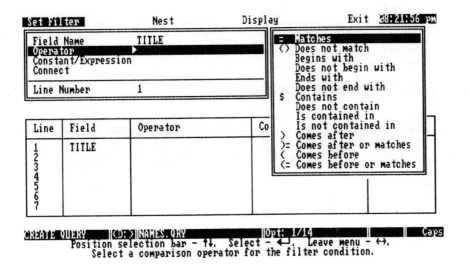

Figure 2-40. III PLUS offers several types of logical operators to use in designing a QRY file filter

CHARACTER values will be returned in the ASCII value if the key-field is greater than the ASCII value of the search key, and DATE values will return with dates that come after the search-key date.

The next step is to determine if the filter is going to involve another condition. The other condition can involve the same field as already used, another field, or a valid III PLUS expression.

An example of using the same field to create a two-level condition would be

TITLE begins with "T" AND ends with "E"

This two-level condition would return all filters and show all records with a TITLE field beginning with T and ending with E, such as TE, That is E, and Teddy E. Using a valid III PLUS expression might be

TITLE begins with "T" AND DATE( ) < 08/07/86

dBASE III PLUS File Types

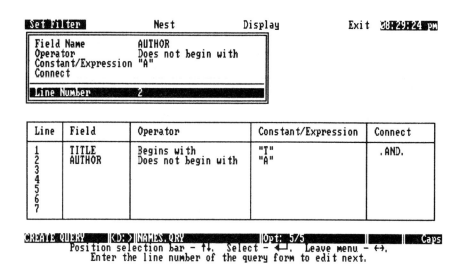

Figure 2-41. This figure shows two separate database fields used to create a specialized filter for the QRY file

Figure 2-41 shows the results of creating a two-level condition using more than one database field. Figure 2-36 shows the Connect option of the SET FILTER menu. In the example, you want to build a somewhat complex QRY that involves several database fields. You need to connect your first line of the QRY with other lines. In particular, as you can see in Figure 2-41, you're interested in connecting your QRY in such a way that two separate fields must hold specific information. Figure 2-41 shows that the AUTHOR field must not begin with A and the TITLE field should begin with T.

The problem with creating several levels of conditions for the QRY file is that not all levels may have the same precedence. You may be more interested in titles that begin with T than you are in titles that begin with T and authors that don't begin with A. The III PLUS ASSIST module and QUERY generator handle that problem with the concept of nesting conditions. Figure 2-42 shows the Nest menu on the QUERY design screen. The conditions that you

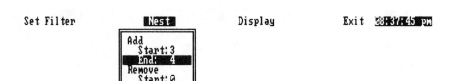

```
Set Filter          Nest          Display          Exit  08:37:45 pm
                 ┌─────────────┐
                 │ Add         │
                 │   Start: 3  │
                 │   End:   4  │
                 │ Remove      │
                 │   Start: 0  │
                 │   End:   0  │
                 └─────────────┘
```

Line	Field	Operator	Constant/Expression	Connect
1	TITLE	Begins with	"T"	.AND.
2	AUTHOR	Does not begin with	"A"	.AND.
3	⟨ CATEGORY	Matches	"Science Fiction"	.OR.
4	CATEGORY	Matches	"Fantasy" ⟩	
5				
6				
7				

```
CREATE QUERY      ⟨D:⟩ NAMES.QRY                    Opt: 2/4              Caps
           Position selection bar - ↑↓.  Select - ◄┘.  Leave menu - ↔.
           Enter the line number of the query form to stop nesting.
```

Figure 2-42. The III PLUS QUERY generator allows you to nest several levels of conditions in each QRY file

want to nest are

CATEGORY = ("Science Fiction" .OR. "Fantasy")

Those conditions, due to the limits of dBASE III PLUS, turn into the two lines

```
CATEGORY matches "Science Fiction" .OR.
CATEGORY matches "Fantasy"
```

That is all there is to designing a QRY. The last two steps are to DISPLAY the results of the QRY's filtering and to SAVE the QRY to disk as a file. Figure 2-43 shows the completed QRY ready for DISPLAY. Figure 2-44 shows the result of letting III PLUS DISPLAY the filtered information. The STATUS line at the bottom of Figure 2-44 shows that the first record to match the conditions listed in Figures 2-43 and 2-44 is record 160 (there are 874 records in this database).

Line	Field	Operator	Constant/Expression	Connect
1	TITLE	Begins with	"T"	.AND.
2	AUTHOR	Does not begin with	"A"	.AND.
3	CATEGORY	Matches	"Science Fiction"	.OR.
4	CATEGORY	Matches	"Fantasy"	
5				
6				
7				

▮CREATE QUERY▮   ▮<D:>▮NAMES.QRY▮   ▮Caps▮
                 Select - ◄┘.   Leave prompt pad - ◄→.
         Display records in the database that meet the query condition.

Figure 2-43.   Once the QUERY is designed, you can DISPLAY all records
                in the database that meet the QRY conditions

You save the QUERY by moving the cursor to the Exit menu
option and selecting the Save option. Could the filter have been constructed without the use of the QUERY generator? Yes, but getting it
right might have taken some effort. Figure 2-34 shows the contents
of the NAMES.QRY file and how the QRY file acts on the III PLUS
system. Note that the QRY designed in this section becomes the filter
shown in Figure 2-34.

This is not the easiest form of filter to create. The QRY file can
be used advantageously when complex standard filters are used in a
system.

The limits to the QRY file aren't many, but they are limits,
nevertheless. First, you can only create up to seven levels of nests or
up to seven conditions in the QRY file. A SET FILTER TO expression command has no such constraint.

Note that the QRY file, and the filter contained in it, are not
concerned with the database in USE as they are with the FIELD in
the in-USE database. The filter and QRY file designed in this section
could be used for any DBF file with a structure similar to the data-

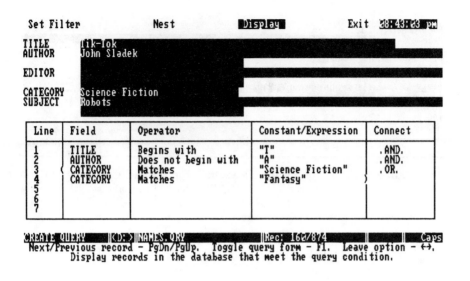

	TITLE	Tik-Tok		
AUTHOR	John Sladek			
EDITOR				
CATEGORY	Science Fiction			
SUBJECT	Robots			

Line	Field	Operator	Constant/Expression	Connect
1	TITLE	Begins with	"T"	.AND.
2	AUTHOR	Does not begin with	"A"	.AND.
3	CATEGORY	Matches	"Science Fiction"	.OR.
4	CATEGORY	Matches	"Fantasy"	
5				
6				
7				

CREATE QUERY   <D:> NAMES.QRY   Rec: 163/874   Caps
Next/Previous record - PgDn/PgUp. Toggle query form - F1. Leave option - ↔,
Display records in the database that meet the query condition.

Figure 2-44. The Display menu option tells III PLUS to show all the records that meet the conditions, such as *Tik-Tok* by John Sladek

base file used in this section. Only one QRY file can be active for any one DBF file, however. You could use ten databases in ten work areas and have a separate QRY file acting on each one of them.

As a final note, you cannot use the command

SET FILTER TO FILE filename

on an existing QRY file to enter that QRY file into the CATALOG. One way to enter an existing QRY file into an active CAT file is through the CREATE QUERY and MODIFY QUERY commands. These two commands drop you into the QUERY design module. Even if you make no changes to the QRY file, exiting from the QUERY design module causes III PLUS to prompt you for a name and associated information for the QRY file.

Figure 2-45 shows another method for getting QRY file data into a CAT file. You use the fact that the CAT file is really a specialized database that can be EDITed. You know what information you need

```
Record No.     13
PATH         :names.qry
FILE_NAME    :names.qry    :
ALIAS        :NAMES        :
TYPE         :qry:
TITLE        :TITLES AND AUTHORS FILTER
             :            :
CODE         :  1:
TAG          :   :
```

Figure 2-45. This figure shows how the QRY file information can be entered into the CATALOG file manually

to place in the CAT file and simply APPEND a BLANK record and then place the necessary information into that record.

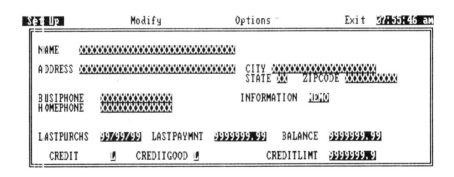

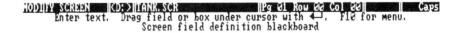

Figure 2-46. The SCR file can be edited with the cursor control keys to create a new FMT file from an old screen image

Filename.SCR—the SCREEN File

There is really not much to say about the SCR file that hasn't been said earlier. The truth of the matter is that the SCR file is something used internally by III PLUS whenever you want to modify an FMT file quickly and easily.

The SCR file is a screen image of a particular screen format, as shown in Figure 2-46. The screen was created earlier in this chapter (Figure 2-13). Here, modifications are made to the original screen layout. These modifications are easily made with the cursor movement keys. Once the changes are made, you can save the new screen image to an SCR file for future use and generate a new FMT file.

Because the SCR files provide a quick and easy way to create and modify custom screen forms, it is a good idea to keep all SCR files with the system they're designed for.

Filename.TXT—the TEXT Output File

The output TXT file is primarily used for generating ASCII files of your database. These ASCII files can then be read into most word processors to use in letters, forms, and memos.

Not every software package looks at data in the same way. Some packages use special field delimiters, and other packages use a compressed data format. The most convenient and realistic way to get every package to communicate with every other package is to get the data into a format every package can read. Once the data is read, it is up to that other package to manipulate the data.

The universal data form is ASCII text. What is ASCII text? Consider Figure 2-47. It is data from an INCOME.DBF file in dBASE III PLUS DISP format. The data looks like it's in ASCII format, but that is because III PLUS knows how the data is stored, what the database file field delimiters are, and how the information should be presented on the screen. Figure 2-48, on the other hand, is a straight file dump of the INCOME.DBF file. No special formatting has been done by III PLUS or DOS to recognize database file field delimiters, data-storage methods and techniques, or screen presentation. Figure

```
-> COPY FILE A:INCOME.DBF TO INCOME.DBF
-> USE INCOME
-> DISP ALL
Record#  RECFOR                                                      DATEDUE  R
ECFROM                                              RECAMOUNT RECDATE
       1 DBASE III ADVANCED PROGRAMMING                                04/27/86 Q
ue Corp                                              2701.04 04/14/86
       2   Reimbursement                                              05/01/86 H
ayden Publishing                                       33.05 04/28/86
       3   Review                                                    05/01/86 L
OTUS Magazine                                        425.00 04/04/86
       4   Article                                                   05/01/86 P
ersonal Computing                                   1000.00 05/01/86
       5 DBASE III ADVANCED PROGRAMMING                                05/27/86 Q
ue Corp                                             1166.98 05/30/86
       6   CONSULTING                                                06/16/86 N
RPC                                                    50.00 05/30/86
       7 DBASE III ADVANCED PROGRAMMING                                06/27/86 Q
ue Corp                                              990.81 06/27/86
->
```

Figure 2-47. This is how III PLUS DISPLAYs the INCOME.DBF file

```
-> TYPE INCOME.DBF
♦U$
◙
                                       19860501Personal Computing
                         1000.0019860501 DBASE III ADVANCED PROGRAMMING
                     19860527Que Corp
           1166.9819860530 CONSULTING
           19860616NRPC
       50.0019860530 DBASE III ADVANCED PROGRAMMING
19860627Que Corp                                                   990.8119
860627

->
```

Figure 2-48. The information in the INCOME.DBF file is not ready for
direct screen output; it must first be formatted

2-49 shows the INCOME.DBF file in an ASCII format known as
SDF, or System Default Format.

There are many ways of creating TXT files, however. Figure 2-
49, for example, was created with the command

COPY TO OUTPUT SDF

```
-> USE INCOME
-> COPY TO OUTPUT SDF
-> TYPE OUTPUT.TXT
DBASE III ADVANCED PROGRAMMING                                        19860427Que Corp
                                                           2701.0419860414
                                                                     19860501Hayden Publi
Reimbursement
shing                                                         33.0519860428
Review                                                               19860501LOTUS Magazi
ne                                                           425.0019860404
Article                                                              19860501Personal Com
puting                                                      1000.0019860501
DBASE III ADVANCED PROGRAMMING                                        19860527Que Corp
                                                           1166.9819860530
CONSULTING                                                           19860616NRPC
                                                             50.0019860530
DBASE III ADVANCED PROGRAMMING                                       19860627Que Corp
                                                            990.8119860627

->
```

Figure 2-49.   The INCOME.DBF file can be written as an ASCII text file
and used by other software programs

```
-> USE INCOME
-> COPY TO OUTPUT DELIM WITH ,
-> TYPE OUTPUT.TXT
,DBASE III ADVANCED PROGRAMMING,,19860427,,Que Corp,,2701.04,19860414
,Reimbursement,,19860501,,Hayden Publishing,,33.05,19860428
,Review,,19860501,,LOTUS Magazine,,425.00,19860404
,Article,,19860501,,Personal Computing,,1000.00,19860501
,DBASE III ADVANCED PROGRAMMING,,19860527,,Que Corp,,1166.98,19860530
,CONSULTING,,19860616,,NRPC,,50.00,19860530
,DBASE III ADVANCED PROGRAMMING,,19860627,,Que Corp,,990.81,19860627

->
```

Figure 2-50.   Figure 2-49 shows the INCOME.DBF output in SDF format. This figure shows the same data output in DELIM
WITH , format

This command tells III PLUS to take the in-USE database and
COPY the fields to a file called OUTPUT in SDF format. The OUT-
PUT file will be created if it doesn't already exist on the target disk.
It will be written over if it does exist. In either case, a new file will be
written.

Figure 2-50 shows a file created using the command

COPY TO OUTPUT DELIMITED WITH ,

This command is similar to the previous command, except you choose how each field will be separated from others in the TXT output file.

Any character can be used as the DELIMITED character in the second version of the command.

Filename.VUE—the VIEW File

The VUE (VIEW) file is similar to the CAT (CATALOG) file in one critical way—it lets you use more than one file at a time and permits only certain methods of using the files simultaneously.

The CATALOG file, as you may remember, contains groups of related files and specifies how those relations work. The VUE file does these same things, but it specifically remembers how certain database files are related and linked together.

To further complicate matters, the VUE file is similar to the QRY file in the way it is created and operates. Remember that the QRY file is used to set up filters that act upon a given database. The VUE file also sets up things that act upon a given database. In the case of the VUE file, however, the information in the file tells III PLUS how two or more DBF files can be linked and used as if they were a single file.

The ability to link several databases and use them as if they were one DBF file is powerful and bears some investigation. The JOIN command can be used to create a new database with selected fields from the fields of two other databases. The VUE file also performs that function, but the two databases never have to be JOINed to create the third file. In truth, the third file is never created.

Programmers sometimes talk of things that exist only in theory as "virtual" parts of the software, hardware, or system in general. The VUE file allows III PLUS to behave as if a new database physically exists, although that database is virtual in nature. It doesn't exist on any disk—unless you place it there with JOIN commands—

and is only active in the RAM of the computer. The VUE file does allow you to see specific field combinations from two or more DBF files, however. This can be likened to three-dimensional viewing in the following way.

Say you have two databases, MSSFILE and MAGAZINE. MSSFILE is INDEXed on the AUDIENCE field. The MAGAZINE database also has the AUDIENCE field in its structure. The two databases have no other fields in common, however. Also, the two databases are composed of information on similar items. MSSFILE contains information on manuscripts and their potential markets, INDEXed by AUDIENCE. The MAGAZINE database contains a list of markets and what their audiences may be.

You can create a VUE file that shows information on the manuscript from the MSSFILE database alongside information from the MAGAZINE database. This file is shown in Figure 2-51.

The VUE file can be created in one of two ways. Both methods will bring you to the VIEW design module. The first method is to use either the command

MODIFY VIEW filename

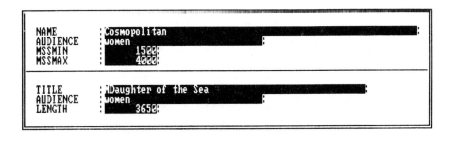

Figure 2-51. The MSSFILE's information on a manuscript's audience is used to match it against possible magazine markets in the MAGAZINE database, showing a three-dimensional relationship

or the command

CREATE VIEW filename

Either of these commands will place you in the VIEW design module, shown in Figure 2-52.

The other method of creating the VUE file is to use the ASSIST program to start you in the VIEW creation process. Through the ASSIST menu, you CREATE a VIEW file by selecting the VIEW option on the CREATE menu. dBASE III PLUS asks you for a filename. You can enter any eight-character name for the VUE file.

Once the DBF and NDX files (if any) have been selected for viewing, III PLUS needs to know the field that will form the causal link from one database to the others. Figure 2-53 shows the Relate menu. Here the TITLE field is used to link the two databases. The screen shows that the TITLE in the SKCBOOKS database will be used as a key in the JDCBOOKS database file.

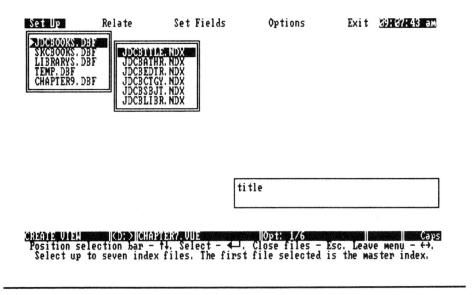

Figure 2-52. The VUE file offers you all available DBF and NDX files for linking

The next step in CREATEing VUE files is to tell III PLUS what fields are going to be shown from the two databases. This is done with the SET FIELDS menu option. You use the cursor to select the DBF file and then use the cursor and RETURN keys to pick the fields from each DBF file that you want shown.

During the CREATEion of the VUE file, remember that you're working with DBF files and establishing links between them. Because you're working with DBF files, it is possible to use FILTER (as in QRY) and FORMAT files. These files are selected through the Options menu. You can create the FILTER on this menu or use the SET FILTER TO FILE filename command outside of the menu system.

Similarly, you can type in the name of a valid FMT file for the FORMAT option. The last step in generating a VUE file is the same as the last step in generating any other menu-created files in this section. You must move the cursor to the Exit menu and select the SAVE option.

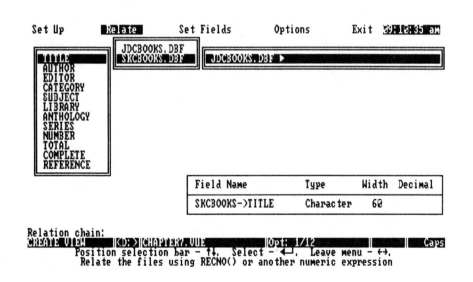

Figure 2-53. The TITLE field is being used to link the SKCBOOKS and JDCBOOKS databases through the VUE file

When all this is done, the VUE file is saved to disk. The VUE file itself is an unprintable file that is a compressed code internal to dBASE III PLUS. The code in the VUE file is equivalent to using the SET RELATION TO expression command. In this case, the RELATION established within this section is that SKCBOOKS is related into JDCBOOKS through the TITLE field.

File-Creation Commands

File-creation commands are all the commands that deal with starting with nothing and ending with something. As you saw in Chapter 2, III PLUS can create a wide variety of files. Here you will get specific information on the individual commands that bring those files into existence.

This chapter details the use of each file-creation command in dBASE III PLUS. Each section offers an explanation of the command, the general use of the command, and, when applicable, advanced uses of the command.

COPY

The COPY command is one of the basic dBASE III PLUS commands. It allows you to transfer information from one database to another database without altering the original file. This ability can be useful when taking records from a masterbase and placing them in a work file.

This chapter covers all uses of the COPY command except its use in creating STRUCTURE EXTENDED files and making copies of non-DBF files. The former topic is covered in the next section, and the latter topic is covered in the COPY FILE command section.

COPY command uses in this section include COPYing to a new file, COPYing only certain fields in the masterbase to the database, COPYing based on certain qualifiers (the FOR and WHILE qualifiers), and COPYing to non-dBASE III PLUS files. dBASE III PLUS uses the COPY command to generate SYLK (Multiplan), WKS (Lotus 1-2-3), DIF (VisiCalc), SDF, and DELIMITED files directly.

Syntax   COPY is one of the most versatile dBASE III PLUS commands. For example, you can mix the order of the COPY qualifiers.

The COPY command follows a syntax-and-use convention. The command, in its simplest form, is

COPY TO dbf file

This use, as well as all uses of the COPY command, creates a new file.

If you want a DBF file called DATAFILE, the general use of the COPY command would be

COPY TO DATAFILE

This would COPY every record and each field in each record in the in-USE database to DATAFILE. You can COPY data to a DBF file with a nonstandard name with commands such as

```
COPY TO DATAFILE.OLD
COPY TO DATAFILE.SAV
COPY TO DATAFILE.TMP
```

although there is no need to limit yourself to those file extensions. Remember that to USE those DBF files later, you must use the same name you used in the COPY command. Nor do you have to limit yourself to a DBF file with an extension. You can just as easily create a DBF file with no extension using

COPY TO DATAFILE.

The period (.) in the above command tells III PLUS to create a database file called "DATAFILE" but not to give it a .DBF extension.

You can specify an exact number of records to COPY with the command

COPY NEXT n TO DATAFILE

Note that III PLUS starts at the current record and COPYs only the NEXT n records. If you are at the last record in the file and ask to COPY the NEXT 100, all you get is one record in the target database.

You can specify specific fields to COPY from the source database to the target database with the command

COPY TO DATAFILE FIELDS field1, field2,...

This version of the COPY command tells III PLUS to COPY only the fields listed after the FIELDS qualifier.

It is possible to select specific records from the source database with the FOR and WHILE qualifiers. COPYing only records that meet some condition (field1 = "condition1" in the following example) can be done with

COPY TO DATAFILE FOR field1 = "condition1"

This tells III PLUS to go through the entire source file and find the records that meet the preceding condition. Then it is told to COPY only those records to the target file. A similar method can be used when an NDX file is open and associated with the source database. The COPY command then becomes

COPY TO DATAFILE WHILE field1 = "condition1"

This assumes the record pointer has been set to the first record to meet the condition with the FIND, SEEK, or LOCATE command. The FOR and WHILE qualifiers can be used together, but be careful in their use. A full explanation of the use of FOR and WHILE when COPYing appears in the next section.

Last, you can create foreign file types with the command

COPY TO DATAFILE TYPE file type

The file type can be in ASCII, VisiCalc, Lotus 1-2-3, or Multiplan format (SDF, DELIM, DIF, WKS, and SYLK, respectively).

These qualifiers can be mixed and matched as necessary. For example, you could

COPY TO DATAFILE FIELDS field1,field6 FOR field3 > 100

This would copy the first and sixth fields from the source database to DATAFILE FOR each record in the source file in which the third field was greater than 100. (See the "Advanced Use" section for more details.)

Use   The first thing to learn about the COPY command is that it will write over an existing file that has the same name. For example, Figure 3-1 shows the COPY command writing over a similarly named existing file unless either the SET SAFETY or CONFIG.DB SAFETY command is on. This writing over will occur even when you are creating foreign file formats.

There are several options to using the COPY command. The most common use is to COPY data from one database to another. That is done by first USEing a database, then COPYing from it, as shown here:

```
USE EXPENSES
COPY TO EXPENSES.OLD
COPY TO OLDEXPNS.
```

COPY TO EXPENSES.OLD, the first version of the COPY command, demonstrates that the COPY command can be used to create DBF files without the .DBF extension. However, to USE that file, you would have to tell III PLUS to

USE EXPENSES.OLD

The second COPY command, COPY TO OLDEXPNS, shows the COPY command being used to create a DBF file with no extension. You would have to enter

USE OLDEXPNS.

to USE that database file. Note the period (.) in the command.

The next method of using the COPY command still assumes you want to COPY data from one database to another database, but in this instance you want to copy only a certain number of records. That command adds the SCOPE qualifier in the form of

NEXT n

where n is some numeric expression. Note that this command

```
-> DIR P*
Database Files    # Records    Last Update    Size
PASSWORD.DBF         8         07/09/86        266
PFSTEST.DBF          1         01/01/80        504
PROMPTS.DBF          4         07/01/86        330

    1100 bytes in     3 files.
5152768 bytes remaining on drive.

-> SET SAFETY ON
-> USE PASSWORD
-> COPY TO PASS2
        8 records copied
-> COPY TO PASS2
PASS2.dbf already exists, overwrite it? (Y/N) No
-> SET SAFETY OFF
-> COPY TO PASS2
        8 records copied
->
```

Figure 3-1.   The COPY command will write over existing files unless the SET SAFETY or CONFIG.DB SAFETY command is ON

COPYs the NEXT n records. If the record pointer is at the end of the file, only one record will be COPYed, no matter what n is (unless n = 0, of course). A source file with 100 records, positioned at record 79, getting the command

COPY NEXT 50 TO DATAFILE

would COPY only 21 records.

The n can be any algebraic function or variable. The important thing is that n must be equated with some definite numeric value. The command form is

COPY TO database NEXT n

Note that the simplest form of the COPY command has no SCOPE option and assumes all records in the masterbase are to be COPYed. It is the functional equivalent of the command

COPY TO database NEXT RECCOUNT( )

when the record pointer is at the beginning of the file. The dBASE III PLUS RECCOUNT( ) function returns the total number of records in the masterbase; hence, the NEXT RECCOUNT( ) scope qualifier COPYs all the records in the masterbase when positioned at the beginning of the file. Different methods of using the scope option can be seen in Figure 3-2.

The next variation on the COPY theme has to do with only COPY-ing specific data from the database. This does not refer to specific data, as in specific records. That is done with the NEXT n scope qualifier. This section is concerned with COPYing data only from specific fields in the database. That is done with the command

COPY TO database FIELDS field1, field2,...

where field1, field2, and so on, represent actual field names in the source database.

This command instructs III PLUS to take information only from specific fields in the masterbase. This is useful when you're using a database in which specific fields contain confidential information.

```
-> USE EXPENSES
-> COPY NEXT 10 TO C10
        10 records copied
-> COPY NEXT 10/2 TO C10
        5 records copied
-> ? RECCOUNT()
        16
-> 1
-> COPY NEXT RECCOUNT() TO C10
        16 records copied
-> 1
-> COPY NEXT RECCOUNT()/10 TO C10
        1 record copied
-> COPY NEXT 100 TO C10
        16 records copied
-> 15
-> COPY NEXT RECCOUNT() TO C10
        2 records copied
->
```

Figure 3-2. The NEXT scope qualifier tells III PLUS how many records to COPY

These confidential fields can be "masked" from the target database using the FIELDS qualifier, as in Figure 3-3.

dBASE III PLUS allows another version of the scope qualifier with the FOR and WHILE qualifiers. These qualifiers can be used in conjunction with each other or separately.

Essentially, the FOR and WHILE qualifiers tell III PLUS to continue COPYing data to the target file as long as some logical condition or conditions are met. This form of the COPY command can take one of three forms, as shown in the following listing:

```
USE CLACCT
COPY TO NYCLACCT FOR STATE = "NY"
USE CLACCT INDE CLCITY
FIND "NYC"
COPY TO NYACCT WHILE CITY = "NYC"
FIND "MANCHESTER"
COPY TO MNHACCT FOR STATE = "NH" WHILE CITY = "MANCHESTER"
```

You can start with the CLACCT.DBF file. This example begins with the assumption that the CLACCT file is a database of national client

```
-> USE EXPENSES
-> COPY FIELDS PAYFOR,PAYTO,PAYAMOUNT TO C10
      16 records copied
-> USE C10
-> DISP NEXT 8
Record#  PAYFOR                                              PAYTO
                                      PAYAMOUNT
        1 *Rental Insurance                                  Allstate
                                        57.00
        2  Auto Expense                                      Allstate
                                       246.00
        3  Rent, Utilities                                   Susan Carr
abis                                   332.89
        4  Office Supplies                                   Susan Carr
abis                                   298.00
        5 *                                                  mileage
                                         0.00
        6  Toll                                              NH Turnpik
e                                        5.00
        7  Office Supplies                                   Computer T
own                                     14.50
        8  Motel                                             Am Ex
                                        39.27
->
```

Figure 3-3.   The FIELDS qualifier tells III PLUS what fields to COPY
                to the destination database

accounts. It is assumed that the database is large enough to be broken up into smaller, regional databases.

Because you started with an unINDEXed database, you can use the FOR qualifier to go through the database in a sequential search. dBASE III PLUS looks at each record, from the first to the last, when you use the FOR option by itself, no matter what command is being FORed. The command

COPY TO NYCLACCT FOR STATE = "NY"

starts at record 1 and checks for the logical condition

STATE = "NY"

in each record. Each record in the CLACCT.DBF file that meets that requirement gets copied to the target file. But using FOR by itself forces dBASE III PLUS to scan every record. This can be time-consuming with a large database file.

The next thing to do is refine the search somewhat using an NDX file. Line 3 tells III PLUS to USE the CLACCT file in conjunction with the CLCITY.NDX file, an index file created by INDEXing CLACCT on the CITY field. INDEXing on the CITY field allows you to use the FIND command and tell III PLUS what specific CITY you're looking for.

If there are no other states — at least in the CLACCT file — that have a city or town named New York City, you can use the COPY command with the WHILE qualifier to COPY only those clients who are in the New York City area.

But how do you make sure you COPY only clients from Manchester, New Hampshire? Note that the last line of the listing uses the FOR and WHILE qualifiers together. The most important thing to notice about the use of these together is the order in which they're used. If you INDEX the CLACCT file on the CITY field, you will find records with like-named cities next to each other as you scan the file. It is imperative that the WHILE qualifier be used on the keyfield. You could not use them as

```
COPY TO MNHACCT WHILE STATE = "NH" FOR CITY = "MANCHESTER"
```

as you would be using the WHILE qualifier incorrectly. The last qualifier, FOR, takes precedence and tells III PLUS to perform a sequential search, even though an NDX file is used with the DBF file. If the first record in the INDEXed DBF file doesn't contain NH in the STATE field, III PLUS will quit COPYing without looking further for possibly useful information.

Back to using the FOR and WHILE qualifiers correctly: You may find several records with CITY = "MANCHESTER", but the STATE field could contain any number of states. What's worse, the STATE field is not part of the INDEX. You might have 25 Manchester, Michigan, records followed by three Manchester, New Hampshire, records followed by one Manchester, Massachusetts, record…

You can't be sure that the CLCITY.NDX file has the STATEs indexed alphabetically. The only way you can guarantee that only the Manchester, New Hampshire, records will be COPYed to the MNHACCT.DBF file is to use the FOR qualifier to limit what to COPY WHILE CITY = "MANCHESTER".

Consider further the situation of using the FOR and WHILE qualifiers in reverse order. The listing shows that the CLACCT.DBF file is INDEXed on the CITY field to the CLCITY.NDX file. Having the CITY field as keyfield allows you to use the WHILE qualifier to limit your COPYing to a specific city. The FOR qualifier allows you to limit your COPYing to some other condition WHILE CITY = "MANCHESTER". You could use the FOR and WHILE qualifiers in reverse order in the COPY command, but you couldn't reverse their use in the command. In other words,

COPY TO MNHACCT WHILE CITY = "MANCHESTER" FOR STATE = "NH"

is allowed and performs the same thing as the last COPY command in the listing.

COPY TO MNHACCT WHILE STATE = "NH" FOR CITY = "MANCHESTER"

would not provide you with a satisfactory COPY. Various examples of this are shown in the following listing. In each case, you FIND "Gas" and set different parameters with the FOR and WHILE qualifiers. Depending on which qualifier comes first in the command, and what is being qualified, you either COPY parts of records or end up with an empty target DBF file.

```
          -> use expenses inde payto
          -> disp all payto,payamount
          Record#   payto
payamount
                1
0.00
                2   Allstate
57.00
                3   Allstate
246.00
                9   Am Ex
39.27
               10   Am Ex
27.95
                8   Computer Town
14.50
               15   Ford Motor Credit
305.33
               12   Gas
6.50
               13   Gas
10.50
                7   NH Turnpike
5.00
               16   Post Office
1.72
                4   Susan Carrabis
332.89
```

```
                5   Susan Carrabis
298.00
                6   mileage
0.00
               11   mileage
0.00
               14   mileage
0.00
      -> find "Gas"
      -> copy to chap10 for payamount > 10 while payto = "Gas"
         1 record(s) copied
      -> find "Gas"
      -> copy to chap10 while payto = "Gas" for payamount > 10
         1 record(s) copied
      -> copy to chap10 for payto = "Gas" while payamount > 10
         No record(s) copied
```

The last COPY command parameter to concern yourself with is the TYPE qualifier. Unlike the other dBASEs, dBASE III PLUS can create foreign data files automatically. The foreign data files III PLUS can create include ASCII (which the other dBASEs could create), Lotus 1-2-3, VisiCalc, and Multiplan.

Note that dBASE III PLUS can create a PFS file, but you must use the EXPORT command to do that (see the EXPORT command later in this chapter).

The TYPE qualifier is actually a wasted word, although the function is anything but wasted. The preferred form of the command is

COPY TO target file TYPE file type

In truth, all you need to type is

COPY TO target file type

The next listing shows several ways of using the COPY command with the TYPE qualifier. (This listing was generated with the SET ALTERNATE ON command.) The data from the EXPENSES.DBF file is shown there. III PLUS has been asked to DISPLAY that data to the screen. No delimiting or trimming is taking place. That same data is then COPYed to several other files, each using a different version of the TYPE qualifier.

```
-> use expenses
-> list
```

```
Record#  PAYTO
PAYFOR
CHECKNUM    PAYAMOUNT PAYDATE   MILEAGE

1


/  /
    2  Allstate                                       Rental
Insurance
tovisa           57.00 07/12/86       0.0
    3  Allstate                                       Auto
Expense
tovisa          246.00 07/12/86       0.0
    4  Susan Carrabis                                 Rent,
Utilities
tovisa          332.89 07/12/86       0.0
    5  Susan Carrabis                                 Office
Supplies
tovisa          298.00 07/12/86       0.0
    6
mileage

0.00 07/11/86   146.0
    7  NH Turnpike
Toll
cash              5.00 07/12/86       0.0
    8  Computer Town                                  Office
Supplies
cash             14.50 07/08/86       0.0
    9  Am Ex

Motel
1316             39.27 07/09/86       0.0
   10  Am Ex
Delphi
1316             27.95 07/09/86       0.0
   11
mileage

0.00 07/03/86    15.0
   12
Gas

cash              6.50 07/03/86       0.0
   13
Gas

cash             10.50 07/05/86       0.0
   14
mileage

0.00 07/07/86     6.0
   15  Ford Motor Credit                             Auto
Expense
1317            305.33 07/10/86       0.0
   16  Post Office
Postage
cash              1.72 07/12/86       0.0
```

```
-> copy to copysdf type sdf
-> copy to copydeli type delim with blank
-> copy to copydw type delim with /
-> copy to copydast delim with *
```

Consider the following listing:

```
Allstate                                    Rental
Insurance
tovisa          57.0019860712       0.0
Allstate                                    Auto
Expense
tovisa          246.0019860712      0.0
Susan Carrabis                              Rent,
Utilities
tovisa          332.8919860712      0.0
Susan Carrabis                              Office
Supplies
tovisa          298.0019860712      0.0
mileage

0.0019860711    146.0
NH Turnpike
Toll
cash            5.0019860712        0.0
Computer Town                               Office
Supplies
cash            14.5019860708       0.0
Am Ex
Motel
1316            39.2719860709       0.0
Am Ex
Delphi
1316            27.9519860709       0.0
mileage

0.0019860703    15.0
Gas

cash            6.5019860703        0.0
Gas

cash            10.5019860705       0.0
mileage

0.0019860707    6.0
Ford Motor Credit                           Auto
Expense
1317            305.3319860710      0.0
Post Office
Postage
cash            1.7219860712        0.0
```

It shows the result of the command

The data is COPYed to a TXT output file in the System Default Format.

What exactly is the System Default Format? Note that each data field in the COPYSDF file has the same length as the original data field in the EXPENSES.DBF file, each record in the COPYSDF file ends with a carriage return (ASCII 13), each record is a fixed length in the COPYSDF file, and there are no delimiters per se. This is a useful format if you need to get dBASE III PLUS data into some other system, such as a telecommunications application that can receive data in fixed-length format. Most often this type of output is used to format dBASE III PLUS data for applications written in languages such as BASIC, FORTRAN, and Pascal. These languages can read data in fixed-length format far more easily than they can read data and look for delimiters.

The second type of TXT data transmission is the DELIMITED WITH BLANK. An example of this command is

COPY TO COPYDELI TYPE DELIM WITH BLANK

The result of this command is shown in the following listing:

```
Allstate Rental Insurance tovisa 57.00 19860712 0.0
Allstate Auto Expense tovisa 246.00 19860712 0.0
Susan Carrabis Rent, Utilities tovisa 332.89 19860712 0.0
Susan Carrabis Office Supplies tovisa 298.00 19860712 0.0
mileage    0.00 19860711 146.0
NH Turnpike Toll cash 5.00 19860712 0.0
Computer Town Office Supplies cash 14.50 19860708 0.0
Am Ex Motel 1316 39.27 19860709 0.0
Am Ex Delphi 1316 27.95 19860709 0.0
mileage    0.00 19860703 15.0
Gas    cash 6.50 19860703 0.0
Gas    cash 10.50 19860705 0.0
mileage    0.00 19860707 6.0
Ford Motor Credit Auto Expense 1317 305.33 19860710 0.0
Post Office Postage cash 1.72 19860712 0.0
```

There was a time when several software programs could determine fields by looking for empty spaces (BLANKS) between the fields. This assumed there were no blank spaces in the data in the fields. Although there are still some systems that make use of this data format, you can see that it would be of little use with the EXPENSES.DBF file.

This doesn't mean you should cast off the DELIMITED WITH BLANK data TYPE easily. It provides a useful method of transmitting data, but be sure there are no blank spaces in the data before you use it. Using data assumed to be in this format but actually containing blanks in the data fields will cause incorrect data input.

You can also use a delimiting character to separate the data fields with the COPY command. This is shown in the following listings:

```
//,//,//,,,
/Allstate/,,/Rental Insurance/,/tovisa/,57.00,19860712,0.0
/Allstate/,,/Auto Expense/,/tovisa/,246.00,19860712,0.0
/Susan Carrabis/,,/Rent,
Utilities/,/tovisa/,332.89,19860712,0.0
/Susan Carrabis/,,/Office
Supplies/,/tovisa/,298.00,19860712,0.0
/mileage/,//,//,0.00,19860711,146.0
/NH Turnpike/,/Toll/,/cash/,5.00,19860712,0.0
/Computer Town/,/Office Supplies/,/cash/,14.50,19860708,0.0
/Am Ex/,/Motel/,/1316/,39.27,19860709,0.0
/Am Ex/,/Delphi/,/1316/,27.95,19860709,0.0
/mileage/,//,//,0.00,19860703,15.0
/Gas/,//,/cash/,6.50,19860703,0.0
/Gas/,//,/cash/,10.50,19860705,0.0
/mileage/,//,//,0.00,19860707,6.0
/Ford Motor Credit/,/Auto
Expense/,/1317/,305.33,19860710,0.0
/Post Office/,/Postage/,/cash/,1.72,19860712,0.0


**,**,**,,,
*Allstate*,*Rental Insurance*,*tovisa*,57.00,19860712,0.0
*Allstate*,*Auto Expense*,*tovisa*,246.00,19860712,0.0
*Susan Carrabis*,*Rent,
Utilities*,*tovisa*,332.89,19860712,0.0
*Susan Carrabis*,*Office
Supplies*,*tovisa*,298.00,19860712,0.0
*mileage*,**,**,0.00,19860711,146.0
*NH Turnpike*,*Toll*,*cash*,5.00,19860712,0.0
*Computer Town*,*Office Supplies*,*cash*,14.50,19860708,0.0
*Am Ex*,*Motel*,*1316*,39.27,19860709,0.0
*Am Ex*,*Delphi*,*1316*,27.95,19860709,0.0
*mileage*,**,**,0.00,19860703,15.0
*Gas*,**,*cash*,6.50,19860703,0.0
*Gas*,**,*cash*,10.50,19860705,0.0
*mileage*,**,**,0.00,19860707,6.0
*Ford Motor Credit*,*Auto
Expense*,*1317*,305.33,19860710,0.0
*Post Office*,*Postage*,*cash*,1.72,19860712,0.0
```

The commands that create these data formats are shown as

```
COPY TO COPYDW TYPE DELIM WITH /
COPY TO COPYAST DELIM WITH *
```

The DELIM WITH character data format always includes a comma (,) between fields. Any ASCII character can be used with this form of the command. This type of data formatting is useful when sending data to another software system that recognizes field breaks using a special character.

So much for TXT TYPE formats. How does dBASE III PLUS handle truly foreign formats such as SYLK, WKS, and DIF files? Quite well, actually. The data shown in earlier listings is shown in Lotus 1-2-3 WKS format in Figures 3-4 and 3-5.

Note how the data is placed into the 1-2-3 spreadsheet. Row 1 of the spreadsheet contains the field names from the original database. The data begins immediately below that. Figures 3-4 and 3-5 show

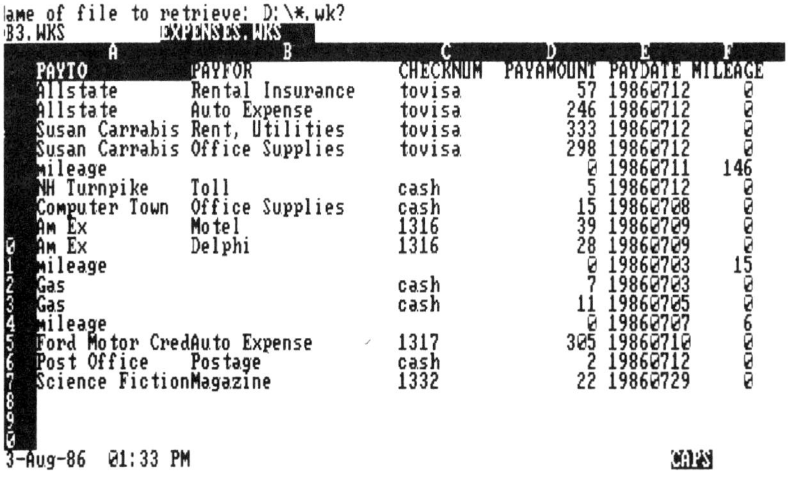

Figure 3-4. dBASE III PLUS creates Lotus 1-2-3 WKS files with the COPY TO destination WKS command

dBASE III PLUS: The Complete Reference

Row 2 as blank. That is due to including a blank record as the first record in the original database.

Note also that dBASE III PLUS produces Lotus 1-2-3 WKS files. The .WKS extension indicates that III PLUS is producing files compatible with 1-2-3 r1. The examples were done using 1-2-3 r2. That should not be a concern to anyone using either r1 or r2 of the 1-2-3. Figure 3-5 shows 1-2-3 r2 performing the conversion from an r1 to r2 spreadsheet format automatically when saving the file.

There are some other things to know about the COPY command. The COPY command assumes it is COPYing to another DBF file unless you specify otherwise with one of the TYPE options. The COPY command automatically creates a file with the .DBF extension unless you specify otherwise. You can specify otherwise either with a TYPE qualifier or by including a period (.) in the target filename in the command. An example of this is

COPY TO NEWFILE.

```
Enter save file name: D:\EXPENSES.WK1
File will be saved as .WK1
        A              B              C          D        E        F
 1  PAYTO          PAYFOR          CHECKNUM  PAYAMOUNT PAYDATE MILEAGE
 2  Allstate       Rental Insurance tovisa        57 19860712       0
 3  Allstate       Auto Expense    tovisa       246 19860712       0
 4  Susan Carrabis Rent, Utilities tovisa       333 19860712       0
 5  Susan Carrabis Office Supplies tovisa       298 19860712       0
 6  mileage                                       0 19860711     146
 7  NH Turnpike    Toll            cash           5 19860712       0
 8  Computer Town  Office Supplies cash          15 19860708       0
 9  Am Ex          Motel           1316          39 19860709       0
10  Am Ex          Delphi          1316          28 19860709       0
11  mileage                                       0 19860703      15
12  Gas                            cash           7 19860703       0
13  Gas                            cash          11 19860705       0
14  mileage                                       0 19860707       6
15  Ford Motor CredAuto Expense    1317         305 19860710       0
16  Post Office    Postage         cash           2 19860712       0
17  Science FictionMagazine        1332          22 19860729       0
18
19
20
13-Aug-86  01:37 PM                                          CAPS
```

Figure 3-5.   Lotus 1-2-3 r2 was used in these examples. 1-2-3 r2 reads in the dBASE III PLUS created WKS file, converts it to WK1 format, and saves the file

The period in the preceding command tells III PLUS to create a new database file but to call the file NEWFILE period. There is no extension on the file. To use the file later, you would have to request the name in the same way. For instance, to COPY to the file and then USE it, you would have to type

```
COPY TO NEWFILE.
USE NEWFILE.
```

Both the COPY and USE commands specify the filename with the period (.).

Also note that any associated DBT files are not included when COPYing to a TXT file (either SDF or DELIM TYPE options). They are included when COPYing to a foreign data format such as SYLK, DIF, or WKS.

Advanced Use   There are several ways to demonstrate advanced use of the COPY command. The example given in the following listing is based on the concept of masking information from a masterbase to a database and can be used in a networking situation with little modification. A networked system assumes this PRG file is being used by the system operator.

```
** C10COPY.PRG -> AN EXAMPLE OF THE COPY COMMAND
** THIS ROUTINE ASSUMES THERE ARE LESS THAN 70 FIELDS IN THE
** DBF
*
CLOSE ALL
SET CATA TO MASTER
USE ?
COPY STRUC EXTE TO SEFILE
SELE 2
USE SEFILE
NUMOFRECS = RECCOUNT()
NUMOFCOLS = 1
*
DO WHIL NUMOFRECS > 22
   NUMOFRECS = NUMOFRECS/2
   NUMOFCOLS = NUMOFCOLS + 1
ENDD
*
CLEA
@ 1,0 TO NUMOFRECS+1, (NUMOFCOLS+1)*10 + (NUMOFCOLS+1)
DOUBLE
ROWNUM = 2
COLNUM = 1
*
```

```
DO WHIL RECNO() < RECCOUNT()
   FIELD = FIELD(1)
   @ ROWNUM,COLNUM SAY &FIELD
*
   IF ROWNUM = NUMOFRECS
      ROWNUM = 2
      COLNUM = COLNUM + 11
   ELSE
      ROWNUM = ROWNUM + 1
   ENDI
*
   SKIP
ENDD
*
COPFIELDS = SPACE(100)
@ 23,0 SAY "FIELDS TO COPY (SEPARATE WITH ',' OR 'ALL')"+;
         " -> " GET COPFIELDS PICT "@S25"
READ
*
IF UPPER(TRIM(COPFIELDS)) = "ALL"
   COPFIELDS = ""
ELSE
   COPFIELDS = "FIELDS " + TRIM(COPFIELDS)
ENDI
*
CLEAR
ACCE "DESTINATION FILE NAME (8 CHAR MAX) -> " TO FILENAME
FILETYPE = SPACE(4)
ACCE "FILE TYPE (SDF, DELI, WKS, SYLK, DIF, " + ;
     "[RETURN FOR DBF]) -> " TO FILETYPE
*
DO CASE
   CASE LEN(TRIM(FILETYPE)) = 0
      FILETYPE = ""
   CASE FILETYPE = "DELI"
      ACCE "DELIMIT WITH (1 CHAR MAX, ' ' FOR BLANK) -> "+;
         TO DELIMCHAR
*
      FILETYPE = IIF(LEN(TRIM(DELIMCHAR) = 0, FILETYPE + ;
                 " WITH BLANK",FILETYPE+"WITH "+DELIMCHAR)
ENDC
*
? "COPY TO " + FILENAME + COPFIELDS + FILETYPE
USE
SELE 1
COPY TO &FILENAME +" "+&COPFIELDS+" "+&FILETYPE
ERAS SEFILE.DBF
*
** EOF
```

This PRG file uses some clever switching methods to build a command. Remember that your goal in working with this PRG file is to create a selective COPY option for the user.

You start by CLOSEing ALL the files. This includes the DBFs,

CATs, NDXes, and so on. Next, you SET the CATALOG file TO MASTER. This assumes the system has some MASTER CATALOG file that contains information on all the databases available to the system. The line

USE ?

is a function of the CAT file. The USE ? command tells III PLUS to list all available DBF files in the CATALOG.

A DBF file is chosen from the MASTER.CAT file via the USE ? command. The STRUCTURE of the chosen DBF file is COPYed to a generic, all-purpose file you call SEFILE (see the next section for more on the STRUCTURE EXTENDED COPY command). The name SEFILE is an acronym for Structure Extended FILE, a file similar to certain TANK files. The SEFILE and TANK files are meant to be used and deleted as necessary.

You can prepare to work on the SEFILE with SELE 2 and USE SEFILE. The SEFILE now has information you need to build your

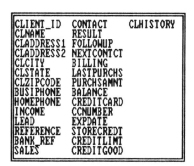

FIELDS TO COPY (SEPARATE WITH ',' OR 'ALL') -> :   :

Figure 3-6.   This screen is built by the two DO WHILE...ENDDO loops in the C10COPY.PRG file

next screen. The NUMOFRECS = RECCOUNT( ) command creates a variable with the number of records in the SEFILE. The number of records in the SEFILE corresponds to the number of fields in the database in work area 1. The two DO WHILE...ENDDO loops that follow build the screen shown in Figure 3-6.

It is pointless to generate a screen unless some information is either coming from or going to the user. This screen lets the user know what fields are available for copying. The @...SAY...GET command uses a SCROLL function in the PICTURE qualifier to the @...SAY...GET command (see Chapter 8 for more on the @... SAY...GET PICTURE command).

The rest of the commands in the listing simply build the rest of the COPY command by asking for a target filename and file type. Note that you don't need to ask for a directory, nor allow for one. That can be easily added. A networked version would also allow for setting access priorities on the fields and records, depending on who would use the target database.

COPY FILE

The COPY FILE command is used for the same reason that the DOS COPY command is used, to make an exact COPY of a source file. Like the DOS COPY command, the target file must have either a new name or be placed in a new directory.

Syntax   The COPY FILE command has the form

COPY FILE source.ext TO target.ext

There are no qualifiers allowed, as the command does not make use of any of dBASE III PLUS's special functions or abilities. It is similar in all ways to the DOS COPY command.

Note that, like the DOS COPY command, this command won't allow you to COPY a FILE to itself. The source and target files must include their extensions. If you want to COPY to or from a FILE that has no extension, you must use the period (.) to tell III PLUS that the particular file has no extension. Also note that the COPY FILE command only copies the FILE named as the source file. It does not COPY associated FILEs to the target.

Use   Use of the COPY FILE command is limited to its one specific function, but that one function is useful in several ways.

First, the COPY FILE command is internal to dBASE III PLUS. You don't have to exit to DOS to COPY files. This feature is useful when you want to make backups and reserve files of non-DBF files.

You can use the COPY command to make a variety of database file clones, but only the COPY FILE command can COPY non-DBF files from inside dBASE III PLUS. Therefore, the COPY command will COPY the associated DBT file.

The COPY FILE command only COPYs the source FILE, however. The command form is

COPY FILE source.ext TO target.ext

to make a copy of the named file. You can use the COPY FILE command to COPY a DBF file, but the COPY FILE command will not COPY any associated DBT (MEMO field) files. Those would need to be COPYed separately.

An example of the use of the COPY FILE command at its best is shown in Figure 3-7. Sometimes the system running III PLUS doesn't have enough memory to RUN an external program, even one as small as DOS' COPY. The solution is to use the COPY FILE command.

Note that the COPY FILE command will use paths and directories when they are given as part of the source and target filenames.

Advanced Use   An advanced use of the COPY FILE command comes from knowing that the COPY FILE command, like the DOS COPY command, is capable of going between directories and disks. This ability can be further enhanced by recognizing that the user may want to COPY associated FILEs as well.

The following routine is similar in many ways to the advanced COPY routine shown in the previous section. You start by DISPLAYing the FILE _NAME field of the MASTER.CAT database file, as it will contain all files relative to a given system. This is a quick and dirty way of showing the user what files are available for COPYing.

```
-> SET TALK ON
-> ! COPY C10.DBF E:
Insufficient memory
       ?
! COPY C10.DBF E:
-> COPY FILE C10.DBF TO E:C10.DBF
   2048 bytes copied
-> COPY FILE C10.DBF TO E:RALPHIE.DBF
   2048 bytes copied
-> COPY FILE EXPENSES.DBF TO G:TIC
   2560 bytes copied
-> ! COPY EXPENSES.DBF G:TIC
Insufficient memory
       ?
! COPY EXPENSES.DBF G:TIC
->
```

Figure 3-7. The COPY FILE command allows you to COPY and FILE without exiting DOS or using the ! command

The user types in the name of the FILE to COPY, the name of the target file, and a drive and directory designator.

```
** C10CFILE.PRG TO USE THE "COPY FILE" COMMAND
*
CLOSE ALL
USE MASTER.CAT
DISP ALL FILE_NAME
FILENAME = SPACE(12)
TARGETNAME = SPACE(8)
DAD = SPACE(20)
CLEA
ACCE "WHAT FILE TO COPY -> " TO FILENAME
ACCE "DESTINATION FILE NAME (8 CHAR MAX) -> " TO TARGETNAME
ACCE "DRIVE AND DIRECTORY (20 CHAR MAX) -> " TO DAD
TARGETNAME = TRIM(DAD) + TRIM(TARGETNAME)
YORN = .F.
@ 10,0 SAY "COPY ASSOCIATED FILES (Y/N) ? -> " ;
       GET YORN PICT "Y"
READ
*
IF YORN
   LOCA FOR UPPER(FILE_NAME) = UPPER(FILENAME)
   FINDER = CODE
   *
   IF FINDER = 0
       FILENAME = LEFT(FILE_NAME,AT(".",FILE_NAME))
```

```
            GOTO 1
            LOCA FOR UPPER(FILE_NAME) = UPPER(FILENAME)
       *
            DO WHILE .NOT. EOF()
                SOURCE = FILE_NAME
                DESTINATION = TARGETNAME + RIGHT(FILE_NAME,;
                            AT(".",FILE_NAME))
                COPY FILE &SOURCE TO &DESTINATION
                CONT
            ENDD
       *
       ELSE
            GOTO 1
            LOCA FOR CODE = FINDER
       *
            DO WHIL .NOT. EOF()
                SOURCE = FILE_NAME
                DESTINATION = TARGETNAME + RIGHT(FILE_NAME,;
                            AT(".",FILE_NAME))
                COPY FILE &SOURCE TO &DESTINATION
                CONT
            ENDD
       *
       ENDI
       *
ELSE
    COPY FILE &FILENAME TO &TARGETNAME
ENDI
*
** EOF
```

The next important step is to find out whether the user wants to COPY only one FILE or all associated files. VUE files summon their own files and have a CATALOG code of 0. Finding files associated with a VUE file involves getting part of the VUE filename and using that as a key to LOCATE like-named files. (Note that it is assumed here that associated files have like names, for this program to work as intended.)

COPYing associated FILEs is much easier if the user calls some other file. The C10CFILE.PRG program uses the CATALOG code value of the source file to LOCATE associated files.

COPY STRUCTURE

The COPY STRUCTURE command is a special case of the COPY command. The COPY STRUCTURE command is not to be confused with the COPY STRUCTURE EXTENDED command, covered in the next section.

Syntax   The syntax of the COPY STRUCTURE command is identical to that of the COPY command, with the exception that only the FIELDS qualifier is valid. The fact that only the FIELDS qualifier is valid is due to the purpose of the COPY STRUCTURE command.

The COPY STRUCTURE command serves the sole purpose of making duplicates of the source database's structure. The structure of any database can be seen by putting a database in USE, then typing

DISPLAY STRUCTURE

as shown in Figure 3-8.

```
-> DISP STRUC
Structure for database: D:7TANK.dbf
Number of data records:       0
Date of last update  :  08/13/86
Field  Field Name  Type        Width    Dec
    1   NAME        Character      30
    2   ADDRESS     Character      30
    3   CITY        Character      20
    4   STATE       Character       2
    5   ZIPCODE     Character      10
    6   BUSIPHONE   Character      14
    7   HOMEPHONE   Character      14
    8   INFO        Memo           10
    9   LASTPURCHS  Date            8
   10   LASTPAYMNT  Numeric        10       2
   11   BALANCE     Numeric        10       2
   12   CREDIT      Logical         1
   13   CREDITGOOD  Logical         1
   14   CREDITLIMT  Numeric        10       2
** Total **                      171

->
```

Figure 3-8.   The DISPLAY STRUCTURE command lists the different fields and their characteristics to the screen

The syntax of the simplest form of the command is

COPY STRUCTURE TO target

You can COPY fields of the source file selectively to the target by including the FIELDS qualifier in the command, as shown.

COPY STRUCTURE TO target FIELDS field1,field2,...

Note that you are only COPYing the STRUCTURE of the source file, not records, nor are you COPYing WHILE certain conditions are met or FOR a particular set of circumstances. Because you are only COPYing the STRUCTURE of the source file, the only valid qualifier is FIELDS. FIELDS tells III PLUS which fields in the source file to COPY to the target file.

Use   Use of the COPY STRUCTURE command is limited to COPYing the STRUCTURE of the source database to the target database. Note that this command cannot be used to COPY files, records, or data in fields. But its limitation is its strength.

A working database system often has need of database shells. That is where the COPY STRUCTURE command shows its strength. Consider the following block of code:

```
USE dbffile1
COPY STRUC TO dbffile1.SHL
USE dbffile2
COPY STRUC TO dbffile2.SHL
USE dbffile3
COPY STRUC TO dbffile3.SHL
  . .       .      .      .      .
  . .       .      .      .      .
  . .       .      .      .      .
```

The block of code is simple and is meant to be used interactively, but at a crucial time. The specific time is when you've finished designing the database files for your application.

You can keep empty versions of your databases on a disk by COPYing their STRUCTUREs to SHeLl files. The SHL file is an empty database made up of nothing more than the structure to some other database. It is the database shell.

An alternative version of the command includes the FIELDS qualifier. The command becomes

COPY STRUC TO target FIELDS field1, field2,...

This use of the COPY STRUCTURE command is similar to the one detailed earlier, except you use an empty masterbase to create the smaller, working databases for the system. The single masterbase is saved on a storage disk and only used when the smaller, working databases are destroyed and the user needs a replacement file. An example of this use is shown in the following listing:

```
USE masterbase
COPY STRUC TO dbffile1 FIELDS
field1,field2,field3,field4,field5
COPY STRUC TO dbffile2 FIELDS
field6,field7,field8,field9,field10
COPY STRUC TO dbffile3 FIELDS
field11,field12,field13,field14,;
   field15,field16,field17,field18,field19,field20,field21
 . .      .      .      .
 . .      .      .      .
 . .      .      .      .
```

Note that fields are grouped together even though you're creating separate files from the masterbase.

Advanced Use   Perhaps the most common use of the COPY STRUCTURE command has to do with data entry. You never want to add data directly to your databases. Adding data, even one record, takes a long time. Adding data directly to a database means having a database open and subject to all the vagaries of fluctuations in line voltage and current, memory failure, disk crashes, overheated board components, and passing electrons. All of these are bad news for your database, as any one of them can destroy a database.

One way to keep this from happening is to add data to a temporary file that does nothing but act as a tank. The following code shows how to use the COPY STRUCTURE command to prevent anything from happening to a database during data addition:

```
COPY STRUC TO TANK
SELE 2
USE TANK
a 20,0 CLEA
a 22,0 SAY "Type CTL-W to save information, " + ;
          "CTL-Q to exit"
```

```
                REPEATER = FIELD(1)
    *
                DO WHIL .T.
                    APPE BLAN
                    DO &GETTER
                    READ
    *
                    IF LEN(TRIM(&REPEATER)) = 0
                        DELE
                        EXIT
                    ENDI
    *
                ENDD
    *
                USE
                SELE 1
                SET DELE ON
                APPE FROM TANK
                SET DELE OFF
                DO &GETTER
                CLEA GETS
                DO EDITMENU
                ERAS TANK.DBF
```

The command of interest starts off the session. The STRUC-
TURE of the primary-use database is COPYed to a temporary TANK
file. That file is then USEd in work area 2. When you finish adding
(APPENDing) records, you exit from the module. The TANK.DBF
file is closed with the naked USE command, work area 1 is again
SELECTed, and the records in the TANK.DBF file are APPENDed
to the primary database.

You SET DELETE ON to make sure the last, empty record is
not APPENDed to your primary database. The reason for the naked
USE command is to ensure that you're able to ERASE the TANK.DBF
file. dBASE III PLUS will not ERASE an in-USE file.

The program also makes use of GETTER files and assumes that
a database is already in USE and a SAY file has been executed. This
method ensures that nothing happens to your databases during the
addition of data.

COPY STRUCTURE EXTENDED

The COPY STRUCTURE EXTENDED command is another single-
use command that follows the syntax of COPY and COPY STRUC-
TURE but is limited in what it can do. Like most things that are

limited, the one thing it does do can be useful and powerful. The "Advanced Use" section shows how to use the COPY STRUCTURE EXTENDED command to customize databases during a work session.

Syntax   The COPY STRUCTURE EXTENDED command is identical to the COPY STRUCTURE command.

COPY STRUCTURE EXTENDED TO target file

It also allows the use of the FIELDS qualifiers, as in

COPY STRU EXTE TO target file FIELDS field1, field2,...

Note that the preceding line uses the dBASE four-letter-word convention.

Use   The COPY STRUCTURE EXTENDED command performs a special COPY operation on the source file. Specifically, it copies information about the fields in the source file to the target database. At this point, it might be useful to show the similarities and differences the COPY STRUCTURE EXTENDED command has with the other types of COPY commands.

Like the COPY and COPY STRUCTURE commands, the COPY STRUCTURE EXTENDED command creates a database. Unlike the other COPY commands, the COPY STRUCTURE EXTENDED target file bears little resemblance to the source file. Like the COPY command, the COPY STRUCTURE EXTENDED command takes information from the source file and places it in the target file. Unlike the COPY command, the COPY STRUCTURE EXTENDED command doesn't COPY data, records, or the individual fields of the source database.

The unique feature of the COPY STRUCTURE EXTENDED command is that it creates a target file that contains only information about the fields in the source file. Note the difference between this command and the COPY STRUCTURE command. The COPY STRUCTURE command COPYs the database fields from the source file to the target file. The COPY STRUCTURE EXTENDED command COPYs only information about the source database's fields to the target file.

Every database created by the COPY STRUCTURE EXTENDED command has the same form, no matter what the source database looks like. The field STRUCTURE of a COPY STRUCTURE EXTENDED target file is shown in Figure 3-9.

This file contains only four fields. Note that the four fields correspond to the information the dBASEs need to know to place a data field in a database. That is the data that the COPY STRUCTURE EXTENDED command places in the target file, as shown in Figure 3-10.

Note that the DISPLAY ALL command used on the COPY STRUCTURE EXTENDED file in Figure 3-10 gives the same information about the source file as Figure 3-8's DISPLAY STRUCTURE command. That is where the power of the command can be put to good use.

The other aspect of the COPY STRUCTURE EXTENDED file worth noting is that you can use the FIELDS qualifier on it. This form of the command allows you to be selective in what fields are COPYed to the STRUCTURE EXTENDED file. In this respect, the

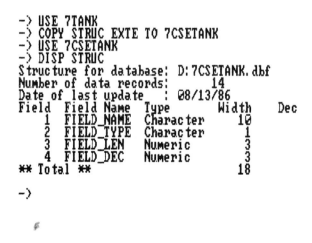

```
-> USE 7TANK
-> COPY STRUC EXTE TO 7CSETANK
-> USE 7CSETANK
-> DISP STRUC
Structure for database: D:7CSETANK.dbf
Number of data records:        14
Date of last update    : 08/13/86
Field  Field Name  Type       Width    Dec
    1  FIELD_NAME  Character      10
    2  FIELD_TYPE  Character       1
    3  FIELD_LEN   Numeric         3
    4  FIELD_DEC   Numeric         3
** Total **                       18

->
```

Figure 3-9. Every file created by the COPY STRUCTURE EXTENDED command contains these four fields, no matter what the source database contains

COPY STRUCTURE EXTENDED command behaves similarly to the COPY STRUCTURE command.

CREATE database

The CREATE command is the basic tool for designing databases. There is no advanced use for the CREATE command. It can be used in the PROGRAMming mode, but it performs clumsily in that arena.

The CREATE command is primarily used in the INTERACTIVE (dBASE prompt) mode.

Syntax   The syntax of the CREATE command is elegant and simple. The form is

CREATE database

```
-> DISP ALL
Record#    FIELD_NAME FIELD_TYPE FIELD_LEN FIELD_DEC
    1      NAME       C                30         0
    2      ADDRESS    C                30         0
    3      CITY       C                20         0
    4      STATE      C                 2         0
    5      ZIPCODE    C                10         0
    6      BUSIPHONE  C                14         0
    7      HOMEPHONE  C                14         0
    8      INFO       M                10         0
    9      LASTPURCHS D                 8         0
   10      LASTPAYMNT N                10         2
   11      BALANCE    N                10         2
   12      CREDIT     L                 1         0
   13      CREDITGOOD L                 1         0
   14      CREDITLIMT N                10         2
->
```

Figure 3-10.   The information in the COPY STRUCTURE EXTENDED file is identical to that shown when the DISPLAY STRUCTURE command is used on the source file

Used as shown, the CREATE command will instruct dBASE III PLUS to start the database design screen. The design screen will appear in one of two formats, depending on the MENU setting. Setting either the SET MENU or CONFIG.DB MENU command ON will cause III PLUS to show the screen in Figure 3-11. Setting MENUs off will show the screen in Figure 3-12. You use the F1 key to toggle the MENU ON or off in either mode.

Note that this command only CREATEs databases. Many of the other CREATE commands are synonymous with their MODIFY counterparts. This is not the case with the CREATE database command. The only way to alter an existing database is through the MODIFY STRUCTURE command (see Chapter 4).

Use   CREATE tells III PLUS to begin designing a DBF file. You must follow the command with a modifier to design anything other than a database (see following sections in this chapter).

There are two basic ways to start the CREATE database part

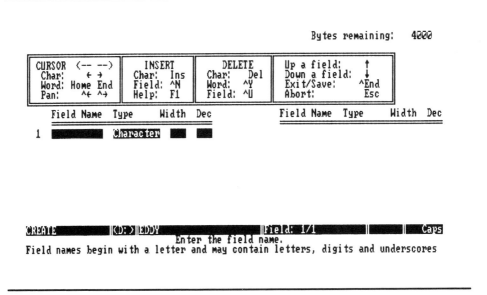

Figure 3-11.   The CREATE design screen with MENUs ON

of III PLUS. The first method is to use the CREATE command from the dBASE prompt as follows:

```
CREATE database
```

dBASE III PLUS assumes the database will have the .DBF extension unless you tell it otherwise. You can create a database without an extension by telling dBASE to

```
CREATE database.
```

The period (.) in the preceding command line is important. It tells III PLUS that the database file will not have an extension. But remember that CREATEing a database without an extension means you'll have to USE the database without an extension, as in

```
USE database.
```

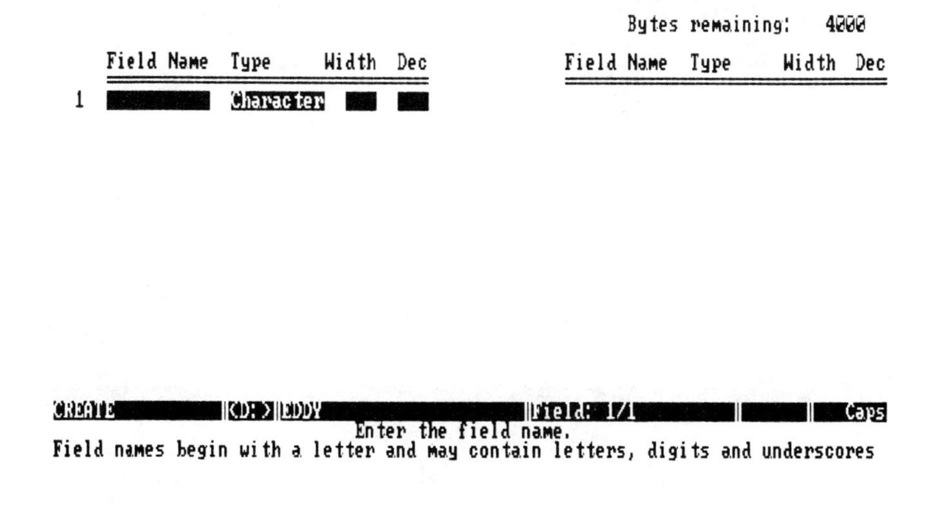

Bytes remaining: 4000
Field Name Type Width Dec
Field Name Type Width Dec
1 Character
CREATE <D:> EDDY Field: 1/1 Caps
Enter the field name.
Field names begin with a letter and may contain letters, digits and underscores

Figure 3-12. The CREATE design screen with MENUs off

Again, the period in the command is important. CREATEing a database without an extension and then trying to USE that database without letting III PLUS know that the DBF file has no extension will cause III PLUS to tell you the database can't be found.

A similar situation can arise when you CREATE a database with a nonstandard extension. III PLUS allows you to use any three-character string as the extension but will look only for database files with the .DBF extension unless you tell it otherwise. You must tell III PLUS the full name of the file to USE if you CREATE a database file with an extension other than .DBF.

The other method for CREATEing databases works through the ASSIST mode shown in Figure 3-13. This is a purely interactive, menu-driven mode. Note that once you've moved the cursor to the CREATE menu and selected DATABASE FILE, you are back in the CREATE design mode.

Command: CREATE

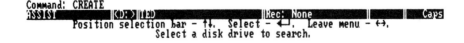

Position selection bar - ↑↓. Select - ↵. Leave menu - ↔.
Select a disk drive to search.

Figure 3-13. The ASSIST mode also allows you to CREATE databases

The COPY STRUCTURE EXTENDED command was described earlier. In that section, it was also mentioned that the other side of the COPY STRUCTURE EXTENDED command is the CREATE FROM command. This command follows the syntax and rules of the CREATE command, except it only works with a structure-extended file. There is no advanced use for this command.

Syntax   The CREATE FROM command is useful in that it allows you to automate the process of database design partially. The syntax of the command is similar to that of the CREATE command.

CREATE database FROM structure extended file

The command has no qualifiers. Note that the command will only create DBF files and that a structure-extended file must be used. (See the "COPY STRUCTURE EXTENDED" section earlier in this chapter for more information on the structure-extended file.)

Use   The CREATE FROM command is used mostly as an interactive command. It cannot be accessed through any menu system. The power of the CREATE FROM command is that it lets you design your own menu systems to create DBF files.

The command takes information from a structure-extended file. All structure-extended files have four fields in common: FIELD_NAME, FIELD_TYPE, FIELD_LEN, and FIELD_DEC (see Figure 3-10). These four fields and the information in them are automatically created when the COPY STRUCTURE EXTENDED command is used.

The records in the structure-extended file contain information about the structure of the source database that was used in the COPY STRUCTURE EXTENDED command. The information in each record is similar to that shown in a DISPLAY STRUCTURE command. The fact that this information is now in an editable DBF form allows you to make changes to the structure of the source database without going through the interactive design screen.

Changes made to the structure-extended file can then be used to modify the structure of the source file with the CREATE FROM command. You will be warned you are going to write over an existing file if you try to CREATE an existing name FROM a structure-extended file. A safer method for using the CREATE FROM command is shown in the following listing:

```
CREATE TANK FROM structure extended file
USE TANK
APPEND FROM source database
RENAME (source database).DBF TO (source database).SAV
RENAME TANK.DBF TO (source database).DBF
```

It shows a method for using the CREATE FROM command that preserves the source database for backup purposes. A temporary TANK database is CREATEd FROM the structure-extended file based on the source database. Data from the source database is APPENDed to TANK.DBF FROM the source database. The source database is RENAMEd TO something else. In this case, the source database was given a .SAV extension. The last step is to RENAME the TANK.DBF file TO the original source filename.

CREATE LABEL

The CREATE LABEL command is an interactive command. It can be accessed either at the dBASE prompt or through the ASSIST module. Like many of the form-creation commands, it can create forms — labels, in this case — that get data from several sources. That ability is shown in the Use section.

Syntax   The syntax of the CREATE LABEL command is

CREATE LABEL label file

This command tells III PLUS to activate the LABEL LBL design menu (Figure 3-14). You must have a database open in the currently selected work area to CREATE a LABEL. III PLUS will ask for a database to USE if one isn't currently open and active.

The CREATE LABEL command is synonymous with the MOD-IFY LABEL command.

Use   LBL files are linked to a particular database at their creation. They do not need to be linked to any one database in particular, as their primary involvement is with the structure of the database and not the database name. This can pose a problem when an LBL file is either created or used when a CAT file is open.

Figures 3-15 and 3-16 show two different databases that share the same structure. The field names, field types, field lengths, and number of decimal places for numeric fields are identical. One LBL file was created for the database shown in Figure 3-15. This one LBL file can be used for any number of similarly structured DBF files.

A problem can occur when you try to use an LBL file for a database other than the one it was created with if a CAT file is open. The CAT file tells III PLUS which files are associated with which other files. This occurs only when you ask the CAT file to tell you what LBL files are available. It is due to the way in which the CAT file keeps track of files. It knows you CREATEd the LABEL file when a certain DBF file was in USE. Unfortunately, the CAT file is not as crea-

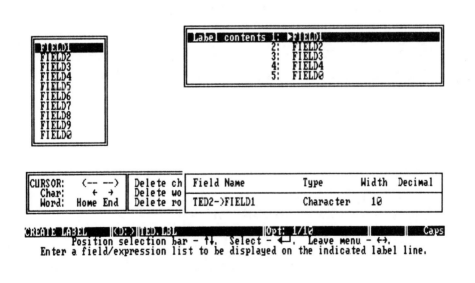

Figure 3-14.   The LABEL design menu. The MENU can be toggled ON and off with the F1 key

```
-> USE TED
-> DISP STRUC
Structure for database: D:TED.dbf
Number of data records:        0
Date of last update   : 08/14/86
Field  Field Name  Type        Width     Dec
    1  FIELD1      Character      10
    2  FIELD2      Character      10
    3  FIELD3      Character      10
    4  FIELD4      Character      10
    5  FIELD5      Character      10
    6  FIELD6      Character      10
    7  FIELD7      Character      10
    8  FIELD8      Character      10
    9  FIELD9      Character      10
   10  FIELD0      Character      10
** Total **                     101

-> LABEL FORM TED
->
```

Figure 3-15. The LBL file was created by first linking it to this database

tive in its use of files as you can be and links that LBL file to that DBF file.

You can access the LBL file for a particular DBF file other than the one you CREATEd it with simply by using the command

LABEL label file

The CAT file, if open, will then ask for information on the LBL file when used with the in-USE DBF file.

Note that either the open database and the LBL file have to be in the same work area or the LBL file should point to the active work area. If they are not in the same work area, III PLUS gives you an error message.

Advanced Use An advanced use of the CREATE LABEL command has to do with the fact that all the form-generating commands

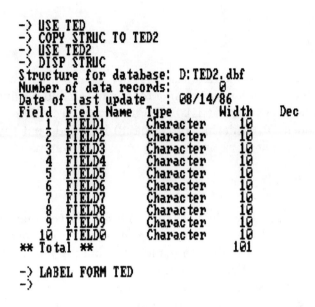

```
-> USE TED
-> COPY STRUC TO TED2
-> USE TED2
-> DISP STRUC
Structure for database: D:TED2.dbf
Number of data records:      0
Date of last update   : 08/14/86
Field  Field Name  Type       Width    Dec
    1   FIELD1      Character      10
    2   FIELD2      Character      10
    3   FIELD3      Character      10
    4   FIELD4      Character      10
    5   FIELD5      Character      10
    6   FIELD6      Character      10
    7   FIELD7      Character      10
    8   FIELD8      Character      10
    9   FIELD9      Character      10
   10   FIELD0      Character      10
** Total **                      101

-> LABEL FORM TED
->
```

Figure 3-16. The LBL file created for Figure 3-15 can be used for any database with a structure similar to the structure of the database shown in Figure 3-15

(LABEL, REPORT, SCREEN, and, of course, VIEW) can be used with more than one open database.

The dBASE III PLUS standard is to use a single database in a single work area. Normally, you would open several DBFs by USEing them in several work areas, as shown in the following listing:

```
SELE 1
USE dba
SELE 2
USE dbb
SELE 3
USE dbc
SELE 4
USE dbd
SELE 5
USE dbe
SELE 6
USE dbf
```

```
SELE 7
USE dbg
SELE 8
USE dbh
SELE 9
USE dbi
```

Note that only nine database files are open in this listing.

The reason for not opening ten databases and placing them in the ten work areas is that III PLUS uses work area 10 for the CAT file. Any open DBF file in work area 10 is closed, and the CAT file is placed in that work area when you use the command

SET CATALOG TO catalog file

You must have the CONFIG.SYS FILES command up to at least 20 to open this many files. A good working number is 25 for the CONFIG.SYS FILES command, especially if you intend to use several DBFs and their NDX files.

Back to advanced LBL files: You can use several open DBFs in the design of your LBL form simply by telling III PLUS in what area specific data lies. For example, you have client-address data in work area 1. That makes up most of the label. You also have routing information in work area 2 and account information in work area 3. A field from each of these two areas also goes on the label. Figure 3-17 shows how you use the work-area designators to tell III PLUS what work area the information lies in. Once the LABEL is CREATEd, it is saved.

Remember that this LBL now needs information from all three databases to work properly, and those three databases must be in the three work areas exactly as they were when the LABEL was CREATEd. If they are not, you'll see an error message.

What does the finished LABEL look like? Look at Figure 3-18.

CREATE QUERY

The CREATE QUERY command is an interactive command much like the CREATE LABEL and CREATE SCREEN commands. These commands generate files that perform actions on the open data-

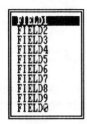

```
┌─────────────┐        ┌──────────────────────────────────┐
│▐FIELD1      │        │Label contents 1: ▶A->FIELD1      │
│ FIELD2      │        │               2:  A->FIELD2      │
│ FIELD3      │        │               3:  A->FIELD3      │
│ FIELD4      │        │               4:  B->FIELD4      │
│ FIELD5      │        │               5:  C->FIELD5      │
│ FIELD6      │        └──────────────────────────────────┘
│ FIELD7      │
│ FIELD8      │
│ FIELD9      │
│ FIELD0      │
└─────────────┘
```

CURSOR:	<-- -->	Delete ch	Field Name	Type	Width	Decimal
Char:	← →	Delete wo				
Word:	Home End	Delete ro	TED->FIELD1	Character	10	

```
CREATE LABEL      |(D:)TEDALL3.LBL           |Opt: 1/10           |          Caps
```
Position selection bar - ↑↓. Select - ⏎. Leave menu - ↔.
Enter a field/expression list to be displayed on the indicated label line.

Figure 3-17. This LBL file pulls information from three databases in work areas 1, 2, and 3

```
-> LABEL FORM TEDALL3
Joseph-David Carrabis        Susan Klink Carrabis        Donna Funteral
32 Foxmoor Circle            32 Foxmoor Circle           Strawberry Bank
Nashua, NH                   Nashua, NH                  Portsmouth, NH
03063                        03063                       03063
CARRJD0001                   CARRSK0001                  FUNTDC0001

Bruce Klink                  Bernadette Perry            John Scullin
24 Danbury Rd                90 Sherborne St             husband of Sandra
Nashua, NH                   Manchester, NH              also in Stoughton
03062                        03105                       02202
KLINBR0001                   PERRBC0001                  SCULJR0001

Sandra Scullin
somewhere in
Stoughton, Ma
02202
SCULSR0001

->
```

Figure 3-18. These are samples of the LABELs created in this section

base. The CREATE QUERY command opens a menu system that prompts you for information necessary to design a filter for use in a work session. The file generated has a .QRY extension. This command is identical to the MODIFY QUERY command.

There is no advanced use of this command, as each QRY file is linked to only one active database in one work area at a time.

Syntax The CREATE QUERY command is an interactive, menu-driven command that allows you to create custom filters for use in your III PLUS applications. The command form is

CREATE QUERY qry file

The CREATE QUERY command needs to know what database it is being designed for and the QUERY filename.

Use The power of the CREATE QUERY command lies in its ability to generate files in a code III PLUS uses to place limits on working databases. The limits, also called filters, tell III PLUS what to look for and what to ignore when working with databases. For example, to find all the active clients in Manchester, New Hampshire, in a database, you could use

DISPLAY ALL FOR ACTIVE .AND. CITY = "MANCHESTER" .AND. ;
    STATE = "NH"

where ACTIVE is a logical field that is either TRUE (the client is active) or FALSE (the client isn't active). Note that you must use the semicolon (;) to tell III PLUS that the command is continued on the next line. This command tells III PLUS to DISPLAY only the records that meet the included condition.

A QRY file that tells III PLUS to meet that same condition is easily generated in the menu system. Figure 3-19 shows how this type of filter appears in the CREATE QUERY menu system.

The CREATE QUERY command allows the designer to set up filters that might be common to a given application. The filter above

ACTIVE .AND. CITY = "MANCHESTER" .AND. STATE = "NH"

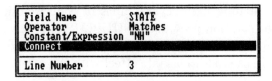

```
┌──────────────────────────────────────────────────┐
│ Field Name            STATE                       │
│ Operator              Matches                     │
│ Constant/Expression   "NH"                        │
│ Connect                                           │
│ ─────────────────────────────────────────────────│
│ Line Number           3                           │
└──────────────────────────────────────────────────┘
```

Line	Field	Operator	Constant/Expression	Connect
1	ACTIVE			.AND.
2	CITY	Matches	"MANCHESTER"	.AND.
3	STATE	Matches	"NH"	
4				
5				
6				
7				

CREATE QUERY   <D:>GREGORY.QRY   Opt: 4/5   Caps
      Position selection bar - ↑↓. Select - ◄─┘. Leave menu - ◄→.
        Select a logical connector for the filter condition.

Figure 3-19.   This QRY will tell III PLUS to show only records that
                 match the condition ACTIVE .AND. CITY = "MAN-
                 CHESTER" .AND. STATE = "NH"

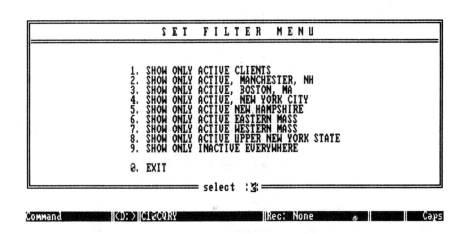

```
            S E T   F I L T E R   M E N U
    ════════════════════════════════════════════════

        1. SHOW ONLY ACTIVE CLIENTS
        2. SHOW ONLY ACTIVE, MANCHESTER, NH
        3. SHOW ONLY ACTIVE, BOSTON, MA
        4. SHOW ONLY ACTIVE, NEW YORK CITY
        5. SHOW ONLY ACTIVE NEW HAMPSHIRE
        6. SHOW ONLY ACTIVE EASTERN MASS
        7. SHOW ONLY ACTIVE WESTERN MASS
        8. SHOW ONLY ACTIVE UPPER NEW YORK STATE
        9. SHOW ONLY INACTIVE EVERYWHERE

        0. EXIT

    ═══════════════ select :█ ═══════════════
```

Command   <D:>GREGORY   Rec: None   Caps

Figure 3-20.   A sample QRY file-selection menu

might be needed throughout a work session. It would be tedious to have to repeat that condition in various commands throughout a work session, and having to include it in several lines of code would be equally frustrating. The solution provided by III PLUS is to use the CREATE QUERY command to design the QRY file with the proper conditions and then call those conditions into effect with the command

SET FILTER TO FILE qry file

The system designer, who can prognosticate 99-100% of the needs of the user, can use the interactive CREATE QUERY command to create several QRY files that can be selected by the user during a work session. An example of a menu system used to select filters is shown in Figure 3-20.

```
-> SELE 1
-> USE TED
-> SELE 2
-> USE TED2
-> SELE 3
-> USE TED3
-> SELE 1
-> REPO FORM TEDREPT RECORD(1)
         Page No.    1
         08/14/86
                              REPORT FORM USING 3 DATABASES

         FIELD1              DBF B FIELD4         DBF C FIELD0

         Joseph-David Carrabi C/O NORTHERN LIGHTS  CARRJD0001
-> 
```

Figure 3-21.   An FRM file created to use three databases in work areas 1, 2, and 3

dBASE III PLUS: The Complete Reference

```
-> SELE 1
-> USE TED
-> SELE 2
-> USE TED2
-> SELE 3
-> USE TED3
-> SELE 2
-> REPO FORM TEDREPT RECORD(1)
        Page No.     1
        08/14/86
                            REPORT FORM USING 3 DATABASES

        FIELD1              DBF B FIELD4        DBF C FIELD0


        7221-889            C/O NORTHERN LIGHTS  CARRJD0001

->
```

Figure 3-22. This FRM is identical to the one shown in Figure 3-21, except that here the second work area is left active

```
-> SELE 1
-> USE TED
-> SELE 2
-> USE TED2
-> SELE 3
-> USE TED3
-> REPO FORM TEDREPT RECORD(1)
        Page No.     1
        08/14/86
                            REPORT FORM USING 3 DATABASES

        FIELD1              DBF B FIELD4        DBF C FIELD0


        CORP BUY            C/O NORTHERN LIGHTS  CARRJD0001

->
```

Figure 3-23. This FRM is identical to the one used in Figures 3-21 and 3-22, but work area 3 is left active

CREATE REPORT

The CREATE REPORT command is an interactive command that is identical in all ways to the CREATE LABEL command except that it produces FRM files. For details, see the CREATE LABEL command earlier in this chapter.

However, the technique of using several open databases with a REPORT FORM has its hazards, as illustrated in Figures 3-21, 3-22, and 3-23. If the databases share similar fields, it doesn't matter where the FRM gets data. All three databases have the same structure; thus, the FRM doesn't have to be called from work area 1 to find a FIELD1 data field. If you design databases such as these (that is, databases that share structures but not data), you must be sure you call the FRM from the correct work area.

Another method for using an FRM file with several open databases is to use the SET VIEW TO and SET RELATION TO commands. Both commands allow REPORTs to be generated with several active related files. More information on relating databases is in the CREATE VIEW command section later in this chapter.

CREATE SCREEN

The CREATE SCREEN command is an interactive command, much like the CREATE QUERY command. Both commands generate files that perform actions on the open database.

This command is also similar to the MODIFY SCREEN command, with the exception that the MODIFY SCREEN command loads an existing FMT file into memory. The CREATE SCREEN command does not.

Syntax The CREATE SCREEN command allows you to create custom @...SAY...GET files easily for transferring data from the user to the database and vice versa. The command form is

CREATE SCREEN fmt file

The CREATE SCREEN command needs to know what database it is being designed for and the SCREEN filename. The CREATE SCREEN command is also accessible through the ASSIST menus. SCREENs are CREATEd on the ASSIST menu through the CREATE FORMAT option.

You must USE a database before you'll be allowed to leave the setup stage of the CREATE SCREEN menu system. A database can be put in USE either before typing the CREATE SCREEN command or from the SETUP DATABASE option.

Set Up　　　　Modify　　　　Options　　　　Exit

```
Screen Field Definition
 Action:   Display/SAY
 Source:   TED
 Content:
 Type:
 Width:
 Decimal:

 Picture Function:
 Picture Template:
 Range:
```

CREATE SCREEN   C:\TEDSCR.SCR   Opt: None
Position selection bar - ↑↓, Select - ↵, Leave menu - ↔, Blackbo

Figure 3-24. The CREATE SCREEN menu system

Use   The power of the CREATE SCREEN command lies in its ability to generate well-designed input/output screens. The CREATE SCREEN command activates the menu system shown in Figure 3-24. The user can move data fields simply by placing the cursor on them and typing RETURN. The system then prompts you for information on where to move the field. This menu system also allows you to add lines and boxes to your screen image through the OPTIONS command on the menu, as shown in Figure 3-25.

Once your screen is designed to your liking, you move the cursor to the EXIT SAVE option. This tells III PLUS to create two files for your future use. The first file has an .SCR extension and a file of the actual screen you've laid out. The second file is the FMT file that translates your screen image into @...SAY and @...GET commands. The MODIFY SCREEN and CREATE SCREEN commands use the SCR file to redesign screen images when you type either

CREATE SCREEN (existing) scr file

or

MODIFY SCREEN (existing) scr file

You should be aware that the CREATE SCREEN command allows you to design custom FMT files more than one screen length long, which is sometimes necessary. The advantage to using FMT files that cover several screen pages is that III PLUS automatically knows how to shuttle between the screens. Either you or the CREATE SCREEN command will place READ commands where you want screen breaks to occur. Then use the PGUP and PGDN keys to shuttle between the screens. Note that you can't shuttle up once you've RETURNed and CONFIRMed the last GET in the last screen.

CREATE VIEW

The CREATE VIEW command offers a means of setting up a file that contains information on what is happening in the dBASE III PLUS system at a specific time. That file could include information

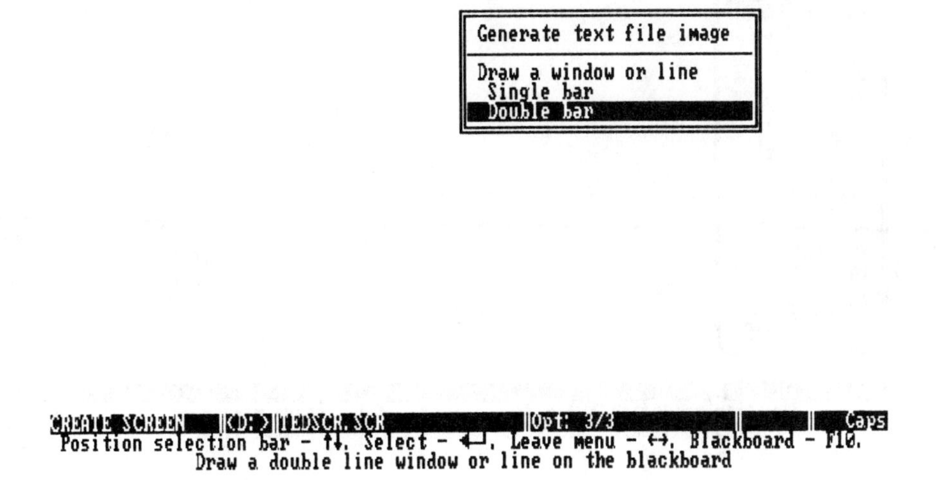

```
┌─────────────────────────────────┐
│ Generate text file image        │
├─────────────────────────────────┤
│ Draw a window or line           │
│    Single bar                   │
│ ▌Double bar                     │
└─────────────────────────────────┘
```

CREATE SCREEN   C:DE>TEDSCR.SCR   Opt: 3/3   Caps
Position selection bar - ↑↓, Select - ←┘, Leave menu - ↔, Blackboard - F10.
           Draw a double line window or line on the blackboard

Figure 3-25.   The CREATE SCREEN menu system allows you to draw boxes and lines through the OPTIONS selection

on active databases and which work areas those databases are in, which format files are in use, which relations have been set up, which index files are active, and which filters have been set, either through the SET FILTER TO or SET FILTER TO FILE command.

Syntax   The CREATE VIEW command generates a VUE file with information on related databases, format files, and filters. The syntax of the CREATE VIEW command is

CREATE VIEW vue file

The CREATE VIEW command is identical to the MODIFY VIEW command (discussed in Chapter 4). The CREATE VIEW command can also be accessed through the ASSIST menu.

Use   Figure 3-26 shows the SETUP option of the CREATE VIEW menu. This menu was entered with the three TED databases

```
►TED.DBF
 EDITDBFL.DBF
 LETTER.DBF
 OTHER.DBF
 PASS2.DBF
 PASSWORD.DBF
 PFSTEST.DBF
 PROMPTS.DBF
 SEFILE.DBF
 TANK2.DBF
 TEMP.DBF
 EXPSORT.DBF
 EXP.DBF
 EXPENSES.DBF
 TANK.DBF
►TED2.DBF
►TED3.DBF
 JOINFILE.DBF
```

CREATE VIEW ▐ ▌(D:)TED.VUE ▐ ▌Opt: 13/30 ▐ ▌ ▌Caps
Position selection bar - ↑↓. Select - ⏎. Leave menu - ↔.
Select database file(s) to be represented in this view.

Figure 3-26.   The SETUP option on the CREATE VIEW menu system
                flags databases that are active when the CREATE VIEW
                command is entered

active, and the SETUP menu option acknowledges that fact by marking them with triangles.

The CREATE VIEW command doesn't need to know what databases are in USE before you put it in use. You can choose the databases to relate from this menu. Note that this SETUP option is
different from SETUP options on other menu systems.

The step after selecting databases is to set their relations and
fields to show how the relations flow into one another. (See Figure
3-27.) This is where some of the power of the VUE file is shown.

You can CREATE VIEW files that determine relations in one of
two ways. The first way is through the use of an NDX file. If the base
file isn't INDEXed, the CREATE MENU system will give an error
message (Figure 3-28). The base file in a VUE or relation is the file
that relates to other files. In this example, TED is the base file. The
error message is

Database is not indexed. Press any key to continue.

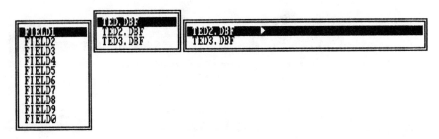

Field Name	Type	Width	Decimal
TED->FIELD1	Character	20	

Relation chain: TED.DBF->TED2.DBF
CREATE VIEW   <D:>TED.VUE   Opt: 1/10   Caps
          Position selection bar - ↑↓. Select - ◄┘. Leave menu - ↔.
          Relate the files using RECNO() or another numeric expression

Figure 3-27. The CREATE VIEW menu system prompts for the databases to relate and how the relations are to be set

Relation chain: TED.DBF->TED2.DBF
CREATE VIEW   <D:>TED.VUE   Opt: 1/10   Caps
          Database is not indexed. Press any key to continue.
          Relate the files using RECNO() or another numeric expression

Figure 3-28. III PLUS won't allow you to CREATE a VIEW using an unINDEXED database as the base file

```
Relation chain: TED.DBF->TED2.DBF
CREATE VIEW          (D:)TED.VUE          |Opt: 1/1|                    Caps
       Enter an expression.  F10 for a field menu.  Finish with ↵.
       Relate the files using RECNO() or another numeric expression
```

Figure 3-29. The CREATE VIEW menu relates databases by record number

III PLUS offers another method of relating files. That method is detailed in the line directly under the error message

Relate the files using RECNO( ) or another numeric expression.

The RECNO( ) function is the III PLUS database record number function. It returns the number of the record currently under the record pointer. Figures 3-29 and 3-30 show the relation being made by a record number.

Note that you can enter a field name as part of the relation, a record number, or a valid dBASE III PLUS numeric expression. Valid numeric expressions INCLUDE such things as

```
10/5
RECNO()/10
ASC(&FIELD1)
VAL("19283")
```

```
-> DISP STAT

Currently Selected Database:
Select area:  1, Database in Use: D:TED.DBF    Alias: TED
     Related into: TED2
     Relation: 2

Select area:  2, Database in Use: D:TED2.DBF   Alias: TED2

Select area:  3, Database in Use: D:TED3.DBF   Alias: TED3
     Format file: D:TEDSCR.FMT

File search path:
Default disk drive: D:
Print destination:  PRN:
Margin =      0
Current work area =    1   Delimiters are ':' and ':'

Press any key to continue...
```

Figure 3-30.   You can use a file's record number as a means of relating databases

The CREATE VIEW command allows several relations to exist at a given time. The relations are limited to a hierarchical structure. The first database in the hierarchy relates to the second database. The first database cannot relate to any other databases once that first relation is established unless the first relation is broken. The second database can relate to a third database, however, and the third to a fourth, and so on. You cannot use this command to create multiple relations from one database to different databases simultaneously.

CREATE VIEW FROM ENVIRONMENT

It is also possible to develop relations with the SET RELATIONS TO command and generate a VUE file with the CREATE VIEW FROM ENVIRONMENT command. This command performs the same function as the CREATE VIEW command, but the manner of file creation differs.

The CREATE VIEW command opens a menu system that guides you through the details of linking open databases, index files, format files, query files, and so on, eventually placing a VUE file on disk. That VUE file contains all the information you entered on the menu. The information is in a compressed form that is read by dBASE III PLUS when and if you ever use the VUE file with the SET VIEW TO command.

CREATE VIEW FROM ENVIRONMENT assumes all relations and files are already established and active in the system. The command then reads this information and places it into a VUE file. III PLUS doesn't care if the information is entered through this command or CREATE VIEW; the file is identical for identical relations and files. There is no advanced use of the command.

Syntax   The command form is

CREATE VIEW FROM ENVIRONMENT

The "environment" mentioned in the command is the working system at the time the command is entered. Any relations defined with the SET RELATION TO command, any NDX files active through the SET INDEX TO or USE dbf INDEX ndx command, any filtering conditions entered with the SET FILTER TO or SET FILTER TO FILE command, and any format files activated with the SET FORMAT TO command are read by the CREATE VIEW FROM ENVIRONMENT command to a new VUE file.

When used in the form just given, the command prompts for a VUE filename. You can avoid the prompt by entering the filename in one of two ways. Both methods are done within the command. The two methods are

CREATE VIEW FROM ENVIROMENT vue file

and

CREATE VIEW vue file FROM ENVIRONMENT

Use   The CREATE VIEW FROM ENVIRONMENT command is useful for the system developer who has to work through a tuning phase before the system is implemented. Such phases are common in the engineering and science disciplines, where lab-report formats, methods of indexing and relating databases, and filters are often fine-tuned before the system is released to the lab or office at large.

An example from real life involves a biotechnology company that needs to produce reports on different patient samples, which are based on the results of different tests, in turn based on different parameters. The reports must relate that data in a historical fashion. Each report, with overlying file and field parameters, if designed through menu systems would take far longer to produce than if the user were to go into the dBASE III PLUS Interactive mode and start with something as simple as

```
USE 1JAN86.PAT INDE J6SUGAR,J6IRON,J6T-CELL
SET FORMAT TO SUGAR
SET FILT TO ALCOHOL < 10
SELE B
USE 1JAN85.PAT INDE J5SUGAR,J5IRON,J5T-CELL
SET RELA TO SUGAR INTO B
```

Note that the dBASE four-letter-word convention is used in the previous example. These commands, taken together, form a working system environment. You could type CREATE VIEW FROM ENVIRONMENT at this point, and III PLUS would write this information to a VUE file. This command prompts for a VUE file-name if one is not given.

As time goes on, this firm will adjust some of the files, decide to use different INDEXing methods, or opt for a different format. Each time the firm makes a change, it can

```
CREATE VIEW FROM ENVIRONMENT
```

and test the new VUE file immediately.

EXPORT TO pfs file [TYPE] PFS

The EXPORT command is a specialized command that allows III PLUS to create PFS:file data files. Creating PFS:file data files is the only function the command has.

Syntax   The command syntax is

EXPORT TO pfs file TYPE PFS

You can use

EXPORT TO pfs file PFS

without causing dBASE III PLUS any problems. This command assumes a database is in USE in the current work area. Note that the PFS:file created with the EXPORT command has the same name as the in-USE dBASE III PLUS DBF file in Figure 3-31. You can give the PFS:file data file any name you wish. PFS:file data files commonly have no extensions. Note that you can tell III PLUS to create a PFS:file data file with either an extension or no extension by typing

EXPORT TO (pfs file).ext PFS

or

EXPORT TO (pfs file). PFS

```
-> USE TED
-> COPY TO PFSTEST
-> EXPORT TO PFSTEST PFS
-> EXPORT TO PFSFILE. PFS
-> EXPORT TO PFSFILE.PFS PFS
-> DIR PFS*.*
PFSFILE           PFSFILE.PFS        PFSTEST        PFSTEST.DBF

   50702 bytes in     4 files.
5124096 bytes remaining on drive.

->
```

Figure 3-31.   The EXPORT command creates PFS:file data files

Use   In many ways the EXPORT command is similar to the COPY TO foreign file FILETYPE command discussed earlier in this chapter. The EXPORT command assumes a database is open and in the current work area and translates that information in that database into a foreign-file format. The EXPORT command is capable of generating PFS:file data files only.

The reason a special command is used to generate PFS files has to do with the way PFS:file data files are created in the PFS system. A PFS:file data file format is intimately linked to how the data is presented on the screen. That is different from dBASE III PLUS, in which the usual data representation lists the rows vertically for general editing and appending procedures (see Figure 3-32).

III PLUS relies on the programmer, developer, or user to place the information on the screen in a pleasing manner. Aesthetic placement of the database information on the screen is done with the FMT files and SET FORMAT TO command in the dBASE III PLUS system. The designer can also use SAY and GET files to customize screens.

PFS:file doesn't have such luxuries. The data is placed on the screen in a specific pattern that is designed when the PFS:file system is first set up. This can be modified later, but involves restructuring

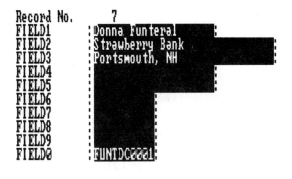

Figure 3-32.   This is the most general representation of dBASE III PLUS data

the database. Redesigning the screen in III PLUS merely involves use of the CREATE SCREEN or MODIFY SCREEN command.

In any case, the PFS:file data file's data is intimately linked to the way that data is presented on the screen. The EXPORT command acknowledges this fact and uses whatever FMT file is open and in the current work area as a basis for creating the PFS:file data file's screen image. Thus, the dBASE III PLUS data screen shown in Figure 3-32 produces an identical PFS:file screen because no FMT file is active. The more bizarre and intricate your FMT file, the more bizarre and intricate the EXPORTed PFS:file screen will be.

Note that III PLUS will warn you if you're about to write over an existing PFS:file data file with the same filename, if either the SET SAFETY or CONFIG.DB SAFETY command is ON.

Advanced Use   Advanced use of the EXPORT command has more to do with how you want the PFS:file screen to appear than how things in III PLUS will behave. The more intricate your FMT file, the more intricate your PFS:file screen.

The EXPORT command doesn't just take the data from the database and translate it into a foreign-file format, as the COPY TO foreign file FILETYPE command does. The file formats that can be COPYed are actually predefined by the destination software package. 1-2-3 WKS files have only one form, Multiplan SYLK files have only one form, and VisiCalc DIF files have only one form. These forms are "hard" coded into their respective packages.

PFS:file does not have a hard-coded data form. The data goes into the database differently depending on where the data appears on the screen. That makes an incredible difference in how much the EXPORT command has to do before it begins writing the new file format.

Enter the FMT file. The FMT file tells III PLUS where the data is supposed to go on a screen. Where data goes on a screen is something the PFS:file data file tells PFS:file. Therefore, each data file EXPORTed will be different, depending on which FMT file is active.

Consider a single database that has four FMT files associated with it. The following command list

```
USE database
SET FORMAT TO fmt1
EXPORT TO dbfmt1 PFS
```

```
SET FORMAT TO fmt2
EXPORT TO dbfmt2 PFS
SET FORMAT TO fmt3
EXPORT TO dbfmt3 PFS
SET FORMAT TO fmt4
EXPORT TO dbfmt4 PFS
```

would create four different PFS:file data files. The four new files would be created with different screen images that mimicked the III PLUS FMT files fmt1, fmt2, fmt3, and fmt4. The PFS:file package also allows the use of the PGDN and PGUP keys for shuttling between screens, much like the FMT files allow shuttling between screens. The EXPORT command acknowledges this and knows when and where to break FMT multi-screen formats in the PFS:file data file's screen image when EXPORTing and formats the PFS:file data file accordingly.

Finally, the EXPORT command writes data to the PFS:file data file according to whatever NDX file is currently active and at the top of the list. For example, the commands

```
USE database INDE ndx1, ndx2, ndx3,..., ndx7
EXPORT TO pfs file PFS
```

would create a PFS:file data file in the index ordered by NDX file ndx1.

IMPORT FROM pfs file
[TYPE] PFS

The sister command of EXPORT is IMPORT. This command is similar to the APPEND FROM foreign file FILETYPE command except it handles only PFS:file data files.

Syntax   The syntax for the IMPORT command is identical to the syntax for the EXPORT command. The command is

IMPORT FROM pfs file TYPE PFS

and can be used as

The IMPORT command, while not having an advanced use, still does a great deal of work. The work is based on the fact that the PFS:file data file is not just data, but data and screen image combined (see the EXPORT section).

Use   The IMPORT command does three things. First, it creates a dBASE III PLUS DBF file from the data in the PFS:file data file. The resulting DBF file can be APPENDed, COPYed, EDITed, and MODIFYed like any other III PLUS DBF file. The IMPORT command also generates an FMT file. This FMT file holds the information on the screen image that was contained in the PFS:file data file. Last, the IMPORT command creates a VUE file to link the FMT file to the DBF file. When III PLUS is through IMPORTing, it SETs the VIEW TO the newly IMPORTed VUE file and USEs the newly IMPORTed DBF.

Note that you do not have to use either the FMT or VUE files in conjunction with the DBF file. These files are generated by the IMPORT command to provide total visual compatibility with PFS:file. Your major concern is actually getting the data from PFS:file, and that data is contained in the new DBF file. You can create your own FMT files for the new DBF file if you wish. A PFS:file data file with records that cover several screens will be IMPORTed with an FMT file that can cover several screens and knows when and where screen breaks should occur, however. That feature can be handy and shouldn't be discarded.

The DBF and associated files all carry the filename of the PFS:file data file. You can tell III PLUS not to use an extension, but that restriction will apply only to the DBF file. Both the FMT and VUE files will have their proper extensions.

INDEX

The dBASE III PLUS INDEX command instructs III PLUS to place a certain order on the in-USE DBF file. The DBF file is ordered on a secondary key to an NDX file.

Syntax The INDEX command can be used in two ways. The first is in the active command

INDEX ON key expression TO ndx file

This form of the command instructs III PLUS to perform several different operations, all of which are designed to determine the value of the key expression in each record of the in-USE database and then determine the order of those values. The key expression can be any valid dBASE III PLUS expression, but it must have meaning for the in-USE database. You could use

```
INDEX ON field1 TO ndx1
INDEX ON field1 + field2 TO ndx12
INDEX ON RIGHT(field1,10) + DTOC(field5) TO ndx15
INDEX ON ASC(field4) TO ndx4
```

to create a variety of order patterns in the NDX files. The key expression can be any NUMERIC, CHARACTER, or DATE data field.

The INDEXing norm is to go from A to Z, 0 to infinity, yesterday to today. This is called least-to-greatest ordering. A variation on the INDEX command is to use the negative sign (−) to indicate INDEX-ing in reverse order.

The INDEX command also allows for automatic generation of UNIQUE NDX files with the UNIQUE qualifier on the INDEX command, as in

INDEX ON key expression TO ndx file UNIQUE

This application of the command causes III PLUS to ignore repeated key expression values when building the NDX file.

The second method of using the INDEX command is as a qualifier when USEing a database, as in

USE database INDEX ndx file

This method instructs III PLUS to open the named NDX file when the named DBF file is opened. The NDX file is then used to supply order to the DBF file. III PLUS allows up to seven NDX files to be opened for each in-USE database. You can open extra files for the active DBF by listing them in the USE command, as in

```
USE database INDEX ndx1, ndx2, ndx3,..., ndx7
```

Use   The INDEX command's general form is

```
INDEX ON key expression TO ndx file
```

This form of the command instructs III PLUS to perform several different operations. The first step taken by III PLUS is to determine the value of the key expression for every record in the database. This step starts by looking at the value of the key expression in record 1. The value of the key expression is then determined for record 2. III PLUS decides which of the two records has the greater key-expression value and places the record numbers next to the key-expression values in the target NDX file.

Next, III PLUS determines the value of the key expression in record 3 and decides where record 3's value goes in relation to the key-expression values in records 1 and 2. It places the key-expression value of record 3 in the NDX file in its proper place. This process continues until the entire database is INDEXed on the key expression.

The key expression used in the INDEX command can be any NUMERIC, CHARACTER, or DATE expression. III PLUS will not INDEX on LOGICAL or MEMO fields. Note that the first part of the key expression determines the expression type. For example, a key expression of

```
ABS(field1)
```

determines that the key expression is going to be a NUMERIC key expression. You could add more precision to the key expression with

```
ABS(field1) + VAL(LEFT(ZIPCODE,5))
```

Note here that two different field types are combined. Field1 is a NUMERIC data type, and ZIPCODE is a CHARACTER type. You first select the left five characters of the ZIPCODE field, then convert them into their numeric VALues to make the entire keyfield expression numeric. Similarly, using the ZIPCODE field first, you would have to write the key expression in one of the two following ways:

```
VAL(LEFT(ZIPCODE,5)) + ABS(field1)
ZIPCODE + STR(FIELD1)
```

The first line in the preceding listing is still a numeric key expression. The second line is of CHARACTER type because the first part of the key expression is character data. You must convert the numeric data in field1 to a character STRing before you can use it.

The INDEX command creates an order based on ascending values. There is a 100-character limit on the size of the key expression.

Advanced Use   There are several advanced ways to use the INDEX command. The first method to investigate is creating descending NDX files through the use of the negative (−) sign. This can obviously be used to create decreasing NDX files when the key expression is numeric in nature. The command is

INDEX ON −numeric key expression TO ndx file

But how does one create a descending NDX file on character data? That involves the use of the ASC function. The ASC function determines the ASCII value of the first character in a character string. You can use the ASC function to create descending character NDX files with

INDEX ON −ASC(character key expression) TO ndx file

Note that this method pays attention to only the first character in the key expression.

The UNIQUE qualifier tells III PLUS to record only the first occurrence of a key expression in the NDX file. An example of the differences in UNIQUE and non-UNIQUE NDX files can be seen in comparing Figures 3-33 and 3-34. The first figure shows that all records are written to the NDX file. The second figure shows that only the first occurrence of a key expression gets written to the NDX file.

```
-> USE EXPENSES
-> INDE ON PAYTO TO EXPALL
-> DISP ALL PAYTO
Record#  PAYTO
       1 Allstate
       2 Allstate
       8 Am Ex
       9 Am Ex
       7 Computer Town
      14 Ford Motor Credit
      11 Gas
      12 Gas
       6 NH Turnpike
      15 Post Office
      16 Science Fiction & Fantasy Workshop
       3 Susan Carrabis
       4 Susan Carrabis
       5 mileage
      10 mileage
      13 mileage
->
```

Figure 3-33. The EXPENSES database is INDEXed on the PAYTO field without the UNIQUE qualifier

```
->
-> USE EXPENSES
-> INDE ON PAYTO TO EXPUNIQ UNIQUE
-> DISP ALL PAYTO
Record#  PAYTO
       1 Allstate
       8 Am Ex
       7 Computer Town
      14 Ford Motor Credit
      11 Gas
       6 NH Turnpike
      15 Post Office
      16 Science Fiction & Fantasy Workshop
       3 Susan Carrabis
       5 mileage
->
```

Figure 3-34. The EXPENSES database is INDEXed on the PAYTO field with the UNIQUE qualifier

This qualifier is useful when creating NDX files for very large databases that have repetitive data in the keyfield. The advantage lies in savings of machine time and disk space. An NDX file for a large database will itself be large. If the key expression's data is highly repetitive, there is no need to keep that information in the NDX file and on disk. Trying to FIND and SEEK information through that NDX file would also take up more time than using a UNIQUE NDX file. The UNIQUE form is

INDEX ON key expression TO ndx file UNIQUE

JOIN

The JOIN command can take data from two different sources and combine that data into one file. This is similar to the VUE file's ability to present data from two or more files simultaneously, but there is an important distinction between the two.

The VUE file presents data from more than one source. This data can be presented via an FMT file or a simple screen dump. The JOIN command physically combines data from two sources into a single file. The SET VIEW TO vue file command doesn't cause III PLUS to generate a new file. The JOIN command does cause III PLUS to generate a new file.

Syntax   The syntax of the JOIN command can be confusing at first; therefore, it is broken into small parts here. The first part of the command is

JOIN WITH database in another work area

This can be shortened somewhat by using the DBF file's alias. The alias for any database in work area 1 is "A"; for any database in work area 2, it is "B"; in work area 3, it is "C"; and so on. You can also specify other aliases if you wish. See Chapter 5 for more on database alias names.

The principal function of the JOIN command is to take data from two different sources. The sources in dBASE III PLUS are DBF files. The JOIN command is issued from one work area where a DBF file is in USE. The DBF file in USE has to be one of the two DBFs that contains data you want to JOIN. In another work area there must be another, open database file. The DBF file in that other area must be in USE for the JOIN command to access the information in that file. Therefore, the first part of the JOIN command, as shown previously, would be used in code as follows:

```
SELE 1
USE AFILE
SELE 2
USE BFILE
JOIN WITH AFILE ...
```

This would tell III PLUS that there are two different DBF files open and in USE in work areas 1 and 2. From work area 2, call the DBF file in work area 1 and JOIN WITH it...

The next part of the command has to do with where the JOINed data is going.

JOIN WITH other dbf TO target

The new part of the command here is "TO target". Several of the III PLUS commands discussed thus far make use of a target file, and JOIN is no different. After collecting data from two DBF files, you'd like to put that data somewhere for future use and reference. Put it in a target file. The target file follows all the III PLUS filenaming conventions, although the JOIN command writes to a DBF file no matter what extension you use. You can specify no extension or an extension other than the DBF database file extension by typing

JOIN WITH other dbf TO (join file).

to specify no file extension or

JOIN WITH other dbf TO (join file).(other extension)

to specify a non-DBF file extension for the target file.

The last part of the command is the qualifier FOR. Most other III PLUS commands (COPY is an example) use the FOR qualifier to limit what III PLUS does during an operation. The JOIN command is different in that the FOR qualifier is a necessary part of the command. If you try to JOIN something without using the FOR qualifier, you'll get an error message. The FOR qualifier tells III PLUS what records in the current file are to be JOINed with records from the other file.

Note that the JOIN command can also use the FIELDS qualifier. The FIELDS qualifier tells III PLUS to JOIN only the named fields. The FIELDS JOINed can be from either of the databases named in the JOIN command. Only the named FIELDS will be included in the target file, however. Specifying no fields instructs III PLUS to use all the fields from both databases in the target file. This can cause a problem if the two databases have more than 128 fields combined. III PLUS truncates the excess fields from the second source file. For example, if the command

JOIN WITH BFILE TO JOINFILE FOR FIELD1 = true condition

were issued from work area 1, where afile merrily sits, and afile has 70 fields per record and bfile has 70 fields per record, JOINFILE would have only 128 fields per record. The actual fields would be the 70 from afile and the first 58 from bfile.

Use   The JOIN command is one of the primitive dBASE commands. The nature of the command is to perform a sequential search on the current database to find records that match the FOR condition. Note that the JOIN command allows only the FOR qualifier. It doesn't allow the WHILE qualifier.

There are several things regarding the use of the JOIN command that the user must be aware of. To begin, take a look at the following two database structures. The first is for the EXPENSES.DBF file and the second is for the TED.DBF file:

```
-> USE EXPENSES
-> DISP STRUC
Structure for database: C:EXPENSES.dbf
Number of data records:       16
Date of last update   : 07/13/86
Field   Field Name   Type        Width      Dec
    1   PAYTO        Character      40
    2   PAYFOR       Character      60
    3   CHECKNUM     Character      10
    4   PAYAMOUNT    Numeric        10        2
    5   PAYDATE      Date            8
```

```
      6  MILEAGE        Numeric         7       1
 **  Total  **                         136

 ->  ?  RECCOUNT()              **  of  EXPENSES.DBF
        16


 ->  USE  TED
 ->  DISP  STRUC
 Structure  for  database:  C:TED.dbf
 Number  of  data  records:        1
 Date  of  last  update     :  01/01/80
 Field    Field  Name    Type         Width      Dec
      1    FIELD1        Character      20
      2    FIELD2        Character      20
      3    FIELD3        Character      20
      4    FIELD4        Character      20
      5    FIELD5        Character      20
      6    FIELD6        Character      10
      7    FIELD7        Character      10
      8    FIELD8        Character      10
      9    FIELD9        Character      10
     10    FIELD0        Character      10
 **  Total  **                        151

 ->  ?  RECCOUNT()              **  of  TED.DBF
        1
```

These two databases are used here specifically because their structures are radically different.

Now, the first thing done here is a "blind" JOIN. There's no need to be terribly specific in how data is JOINed. The process is shown here:

```
 ->  USE  EXPENSES          **  has  16  records
 ->  SELE  2
 ->  USE  TED               **  has  1  record
 ->  SELE  1
 ->  JOIN  WITH  TED  FOR  PAYTO  =  "C"  TO  JOINFILE
          1  record  joined
 ->  JOIN  WITH  TED  FOR  PAYTO  =  "m"  TO  JOINFILE
          3  records  joined
```

The first thing to be aware of is that, according to Figure 3-33, there is one record in the EXPENSES.DBF file in which the PAYTO field has a value of "C" (the record with PAYTO = "Computer Town"). Because there is only one record in which the condition

PAYTO = "C"

is met, only one record is JOINed. Next,

Again, according to Figure 3-33, there are three records that meet the condition

PAYTO = "m"

(the three with PAYTO = "mileage"). This time, because three records in the current database match the condition, three records are JOINed from the two databases. All well and good. The JOIN command is performing a multiplication of records. There is only one record in the TED.DBF file, and it is being used for each correct conditional match in the EXPENSES.DBF file. The result of the last JOIN command in the preceding listing is shown here:

```
-> USE JOINFILE
-> DISP ALL
Record#   PAYTO
PAYFOR
CHECKNUM     PAYAMOUNT PAYDATE   MILEAGE FIELD1
FIELD2                 FIELD3
FIELD4                 FIELD5                 FIELD6
FIELD7     FIELD8      FIELD9      FIELD0
        1
mileage

0.00 07/11/86    146.0 Joseph Carrabis       32 Foxmoor
Circle     Nashua, NH 03063     USA                   (603)
881-9390
071786
        2
mileage

0.00 07/03/86     15.0 Joseph Carrabis       32 Foxmoor
Circle     Nashua, NH 03063     USA                   (603)
881-9390
071786
        3
mileage

0.00 07/07/86      6.0 Joseph Carrabis       32 Foxmoor
Circle     Nashua, NH 03063     USA                   (603)
881-9390
071786
```

Note that the information in the TED.DBF fields in each record is identical. The only different information is that JOINed from the EXPENSES.DBF file. The TED.DBF information is repeated three

times because there were three occurrences of PAYTO = "m" in the
EXPENSES.DBF. To further illustrate, consider JOINFILE's structure, shown here:

```
-> USE JOINFILE
-> DISP STRUC
Structure for database: C:JOINFILE.dbf
Number of data records:      3
Date of last update   : 01/01/80
Field   Field Name   Type        Width     Dec
    1   PAYTO        Character      40
    2   PAYFOR       Character      60
    3   CHECKNUM     Character      10
    4   PAYAMOUNT    Numeric        10        2
    5   PAYDATE      Date            8
    6   MILEAGE      Numeric         7        1
    7   FIELD1       Character      20
    8   FIELD2       Character      20
    9   FIELD3       Character      20
   10   FIELD4       Character      20
   11   FIELD5       Character      20
   12   FIELD6       Character      10
   13   FIELD7       Character      10
   14   FIELD8       Character      10
   15   FIELD9       Character      10
   16   FIELD0       Character      10
** Total **                        286
```

The fields are JOINed from the EXPENSES.DBF file first, followed by the TED.DBF fields. All the fields are JOINed because no
fields with the FIELDS qualifier were specified.

If you were to reverse the command, as shown in Figure 3-35,
how many records would you expect the JOINFILE to have? The
answer is shown here:

```
-> SELE 1
-> USE EXPENSES
-> SELE 2
-> USE TED
-> DISP ALL
Record#   FIELD1                    FIELD2
FIELD3                    FIELD4
FIELD5                    FIELD6      FIELD7      FIELD8
FIELD9       FIELD0
       1   Joseph Carrabis          32 Foxmoor Circle      Nashua,
NH 03063     USA                (603)
881-9390
071786
-> JOIN WITH EXPENSES FOR FIELD1="J" TO JOINFILE
      16 records joined
```

```
-> SELE 1
-> USE EXPENSES
-> SELE 2
-> USE TED
-> JOIN WITH A FOR FIELD1 = "J" TO JOINFILE
      16 records joined
->
```

Figure 3-35. The JOIN command multiplies one database's records by the other database's records

Note that the DBF alias name is used here. The listing shows that, although there is only one record in the TED.DBF file, that one record is multiplied by each record in the other file (EXPENSES, in this example) to write a total of 16 records in the JOINed file. This new JOINFILE has the data from TED repeated 16 times, one time for each of the 16 records in the EXPENSES database.

Needless to say, JOINing data from two large databases, with the current file having several records that meet the FOR condition can cause III PLUS to write an incredibly large file. A strong recommendation is that you determine the size of your JOINed file before attempting to write it to disk. An example of a dBASE III PLUS code that determines the size of the JOINed file is given in the "Advanced Use" section.

The FIELDS qualifier tells III PLUS what fields to take from each database and place in the JOINed file. For example, the next listing shows the JOIN command used as before, but this time only one field is mentioned in the command. The one field is from the TED database. The JOINFILE is essentially a copy of the one field from TED, repeated 16 times. But you can take fields from both databases and place them in the JOINed file.

```
-> JOIN WITH A FOR FIELD1 = "J" TO JOINFILE FIELD FIELD1
      16 records joined
-> USE JOINFILE
-> DISP STRUC
```

```
Structure for database: C:JOINFILE.dbf
Number of data records:      16
Date of last update   : 01/01/80
Field  Field Name  Type       Width    Dec
    1  FIELD1      Character      20
** Total **                       21
```

The next listing shows a field from TED and a field from EXPENSES combined in the JOINFILE. Note that the JOIN command has still performed a multiplication of data. The data in FIELD1 of the single record in the TED.DBF file has been repeated 16 times—each time the data from a PAYTO field in the EXPENSES.DBF file has been JOINed to it.

```
-> USE TED
-> JOIN WITH A FOR FIELD1 = "J" TO JOINFILE FIELD
FIELD1,PAYTO
     16 records joined
-> USE JOINFILE
-> DISP STRUC
Structure for database: C:JOINFILE.dbf
Number of data records:      16
Date of last update   : 01/01/80
Field  Field Name  Type       Width    Dec
    1  FIELD1      Character      20
    2  PAYTO       Character      40
** Total **                       61

-> DISP ALL
Record#  FIELD1                 PAYTO
     1   Joseph
Carrabis
     2   Joseph Carrabis
Allstate
     3   Joseph Carrabis
Allstate
     4   Joseph Carrabis        Susan
Carrabis
     5   Joseph Carrabis        Susan
Carrabis
     6   Joseph Carrabis
mileage
     7   Joseph Carrabis        NH
Turnpike
     8   Joseph Carrabis        Computer
Town
     9   Joseph Carrabis        Am
Ex
    10   Joseph Carrabis        Am
Ex
    11   Joseph Carrabis
mileage
    12   Joseph Carrabis
```

```
Gas
     13   Joseph Carrabis
Gas
     14   Joseph Carrabis
mileage
     15   Joseph Carrabis        Ford Motor
Credit
     16   Joseph Carrabis        Post
Office
```

Advanced Use   The following advanced way to use the JOIN command is based on typical complaints from programmers. The problem is that you can start to JOIN files and not know if you have enough room on the disk to receive the information. A simple remedy, one that you can easily customize for your applications, is shown here:

```
SELE 1
USE afile
COUNT FOR condition TO AJOINRECS
JOINRECS = AJOINRECS * RECSIZE() + aheadersize
SELE 2
USE bfile
COUNT TO BJOINRECS
JOINRECS = JOINRECS + BJOINRECS * RECSIZE() + bheadersize
*
IF JOINRECS < DISKSPACE()
   JOIN WITH afile FOR condition TO JOINFILE
ENDI
*
```

This example uses two undeclared DBF files, afile and bfile, and two undeclared variables, aheadersize and bheadersize. There are several assumptions made in this code, so it is important that you customize it for your own applications.

It works by first determining the file size of the database that is going to be JOINed. AJOINRECS is an acronym for afile JOINed RECordS—in other words, the number of records in the afile that are going to be JOINed. The FOR condition in the COUNT command is the same one that you'll use in the actual JOIN command.

The number of records that are going to be JOINed (AJOIN-RECS) is multiplied by the size of a record (RECSIZE()). That value is added to aheadersize, which is the size of the afile file header. The result of that arithmetic is placed in the JOINRECS variable.

You do this same bit of arithmetic with the bfile. After you've performed this arithmetic with afile and bfile, determine the possible size of the JOINed file. If the size of the JOINed file (JOINRECS, in the IF command) is less than the available disk space (DISK-SPACE( )), then JOIN the files.

Modifications to this code would be error messages, user prompts for source and target disks, and better determination of the record and field sizes.

MODIFY COMMAND prg file

The MODIFY COMMAND command is a specialized use of the MODIFY FILE command, which is shown in the next section. The MODIFY COMMAND command has no advanced use and both creates and edits PRG files in the III PLUS system.

Syntax   The syntax of the command is

MODIFY COMMAND prg file

The reason MODIFY COMMAND is a specialized case of MODIFY FILE is based on the files the two commands work with. The MODIFY COMMAND command defaults to working with PRG files. The MODIFY FILE command works with any ASCII text file; you normally supply an extension. You can use the commands interchangeably, so long as you remember to use a file extension when using the two commands.

Use   The MODIFY COMMAND command is used primarily to edit PRG files in the dBASE III PLUS system. You can use the command to edit and create any kind of ASCII text file.

Note that you can activate the EDITing menu by typing F1 when in the MODIFY COMMAND mode. Figure 3-36 shows the menu and an error message at the top of the screen. You must supply III PLUS with the complete filename when using the CTRL-KR key combination to read another file into the currently edited file. Users familiar with WordStar's editing functions will be comfortable with the III PLUS Text Editor, which III PLUS uses for the MODIFY COMMAND command and several other editing functions.

File does not exist (press SPACE)

```
CURSOR:   <-- -->    ║         UP  DOWN   ║  DELETE       ║ Insert Mode:     Ins
Char:     ← →        ║ Line:    ↑   ↓     ║ Char:   Del   ║ Insert line:     ^N
Word:   Home End     ║ Page: PgUp PgDn    ║ Word:   ^T    ║ Save: ^W Abort: Esc
Line:    ^← ^→       ║ Find:   ^KF        ║ Line:   ^Y    ║ Read file:       ^KR
Reformat: ^KB        ║ Refind: ^KL        ║               ║ Write file:      ^KW
```

Figure 3-36.   The MODIFY COMMAND/MODIFY FILE menu. Attempting to read in a nonexisting file produces an error message

MODIFY FILE ASCII file

The MODIFY FILE command is III PLUS's general-purpose text-editing command. The command can be used for just about any type of text editing, provided the file you wish to edit is ASCII text. The MODIFY FILE command both edits and creates text files and has no advanced use.

Syntax   The syntax of the command is

MODIFY FILE filename.ext

Note that, unlike the MODIFY COMMAND command shown in the previous section, the file named in the MODIFY FILE command must have an extension.

Use   The MODIFY FILE command serves the function of a general-purpose text processor in the III PLUS system. You can use this command to edit FMT, PRG, PRC, TXT, and other ASCII text files. It is identical to the MODIFY COMMAND command shown in the previous section, with the added provision that MODIFY FILE needs to know the file extension. The MODIFY COMMAND command assumes the .PRG extension but can be used to edit or create any ASCII text file. The MODIFY FILE command makes no assumptions and doesn't automatically add the .PRG extension to every file it creates.

Actually, it's not strictly true that you must include an extension. What you must include is some indication of the file extension when using the MODIFY FILE command. You can tell III PLUS to create a file with no file extension by typing

MODIFY FILE filename.

The period (.) in the preceding command tells III PLUS that the file being edited or created has no extension. Note that a file with no extension must be referenced in the same way throughout any III PLUS work session.

SAVE TO mem file
[ALL LIKE/EXCEPT <skeleton>]

The SAVE command is used to create and update MEM files. MEM files are files that contain memory variables used during a work session. These variables are sometimes stored at the end of one work session and retrieved at the start of the next work session. They serve the purpose of determining system defaults.

Syntax   The syntax of the SAVE command is

SAVE TO mem file

This form instructs III PLUS to SAVE TO the named MEM file all memory variables in the system. The MEM file follows the standard III PLUS filenaming conventions. The SAVE command defaults to a .MEM extension on the file it SAVEs. You can override this default by specifying either a non-.MEMfile extension or no extension by including a period (.) at the end of the filename. An example of this last would be

SAVE TO (mem file).

The SAVE command allows for SAVEing memory variables by using the ALL, LIKE, and EXCEPT qualifiers. Note that SAVE defaults to the ALL qualifier unless something else is specified.

The ALL qualifier tells III PLUS to SAVE every active memory variable to the MEM file. The command

SAVE TO mem file ALL LIKE example

tells III PLUS to SAVE only those memory variables that fit into the example pattern. The example pattern can be W*, WAIT*, ???c*, and so on. These patterns tell III PLUS to SAVE only memory variables that begin with *W*, only memory variables that begin with *WAIT*, and only memory variables that have *C* as the fourth letter in their name, respectively.

You can fine-tune the SAVE function with the EXCEPT qualifier, as in

SAVE TO mem file ALL LIKE example EXCE variable1, variable2,...

Note that the dBASE III PLUS four-letter-word convention is used in the above command. This version of the command tells III PLUS to save all memory variables that fit the example pattern, but to exclude the memory variables named after the EXCEPT qualifier.

Use   The SAVE command is most often used to tidy up machine memory. Each memory variable left active in the machine causes some memory to be lost to other activities. The number of memory variables that are needed in a full-blown system can be staggering and might use several thousand bytes of memory space.

That is where the SAVE command comes in. It allows you to store memory variables selectively. These SAVEd memory variables can be RESTOREd later in the same work session or in another work session entirely.

Advanced Use   The SAVE command can be used to SAVE system defaults to a MEM file. Figure 3-37 shows such a file. As you can see, alphanumeric characters, graphics characters, and numeric data have been included in the WRITE.MEM file. You can also include LOGICAL and DATE data.

```
-> CLEAR MEMO
-> REST FROM WRITE
-> DISP MEMO
CDRIVE      pub  C   "C:"
CPATH       pub  C   "c:\db3\write"
DLINE       pub  C   "═══════════════════════════════════

                    ="
FRAME       pub  C   "┌─┤┘═└┤"
SETDATE     pub  N          2 (          2.00000000)
SLINE       pub  C   "_____

                    _"
WAITLENGTH  pub  N          2 (          2.00000000)
WAITTIME    pub  N         10 (         10.00000000)
      8 variables defined,    215 bytes used
    248 variables available,  5785 bytes available

->
```

Figure 3-37. The variables listed in this figure, SAVEd to C:\WFAL\ WRITE, are system defaults for the WFAL vertical market package

You can either use the ALL LIKE and EXCEPT qualifiers in your SAVE command or use the RELEASE command.

SET ALTERNATE TO txt file

The SET ALTERNATE TO command is used to create an ASCII text file that records all the information III PLUS sends to the screen and all commands, queries, and so on that you type into III PLUS. This section covers the SET ALTERNATE TO command and shouldn't be confused with the SET ALTERNATIVE on/OFF command covered in Chapter 11.

Syntax   The command syntax is

SET ALTERNATE TO txt file

III PLUS uses the standard filenaming conventions, with the default file extension being .TXT. You can SET the ALTERNATE file TO any file extension or TO no extension with

SET ALTER TO (txt file).(non-.TXT extension)

for an extension other than .TXT or

SET ALTER TO (txt file).

for no extension. Note that the III PLUS four-letter-word convention is used in the preceding two commands. The SET ALTERNATE TO command also closes the currently open and active ALTERNATE file. That is done by not specifying any target file in the command, as in

SET ALTERNATE TO

Note that III PLUS needs to know where the ALTERNATE file is supposed to go if you wish to write the file somewhere other than the default disk. For example, if you're using drive B as your default and you want the ALTERNATE file written to drive A, you must enter the command as

SET ALTER TO A:(txt file)

Use   The SET ALTERNATE TO command is useful in creating ASCII text files that can be printed and used in reports and classes. Most of the listings in this book were created as ALTERNATE files.

What is an ALTERNATE file? The file would more properly be called a SCREEN DUMP TO DISK file. The ALTERNATE file captures any information that goes to the screen when SET ALTERNATE is ON. The information can be what you type in or what III PLUS sends out—so long as it goes to the screen.

Now that you've accepted the fact that anything that goes to the screen gets into the ALTERNATE file, here's the exception: No full-screen mode will go to the ALTERNATE file. Full-screen mode operations include any file that is opened with the SET FORMAT TO command.

Note that III PLUS will not tell you if you're writing over an existing ALTERNATE file.

Advanced Use   A primary use for the ALTERNATE file is as a remote debugging aid when doing consulting work for a client. Debugging over the phone is an agony. III PLUS offers many venues for debugging, but most of these would be annoying to the user during a work session. The one method that is not annoying is one the user never sees. That is where the SET ALTERNATE TO command comes in.

If you were to do this type of consulting, you could include the SET ALTERNATE TO txt file and SET ALTERNATE ON commands as the first two commands in any system you wrote and sent out for use. You could have this command stay in the main program until a client hadn't called you for a period of six months. Whenever the client called with a problem, your first task would be to determine if the problem could be solved easily over the phone. If it couldn't, your next task would be to guide the user to the COPY FILE command. You would have the user

```
COPY FILE NLCALTER.TXT TO A:(company name).TXT
```

This command makes some assumptions. First, realize that the SET ALTERNATE commands you include in each system sent out are

```
SET ALTER TO NLCALTER
SET ALTER ON
```

Second, drive A is not the system default. Third, III PLUS automatically truncates any company name that is more than eight characters long. An example of the information that can be captured by an ALTERNATE file is given here:

```
-> DO LIBRARY
The available library files are
Record#   TITLE
      1   All of Joseph's
```

```
books
     2  All of Susan's
Books

Which LIBRARY do you wish to use? (#) -> 1
FIND Author, Editor, Title, Category, Subject, or Library?
-> subject
Find SUBJECT > Mystery
```

SET CATALOG TO cat file

The SET CATALOG TO cat file command instructs III PLUS to open a CAT file. The CATALOG files are used by III PLUS as a means of filtering files from the system. Information on CAT files can be found in Chapter 2.

There are two variations on the SET CATALOG command. This section deals with SETting the CATALOG file. Information on SETting the CATALOG ON and off can be found in Chapter 11. There is no advanced use of the command.

Syntax   The syntax of the command is

SET CATALOG TO cat file

where cat file follows the standard III PLUS file naming conventions. III PLUS assumes a file extension of .CAT unless you specify some other extension.

This command serves two purposes. It can be used to create a new CAT file or open an existing CAT file. III PLUS looks for the CAT filename on the default disk unless you include a drive designator in the command, such as

SET CATA TO DN:(cat file)

Note that the III PLUS four-letter-word convention is used in the preceding command. The *DN:* stands for Drive Name:. You would open a CAT file on drive A by typing

SET CATA TO A:(cat file)

assuming drive A was not the system default.

You can close CAT files with the command by not specifying any CAT filename, as in

SET CATA TO

This closes any open CAT file.

Use   The SET CATALOG TO cat file command opens and closes a special type of III PLUS database that has the .CAT file extension. Note that the user can open and close only one CAT file at a time, even though III PLUS keeps two CAT files active and always keeps one CAT file for itself.

You can open and close CAT files that you have created for your own purposes. III PLUS also keeps a CATALOG.CAT file for itself. This reserved CAT file is the master CAT file for the system and is used by III PLUS to tell you what CAT files are available. You can query III PLUS on available CAT files with

SET CATALOG TO ?

This command causes III PLUS to look in the CATALOG.CAT file for the names of all the CAT files ever created.

The CATALOG.CAT file can be EDITed, APPENDed, and COPYed just like any other DBF file. If no CAT file exists on the default drive with the given name, III PLUS will create a new CAT file and add the name of the new CAT file to the CATALOG.CAT file.

All CAT files, with the exception of the CATALOG.CAT file, are placed in work area 10 when the SET CATALOG TO cat file command is entered. Note that this leaves you one fewer work area to use with your system.

SORT

The SORT command performs the same function as the INDEX command discussed earlier in this chapter. There are a few minor differences between the two commands as far as execution goes, but the major thing to know is that the INDEX command creates an NDX file that orders the DBF file according to some methodology you impose. The NDX file contains the secondary keys that you use to tell III PLUS what primary keys to look at in the DBF file.

The SORT command doesn't create any NDX files. Instead, it creates a brand new DBF file that contains the records physically ordered according to your methodology.

Syntax   The SORT command has a somewhat involved syntax. The first part of the command is

SORT TO target file

This command assumes some DBF file is open and active in the current work area. The target file is a DBF file and follows the standard III PLUS filenaming conventions. You can tell III PLUS either to use a different file extension or no extension. III PLUS gives the target file a .DBF extension unless you tell it otherwise.

Once you've decided what to call your SORTed file, you have to tell III PLUS what the ordering method is going to be. That is done by specifying the FIELDS to SORT ON, as in

SORT TO target file ON field1

This specifies one field, "field1", as the field you really want to know about. A similar INDEX command would be

INDEX ON field1 TO target file

An example of this type of SORT is shown in Figures 3-38 and 3-39. Figure 3-39 shows a sample of the data from a book database exactly as it was entered. There isn't much order there. The command

SORT ON TITLE TO BOOKS2

tells III PLUS to impose an order on the TITLE field in the BOOK database and write the resulting order to a new file called BOOKS2. There are three things to note here. First, the user didn't have to tell III PLUS to perform an ASCENDING SORT. That was automatic.

```
-> USE BOOKS
-> DISP ALL
Record#  TITLE
      1  ROGET'S UNIVERSITY THESAURUS
      2  OXFORD AMERICAN DICTIONARY
      3  Words
      4  American Heritage Dictionary
      5  Webster's New World Dictionary
      6  BOOK OF JARGON, THE
      7  BARTLETT'S FAMILIAR QUOTATIONS
      8  Handbook of Good English, The
      9  Roget's International Thesaurus
     10  DICTIONARY OF PHILOSOPHY AND RELIGION
     11  METAMAGICAL THEMAS
     12  Guardian
     13  History of Witchcraft and Demonology, The
     14  Soul of CP/M
     15  OTHER WORLDS
     16  GODEL, ESCHER, BACH
     17  Connections
     18  Essential Talmud, The
     19  Acts and Letters of the Apostles
-> 
```

Figure 3-38. This BOOK database is used in this section to show the type of ordering methods available with the SORT command

Second, the key difference between SORT and INDEX is that the INDEX command creates a secondary key file according to your ordering methods. The SORT command creates a primary key file according to your ordering methods. Third, the placement of words is mixed in the command. It doesn't matter if you TO or ON first. III PLUS can figure it out.

III PLUS automatically performs an ASCENDING SORT on your data. You can specify a DESCENDING SORT with

SORT ON field name /D TO target file

Performing a DESCENDING SORT on the BOOKS database is done with

SORT ON TITLE /D TO BOOKS3

```
-> SORT ON TITLE TO BOOKS2
-> USE BOOKS2
-> DISP ALL
Record#   TITLE
       1  Acts and Letters of the Apostles
       2  American Heritage Dictionary
       3  BARTLETT'S FAMILIAR QUOTATIONS
       4  BOOK OF JARGON, THE
       5  Connections
       6  DICTIONARY OF PHILOSOPHY AND RELIGION
       7  Essential Talmud, The
       8  GODEL, ESCHER, BACH
       9  Guardian
      10  Handbook of Good English, The
      11  History of Witchcraft and Demonology, The
      12  METAMAGICAL THEMAS
      13  OTHER WORLDS
      14  OXFORD AMERICAN DICTIONARY
      15  ROGET'S UNIVERSITY THESAURUS
      16  Roget's International Thesaurus
      17  Soul of CP/M
      18  Webster's New World Dictionary
      19  Words
-> 
```

Figure 3-39. The BOOK database is SORTed on the TITLE field in ASCENDING order TO the BOOKS2 database to produce this listing

and is shown in Figure 3-40.

You can also tell III PLUS to note the differences between UPPERCASE and lowercase letters with the /C option. An example of this is shown in Figures 3-41 and 3-42.

Up to ten fields can be included in the SORT command. Each field can be qualified with the /A (ASCENDING, the default), /D (DESCENDING), /C (CASE), or the combinations /AC (ASCENDING CASE) or /DC (DESCENDING CASE). The first field listed is the primary SORT key, the second field is the secondary SORT key, and so on for the ten fields if listed. For example, the command

SORT ON field1/DC, field2/C, field3/AC TO target file

```
-> SORT ON TITLE /D TO BOOKS3
-> USE BOOKS3
-> DISP ALL
Record#  TITLE
       1  Words
       2  Webster's New World Dictionary
       3  Soul of CP/M
       4  Roget's International Thesaurus
       5  ROGET'S UNIVERSITY THESAURUS
       6  OXFORD AMERICAN DICTIONARY
       7  OTHER WORLDS
       8  METAMAGICAL THEMAS
       9  History of Witchcraft and Demonology, The
      10  Handbook of Good English, The
      11  Guardian
      12  GODEL, ESCHER, BACH
      13  Essential Talmud, The
      14  DICTIONARY OF PHILOSOPHY AND RELIGION
      15  Connections
      16  BOOK OF JARGON, THE
      17  BARTLETT'S FAMILIAR QUOTATIONS
      18  American Heritage Dictionary
      19  Acts and Letters of the Apostles
-> 
```

Figure 3-40. The BOOK database is SORTed on the TITLE field in DESCENDING order TO the BOOKS3 database to produce this listing

tells III PLUS that field1 is the most important field to SORT ON, and to perform a DESCENDING CASE SORT ON that field. Once III PLUS has SORTed on field1, it is told to perform a secondary SORT ON field2 and pay attention to CASE. When III PLUS is done with field2, it is to perform a tertiary SORT on field3 in ASCENDING CASE order. When III PLUS has finished the three SORTs, it is told to write the resulting DBF file as the named target file.

The next part of the SORT command is the ever-popular SCOPE option. The SCOPE option tells III PLUS how many records in the source database to SORT into the target file. SORTing only the first ten records in a database would be done with

SORT ON field TO target file NEXT 10

```
-> USE BOOKS
-> DISP ALL
Record#   TITLE
       1  ROGET'S UNIVERSITY THESAURUS
       2  OXFORD AMERICAN DICTIONARY
       3  Words
       4  American Heritage Dictionary
       5  Webster's New World Dictionary
       6  BOOK OF JARGON, THE
       7  BARTLETT'S FAMILIAR QUOTATIONS
       8  Handbook of Good English, The
       9  Roget's International Thesaurus
      10  DICTIONARY OF PHILOSOPHY AND RELIGION
      11  METAMAGICAL THEMAS
      12  Guardian
      13  History of Witchcraft and Demonology, The
      14  Soul of CP/M
      15  OTHER WORLDS
      16  GODEL, ESCHER, BACH
      17  Connections
      18  Essential Talmud, The
      19  Acts and Letters of the Apostles
   ->
```

Figure 3-41. The BOOK database, having a few records changed to
UPPERCASE, is SORTed to produce this listing

III PLUS assumes every record is going to be SORTed unless you
specify otherwise.

The last part of the SORT command involves the FOR and
WHILE qualifiers. You can instruct III PLUS to SORT only records
that meet conditions specified by the FOR and WHILE qualifiers.
The FOR qualifier performs a sequential search for matching
records, and WHILE performs a logical search. In this aspect, both
FOR and WHILE perform identically with their COPY counterparts.

The FOR and WHILE qualifiers are not mutually exclusive. You
should recognize that the WHILE qualifier is best used when an
NDX file is active.

SORTing records that meet some condition (field1 = "condition1"
in the following example) can be done with

```
-> SORT ON TITLE /C TO BOOKS4
-> USE BOOKS4
-> DISP ALL
Record#  TITLE
        1  Acts and Letters of the Apostles
        2  American Heritage Dictionary
        3  BARTLETT'S FAMILIAR QUOTATIONS
        4  BOOK OF JARGON, THE
        5  Connections
        6  DICTIONARY OF PHILOSOPHY AND RELIGION
        7  Essential Talmud, The
        8  GODEL, ESCHER, BACH
        9  Guardian
       10  Handbook of Good English, The
       11  History of Witchcraft and Demonology, The
       12  METAMAGICAL THEMAS
       13  OTHER WORLDS
       14  OXFORD AMERICAN DICTIONARY
       15  Roget's International Thesaurus
       16  ROGET'S UNIVERSITY THESAURUS
       17  Soul of CP/M
       18  Webster's New World Dictionary
       19  Words
-> 
```

Figure 3-42.   The BOOK database used in Figure 3-41 is SORTed again, but this time using the /C option to tell III PLUS to differentiate between UPPERCASE and lowercase data

SORT ON fields TO target file FOR field1 = "condition1"

This tells III PLUS to go through the entire source file and find the records that meet the preceding condition. III PLUS is to SORT only those records to the target file. A similar method can be used when an NDX file is open and associated with the source database. The SORT command then becomes

SORT ON fields TO target file WHILE field1 = "condition1"

This assumes the record pointer has been set to the first record to meet the condition with the FIND, SEEK, or LOCATE command. The FOR and WHILE commands can be used together, but you should be careful in their use. A full explanation of FOR and WHILE when SORTing is in the next section.

Use   The SORT command can be used when data needs to be presented according to some orderly pattern, but is rarely APPENDed, INSERTed, or EDITed. This is the best command to use when it is necessary to produce a saleable mailing list. You can provide SORTs on up to ten fields according to your client's needs. An example of mail-list SORTs is shown in the "Advanced Use" section.

Most often, the SORT command is used in much the same way that someone would post time-related listings. The IRS likes things posted quarterly. In essence, it asks for a quarterly SORT of information. The SORT stays in effect until the next posting period. Another SORT is done at that time.

The SORT command does not warn you when it is about to write over an existing file unless either the SET SAFETY or CONFIG.DB SAFETY command is ON.

There are other similarities between the INDEX and SORT commands. For instance, both are unable to create orders on either LOGICAL or MEMO fields. Both update any CAT file in effect. Note that the SORT command cannot SORT a database to itself. This produces an error message. You should also note that you can't SORT on functions or other normally valid dBASE III PLUS expressions. The SORT command is valid only with actual field names from the source database.

The last aspect of SORTing to discuss deals with the FOR and WHILE qualifiers. The FOR and WHILE qualifiers are another version of the SCOPE qualifier shown in the "Syntax" section. These qualifiers can be used in conjunction with each other or separately.

Essentially, the FOR and WHILE qualifiers tell III PLUS to continue SORTing data to the target file as long as some logical condition or conditions are met. You can

SORT ON fields TO target file FOR condition

III PLUS will perform the SORT operation on every record in the source file that meets the FOR condition in the command. The condition can be any valid III PLUS expression. Because you start with an unINDEXed database, you can use the FOR qualifier to go through the database in a sequential search. dBASE III PLUS looks at each record, from the first to the last, when you use the FOR option by itself no matter what command is being FORed. An example of WHILE is

SORT ON fields TO target file WHILE condition

This command assumes that the source file is INDEXed on some field that is part of the condition and that the record pointer is at the first record that meets that condition. You can use the SORT command with the WHILE qualifier to SORT only those records that meet the condition entered with the command. Note that the WHILE command must be used on the keyfield for it to work correctly.

Advanced Use   One type of work where the SORT command is invaluable is that done by the company that makes its living through the mail. The firm's principal tool is the mailing list. It can create its own mailing list or buy someone else's. Invariably, the company that develops its own mailing list decides to sell it to other companies.

But each company that purchases a mailing list has different needs, based on its product, its distribution channels, and its marketing efforts. For example, consider a local mail-order company that had developed a large list of names and addresses in a short period of time. Unfortunately, the firm wasn't having much luck marketing its products. Nevertheless, it did have an extensive list of names throughout the U.S. and Canada. Someone suggested that the company see if any other similar companies (but ones that were turning a profit) would be interested in getting semiannually updated mailing lists, complete with labels.

TOTAL

The last command covered in this chapter is TOTAL. The TOTAL command writes a DBF file that contains TOTALs of all numeric fields in the source database.

Syntax   The TOTAL command, like the TOTAL command in the previous section, as well as several other III PLUS commands, has a somewhat complex syntax. The basic syntax for the TOTAL command is

TOTAL ON keyfield TO target file

The target file is a III PLUS DBF file and follows all the naming conventions discussed elsewhere in this chapter. The new part of the command is the KEYFIELD qualifier.

The TOTAL command looks at one field in the entire database. It looks at the same field in each record, much as a simple INDEX command would do. That one field is called the keyfield. The Use section explains why the keyfield is so important to the TOTAL command.

The next part of the TOTAL command to concern yourself with is the SCOPE qualifier. The TOTAL command will only TOTAL as many records as you tell it to TOTAL. You can TOTAL the NEXT ten records in the source file with

TOTAL ON keyfield TO target file NEXT 10

You should note that the NEXT qualifier doesn't care where in the source file you issue the command. If you're at the beginning of the file and have 1000 records, you can TOTAL ON the NEXT 10 with relative surety of achieving your goal. If you're positioned at record 996, however, the same command will only TOTAL the last four records in the database.

Because the TOTAL command operates on fields in the source database, you have the option of telling it which fields you want included in the TOTAL. You can tell III PLUS what fields to TOTAL with

TOTAL ON keyfield TO target file FIELDS field1, field2,...

Each field listed after the FIELDS qualifier becomes a TOTALed field in the target file. For instance, the EXPENSES.DBF structure shown in the following listing lists two numeric data fields, PAY-AMOUNT and MILEAGE:

```
-> USE EXPENSES
-> DISP STRUC
Structure for database: C:EXPENSES.dbf
Number of data records:       16
Date of last update   : 07/13/86
Field  Field Name  Type        Width     Dec
    1  PAYTO       Character      40
    2  PAYFOR      Character      60
    3  CHECKNUM    Character      10
    4  PAYAMOUNT   Numeric        10        2
    5  PAYDATE     Date            8
    6  MILEAGE     Numeric         7        1
** Total **                     136
```

Assuming you had INDEXed or TOTALed the EXPENSES.DBF file on the PAYFOR field, you could instruct III PLUS to TOTAL both numeric data fields with

TOTAL ON PAYTO TO target file FIELDS PAYTO, MILEAGE

An example of this appears in the "Advanced Use" section.

The last part of the TOTAL command involves the FOR and WHILE qualifiers. You can instruct III PLUS to TOTAL records only that meet conditions specified by the FOR and WHILE qualifiers. The FOR qualifier performs a sequential search for matching records, and WHILE performs a logical search. In this aspect, FOR and WHILE perform identically with their COPY and SORT counterparts. The FOR and WHILE qualifiers are not mutually exclusive. You should recognize that the WHILE qualifier is best used when an NDX file is active.

TOTALing records that meet some condition (field1 = "condition1" in the following example) can be done with

TOTAL ON keyfield TO target file FOR field1 = "condition1"

This tells III PLUS to go through the entire source file and find the records that meet this condition. It is to TOTAL only those records to the target file. A similar method can be used when an NDX file is open and associated with the source database. The TOTAL command then becomes

TOTAL ON keyfield TO target file WHIL field1 = "condition1"

Note that the dBASE III PLUS four-letter-word convention is

used in the command. The preceding TOTAL command assumes the record pointer has been set to the first record to meet the condition, with the FIND, SEEK, or LOCATE commands. The FOR and WHILE commands can be used together, but you should be careful in their use. A full explanation of FOR and WHILE when TOTALing follows.

Use   The TOTAL command has a limit imposed on it by III PLUS. The TOTAL command has to work with either an INDEXed or SORTed DBF file. It works by looking at one field in the entire DBF. It operates on several fields, if told to, but it searches for only one field while it operates on the several.

Like the INDEX and SORT commands, the TOTAL command looks for differences in the one keyfield that it is searching for in the source DBF. Every time it finds a record with a keyfield identical to the keyfield in the last record it operated on, III PLUS adds the numeric fields in the new record to those in the old record. This summation is called TOTALing. A practical example of TOTALing is shown in the "Advanced Use" section.

The topics of the NEXT qualifier and FIELDS have been covered well enough in the "Syntax" section to go directly into the FOR and WHILE qualifiers here. These qualifiers are often used to create smaller TOTALed files.

The FOR and WHILE qualifiers are another version of the scope qualifier shown in the "Syntax" section. These qualifiers can be used in conjunction with each other or separately.

Essentially, the FOR and WHILE qualifiers tell III PLUS to continue TOTALing data to the target file as long as some logical condition or conditions are met. You can

TOTAL ON field TO target file FOR condition

III PLUS will perform the TOTAL operation on every record in the source file that meets the FOR condition in the command. The condition can be any valid III PLUS expression. Because you start with an unINDEXed database, you can use the FOR qualifier to go through the database in a sequential search. dBASE III PLUS looks at each record, from the first to the last, when you use the FOR option by itself, no matter what command is being FORed. An example of WHILE is

This command makes the assumption that the source file is INDEXed on some field that is part of the condition and that the record pointer is at the first record that meets that condition. You can use the TOTAL command with the WHILE qualifier to TOTAL only those records that meet the condition entered with the command. The WHILE command must be used on the keyfield for it to work correctly.

Advanced Use   A practical example of the TOTAL command is one that is used to organize information for the IRS 1040-SE schedule. Every quarter, the IRS wants to know how much money you've made and how you made it. The code in the following listing shows how that data is TOTALed from the EXPENSES.DBF file shown earlier in the TOTAL section.

```
USE EXPENSES INDE PAYFOR
TOTA ON PAYFOR TO TANK FIELDS PAYAMOUNT
SELE 2
USE TANK
SELE 3
USE EXPTTLS INDE EXPTTLS
UPDA ON PAYFOR FROM B REPL PAYAMOUNT WITH ;
      PAYAMOUN + B->PAYAMOUNT RANDOM
SELE 2
GOTO 1
*
DO WHIL .NOT. EOF()
   SELE 3
   SEEK B->PAYFOR
*
   IF .NOT. FOUND()
      APPE BLANK
      REPL NEXT 1 PAYFOR WITH B->PAYFOR, ;
      PAYAMOUNT WITH B->PAYAMOUNT
   ENDI
*
   SELE 2
   SKIP
ENDD
*
SELE 3
USE
SELE 2
USE
ERAS TANK.DBF
SELE 1
```

The source database is EXPENSES INDEXed on the PAYFOR fields. You TOTAL the EXPENSES database ON PAYFOR as the keyfield TO a temporary TANK.DBF file. Next, you SELECT and USE the TANK file and a third file, EXPTTLS, INDEXed on the PAYFOR field to EXPTTLS.NDX. "EXPTTLS" is an acronym for EXPense ToTaLS. You then UPDATE the EXPTTLS file on PAYFOR.

There is always the possibility that you will have expenses this quarter that you didn't incur last quarter. You add those new expenses to the EXPTTLS file in the DO WHILE...ENDDO loop. This is necessary because the UPDATE command only works on identical field values. No new PAYFOR values will be included in the UPDATE. This way, you can assure yourself that new items are included in the yearly and quarterly printouts. The rest of the listing does simple housekeeping.

What you should observe about this block of code is how it uses the TOTAL command to generate a database, shown in the following listing, that contains the TOTALed data. This one command saves the developer/programmer/user several steps of code if that user is limited to only the SUM and COPY commands.

The TOTAL command creates the TOTALed DBF file with the desired fields, organized on the keyfield, with numeric fields summed in one operation.

```
-> USE EXPTTLS
-> DISP STRUC
Structure for database: C:EXPTTLS.dbf
Number of data records:        21
Date of last update   : 07/13/86
Field  Field Name  Type        Width   Dec
    1  PAYFOR      Character     60
    2  PAYAMOUNT   Numeric       10      2
** Total **                     71

-> LIST PAYAMOUNT, TRIM(PAYFOR)
Record#    PAYAMOUNT TRIM(PAYFOR)
    1          0.00
    2         29.70 Advertising
    3        778.82 Auto Expense
    4        236.12 Books
    5        157.50 Education
    6       1901.53 Equipment
    7        260.00 Legal
    8         58.22 Magazine
    9         49.22 Meals Out
   10         43.25 Motel
```

```
11    1409.12 Office Equipment
12     679.53 Office Supplies
13       8.00 Parking fee
14     143.72 Phone
15     241.55 Postage
16     304.80 Rent, Utilities
17      15.00 Research
18       6.50 Toll
19     320.50 Travel
20       0.00 Rental Insurance
21       0.00 Delphi
```

File Modifying Commands

This chapter covers all the commands that alter what a file is or what it does; that is, it discusses "Modifying" commands. These commands allow you to change a database file in some way other than adding data (see Chapter 6 for data addition commands). An example of such a command is SET ALTERNATE ON/off, discussed later in this chapter. This command doesn't create a new ALTERNATE file, but it does modify the file by placing more screen information in it.

DELETE FILE

The DELETE FILE command is synonymous with another command in this chapter, ERASE. Both commands can be used to remove files from the disk. That, of course, means there is a danger of removing valuable files. The "Advanced Use" section lists a program that avoids this danger.

Syntax   The command syntax is

DELETE FILE filename.ext

Note that the command needs the full filename. You cannot

DELETE FILE filename

because III PLUS will not know what you're doing and will give you an error message. Also, the command will accept drive and path designators as part of the filename. To DELETE the "PROSPECT.DBF" FILE in the C:\DB3\COMPLETE directory, you have to enter

This assumes C: \DB3 \COMPLETE is not the default drive and directory. III PLUS assumes the default drive and directory when no others are included in the filename.

Use   Use of the DELETE FILE command is fraught with dangers. The most obvious danger is that the user might remove a valuable file from the disk when executing this command.

The command also tells you if it can't find the FILE you want to DELETE (see Figure 4-1). The "Advanced Use" section shows a programmatic way of DELETEing FILES.

Advanced Use   The method of advanced use described here shows how you can selectively DELETE FILEs from a disk. The code, shown in the following listing, uses two databases, FILETANK and FILE1.

```
** DELETER.PRG TO DELETE DISK FILES UNDER USER CONTROL
*
CLEA
CLOSE ALL
SELE 2
USE FILE1
SELE 1
USE FILETANK
SET CONS OFF
SET ALTER TO FILETANK
SET ALTER ON
LIST FILES LIKE *.*
CLOSE ALTER
SET CONS ON
APPE FROM FILETANK SDF
1
DELE NEXT 2
GOTO RECCOUNT() - 4
DELE NEXT 5
PACK
*
DO WHIL .NOT. EOF()
    SELE 2
    APPE BLAN
    REPL NEXT 1 FILENAME WITH SUBSTR(A->FILES,1,13)
    APPE BLAN
    REPL NEXT 1 FILENAME WITH SUBSTR(A->FILES,20,13)
    APPE BLAN
    REPL NEXT 1 FILENAME WITH SUBSTR(A->FILES,39,13)
    APPE BLAN
    REPL NEXT 1 FILENAME WITH SUBSTR(A->FILES,58,13)
    SELE 1
    SKIP
```

```
ENDD
*
SELE 2
LOCA FOR FILENAME = "FILETANK.DBF"
DELE
LOCA FOR FILENAME = "FILE1.DBF"
DELE
LOCA FOR FILENAME = "FILE2.DBF"
PACK
SORT ON FILENAME TO FILE2
USE FILE2
ACCE "FILE TO DELETE ('ALL', 'EXT', 'FILENAME', 'LIST')? ->
" TO KILLS
KILLS = UPPER(KILLS)
*
DO CASE
   CASE KILLS = 'ALL'
        1
*
      DO WHIL .NOT. EOF()
         KILLS = + FILENAME

         ? "DELETING " + FILENAME
         DELE FILE &KILLS
         SKIP
      ENDD
*
   CASE KILLS = 'EXT'
      ACCE "WHAT IS THE EXTENSION (3 CHAR MAX)? -> " TO KILLS
      KILLS = "." + KILLS
      LOCA ALL FOR AT(KILLS,FILENAME) # 0
*
      DO WHIL .NOT. EOF()
         THISONE = FILENAME
         ? "DELETING " + FILENAME
         DELE FILE &THISONE
         CONT
      ENDD
*
   CASE KILLS = 'FILENAME'
      ACCE "WHAT IS THE FILENAME (8 CHAR MAX)? -> " TO KILLS
      KILLS = KILLS + "."
```

```
-> DELE FILE C10.DBF
File has been deleted.
-> DELE FILE DOLORS.BAK
File has been deleted.
-> DELE FILE C10.HMM
File does not exist
->
```

Figure 4-1.   The DELETE FILE command tells you when you're trying
to DELETE a nonexistent FILE

```
          LOCA ALL FOR AT(KILLS,FILENAME) # 0
*
       DO WHIL .NOT. EOF()
          THISONE = FILENAME
          ? "DELETING " + FILENAME
          DELE FILE &THISONE
          CONT
       ENDD
*
    CASE KILLS = 'LIST'
       CLEA
       YORN = .T.
       LOOPER = 1
       1
*
       DO WHIL .NOT. EOF()
          @ RECNO()/LOOPER,0 SAY FILENAME + " Y/N -> ";
                                       GET YORN PICT "Y"

          READ
*
          IF YORN
             KILLS = FILENAME
             DELE FILE &KILLS
             @ RECNO()/LOOPER,13 SAY "HAS MET MAGNETIC DEATH"
          ENDI
*
          IF RECNO()/LOOPER > 23
             LOOPER = LOOPER + 1
          ENDI
*
          SKIP
       ENDD
*

ENDC
*
ZAP
USE FILE1
ZAP
SELE 1
ZAP
CLOSE ALL
*
** EOF
```

The FILE1 database is SORTed to another database, FILE2. The
following listing shows the structure for FILETANK and FILE1:

```
-> USE FILETANK
-> DISP STRUC
Structure for database: C:FILETANK.dbf
Number of data records:      0
Date of last update   : 07/22/86
Field  Field Name  Type       Width    Dec
    1  FILES       Character     80
** Total **                     81

-> USE FILE1
```

```
-> DISP STRUC
Structure for database: C:FILE1.dbf
Number of data records:        0
Date of last update    : 07/22/86
Field  Field Name  Type      Width     Dec
    1  FILENAME    Character    12
** Total **                     13
```

The DELETER.PRG file works very simply. It starts by CLOSEing ALL open files. This allows III PLUS to DELETE all the FILEs. You USE FILE1 first, because you need that file eventually and want to get it out of the way early in the program.

Your next step is to USE the FILETANK.DBF, which is structured as one 80-character-wide field. You create a FILETANK.TXT ALTERNATE file. All ALTERNATE files are 80 characters wide. The ALTERNATE file stays open only long enough to receive a specific LISTing of FILES LIKE *.*. In other words, you want the FILETANK.TXT ALTERNATE file to get a directory listing.

Remember that FILETANK.DBF is still in USE and in the current work area. You APPEND the System Default Format FILE-TANK.TXT file. The following listings show the information in the ALTERNATE and DBF file formats, respectively. You'll notice that there are some wasted records in the DBF file. Those are taken care of with the two DEL commands. You PACK after DELETEing to ensure that you will only have records in the FILETANK.DBF file that contain the names of files on the disk.

```
   -> TYPE FILETANK.TXT

    7CSETANK.DBF        PASSWORD.DBT        PROMPTS.DBF
PROMPTER.TXT
    PASSWORD.NDX        TANK.VUE            TANK.SCR
TEMP.TXT
    TEMP.SCR            TEMP.FMT            TANK.LBL
PASSWORD.DBF
    TANK2.DBF           DELIMS.PRG          TED.STR
ALTER.TXT
    CHAPTER9.DBF        CHAPTER9.DBT        CHAPTER9.SCR
CHAPTER9.FMT
    TANK.DBT            TANK.TXT            TEMP.DBF
TANK.FMT
    CITYTANK.FRM        CITYTANK.NDX        CHAPTER9.TXT
SAVETANK.DBT
    C9SECURE.TXT        TEMP.DBT            EDITDBFL.SCR
CHAPTER9.1
    C9SECURE.SCR        C9SECURE.FMT        C9EDITNG.PRG
CLACCT.DBF
    CPYSTREX.PRG        7TANK.DBT           7TANK.TXT
7TANK.SCR
    7TANK.FMT           -UN1CTGY.NDX        ART.FMT
```

```
CHAPTER7.FMT
      CHAPTER7.SCR          CHAPTER7.TXT          CHAPTER7.VUE
NAMES.QRY
      EDITDBFL.BAK          UNIQCTGY.NDX          EDITDBFL.DBF
PASS2.DBF
      CITYSTAT.NDX          NAME.NDX              OUTPUT.TXT
OUTPUT2.TXT
      PASS2.DBT            MASTER.CAT            CATALOG.CAT
CHAPTER9.VUE
      DB3.WKS              EXPENSES.DBF          EXPENSES.WKS
EXPENSES.NDX
      C10.DBF              C10-1.TXT            TED.OLD
C10-1.FW2
      SEFILE.DBF           C10CTEST.DBF          C10CT2.DBF
COPYDELI.TXT
      ERASER.BAK           C10CT2.DBT           C10COPY.PRG
ERASER.PRG
      C10CFILE.PRG         DELIMB.TXT           TED.BAK
EDITDBFL.FMT
      TED.LBL              TED2.DBF             TED3.DBF
TEDALL3.LBL
      TED.DBF              TED2.NDX             TED3.NDX
C10CQRY.DBF
      C10CQRY.QRY          FILTSET.MEM          FILTSET.PRG
TEDREPT.FRM
      TEDSCR.SCR           TEDSCR.FMT           TEST.VUE
TED.VUE
      FRED.VUE             FRED2.VUE            TED
PFSTEST.DBF
      PFSTEST             PFSFILE              PFSFILE.PFS
PFSTEST.SCR
      PFSTEST.FMT          PAYTO.NDX            EXPALL.NDX
EXPUNIQ.NDX
      OTHER.DBF            JOINTANK.DBF          JOINFILE.DBF
C10TEST.PRG
      C10TEST             C10.PRG              C10.MEM
TEST.TXT
      C10TEST.TXT          C10.TXT              BOOKS.DBF
BOOKS2.DBF
      BOOKS3.DBF           BOOKS4.DBF            FILETANK.DBF
FILE2.DBF
      FILE1.DBF            FILETANK.TXT

      354888 bytes in    126 files.
     3346432 bytes remaining on drive.



-> USE FILETANK.DBF
-> LIST ALL
Record#  FILES
     1

     2  7CSETANK.DBF         PASSWORD.DBT          PROMPTS.DBF
PROMPTER.TXT
     3  PASSWORD.NDX         TANK.VUE             TANK.SCR
TEMP.TXT
     4  TEMP.SCR             TEMP.FMT             TANK.LBL
```

```
PASSWORD.DBF
        5   TANK2.DBF       DELIMS.PRG        TED.STR
ALTER.TXT
        6   CHAPTER9.DBF    CHAPTER9.DBT      CHAPTER9.SCR
CHAPTER9.FMT
        7   TANK.DBT        TANK.TXT          TEMP.DBF
TANK.FMT
        8   CITYTANK.FRM    CITYTANK.NDX      CHAPTER9.TXT
SAVETANK.DBT
        9   C9SECURE.TXT    TEMP.DBT          EDITDBFL.SCR
CHAPTER9.1
       10   C9SECURE.SCR    C9SECURE.FMT      C9EDITNG.PRG
CLACCT.DBF
       11   CPYSTREX.PRG    7TANK.DBT         7TANK.TXT
7TANK.SCR
       12   7TANK.FMT       -UNICTGY.NDX      ART.FMT
CHAPTER7.FMT
       13   CHAPTER7.SCR    CHAPTER7.TXT      CHAPTER7.VUE
NAMES.QRY
       14   EDITDBFL.BAK    UNIQCTGY.NDX      EDITDBFL.DBF
PASS2.DBF
       15   CITYSTAT.NDX    NAME.NDX          OUTPUT.TXT
OUTPUT2.TXT
       16   PASS2.DBT       MASTER.CAT        CATALOG.CAT
CHAPTER9.VUE
       17   DB3.WKS         EXPENSES.DBF      EXPENSES.WKS
EXPENSES.NDX
       18   C10.DBF         C10-1.TXT         TED.OLD
C10-1.FW2
       19   SEFILE.DBF      C10CTEST.DBF      C10CT2.DBF
COPYDELI.TXT
       20   ERASER.BAK      C10CT2.DBT        C10COPY.PRG
ERASER.PRG
       21   C10CFILE.PRG    DELIMB.TXT        TED.BAK
EDITDBFL.FMT
       22   TED.LBL         TED2.DBF          TED3.DBF
TEDALL3.LBL
       23   TED.DBT         TED2.NDX          TED3.NDX
C10CQRY.DBF
       24   C10CQRY.QRY     FILTSET.MEM       FILTSET.PRG
TEDREPT.FRM
       25   TEDSCR.SCR      TEDSCR.FMT        TEST.VUE
TED.VUE
       26   FRED.VUE        FRED2.VUE         TED
PFSTEST.DBF
       27   PFSTEST         PFSFILE           PFSFILE.PFS
PFSTEST.SCR
       28   PFSTEST.FMT     PAYTO.NDX         EXPALL.NDX
EXPUNIQ.NDX
       29   OTHER.DBF       JOINTANK.DBF      JOINFILE.DBF
C10TEST.PRG
       30   C10TEST         C10.PRG           C10.MEM
TEST.TXT
       31   C10TEST.TXT     C10.TXT           BOOKS.DBF
BOOKS2.DBF
       32   BOOKS3.DBF      BOOKS4.DBF        FILETANK.DBF
FILE2.DBF
       33   FILE1.DBF       FILETANK.TXT
```

File Modifying Commands

```
34

35    354888 bytes in    126 files.

36   3346432 bytes remaining on drive.
```

The DO WHILE...ENDDO loop is where you once again make use of the FILE1.DBF file. You first APPEND a BLANK record and then REPLACE the FILENAME field (the FILENAME field is the only one in each record) with the first filename in the FILES field in the FILETANK.DBF file.

This surgical editing of filenames in the FILES field is done with the SUBSTR( ) function. This function allows you to specify a starting and ending point for a string truncation.

Once all the filenames are transferred from the FILETANK database to the FILE1 database, you should make sure you don't try to DELETE any FILEs that will be in USE during the present and any future execution of the program. You LOCATE the records that contain the filenames FILETANK .DBF, FILE1.DBF, and FILE2 .DBF. Those three records are permanently taken out of harm's way by PACKING the FILE1 database. The remaining records are SORTed TO FILE2.DBF.

FILE2.DBF is then USEd. You decide whether you want to DELETE all FILES, files by extension, or files by filename, or whether you want to list the files and decide whether to DELETE them as you go along.

The DO CASE...ENDCASE statement takes the user's choice and operates by selectively DELETEing the intended FILES. Note that III PLUS doesn't allow you to use a field name in the DELETE FILE command. You can use a macro command in the DELETE FILE command without problems, however. Here, you can use

```
DELETE FILE &THISONE
```

as the macro substitution.

It is worth noting that this program is designed to work with the SAFETYs off. The program would be better if it allowed the user to verify each file's deletion in each of the CASEs.

ERASE

The ERASE command is identical to the DELETE FILE command. The command works and functions in exactly the same way as DELETE FILE. As such, the text will not go into great detail about the command's workings. In all cases, you can use the two commands interchangeably.

Syntax   The command syntax is

ERASE filename.ext

Note that the command needs the full filename. (Note also that, unlike the DELETE FILE command, ERASE does not include the word FILE.) You cannot

ERASE filename

because III PLUS will not know what you're doing. You will get an error message. Also, the command will accept drive and path designators as part of the filename. To ERASE the PROSPECT.DBF FILE in the C:\DB3\COMPLETE directory, you would have to enter

ERASE C:\DB3\COMPLETE\PROSPECT.DBF

This assumes C:\DB3\COMPLETE is not the default drive and directory. III PLUS assumes the default drive and directory when no others are included in the filename.

Use   It is easy to remove a valuable file from the disk when using the ERASE command.

This command also tells you if it can't find the file you want to ERASE. It does so in exactly the same way the DELETE FILE command would perform such a task (see Figure 4-1).

Advanced Use   To show how similar in both function and syntax the ERASE and DELETE FILE commands are, you can take the DELETER.PRG file and use a word processor to change every occurrence of DELETE FILE to ERASE; the program will work perfectly.

MODIFY COMMAND

The MODIFY COMMAND command was covered in detail in Chapter 3. The command itself is a special case of the MODIFY FILE command. MODIFY COMMAND has no advanced use.

Syntax   The syntax for this command is

MODIFY COMM prg file

The command itself can be used to make changes to any ASCII text file. III PLUS assumes that you are going to be working with PRG files when you use this command, however, so you could edit the ACCOUNTS.PRG file by entering

MODI COMM ACCOUNTS

Note that the text uses the dBASE III PLUS four-letter-word convention in the preceding command. You could also edit any other text file simply by including the proper extension.

You can use the MODIFY COMMAND command to alter FMT files without going through the MODIFY SCREEN command. For example, you could edit the TED.FMT file by entering

MODIFY COMMAND TED.FMT

This would allow you to edit the FMT file without using the intermediate SCR file and associated menu system.

Use   Use of the MODIFY COMMAND command is not limited to editing PRG files. Any text file can be used when III PLUS is given the extension. This allows you to be quite creative in making filenames that fit their purpose. For example, you can

MODI COMM ACCOUNTS.PRC

and edit the ACCOUNTS system's PROCEDURE file. Note that this file would have to be accessed with

SET PROC TO ACCOUNTS.PRC

in a program. Using varied extensions puts some housekeeping responsibility on the user. If you want to edit ACCOUNTS.FMT and instead type

MODI COMM ACCOUNTS

III PLUS will place you in the ACCOUNTS.PRG file. III PLUS will create a new file if the named file doesn't exist on the default drive and directory.

You can use drive and directory designators in the command without confusing III PLUS. For example, to edit the ACCOUNTS .PRG file located in C:\DB3\ACCOUNTS\GENERAL, you enter

MODI COMM C:\DB3\ACCOUNTS\GENERAL\ACCOUNTS

This assumes C:\DB3\ACCOUNTS is not the default drive and directory. III PLUS assumes the default drive and directory when no others are included in the filename.

MODIFY FILE

The MODIFY FILE command was covered in Chapter 3. This section briefly touches on the command because you can use it as an on-board text editor in dBASE III PLUS.

Syntax   The syntax of the command is

MODIFY FILE filename.ext

and must include the extension if one is going to be used. Entering

MODIFY FILE filename

with no extension causes III PLUS to write a file with no extension. This is different from the MODIFY COMMAND command discussed in the previous section and in Chapter 3. The MODIFY COMMAND command assumes a .PRG extension. The MODIFY FILE command assumes no extension.

Use   The MODIFY FILE command serves III PLUS as a general-purpose text editor. The ability it offers you to write any kind of file can be put to good use. You can use it to create text when memory is too low to allow the use of an external word processor. MODIFY FILE allows the use of macro substitutions; this is shown in the next section.

Advanced Use   In Chapter 3, it was asserted that the MODIFY FILE command has no advanced use. That is basically the case, but you can stretch the truth by demonstrating that the command can be used to develop a word-processing environment in the III PLUS system.

You must, however, start with the caveat that there are more elegant word processors that you can use in III PLUS if you use the RUN and ! commands. The following listing allows you to use the MODIFY FILE command as a text editor when, after loading in several memory-resident packages, there isn't enough memory left over to make use of external word processors.

```
** EDITOR.PRG USING THE MODIFY FILE COMMAND
*
SET TALK OFF
SET BELL OFF
SET SCORE ON
*
DO WHILE .T.
   CLEAR
   @ 2, 0 TO 13,79 DOUBLE
   @ 3,24 SAY [W R I T E / E D I T   M O D U L E]
   @ 4,1 TO 4,78 DOUBLE
   @ 7,33 SAY [1. WRITE/EDIT TEXT]
   @ 8,33 SAY [2. MAILMERGE]
   @ 9,33 SAY [3. MAKE LABELS]
   @ 11, 33 SAY '0. EXIT'
   STORE 0 TO selectnum
   @ 13,33 SAY " select      "
   @ 13,42 GET selectnum PICTURE "9" RANGE 0,3
   READ
*
   DO CASE
      CASE selectnum = 0
         RETURN
      CASE selectnum = 1
         @ 20,0 CLEA
         ACCE "FILE TO EDIT -> " TO FILENAME
```

```
            SET MENU ON
            MODI FILE &FILENAME
            SET MENU OFF
       CASE selectnum = 2
            @ 20,0 CLEA
            ACCE "FILE TO MERGE -> " TO FILENAME
            ACCE "CONDITION FOR MERGE (FIELD = 'CONDITION') -> " ;
                 TO CONDITION
            USE LETTER
            APPEN FROM &FILENAME SDF
            SELE 2
            USE CLIENTS
            LOCA FOR &CONDITION
*
            DO WHIL .NOT. EOF()
               SELE 1
               1
               SET PRINT ON
               ? LINE
               SKIP
               SELE 2
               ? NAME
               ? ADDRESS1
               ? ADDRESS2
               ? CITY + ", " + STATE + "        " + ZIPCODE
               ? COUNTRY
               SELE 1
*
               DO WHIL .NOT. EOF()
                  ? LINE
                  SKIP
               ENDDO
*
               SELE 2
               CONT
            ENDD
*
       CASE SELECTNUM = 3
            @ 20,0 CLEA
            ACCE "CONDITION FOR LABELS (FIELD = 'CONDITION') -> " ;
                 TO CONDITION
            LABEL FORM ADDRESS FOR &CONDITION
       ENDCASE
*
ENDDO T
*
** EOF: EDITOR.PRG
```

The menu system is self-explanatory. Skip through that to the second CASE, where selectnum = 1.

You specify the name of the file you want to edit. As long as you include the drive and directory designators, any filename is valid. You could respond to the ACCE prompt with

A:\CLIENTS\NH\OVERDUE.LTR

and III PLUS would use that as the macro substitution in the command

MODI FILE &FILENAME

Note that you should SET MENUs ON before you begin editing the file and SET MENUs OFF when you're finished. The MODIFY FILE command and its associated text editor are simplistic, so you need as much help as you can get.

For what it's worth, the third option (selectnum = 2) performs as a rudimentary mail merge by LOCATEing all records in the CLIENT database that meet a certain condition. The strategy for this program is quite similar to that used in the DELETER.PRG program listed earlier in this chapter.

The important part of the CLIENT.DBF file's structure is evident from the data used in the merge. The LETTER.DBF file has only one field per record. The one field, LINE, is 80 characters long.

The file that is actually edited with the MODIFY FILE command is used as an SDF file and APPENDed into the LETTER database. This database, as mentioned above, has only one field per record. Each record is one line of the original text. Of course, the LETTER.DBF file isn't USEd unless you want to mail merge your text file with something from your CLIENT database.

The third option allows you to tell III PLUS what CONDITION to use as the LOCATE argument. Note that you don't use FIND or SEEK at this point, although you could. Doing so would necessitate the use of much more code, which would be designed to gather information on what FIELD, what CONDITION, and so on. It is much simpler to use the LOCATE FOR command and let the computer do the work. In this case, even with a large database, the printer would be printing out one letter while III PLUS was searching for and formatting the next one.

Improvements to this code would be the ability to delimit fields in the text file and have III PLUS search for those fields and replace them with specific information in the CLIENT database. Actually, that process is shown in Chapter 21, using the SUBSTR( ) function.

MODIFY LABEL

The MODIFY LABEL command is identical to and interchangeable with the CREATE LABEL command described in Chapter 3. This command is used both to design new LBL forms and alter old ones. These LBL forms are used by III PLUS with the LABEL FORM command to generate mailing labels. The labels can be sent to both screen and printer.

The command form is

MODIFY LABEL lbl file

and uses a menu-driven form generator.

MODIFY QUERY

The MODIFY QUERY command is interchangeable with and identical to the CREATE QUERY command discussed in Chapter 3. The command form is

MODIFY QUERY qry file

This command opens a menu-driven design system that allows you to create custom QRY files. You then use these QRY files with the SET FILTER TO FILE command to tell III PLUS what information to mask in the database.

MODIFY REPORT

The MODIFY REPORT command is identical to and interchangeable with the CREATE REPORT command discussed in Chapter 3. This command either creates or edits FRM files that are then used to display information from the in-USE databases to the screen or printer. The command form is

MODIFY REPORT frm file

MODIFY SCREEN

The MODIFY SCREEN command is identical to and interchangeable with the CREATE SCREEN command discussed in Chapter 3. MODIFY SCREEN tells III PLUS to open a menu-driven design system. The menu system allows you to create new or edit old FMT files. The actual FMT files aren't edited, however.

An intermediate SCR file is edited with the MODIFY SCREEN and CREATE SCREEN commands. This SCR file is the screen image of the FMT file that is used with the SET FORMAT TO command. The MODIFY SCREEN and CREATE SCREEN commands allow editing of this intermediate SCR file. You have the option upon exiting from the MODIFY SCREEN and CREATE SCREEN commands of telling III PLUS to save the SCR file in FMT format or abandon the operation (see Figure 4-2).

Saving the SCR file tells III PLUS to write a new FMT file based on the editing done on the SCR file. The command form is

MODIFY SCREEN scr file

MODIFY STRUCTURE

The MODIFY STRUCTURE command is used identically with the CREATE dbf file command, but the two commands are not interchangeable. The CREATE dbf file command tells III PLUS to generate a new DBF file. It can't be used to edit an existing DBF file. Using the CREATE dbf command to edit an existing file forces III PLUS to erase the old file and start anew. Unless one of the SAFETY commands is on, this erasing of the old DBF file is done without warning you of the DBF file's potential destruction. However, the

MODIFY STRUCTURE command lets you edit the DBF file structure without deleting the old file.

Syntax   The syntax of the MODIFY STRUCTURE command is typical of commands designed to work with DBF files.

MODIFY STRUCTURE

Note that the command doesn't mention any other files when you enter it. III PLUS assumes some DBF file is in USE and is in the current work area when the command is entered. III PLUS prompts you for a DBF file if none are in USE in the current work area.

Use   The MODIFY STRUCTURE command opens up a menu-driven system identical with the CREATE dbf file command (see

Set Up   Modify   Options

MODIFY SCREEN   [D:]TEDSCR.SCR   Opt: 1/2   Caps
Position selection bar - ↑↓, Select - ↵, Leave menu - ←→, Blackboard - F10,
                    Exit and save changes.

Figure 4-1.   The MODIFY SCREEN command opens a menu-driven system that asks you to either save or abandon the changes made to the SCR and FMT files

File Modifying Commands   **179**

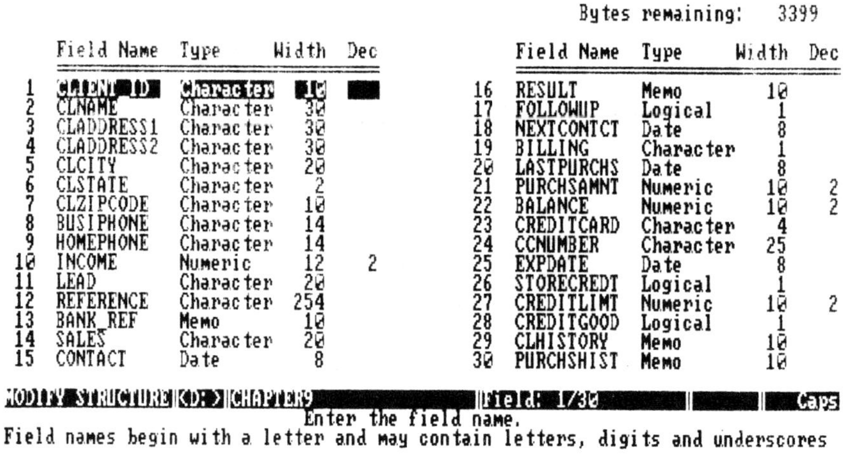

	Field Name	Type	Width	Dec		Field Name	Type	Width	Dec
1	CLIENT_ID	Character	10		16	RESULT	Memo	10	
2	CLNAME	Character	30		17	FOLLOWUP	Logical	1	
3	CLADDRESS1	Character	30		18	NEXTCONTCT	Date	8	
4	CLADDRESS2	Character	30		19	BILLING	Character	1	
5	CLCITY	Character	20		20	LASTPURCHS	Date	8	
6	CLSTATE	Character	2		21	PURCHSAMNT	Numeric	10	2
7	CLZIPCODE	Character	10		22	BALANCE	Numeric	10	2
8	BUSIPHONE	Character	14		23	CREDITCARD	Character	4	
9	HOMEPHONE	Character	14		24	CCNUMBER	Character	25	
10	INCOME	Numeric	12	2	25	EXPDATE	Date	8	
11	LEAD	Character	20		26	STORECREDT	Logical	1	
12	REFERENCE	Character	254		27	CREDITLIMT	Numeric	10	2
13	BANK_REF	Memo	10		28	CREDITGOOD	Logical	1	
14	SALES	Character	20		29	CLHISTORY	Memo	10	
15	CONTACT	Date	8		30	PURCHSHIST	Memo	10	

MODIFY STRUCTURE |<D:>|CHAPTER9 |Field: 1/30 | |Caps
Enter the field name.
Field names begin with a letter and may contain letters, digits and underscores

Figure 4-3.   The MODIFY STRUCTURE command opens up a screen that is identical with the CREATE dbf file command

Figure 4-3). The command assumes a DBF file is accessible. Normally, the command is used in the interactive mode as

```
USE dbf file
MODI STRUC
```

MODIFYing a database STRUCTURE actually causes several things to happen. First and foremost, III PLUS makes a backup copy of the database in USE. This backup copy is actually a temporary file that is used to prevent III PLUS from damaging the valued DBF file by accident. Changes are then made to the STRUCTURE of the DBF file.

When you are finished making changes, III PLUS asks for confirmation and, once that is given, tells you that only data fields with similar names will be copied from the old DBF file to the MODIFYed one (Figure 4-4). You can specify data COPYing from all fields, regardless of field name changes. III PLUS does this by matching field names first and then matching field positions.

	Field Name	Type	Width	Dec		Field Name	Type	Width	Dec
1	RALPH	Character	10		16	RESULT	Memo	10	
2	CLNAME	Character	30		17	FOLLOWUP	Logical	1	
3	CLADDRESS1	Character	30		18	NEXTCONTCT	Date	8	
4	CLADDRESS2	Character	30		19	BILLING	Character	1	
5	CLCITY	Character	20		20	LASTPURCHS	Date	8	
6	CLSTATE	Character	2		21	PURCHSAMNT	Numeric	10	2
7	CLZIPCODE	Character	10		22	BALANCE	Numeric	10	2
8	BUSIPHONE	Character	14		23	CREDITCARD	Character	4	
9	HOMEPHONE	Character	14		24	CCNUMBER	Character	25	
10	INCOME	Numeric	12	2	25	EXPDATE	Date	8	
11	LEAD	Character	20		26	STORECREDT	Logical	1	
12	REFERENCE	Character	254		27	CREDITLIMT	Numeric	10	2
13	BANK_REF	Memo	10		28	CREDITGOOD	Logical	1	
14	SALES	Character	20		29	CLHISTORY	Memo	10	
15	CONTACT	Date	8		30	PURCHSHIST	Memo	10	

MODIFY STRUCTURE <DB> CHAPTER9   Field: 1/30   Caps
Press ENTER to confirm. Any other key to resume.
Database records will be APPENDED from backup fields of the same name only!!

Figure 4-4. The MODIFY STRUCTURE command only copies data fields from the old DBF file to the MODIFYed DBF file that have the same field name in both

MODIFY VIEW

The MODIFY VIEW command is identical to and interchangeable with the CREATE VIEW command. Both commands can create and edit new or existing VUE files. Information on the CREATE VIEW command can be found in Chapter 3.

Syntax   The syntax of the command is identical to that of the CREATE VIEW command and is

MODIFY VIEW vue file

This tells III PLUS to open the menu-driven design system. Note that the command asks for a VUE file if none is given when the command is entered.

Use   One use of the MODIFY VIEW command that is not documented has to do with the ability to

MODIFY VIEW FROM ENVIRONMENT

This form of the command makes it useful and powerful when you want to alter the design and use of existing VUE files. In Chapter 3 it was shown that there are times when it is necessary to fine-tune a VUE file through the development stage of a system. This command simplifies that process somewhat by accepting the existing VUE file parameters and altering them according to changes made in the working environment.

RENAME

The RENAME command is the dBASE III PLUS counterpart to the DOS REName command. Both commands allow you to change the name of a file. The advantage to the III PLUS RENAME command is that you don't have to exit to DOS or run the risk of getting a memory error message when ! RENaming a file.

Syntax   The RENAME command form is

RENAME existing file TO new filename

In many ways, the RENAME command is similar to the COPY FILE command. Both commands require the use of complete filenames to function properly. For example,

RENAME TED TO JOHN

would produce an error message if you wanted to RENAME TED.DBF, TED.FMT, TED.SCR, and so on, or give the file a new name of JOHN.DBF, JOHN.FMT, or JOHN.SCR. What the preceding command does tell III PLUS to do is find a file named TED on the default drive and directory. III PLUS will not look for TED.DBF, TED.FMT, or any other variation on the name. It will only look for TED. Further, if III PLUS manages to find a file with the name TED and no extension, it will RENAME that file JOHN, also with no extension.

You can RENAME a file with an extension TO a file without an extension with

RENAME filename.ext TO filename

Likewise, you can RENAME a file without an extension TO a file with an extension with

RENAME filename TO filename.ext

Use   The RENAME command is useful as a backup device and as a method to prevent III PLUS from writing over existing files. Note that, unlike the DOS REName command, III PLUS won't allow wildcards such as ? and * as part of the filename. In other words, you can't

RENAME TED.* TO JOHN.*

III PLUS will give you an error message. Also note that the command accepts drive and directory designators as part of the filename. You can

RENAME C: \DB3 \COMPLETE \TED.DBF TO C: \DB3 \COMPLETE \JOHN.DBF

III PLUS assumes the default drive and directory when none are included in the filename. Note that you can't RENAME an in-USE DBF file, even when the file is not in the current work area.

Advanced Use   The best use of the RENAME command comes when you're using menu systems that create files. An example of such a system appears in the following listing:

```
** CREATOR.PRG FILE TO DEMONSTRATE RENAME AND MODIFY
** COMMANDS
*
DO WHILE .T.
   CLEAR
   @ 2, 0 TO 18,79 DOUBLE
@ 3,18 SAY [C R E A T E / M O D I F Y   F I L E   M E N U]
   @ 4,1 TO 4,78 DOUBLE
   @  7,25 SAY [1. GET FILENAME]
   @  8,25 SAY [2. CREATE DATABASE]
   @  9,25 SAY [3. MODIFY DATABASE STRUCTURE]
   @ 10,25 SAY [4. CREATE/MODIFY SCREEN FORMAT]
   @ 11,25 SAY [5. CREATE/MODIFY REPORT]
   @ 12,25 SAY [6. CREATE/MODIFY LABEL]
   @ 13,25 SAY [7. CREATE/MODIFY QUERY]
   @ 14,25 SAY [8. CREATE/MODIFY VIEW]
```

```
    a 16, 25 SAY '0. EXIT'
    STORE 0 TO selectnum
    a 18,33 SAY " select     "
    a 18,42 GET selectnum PICTURE "9" RANGE 0,8
    READ
    FILENAME = SPACE(80)
    YORN = .T.
*
    IF SELECTNUM > 1 .AND. LEN(TRIM(FILENAME) = 0
       a 20,0 SAY "SORRY, I NEED A FILENAME TO DO THAT."
       WAIT
       LOOP
    ENDI
*
    DO CASE
       CASE selectnum = 0
          RETURN
       CASE selectnum = 1
*
          DO WHIL .T.
             a 20,0 SAY "WHAT IS THE FILE NAME ([DRIVE:]"+;
    [\DIRECTORY(s\)][NAME][.EXT], RETURN TO EXIT)? -> " ;
             TO FILENAME
             a 21,0 GET FILENAME
             READ
*
             DO CASE
                CASE LEN(TRIM(FILENAME)) = 0
                   EXIT
                CASE FILE("&FILENAME")
                   a 20,0 SAY "THAT FILE EXISTS. "+;
                   "RENAME IT (Y/N)? -> " GET YORN PICT "Y"
                   READ
*
                   IF .NOT. YORN
                      EXIT
                   ELSE

                      ACCE "NEW FILE NAME? -> " TO FILENAME2
                      RENAME &FILENAME TO &FILENAME2
                   ENDI
*
                CASE .NOT. FILE("&FILENAME")
                   EXIT
             ENDCASE
*
          ENDD
*
       CASE selectnum = 2
          CREATE &FILENAME
       CASE selectnum = 3
          USE &FILENAME
          MODIFY STRUC
       CASE selectnum = 4
          MODIFY SCREEN &FILENAME
       CASE selectnum = 5
          MODIFY REPORT &FILENAME
       CASE selectnum = 6
          MODIFY LABEL &FILENAME
```

```
    CASE selectnum = 7
        MODIFY QUERY &FILENAME
        CASE selectnum = 8
            MODIFY VIEW &FILENAME
    ENDCASE
*
ENDDO T
*
** EOF: CREATOR.PRG
```

The menu itself is generated with the APPSGEN utility. The RE-NAME command is used in the second menu option (selectnum = 1).

The program allows you to create any type of files available to the III PLUS system. All it needs to know is the name of the new file. However, before a new file is created, the program checks to make sure no file already exists with the same filename. That is done in the DO WHILE...ENDDO loop in the second menu selection. If a file is found with the same filename, you are given the option of RENAME-ing the old file. Note that the RENAME command allows the use of macro substitutions, as shown in

RENAME &FILENAME TO &FILENAME2

Also, CREATE or MODIFY will not execute unless a file is first specified with menu option 1.

There is an obvious addition that can be made to this program. No check is made to determine if the RENAMEd filename already exists.

SET ALTERNATE ON/off

The SET ALTERNATE ON/off command has one function in the III PLUS system. It is used to have III PLUS SEND/not send screen listings to whatever ALTERNATE file is declared in the SET ALTERNATE TO command.

Syntax   The syntax of the command is

SET ALTERNATE ON/off

III PLUS assumes an ALTERNATE file has been declared with the SET ALTERNATE TO command when this command is entered. III PLUS doesn't tell you if no ALTERNATE file is in effect, nor will III PLUS send screen information anywhere.

III PLUS sends screen listings to the ALTERNATE file whenever SET ALTERNATE is ON and doesn't send screen listings to the ALTERNATE file when SET ALTERNATE is off.

Use   The SET ALTERNATE ON/off command's use was discussed in Chapter 3. The primary function of the command is to provide an unobtrusive method of debugging programs in the field. The command can also be used to translate III PLUS screen listings into DBF files, as shown in this chapter. A third use, partially acknowledged in the listings shown with the DELETE FILE command, is to capture information selectively from the screen to a TXT file. You do this by using the command

```
SET ALTER ON
```

directly before the capture, followed by the command

```
SET ALTER OFF
```

once the capture is complete. Note that the III PLUS four-letter-word convention is used in the above commands.

File Manipulation Commands

All the commands in this chapter deal with some aspect of manipulating files. None of them is used for file modification or creation.

CLEAR ALL

The CLEAR ALL command is a special case of the CLEAR command. The CLEAR command by itself erases the screen. In its other guises, the CLEAR command can release fields specified with the SET FIELDS TO command, release GETs in memory waiting to be READ, CLEAR out the memory-variable buffer, and CLEAR out pending keys in the typeahead buffer.

This section will concern itself with the CLEAR ALL command's ability to reset the dBASE III PLUS system to its default values.

Syntax   The syntax of the command is

CLEAR ALL

This tells III PLUS to reset to the opening default values. The command is primarily designed for interactive use but can also be used in a PRG file.

Use   The CLEAR ALL command does three specific things when entered into the III PLUS system. Those three things are

```
1. Close all open database and associated files. This
includes any CAT file opened with the SET CATALOG TO
command. No files are left active after the CLEAR ALL
command because all files must be associated with DBF files
in some way, and the CLEAR ALL command closes ALL DBF files.

2. Flush the memory buffer. This effectively erases all
memory variables in the system when the CLEAR ALL command is
entered. No memory variables are SAVEd to a MEM file when
the CLEAR ALL command is entered unless the user first
enters a SAVE TO mem file command.

3. Work area 1 is SELECTed, no matter what work area the
CLEAR ALL command is issued from.
```

Note that these three things essentially interact with III PLUS's storage memory and not its program memory.

The general use of the CLEAR ALL command is in the Interactive mode, where you can enter the command from the dBASE prompt. It can be used in PRG files, but you should exercise extreme caution when doing so. A general policy you might follow is to use the CLEAR ALL command as the first command in the first PRG file in a system. This allows your system to make some assumptions before it begins juggling DBFs and other files.

The following listing shows the Library System main module.

```
** LIBRARY.PRG MAIN MODULE FOR PERSONAL LIBRARIES
** COPYRIGHT 1984, 1985, 1986 JOSEPH-DAVID CARRABIS
*
CLOS ALL
CLEA ALL
*
* THINGS TURNED ON
SET DELI ON
SET ESCA ON
SET INTE ON
*
* THINGS TURNED OFF
SET BELL OFF
SET CONF OFF
SET STAT OFF
SET SAFE OFF
SET TALK OFF
*
REST FROM LIBRARY
SET PATH TO &CPATH
SET DEFA TO &CDRIVE
SET PROC TO LIBPROC.PRC
```

```
SET DELI TO '><'
*
ON ERROR DO ERRORMSS
*
NEWDRIVE = CDRIVE
NEWPATH = CPATH
DBFILE = SPACE(10)
PLACE = 0
*
DO WHILE .T.
   CLEAR
   @ 2, 0 TO 14,79 DOUBLE
   @ 3,26 SAY "PERSONAL LIBRARY SYSTEM"
   @ 4,1 TO 4,78 DOUBLE
   @  7,20 SAY [1. SELECT LIBRARY TO USE (CURRENT IS ] +;
                 NEWDRIVE + DBFILE + [)]
   @  8,20 SAY [2. EDITING MENU]
   @  9,20 SAY [3. REPORTS MENU]
   @ 10,20 SAY [4. LIBRARY PROGRAM UTILITIES]
   @ 12,20 SAY '0. EXIT'
   STORE 0 TO selectnum
   @ 14,33 SAY " select        "
   @ 14,41 GET selectnum PICTURE "9" RANGE 0,4
   READ
*
   IF LEN(TRIM(DBFILE)) = 0 .AND. SELECTNUM > 1
      @ 0,0 SAY "You must choose a LIBRARY before you do "+;
                 "anything else."
      DO POOL
      LOOP
   ENDIF
*
   DO CASE
      CASE selectnum = 0
         SAVE TO LIBRARY
         QUIT
      CASE selectnum = 1
         DO GETLIBR
      CASE selectnum = 2
         DO LIBSAY
         DO LIBFILL
         DO LIBEDIT
      CASE selectnum = 3
         DO LIBREPT
      CASE selectnum = 4
         DO LIBUTILM
   ENDCASE
ENDCASE
*
ENDDO T
* EOF: LIBRARY.PRG
```

Note that the first and second executable commands in the program
are

```
CLOS ALL
CLEA ALL
```

These commands (much of the file, actually) make use of the dBASE III PLUS four-letter-word convention. The CLEAR ALL command tells III PLUS to do everything else from work area 1, start with no open DBF files in any work areas, and flush the memory to make room for everything this program will be putting there.

You can use the CLEAR ALL command elsewhere in a PRG file, but you should do so judiciously. You could accidentally flush some necessary memory variables from the system or find yourself without a means to reopen some necessary DBF and associated files.

Note that the CLEAR ALL command has the same effect as

SET CATALOG TO

on any CATALOG files in work area 10.

CLOSE (file type)

The CLOSE command, like the CLEAR command, has many guises. Unlike the CLEAR command, the CLOSE command must be qualified. The qualifiers include ALL, ALTERNATE, DATABASES, FORMAT, INDEX, and PROCEDURE. The qualifiers are discussed in the "Syntax" and "Use" sections.

The CLOSE command has no advanced uses.

Syntax   The CLOSE command has a rich variety of qualifiers, but the syntax of the command never changes. You will always

CLOSE something

You can

```
CLOSE ALL
CLOSE ALTERNATE
CLOSE DATABASES
CLOSE FORMAT
CLOSE INDEX
CLOSE PROCEDURE
```

The CLOSE command can be used with the III PLUS four-letter-word convention. The preceding commands then become

```
CLOS ALL
CLOS ALTE
CLOS DATA
CLOS FORM
CLOS INDE
CLOS PROC
```

All versions of the CLOSE command can be used interactively or in PRG files.

Use   The CLOSE command is similar to the CLEAR command in many ways. The CLEAR command, in its many guises, affects memory. The CLOSE command, in all its guises, affects files in memory. Note that not one of the CLOSE commands affects anything except open files. Even the

CLOS ALL

command only CLOSEs open files related to databases. It isn't particularly important which files are open, but if they are related to DBFs in any way, the CLOSE ALL command CLOSEs them. Note that the CLOSE ALL command doesn't affect open PRG files. If it did, it could not be used as the first executable command. It does make sure there is nothing open that you can possibly damage.

The CLOSE PROCEDURE command does CLOSE open PROCEDURE files, though. It doesn't matter what extension you've given a PROCEDURE file. III PLUS recognizes PROCEDURE files by their use in the SET PROCEDURE TO prc file command, not by file extension.

CLOSE ALL

This command takes all database (DBF), index (NDX), format (FMT), report form (FRM), label form (LBL), view (VUE), query (QRY), alternate (TXT), and MEMO field (DBT) files out of the active system. The only files not affected by the CLOSE ALL command are catalog (CAT), memory variable (MEM), and program (PRG) files.

Note that, unlike the CLEAR ALL command, the CLOSE ALL command doesn't CLOSE any CAT file in work area 10 if the CAT file was accessed with the SET CATALOG TO cat file command. Once a file is CLOSEd, you have to open it in the standard dBASE

III PLUS manner (the USE and INDEX commands for DBF, DBT, and NDX files, and the appropriate SET command for TXT, FMT, NDX, and PRC files).

CLOSE ALTERNATE

This command only affects active ALTERNATE files. There is a hidden caveat in this. The ALTERNATE file doesn't have to be open to be active. ALTERNATE files are made active with the SET ALTERNATE TO txt file command. They are made open (screen information is sent to them and stored there) with the SET ALTERNATE ON command. The CLOSE ALTERNATE command affects any file made active with the SET ALTERNATE TO txt file command, regardless of whether the ALTERNATE file is SET ON or SET off. Once the ALTERNATE file is CLOSEd, you have to enter another SET ALTERNATE TO txt file command, followed by a SET ALTERNATE ON command, to have screen information dumped into the ALTERNATE file again.

CLOSE DATABASES

This command CLOSEs any open and in-USE databases. It also closes any associated NDX and FMT files. No matter what work area the databases are in, this command will find them and CLOSE them and their associated files. This command will not affect any CAT files in work area 10 if the CAT file was accessed with a SET CATALOG TO cat file command. If the CAT file is accessed like a regular database with a USE cat file command, the CLOSE DATABASES command will close it. Note that III PLUS doesn't identify databases by their names or extensions, but by whether or not they are USEd.

CLOSE FORMAT

Format (FMT) files are the files that are created and modified with the CREATE SCREEN and MODIFY SCREEN commands. You can also create and modify an FMT file with the MODIFY COMM filename.fmt and MODIFY FILE filename.fmt commands. These files are linked to specific DBF files.

You can have ten FMT files open, one for each DBF file in each work area. Each DBF can only have one open FMT file at a time, however. The CLOSE FORMAT command tells III PLUS to CLOSE the FMT file in the current work area. You have to SET FORMAT TO fmt file to open or reopen an FMT file once the CLOSE FORMAT command has been entered.

Note that this command, unlike the CLOSE DATABASES and CLOSE ALL commands, only affects the current work area. It doesn't affect any FMT files in noncurrent work areas. For example, if you are working in work area 1 and enter CLOSE FORMAT, the only FMT file that will be CLOSEd is the one in work area 1. No open FMT files in work areas 2 through 10 will be affected.

CLOSE INDEX

Each separate DBF file can have up to seven open NDX files associated with it. Like FMT files, the NDX files are linked to a specific work area. The CLOSE INDEX command will CLOSE any and all NDX files in the current work area. It behaves just as the CLOSE FORMAT command does in this respect.

The CLOSE INDEX command will close all seven NDX files if seven NDX files are open in the current work area. If there are 70 NDX files open, seven in each work area, it will leave 63 NDX files open, seven in each of the nine remaining work areas.

Use the CLOSE DATABASES command to CLOSE all the NDX files in every work area in the system. Of course, that also CLOSEs all DBF and FMT files.

CLOSE PROCEDURE

This command only affects one file at a time: the file accessed with the SET PROCEDURE TO prc file command. This command can only be used in the PROGRAM mode, because III PLUS will not allow you to SET a PROCEDURE and then use modules in it unless you are in PROGRAM mode.

The CLOSE PROCEDURE command doesn't care what work area you are currently in; it will seek out the open PRC file and CLOSE it. This is most interesting when the program that opened the PRC file has switched to a different work area from the one in which it started.

REINDEX

The REINDEX command complements the INDEX, SET INDEX TO, and SET ORDER TO commands: these commands tell III PLUS to create (INDEX), activate (SET INDEX TO), or change the priority of (SET ORDER TO) the NDX files associated with a particular database file; only the REINDEX command has the ability to use the key expressions defined for an existing NDX file and perform the INDEXing operation again. This effectively manipulates any NDX files in the current work area by forcing the INDEX operation again.

Syntax   The REINDEX command has no qualifiers or filenames associated with it. The command is

REINDEX

The REINDEX command only affects the NDX files active in the current work area. For example, the command sequence

```
SELE 1
USE afile INDE andx1, andx2
SELE 2
USE bfile INDE bndx1
SELE 3
USE cfile INDE cndx1, cndx2, cndx3
SELE 6
USE ffile INDE fndx1, fndx5
REINDEX
```

tells III PLUS to perform an INDEX only on ffile in work area 6. Further, the REINDEX command tells III PLUS to find the key expression used in fndx1 and INDEX ffile on that key expression to the fndx1 NDX file and then find the key expression used in fndx5 and INDEX ffile on that key expression to the fndx5 NDX file.

The command as shown in this listing will not force an INDEX on work areas 1, 2, or 3, nor will it affect any NDX files opened in those areas.

Use   The REINDEX command provides a simple method of keeping NDX files intact whenever problems have occurred. Consider a situation in which a system has been designed with several DBF and NDX files, such as that shown in the preceding listing. Suppose that the integrity of some or all of the NDX files comes into question. This can occur if the INDEXing operation is interrupted, if an APPEND to an INDEXed file is interrupted, or if you UPDATE on a key expression and are interrupted, for example.

The DBF files have already been placed in USE in the separate work areas with the commands shown in the listing. The problem now is to validate the integrity of the NDX files. Without the REINDEX command, you would have to enter

```
SELE 1
INDEX ON key expression a1 TO andx1
INDEX ON key expression a2 TO andx2
SELE 2
INDEX ON key expression b1 TO bndx1
SELE 3
INDEX ON key expression c1 TO cndx1
INDEX ON key expression c2 TO cndx2
INDEX ON key expression c3 TO cndx3
SELE 6
INDEX ON key expression f1 TO fndx1
INDEX ON key expression f5 TO fndx5
```

That is a lot of code not doing much of anything except taking up time and space. The same results are obtained with the REINDEX command with the code shown in this listing:

```
SELE 1
REIN
SELE 2
REIN
SELE 3
REIN
SELE 6
REIN
```

Note that the REINDEX command works on all NDX files in the current work area. It ignores ORDER priorities as far as performing more accurate INDEXings, but it does REINDEX the NDX files in the ORDER they are listed in the USE, SET INDEX TO, and SET ORDER TO commands.

Advanced Use   The "Use" section noted the occasional need to REINDEX if problems occur with the NDX files. The ability to REINDEX can be coded into programs easily; the procedure can be made automatic if the programmer makes use of the ERROR( ) function. Such a case is shown in this section.

```
** FROM LIBPROC.PRC FILE FOR LIBRARY SYSTEM
** COPYRIGHT 1984,1985,1986 JOSEPH-DAVID CARRABIS
*
PROC ERRORMSS
*
DO CASE
   CASE ERROR() = 1
      @ 0,0 SAY "That file doesn't exist on drive "+NEWDRIVE
      DO POOL
      RETU TO MASTER
   CASE ERROR() = 4
      @ 24,50 say "Record Number -> END   "
      @ 0,0 SAY "You're at the end of the file now. "
   CASE ERROR() = 5
      @ 24,50 say "Record Number -> END   "
      @ 0,0 SAY "You can't CONTINUE any further. "+;
                     "You're at the end."
   CASE ERROR() = 38
      @ 24,50 say "Record Number -> 0    "
      @ 0,0 SAY "You can't go any further. "+;
                     "You're at the beginning now. "
   CASE ERROR() = 42
      @ 0,0 SAY "You must LOCATE before you can CONTINUE. "
   CASE ERROR() = 114
      CLEAR
      @ 10,10 TO 20,70 DOUBLE
      @ 15,15 SAY "The INDEX file is damaged, "+;
                      "excuse me while I REINDEX."
      REIN
   CASE ERROR() = 125
      @ 0,0 SAY "Please turn the PRINTER ON."
   OTHE
      @ 0,0 SAY "I'VE ENCOUNTERED AN UNKNOWN ERROR. "+;
                     "PLEASE TRY AGAIN."
ENDC
*
DO POOL
*
PROC POOL
LAPS = 0
*
DO WHILE LAPS < WAITTIME
   LAPS = LAPS + 1
ENDD
*
RETU
*
* END OF LIBPROC.PRG PROCEDURE FILE
```

The preceding listing shows the ERRORMSS (ERROR MeSSages) PROCEDURE from the LIBPROC.PRC file used in the Library System. Its principal purpose is to tell the user that some error has occurred in the system and then to take action based on that error. dBASE III PLUS has many types of ERROR( ) flags available to it; only a few are used here.

Close to the bottom of the listing you'll notice

```
CASE ERROR( ) = 114
```

The 114 comes from the *Learning and Using dBASE III PLUS* documentation in the "Error Messages" section.

ERROR( ) 114 occurs whenever an NDX file that has been accessed by the system is damaged. III PLUS doesn't care why the NDX file has been damaged, nor is it particularly interested in how the file was damaged. All it cares about when ERROR( ) 114 occurs is that the NDX file is damaged.

The only time III PLUS finds out if an NDX file is damaged is when the command

```
SET INDEX TO ndx file(s)
```

or

```
USE database INDE ndx file(s)
```

is used. Hence, the NDX file, its key expression, and the associated DBF files are all active and current in the system. The ERROR( ) found, III PLUS performs the ERRORMSS PROCEDURE. Note that earlier, in the Library System main module, the command

```
ON ERROR DO ERRORMSS
```

is used. This command need only be issued once in a system to tell III PLUS to DO ERRORMSS whenever *any* dBASE III PLUS detectable error occurs.

Back to the immediate topic of interest. The DBF, NDX, and key expression are immediately available, even if the NDX is damaged. Therefore, you can REINDEX the immediately open and in-USE files.

The SELECT command is used to switch between work areas in the dBASE III PLUS system. There are ten work areas available, and each work area can hold a separate database and its associated files.

Syntax There are two forms of the SELECT command. The first form uses a numeric value between 1 and 10, as in

SELECT 1

or

SELECT 10

The SELECT command doesn't allow a numeric expression, however. The command

SELECT 100/10

causes III PLUS to give an error message (see the following listing).

```
-> SELE 1
-> SELE A
-> SELE J
-> NUMBER = 1
1
-> SELE (NUMBER)
ALIAS not found
        ?
SELE (NUMBER)
-> SELE NUMBER
ALIAS not found
              ?
SELE NUMBER
-> WORD = "A"
A
-> SELE WORD
ALIAS not found
            ?
SELE WORD
-> SELE &WORD
-> BIGWORD = "JUNIPER"
JUNIPER
-> SELE &BIGWORD
ALIAS not found
              ?
SELE JUNIPER
-> SELE LEFT(BIGWORD,1)
```

```
ALIAS not found
       ?
SELE LEFT(BIGWORD,1)
-> PART = LEFT(BIGWORD,1)
J
-> SELE &PART
-> SELE 100/10
Cannot select requested database
       ?
SELE 100/10
-> SELE (100/10)
ALIAS not found
       ?
SELE (100/10)
-> SELE 10
```

The SELECT command also allows you to use the first ten letters of the alphabet as designators for the separate work areas. You
can

SELE A

to get work area 1 instead of typing its equivalent

SELE 1

The alphabetic work-area designators are the letters A through
J. These alphabetic designators are the equivalents of 1 through 10,
respectively.

Use   The SELECT command is the III PLUS command that
allows you to open and USE more than two databases at the same
time. Users familiar with dBASE II may remember the commands

SELECT PRIMARY
SELECT SECONDARY

in that language. Those two commands allowed dBASE II to open
and USE two different databases simultaneously. Users need to juggle more than two files at once, however.

Enter dBASE III and dBASE III PLUS. These systems allow
you to open and USE up to ten different databases and work on them
simultaneously. You can shuttle between the different work areas
with the SELECT command.

The "Syntax" section described the ability of III PLUS to use the
first ten letters of the alphabet as work-area designators. These first

ten letters, when used to specify work areas to the III PLUS SELECT command, are called aliases. An alias is associated not with the work area but with the database that is in USE in a separate work area. For instance, the commands

```
SELE 1
USE afile
```

tell III PLUS to make work area 1 the current work area and open afile in that area. From then on, in any command that asked for information from afile, you could just as easily use the letter A. III PLUS would know you meant afile.

Suppose you have afile in USE in work area 1 and bfile in USE in work area 2. Suppose further that you want to take some information in bfield1 and REPLACE it with information from afield1. You could

REPL NEXT 1 B—>bfield1 WITH A—>afield1

III PLUS would know that it should retrieve information from afile's afield1 and place that information in bfile's bfield1. The concept of aliases goes beyond the use of A, B, C, D, and so on as designators to pinpoint the work area you're interested in. Using the previous example, you could also write

REPL NEXT 1 BFILE—>bfield1 WITH AFILE—>afield1

where the database aliases aren't really aliases in the true sense of the word. You can enter

```
SELE 1
USE afile ALIAS ABERNATHY
SELE 2
USE bfile ALIAS BERNARD
```

and actually give your database files true aliases. The REPLACE command could then become

REPL NEXT 1 BERNARD—>bfield1 WITH ABERNATHY—>afield1

Again, III PLUS would know exactly what you're trying to do.

Advanced Use   The advanced use of the SELECT command has to do with aliases, as mentioned in the "Use" section. Consider the following listing:

```
-> USE TED
-> SELE 2
-> USE CHAPTER9
*> SELE 3
-> USE FILETANK
-> SELE 4
-> USE BOOKS4
*> DISP STAT
```

Select area: 1, Database in Use: C:TED.dbf   Alias: TED

Select area: 2, Database in Use: C:CHAPTER9.dbf   Alias:
CHAPTER9
    Memo file: C:CHAPTER9.dbt

Select area: 3, Database in Use: C:FILETANK.dbf   Alias:
FILETANK

Currently Selected Database:
Select area: 4, Database in Use: C:BOOKS4.dbf   Alias:
BOOKS4

```
-> SELE TED
-> DISP STAT
```

Currently Selected Database:
Select area: 1, Database in Use: C:TED.dbf   Alias: TED

Select area: 2, Database in Use: C:CHAPTER9.dbf   Alias:
CHAPTER9
    Memo file: C:CHAPTER9.dbt

Select area: 3, Database in Use: C:FILETANK.dbf   Alias:
FILETANK

Select area: 4, Database in Use: C:BOOKS4.dbf   Alias:
BOOKS4

```
-> SELE FILETANK
-> DISP STAT
```

Select area: 1, Database in Use: C:TED.dbf   Alias: TED

Select area: 2, Database in Use: C:CHAPTER9.dbf   Alias:
CHAPTER9
    Memo file: C:CHAPTER9.dbt

Currently Selected Database:
Select area: 3, Database in Use: C:FILETANK.dbf   Alias:
FILETANK

Select area: 4, Database in Use: C:BOOKS4.dbf   Alias:
BOOKS4

```
-> SELE BOOKS4
-> DISP STAT
```

Select area: 1, Database in Use: C:TED.dbf   Alias: TED

```
Select area:  2, Database in Use: C:CHAPTER9.dbf   Alias:
CHAPTER9
    Memo  file: C:CHAPTER9.dbt

Select area:  3, Database in Use: C:FILETANK.dbf   Alias:
FILETANK

Currently Selected Database:
Select area:  4, Database in Use: C:BOOKS4.dbf   Alias:
BOOKS4

·> SELE TED
·> DISP STAT

Currently Selected Database:
Select area:  1, Database in Use: C:TED.dbf   Alias: TED

Select area:  2, Database in Use: C:CHAPTER9.dbf   Alias:
CHAPTER9
    Memo  file: C:CHAPTER9.dbt

Select area:  3, Database in Use: C:FILETANK.dbf   Alias:
FILETANK

Select area:  4, Database in Use: C:BOOKS4.dbf   Alias:
BOOKS4
```

This listing shows the use of aliases in their purest form. Once a database has been put in USE, you can SELECT a particular database's work area by using the name or alias of the database in the SELECT command. For example, you USE four different databases in the first four work areas. You can then SELECT any one of the work areas with

SELECT alias name

Note that the alias name doesn't have to be the given name of the database. Information on giving databases alias names is in the next section on the USE command.

USE

The USE command is a virtual coelacanth in the dBASE system. It is the only command in the III PLUS system that can open and close individual databases.

Syntax   The USE command has two basic forms. The first and most obvious form is used to make a database active in the current work area.

USE database

The second form of the USE command is used to close databases in the current work area. That form of the command is the naked command

USE

Note that it only closes the current work area's database and associated files. CLOSEing all the databases in all the work areas is done with the CLOSE DATABASES command discussed earlier.

Use   The USE command makes a named database file accessible to III PLUS operations. The USE command can be qualified with the INDEX command. The INDEX command allows III PLUS to associate up to seven NDX files with the database file being put into USE. That form of the USE command is

USE database INDEX ndxl, ndx2, . . . , ndx7

Note that the USE command makes the entire database available for any valid III PLUS DBF operations. This means that no filters are set, no fields are masked, and DELETEd records are shown (unless either the SET DELETE or CONFIG.DB DELETE command is ON).

You can also enter the USE command without a database filename if a CATALOG is active in work area 10. The command

USE ?

instructs III PLUS to provide a list of all available DBF files in the CATALOG. Note that you won't necessarily be able to USE all the DBF files on the disk—just the ones logged in the CATALOG file.

Last, the USE command by itself closes the currently active DBF file. For example, if you were in work area 1 and had the TED.DBF file in USE, entering

USE

would close the TED.DBF file. The exception to this rule occurs when you try to close a CAT file activated with the SET CATALOG TO cat file command. You can SELE 10 and USE, but the CAT file will not close. You have to use the SET CATALOG TO command to close the CAT file.

Advanced Use   The advanced use of the USE command described here has to do with assigning alias names to databases. Your choice of an alias name isn't important. The alias name can be longer than eight characters, but it cannot use an extension. Also note that it is wasted effort to use the work-area designators A through J as aliases because III PLUS does that automatically. The alias form of the USE command is

USE database ALIAS alias name

You can use alias names with the USE and INDEX commands as

USE database INDE ndxl, ndx2,... ALIAS alias name

As demonstrated earlier, the alias name doesn't have to resemble remotely the actual database name. If such is the case, why use alias names?

Consider a situation in which you have different databases used by the same system simultaneously. You want the different databases to share similar filenames but want to differentiate them from one another by function in the actual system. The following code offers a solution.

```
SELE 1
USE CLIENT1 ALIAS ADDRESSES
SELE 2
USE CLIENT2 ALIAS CREDITINFO
SELE 3
USE CLIENT3 ALIAS SALESHISTORY
```

The aliases listed with the databases are far more descriptive than the actual database names. The aliases also afford the programmer the luxury of not having to remember what was in work area 1, what was in work area 2, and so on. All the programmer has to do to switch from some work area to the work area with the client credit information is to enter

This immediately puts the system in work area 2 with the CLIENT2 database. Further, the programmer can use code such as

```
SELE CREDITINFO
REPL NEXT 1 BALANCE WITH BALANCE + SALESHISTORY->PURCHASE
```

This obviously spares the system developer/programmer a lot of memory work.

Data Addition Commands

This chapter deals with commands that are used to get data into a database. These commands, with the exception of READ, are not used for getting data into memory variables, nor are any of these commands used for editing existing data in a database or memory.

APPEND

The APPEND command has three forms: APPEND, APPEND BLANK, and APPEND FROM. This section deals with the APPEND command.

The plain APPEND command is used for full-screen data entry. A DBF file has to be in USE and in the current work area for the command to work. There isn't any advanced use of the command.

Syntax   The command form is the single word

APPEND

No qualifiers or filenames are necessary. Note that this form is for the naked APPEND command, not APPEND BLANK or APPEND FROM.

Use   The APPEND command is a full-screen editing command that is most often used when full-screen operations are in effect. These operations are put into effect whenever an FMT file is called from disk to memory with the SET FORMAT TO fmt file command or a DBF file is placed in USE in the INTERACTIVE mode.

For example, you can enter data to a DBF file by entering

```
USE afile
APPEND
```

This combination of commands tells III PLUS to put afile in USE, then put a blank record at the end of the file, position the record pointer at the blank record, and open that record for input. The APPEND command adds records in straight field format unless an FMT is active; these differences are demonstrated in Figures 6-1 and 6-2.

Figure 6-1 shows APPEND full-screen editing in the fields format, and Figure 6-2 shows APPEND full-screen editing in the FMT format.

Because it activates a full-screen editing mode, the APPEND command is primarily a one-pass operation. In other words, repeated data entry isn't easily negotiated with the APPEND command.

Each APPENDed record tells III PLUS if data is being entered by testing the first data field for information. This means that leaving the first data field blank causes III PLUS to exit from the APPEND mode. You can, of course, use the DOWN ARROW key to

Figure 6-1. A fields format full-editing APPEND screen

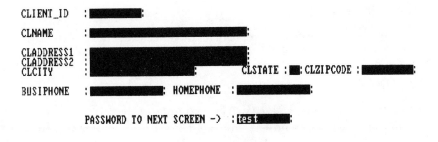

```
CLIENT_ID  :████████:
CLNAME     :████████████████:
CLADDRESS1 :
CLADDRESS2 :████████████████:
CLCITY     :████████████:  CLSTATE :██: CLZIPCODE :████████:
BUSIPHONE  :████████████: HOMEPHONE :████████████:

        PASSWORD TO NEXT SCREEN -> :test█████:
```

Figure 6-2.   An FMT format full-editing APPEND screen

place the cursor in the second data field. You may find this unsatis-factory, however.

You may want to enter data to the third and fifth fields and none of the others. Using the RETURN key to move the cursor to the third field would force III PLUS to exit from the APPEND mode.

Using the cursor keys to move the cursor to the third field would be slightly inelegant in a fully developed system. As long as data is being entered into the first field of every record APPENDed to the database, however, this command is an excellent means of adding data to a DBF file.

Note that the APPEND command automatically sets the record pointer at the APPENDed record. This command also updates an NDX file if one is in use.

APPEND BLANK

The APPEND BLANK command is used to create an empty record in a database file, much like the naked APPEND command explained in the last section. The difference between the APPEND and APPEND BLANK commands has to do with how data is entered. The DBF file has to be in USE and in the current work area for APPEND BLANK to work.

Syntax   The syntax of the APPEND BLANK command is simply

APPEND BLANK

You can use the four-letter-word convention to shorten the command to

APPE BLAN

Use   The APPEND BLANK command, like the APPEND command, works only on the current DBF file. There is a difference in how the two commands handle the problem of data entry, however.

The APPEND command drops you into a full-screen editing mode, as shown in Figures 6-1 and 6-2. The APPEND BLANK command merely adds a BLANK record to the end of the in-USE database. It doesn't activate a full-screen editing mode nor does it set you up for immediate data entry; it simply adds a BLANK record to the end of the database. It does update any NDX files in use, even when the only information entered is a BLANK record.

The last section mentioned that the APPEND command could prove troublesome if you didn't want to enter data to the first field in every record you APPENDed to the database. This is because the naked APPEND command needs information in the first field of each APPENDed record to tell III PLUS that more data is being added and not to exit from the APPEND mode.

The APPEND BLANK command provides an elegant solution to that problem, in the PROGRAM mode. This solution is shown in the "Advanced Use" section. The key to APPEND BLANK's use is its lack of concern with data entry. The APPEND BLANK command is more concerned with adding a BLANK record to the end of the database.

Advanced Use   The APPEND BLANK command has one great advantage over the APPEND command: its ability to add a blank record to the end of the in-USE database. Like the APPEND command, the APPEND BLANK command positions the record pointer to the newly APPENDed record. The following code makes use of the APPEND BLANK command's features for data entry.

```
USE afile
REPEATER = FIELD(1)
*
```

```
DO WHIL .T.
    APPE BLAN
    DO SAYS
    DO GETS
    READ
*
    IF LEN(TRIM(&REPEATER)) = 0
        DELE
        EXIT
    ENDI
*
ENDD
```

The beginning of the code segment places a file in USE. Here afile is USEd. Then the FIELD( ) function is used to create a variable, REPEATER, which has the value of afile's first field name. You can use any field in the database for the REPEATER.

The next step is to create a DO WHILE...ENDDO loop that APPENDs a BLANK record, puts up a SAY screen, puts up a GET screen, and then READs the GETs. The IF...ENDIF conditional phrase is where you really make use of the APPEND BLANK command's unique abilities.

You next check to see IF the LENgth of the TRIMmed data field referenced in the REPEATER variable is 0. IF it is, then DELETE the last APPENDed BLANK record and EXIT the DO WHILE ...ENDDO loop. If the length of that field is not 0, continue through the loop.

How is this action fundamentally different from the APPEND command? Remember, you can use the FIELD( ) function to specify any field name for the REPEATER variable. That being the case, you don't need to be sure the user adds data to the first data field for each record, nor do you have to worry about dropping out of the APPEND mode if no data is added to the first field. The FIELD( ) function can be used to specify the most important field in the DBF file, even if that field isn't the first field listed.

APPEND FROM file
[FILETYPE] FOR condition

The last form of the APPEND command discussed in this chapter has to do with the addition of large amounts of data from other files.

Note that this includes adding data from foreign file types with the use of the TYPE qualifier.

Syntax The APPEND FROM command has a number of forms. In each form, note that data will only be APPENDed FROM the source file from fields that have the same field names as those in the current file. For example, the databases shown in the following listings share some field names. III PLUS will only add records and APPEND fields FROM the JDCBOOKS.DBF file that have the same name as fields in the BOOKS.DBF file. You can APPEND FROM a source DBF file with 100 fields per record to a target DBF file with only ten fields per record, but only ten fields per APPENDed record will be added to the target file.

```
·> USE JDCBOOKS
·> DISP STRUC
Structure for database: C:JDCBOOKS.dbf
Number of data records:      874
Date of last update   : 07/08/86
Field   Field Name   Type        Width      Dec
    1   TITLE        Character      60
    2   AUTHOR       Character     100
    3   EDITOR       Character     100
    4   CATEGORY     Character      30
    5   SUBJECT      Character     100
    6   LIBRARY      Character      20
    7   ANTHOLOGY    Logical         1
    8   SERIES       Logical         1
    9   NUMBER       Numeric         4
   10   TOTAL        Numeric         4
   11   COMPLETE     Logical         1
   12   REFERENCE    Character     254
** Total **                       676


·> USE BOOKS
·> DISP STRUC
Structure for database: C:BOOKS.dbf
Number of data records:      874
Date of last update   : 07/08/86
Field   Field Name   Type        Width      Dec
    1   TITLE        Character      60
    2   AUTHOR       Character     100
    3   EDITOR       Character     100
    4   CATEGORY     Character      30
    5   SUBJECT      Character     100
** Total **                       390
```

The simplest form of the command is used to add data from some other dBASE III PLUS DBF file.

APPEND FROM dbf file

Note that the named file must not be in USE in any work area.

The second form of the command comes from the fact that the user may want to specify certain conditions for APPENDing. You may not want to APPEND all the records from the source database to the target database; you may only want to APPEND records

FOR CITY = "Newport"

The FOR qualification of the APPEND command is

APPEND FROM dbf file FOR condition

The condition must be a valid dBASE III PLUS expression that has relevance in the source file. In other words, you can't enter a FOR condition that applies only to the target file.

Consider a situation in which you want to APPEND records FROM a database of New England clients, NECLIENTS, some of whom are from New Hampshire, to a database of only New Hampshire clients, NHCLIENTS. You could enter

APPEND FROM NECLIENTS FOR STATE = "NH"

This would tell III PLUS to scan NECLIENTS for all occurrences of STATE = "NH" and add only those records that meet that condition to the end of the NHCLIENTS.DBF file.

The next case of the APPEND FROM command to consider is the TYPE qualifier. The APPEND FROM command becomes the antithesis to the COPY TO command when used with the TYPE qualifier.

III PLUS can APPEND the current DBF file from a variety of foreign file types. In particular, the file types are ASCII (as DELI and SDF), Lotus 1-2-3 WKS file format, VisiCalc DIF file format, and Multiplan SYLK file format. This form of the APPEND command is

APPEND FROM foreign file TYPE file type

Note that you can use the command without the TYPE qualifier without causing any problems. For example, you can tell III PLUS to APPEND from the TAXES.WKS file with

APPEND FROM TAXES WKS

and III PLUS will know that you mean the TAXES.WKS file in 1-2-3 format.

You can include the drive and directory designators in the filename in any of the APPEND FROM forms without causing problems. III PLUS assumes the default drive and directory unless another one is specified.

Last, you can mix and match any of the qualifiers without confusing III PLUS. This feature is useful when you want to APPEND only specific information from a foreign format, as in

```
APPEND FROM TAXES WKS FOR INCOME > 35000
```

Use There is a variety of uses for the APPEND FROM command, all of which have to do with getting data from one file into the current one. The APPEND FROM command only adds records to the end of the current database. It is also aware of active NDX files in the current work area.

For example, the commands

```
USE afile INDE andx1, andx2,...
APPEND FROM bfile
```

cause III PLUS to update the active NDX files. The records are still physically entered at the end of the DBF file, but the NDX files place the keyfield values in their proper places in the key-expression list.

The APPEND FROM command can be selective in what is APPENDed. The FOR command is actually all you need. The basis for this is the APPEND FROM command's default need to look through source files sequentially. The APPEND FROM command doesn't have the NEXT or WHILE qualifiers, but you can build an extensive FOR list such as

```
FOR CITY="MANCHESTER" .AND. STATE = "MA" .AND.
AT("JOSEPH",NAME)
```

The preceding FOR condition would copy only the names of clients in Manchester, New Hampshire, with "JOSEPH" somewhere in their names. Why use this type of qualifier and no others with APPEND?

The APPEND command can also read foreign file formats. You can use the FOR qualifier with all the foreign file formats. It is a difficult piece of software engineering to get III PLUS to read and APPEND FROM various file formats. No one can guarantee how the foreign files are ordered, indexed, sorted, and so on. The solution is to limit the APPEND FROM operation to the FOR qualifier.

Advanced Use   The advanced use of the APPEND FROM command shown here is the APPEND version of the COPY TO program written in Chapter 3.

```
** AN EXAMPLE OF THE APPEND COMMAND
** THIS ROUTINE ASSUMES THRE ARE LESS THAN 70 FIELDS IN THE
** DBF
*
CLOSE ALL
SET CATA TO MASTER
USE ?
COPY STRUC EXTE TO SEFILE
SELE 2
USE SEFILE
NUMOFRECS = RECCOUNT()
NUMOFCOLS = 1
*
DO WHIL NUMOFRECS > 22
   NUMOFRECS = NUMOFRECS/2
   NUMOFCOLS = NUMOFCOLS + 1
ENDD
*
CLEA
@ 1,0 TO NUMOFRECS+1, (NUMOFCOLS+1)*10 + (NUMOFCOLS+1)
DOUBLE
ROWNUM = 2
COLNUM = 1
*
DO WHIL RECNO() < RECCOUNT()
   FIELD = FIELD(1)
   @ ROWNUM,COLNUM SAY &FIELD
*
   IF ROWNUM = NUMOFRECS
      ROWNUM = 2
      COLNUM = COLNUM + 11
   ELSE
      ROWNUM = ROWNUM + 1
   ENDI
*
   SKIP
ENDD
*
CONDITION = SPACE(100)
CLEAR
@ 5,0 SAY "CONDITION FOR APPEND ([RETURN] FOR NO "+;
            "CONDITION) -> " GET CONDITION "@S25"
```

```
READ
CONDITION = IIF(LEN(TRIM(CONDITION)) = 0,;
              CONDITION = "", CONDITION = "FOR " + CONDITION)
ACCE "SOURCE FILE NAME (8 CHAR MAX) -> " TO FILENAME
FILETYPE = SPACE(4)
ACCE "FILE TYPE (SDF, DELI, WKS, SYLK, DIF, "+;
   "[RETURN FOR DBF]) -> " TO FILETYPE
*
DO CASE
   CASE LEN(TRIM(FILETYPE)) = 0
      FILETYPE = ""
   CASE FILETYPE = "DELI"
      ACCE "DELIMIT WITH (1 CHAR MAX, ' ' FOR BLANK) -> "+;
           TO DELIMCHAR
*
      FILETYPE = IIF(LEN(TRIM(DELIMCHAR) = 0, FILETYPE +;
                    " WITH BLANK", FILETYPE + "WITH" +;
                    DELIMCHAR)
ENDC
*
? "APPEND FROM " + FILENAME + FILETYPE
SELE 1
APPE FROM &FILENAME + " " + &FILETYPE + " " + &CONDITION
*
** EOF
```

The program works almost identically to the C10COPY.PRG file shown in Chapter 3. It starts with a catalog file to offer you a choice of DBF files and helps take care of housekeeping. Once a DBF file is USEd, you are shown the fields (the DO WHILE...ENDDO loop), and a FOR condition is requested, as in

APPEND FROM dbf file FOR condition

You can enter a condition or not. The IIF( ) function immediately after the field listing determines whether or not the APPEND command will have a FOR qualifier. Next, you ask the name of the source file and get the source file's TYPE. All of this is then built into an APPEND FROM command using macro substitutions in the last executable line of the program,

APPE FROM &FILENAME + " " + &FILETYPE + " " + &CONDITION

Note that the entire command line is a series of macro substitutions. III PLUS can use the command as written and will APPEND whatever is requested.

The BROWSE command is one of the richest commands in the III PLUS system. It has the ability to add data, edit data, view data, mask fields, scan the database, generate screen reports (although not as elegantly as the REPORT FORM command), and perform instantaneous updates of NDX files.

The standard BROWSE display mode is all fields in a record, each field displayed first to last from left to right across one or more screens, all records in the database, and each record displayed first to last from top to bottom down one or more screens.

Syntax   The BROWSE command has a rich and powerful syntax that builds on the simple command

BROWSE

The command assumes a DBF is in USE in the current work area. A simple BROWSE screen is shown in Figure 6-3. This figure shows the BROWSE command with the SET MENU and CONFIG.DB MENU commands OFF.

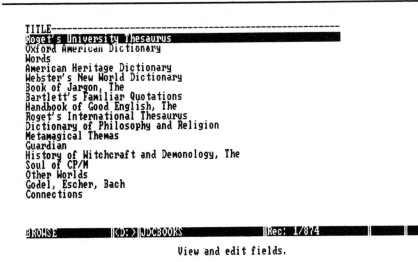

```
TITLE-------------------------------------------------------
Roget's University Thesaurus
Oxford American Dictionary
Words
American Heritage Dictionary
Webster's New World Dictionary
Book of Jargon, The
Bartlett's Familiar Quotations
Handbook of Good English, The
Roget's International Thesaurus
Dictionary of Philosophy and Religion
Metamagical Themas
Guardian
History of Witchcraft and Demonology, The
Soul of CP/M
Other Worlds
Godel, Escher, Bach
Connections


BROWSE         KD: >DDCBOOKS              Rec: 1/874              Caps
                       View and edit fields.
```

Figure 6-3.   A simple BROWSE screen

The FIELD name is listed and the data in the first field in the first 17 records is displayed. The STATUS line tells you you're in BROWSE mode on drive C USEing the JDCBOOKS.DBF file, with the cursor on the first of 874 records. This display comes from the naked BROWSE command.

You can press the F10 key to see menus that tell you how to move through the DBF file you're BROWSEing (Figure 6-4). On this menu, Top and Bottom take you to the first and last record in the database. Lock tells III PLUS how many columns to keep fixed on the left of the screen. Record No. allows you to tell III PLUS to display a specific record. Freeze tells III PLUS to allow editing to only one field. You can freeze several fields, one at a time, by repeatedly typing F or moving the cursor to Freeze and typing RETURN, and then entering the name of each field you'd like to freeze. An example of such a field, LIBRARY, is shown in Figure 6-5. Note that it is the only data field highlighted by a cursor in the record.

Note that the Bottom, Top, Record No., Lock, and Freeze options are available when two conditions are met. First, the F10 key must be typed. Second, the DBF file in USE must *not* be associated with an NDX file. If an NDX file is active, the menu shown in Figure 6-6 appears.

The new item on this menu is the Find option. This option works identically to the III PLUS FIND command, except the BROWSE F10 Find option is menu-driven. You can find information in the INDEXed DBF file either by typing F or moving the cursor to the Find option and typing RETURN. III PLUS then prompts you for a search string.

There are different ways of entering the BROWSE command from the dBASE prompt. Figure 6-7 shows the JDCBOOKS.DBF file in the BROWSE mode when the command is entered as

BROWSE

You can use the BROWSE WIDTH command with a WIDTH qualifier.

BROWSE WIDTH 20

tells III PLUS to display as many fields as possible at 20 characters per field. The WIDTH qualifier can be any valid numeric expression in III PLUS.

dBASE III PLUS: The Complete Reference

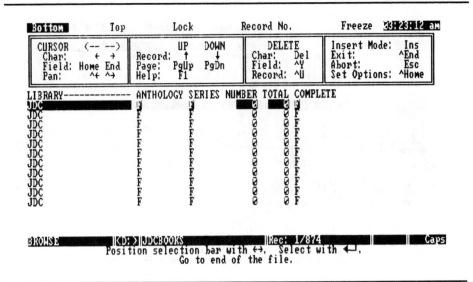

Figure 6-4. The F10 Movement menu in the BROWSE mode

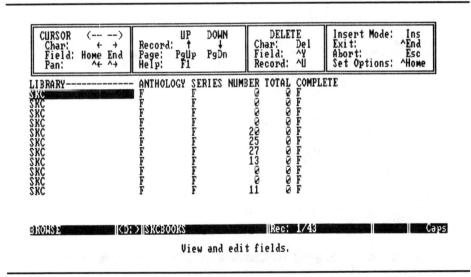

Figure 6-5. One field in the database after a Freeze

Figure 6-6. This F10 menu results when the current DBF file has an active associated NDX file

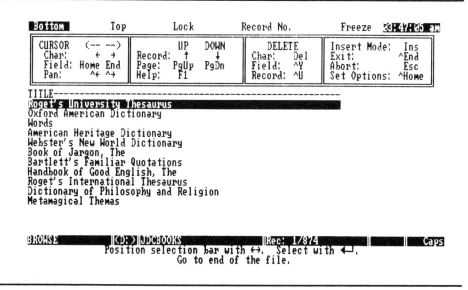

Figure 6-7. The JDCBOOKS.DBF file in the standard BROWSE display mode

The next qualifier to consider is the FIELDS qualifier.

BROWSE FIELDS field1, field2,...

tells III PLUS to display only the fields listed after the FIELDS qualifier. The FIELDS qualifier also tells III PLUS to display the listed
fields in the order they are listed.

The BROWSE command also allows you to specify a LOCK
expression, identical to the Lock feature available on the F10 BROWSE
menu, from the command line as

BROWSE LOCK n

where n is a valid dBASE III PLUS numeric expression. This command tells III PLUS to LOCK on the left of the BROWSE display the
number of fields specified by n. For example, to LOCK the first two
fields in the database to the left of the BROWSE display, you'd enter

BROWSE LOCK 2

The combination of the FIELDS and LOCK qualifiers can be
useful in many ways. For example, you can specify which fields you
want displayed, and where and how you want them displayed as in

BROW FIELDS field10, field9,...LOCK 1

This tells III PLUS to keep the data in field10 of each record on the
left of the BROWSE display, no matter where else the user moves the
cursor to in a given record.

The FREEZE command is identical to the F10 BROWSE menu
Freeze option. Figure 6-8 shows how the BROWSE command works
when entered as

BROWSE FIELDS TITLE, AUTHOR WIDTH 30

There are three remaining qualifiers to the BROWSE command:
NOFOLLOW, NOAPPEND, and NOMENU. The last two qualifiers
are rather straightforward; the text will discuss them first.

The NOMENU command tells III PLUS to set up the BROWSE
display without the F10 menu. This command overrides the SET
MENU and CONFIG.DB MENU ON commands.

The NOAPPEND qualifier is used to tell III PLUS whether or
not to let the user add records to the end of the database. The
BROWSE command defaults to APPENDing records to the end of

```
TITLE----------------------- AUTHOR--------------------------
Fundamentals of Physics     David Halliday, Robert Resnick
Quanta: Essays in Theoretical
Black Holes and Warped Spaceti William J. Kaufmann, III
Electromagnetism: Principles a Paul Lorrain, Dale R. Corson
Magnetic Resonance          Robert T. Schumacher
Scale and Conformal Symmetry i
Iliad, The                  Homer
Differential and Integral Calc Love
Relativity: The Special and th Albert Einstein
Electromagnetic Theory      Stratton
Nonlinear Ordinary Differentia D.W. Jordan, P. Smith
Programmers at Work
CD ROM: The New Papyrus
Your Home
Canticle for Leibowitz, A   Walter M. Miller, Jr.
1-2-3 Business Formula Handboo Ron Person
1-2-3 Financial Macros      Thomas Carlton
```

BROWSE   D:>JDCBOOKS   Rec: 844/874   Caps
View and edit fields.

Figure 6-8.   Two fields in the database are displayed for all BROWSE
operations with the FIELDS qualifier

the BROWSEd database. Changing the BROWSE command to

BROWSE NOAPPEND

tells III PLUS not to let the user add records to the end of the
database.

The NOFOLLOW qualifier is used only when NDX files are
active with the current BROWSEd database. To understand what the
NOFOLLOW qualifier does, you need to understand what it stops the
BROWSE command from doing.

The normal working of the BROWSE command when an NDX
file is active is simple enough: You change the value of the keyfield,
and III PLUS changes the record's position in the BROWSE display.
That makes sense. The database is INDEXed on the keyfield. When
the value of an individual record's keyfield is changed, that record's
position in the NDX file is changed. BROWSE lists records in its
display in the order they're presented in the DBF file or NDX file,
when one is active. When you change the order in the active file, that
change is echoed in the BROWSE display.

When III PLUS changes the order of records in the BROWSE display based on changes made in the keyfield of the active NDX file, the action is called FOLLOWing. The NOFOLLOW qualifier tells III PLUS *not* to make changes in the order shown in the BROWSE display based on changes in the keyfield of the active NDX file.

Use   As the text has already explained the syntax of the BROWSE command, this section will only highlight the command's use.

One of the drawbacks to the BROWSE command is its inability to place fields on the display where you want those fields to show up. Even though the BROWSE command is powerful in the INTERAC-TIVE mode, it is impractical to use for repetitive data addition and editing because of its cumbersome method of placing fields on the screen in a logical input/output fashion. You can alter the screen display somewhat with

BROWSE FIELDS field list

and

BROWSE FIELDS field list WIDTH n LOCK m

where both m and n are valid dBASE III PLUS numeric expressions.

Another drawback to the BROWSE command has to do with large fields and the LOCK command. The JDCBOOKS.DBF file has several data fields that are more than 50 characters wide. LOCKing any of those fields would force III PLUS to keep the field constantly in the display, hence showing none of the other fields that were more than 20 characters wide (the BROWSE command assumes a 70-character-wide screen; 5 characters on each side are for borders). One way to use the LOCK qualifier with large data fields is

BROWSE WIDTH 20 LOCK 1

or

BROWSE WIDTH 20 FIELDS field list LOCK n

You can use the WIDTH qualifier without fear of truncating information in the fields because the fields are scrolled through the WIDTH. A 100-character-wide field qualified by WIDTH 20 only shows 20 characters at a time, but you can scroll through all 100 characters by using the cursor keys if necessary.

The default of the BROWSE command is to allow data entry. The command pays attention to whether or not an NDX file is active with the current database and knows that data should be APPENDed at either the logical or physical bottom of the database. Data is APPENDed at the physical end of file when no NDX file is active. This is done by moving to the bottom of the file (the last displayed record) and pressing the DOWN ARROW key.

III PLUS asks if you want to "Add new records? (Y/N)" Typing **Y** causes III PLUS to APPEND a BLANK record at the physical end of the DBF file and set the record pointer to the newly APPENDed record. An active NDX file causes III PLUS to APPEND records at the logical end of file.

INSERT [BLANK] [BEFORE]

The INSERT command is similar to the APPEND command in several ways. Both can be used to add data to the current DBF file. Both can add BLANK records to the current DBF file. The big difference between the two commands is that the INSERT command is a one-shot deal; it can add only a single record to the current database. The APPEND command can add one to several records to the current database.

There is no advanced use of the command.

Syntax   The command has three forms. The first and most basic form is

INSERT

This tells III PLUS to add a blank record immediately after whatever record the pointer is currently set at. For example, if the record pointer is positioned at record 345, typing INSERT will open a blank record at position 346. Each of the remaining records, from 346 to the end of the database, is bumped up one.

The second form of the command is

INSERT BEFORE

This is identical in all ways to the INSERT command just listed, but the blank record is added before the record currently under the pointer. In other words, if the record pointer is currently at record 345, typing INSERT BEFORE tells III PLUS to add a blank record at record 345 and bump all records from 345 to the end of the file up one. Both of these commands share the full-screen EDITing mode.

The last form of the INSERT command is

INSERT BLANK

This can be modified to

INSERT BLANK BEFORE

which places a BLANK record before the current record. The key difference between the INSERT BLANK and INSERT commands is that the INSERT BLANK command doesn't access the full-screen EDITing mode.

Use   Both INSERT BEFORE and INSERT open the full-screen EDITing mode, through either the field-format or FMT-format modes. The difference between these commands and the similar APPEND commands is that APPEND can handle a variety of file formats and large amounts of data at once. The INSERT command is a single-pass command that can enter only a single record at a given time. The INSERT BLANK command does not activate any editing or menu modes and is ideal for creating single, empty records for later data addition.

READ

The READ command can get data from the user for both memory and database entry, but it has to be accompanied by at least one GET to function as intended.

Syntax   The READ command appears as

READ

and is used to get information from the user into the system. A variation on this theme is the command

This tells III PLUS not to clear the GETs that are being READ. If you READ SAVE a group of GETs, those GETs will still be active next time you READ. The GETs will not remain active if the record pointer is moved before the next READ is entered into the system.

Use   The READ command offers the primary means of clearing GETs from the III PLUS system and taking the data from the user to either a database or memory. Anytime a variable is declared with either

```
STORE value TO variable
```

or

```
variable = value
```

or a database field becomes available for data entry, that data can be entered by using

```
a X,Y GET field
READ
```

or

```
a X,Y GET variable
READ
```

The central variation on the READ command is

READ SAVE

The principal difference between READ and READ SAVE has to do with the clearing of all the GETs in memory. Any GETs placed in a system are active from one READ to the next. That makes it difficult to use those same GETs repeatedly for repeated data entry in a system.

The READ SAVE command allows you to perform repeated data entry, an example of which is shown in the "Advanced Use" section. The READ SAVE command is best used when the same set of variables or data fields are repeatedly entered into the system. The reason for this is the READ SAVE command doesn't clear memory as the READ command does. READ SAVE leaves all GETs active and available to the system.

Advanced Use READ SAVE is useful in designing systems in its ability to pass data from various constantly used variables to different databases. The code shown here demonstrates how the READ SAVE command allows you to get information to a variety of places in memory without juggling databases and memory more than is necessary.

To start, you assume there are seven databases in USE. The databases are in work areas 2-8. The current work area is 1, and that is where all of your work is done. In this case, all the databases are identical and will be sent to various remote offices of the same company.

```
** PRG TO ENTER REPEATED DATA TO SEVERAL DBFS
*
STORE SPACE(30) TO NAME, ADDRESS1, ADDRESS2, CITY, COUNTRY
STATE = "  "
ZIPCODE = SPACE(10)
STORE SPACE(14) TO HOMEPHONE, BUSIPHONE
*
DO WHIL .T.
   DO MEMSAY
   DO MEMGET
   READ SAVE
*
   IF LEN(TRIM(M->NAME)) = 0
      CLEAR GETS
      EXIT
   ENDI
*
   COUNTER = 65
*
   DO WHIL COUNTER < 76
      WORKAREA = CHR(COUNTER)
      SELE &WORKAREA
      APPE BLANK
      REPL NEXT 1 NAME WITH M->NAME
      REPL NEXT 1 ADDRESS1 WITH M->ADDRESS1
      REPL NEXT 1 ADDRESS2 WITH M->ADDRESS2
      REPL NEXT 1 CITY WITH M->CITY
      REPL NEXT 1 STATE WITH M->STATE
      REPL NEXT 1 ZIPCODE WITH M->ZIPCODE
      REPL NEXT 1 HOMEPHONE WITH M->HOMEPHONE
      REPL NEXT 1 BUSIPHONE WITH M->BUSIPHONE
      REPL NEXT 1 COUNTRY WITH M->COUNTRY
      COUNTER = COUNTER + 1
   ENDD
*
   SELE 1
*
ENDD
*
** EOF
```

What does the file do and how does it do it? The purpose of the file is to make several copies of data at the time of input. The assumption is that the data is not only repeated in several databases but is also repetitive in values. The READ SAVE command keeps the memory variables, specified by the M—> work-area qualifiers, at their default values. The only time the values of the memory variables change is when the user enters new data to them. At any other time, the data left from the last entry is used for the REPLACE-ments in the different databases.

Data Editing
Commands

This chapter deals with all the dBASE III PLUS commands that can be used to edit data in a database. It does not include any commands that can be used to edit memory variables.

All of these commands, with the exception of CLEAR GETS, GET, and READ, are used exclusively with either active or current databases. CLEAR GETS, GET, and READ can be used with memory variables as well.

BROWSE

The BROWSE command was covered thoroughly in Chapter 6. Refer to Chapter 6 for information on that command.

CHANGE

The CHANGE command is used to tell III PLUS to allow editing to specific fields in a database. It is similar to the REPLACE command, except the CHANGE command allows direct user input. It is most often used in conjunction with an FMT file. Note that the EDIT command is identical in all respects to the CHANGE command.

Syntax The CHANGE command is similar to the REPLACE command in many ways. Both commands allow you to edit several records in a database at a given time. The difference between the two commands is that CHANGE is a full-screen editing command. It is more often used in an interactive mode and with an associated FMT file, whereas REPLACE finds more applications in programmatic work.

The CHANGE command's syntax has several facets. The simplest form of the command is

CHANGE

Note that this assumes some database is current and active. The above form of the CHANGE command tells III PLUS to allow full-screen editing of all the fields in each record of the database. This is a valid use of the command, but it isn't the best tool for the job and is indelicate in its execution. The first qualifier to use with the CHANGE command specifies how many records in the database are going to be edited. The form is

CHANGE NEXT n

where n is a valid dBASE III PLUS numeric value. This form of the command is useful when the current database has been sorted or otherwise ordered and the user or programmer knows exactly how many records require CHANGEing. For example, if you know you only need to change the NEXT 20 records in the database, you'd use the command

CHANGE NEXT 20

Note that the NEXT qualifier begins counting the NEXT n records at the current record. If you are working with a database of 100 records and are currently positioned at record 95, the above command would only allow you to CHANGE the next 5 records.

A more succinct method of telling III PLUS how many records need CHANGEing is to let it decide the number to edit. You tell it to do this with the FOR and WHILE qualifiers. FOR is III PLUS's random qualifier and tells III PLUS to CHANGE any records in the DBF file that meet a specific condition. III PLUS recognizes that the records that meet the condition might not be contiguous and scans the database from first record to last record, only allowing

CHANGEs to the records that meet the condition. The command form is

CHANGE FOR condition

Examples of valid conditions are PAYFOR = 'Auto Expense' and PAYAMOUNT > 100.

WHILE is III PLUS's sequential qualifier. It tells III PLUS to CHANGE records WHILE a certain condition is met. Note that this assumes the current record meets the condition. For example, you could use the command

CHANGE WHILE PAYAMOUNT > 100

but if the current record's PAYAMOUNT field is less than or equal to 100, no CHANGEing will be done. The WHILE qualifier will let the user make CHANGEs only WHILE the condition is met and is most often used when the database has been either INDEXed or SORTed. Both INDEXing and SORTing create sequential files that contain like values in keyfields.

It is possible to mix and match these three qualifiers in several ways. For example, you could tell III PLUS to

CHANGE NEXT 100 FOR condition1 WHILE condition2

This tells III PLUS to allow CHANGEs to the NEXT 100 records from the location of the record pointer at present, to CHANGE only the NEXT 100 records FOR some condition, and only WHILE some other condition. This grouping of qualifiers can give you precise control over what data in what records will be CHANGEd.

Of course, these qualifiers still let you edit every field in the database. The qualifiers allow the programmer/developer some finesse, but not enough.

The last qualifier to discuss is FIELDS. This qualifier tells III PLUS what FIELDS the user will be allowed to CHANGE. The command form is

CHANGE FIELDS field1, field2,...

Note that the plain CHANGE command is the same as listing each of the current database's fields in the FIELDS qualifier. Be careful when using the CHANGE command with the FIELDS qualifier; it has no effect on fields in an active FMT file.

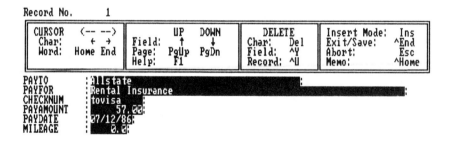

```
Record No.      1
 ┌────────────────────────────────────────────────────────────────────────────┐
 │ CURSOR    <-- -->          UP   DOWN     DELETE       Insert Mode:   Ins     │
 │  Char:     ←   →    Field:  ↑    ↓       Char:   Del  Exit/Save:    ^End     │
 │  Word:   Home End   Page: PgUp PgDn      Field:  ^Y   Abort:        Esc      │
 │                     Help:  F1            Record: ^U   Memo:        ^Home     │
 └────────────────────────────────────────────────────────────────────────────┘
 PAYTO       :Allstate                                  :
 PAYFOR      :Rental Insurance                                      :
 CHECKNUM    :tovisa
 PAYAMOUNT   :     57.00:
 PAYDATE     :07/12/86:
 MILEAGE     :     0.0:
```

Figure 7-1.   The CHANGE command can use the F1 key to activate the full-screen editing menu

The CHANGE command shares all the full-screen editing features of the BROWSE command. Figure 7-1 shows the menu feature active in a CHANGE screen. Note that this is shown without an active FMT file. The F1 menu toggle has no effect when CHANGEs are made through an FMT file.

Use   Consider a situation in which several but not all records in a database should be CHANGEd to meet some recent conditions. One example from real life involves mare management and foaling information. This information is both confidential and highly conditional. Each season's information has to be entered, and no two records should have the same data.

You don't use an FMT file because of the lack of FIELD control, but you can enter

CHANGE FIELD BLOODSTAT WHILE SEX = "F" FOR DATE( ) − DOB > 1200

This command makes a few assumptions. First, three of the fields in the database are BLOODSTAT (BLOODline STATistics), SEX (mare = "F", stallion = "M", gelding = "G"), and DOB (Date Of Birth). You're only interested in changing the BLOODSTAT field based on which mare was serviced by which stallion. The WHILE qualifier is used because the database is INDEXed on SEX. The FOR qualifier makes sure you can only CHANGE records for mares that are more than three years old. Note that the standard positions of the

FOR and WHILE qualifiers are altered in the preceding command. III PLUS knows how to parse the command and places the correct conditions with the correct qualifiers.

Advanced Use   So far everything you've been told about the CHANGE command has to do with its acting on the current database. You can tell it to work on any active database, however, by modifying the command to

CHANGE FIELDS A—>fielda, B—>fieldb,...

where A and B are work-area aliases. Be aware that databases must be open in the work areas given in the aliases. You do not have to list the current work area with an alias. For example, this list of commands

```
SELE A
USE EXPENSES
SELE B
USE CHAPTER9
SELE C
USE SALES
CHANGE FIELDS A->PAYTO, B->CLNAME, SALESID
```

uses the A and B aliases because the current work area is C. Note that only the current work area's record pointer changes as each record is CHANGEd. SETting RELATIONS causes III PLUS to track all the databases.

CLEAR GETS

The CLEAR GETS command can be used either for database-field or memory-variable work. It operates the same way in both instances. The only difference between the two types of work lies in what III PLUS is GETting at a given time.

The command itself is a combination of the CLEAR and GET commands. The CLEAR command can take several qualifiers, depending on what is being CLEARed. One of the qualifiers is GETS. The GET command tells III PLUS to GET information from the user, the database, or the memory variable. Naturally, the combination tells III PLUS to CLEAR whatever it GETted.

Syntax   The syntax of this command is straightforward. You use the command in both interactive and programmatic modes as

CLEAR GETS

Note that this command doesn't erase the screen. It CLEARs the input buffer in memory.

Use   The CLEAR GETS command finds its best application in large programming environments that require a lot of memory management. The command is usually seen in systems that have the CONFIG.DB command

GETS = n

The GET command serves two basic purposes in III PLUS. It can either take information from the user and place it in memory or get information from memory and display it for the user. Memory can be either memory variables or database fields. Editing data involves both of the GET operations on both memory variables and database fields. You have a command or group of commands that GET information from something and send it somewhere else.

GETs all by themselves will only GET data from memory and display it wherever the x and y coordinates tell it to. The GET commands will send information to a record when the READ command is used after the GETs.

The READ command is significant in many ways. First, it tells III PLUS to allow editing of whatever GETs are on the screen. And where do the GETs go when they are being edited? They can't go to the database fields or memory variables directly. If they did, you wouldn't be able to press the ESC key to quit editing without changing anything.

III PLUS sends things to a temporary input buffer whenever anything is READ. "Temporary" doesn't mean the buffer exists only when data is being edited or entered. The buffer is always in machine memory. It is temporary in the sense that the information in the buffer changes constantly. Like most machine-memory buffers, it is finite in size. It can only hold so much information. Whenever too much information is sent to the buffer, some of the older information in the buffer gets thrown out to make room for the newer information. The process that is used to determine which information gets tossed out is familiar to some people as FIFO—First In, First Out. The process takes whatever information was sent to the buffer first, as in First In, and throws that information out when more room is needed.

That process may be all well and good in some instances, but chances are you'd like to do something with whatever information you send to the dBASE III PLUS input buffer. III PLUS allows you a method of making sure the input buffer has enough room for all the information you're likely to send it at a given time. The method of ensuring that the input buffer is large enough for the tasks at hand involves use of the CONFIG.DB GETS = n command, where n is some integer value between 35 and 1023. These values are the minimum and maximum number of GETs you can keep active in the input buffer before you have to flush the buffer. For example, the CONFIG.DB command

GETS = 50

tells III PLUS to set aside enough machine memory for the input buffer to hold 50 GETs. What happens when you try to put 51 GETs in the top of the buffer? You lose the first GET you put in the buffer.

The way to tell III PLUS to ignore some of the GETs and keep the present input buffer intact is to use the command

CLEAR GETS

For example, you might want to send data to the screen and have it appear at predescribed x and y positions. You would use the command

@ x,y GET field

To tell III PLUS to ignore those GETs and not let the user edit information there, you would use CLEAR GETS immediately after the GET commands.

Advanced Use   III PLUS doesn't particularly care how the GETs are used when a CLEAR GETS command follows them. This is a useful fact when you are developing systems and you need to conserve space on disk or in memory. The following listing shows part of a PROCEDURE file for a poorly constructed system. Note that both

PROC LIBFILL and PROC LIBGETS use most of the same code except for the last few lines. The last line of the LIBFILL PROCE-DURE merely tells III PLUS to deny the user access to the data. The last lines of the LIBGETS PROCEDURE tell III PLUS to make sure there is something to READ before trying to READ past EOF and blowing up when nothing's there.

```
PROC LIBFILL
@  4, 12  GET  TITLE
@  6, 12  GET  AUTHOR    FUNCTION "S60"
@  7, 12  GET  EDITOR    FUNCTION "S60"
@  9, 12  GET  CATEGORY
@ 10, 12  GET  SUBJECT   FUNCTION "S60"
@ 12, 12  GET  LIBRARY
@ 14, 13  GET  ANTHOLOGY   PICTURE "y"
@ 14, 23  GET  SERIES    PICTURE "y"
@ 14, 33  GET  NUMBER
@ 14, 45  GET  TOTAL
@ 14, 60  GET  COMPLETE   PICTURE "y"
@ 16, 13  GET  REFERENCE   FUNCTION "S60"
@ 24, 50  SAY "Record Number -> " + STR(RECNO(),4,0)
CLEA GETS
*
PROC LIBGETS
@  4, 12  GET  TITLE
@  6, 12  GET  AUTHOR    FUNCTION "S60"
@  7, 12  GET  EDITOR    FUNCTION "S60"
@  9, 12  GET  CATEGORY
@ 10, 12  GET  SUBJECT   FUNCTION "S60"
@ 12, 12  GET  LIBRARY
@ 14, 13  GET  ANTHOLOGY   PICTURE "y"
@ 14, 23  GET  SERIES    PICTURE "y"
@ 14, 33  GET  NUMBER
@ 14, 45  GET  TOTAL
@ 14, 60  GET  COMPLETE   PICTURE "y"
@ 16, 13  GET  REFERENCE   FUNCTION "S60"
@ 24, 50  SAY "Record Number -> " + STR(RECNO(),4,0)
*
    IF ERROR() <> 5
       READ
    ENDI
*
```

These two PROCEDUREs are wasteful side by side. They are repetitive and take up machine-memory space that could be put to better use. The solution is to use the last lines of both PROCEDUREs as part of the calling program. For example, if you know that a certain part of the application calls for a data display without user access, you can write the calling code as

```
DO LIBGETS
CLEAR GETS
```

and make similar modifications if you know you want to allow user access in the calling code.

DELETE

The DELETE command is another III PLUS command with several qualifiers. The function of the DELETE command is not to remove records from the current database, but to mark records for removal. There is a significant difference there. Records marked for DELETE aren't physically removed from the database; they are only flagged in a certain way.

There are several ways to use that DELETE flag, however, and many of them have nothing to do with removing records from a database physically.

Syntax　　The DELETE command works on records in a database. It edits them in the sense that it can mark the records for the most permanent kind of change available: physical removal from the database.

The simplest form of the command is

DELETE

This tells III PLUS to mark the current database record for removal. Note that this is a logical internal flag used by III PLUS to mark records. The DELETE command doesn't make use of a database field, nor does it rely on you to enter a Y or N value. A fuller explanation of internal and external flags appears in the "Use" section.

You can also tell III PLUS to DELETE a certain number of contiguous records with the NEXT scope qualifier. Like all commands that use the NEXT qualifier, DELETE starts at the current record and works on the NEXT n records. The command form is

DELETE NEXT n

where n is a valid dBASE III PLUS numeric expression. You could DELETE the NEXT 20 records by entering

DELETE NEXT 20

Note that this works on the NEXT n records. If you were USE-ing a 500-record database, and the record pointer were on record 485, the preceding DELETE would only mark records 485 through 500. This means there are only 15 records marked for DELETE.

The DELETE command also allows use of the FOR and WHILE qualifiers. FOR is III PLUS's random qualifier. It tells III PLUS to DELETE any records in the DBF file that meet a specific condition. III PLUS recognizes that the records that meet the condition might not be contiguous and scans the database from first record to last record, only marking the records that meet the condition. The command form is

DELETE FOR condition

Valid conditions might be PAYFOR = 'Auto Expense' or PAY-AMOUNT > 100.

WHILE is III PLUS's sequential qualifier. It tells III PLUS to DELETE records WHILE a certain condition is met. Note that this assumes the current record meets the condition. For example, you could use the command

DELETE WHILE PAYAMOUNT > 100

but if the current record's PAYAMOUNT field has a value less than or equal to 100, no DELETEing will be done.

The WHILE qualifier will let the user make DELETEs only WHILE the condition is met and is most often used when the data-base has been either INDEXed or SORTed. Both INDEXing and SORTing create sequential files that contain like values in keyfields.

It is possible to mix and match these three qualifiers in several ways. For example, you could tell III PLUS to

DELETE NEXT 100 FOR condition1 WHILE condition2

This tells III PLUS to mark the NEXT 100 records from where the record pointer is at present and to only mark for DELETE the NEXT 100 records FOR some condition and only WHILE some other condition exists. This grouping of qualifiers can give you precise con-trol over which records will be DELETEd.

An undocumented use of the DELETE command makes use of the RECORD qualifier. Normally, the DELETE command only acts on the current record in the database. You would mark record 15 for DELETE if record 15 were the current record when you entered the DELETE command. Sometimes you want to DELETE a record other than the current one. That is done with the command

DELETE RECORD n

where n is a valid dBASE III PLUS numeric expression and is within the range of the database. You can't enter

DELETE RECORD 100

if the database only has 90 records. This form of the command allows you to mark for DELETE any record in the database, regardless of where the record pointer rests.

The last form of the command is a global DELETE of records. The form is

DELETE ALL

This tells III PLUS to mark every record in the database for DELETE. It doesn't matter where the record pointer is when this command is entered. All records will be marked for DELETE.

Use   The DELETE command uses an internal flag. What is an internal flag?

An internal flag is something that the user has no direct control over. For example, you could create a logical field in the database and call that field DELETED. You could then enter a Y to mark that record for DELETE or an N to tell III PLUS you want to keep that record in the database. Because you created the field and you enter the mark yourself, the DELETED field is an external flag. An example of code to go along with this example would be

```
YORN = .F.
a 10,10 SAY "DELETE THIS RECORD (Y/N) -> " GET YORN PICT "Y"
READ
REPL NEXT 1 DELETED WITH YORN
```

There is an interesting aspect to this code that should be noted by the reader. The logical variable YORN is used to do two things. First, YORN holds the user's response to the prompt "DELETE THIS RECORD (Y/N)—> ". Second, the value the user gives YORN is directly applied to the DELETED field in the database. This is more efficient than alternate programming methods, as less memory space is used for ancillary variables and less code is used to do the job of externally flagging the record.

III PLUS uses an internal flag when you mark a record for DELETE. Code similar to that in the previous listing, but using the III PLUS internal flag, would be

```
YORN = .F.
@ 10,10 SAY "DELETE THIS RECORD (Y/N) -> " GET YORN PICT "Y"
READ
*
IF YORN
    DELE
ENDI
*
```

This is more code than was used for the external flag. What is gained by using the internal flag?

Each DELETED field in the database takes up one more byte in each record. This doesn't include the extra space needed to tell III PLUS where the DELETED field is in the record and other assorted housekeeping information. A database with 1024 records will be slightly over 1K larger because of the DELETED field, regardless of whether the field is used or not (both .T. and .F. take up one byte in the file). What is 1K in a file? Not much, but if you plan on doing some serious applications, the single K will grow rapidly.

On the other hand, the internal DELETE flag takes up no room on disk or in the file. Only III PLUS knows the record is marked, and it only knows it internally.

Advanced Use   Sometimes you want to delete a record only to mask it from some other operations that will follow later in the program. Likewise, when considering physically removing the records from the database, you have to ask if you're going to wipe out all the records or only certain ones. dBASE III PLUS uses the DELETE, SET DELETED ON, PACK, and ZAP commands and the DELETED( ) function to do most of this.

You can DELETE a record from a database, but that DELETE doesn't physically remove the DELETEd record from the database. In fact, it doesn't do anything other than mark the record. If you DISPLAY a database with DELETEd records, those records will still show up, as they do in Figure 7-2.

```
-> DELE RECO 3
-> DELE RECO 7
-> DELE RECO 10
-> DELE RECO 12
-> DISP ALL PAYFOR
Record#  PAYFOR
       1  Rental Insurance
       2  Auto Expense
       3 *Rent, Utilities
       4  Office Supplies
       5
       6  Toll
       7 *Office Supplies
       8  Motel
       9  Delphi
      10 *
      11
      12 *
      13
      14  Auto Expense
      15  Postage
      16  Magazine
-)
```

Figure 7-2. DELETEd records are not removed from a database by the act of DELETEing them. They are marked for deletion

Compare Figure 7-2 with Figure 7-3 and you'll see the difference between simply marking a record for DELETE and telling III PLUS to pay attention to those internal flags.

You can "hide" DELETEd records from certain commands by using the SET DELETED ON command, as shown in Figure 7-3. This command tells dBASE III PLUS to behave as if the DELETEd records didn't exist in the database. You have, in effect, filtered the database to a process similar to filtering with the SET FILTER TO command. The SET DELETED ON command is a specialized filter in the sense that the filtering mechanism is built into the dBASE III PLUS system.

DELETED( ) is a logical function that tells the user if a particular record has been DELETEd. It can be used as a reverse filter to SET DELETED ON.

There will be times when you want to physically remove the

```
-> SET DELE ON
-> DISP ALL PAYFOR
Record#  PAYFOR
      1  Rental Insurance
      2  Auto Expense
      4  Office Supplies
      5
      6  Toll
      8  Motel
      9  Delphi
     11
     13
     14  Auto Expense
     15  Postage
     16  Magazine
-)
```

Figure 7-3. The SET DELETED ON command tells dBASE III PLUS to "hide" DELETEd records from certain commands, such as DISPLAY. This doesn't mean the records have been removed from the database; they are simply transparent to certain commands

DELETEd records from the database. This is done with the PACK command (discussed later in this chapter). PACK is a destructive, non-reversible command that physically changes the size of the database by removing all records marked as DELETEd. All records that aren't DELETEd are preserved during a PACK.

Lastly, dBASE offers the ZAP command (also discussed later in this chapter). This is a destructive, non-reversible command that physically removes *all* records from a database, *regardless of whether they are marked for deletion or not!*

These options provide several methods by which the user can hide or delete data from the database. Your task in designing a kernel to DELETE records from a database is to recognize that the user

```
1) may want to "hide" records for a while, but not DELETE
them permanently.
2) may want to "hide" records, but not DELETE all the
"hidden" records.
3) may want to DELETE records permanently.
4) may want to DELETE all the records permanently.
```

5) will be allowed to DELETE only one record at a time.
6) will know whether the record is going to be a permanent DELETEion or a temporary one. In other words, the user will know if the record can be physically removed from the database or only hidden temporarily.
7) will make no physical removal of records at this time.

Assumption 7 is vital. It provides a safety measure against permanent deletion.

You also assume the screen has been SAYed and FILled as necessary to assure users that they are DELETEing the correct record.

You start by adding a new field at the end of your database structure. Using the EXPENSES database structure, you add the logical field PERM (Figure 7-4).

What does the kernel look like?

```
* DELETE KERNEL
DELE
@ 20,0 CLEA
@ 22,0 SAY "Is this a PERMANENT deletion? ";
   GET PERM PICTURE "N"
READ
DELFLAG = .T.
* END OF DELETE KERNEL
```

Bytes remaining: 3864

	Field Name	Type	Width	Dec		Field Name	Type	Width	Dec
1	PAYTO	Character	40						
2	PAYFOR	Character	60						
3	CHECKNUM	Character	10						
4	PAYAMOUNT	Numeric	10	2					
5	PAYDATE	Date	8						
6	MILEAGE	Numeric	7	1					
7	PERM	Logical	1						
8		Character							

MODIFY STRUCTURE <D:> EXPENSES   Field: 8/8   Caps
Enter the field name.
Field names begin with a letter and may contain letters, digits and underscores

Figure 7-4.   The only change to this database is the addition of the logical PERM field at the bottom of the structure

There it is, a simple, elegant tool that allows you to consider several options. How do you know which records are marked and what they are marked for? The only time you need to know that a record is marked is when you are either GETting or FILling the screen. You can add two lines to the calling program that will handle that situation. The two lines are executed before the GET file is called.

```
DELEMSS = IIF(DELETED(),"DELETED ",SPACE(8)) +;
IIF(PERM,"PERMANENT",SPACE(9))
@ 2,60 SAY DELEMSS
```

These two lines tell you if the record is marked for DELETE and if the DELETE is going to be PERManent.

The text hasn't explained the command

```
DELFLAG = .T.
```

in our kernel yet. Condition 7 implies that permanent DELETEs are not made at this time. True. At the end of a work session, the calling program can check the DELFLAG variable to prompt the user regarding making permanent DELETEs with the following code:

```
IF DELFLAG
   CLEA
   ACCE "Deletions have been made. Make them "+;
   "PERMANENT? (Y/N) -> " TO DELFLAG
*
   IF DELFLAG
       RECA FOR .NOT. PERM
       PACK
   ENDI
*
ENDI
```

Here you use the combination of the DELETEd flag and the PERM field to PACK only those records that are to be permanently removed from the database with the RECALL FOR condition and PACK. These two commands RECALL all database records that don't meet the condition (.NOT. PERM), leaving only the records you do wish to remove physically.

The careful reader will wonder why the text now includes a logical field when that action was termed a bad idea in the "Use" section. Well, it is and it isn't. It is a bad idea to create a logical field if all that field is going to do is serve as an external DELETE flag. The logical field PERM used in this example doesn't serve entirely as an external DELETE flag. It serves to tell III PLUS if a DELETEd record is merely being masked from the system or is to be removed physically from the system.

EDIT

The EDIT command is identical to the CHANGE command discussed earlier in this chapter. Refer to that section for a discussion of its syntax and use.

GET

The GET command is unique in that it serves to transfer information to and from database fields and memory variables to the user. Additional information on the GET command can also be found in the section on CLEAR GETS earlier in this chapter. GET can be considered a qualifier for the @ command, as you must use the GET command after an @, as in

@ x,y GET data

where x and y represent screen coordinates. Note that this command can only be used on screen. You cannot GET information from an @ x,y printer position.

Syntax   The GET command must be used with the @ x,y coordinate marker. This tells III PLUS where to GET information from.

The GET command can take several qualifiers. These qualifiers can be used to tell both the user and III PLUS what valid data looks like and when it has been entered.

The standard form of the GET command is

@ x,y GET data

III PLUS doesn't care if the "data" is a database field or a memory variable. Note that III PLUS will GET data either for or from the current database record's fields or an existing memory variable. III PLUS will send you an error message if you try to GET something from an undeclared memory variable or a nonexistent database field.

The first qualifier to the GET command is PICTURE. This is used to tell III PLUS what the GETted data should look like. For example:

```
a   4, 14   GET   PAYTO
a   5, 14   GET   PAYFOR
a   7, 14   GET   CHECKNUM
a   9, 14   GET   PAYAMOUNT PICT "$$$$$$.$$"
a   9, 42   GET MILEAGE
a  10, 14   GET   PAYDATE
READ
```

The addition of the PICTURE qualifier on the GET PAYAMOUNT command tells III PLUS to show the user a screen such as that shown in Figure 7-5. This method of using the PICTURE qualifier is called templating. III PLUS allows the following templates in a PICTURE qualifier:

```
9 - ALLOWS ONLY DIGITS AND VALUE SIGNS
# - ALLOWS DIGITS, VALUE SIGNS AND BLANK SPACES
A - ALLOWS ON LETTERS
L - ALLOWS ONLY T, F, Y, N, y, OR n LOGICAL DATA TYPES
Y - ALLOWS ONLY Y, N, y, OR n LOGICAL DATA TYPES
N - ALLOWS ONLY ALPHANUMERIC INPUT
X - ACCEPTS ANY CHARACTER AS INPUT
! - CONVERTS ANY LOWER CASE TO UPPER CASE DURING INPUT
$ - REPLACES LEADING ZEROES WITH "$" IN NUMERIC INPUT
* - REPLACES LEADING ZEROES WITH "*" IN NUMERIC INPUT
. - FORCES A DECIMAL POINT (".")
, - SHOW APPROPRIATE COMMA (",") IF NUMERIC INPUT IS OVER
100
```

Each of the templates serves a specific purpose in a GET PICTURE function. Explanations of the individual template options are given in the "Use" section.

These templates are only part of what the PICTURE qualifier to the GET command can do. There are several ways to use the PICTURE qualifier. Each way is called a PICTURE FUNCTION. These PICTURE FUNCTIONs give III PLUS and the user specific information about the data being entered. The separate FUNCTIONs are

```
B - NUMBERS ARE LEFT JUSTIFIED
Z - NUMERIC 0 IS DISPLAYED AS BLANK
D - DATE IS "MM/DD/YY"
E - DATE IS "DD/MM/YY"
```

```
A - ACCEPT ONLY ALPHA CHARACTERS
! - CONVERT LETTERS TO UPPER CASE
R - USED TO PLACE NON DATA CHARACTERS INTO THE PICTURE
S - SCROLL OVER DATA
```

Not listed are the PICTURE FUNCTIONs C, X, and ((the left parenthesis). These FUNCTIONs can only be used with the SAY qualifier (see Chapter 8). Each of the FUNCTIONs listed in the preceding listing works with the GET command. Explanations of the separate FUNCTIONs are in the "Use" section.

The last part of the GET command's syntax to investigate is the RANGE qualifier. This qualifier tells III PLUS what upper and lower bounds to put on data entry. You tell III PLUS the upper and lower bounds with

@ x,y GET data RANGE low,high

where "low" and "high" represent the minimum and maximum values allowed for data entry. You can also specify single boundaries by placing a single minimum value to the left of the comma. An example is

@ x,y GET data RANGE low,

```
PAYTO         :                                     :
PAYFOR        :                                            :

CHECKNUM      :            :

PAYAMOUNT     :9999999.99:    MILEAGE    :        :
PAYDATE       :  /  /  :
```

Record Number -> 17

Figure 7-5.   The addition of the PICTURE qualifier gives the user a better idea of what information goes in each field

This tells III PLUS to put only a minimum boundary on data input. You could use the command

@ x,y GET data RANGE 0,

to tell III PLUS that no negative numbers will be accepted as valid entry data. Similarly, you can specify a maximum data-entry value with

@ x,y GET data RANGE ,high

This tells III PLUS there is an upper limit on valid input data. You could specify no values over 100 with

@ x,y GET data RANGE ,100

Note that any valid dBASE III PLUS numeric expressions can be used as RANGE limits.

Use   The "Syntax" section described the PICTURE qualifier's templates but didn't list what the templates do during data entry. Starting at the top, then:

9   Place the number 9 in the PICTURE qualifier to tell III PLUS that only numeric values are allowed as input. This doesn't mean you can't use character input, as 0 through 9 are valid numeric character data. For example, a car registration might be CARRJOSD99871. That could be placed in a PICTURE qualifier as

@ x,y GET CARREG PICT "AAAAAAAA99999"

This tells III PLUS to accept only the numeric characters 0, 1, 2, 3, 4, 5, 6, 7, 8, and 9 for the last five characters of the CARREG field. The exception to this is when the 9 template is used with numeric memory variables or database fields. In that case you can also use plus, minus, and a blank space (+, − and , respectively) as valid numeric-data input.

This template is used exclusively with number input. It tells III PLUS to allow only the digits 0 through 9, plus, minus, and a blank space (+, − and , respectively) as valid numeric-data input.

A   The A character tells III PLUS to allow only alpha characters as valid input. Note that this doesn't allow alphanumeric input; only the

UPPERCASE and lowercase A through Z characters will be accepted.

L III PLUS shows the concepts of TRUE and FALSE in four basic ways. The TRUE/FALSE pairs are T/F, t/f, Y/N, and y/n. These last two pairs correspond to logical YES and NO groups. The L template tells III PLUS to accept only input from one of the logical pairs. You could input T, t, Y, or y as TRUE data and F, f, N, or n as FALSE data. Note the difference between this template and the next one.

Y This template follows the logic patterns that were shown in the L template. The only difference is that this template only accepts Y and y for TRUE and N and n for FALSE. Note that it also converts the lowercase y and n to UPPERCASE characters when they are entered.

N The N template is similar to the A template except it allows all alphanumeric characters as input.

X The X template allows you to input any character. It doesn't care if the field is numeric, character, or logical data. Note that III PLUS might argue with this if the data being entered were not the same as the field or variable the data were being entered to. In other words, III PLUS will still stop you from entering ABCDE to a numeric-data type.

! This template affects only alpha input. It converts all lowercase letters to UPPERCASE once they are entered. For example, you might enter the name Joseph-David Carrabis. III PLUS would convert your input to JOSEPH-DAVID CARRABIS after you went to the next input field.

$ This template is most often used when the field or variable holds numeric data and the data is currency. The $ is used to tell III PLUS to lead the entered value with the dollar-sign symbol ($). Entering 45.67 in a numeric field that is ten characters wide would result in $$$$$45.67.

* The * template functions identically to the $ template, except leading zeros are replaced with an asterisk (*). The example then becomes *****45.67.

. The . template is used in numeric data input to tell the user where the decimal point (.) is in the input field.

, The , template is used in numeric data input much as the . template. The difference is that the comma (,) is used to ease reading of numbers larger than 100.

The text has not provided information on the PICTURE qualifier's functions. Starting at the top:

B The B function tells III PLUS to left-justify data during display and input.

Z The Z function tells III PLUS to display numeric 0 value data as a blank string.

D The D function tells III PLUS to display dates in the standard American manner of MM/DD/YY (month/day/year format). Note that III PLUS will not allow you to leave the DATE field unless a valid date has been entered in the proper form.

E The E function tells III PLUS to display dates in the European manner of DD/MM/YY (day/month/year format). Note that III PLUS will not allow you to leave the DATE field unless a valid date has been entered in the proper form.

A The A function is identical to the A template symbol. It only allows alpha characters as valid input. Note that it doesn't allow alphanumerics, only alpha input.

! The ! function is identical to the ! template symbol. It only affects character input and converts all lowercase input to UPPERCASE characters as the data is entered.

R The R function allows the programmer/designer to place characters in the GET field that will not be used as part of the data when the GET is READ into memory or the database. This feature requires some explaining. First, it only works with character data. Say you wanted data entered and the data had to be ten characters wide. You don't want someone to enter eight characters; you want ten. How do you let the user know that ten characters have to be entered? You could use

```
@ x,y GET data PICT "@R —> 99999 <—"
```

to tell III PLUS to format some alphanumeric data in a special way. Or you could include an enlivening prompt with the command

@ x,y GET data PICT "@R HEY, YOU AWAKE OR WHAT   "

Examples of both of these appear in Figure 7-6. Can you figure out why the comma and A's are missing from the bottom of the screen? (Both are templates.)

S The last function to discuss is S. The problem solved by the S function has to do with the aesthetics of GETting information on the screen when the variable or field is larger than you'd like. In other words, how do you fit a 200-character-wide field or variable into a 50-character-wide slot? You do it with the S function. S is used as

@ x,y GET data PICT "@Sn"

where n is a number. You could use a number as high as your field is wide for n, but that wouldn't accomplish much. The S function allows you to use the LEFT and RIGHT ARROW keys, the HOME and END keys, and CTRL-A and CTRL-F to move through an entry quickly. III PLUS automatically scrolls the field's or variable's contents from right to left as you move with the cursor through the entry. No information is lost during this operation.

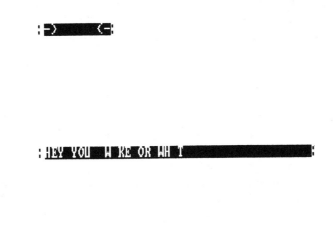

Figure 7-6.   The top GET shows the use of the "—> 999 <—" R FUNC-TION. The bottom GET is more whimsical

You've learned about the PICTURE functions and templates that can be used with the GET command. Now I'll described their use.

Templates are used in a literal sense. You tell III PLUS that a particular entry is going to be ten alpha characters wide with

@ x,y GET data PICT "AAAAAAAAAA"

You could use a similar expression for a ten-digit numeric field:

@ x,y GET data PICT "9999999999"

PICTURE functions are handled a little differently. You can tell III PLUS to use a function in either of the following ways:

```
a X,Y GET data PICT "t" FUNC "f"
a X,Y GET data PICT "af t"
```

The examples above are identical in what they do. The main difference is their length. The text uses f to represent any function and t to represent any template. Note the use of the at symbol (@) in the second form of the command. The at symbol is necessary to tell III PLUS that the next letter in the PICTURE qualifier is actually a function and not a template.

Advanced Use   Advanced uses of the GET command come directly from mixing the qualifiers. The PICTURE and RANGE qualifiers allow much finesse in what will be entered and how.

You can mix and match the templates. Each template symbol only affects the space it occupies in the PICTURE qualifier. For example, the command

@ x,y GET data PICT "AX!!!999A"

tells III PLUS to allow only alpha input for the first character, allow any character for the second input character, convert the next three characters to UPPERCASE only if they are entered as lowercase alpha characters, allow only numeric input for the next three characters, and allow only alpha input for the last character. That is a bizarre example, but you could combine the templates to something much more useful such as

@ x,y GET data PICT "$$$$$.99"

This tells III PLUS to replace any leading zeros with the dollar sign ($), force a decimal point (.) before the last two digits, and leave the two digits after the decimal point in standard numeric form.

Note also that the function and template are separated with a blank space. This is because you can group functions in the second form of the command. For example, you could tell III PLUS to left-justify numeric input and leave zero values blank with

@ x,y GET data PICT "@BZ"

You could further tell III PLUS that the numeric field or variable is exactly ten characters wide and should have leading zeros replaced with dollar signs by adding

@ x,y GET data PICT "@BZ $$$$$$$.99"

Note that the dBASE III PLUS four-letter-word convention has been used exclusively in the preceding discussion.

You can also mix and match PICTURE and RANGE qualifiers as you like. An example might be displayed as

@ x,y GET INCOME PICT "@SI0B $$$$$$$.99" RANGE 9999999,

This tells III PLUS to left-justify, allow scrolling through all 19 allowable digits even though only 10 will show in the input field, replace leading zeros with a dollar sign, force a decimal point before the last two digits, show the last two digits as numeric data, and permit no entry less than $9,999,999.00.

PACK

The PACK command is a one-shot dBASE III PLUS command that permanently removes records physically marked for DELETEion with the DELETE command. You should be cautious when using this command, as it is a nonrecoverable destructive command.

Syntax   There is nothing special or unique about the syntax of the PACK command. It can be used either interactively or programmatically as

This causes all records marked for DELETE in the current database to be physically removed from the database.

Use PACK has one purpose: to remove records from a database. Its potential danger cannot be overemphasized. Following is a block of code that detects DELETEd records and removes them.

```
* PACKER.PRG
*
CLEA
a 4,0 TO 10,79 DOUBLE
a 6,20 SAY [0. QUIT WITHOUT CHANGING ANYTHING]
a 7,20 SAY [1. REMOVE DELETED ENTRIES]
a 8,20 SAY [2. REMOVE ALL ENTRIES]
a 10,33 SAY " select        "
a 10,42 GET selectnum PICTURE "9" RANGE 0,2
READ
*
DO CASE
   CASE selectnum = 2
      ZAP
   CASE selectnum = 1
      CLEA
      SET TALK ON
      ? "PACKING DATABASE TO REMOVE DELETED RECORDS"
      PACK
      SET TALK OFF
ENDC
*
** EOF PACKER
```

This code makes use of several of the properties of III PLUS during the PACKing procedure. First, it CLEARs the screen and puts up a menu. The safest option is "0. QUIT WITHOUT CHANGING ANYTHING." The second safest option is "1. REMOVE DELETED ENTRIES." The last option, "2. REMOVE ALL ENTRIES," will be discussed in the ZAP section.

Assuming you want to REMOVE DELETED ENTRIES, III PLUS CLEARs the screen, SETs TALK ON to let you know what you're losing, and puts up a couple of messages to that effect. This results in a display similar to the one in Figure 7-7.

This is an example of the PACK command used in a programmatic way. But it has a fatal flaw: You can't stop the PACKing operation once it is started. You can press the ESC key—an action that normally interrupts any dBASE III PLUS process—but doing so during PACKing could cause a great deal of harm to your database.

The "Advanced Use" section shows some code that eliminates the need to press the ESC key.

Advanced Use   The problem with PACK is that it is a one-directional, one-shot deal. You PACK a database, you lose records. A programmatic way to make sure you can still find those PACKed records is to create a BACKUP file. The code to do that follows:

```
** BACKUP PRG TO BE USED BEFORE PACKING
*
CLEAR
FILENAME1 = DBF()
FILENAME2 = LEFT(DBF(),AT(".",DBF())) + "BAK"
? "CHECKING FOR EXISTING BACKUP FILES"
*
IF FILE("&FILENAME2")
    YORN = .F.
    @ 10,0 SAY "A BACKUP FILE ALREADY EXISTS. QUIT (Y/N) ->";
           GET YORN PICT "Y"
    READ
*
    IF YORN
        RETURN
    ENDI
*
ENDI
*
? "MAKING BACK UP FILE"
USE
RENAME &FILENAME1 TO &FILENAME2
USE &FILENAME2
SET DELETED ON
? "CREATING NEW WORK FILE"
COPY TO &FILENAME1
SET DELETED OFF
USE &FILENAME1
*
** EOF
```

```
PACKING DATABASE TO REMOVE DELETED RECORDS
No records copied
REINDEXING DATABASE



    ->
```

Figure 7-7.   This screen results from PACKing with the code shown in the preceding "Use" section

The first thing to note about the preceding code is that the PACK command doesn't appear in it. The PACK command is so lethal that you might often want not to use it and to code around it. The preceding code is an example of that. You can make use of the COPY command's ability to ignore DELETEd records during a COPY session to "PACK" the database.

The preceding code creates a backup file on the same disk as the work disk. This may not be a good idea, depending on how much room you have available on the work disk. Elsewhere this book shows a block of code that can be used to determine if there is enough space on a disk for a file copy. That code can be dropped in here to act as a safety switch if no room is available for the COPY.

READ

All information that is relevant to the READ command in editing data has already been given in Chapter 6 and earlier in this chapter.

RECALL

The RECALL command is the antithesis of the DELETE command. You can think of RECALL as a reprieve. RECALL tells III PLUS to unmark a record for deletion. This causes III PLUS to reset the internal DELETE flag.

The RECALL command is another III PLUS command with several qualifiers. Records unmarked by RECALL can only be unDELETEd before the database is PACKed.

The nature of the RECALL command doesn't lend itself to advanced uses.

Syntax   The RECALL command works on records in a database. It edits them in the sense that it can bring the records back from the brink of PACKed destruction.

The simplest form of the command is

RECALL

This tells III PLUS to RECALL the current database record. Note that this works on the logical internal flag used by III PLUS to mark records. The RECALL command doesn't make use of a database field, nor does it rely on you to enter a Y or N value. A fuller explanation of internal and external flags appears in the "Use" section of this command later in this chapter.

You can also tell III PLUS to RECALL a certain number of contiguous records with the NEXT qualifier. Like all commands that use the NEXT qualifier, RECALL starts at the current record and works on the NEXT n records. The command form is

RECALL NEXT n

where n is a valid dBASE III PLUS numeric expression. You could RECALL the NEXT 20 records by entering

RECALL NEXT 20

Note that this works on the NEXT n records. If you were USE-ing a 500-record database, and the record pointer were on record 485, the above RECALL command would only unmark records 485 to 500. This is only 15 records unmarked by RECALL.

The RECALL command also allows use of the FOR, WHILE, RECORD, and ALL qualifiers, just as the DELETE command does. (For details, see the DELETE command earlier in this chapter.)

Use   In the DELETE command section, you were shown how to use external and internal flags to DELETE records. Here, you will see how to use similar code for RECALLing records.

Going along with the example of a logical field called DELETED, an N entered in that field would tell III PLUS one of two things. Either the record hasn't been marked for DELETE or it is to be RECALLed. An example of code to go along with this example would be

```
YORN = .F.
@ 10,10 SAY "RECALL THIS RECORD (Y/N) -> " GET YORN PICT "Y"
READ
REPL NEXT 1 DELETED WITH YORN
```

Note that the logical variable YORN is used to do two things. First, YORN holds the user's response to the prompt "RECALL THIS RECORD (Y/N) —>". The value the user gives YORN is directly applied to the DELETED field in the database. This is more efficient than alternate programming methods, as less memory space is used for ancillary variables and less code is used to do the job of flagging the record externally.

Code similar to the preceding, but using the III PLUS internal flag, would be

```
YORN = .F.
a 10,10 SAY "RECALL THIS RECORD (Y/N) -> " GET YORN PICT "Y"
READ
*
IF YORN
   RECA
ENDI
*
```

The internal flag takes up no room on disk or in the file. Only III PLUS knows whether the record is marked or not, and it only knows that internally.

REPLACE

The REPLACE command is the programmatic version of the CHANGE command described earlier in this chapter. The REPLACE command is programmatic in the sense that no FMT files or direct user input is required for the command to function properly. The CHANGE command allows direct user input.

Syntax   The REPLACE command is similar to the CHANGE and EDIT commands in many ways. All three commands allow you to edit several records in a database at a given time. The difference between REPLACE and the CHANGE and EDIT commands is that the latter two are both full-screen editing commands. They are often used in an interactive mode and with an associated FMT file, whereas REPLACE finds more applications in programmatic work.

The REPLACE command's syntax has several facets. The command can be used in the INTERACTIVE mode, but because it doesn't allow full-screen editing, more responsibility is forced on the user/programmer/developer. The simplest form of the command must include a list of fields that are going to be REPLACEd.

```
REPLACE field1 WITH value1, field2 WITH value2,...
```

Note that this assumes some database is current and active. The preceding form of the command tells III PLUS to REPLACE whatever is in field1 with value1, whatever is in field2 with value2, and so on. You can use this form of the command to REPLACE every field in the current record with some new value, or a single field with a single value.

The preceding command tells III PLUS to REPLACE only the fields in the current record in the current database. If the record pointer is on record 10, only the fields in record 10 will be replaced.

III PLUS allows you to make REPLACEments to the fields in several records with the NEXT, FOR, and WHILE qualifiers in the same way that you use the CHANGE command (for details, see the CHANGE command section earlier in this chapter).

It is possible to mix and match these three qualifiers in several ways. For example, you could tell III PLUS to

```
REPLACE NEXT 100 field1 WITH value1, ;
                 field2 WITH value2, ... ;
                 FOR condition1 WHILE condition2
```

This tells III PLUS to make REPLACEments to the listed fields in the NEXT 100 records following the record pointer's current location and only to make REPLACEments FOR some condition (condition1) WHILE some other condition (condition2). This grouping of qualifiers can give you precise control over what fields in which records will be REPLACEd.

The last form of the command is a global REPLACEment of fields in all the records in the current database. The form is

```
REPLACE ALL field1 WITH value1, field2 WITH value2,...
```

This tells III PLUS to REPLACE the listed fields with the listed values for every record in the database. It doesn't matter where the record pointer is when this command is entered. All records will be affected by the ALL qualifier in the REPLACE command.

Use   While it is true that the REPLACE command can be used in the INTERACTIVE mode, it finds most of its use in the programming environment. An example of how the REPLACE command can be used in programs comes from the world of sales management.

For example, one of the fields in a database may be SALES. That field holds the name of the salesperson servicing this client's account. What happens when a salesperson's client list grows too large for a single individual to handle? One of two things. First, you can recognize that the salesperson is doing an excellent job and you should promote that salesperson out of that job. The second option is to break the salesperson's territory into smaller territories and dish these smaller territories out to other members of the sales force.

The example used here assumes a single salesperson services all of New England. The geographic area doesn't grow, but the salesperson's client list does, until it is more than that salesperson can reasonably handle. You, the sales manager, decide to break the New England territory into six state regions. You are going to use the following information in the REPLACEments:

```
All NH clients will go to Nancy Haagen.
All MA clients will go to Mike Allenby.
All RI clients will go to Roberta Ignatouski.
All CN clients will go to Carl Nugent.
All VT clients will go to Vera Trombly.
All ME clients will go to Martin Edwards.
The LEAD field in each of the affected records will be
REPLACED with Donna Acker, the salesperson you're promoting
out of the job.
```

You can use the following block of code from the dBASE prompt to make the necessary REPLACEments.

```
REPL ALL SALES WITH "Nancy Haagan", ;
        LEAD WITH "Donna Acker" FOR STATE = "NH"
REPL ALL SALES WITH "Mike Allenby", ;
        LEAD WITH "Donna Acker" FOR STATE = "MA"
REPL ALL SALES WITH "Roberta Ignatouski", ;
        LEAD WITH "Donna Acker" FOR STATE = "RI"
REPL ALL SALES WITH "Carl Nugent", ;
        LEAD WITH "Donna Acker" FOR STATE = "CN"
REPL ALL SALES WITH "Vera Trombly", ;
        LEAD WITH "Donna Acker" FOR STATE = "VT"
REPL ALL SALES WITH "Martin Edwards", ;
        LEAD WITH "Donna Acker" FOR STATE = "ME"
```

A programmatic version of this is shown in the "Advanced Use" section.

Another method of using the REPLACE command comes from having several databases active but not current. You can use informa-

tion from databases in other work areas to provide the REPLACE-
ment values of the fields in the current database. An example of this
would be

REPL NAME WITH A—>NAME

This tells III PLUS to REPLACE the value in the current database's
NAME field with whatever is found in the NAME field in whatever
database is in work area 1 (A is the default alias for any database in
work area 1). There is no limit to how many different databases can
be used in this type of REPLACEment. You could use

```
REPL field1 WITH A->fielda, field2 WITH B->fieldb, ;
   field3 WITH C->fieldc, ...
```

where fielda, fieldb, and fieldc represent any fields in the other work
area's databases. You don't have to REPLACE field1 in work area 2
with field1 from work area 1.

The preceding command only REPLACEs the current record's
fields in the current database. If you were to change the command to

```
REPL ALL field1 WITH A->fielda, field2 WITH B->fieldb, ;
   field3 WITH C->fieldc, ...
```

the current database's record pointer would move. You would be
REPLACEing each of the current database record fields with data
from the same, single record in each of the other work areas.

Advanced Use   The following REPLACE routine is applicable to
any database, as the user picks the database:

```
** GENERAL PURPOSE REPLACER PROGRAM
*
CLEAR
SET CATA TO MASTER
USE
*
DO WHIL .T.
   VALUE = SPACE(20)
   ACCE "WHAT FIRST FIELD TO REPLACE (? FOR FIELD LIST, " +;
      "RETURN TO QUIT)? -> " TO FIELD1
*
   IF LEN(TRIM(FIELD1)) = 0
      RETURN TO MASTER
   ELSE
*
```

```
        IF FIELD1 = "?"
            DISP STRUC
            ACCE "WHAT FIRST FIELD TO CHANGE? -> " TO FIELD1
        ENDI
*
    ENDI
*
    ACCE "FIRST FIELD'S NEW VALUE (20 CHAR MAX)? -> " ;
        TO VALUE1
    REPL &FIELD1 WITH VALUE
ENDD
*
** EOF
```

This code segment makes use of the CATALOG file to let the user pick a database and then lists the fields in the database (through the DISP STRUC command) should the user forget what fields are available. There are many ways to improve on this code. The two obvious ways are to write the code to make REPLACEments on several fields at once and to include an error check should the user's field selection not be in the selected database.

UPDATE

The UPDATE command is a unique command that allows the user to make changes in the current database with data from a database in another work area. The command uses REPLACE as part of its syntax.

There is little differentiation between use and advanced use of the UPDATE command. It is a high-level dBASE III PLUS command, in any case.

Syntax The UPDATE command has a special purpose in the dBASE III PLUS system and is the top end of a certain set of editing commands. At the low end are the CHANGE and EDIT commands. These two commands rely heavily on the user's immediate interaction to work properly. The user must enter the edited information at each record. The middle-level command is REPLACE.

The REPLACE command can be used either interactively or programmatically and edits data in one or more records, but doesn't rely on the user's immediate interaction to do the editing. The user can tell III PLUS what information to edit when the command is entered. This makes the REPLACE command excellent for lengthy editing on selected fields, but the user still has to know what information to place in the command when it is entered. At the top of the list is the UPDATE command. It is the only command that can make changes to one database based on data from another database and do it automatically. The user doesn't need to tell III PLUS what information is being UPDATEd. All that is necessary is that the user know what database holds the UPDATEd information.

Because the UPDATE command edits information automatically in the current database, using information from another database, it makes use of the REPLACE command in its syntax. The previous section showed how data from one database could be used to REPLACE data in the current database. The command was

REPLACE field WITH A—>fielda

(If the above is confusing to you, read the previous section on the REPLACE command.)

The UPDATE command uses a similar syntax, but before you tell III PLUS what to REPLACE, you must tell it where to UPDATE FROM.

UPDATE ON keyfield FROM alias

Note that the preceding is not the full form of the command; it does show the UPDATE command's syntax, however. The expressions "keyfield" and "alias" in the command have the same meanings here as they've had elsewhere in this book, but their importance is magnified in the UPDATE command. The keyfield mentioned in the UPDATE command *must* follow these rules:

1) IT MUST BE THE FIELD ON WHICH THE CURRENT DATABASE IS EITHER INDEXED OR SORTED AND
2) IT MUST HAVE THE SAME NAME AS A FIELD IN THE SOURCE DATABASE

If either of these rules is ignored, you will not be able to UPDATE from the source database. The alias in the above command is the name or work area of the source database. Remember that the alias can be the name of the database, the alpha code for the work area (A-J, for work areas 1-10 respectively), or a name you assign the database in the USE command (see the USE command in Chapter 5 for more information on work areas and database aliases). The preceding command is combined with the appropriate REPLACE command to form the complete UPDATE command.

UPDATE ON keyfield FROM alias REPLACE field1 WITH value1

Note that the REPLACE part of the command behaves exactly as the simple, unqualified form of the REPLACE command. You can extend the UPDATE command to REPLACE several fields in the current database with

```
UPDA ON key field FROM alias REPL field1 WITH value1, ;
                                   field2 WITH value2, ;
                                   field3 WITH value3, ...
```

Note that the semicolon (;) is used to tell III PLUS that the above UPDATE command is continued on the next line.

The UPDATE command does have one qualifier, but it is not one you would have seen used with either the EDIT/CHANGE or REPLACE command. The qualifier is RANDOM and has to do with the UPDATE command's working on databases rather than user-supplied data.

In addition to these two absolute musts for using the preceding UPDATE command, there is a third must, but it is not absolute. This third must comes from the fact that the UPDATE command prefers to work with INDEXed databases. The third must would be

3) THE SOURCE DATABASE MUST BE INDEXED ON THE SAME KEY FIELD AS THE TARGET DATABASE

The preceding listing does indeed show a must *if* the source database is INDEXed at all. If the source database is INDEXed at all, it must be INDEXed on the same field as the target database to work with the unqualified UPDATE command. If the target file is INDEXed on "NAME", the source file must also be INDEXed on "NAME"; if the target file is INDEXed on "SALESNUM", the source file must also be INDEXed on "SALESNUM", and so on. This also holds if the target database has been SORTed.

Note that the target file must be either INDEXed or SORTed according to the three listed musts. It doesn't say that the source file must be INDEXed or SORTed to be used by the qualified UPDATE command. The RANDOM qualifier is a way around the need for INDEXed or SORTed source databases. The command form is

UPDA ON keyfield FROM alias REPL field1 WITH value1 RANDOM

As before, you can REPLACE as many fields as you wish in the UPDATE command.

The RANDOM qualifier tells III PLUS that the source file isn't INDEXed or SORTed. Of course, this means III PLUS does a sequential search of the source file. Whenever it encounters a keyfield value in the source file that matches the value of a keyfield in the target file, it REPLACEs the listed fields with the listed values.

Use   The UPDATE command is a powerful, upper-level database management tool and can be used in several ways.

The action of the UPDATE command is a highly automated process that starts when you enter the command and then runs as long as there is information available to the system. A standard program block that makes use of the UPDATE command would be

```
SELE A
USE adatabase INDE andx1, andx2, andx3, ...
SELE B
USE bdatabase INDE bndx1, bndx2, bndx3, ...
UPDA ON common key field FROM A REPL bfield1 WITH ;
    bfield1 + afield1, bfield2 WITH afield2, ...
```

This block of code first opens a database in work area 1 (alias "A"). The database opened in work area 1 can have up to seven NDX files associated with it, but the most important NDX file for the UPDATE command is the primary NDX file.

Work area 2 (alias "B") is then SELECTed, and another database is opened up. That database can also have seven associated NDX files, but the most important NDX file is the primary NDX file, the first one listed in the command. The importance of the primary NDX files is that both ANDX1 and BNDX1 must have the same field as their keyfield. An example of this is

```
-> USE CHAPTER9
-> LIST STRUC
Structure for database: C:CHAPTER9.dbf
Number of data records:         2
Date of last update    : 08/05/86
```

```
Field  Field Name   Type         Width    Dec
    1  CLIENT_ID    Character      10
    2  CLNAME       Character      30
    3  CLADDRESS1   Character      30
    4  CLADDRESS2   Character      30
    5  CLCITY       Character      20
    6  CLSTATE      Character       2
    7  CLZIPCODE    Character      10
    8  BUSIPHONE    Character      14
    9  HOMEPHONE    Character      14
   10  INCOME       Numeric        12        2
   11  LEAD         Character      20
   12  REFERENCE    Character     254
   13  BANK_REF     Memo           10
   14  SALES        Character      20
   15  CONTACT      Date            8
   16  RESULT       Memo           10
   17  FOLLOWUP     Logical         1
   18  NEXTCONTCT   Date            8
   19  BILLING      Character       1
   20  LASTPURCHS   Date            8
   21  PURCHSAMNT   Numeric        10        2
   22  BALANCE      Numeric        10        2
   23  CREDITCARD   Character       4
   24  CCNUMBER     Character      25
   25  EXPDATE      Date            8
   26  STORECREDT   Logical         1
   27  CREDITLIMT   Numeric        10        2
   28  CREDITGOOD   Logical         1
   29  CLHISTORY    Memo           10
   30  PURCHSHIST   Memo           10
** Total **                      602

-> COPY TO C9SALES FIELDS CLNAME, CLADDRESS1, CLCITY,
CLSTATE, CLZIPCODE, BUSIPHONE, SALES, BILLING,
PURCHSAMNT, PURCHSHIST

-> USE C9SALES
-> LIST STRUC
Structure for database: C:C9SALES.dbf
Number of data records:     2
Date of last update   : 08/06/86
Field  Field Name   Type         Width    Dec
    1  CLNAME       Character      30
    2  CLADDRESS1   Character      30
    3  CLCITY       Character      20
    4  CLSTATE      Character       2
    5  CLZIPCODE    Character      10
    6  BUSIPHONE    Character      14
    7  SALES        Character      20
    8  BILLING      Character       1
    9  PURCHSAMNT   Numeric        10        2
   10  PURCHSHIST   Memo           10
** Total **                      148
```

The use investigated here comes from the example of sales management. The sales force has been out in the field with portable computers. Now the sales force members have returned or mailed their order disks back to the home office so that the orders can be processed.

The first thing to note is that the salespeople don't have the complete structure of the CHAPTER9 database with them while they're making sales calls. That would be inefficient. They don't need all those fields.

The CHAPTER9 database is used here to create sales-force databases, C9SALES. These databases aren't exemplary of regional sales-force databases; they merely serve as examples here. These databases obviously share several fields.

Assume you're going to UPDATE the CHAPTER9 database from the C9SALES databases. To make proper use of the UPDATE command, you would have to INDEX the CHAPTER9 database on any of the non-MEMO fields (you can't INDEX a database on a MEMO field). You choose to INDEX on the SALES field. Both databases have the SALES field, but the target file (CHAPTER9, in this example) must be either INDEXed or SORTed on a specific field for the UPDATE command to function properly. It is not necessary to INDEX the C9SALES database on the SALES field. You will see how to perform UPDATES with INDEXed or SORTed source files shortly.

So far, you have the following:

```
1) we're going to UPDATE CHAPTER9 FROM C9SALES
2) we're going to UPDATE CHAPTER9 ON SALES
3) the C9SALES database is INDEXed on the SALES field
4) the CHAPTER9 database is INDEXed on the SALES field
5) we want to REPLACE the CHAPTER9 PURCHSAMNT field WITH
CHAPTER9 PURCHSAMNT + C9SALES PURCHSAMNT
```

Using the above information, the UPDATE command is

```
UPDA ON SALES FROM C9SALES REPL PURCHSAMNT WITH ;
    PURCHSAMNT + B->PURCHSAMNT
```

Note the use of the dBASE III PLUS four-letter-word convention and the semicolon to tell III PLUS the UPDATE command is continued on the next line. All of the above is done and shown next.

```
-> SELE 2
-> USE C9SALES
-> INDEX ON SALES TO C9SALES
-> SELE A
-> USE CHAPTER9
-> INDEX ON SALES TO CHAPTER9
-> UPDATE ON SALES FROM C9SALES REPLACE PURCHSAMNT WITH
PURCHSAMNT+B->PURCHSAMNT
```

An alternative form of the preceding command making use of alias names is

```
UPDA ON SALES FROM B REPL PURCHSAMNT WITH PURCHSAMNT +;
B->PURCHSAMNT
```

Note that both databases are INDEXed in this example. You can use the UPDATE command when the source database isn't INDEXed or SORTed by including the RANDOM qualifier. The command then becomes

```
UPDA ON SALES FROM B REPL PURCHSAMNT WITH PURCHSAMNT +;
   B->PURCHSAMNT RANDOM
```

Note that the provision to using the RANDOM qualifier is that the source database not be INDEXed on the same keyfield as the target database. This doesn't mean the source file can't be INDEXed or SORTed at all; it merely means the source file doesn't have to be INDEXed or SORTed on the same keyfield as the target file. You could use two databases that share a common field, the target file INDEXed or SORTed on that common field, and the source file INDEXed or SORTed on another field or not INDEXed or SORTed at all, and use the RANDOM qualifier to perform the UPDATE without problems.

ZAP

Now you come to the demon of the dBASE III PLUS system, the ZAP command. This is perhaps the most dangerous of the III PLUS commands. It removes records completely from the database. If you have a 2000-record database and you ZAP it, you *had* a 2000-record database. Now you have a database with no records.

Syntax   III PLUS equates ZAP to the code

```
DELETE ALL
PACK
```

However, using the preceding code would give you a second chance. You could use the RECALL ALL command before you entered PACK. The ZAP command syntax is

```
ZAP
```

and that is it. When you use it, you permanently remove every record in your database. The structure of the database won't be affected, but every record is gone. Note especially that the ZAP command doesn't need the DELETE ALL command to remove every record physically. The ZAP command will remove records whether they're marked for DELETE or not.

Use   A reasonable means of thwarting the ZAP danger is shown in the "Advanced Use" section. A standard method is to use either the CONFIG.DB or SET SAFETY command to make sure SAFETY is ON. Having SAFETY ON tells III PLUS to query the user before any ZAPping is started. This setting is shown in Figure 7-8.

Advanced Use   Because ZAP is so dangerous, you should make it a point to force a database-file backup before the actual ZAP occurs. The following code does exactly that. You should include the concept, if not the code, in your own work.

```
-> SET SAFETY ON
-> ZAP
Zap D:CHAPTER9.dbf? (Y/N)
```

Figure 7-8.   ZAPping with SAFETY ON forces a query before removing records

```
** BACKUP PRG TO BE USED BEFORE ZAPPING
*
CLEAR
FILENAME1 = DBF()
FILENAME2 = LEFT(DBF(),AT(".",DBF())) + "BAK"
? "CHECKING FOR EXISTING BACKUP FILES"
*
IF FILE("&FILENAME2")
   YORN = .F.
   ARECS = RECCOUNT()
   ALUPD = LUPDATE()
   SELE 2
   USE &FILENAME2
   CLEA
   ? SPAC(16)+"FILE TO ZAP            EXISTING BACKUP FILE"
   ? " LAST UPDATE -> "+DTOC(ALUPD)+SPACE(13)+DTOC(LUPDATE()
   ? " TOTAL RECORDS -> " + STR(ARECS,8) + SPAC(13) + ;
     STR(RECC(),8)
@ 10,0 SAY "A BACKUP FILE ALREADY EXISTS. QUIT (Y/N) -> " ;
          GET YORN PICT "Y"
   READ
*
   IF YORN
      RETURN
   ENDI
*
ENDI
*
? "MAKING NEW BACK UP FILE"
USE
SELE 1
COPY TO &FILENAME2
? "CREATING NEW WORK FILE"
SET SAFETY ON
ZAP
SET SAFETY OFF
*
** EOF
```

The above code is similar to the code shown in the section on using the PACK command. The major differences are the listing of current and backup-file information for the user with the LUP-DATE( ) and RECCOUNT( ) commands. Also note that you should SET SAFETY ON before you ZAP.

This code could be improved by determining available disk space before COPYing begins and allowing the user to choose the target drive.

Data Display
Commands

This chapter covers the dBASE III PLUS commands that can be used to display data from a database, memory, or a file to either the screen or printer. These commands are grouped because they all give information about data fields or memory variables. The DISPLAY MEMORY command is in this chapter because it tells the user the values of variables in memory. That command and two others, DISPLAY STATISTICS and DISPLAY STRUCTURE, are located in Chapter 15, "Debugging Commands," because they tell the user something about the III PLUS system. Some of the commands discussed in this chapter generate information in the form of reports and labels; others do straight dumps (LIST, TYPE).

@

The @ command is not actually a command. By itself, it does nothing except confuse dBASE III PLUS. It must be qualified. One of the qualifiers, GET, was mentioned in Chapter 7 and is only referenced here. The other qualifiers are

```
@ SAY
@ TO
@ CLEAR
```

Each of the qualifiers has a specific purpose. The last two, @...TO and @...CLEAR, don't actually display data so much as they "prettify" the display field (the screen) by CLEARing it and allowing you to draw lines and boxes.

Syntax Three of the @ command's qualifiers, SAY, TO, and CLEAR, will be discussed here. The fourth qualifier, GET, was discussed in the previous chapter as a separate command.

The first qualifier to cover is the SAY command. This command provides the primary III PLUS method of getting information to the screen or printer at a specific point on the display. The command form is

@ x,y SAY something

where the x,y coordinate pair is measured with x going from top to bottom and y going from left to right. The "something" can be any valid dBASE III PLUS data field or variable. You would tell III PLUS to position a NAME field of a hypothetical current database at screen coordinates (10,30) with

@ 10,30 SAY NAME

Likewise, you could tell III PLUS to position the AMOUNT field of your hypothetical current database at screen coordinates (10,30) with

@ 10,30 SAY AMOUNT

Note that NAME and AMOUNT are used here only for example purposes. III PLUS will tell you if it can't find what you want to SAY.

Also note that using the two preceding commands in the order presented would cause the AMOUNT value to write over some portion of the NAME string. For example, if the AMOUNT field is ten characters wide and the NAME field is 30 characters wide, the above combination of commands gives you ten digits of AMOUNT followed by the remaining 20 characters of NAME. You can use the @...SAY commands to send information to the printer with either of the following:

```
SET PRINTER ON
SET DEVICE TO PRINT
```

These commands are also covered in this chapter.

You can alter the appearance of what you SAY by using a PICTURE qualifier. The PICTURE qualifier can be broken down into functions and templates. Many of these functions and templates were mentioned in Chapter 7 and are only listed in this section. However, there are three functions that work only with the SAY command:

```
C - DISPLAY "CR" (CREDIT) AFTER POSITIVE NUMBER
X - DISPLAY "DB" (DEBIT) AFTER NEGATIVE NUMBER
( - ENCLOSE NEGATIVE NUMBERS IN PARENTHESES ()
```

Each of these PICTURE functions can be used in either of the following forms:

```
@ X,Y SAY something PICT "@f"
@ X,Y SAY something FUNC "f"
```

Note that the dBASE III PLUS four-letter-word convention is used here and that "f" is used to represent any function argument in the preceding listing. The effects of the three functions are shown in Figure 8-1.

The commands that produced the different types of output are shown in the following listing:

```
-> @ 10,10 SAY AMOUNT FUNC "C"
-> @ 12,10 SAY -AMOUNT
-> @ 14,10 SAY -AMOUNT FUNC "X"
-> @ 16,10 SAY -AMOUNT FUNC "("
```

Note that you could mix functions and templates as was done in Chapter 7. For example, you could cover every possibility for Figure 8-1 with the single command

```
@ x,y SAY something FUNC "XC"
```

You couldn't use FUNC "XC(", as the last function in the list takes precedence, and a negative value would be displayed with parentheses ( ) instead of DB.

```
1234567890 CR
-1234567890
1234567890 DB
( 1234567890)
```

Figure 8-1.   From the top to the bottom: the C function, the standard, unqualified negative value, the X function, and the (function

The remaining PICTURE functions are

```
B - NUMBERS ARE LEFT JUSTIFIED
Z - NUMERIC 0 IS DISPLAYED AS BLANK
D - DATE IS "MM/DD/YY"
E - DATE IS "DD/MM/YY"
A - ACCEPT ONLY ALPHA CHARACTERS
! - CONVERT LETTERS TO UPPER CASE
R - USED TO PLACE NON DATA CHARACTERS INTO THE PICTURE
S - SCROLL OVER DATA
```

The PICTURE templates are

```
9 - ALLOWS ONLY DIGITS AND VALUE SIGNS\j\
# - ALLOWS DIGITS, VALUE SIGNS AND BLANK SPACES
A - ALLOWS ON LETTERS
L - ALLOWS ONLY T, F, Y, N, y, OR n LOGICAL DATA TYPES
Y - ALLOWS ONLY Y, N, y, OR n LOGICAL DATA TYPES
N - ALLOWS ONLY ALPHANUMERIC INPUT
X - ACCEPTS ANY CHARACTER AS INPUT
! - CONVERTS ANY LOWER CASE TO UPPER CASE DURING INPUT
$ - REPLACES LEADING ZEROES WITH "$" IN NUMERIC INPUT
* - REPLACES LEADING ZEROES WITH "*" IN NUMERIC INPUT
. - FORCES A DECIMAL POINT (".")
, - SHOW APPROPRIATE COMMA (",") IF NUMERIC INPUT IS OVER
100
```

Information on them can be found in Chapter 7.

Remember that the SAY command doesn't highlight the field or variable being SAYed when used in the default III PLUS mode. Fields and variables are normally highlighted only during a GET command.

The next two forms of the command to investigate aren't really data-display commands. The @ ...TO and @ ...CLEAR are "prettifiers" because they do things to the display screen but don't display any valuable information.

The first of the two commands, @...TO, tells III PLUS to create either a single- or double-lined box. Figure 8-2 shows a double-lined box, a single-lined box, and two very thin boxes, also known as lines. The commands that generated those figures are

```
-> @ 1,1 TO 10,10 DOUBLE
-> @ 1,11 TO 10,21
-> @ 15,0 TO 15,79 DOUBLE
-> @ 18,0 TO 18,79
```

The standard form to create a box of any kind is

```
@ x1,y1 TO x2,y2
```

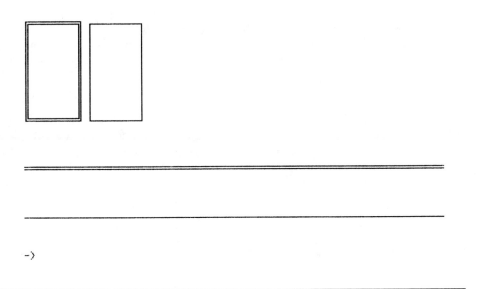

-⟩

Figure 8-2. These are examples of the III PLUS @...TO command

The default is a single-line box. You can specify a double-line box by modifying the command to

@ x1,y1 TO x2,y2 DOUBLE

Note that x2 must be greater than or equal to x1, and y2 must be greater than or equal to y1. Also note that you can't declare an x1 or x2 less than 0 or greater than 24, nor a y1 or y2 less than 0 or greater than 79.

Straight lines are generated by making either the y's or the x's equal in value. A straight horizontal line is made with a command such as

@ x1,y1 TO x2,y1

Note that the y values in the preceding command are equal. A vertical line is created with

@ x1,y1 TO x1,y2

The x values in the preceding command are equal. You can create a double line as you created a double box, simply by including the DOUBLE qualifier in the command line.

As a point of interest, you can create a single- or double-lined "dot" by leaving the x values equal and the y values equal, as in

```
@ xl,yl TO xl,yl
```

It's a lot of work to create either an equal sign (=, the double dot) or a minus sign (−, the single dot), but you can do it if you want. Note that no form of the box and line drawing commands will send boxes or lines to the printer.

The @...CLEAR command is a variation of the CLEAR command. The CLEAR command tells III PLUS to erase the screen. The @...CLEAR command tells III PLUS to erase a specific portion of the screen. The form is

```
@ x,y CLEAR
```

This tells III PLUS to erase everything to the right and under screen coordinates (x,y). The command

```
@ 15,5 CLEAR
```

creates an empty box on the screen by erasing the area from 15,5 to 24,79 (the lower right corner of the screen).

A variation on this is to erase an actual box. You can create an actual box with the command

```
@ xl,yl CLEAR TO x2,y2
```

This is shown in Figure 8-3. The actual command used is

```
@ 10,10 CLEAR TO 20,20
```

Use   Before you start drawing lines and boxes and SAYing things, note the physical restrictions your equipment puts on you. Most computer screens are 80 columns wide by 25 columns long. III PLUS will remind you if you happen to forget. The following listing shows attempts to write to the 80th column and the 25th row as failures, right?

```
·> @ 10,80 SAY PAYTO
Position is off the screen
              ?
```

```
@ 10,80 SAY PAYTO
-> @ 25,10 SAY PAYTO
Position is off the screen
                          ?
@ 25,10 SAY PAYTO
```

No, not quite. The upper-left corner of the screen, which many users would call coordinate position (1,1), is actually coordinate position (0,0). This means that a 25-row screen goes from row 0 to row 24. Likewise, an 80-column screen goes from column 0 to 79. An example of this is shown in Figure 8-4. Any valid dBASE III PLUS numeric expression can be used for the x and y coordinates.

There is a use of the @ command that isn't listed but is useful. The only caveat to it is that it only works in the PROGRAM mode. You can enter it in INTERACTIVE mode, but you'll always return to the dBASE prompt. The command is

@ x,y

This command tells III PLUS to place the cursor at coordinates (x,y). You could position the cursor at coordinates (10,10) with

@ 10,10

```
*
STOR 0 TO WIDE,LONG
STOR 1 TO STARTX,STARTY
CLEA
@ 10,0 SAY "HOW LONG DO YOU WANT THE BOX (1-20)? -> " GET LONG RANG 1,20
@ 11,0 SAY "HOW WIDE DO YOU WANT THE BOX (1-10)? -> " GET WIDE RANG 1,10
READ
CLEA
*
DO WHIL ST            79
*
   IF STAR           3
      STAR           +WIDE
      STAR
   ENDI
*
   @ STAR            0 STARTX+LONG,STARTY+WIDE DOUBLE
     STARTX
     STARTY
ENDD
*
** EOF

-> @ 10,10 CLEAR TO 20,20
->
```

Figure 8-3. The @ 10,10 CLEAR TO 20,20 command is used to carve a box out of the screen contents

Data Display Commands

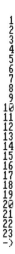

```
                  11111111112222222222333333333344444444445555555555566666666667777777777
1
2
3
4
5
6
7
8
9
10
11
12
13
14
15
16
17
18
19
20
21
22
23
->
```

Figure 8-4.   This screen was generated to prove that a normal 80-column×25-row screen is actually 0-24×0-79

This is useful when you want to place an ACCEPT, INPUT, or WAIT command at a specific place on the screen. For example, you could place any of the three previous commands at position 11,0 with the following:

```
@ 10,0
ACCE "string" TO variable
```

Note that the command (an ACCEPT command, in this case) has been placed at coordinates (11,0), with the cursor first positioned at coordinates (10,0).

Advanced Use   The "Syntax" section noted that you can use the @...SAY command to display variables and data from the current database. You can also use it to display data from any database in any work area, whether or not that database is current. The command form is

```
@ x,y SAY alias—>FIELD
```

where alias signifies the alias name of the database. Remember that each work area has the default alias of A through J (work areas 1 through 10, respectively), the name of the database in USE in each work area, or a name you give each database in each work area in the USE command (see Chapter 5).

Another use of the @...SAY command comes from mixing data types. You would normally get an error message if you tried to SAY something such as

@ x,y SAY string+number+date

This is shown in Figure 8-5. There will be times, however, when you want to mix data types in an output line. III PLUS lets you do this with the following four functions:

```
VAL() - CONVERTS ALPHA DIGITS TO NUMERIC DIGITS
STR() - CONVERTS NUMERIC DIGITS TO ALPHA DIGITS
DTOC() - CONVERTS DATE TO ALPHA
CTOD() - CONVERTS ALPHA TO DATE
```

The first function, VAL( ), converts character-type digits to numeric-type digits. For example, "1983" is a character string, but

VAL("1983")

is a numeric data type. The reverse procedure is handled by the STR( ) function. The number 152 is numeric data, but

---

```
-> DISP MEMO
TRUTH       pub  L  .T.
AMOUNT      pub  N  1234567890  (1234567890.00000000)
NAME        pub  C  "ABCDEFGHIJKLMNOPQRSTUVWXYZABCD"
TODAY       pub  D  09/26/86
      4 variables defined,      52 bytes used
    252 variables available,  5948 bytes available

-> @ 10,10 SAY AMOUNT+TODAY+NAME
Data type mismatch.
                            ?
@ 10,10 SAY AMOUNT+TODAY+NAME
->
```

Figure 8-5.   III PLUS won't let you SAY different data types in a single expression

STR(152)

is a text string. The last two functions are date functions. The first one, DTOC( ), converts Dates TO Characters. The day's date might be 06/08/86, but

DTOC(06/08/86)

is a character string. The opposite function is CTOD( ), Character TO Date. The text string "06/08/86" is made into a date-type variable with

CTOD("06/08/86")

Note that there isn't any function to convert either logical- or memo-type data into another data type. You can mix the functions to display dates with numeric data. One method of entering the preceding command might be

@ x,y SAY string+STR(number)+CTOD(date)

? and ??

This section covers the question-mark data-display prompt (?) and its other form, the double question mark (??).

Syntax   The ? and ?? data-display prompts were developed early in dBASE's career. They are simple to use and powerful. They are simple to use because all you do is enter the question mark

?

Remember that III PLUS considers anything after the question mark a query to the system. A question mark by itself says that you are querying nothing. III PLUS therefore returns nothing. That is, a question mark tells III PLUS to throw a carriage return back at you. Simple and elegant.

The command is of more use when you're asking for information. Any properly formatted query will be answered on the line immediately following the query, as shown in Figure 8-6.

```
-) X = 10
-) Y = 20
-) Z = 30
-) NAME = "JOSEPH-DAVID"
-) CITY = "NASHUA"
-) TODAY = DATE()
-) RIGHTNOW = TIME()
-) ? X
              10
-) ? Y
              20
-) ? NAME
JOSEPH-DAVID
-) ? NAME + STR(X)
JOSEPH-DAVID          10
-) ? RIGHTNOW
09:09:38
-) ? DTOC(TODAY) + CITY
09/26/86NASHUA
-) ? TODAY + TIME
Variable not found.
                  ?
? TODAY + TIME
-)
```

Figure 8-6.   The ? prompt tells III PLUS to answer the question on the line following the prompt

Note that you can mix data types in the query by using the proper functions, and that each response is on the line following the query.

The ?? prompt's syntax is identical to that of the ? prompt. The only difference between the two is in what they do. They both answer any properly formatted queries asked of them. The ?? prompt doesn't answer on the next line, however. It answers the query on the same line that the query is asked, as shown in Figure 8-7. The order of queries is the same as that asked in Figure 8-6. The only difference between the two representations is in the placement of the response. This difference, however, can be significant. Note that some responses don't completely cover their queries.

As a final note, neither the ?? nor the ? prompt can tell you about something they don't know about. Both Figures 8-6 and 8-7 list the command

```
                    10
                    20
JOSEPH-DAVID
JOSEPH-DAVID          10
09:09:38GHTNOW
09/26/86NASHUAAY) + CITY
-> ?? TODAY + TIME
Variable not found.
                    ?
?? TODAY + TIME
->
```

Figure 8-7.   The ?? prompt tells III PLUS to answer the question on the same line as the prompt

TODAY + TIME

But TIME isn't a term III PLUS is familiar with. An error message is returned when you ask for something III PLUS doesn't understand.

Use   Although you might not expect it from such a simple command, the ? and ?? prompts can be significant when used shrewdly. They can be used extensively in the INTERACTIVE mode as a means of determining data-field and memory-variable values. Assuming the current database has a NAME field in it, you can query III PLUS on the contents of the current record with

? NAME

Further, if there is more than one database in USE in the system, you can query III PLUS on any field in any in-USE work area by including the work area's alias, as in

? n—>field

where n is the alias name and field is the name of any field in the database in work area n. For example, to find the contents of the PAYMENT field of the current record in the database in work area C, you'd enter

? C—>PAYMENT

III PLUS would respond with the value in that field. Note that you can use the ?? prompt in each of the preceding cases. The results would only be altered as described in the "Syntax" section.

AVERAGE

The AVERAGE command is a useful tool in that it determines the arithmetic mean of a field over an entire database. You can use it to determine the mean of a single field, a group of fields, or the sum of a group of fields. The fields must be valid dBASE III PLUS numeric expressions.

Syntax   The AVERAGE command has a rather full syntax for a command that only does one thing. The reason for this is that there are many ways to determine an average. Consider the following listing:

```
-> SET TALK ON
-> AVERAGE
     39 records averaged
 PAYAMOUNT MILEAGE
     89.30    31.1
```

The standard command form is

```
AVERAGE
```

The plain AVERAGE command tells III PLUS to determine the arithmetic mean of every numeric field over the entire database. The example given here uses the EXPENSES database. This database has only two numeric fields, PAYAMOUNT and MILEAGE. You can determine the means of both with the plain AVERAGE command.

The next variation on the theme is to specify which fields you'd like AVERAGEd. This is done with

```
AVERAGE field1, field2,...
```

You can list a single numeric field, any number of numeric fields, or all the numeric fields in the database. This is shown in the following listing. The operative word is, of course, *numeric*. The AVERAGE command doesn't work on nonnumeric data types.

```
-> USE EXPENSES
-> SET TALK ON
-> AVERAGE PAYAMOUNT
     39 records averaged
PAYAMOUNT
    89.30
-> AVERAGE PAYAMOUNT, MILEAGE
     39 records averaged
PAYAMOUNT MILEAGE
    89.30    31.1
```

Note that III PLUS has been asked to AVERAGE the PAYA-
MOUNT and MILEAGE fields. This is equivalent to the plain
AVERAGE command shown in the previous listing, because these
are the only two numeric fields in the database.

The AVERAGE command also makes use of the same qualifiers
any database-ranging command does. The first one to explore is
NEXT. The command form is either

```
AVERAGE NEXT n
```

or

```
AVERAGE field1, field2,... NEXT n
```

where n is a valid dBASE III PLUS numeric expression. The first
form of the command tells III PLUS to AVERAGE every numeric
field in the database for the NEXT n records. The second form tells
III PLUS to AVERAGE the listed fields for the NEXT n records.
The following listing shows the effects of each of these command
forms.

```
-> USE EXPENSES
-> SET TALK ON
-> AVERAGE PAYAMOUNT NEXT 5
      5 records averaged
PAYAMOUNT
   186.78
-> AVERAGE PAYAMOUNT NEXT 105
     35 records averaged
PAYAMOUNT
    72.82
-> AVERAGE PAYAMOUNT NEXT 1
No records averaged
```

```
PAYAMOUNT
       0.00
-> 1
-> AVERAGE PAYAMOUNT NEXT 1
       1 record averaged
PAYAMOUNT
      57.00
```

The first thing to remember is that III PLUS only AVERAGEs the NEXT n records from where the current record pointer is. The EXPENSES database used in this example has 39 records in it. You will start at record 1 when you first USE a database, but any operation that changes the record pointer will change how many NEXT records you'll be able to operate on. Note that you can ask to AVERAGE as many records as you like; III PLUS will only AVERAGE as many records as it has available. The single digit, 1, in the listing is used to position the record pointer to the first record in the database.

Next, consider the range qualifiers FOR and WHILE. Several of III PLUS's commands make use of these two qualifiers. The AVERAGE command makes use of FOR to do sequential searches on the database. It finds records that meet some condition and AVERAGEs their numeric fields. The command form is

AVERAGE FOR condition

This operation is shown in the following listing. The FOR qualifier tells III PLUS to scan the entire database for records that meet the condition listed in the command. This works well for use with databases of fewer than 100 records, but the process can be time-consuming when using databases with more than 500 records, especially if you're AVERAGEing several fields in the database.

```
-> USE EXPENSES
-> SET TALK ON
-> AVERAGE PAYAMOUNT FOR PAYFOR = "Office Supplies"
       4 records averaged
PAYAMOUNT
      96.86
-> AVERAGE PAYAMOUNT FOR PAYFOR = "Office Equipment"
       1 record averaged
PAYAMOUNT
    1639.00
```

The WHILE qualifier speeds up AVERAGEing because it works with indexed files. The WHILE qualifier form is identical to the FOR qualifier form.

Note that III PLUS assumes that the current record meets the WHILE condition. This may not be the case, as shown in the following listing. III PLUS doesn't AVERAGE anything when the current record doesn't meet the WHILE condition. It doesn't matter whether the database is INDEXed or SORTed in this instance. The last part of this listing shows a failed AVERAGE even though the database has been INDEXed. The AVERAGE failed because the current record didn't meet the WHILE condition. You have to FIND or SEEK the first occurrence of the condition you want to WHILE, then enter the AVERAGE command.

```
-> USE EXPENSES
-> SET TALK ON
-> AVERAGE PAYAMOUNT WHILE PAYFOR = "Office Equipment"
No records averaged
 PAYAMOUNT
      0.00
-> 1
-> AVERAGE PAYAMOUNT WHILE PAYFOR = "Office Equipment"
No records averaged
 PAYAMOUNT
      0.00
-> INDEX ON PAYFOR TO PAYFOR
   00% indexed    100% indexed            39 Records indexed
-> AVERAGE PAYAMOUNT WHILE PAYFOR = "Office Equipment"
No records averaged
 PAYAMOUNT
      0.00
-> FIND "Office Equipment"
-> AVERAGE PAYAMOUNT WHILE PAYFOR = "Office Equipment"
      1 record averaged
 PAYAMOUNT
   1639.00
-> FIND "Office Supplies"
-> AVERAGE PAYAMOUNT WHILE PAYFOR = "Office Supplies"
      4 records averaged
 PAYAMOUNT
     96.86
```

You can use the WHILE qualifier on a SORTed database. However, you cannot FIND or SEEK anything in a SORTed database, as those commands work only with INDEXed files. You can use the LOCATE command on a SORTed database with no problem. In each of these instances, it is assumed the database is either INDEXed or SORTed on the field that contains the condition. For example, the previous listing shows the EXPENSES.DBF file INDEXed on the PAYFOR field. The WHILE condition is also based on values in the

PAYFOR field. The condition after the WHILE qualifier should be based on a known or suspected value in the keyfield. You are likely to AVERAGE nothing if you use some other field condition in the WHILE qualifier.

Each of the preceding listings shares something other than USE-ing the EXPENSES database and demonstrating some aspect of the AVERAGE command. Each listing SETs TALK ON. The AVERAGE command won't tell you what it found out or how it's progressing unless TALK is ON. You can turn TALK ON with either CONFIG.DB or SET TALK ON. It is assumed you wouldn't want to AVERAGE something unless you wanted to know the average value. You can use AVERAGE with TALK OFF as follows:

AVERAGE TO variable

where variable is a valid dBASE III PLUS variable name. An example of this command is shown here:

```
-> USE EXPENSES
-> SET TALK OFF
-> AVERAGE PAYAMOUNT
-> AVERAGE PAYAMOUNT TO MEAN
-> ? MEAN
        89.30
-> AVERAGE PAYAMOUNT, MILEAGE TO PAYMEAN, MILEMEAN
-> ? PAYMEAN, MILEMEAN
        89.30           31.1
```

III PLUS will either create a new variable or use an existing variable in the AVERAGE command. Note that you can AVERAGE several fields to several variables with the command form

AVERAGE field1, field2,...TO variable1, variable2,...

There are some other aspects of the AVERAGE command that are worth noting. First, you can tell III PLUS to AVERAGE an individual record with the command

AVERAGE RECORD(n)

where n is a valid dBASE III PLUS numeric expression and equates with a valid record number for the current database. This only AVERAGEs the single record you include in the command. If you try to AVERAGE a nonnumeric field, III PLUS returns the message "Not a numeric expression."

Use   The "Syntax" section spends a great deal of time showing you how to use the AVERAGE command on a single field at a time. You can also use the AVERAGE command to determine the mean sum of fields. Consider the following listing:

```
.> AVERAGE PAYAMOUNT+MILEAGE
    39 records averaged
PAYAMOUNT+MILEAGE
           120.35
```

Again, this example uses the EXPENSES database, which has only two numeric fields. You can fine-tune this mean-sum form of the AVERAGE command by using qualifiers to specify certain conditions or the scope of records.

You can also mix and match AVERAGE's qualifiers; you might use the FOR and WHILE qualifiers, for instance. For example, you can use an INDEXed database and FIND a specific condition before using the WHILE qualifier. Also note that the WHILE qualifier can be used on the keyfield of the NDX file.

```
.> USE EXPENSES
.> SET TALK ON
.> INDEX ON PAYFOR TO PAYFOR
    00% indexed    100% indexed              39 Records indexed
.> FIND "Office Supplies"
.> AVERAGE PAYAMOUNT WHILE PAYFOR = "Office Supplies" FOR
PAYDATE < DATE()
       4 records averaged
 PAYAMOUNT
     96.86
.> AVERAGE PAYAMOUNT WHILE PAYFOR = "Office Supplies" FOR
PAYDATE < DATE()-100
No records averaged
 PAYAMOUNT
      0.00
```

Advanced Use   There are times when you need to determine AVERAGEs of nonnumeric data. For the sake of example, consider the following listing:

```
.> ? SUBSTR(DTOC(PAYDATE),4,2)
12
.> AVERAGE VAL(SUBSTR(DTOC(PAYDATE),4,2))
    39 records averaged
VAL(SUBSTR(DTOC(PAYDATE),4,2))
                        16.28
```

Again using the EXPENSES database, remember that the

PAYDATE field is a date-type expression. You normally can't AVERAGE a DATE field. But, through clever programming and use of III PLUS's diverse functions, you can determine that you paid all your bills on the 16.28th day of the month. The reason the SUBSTRing function is used to retrieve the fourth and fifth characters from the PAYDATE field is that the American date format (MM/DD/YY) is used here. If you use the European date format, the AVERAGE command becomes

AVERAGE VAL(LEFT(DTOC(PAYDATE),2))

Note that the preceding command first converts a date-type field to a character expression, then converts the character expression to a numeric data type. All of AVERAGE's qualifiers can be used with this type of command.

BROWSE

The BROWSE command allows data display by creating a spreadsheet-like display of the current database. The cursor keys and special menus can be used to move through the database in the BROWSE mode. The command itself can be used in any of the following forms:

```
BROWSE
BROWSE FIELDS field1, field2, ...
BROWSE FIELDS field list LOCK n
BROWSE FIELDS field list LOCK n WIDTH m
BROWSE FIELDS field list LOCK n WIDTH m FREEZE field
BROW FIEL field list LOCK n WIDT m FREE field NOFOLLOW
BROW FIEL field list LOCK n WIDT m FREE field NOFO NOAPPEND
BROW FIEL field list LOCK n WIDT m FREE field NOFO NOAP
NOMENU
```

Note that field1 and field2 represent any non-MEMO fields in the current database; field list represents any group of fields in the current database separated by commas (,); n and m represent valid dBASE III PLUS numeric expressions; field represents any single field in the current database; and the last three forms of the command use the dBASE III PLUS four-letter-word convention.

You can mix and match any of the listed qualifiers. The BROWSE command is covered in detail in Chapter 6.

The COUNT command shares many features with the AVERAGE command. Both perform some arithmetic on the current database. The AVERAGE command determined the arithmetic mean of all or some records in the current DBF file. The COUNT command also works on all or some records in the current database, but the COUNT command only determines the number of records in the database.

Syntax   The COUNT command's operation is straightforward. Its sole purpose is to determine the number of records that meet a specific condition. The condition might be nonexistent in the database, in which case the COUNT command determines the number of records in the database. The basic command form is

COUNT

This tells III PLUS to determine the total of all records in the database. An example of this is shown in the following listing, where there are only 39 records in the entire database. Using an unqualified COUNT command has the same effect as using the RECCOUNT( ) function. The difference in operation between these two is tremendous, however. The COUNT command counts each record sequentially, actually reading each record although no conditions have been specified. The RECCOUNT( ) function merely looks at the database file header and reads the header field that tells III PLUS how many records are in the entire database. The speed difference, especially in a large database, is impressive.

```
·> USE EXPENSES
·> SET TALK ON
·> COUNT
     39 records
·> ? RECCOUNT()
       39
```

One might guess that part of the COUNT command's power comes from its ability to be qualified. True. It uses the NEXT, FOR, and WHILE qualifiers to specify a scope or conditions on COUNTing. The command form is

COUNT NEXT n

where n is a valid dBASE III PLUS numeric expression. The COUNT command won't COUNT anything beyond the end of the file, so a command such as

COUNT NEXT 200

in a database of 60 records is pointless. It's also pretty useless, because you're *telling* III PLUS how many records to count. Every other dBASE III PLUS command that can be qualified by NEXT operates the same way.

If you further qualify COUNT with either FOR or WHILE, the command gains in utility. Consider the following listing:

```
·> USE EXPENSES
·> SET TALK ON
·> COUNT FOR PAYFOR = "Auto Expense"
      5 records
·> 1
·> COUNT FOR PAYFOR = "Auto Expense"
      5 records
·> COUNT NEXT 10 FOR PAYFOR = "Auto Expense"
No records
·> 1
·> COUNT NEXT 10 FOR PAYFOR = "Auto Expense"
      1 record
```

Initially, you COUNT the entire database FOR a specific condition. The command form is

COUNT FOR condition

This tells III PLUS to return the total number of records in the database that meet the specific condition. Note that the FOR qualifier starts at the top of the database and works down sequentially through every record in the database, until it reaches the end of the file.

When you combine the NEXT and FOR qualifiers, you can begin to perform some sophisticated COUNTs. The command form becomes

COUNT NEXT n FOR condition

where n is a valid dBASE III PLUS numeric expression. This command tells III PLUS to search only the NEXT n records FOR a specific condition. This form of the COUNT command is covered in the "Use" section.

The WHILE qualifier can speed up COUNTing because it works with indexed files. The WHILE qualifier form is identical to the FOR qualifier form.

III PLUS assumes the current record meets the WHILE condition. III PLUS doesn't COUNT anything when the current record doesn't meet the WHILE condition, whether or not the database is INDEXed. You must FIND or SEEK the first occurrence of the condition you want to WHILE, then enter the COUNT command.

You can use the WHILE qualifier on a SORTed database. However, you cannot FIND or SEEK anything in a SORTed database, as those commands only work with INDEXed files. You can use the LOCATE command on a SORTed database with no problem. In each of these instances, it is assumed the database is either INDEXed or SORTed on the field that contains the condition. For example, the following listing shows the EXPENSES.DBF file using an NDX file created earlier. The WHILE condition is based on values in the PAYFOR field. The condition after the WHILE qualifier should be based on a known or suspected value in the keyfield. You are likely to COUNT nothing if you use some other field condition in the WHILE qualifier.

```
-> USE EXPENSES
-> SET TALK ON
-> SET INDE TO PAYFOR
-> FIND "Auto"
-> COUNT WHILE PAYFOR = "Auto"
      5 records
-> FIND "Auto"
-> COUNT WHILE PAYFOR = "Auto" FOR PAYTO = "Sears"
      1 record
```

You can also mix and match AVERAGE's qualifiers. Note that this listing makes use of an INDEXed database and FINDs a specific condition before using the WHILE qualifier. Also note that the WHILE qualifier is used on the keyfield of the NDX file.

The preceding listings share something other than USEing the EXPENSES database and demonstrating some aspect of the COUNT command. Each listing SETs TALK ON. The COUNT command won't tell you what it found out or how it's progressing unless TALK is ON. You can turn TALK ON with either the CONFIG.DB or SET TALK ON command. It is assumed you wouldn't want to COUNT something unless you wanted to know the COUNT value. You can still COUNT things with TALK OFF by using the command form

dBASE III PLUS: The Complete Reference

COUNT TO variable

where variable is a valid dBASE III PLUS variable name. An example of this command is shown here. III PLUS will either create a new variable or use an existing variable in the COUNT command.

```
-> USE EXPENSES
-> SET TALK OFF
-> COUNT
-> COUNT TO NUMOFRECS
-> ? NUMOFRECS
        39
-> COUNT TO AUTORECS FOR PAYFOR = "Auto"
-> ? AUTORECS
         5
```

There are some other aspects of the COUNT command that are worth noting. First, you can tell III PLUS to COUNT an individual record with the command

COUNT RECORD(n)

where n is a valid dBASE III PLUS numeric expression and equates with a valid record number for the current database. This COUNTs only the single record you include in the command.

Use   The COUNT command mixes common use and advanced use. The code given here testifies to that fact. The code is designed to transfer data selectively from an existing database to a new database. The code itself is called a *transfer kernel.*

Transferring data from one file to another is useful when small portions of large databases are to be investigated or when some portion of a database file is going to be archived. This sort of procedure is often used with accounting systems, when monthly or yearly data is transferred from the working database to a historical database.

The important aspects of transferring data are

```
1) knowing what has to be transferred.
2) knowing where the transferred data is supposed to go.
3) knowing where the transferred data is coming from.
4) knowing if we are creating a new target database,
rewriting an old target database, or appending to an old
target database.
5) the source database is already selected before the
TRANSFER kernel is engaged.
```

```
6) we assume the user will either be allowed to tell the
system what the transfer parameters are, or that the entire
situation is automated to the point where the user merely
selects the TRANSFER option.
```

Three dBASE III PLUS commands make up the heart of the transfer kernel. Those three commands are COPY, APPEND, and, of course, COUNT. The complete code for the transfer kernel is listed at the end of this section. To save space, it will not be shown here.

The transfer kernel begins by clearing the screen and getting the name of a target file. If the user gives the target file a name similar to that of an existing file, that user is given several options. The user can enter another name, APPEND to the existing file, DELETE the existing file and write a new file, or quit the transfer kernel completely. All of these options are handled in a DO CASE...OTHERWISE...ENDCASE statement. If the user presses a RETURN, which dBASE interprets as having an ASCII value of 0, the transfer kernel RETURNSs to the calling program. Typing a D ERASEs the existing file. Typing an A tells dBASE to prepare for an APPEND by getting the name of the in-USE database and then to EXIT from the DO WHILE...ENDDO loop. The OTHERWISE condition of the DO CASE...OTHERWISE...ENDCASE statement handles renaming the target database.

Once that loop is passed, you check to see if the user is transferring to another disk drive. If so, SET the DEFAULT to that new drive. The $ function is equivalent to the AT( ) function. Both determine if the first expression is contained in the second expression (see Chapter 21 on string functions for more information).

You accept the target file and switch drives (if necessary). Now get the transfer conditions. If the conditions are not valid (if they are unknown to dBASE), either get new conditions or quit the kernel.

Now you come to the COUNT command. The COUNT command is actually the most important part of this code, as it tells III PLUS how much of the source file is being transferred to the target file. The DO WHILE...ENDDO loop checks to make sure there is enough room on the target disk to hold all the data being transferred. You COUNT how many records in the source database meet the desired conditions. (DO) WHILE the number of desired records times the size of a single record plus 89 plus the number of fields times 32 is greater than the available disk space: put up the error message.

At this point, the user can exit from the transfer kernel simply by typing any key other than T. The option of transferring the entire source database to the target file is not offered. That is unnecessary as it is already handled by the DOS COPY command. Programmers familiar with dBASE III PLUS may wonder why you don't need to check for available disk space with the ERROR(56) function. That function works only once the transfer of data has started. No one wants to be 99% of the way through an APPEND or COPY and then find out that there isn't enough room on the target disk.

The actual transfer of information occurs in the IF... ELSE...ENDIF statement at the end of the kernel. IF the desired ARCHIVE file existed and was to be APPENDed, you USE the existing target file and APPEND from the source database FOR the desired conditions. If you're not APPENDing, COPY the desired information to the ARCHIVE file.

Using an INDEXed database can improve the efficiency of this kernel immensely if the user wants transfer conditions based on the INDEXed field. The consideration is whether you want to let the user transfer from one NDX, several NDXes, or none. If the source database is indexed with only one NDX file, the user must know that instead of typing in a complete condition statement such as

PAYTO = "Sears"

that user only needs to type in "Sears" (assuming the database is INDEXed on the PAYTO field). The program must also determine if the user typed in something that wasn't valid data for the INDEXed field.

There's always the chance that what the user wants as the CONDITION doesn't exist in the source database; the IF...ENDIF statement takes care of that possibility.

FIND "&CONDITIONS"

before the actual transfer statements repositions the record pointer to the start of the desired records.

The finished transfer kernel for an INDEXed database is

```
** TRANSFER KERNEL FOR AN INDEXED DATABASE
*
CLEA
ACCE "What is the name of the target database? -> ";
```

```
         TO ARCHIVEFILE
ARCHIVEFILE = ARCHIVEFILE + ".DBF"
*
DO WHIL FILE(ARCHIVEFILE)
   OLDFILE = ARCHIVEFILE
   CLEA
   ACCE "That file exists. Type another name, "+;
      "A(ppend) to the existing file, or "+;
      "D(elete) the existing file, or RETURN "+;
      "to quit." TO ARCHIVEFILE
*
   DO CASE
    CASE ASC(ARCHIVEFILE) = 0
         RETU
      CASE UPPER(ARCHIVEFILE) = "D"
         ERAS &OLDFILE
         ARCHIVEFILE = OLDFILE
         EXIT
    CASE UPPER(ARCHIVEFILE) = "A"
         DATABASE = DBF()
         EXIT
     OTHE
         ARCHIVEFILE = ARCHIVEFILE + ".DBF"
   ENDC
*
ENDD
*
IF ":"$ARCHIVEFILE
   DEFAULT = LEFT(ARCHIVEFILE,1)
   SET DEFA TO &DEFAULT
ENDI
*
CLEA
ACCE "What are the transfer conditions? -> ";
   TO CONDITIONS
*
DO WHIL TYPE("&CONDITIONS") = TYPE(INDEXFIELD)
   CLEA
   ACCE "Those are not valid conditions. Type "+;
   "them again or RETURN to exit." TO CONDITIONS
*
   IF ASC(CONDITIONS) = 0
      RETU
   ENDI
*
ENDD
*
FIND "&CONDITIONS"
*
IF .NOT. FOUND()
   WAIT "There are no matching conditions. Type "+;
      "any key to exit."
   RETU
ENDI
*
COUNT WHIL &CONDITIONS TO TRANSCASE
*
```

```
DO WHIL TRANSCASE * RECS() + 89 + (NUMFIELDS * 32) > DISK()
   WAIT "There isn't enough room on the disk. "+;
      "(Q)uit or put a new disk in and "+;
      "T(ry again) -> " TO ANSWER
*
   IF UPPER(ANSWER) <> 'T'
      RETU
   ENDI
*
ENDD
*
FIND "&CONDITIONS"
*
IF UPPER(ARCHIVEFILE) = "A"
   USE &OLDFILE
   APPE FROM &DATABASE WHIL &CONDITIONS
ELSE
   COPY TO &ARCHIVEFILE WHIL &CONDITIONS
ENDI
*
** END OF TRANSFER KERNEL FOR INDEXED DATABASE
```

TRANSCASE -> a variable I create to hold the number of records to transfer
RECS() -> a dBASE III PLUS function that returns the size of a source record in bytes
89 -> the size of a dBASE III Plus database file header block, in bytes (the number is valid, don't worry about how I got it)
NUMFIELDS -> the number of fields per record. You must place this number in the TRANSFER kernel, as it depends on the database being transferred. If the TRANSFER kernel is going to be used for a number of databases, NUMFIELDS can be a SAVEd MEMORY variable.
32 -> the size, in bytes, of a database field descriptor (again, don't worry about how I got it, the number is valid)
DISK() -> a dBASE III PLUS function that returns the amount of free space on the default drive, in bytes (we SET the DEFAULT to the target drive earlier)

DISPLAY

The DISPLAY command appeared in the original dBASE. It is one of the class of commands you could call the "coelacanths" and can be used to send information to the screen and the printer. The basic function of the command is given by its name: it DISPLAYs information.

Syntax   DISPLAY has a rather full syntax for a command that serves only one purpose. The standard command form is

DISPLAY

The plain DISPLAY command tells III PLUS to place on the screen the name of every field in the database and then place the contents of the current record's field directly under the field's name. Unless you routinely use small field names and few fields in a database, this can get confusing. All the information is there, but it is difficult to find.

The next variation on the theme is to specify which fields you'd like DISPLAYed. This is done with

DISPLAY field1, field2,...

You can list a single field, a number of fields, or all the numeric fields in the database. The DISPLAY command also makes use of the same qualifiers any database-ranging command does. The first one to explore is NEXT. The command form is either

DISP NEXT n

or

DISP NEXT n field1, field2, ...

where n is a valid dBASE III PLUS numeric expression and field1 and field2 are the names of fields in the current database. The first form of the command tells III PLUS to DISPLAY every field in the database for the NEXT n records. The second form tells III PLUS to DISPLAY the listed fields for the NEXT n records.

You should note that III PLUS only DISPLAYs the NEXT n records from the point where the current record pointer is located. You will start at record 1 when you first USE a database, but any operation that changes the record pointer will change the number of NEXT records you'll be able to operate on. Although you can ask to DISPLAY as many records as you like, III PLUS will only DISPLAY as many records as it has available.

Next you should consider the range qualifiers FOR and WHILE. The DISPLAY command makes use of FOR to do sequential searches on the database to DISPLAY records that meet some condition. The command form is

Examples of DISPLAYing with the FOR qualifier are shown in the following listing. The FOR qualifier tells III PLUS to scan the entire database for records that meet the condition listed in the command.

```
-> DISP FOR PAYFOR = "Auto"
Record#  PAYTO
PAYFOR
CHECKNUM    PAYAMOUNT PAYDATE  MILEAGE
      2  Allstate                                      Auto
Expense
tovisa          246.00 07/12/86     0.0
     14  Ford Motor Credit                             Auto
Expense
1317            305.33 07/10/86     0.0
     22  Sears                                         Auto
Expense
1323             42.99 07/19/86     0.0
     30  Camps Car Wash                                Auto
Expense
cash             4.50 07/07/86      0.0
     31  Texaco                                        Auto
Expense
1321             47.50 07/15/86     0.0
-> DISP PAYTO FOR PAYFOR = "Auto"
Record#  PAYTO
      2  Allstate
     14  Ford Motor Credit
     22  Sears
     30  Camps Car Wash
     31  Texaco
```

The WHILE qualifier speeds up DISPLAYing because it works with INDEXed files. This is shown in the next listing. The WHILE qualifier form is identical to the FOR qualifier form.

DISPLAY WHILE condition

Note that III PLUS assumes the current record meets the WHILE condition. III PLUS doesn't DISPLAY anything when the current record doesn't meet the WHILE condition. You have to FIND or SEEK the first occurrence of the condition you want to WHILE, then enter the DISPLAY command.

```
-> SET INDE TO PAYFOR
-> FIND "Auto"
-> DISP PAYTO WHILE PAYFOR = "Auto"
Record#  PAYTO
```

```
 2   Allstate
14   Ford Motor Credit
22   Sears
30   Camps Car Wash
31   Texaco
```

Note that you can use the WHILE qualifier on a SORTed database. You cannot FIND or SEEK anything in a SORTed database, however, as those commands work only with INDEXed files. You can use the LOCATE command on a SORTed database with no problem. In each of these instances, it is assumed the database is either INDEXed or SORTed on the field that contains the condition. For example, the preceding listing shows the INDEX SET TO PAYFOR. The WHILE condition is also based on values in the PAYFOR field. The condition after the WHILE qualifier should be based on a known or suspected value in the keyfield. You aren't likely to DISPLAY anything if you use some other field condition in the WHILE qualifier.

Some other aspects of the DISPLAY command are worth noting. You can tell III PLUS to DISPLAY an individual record with

DISPLAY RECORD(n)

where n is a valid dBASE III PLUS numeric expression and equates with a valid record number for the current database. Note that this only DISPLAYs the single record you include in the command. It is also possible to create a meaningless DISPLAY. III PLUS, thinking you know what you're doing, dutifully tells you the value of the meaningless DISPLAY. For example, the command

DISPLAY ALL 5

produces the meaningless DISPLAY value "5" for every record in the database.

You can also qualify the command with ALL.

DISPLAY ALL

This form tells III PLUS to DISPLAY all the fields in all the records in the database. It doesn't matter where the record pointer is when this command is entered. All records will be DISPLAYed. You can also limit which fields are DISPLAYed by including the field names, as with

DISPLAY ALL field1, field2,...

Further, note that you can use any of the other qualifiers with the ALL command. This use can be redundant, however. You don't want to

DISPLAY ALL FOR condition

for example. The FOR qualifier automatically covers ALL the records in the database.

There is another qualifier that has not been mentioned that is introduced with the DISPLAY command. It is OFF, and it tells III PLUS not to list the record numbers when DISPLAYing information. The command form is

DISPLAY field list qualifiers OFF

where field list contains the names of fields in the current database and qualifiers can be any logical mix of the qualifiers listed so far in this section. An example of the OFF qualifier used alone and with both qualifiers and field lists is shown in the following listing.

```
-> DISP OFF
  PAYTO
PAYFOR
CHECKNUM     PAYAMOUNT PAYDATE   MILEAGE
  Indian Head National Bank                   Bank Loan
Fee
cash              16.00 07/17/86      0.0
  -> DISP NEXT 2 OFF
  PAYTO
PAYFOR
CHECKNUM     PAYAMOUNT PAYDATE   MILEAGE
  Allstate                                    Rental
Insurance
tovisa            57.00 07/12/86      0.0
  NH Turnpike
Toll
cash               5.00 07/12/86      0.0

  -> DISP NEXT 10 PAYTO,CHECKNUM OFF
  PAYTO                                       CHECKNUM
  Allstate                                    tovisa
  Allstate                                    tovisa
  Susan Carrabis                              tovisa
  Susan Carrabis                              tovisa
  mileage
  NH Turnpike                                 cash
  Computer Town                               cash
  Am Ex                                       1316
  Am Ex                                       1316
  mileage
```

The last thing to know about the DISPLAY command is that you can send the DISPLAY to the printer with another qualifier, TO PRINT. The command is

DISPLAY field list qualifiers TO PRINT

where field list and qualifiers are defined as they were in the previous example. The TO PRINT qualifier doesn't stop information from going to the screen. It merely sends information TO the PRINTer as well.

Use   You can mix and match DISPLAY's qualifiers. For example, you can use the FOR and WHILE qualifiers to create specific DISPLAYs. This is shown in the next listing. The first part of the listing shows what happens when you enter the DISPLAY command when the WHILE condition isn't met. The listing shows that you must use an INDEXed database and FIND a specific condition before using the WHILE qualifier. Also note that the WHILE qualifier is used on the keyfield of the NDX file.

```
-> DISP PAYTO WHILE PAYFOR = "Auto" FOR PAYAMOUNT > 10
Record#  PAYTO

-> FIND "Auto"
-> DISP PAYTO WHILE PAYFOR = "Auto" FOR PAYAMOUNT > 10
Record#  PAYTO
       2  Allstate
      14  Ford Motor Credit
      22  Sears
      31  Texaco

-> FIND "Auto"
-> DISP PAYTO WHILE PAYFOR = "Auto" FOR PAYAMOUNT < 10
Record#  PAYTO
      30  Camps Car Wash
```

You can also use the DISPLAY command to show information not in the current work area. The next listing shows two databases, EXPENSES and CHAPTER9, being put in USE in work areas A and B, respectively. The CHAPTER9 database has only two records. Even though the information is meaningless in this example, you can DISPLAY data in work area 1 from work area 2.

```
-> SELE A
-> USE EXPENSES
-> SELE B
```

```
-> USE CHAPTER9
-> ? RECCOUNT()
         2
-> DISP A->PAYTO
Record#   A->PAYTO
       1  Allstate
-> DISP NEXT 10 A->PAYTO
Record#   A->PAYTO
       1  Allstate
       2  Allstate
```

Note that III PLUS moves the record pointer only in the current work area. The listing shows the record pointer moving in work area B but not moving in work area 2. This leads to a useful application for this ability. You can DISPLAY data in the current work area and compare it to a single variable in another work area. The command form would be

DISPLAY current field list, noncurrent field list qualifiers

where current field list is a list of the fields in the current database, noncurrent field list is a list of fields from some other work area, and qualifiers are valid dBASE III PLUS DISPLAY qualifiers as listed in the "Syntax" section.

Another use of the DISPLAY command is to combine a memory variable with the contents of fields in the database. This can be done with the command form

DISPLAY field1+variable1, field2+variable2,...qualifiers

where field1, field2, and qualifiers have their previous definitions. The new terms are variable1 and variable2. These can be any valid dBASE III PLUS memory variables that are of the same data type as the fields they're being combined with. Numeric-data types can make use of all the arithmetic functions (+, −, *, /, etc.) to form combinations. String-data types can be combined with the plus (+) function. This ability infers that you can DISPLAY fields and memory variables together without having to combine them. This is true. The command looks as you might expect:

DISPLAY field list, variable list

Note that you can mix fields with variables and the same value for the variables will be shown in each line of the display.

Advanced Use   As you might guess, an advanced use of the DISPLAY command involves being able to DISPLAY anything relevant to the current system. That is done by the following block of versatile and transportable code.

```
CLEA
STOR SPACE(10) TO DISPLAYWHAT, DISPLAYFOR
a 21,0 SAY "Display What -> "
*
DO WHIL .T.
   WHAT = SPACE(60)
   a 23,0 SAY "Display? " GET WHAT
   READ
*
   IF LEN(TRIM(WHAT)) = 0
      EXIT
   ENDI
*
   DISPLAYWHAT = IIF(DISPLAYWHAT = SPACE(10), TRIM(WHAT),;
                     DISPLAYWHAT + ", " + TRIM(WHAT))
   a 21, 18 SAY DISPLAYWHAT
ENDD
*
a 22,0 SAY "Display For -> "
*
DO WHIL .T.
   WHAT = SPACE(60)
   a 23,0 SAY "For?      " GET WHAT
   READ
*
   IF LEN(TRIM(WHAT)) = 0
      EXIT
   ENDI
*
   DISPLAYFOR = IIF(DISPLAYFOR = SPACE(10), TRIM(WHAT),;
                     DISPLAYFOR + ".AND. " + TRIM(WHAT))
   a 22, 18 SAY DISPLAYFOR
ENDD
*
CLEA
*
IF LEN(TRIM(DISPLAYFOR)) = 0
   DISP ALL &DISPLAYWHAT
   WAIT
ELSE
   DISP &DISPLAYWHAT FOR &DISPLAYFOR
   WAIT
ENDI
*
CLEA
```

This code isn't as complicated as it looks. The ultimate goal of the entire code segment is to build a DISPLAY command based on user prompts. This code segment can be dropped into any program system and be used to DISPLAY data. For example, you might have a menu option that lets the user list specific information to the screen. The information that is listed is based on user requests. That could be done with the preceding code block.

Realize some built-in niceties of the code—you can use the OFF, TO PRINT, RECORD(n), and WHILE qualifiers by including them in the DISPLAYFOR variable.

DISPLAY MEMORY

The DISPLAY MEMORY command serves two purposes in dBASE III PLUS. In both cases it does the same thing—it DISPLAYs the values assigned any MEMORY variables in the system. The use of the command covered in this chapter has to do with straight dumping of memory variables to the screen and printer. The command is also mentioned in Chapter 15, "Debugging Commands," as it can be used as a debugging tool. There is no advanced use of the command.

Syntax   The standard form of the command is

DISPLAY MEMORY

This form of the command tells III PLUS to send to the screen the name and value of every user-created memory variable in the system. III PLUS will not list any internal variables it has created. If you aren't sure of the difference between internal and external variables, don't worry. You'll never be affected by them. For the curious, an internal variable is something III PLUS creates for its own use. An external variable is one the user creates for his or her use.

The only variation on the command involves the TO PRINT qualifier. The command is

DISPLAY MEMORY TO PRINT

This tells III PLUS to dump the information to the PRINTer.

Use   There isn't much to say about the DISPLAY MEMORY command. It does one thing well. The memory-variable listing can be useful, especially if you want to keep a list of all user-defined variables in the system at a given time.

LABEL FORM

The LABEL command was discussed briefly in Chapters 3 and 4. This section doesn't describe how to CREATE or MODIFY LABELs. It deals only with using the LABEL command to generate LABEL forms on the screen and printer.

Syntax   The LABEL FORM command works by performing searches on a database. It doesn't search for data values, however. It searches for data field names. It looks at the names of the fields in each record in a database and selects the fields chosen in the CREATE and MODIFY LABEL commands to use on the LABEL form. The simplest form of the command is

LABEL FORM lbl filename

This tells III PLUS to generate a LABEL for every record in the current database. Note that the preceding command assumes a database has already been placed in USE in the current work area. III PLUS will prompt you for a database to USE if one hasn't been selected in the current work area. The operative word is *current*. You can use the LABEL FORM command to create LABELs using data from other work areas, but it will not work unless the current work area has an active database.

Like many other III PLUS commands, the LABEL FORM command also allows use of the REST, NEXT, FOR, and WHILE qualifiers. (For details, see the DELETE command in Chapter 7.)

The LABEL FORM command defaults to sending LABELs to the screen unless told otherwise. You send LABELs to the printer with another qualifier, TO PRINT. The command is

LABEL FORM lbl filename qualifiers TO PRINT

where qualifiers are any of the LABEL FORM qualifiers (NEXT, FOR, and WHILE). The fact that you can print the LABELs brings up the fact that you need to make sure the LABELs are properly laid out on your particular LABEL forms. There are two ways to do that. The first method is to use the command

LABEL FORM lbl filename SAMPLE

This command tells III PLUS to first send a filled LABEL form to the screen, to give you the opportunity to position your printer labels with III PLUS's idea of where they should be.

The printer isn't the only place you can send LABELs with the LABEL FORM command. You can also create a disk file for permanent storage. This is excellent when you need to create a reusable file for printing LABELs. III PLUS generates an ASCII text file with the extension and the filename you supply. The command sends information to both the screen and the named file. This file can then be used on any PC regardless of whether that PC uses dBASE III PLUS or not. You would print the TXT file with the DOS command

PRINT txt file

You can modify this form of the LABEL FORM command to include the target file's name with

LABEL FORM frm filename qualifiers TO file txt filename

where qualifiers is defined as previously. Note that the txt filename doesn't need the .TXT extension, as III PLUS supplies that extension automatically. You can create a file with another extension by including the full filename. For example, you could create a LABEL FORM file called LABEL.STF with the command

LABEL FORM frm filename qualifiers TO FILE LABEL.STF

An unlisted use of the LABEL FORM command uses the RECORD qualifier. You could generate a LABEL for any valid record if you entered

LABEL FORM lbl filename RECORD(n)

where n is a valid dBASE III PLUS numeric expression and is within the range of the database. You can't enter

LABEL FORM lbl filename RECORD(100)

if the database has only 90 records. This form of the command allows you to generate LABELs for any record in the database regardless of where the record pointer rests.

Use   The LABEL FORM command's use is described in the "Syntax" section. One other thing worth knowing is that you can use the ? query if a CATALOG file has been SET TO. The command form is

LABEL FORM ?

Note that this assumes a CAT file has been made active with the SET CATALOG TO cat file command.

Advanced Use   Advanced uses of the LABEL FORM command come from CREATEing or MODIFYing the LABEL FORM to handle data from databases in different work areas. See Chapter 3 for information on that topic.

Note that the technique of using several open databases with a LABEL FORM has its hazards. If the databases chosen for your LABEL FORM share similar fields, III PLUS won't be choosy about where it gets data. When all the databases have the same structure, the LABEL file doesn't have to be called from work area 1 to find a field name that it needs to generate the LABEL. If you design databases such as these (that share structures but not data), you must be sure you call the LABEL from the correct work area.

LIST

The LIST command is identical in almost every way to the DISPLAY command. The DISPLAY command stops after a screen of information has been presented and prompts you with

Press any key to continue...

and defaults to showing the current record. The LIST command defaults to showing all the records in the database and doesn't stop after filling a screen. It continues without stopping, scrolling information off the top of the screen. To suspend scrolling, press CTRL-S. To start scrolling again, press CTRL-S a second time.

For information on the syntax and use of the LIST command, see the DISPLAY command earlier in this chapter.

The REPORT FORM command is similar to the LABEL FORM command in many ways. The big difference is that the REPORT FORM command generates full REPORTs instead of just LABELs. You can include several of the CREATE and MODIFY REPORT FORM options in the REPORT FORM command itself. Information on CREATEing and MODIFYing REPORT FORMs can be found in Chapters 3 and 4.

Syntax   The REPORT FORM command works by performing searches on a database. It searches primarily for data field names. It looks at the names of the fields in each record in a database and selects the fields chosen in the CREATE and MODIFY REPORT commands to use on the FRM form. The simplest form of the command is

REPORT FORM frm filename

This tells III PLUS to generate a REPORT for every record in the current database. Note that the preceding command assumes a database has already been placed in USE in the current work area. III PLUS will prompt you for a database to USE if one hasn't been selected in the current work area. The operative word is *current*. You can use the REPORT FORM command to create REPORTs using data from other work areas, but it will not work unless the current work area has an active database.

Like many other III PLUS commands, the REPORT FORM command allows use of the REST, NEXT, FOR, and WHILE qualifiers. (For details, see the DELETE command in Chapter 7.)

The REPORT FORM command defaults to sending REPORTs to the screen unless told otherwise. You send REPORTs to the printer with another qualifier, TO PRINT. The command is

REPORT FORM frm filename qualifiers TO PRINT

where qualifiers are any of the REPORT FORM qualifiers listed previously in this section. The PRINTer isn't the only place you can send REPORTs with the REPORT FORM command. You can also create a disk file for permanent storage. III PLUS generates an ASCII text file with the extension and the filename you supply.

```
-> REPO FORM TED TO FILE
Enter destination file name:
```

The command sends information to both the screen and the named file. This file can then be used on any PC regardless of whether that PC uses dBASE III PLUS. (See the LABEL FORM command earlier in this chapter for details.)

You can also use the REPORT FORM command with the RECORD qualifier, as discussed in the LABEL FORM command section.

You can generate a REPORT for any record in the database regardless of where the record pointer rests. An example of this is shown here:

```
-> REPO FORM TEDREPT
        Page No.       1
        08/08/86
                                REPORT FORM USING 3 DATABASES

        FIELD1                  DBF B FIELD4          DBF C
FIELD0

        Joseph Carrabis         c/o Northern Lights   071786
        Susan Klink Carrabis    c/o Northern Lights   071786
        Bernadette Perry        c/o Northern Lights   071786
        John & Sandra Sculli    c/o Northern Lights   071786
        Jean Stein              c/o Northern Lights   071786
        Liz Fisher              c/o Northern Lights   071786


-> REPO FORM TEDREPT RECORD(3)
        Page No.       1
        08/08/86
                                REPORT FORM USING 3 DATABASES

        FIELD1                  DBF B FIELD4          DBF C
FIELD0


        Bernadette Perry        c/o Northern Lights   071786

-> REPO FORM TEDREPT RECORD(1)
        Page No.       1
        08/08/86
                                REPORT FORM USING 3 DATABASES

        FIELD1                  DBF B FIELD4          DBF C
FIELD0


        Joseph Carrabis         c/o Northern Lights   071786
```

This listing has three distinct sections. The top of the listing shows the standard REPORT FORM command, including all the records in the work area 1 database. The middle of the listing shows the REPORT FORM command entered only for RECORD(3). The bottom of the listing shows the REPORT FORM command entered only for RECORD(1).

The REPORT FORM command also has some qualifiers that are specific to it. These include PLAIN, HEADING, NOEJECT, and SUMMARY. The NOEJECT qualifier stems from III PLUS's default desire to throw a page from the printer whenever you try TO PRINT a REPORT. The command form is

REPO FORM frm filename qualifiers TO PRINT NOEJECT

where qualifiers are any of the qualifiers. This form of the command tells III PLUS to begin printing the REPORT on the present page and not to go to the top of the next page. Note that the NOEJECT qualifier is useless unless accompanied by TO PRINT. The equivalent CREATE and MODIFY REPORT FORM menu command is shown in Figure 8-8.

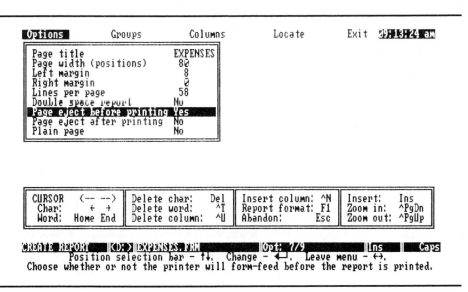

Figure 8-8.   The highlighted CREATE and MODIFY REPORT FORM menu command is equivalent to the REPORT FORM NO-EJECT qualifier

The next two qualifiers, PLAIN and HEADING, have to do with what the REPORT looks like. The PLAIN qualifier tells III PLUS to generate a REPORT without page numbers and date at the top of each page. Further, the report itself isn't broken up into pages when it is sent to the printer, screen, or file. This makes the PLAIN qualifier excellent for creating REPORTs that are going to be shown only on the screen, including REPORTs that are first sent to disk to be read on a screen at a later time. The command form is

REPO FORM frm filename qualifiers PLAIN

where qualifiers is defined as in the previous example.

The equivalent CREATE and MODIFY REPORT FORM menu command is shown in Figure 8-9.

The PLAIN qualifier strips information from the top of the REPORT FORM, but the HEADER qualifier places more information on top of the form. This is useful when you want to include a

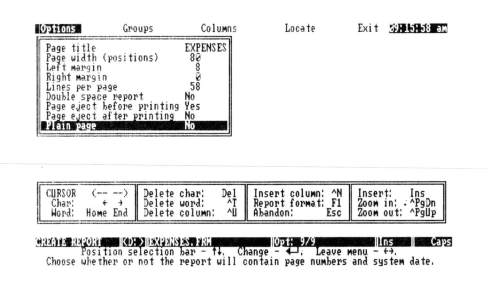

Figure 8-9. The highlighted CREATE and MODIFY REPORT FORM menu command is equivalent to the REPORT FORM PLAIN qualifier

custom message at the time the REPORT is generated, regardless of when the REPORT is viewed or read. The command form is

REPO FORM frm filename qualifiers HEADER "expression"

where qualifiers is defined as shown in the preceding example. III PLUS allows any valid text expression as a HEADER. You can type a literal expression for the HEADER, or you can use a string variable with the & macro symbol. You must still enclose the HEADER expression in valid delimiters even if you're using a macro expression. Valid dBASE III PLUS delimiters include quotes (" "), single quotes (' '), and square brackets ([ ]).

The last qualifier is SUMMARY. This qualifier can be found in the CREATE and MODIFY REPORT FORM menu systems, as well. It tells III PLUS to list only the end results of the data. The equivalent CREATE and MODIFY REPORT FORM menu command is shown in Figure 8-10. The command form is

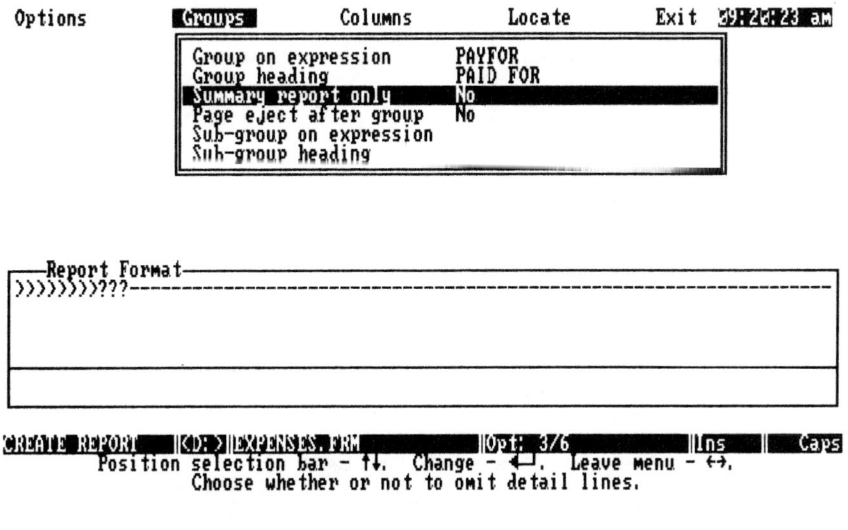

```
Options        Groups       Columns       Locate      Exit  9:24:23 am
              ┌──────────────────────────────────────┐
              │ Group on expression    PAYFOR         │
              │ Group heading          PAID FOR       │
              │ Summary report only    No             │
              │ Page eject after group No             │
              │ Sub-group on expression               │
              │ Sub-group heading                     │
              └──────────────────────────────────────┘



   ┌─Report Format─────────────────────────────────────────────────────┐
   │>>>>>>>???──────────────────────────────────────────────────────── │
   │                                                                     │
   │                                                                     │
   │                                                                     │
   └─────────────────────────────────────────────────────────────────── ┘
 CREATE REPORT   |<D: >|EXPENSES.FRM            |Opt: 3/6       |Ins |  Caps
        Position selection bar - ↑↓.  Change - ←┘.  Leave menu - ↔.
                 Choose whether or not to omit detail lines.
```

Figure 8-10. The highlighted CREATE AND MODIFY REPORT FORM menu command is equivalent to the REPORT FORM SUMMARY qualifier

where qualifiers is defined as in the preceding example. SUMMARY is a good tool when you wish to create capsule REPORTs. The following shows the effect of SUMMARY on a REPORT FORM. The top of the listing is on a nonSUMMARYzed EXPENSE REPORT. Note that each record's information is listed under each GROUP heading as to what the expense was for and under AMOUNT as to the actual expense. This is good if you want to track down a single expense. The bottom of the listing shows the same REPORT SUMMARYzed. No specific information is given regarding individual expenses. The subtotals for each GROUPing are listed. Also note the space saving in screen, file, and printer output.

As a final point of interest, note that several REPORT FORM qualifiers are combined in this listing.

```
-> REPO FORM EXPENSES NEXT 10 PLAIN
                                    EXPENSES REPORT FORM

            PAID TO                 AMOUNT DATE PAID


            ** PAID
FOR
            Gas                       6.50 07/03/86
            Gas                      10.50 07/05/86
            ** Subtotal **
                                     17.00

            ** PAID FOR
Advertising
            Accurate Printing Co     26.95 07/18/86
            ** Subtotal **
                                     26.95

            ** PAID FOR Auto
Expense
            Allstate                246.00 07/12/86
            ** Subtotal **
                                    246.00
            *** Total ***
                                    289.95

-> REPO FORM EXPENSES NEXT 10 PLAIN SUMMARY
                                    EXPENSES REPORT FORM

            PAID TO                 AMOUNT DATE PAID


            ** PAID
```

```
FOR
        ** Subtotal **
                                                17.00


        ** PAID FOR
Advertising
        ** Subtotal **
                                                26.95


        ** PAID FOR Auto
Expense
        ** Subtotal **
                                               246.00
        *** Total ***
                                               289.95
```

Use   The REPORT FORM command's use is described in the "Syntax" section. You should be aware that you can use the ? query if a CATALOG file has been SET TO. The command form is

REPORT FORM ?

Note that this assumes a CAT file has been made active with the SET CATALOG TO cat file command. In any case, III PLUS will ask you for the name of a database to place in USE in the current work area if a DBF file isn't in USE when the REPORT FORM command is entered.

Much of how the REPORT FORM command behaves is based on how the FRM file was originally designed. Refer to the CREATE REPORT command in Chapter 3 for a discussion of using FRM and CAT files with this command; CREATE REPORT works the same way as the REPORT FORM command in this respect.

Another method for using a FRM file with several open databases is to use the SET VIEW TO and SET RELATION TO commands. Both commands allow REPORTs to be generated with several related files active. More information on relating databases is also given in Chapter 3.

Advanced Use   One advanced use of the REPORT FORM command has to do with the HEADER qualifier. Most every aspect of III PLUS recognizes the semicolon (;) as a forced carriage return. This means that III PLUS will respond with a carriage return whenever it encounters a semicolon in a command or text string. You can make

use of this ability to create multiline headers for your REPORT
FORMs, as shown here:

```
-> HEADER = "THIS IS A TEST ; OF AN EMERGENCY ; SEMI:COLON
INCLUSION"
-> REPO FORM EXPENSES NEXT 10 HEADING "&HEADER"
          Page No.      1                  THIS IS A TEST
                                           OF AN EMERGENCY
                                        SEMI:COLON INCLUSION
          08/08/86
                                         EXPENSES REPORT FORM
```

The command that creates the multiline header is

HEADER = "text string"

found at the top of the listing. Notice the semicolons in the string
equation and the placement of carriage returns in the heading on the
REPORT FORM.

SET DEVICE TO

The SET DEVICE TO command is a parameter-control command
that allows you to tell III PLUS whether or not certain things are to
go to the screen or printer. There isn't any true advanced use of this
command.

Syntax   The SET DEVICE TO command has the basic form of all
the SET parameter-control commands:

SET DEVICE TO device

where device can be either screen or printer. This command is identical to the SET parameter menu command shown in Figure 8-11.

Use   The SET DEVICE TO command tells III PLUS to send
information to either the screen or printer. The specific information
that is sent to either the screen or printer is whatever is SAYed in the
@...SAY commands. Note that this command is not identical with
the SET PRINT ON/off command discussed in the next section.
    The SET DEVICE TO command tells III PLUS to send only

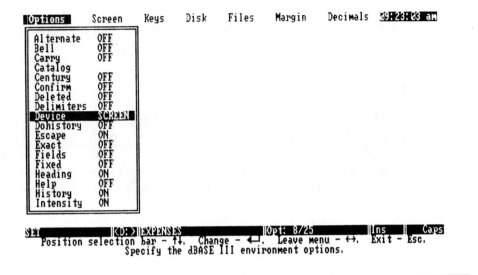

```
 Options    Screen   Keys   Disk   Files   Margin   Decimals  09:23:03 am
 Alternate   OFF
 Bell        OFF
 Carry       OFF
 Catalog
 Century     OFF
 Confirm     OFF
 Deleted     OFF
 Delimiters  OFF
 Device      SCREEN
 Dohistory   OFF
 Escape      ON
 Exact       OFF
 Fields      OFF
 Fixed       OFF
 Heading     ON
 Help        OFF
 History     ON
 Intensity   ON



 SET                    <D:> EXPENSES              Opt: 8/25        Ins      Caps
 Position selection bar - ↑↓.  Change - ⏎.  Leave menu - ↔.  Exit - Esc.
              Specify the dBASE III environment options.
```

Figure 8-11. The SET parameters menu system

@...SAY commands to the listed device. This can be useful in the
correct applications. For example, the following listing shows the
results of trying to SAY things at positions off the screen.

```
-> SET DEVI TO SCRE
-> @ 1,120 SAY 'HELLO'
Position is off the screen
                    ?
@ 1,120 SAY 'HELLO'
-> SET DEVI TO PRIN
-> @ 1,120 SAY 'HELLO'
-> SET DEVI TO SCRE
-> @ 55,10 SAY "WHAT'S NEW?"
Position is off the screen
                      ?
@ 55,10 SAY "WHAT'S NEW?"
-> SET DEVI TO PRIN
-> @ 55,10 SAY "WHAT'S NEW?"
-> SET DEVI TO SCRE
-> @ 55,120 SAY "WAY OFF THE SCREEN"
Position is off the screen
                            ?
@ 55,120 SAY "WAY OFF THE SCREEN"
-> SET DEVI TO PRIN
-> @ 55,120 SAY "WAY OFF THE SCREEN"
```

Data Display Commands

Coordinates (1,120), (55,10), and (55,120) are all off the usual 80×25 screen display. They are not off the ends of what can be displayed with a printer. Even an 80-column printer can send information to those coordinates through COMPRESSED mode, through overwrites, and so on. You can make use of the ability to

SET DEVI TO PRIN

to create wide-carriage printed reports and display formats. Note the use of the dBASE III PLUS four-letter-word convention. Two notes about the SET DEVICE TO command: first, this command affects the output of @...SAY commands only. It doesn't affect the output of ? and ?? commands. Second, items may not print out immediately after this command is entered and an @...SAY is encountered because there may be print buffers in operation.

SET PRINT

The SET PRINT command covered in this chapter is used to turn the PRINTER on and OFF. It is not the SET PRINTER TO command, which is covered in Chapter 11. The command doesn't have an advanced use.

Syntax   The SET PRINT command is one of the dBASE III PLUS system toggles. In this case, the toggle turns the printer on and OFF. The system default is OFF. The command form is

SET PRINT on/OFF

This command affects only whether what is entered on the screen and displayed with the ? and ?? prompts will be echoed at the printer. This command doesn't send @...SAY commands to the printer.

Use   The SET PRINTER on/OFF command has several useful features. The first is its ability to flush the printer buffer, if one exists. In this instance, printer buffer refers to the physical buffer common to most modern printers.

Every printer, regardless of printing speed, print quality, and so on, makes uses of some kind of buffer. Buffer capacities range from 256 characters (1/4K) to 256K. The purpose of a printer buffer is to take over the task of sending information to the printer.

The SET PRINT ON command flushes these hardware types of buffers. Flushing the buffer means III PLUS tells the printer to print every character in the buffer and leave the buffer empty. Why would III PLUS do this?

Some printer buffers don't print everything that's in them when they receive it. They actually store the information until a certain number of characters are assembled. For example, a buffer might not print until at least 500 characters are entered. Five hundred characters is about 11 lines of print. The SET PRINT ON command would tell the printer to print this information even if no more characters were being sent to the printer. In truth, most printers will print once a string of text—demarcated by a carriage return—is sent. The SET PRINT ON command tells these printers to print this information even if no more information is coming into the printer from the computer.

Another feature of the SET PRINT ON command is that it echoes whatever is being entered on the screen. In other words, you could type in

? "Hello"

and III PLUS would send the following to the printer:

```
? "Hello"
Hello
```

This is because the SET PRINT ON command echoes all screen input and echoes the output of ? and ?? commands. Note that the SET PRINT ON command doesn't echo the output of @...SAY commands. For instance, entering

@ 10,15 SAY "Hello"

would cause III PLUS to print out only the command as just listed. It would not print out "Hello" at coordinates (10,15).

A final note on this command comes from the old days of CP/M (an 8-bit operating system) and all versions of PC-DOS and MS-DOS. The SET PRINT on/OFF command acts as a toggle to turn the printer on and off, as mentioned earlier. In that way it is identical to the CTRL-P system command and can be used in conjunction with it. You can turn the printer on with CTRL-P and then, at some later time, turn the printer off with SET PRINTER OFF, without damaging anything in III PLUS or the system. Likewise, the SET PRINTER on/OFF command can be bypassed in the INTERACTIVE mode simply by typing CTRL-P once to turn the printer on and a second time to turn the printer off. You cannot use the CTRL-P key combination in a program. Only the SET PRINTER on/OFF form works in the dBASE III PLUS PROGRAM mode.

SUM

The SUM command is a useful tool in that it determines the arithmetic total of a numeric field over the entire current database. You can determine the total of a single field, a group of fields, or the total of a sum of fields. The fields must be valid dBASE III PLUS numeric expressions to work with the SUM command.

Syntax and Use   The operation and syntax of the SUM command are identical to those of the AVERAGE and COUNT commands discussed earlier in this chapter. Refer to those sections for details.

TYPE

The TYPE command discussed here is not the TYPE( ) function. This command is used to dump text files to either the screen or the printer. The TYPE( ) function is discussed in Chapter 23.

Syntax   The TYPE command's syntax is identical to that of the DOS TYPE command.

TYPE filename.ext

Note that the preceding command includes the file's full name (the filename and extension). You must enter the file's full name to have it listed.

The TYPE command will dump any ASCII text file, regardless of how the file is created, to the screen or printer. To list the contents of a file named BOXER.PRG to the screen, you'd enter

TYPE BOXER.PRG

You could not enter

TYPE BOXER

and have III PLUS list the same file to the screen. Nor will III PLUS allow you to use wild cards (the ? and * used in DOS-level TYPE commands) to list a group of files.

You can have things listed to the printer by modifying the command to

TYPE filename.ext TO PRINT

This form of the command sends the contents of the file to both screen and printer.

Use   The TYPE command has some odd features that you should be aware of. First, you can send the contents of a file to the printer by modifying the command as discussed in the "Syntax" section. That command

TYPE filename.ext TO PRINT

sends the contents of the named file to both the screen and printer. To suspend sending information to the screen or printer, press CTRL-S. To start sending information to the display again, enter another CTRL-S.

You should also know that the TYPE command is a straight dump of text. It doesn't perform any formatting whatsoever and will even print things over the perforations when sent to the printer. You can use the TYPE command to dump nontext files, but the results aren't usually informative.

As a final note, you can use the & macro substitution command to TYPE a file named in a variable. An example is

FILENAME = "FRED.TXT"
TYPE &FILENAME

Data Location Commands

This chapter covers an important class of commands; you use them to find a specific item in the database. Without such commands, no DBMS would be worth the effort to learn.

The data-location command n is included in this chapter. You can tell III PLUS to set the record pointer at record n simply by entering the record number at the prompt.

CONTINUE

The CONTINUE command is actually the second half of the LOCATE CONTINUE command pair. It cannot be used unless the LOCATE command is entered first. (The LOCATE command is discussed later in this chapter.)

Syntax   The CONTINUE command's syntax is the single word

CONTINUE

This command has no modifiers. The CONTINUE command assumes a LOCATE command has already been issued and that a database is ctive in the current work area.

Use   The CONTINUE command is the second half of LOCATE (covered later in this chapter). The LOCATE command is used to find a specific item in a nonindexed database. However, the LOCATE command finds only the first occurrence of the desired item. In that sense it is similar to the FIND and SEEK commands, which are also discussed later in this chapter. FIND, SEEK, and LOCATE find only the first occurrence of the desired item. But you may not be interested in just the first occurrence. For example, if you want to find one book among the several by a given author in a Personal Library System, you would first enter the command

LOCATE FOR AUTHOR = "James Blish"

This would get you to the first record in the database that met that condition. Perhaps you don't want the first book. You would then enter the command

CONTINUE

and III PLUS would find thae next record that met the LOCATE condition. An example of this is shown in the following listing:

```
-> USE C:\LIBRARY\JDCBOOKS
-> LOCATE FOR AUTHOR = "James Blish"
Record =      257
-> DISP TITLE
Record#  TITLE
    257  Black Easter

-> CONT
Record =      258
-> DISP TITLE
Record#  TITLE
    258  Triumph of Time, The

-> CONT
Record =      259
-> DISP TITLE
Record#  TITLE
    259  VOR

-> CONT
Record =      260
-> DISP TITLE
Record#  TITLE
    260  Seedling Stars, The

-> CONT
Record =      261
-> DISP TITLE
Record#  TITLE
    261  A Case of Conscience

-> CONT
Record =      262
-> DISP TITLE
Record#  TITLE
    262  Triumph of Time, The

-> CONT
Record =      670
-> DISP TITLE
Record#  TITLE
    670  They Shall Have Stars

-> CONT
Record =      671
```

```
-> DISP TITLE
Record#  TITLE
    671  Galactic Cluster

-> CONT
End of LOCATE scope
```

Take a minute to understand how the CONTINUE command operates. First, the LOCATE command has already been entered. In particular, it has been entered once, before any CONTINUE commands are entered. Second, the LOCATE command finds the first occurrence of the desired condition in the database. This database isn't indexed or sorted in any way. Third, the CONTINUE command finds the next occurrence of the LOCATE condition. The LOCATE command found the desired condition in record 257. The CONTINUE command found the next occurrence of the desired condition in record 258. (The reason some simultaneous records meet the LOCATE condition is due to the order in which they were entered. There is nothing unique about the database or the LOCATE and CONTINUE commands.) Fourth, the CONTINUE command tells you only what record meets the condition if SET TALK is ON. You aren't told anything if SET TALK is OFF. Fifth, you must still DISPLAY or otherwise show information about the record you have CONTINUEd to. Last, the CONTINUE command will tell you when you've fallen into the abyss. In this case, there was no scope specified in the LOCATE command. The default is to LOCATE over the entire database. The CONTINUE command CONTINUEd trying to LOCATE the condition until it reached the end of the file; hence the message

End of LOCATE scope

appeared. Note again that III PLUS will not tell you it has reached the "End of LOCATE scope" unless SET TALK is ON.

You can have different LOCATE commands active in each work area. This means you can also have different CONTINUEs active in each work area. Shifting work areas doesn't affect the status of the CONTINUE command in any work area other than the work area you're in. As a final note, if you change the LOCATE condition in a particular work area, you'll have changed the CONTINUE condition as well.

Advanced Use   The advanced use discussed here is actually intended as the second half of a LOCATE command (see the LOCATE command later in this chapter).

```
CASE ANSWER = 'C'
   SET ORDER TO 0
   CONT
   DO LIBGETS
   CLEA GETS
   SET ORDER TO 1
   LOOP
```

First note that this code is part of a DO CASE...ENDCASE block. It is intended to be part of a menu system that allows you to move through a current database. In this case, entering a C at some prompt brings you to this block of code. This block also assumes that some NDX files are active (the SET ORDER TO commands can be used only with NDX files).

The actual CONTINUE command is used after the LOCATE condition has been entered. The NDX files are shut off before you CONTINUE. You shut the NDX files off because you aren't using them to LOCATE or CONTINUE. In fact, active NDX files can slow down LOCATE and CONTINUE commands. The reason for this has to do with the way LOCATE and CONTINUE work.

Both LOCATE and CONTINUE perform sequential searches on a database. They start at a given record and look at the next one, then the next one, then the one after that, and so on. That's easy when the database is ordered by record number (1, 2, 3, 4, 5,...100, 101, 102,...900, 901,...). But an indexed database isn't ordered by record number; it is ordered by something that you might find useful and the computer finds incorrigible. For example, the following listing shows the difference between the JDCBOOKS database with no NDX files active and with the same database indexed on AUTHOR. Note the difference in the first ten record numbers.

```
-> GOTO TOP
-> LIST TRIM(AUTHOR) NEXT 15
Record#   TRIM(AUTHOR)
      1
      2
      3   Paul Dickson
      4
      5
      6   Don Ethan Miller
      7   John Bartlett
```

```
    8   Edward D. Johnson
    9
   10   W.L. Reese
   11   Douglas R. Hofstadter
   12   Thomas F. Monteleone
   13   Montague Summers
   14   Mitchell Waite, Robert Lafore
   15   Paul Davies
-> SET INDE TO C:\LIBRARY\JDCBATHR
-> GOTO TOP
-> LIST TRIM(AUTHOR) NEXT 15
Record#   TRIM(AUTHOR)
   869
   164
   249
   247
   169
   170
    64
   783
   873
    55
   168
   868
   356   A.D. Woosley
   287   A.E. Van Vogt
   286   A.E. Van Vogt
```

Trying to LOCATE or CONTINUE over an indexed database forces III PLUS to jump from record to record according to the indexing scheme. That's an incredible amount of disk work in anything with more than 200 records, so shut the NDX files off.

Remember that CONTINUE only tells you the record number where it stops, and only that if TALK is ON. You tell III PLUS to tell you something about the record CONTINUE has stopped at with

```
DO LIBGETS
CLEAR GETS
```

The LIBGETS file is the GET file for the Library System. You CLEAR GETS because you don't want to do any editing here; you just want to see the information. You're through CONTINUEing, so SET the ORDER of the NDX files back to their original order. The last command tells III PLUS to loop back to the beginning of the code this small block is in, as nothing past this block is relevant to what was asked.

Have you noticed that there is no way to tell the user if the end of the file has been reached (assuming TALK is OFF)? You can include that ability easily with

```
*
IF .NOT. FOUND()
   a 23,0
   WAIT "No more to LOCATE. Press any key to continue"
ENDI
*
```

The FOUND( ) function is either true or false, depending on
whether or not III PLUS could LOCATE, FIND, SEEK, or CON-
TINUE to whatever you asked for. The preceding code tells III PLUS
to put up an error message if what you asked for could not be found.

FIND

The FIND command is one of two dBASE III PLUS commands that
work exclusively with NDX files. The other command is SEEK,
covered later in this chapter.

Syntax   The FIND command has only one form and no qualifiers.

FIND "condition"

Note that, in this instance, the condition is delimited with quotes
(" "). This is necessary only if you are going to FIND a literal character string. Consider the following listing:

```
-> DISP STAT

Currently Selected Database:
Select area:  1, Database in Use: C:\LIBRARY\JDCBOOKS.dbf
Alias: JDCBOOKS
     Index file: C:\LIBRARY\JDCBATHR.ndx  Key:
trim(left(author,50))+upper(trim(left(title,50)))

-> FIND "Kenneth Robeson"
-> DISP TITLE
Record#  TITLE
    156  Brand of the Werewolf

-> FIND "Kenneth Robeson"
-> DISP TITLE
Record#  TITLE
    156  Brand of the Werewolf

-> SKIP
```

```
Record No.    694
-> DISP TITLE,AUTHOR
Record#  TITLE
    AUTHOR
    694  Man of Bronze
    Kenneth Robeson

-> SKIP
Record No.    154
-> DISP TITLE,AUTHOR
Record#  TITLE
    AUTHOR
    154  Resurrection Day
    Kenneth Robeson

-> SKIP
Record No.    155
-> DISP TITLE,AUTHOR
Record#  TITLE
    AUTHOR
    155  Man of Bronze, The
    Kenneth Robeson

-> SKIP
Record No.    590
-> DISP TITLE,AUTHOR
Record#  TITLE
    AUTHOR
    590  Other Side of the Mountain
    Michel Bernanos
```

You want to FIND "Kenneth Robeson" in the AUTHOR NDX file. You use the command

FIND "Kenneth Robeson"

III PLUS brings you to the first occurrence of "Kenneth Robeson" in the database (record 156). Repeating the command, however, doesn't change anything. III PLUS sends you right back to record 156. You can SKIP and get to the next occurrence of "Kenneth Robeson" in the NDX file (record 694). (In case you're wondering why this example skips from 156 to 694 to 154 and so on, note that the NDX file is indexed on AUTHOR and TITLE. The titles shown in the listing are in alphabetical order.) In any case, III PLUS will always send you to the first occurrence of what you want to FIND, no matter how many times you try to FIND it. You must then SKIP from record to record to find other occurrences, if any. III PLUS automatically brings you to the next occurrence of what you want to FIND because the database is indexed on the field of interest. You can continue SKIPping until you come to a record that doesn't meet your FIND condition (record 590, in this case).

The next thing to consider is what happens when you can't FIND something. III PLUS will tell you it can't FIND something if either the CONFIG.DB or SET TALK commands are ON, as shown here:

```
-> FIND "Cygnus the Swan"
No find
```

Use   The FIND command needs the FIND condition delimited before it can be used properly. The next listing shows this, especially in the use of memory variables: it uses the memory variable NAME and assigns it the value "Paul Dickson". Can III PLUS FIND that NAME?

```
-> NAME = "Paul Dickson"
Paul Dickson
-> FIND NAME
No find
-> FIND &NAME
-> DISP TITLE,AUTHOR
Record#  TITLE
     AUTHOR
     532  Official Rules
     Paul Dickson
```

No, it can't. III PLUS assumes you want to FIND the expression NAME, not what's inside NAME. You have to use the III PLUS macro & command to tell it there's a substitution going on. III PLUS can't FIND NAME, but it can

FIND &NAME

You can also tell III PLUS whether or not to look for a close match to what you want or exactly what you want. This is done with the command

SET EXACT ON/off

as shown in the next listing. Note that using this command is identical to using the CONFIG.DB EXACT = ON command.

```
-> NAME = "Hans"
Hans
-> FIND &NAME
```

```
-> DISP TITLE,AUTHOR
Record#   TITLE
    AUTHOR
    463  Gravitation and Spacetime
    Hans C. Ohanian

-> SET EXACT ON
-> FIND &NAME
No find
```

This example demonstrates the SET EXACT ON command being used with a memory variable, but the effect is the same regardless of whether a memory variable is being used or not.

You start with SET EXACT OFF, the dBASE III PLUS default. You want to FIND "Hans". You know there are at least two books in the database that meet that criterion. III PLUS brings you to the first occurrence of "Hans" in the AUTHOR field. However, if EXACT is ON, there is no "Hans" in the database. You can ask for either of the EXACT names, "Hans C. Ohanian" or "Hans Kung", and III PLUS will FIND them, but it will not find "Hans" when EXACT is ON.

```
->  FIND "Hans"
-> DISP TRIM(TITLE),TRIM(AUTHOR) WHILE AUTHOR = "Hans"
Record#   TRIM(TITLE)
    TRIM(AUTHOR)
    463  Gravitation and Spacetime
    Hans C. Ohanian
    796  Challenge, The
    Hans Kung


-> SET EXACT ON
-> FIND "Hans C. Ohanian"
-> DISP TRIM(TITLE),TRIM(AUTHOR)
Record#   TRIM(TITLE)
    TRIM(AUTHOR)
    463  Gravitation and Spacetime
    Hans C. Ohanian

-> FIND "Hans Kung"
-> DISP TRIM(TITLE),TRIM(AUTHOR)
Record#   TRIM(TITLE)
    TRIM(AUTHOR)
    796  Challenge, The
    Hans Kung
```

So far the text has used FIND with character strings exclusively. You can also use FIND with numeric data. But be aware that III

PLUS will limit how well you can do this. The FIND command becomes

```
FIND n
```

when used to FIND a numeric value. Note that this isn't for alphanumeric numeric characters, but numeric data in numeric fields. The n in the above command is any value dBASE III PLUS numeric expression. It cannot be an evaluated expression. In other words, .73 is allowed, but 730/1000 is not.

You can FIND the actual numeric value entered as a condition, provided that condition exists in the keyfield in the database. However, the FIND command doesn't allow you to use memory variables in any way when trying to FIND a numeric expression. Each time you try to FIND something using a memory variable, you get dumped into the first record in the indexed database. Note that this record doesn't necessarily meet the FIND condition. You can use a numeric memory variable as the condition with the SEEK command (discussed later in this chapter).

Advanced Use   The advanced use described here comes from a vertical market package. It is designed to use any number of databases, but the databases must fall into one of two conditions for the code as written. Only databases with either one or seven NDX files are allowed. The basic form of the code block is

```
CASE ANSWER = 'F'
   a 20,0 CLEAR
*
   IF LEN(TRIM(NDX(2))) = 0
      INDEXKEY = FIELD(1)
      ACCE "Find &INDEXKEY > " TO TOFIND
   ELSE
      TOFIND = 0
      a 20,0 SAY "Find 1-" + FIELD(1) + ", 2-" + FIELD(2) +;
         ", 3-" + FIELD(3) + ", 4-" + FIELD(4) + ", 5-" +;
         FIELD(5) + ", 6-" + FIELD(6) + " or 7-" + FIELD(7) +;
         " -> " GET TOFIND PICT "9" RANGE 1,7
      SET ORDE TO TOFIND
      TOFIND = SPACE(30)
      ACCE "Find > " TO TOFIND
   ENDI
*
   FIND &TOFIND
*
   IF .NOT. FOUND()
      a 23,0 CLEA
```

```
    WAIT "Can't FIND it. Try LOCATE. Press any key to
continue"
    ENDI
  *
    DO &GETTER
    CLEA GETS
    SET ORDE TO 1
    LOOP
```

As with the CONTINUE command described in the last section, this code is part of a menu system; hence, it starts with

CASE ANSWER = 'F'

for FIND. It CLEARs the lower part of the screen, under some hypothetical data display, and then selects the prompts based on which database is active.

The first prompt is for databases with a single NDX file. The code determines that only one NDX file is active with the line

IF LEN(TRIM(NDX(2))) = 0

The NDX function tells III PLUS the name of the active NDX file whose priority is given in the function argument. The preceding command asks for the second NDX file. The function NDX(7) would ask for the seventh NDX file active for a given database. Note also that you must assume the first field in the database is the one the database is indexed on, as shown with the command

INDEXKEY = FIELD(1)

But what if the database does have more than one NDX file? You can give the user a chance to select which NDX file to use with the prompt

@ 20,0 SAY "Find..."

Again, you're assuming the first seven fields are going to be used to create the seven NDX files. You use the answer to this prompt to SET the ORDER of the NDX files. In other words, if the user selects 7, you

SET ORDER TO 7

This tells III PLUS to make the seventh active NDX file the primary NDX file for the given database. You then prompt the user for something to FIND, FIND it (through a macro substitution, as discussed in the "Use" section), and place the information for the FINDed record on the screen.

You might include an error trap if what is asked for is not found. Note that you reSET the order of the NDX files before you loop back to the top of the menu. Users interested in knowing how you can handle numeric FINDs should refer to the section on the SEEK command later in this chapter.

One last point: note the command

```
ACCE "Find &INDEXKEY > " TO TOFIND
```

You must not write that command as

```
ACCE "Find &INDEXKEY—> " TO TOFIND
```

The difference is subtle. In the former, you see ">". The latter uses "—>". That slight difference will make III PLUS think there might be an alias name floating around. Using the wrong command form might not bring you to a screeching halt, but it could cause major debugging problems.

This code is written for databases with either one or seven active NDX files. You can use databases with two to six NDX files with this code, but the screen can be confusing in such cases.

GO/GOTO

The GO and GOTO commands are identical. This is the direct positioning command in dBASE III PLUS. You GO/GOTO a record.

Syntax   The GO/GOTO command is used for direct positioning in the dBASE III PLUS system. Its roots go back to dBASE II, and it is largely kept on for users who have grown accustomed to GOing somewhere. You can also move the record pointer to a given record simply by entering the desired record's number (see the section on the n data-location command later in this chapter).

The basic form of the command is

```
GO n
```

where n is a valid dBASE III PLUS numeric expression. GO/GOTO has some advantages over the direct number method described in the section on the n command because you can use any valid dBASE III PLUS numeric expression for n instead of an actual number. You can tell III PLUS to GO/GOTO somewhere that is determined by a numeric expression as

GO 20/10

The only caveat is that the evaluated expression has to equate with a record number in the current database. You can't GO 8000 if the database only has 100 records in it, nor can you

GO 2^{10}

if there are fewer than 2^{10} records in the current database (see Figure 9-1). The GO/GOTO command does allow you to use memory variables as the command's argument. This is shown in Figure 9-1.

Note that GO/GOTO will determine the integer portion of a numeric expression automatically. III PLUS couldn't normally GO/GOTO record (20/6), but it will GO/GOTO INT(20/6) without needing the INTEGER function entered by the user.

The GO/GOTO command also has some qualifiers. The first is RECORD(n). The text won't spend any time on this qualifier because it behaves no differently from the unqualified GO/GOTO command. In other words, the commands

```
GO 10
GO RECORD(10)
GO 100/10
GO RECORD(100/10)
```

are identical. They can both use numbers, numeric expressions, and variables as arguments.

GO/GOTO's other two qualifiers are TOP and BOTTOM. They do exactly as you might expect. The command

GO TOP

positions the record pointer at the top of the database. Note that this doesn't say "the first record in the database." Likewise, this doesn't mean that GO BOTTOM positions the record pointer at "the last record in the database." The GO BOTTOM command positions the record pointer at the bottom of the database.

```
-> GO 20/10
-> DISP PAYTO
Record#  PAYTO
       2  Allstate
-> GO 8000
Record is out of range
        ?
GO 8000
-> GO 2^10
Record is out of range
        ?
GO 2^10
-> RECORDNUM = 20
20
-> GOTO RECORDNUM
-> DISP PAYTO
Record#  PAYTO
      20  *mileage
-> GO RECORDNUM/2.5
-> DISP PAYTO
Record#  PAYTO
       8  Am Ex
->
```

Figure 9-1.   You can use numeric expressions and memory variables as GO/GOTO's arguments

Use   Why did Ashton-Tate include two methods for moving the record pointer to a specific record? You answer that by learning the difference between GO/GOTO and simply entering the record number, n. You can GO/GOTO a numeric expression or function, but you can enter the direct record only as a number. You can't use an expression or function to move the record pointer in the direct-entry method. You couldn't enter

100/10

at the dBASE prompt and expect to get anything other than an error message.

The next thing to cover is the difference between TOP and record 1 and BOTTOM and whatever the last record in the file is. The differences become apparent when using NDX files. Normally, the first record in a database is located at the TOP of the file and the last record in the database is located at the BOTTOM of the file. This is because III PLUS is using the record number to order the database. But what if you tell III PLUS to use an NDX file to order the database? The first physical record in the database may not be on TOP of the NDX file, nor may the last physical record in the database be on the BOTTOM of the NDX file. This is demonstrated in the following listing:

```
-> USE EXPENSES
-> GOTO TOP
-> DISP PAYTO,PAYFOR,PAYAMOUNT
Record#   PAYTO                          PAYFOR
                                         PAYAMOUNT
        1 *Allstate                      Rental
Insurance                                57.00
-> GOTO BOTTOM
-> DISP PAYTO,PAYFOR,PAYAMOUNT
Record#   PAYTO                          PAYFOR
                                         PAYAMOUNT
       39   New England Telephone        Phone
                                         63.31


-> SET INDE TO PAYTO
-> GOTO TOP
-> DISP PAYTO,PAYFOR,PAYAMOUNT
Record#   PAYTO                          PAYFOR
                                         PAYAMOUNT
       28   Accurate Printing Co         Advertising
                                         26.95
-> GOTO BOTTOM
-> DISP PAYTO,PAYFOR,PAYAMOUNT
Record#   PAYTO                          PAYFOR
                                         PAYAMOUNT
       38   mileage
                                         0.00


-> SET INDE TO PAYFOR
-> GOTO TOP
-> DISP PAYTO,PAYFOR,PAYAMOUNT
Record#   PAYTO                          PAYFOR
                                         PAYAMOUNT
        5 *mileage
                                         0.00
-> GOTO BOTTOM
-> DISP PAYTO,PAYFOR,PAYAMOUNT
Record#   PAYTO                          PAYFOR
                                         PAYAMOUNT
        6   NH Turnpike                  Toll
                                         5.00


-> SET INDE TO PAYAMOUNT
-> GOTO TOP
```

```
-> DISP PAYTO,PAYFOR,PAYAMOUNT
Record#   PAYTO                              PAYFOR
                                             PAYAMOUNT
       5 *mileage
                                             0.00
-> GOTO BOTTOM
-> DISP PAYTO,PAYFOR,PAYAMOUNT

Record#   PAYTO                              PAYFOR
                                             PAYAMOUNT
      23   White Mountain Computer           Office
Equipment                                    1639.00
```

The start of the listing shows the EXPENSES database active without an NDX file. The TOP of the nonindexed database is record 1 and the BOTTOM is record 39 (there are only 39 records in the file).

The second part of the listing shows what happens to TOP and BOTTOM when you SET INDEX TO PAYTO. The PAYTO.NDX file uses the EXPENSES' PAYTO field as the keyfield. The TOP of the PAYTO field index is record 28; the BOTTOM is record 38. The third part of the listing uses the PAYFOR field as a keyfield. Now record 5 has become the TOP record and record 6 assumes the BOTTOM position. Similar logic follows for the last part of the listing, using the PAYAMOUNT field to order the database.

Advanced Use   There is a method of using the GO/GOTO command that could be considered advanced. You can use the GO/GOTO command to GO/GOTO somewhere in the current database based on the value of a field in another database. In other words, you can

GO A—>fieldname

where A is the alias for work area 1 and fieldname is the name of a numeric field in the database in work area 1. You can GO/GOTO a record based on a nonnumeric field if the character field can be converted to a numeric expression, as in

GO VAL(A—>fieldname)

This ability allows you to GO/GOTO somewhere in your current work area based on expressions, fields, and evaluations located in other work areas.

The LOCATE command can find specific data in any record in the current database. It is the first half of the LOCATE CONTINUE command pair.

Syntax   The LOCATE command has a convoluted syntax. The basic command form is

LOCATE FOR condition

where condition is some valid dBASE III PLUS condition based on the fields in the active database. The EXPENSES database would allow conditions such as PAYTO = "Allstate" and PAYAMOUNT < 100. This tells III PLUS to search every record in the database for the listed condition starting at record 1. Even if you were positioned at record 100 in a database of 200 records, the preceding form of the command would send you back to record 1 to start LOCATEing. III PLUS will stop at the first record that meets the listed condition. You can use the CONTINUE command to LOCATE the next several occurrences of the listed condition. This LOCATE CONTINUE command pair works well with databases that contain fewer than 100 records but may take too much time with databases having more than 500 records.

You can use the LOCATE command without any FOR, as shown in Figure 9-2.

It doesn't matter what database is active when you LOCATE nothing. III PLUS will always drop you at the first record in the database (or the top of an indexed file). Why? You asked for nothing in particular, and III PLUS is telling you it LOCATEd nothing in particular at the first record. But note that this doesn't always happen. The last LOCATE in Figure 9-2 returns the message

End of LOCATE scope

because the active database has no records in it.

You can tell III PLUS how many records to LOCATE over with

```
-> USE EXPENSES
-> LOCATE
Record =        1
-> USE CHAPTER9
-> LOCATE
Record =        1
-> USE C10
-> LOCATE
Record =        1
-> USE JOINFILE
-> LOCATE
Record =        1
-> USE CLACCT
-> LOCATE
End of LOCATE scope
->
```

Figure 9-2. III PLUS will drop you at the first record in a database if you don't want to LOCATE anything

the NEXT qualifier. The command form is

LOCATE NEXT n FOR condition

where n is a valid dBASE III PLUS numeric expression and condition is as just described. This tells III PLUS to LOCATE FOR the listed condition in the database for the NEXT n records. Note that you might end up limiting the scope of your LOCATE too much when you use this form of the command.

III PLUS will only LOCATE over the NEXT n records from where the current record pointer is. The EXPENSES database used in this example has 39 records in it. You will start at record 1 when you first USE a database, but any operation that changes the record pointer will change the number of NEXT records you'll be able to operate on. Note that you can ask to LOCATE over as many records as you like; III PLUS will search only as many records as it has available.

LOCATE also makes use of the WHILE qualifier. This qualifier is usually listed with commands that make use of NDX files. It is true you can use LOCATE on any indexed database, although that is not where the command's strength lies. An example of LOCATEing over an indexed database is shown in the "Use" section.

The WHILE qualifier form builds on the FOR qualifier form

LOCATE FOR condition1 WHILE condition2

where condition1 and condition2 are valid dBASE III PLUS arguments such as those just listed. Note that III PLUS assumes the current record meets the WHILE condition. III PLUS doesn't LOCATE anything when the current record doesn't meet the WHILE condition. This is true whether the database is indexed or sorted. Remember that you're working with an indexed database when you WHILE something. You have to FIND or SEEK the first occurrence of the condition you want to WHILE before entering the LOCATE FOR...WHILE command. The condition after the WHILE qualifier should be based on a known or suspected value in the keyfield. (This topic is covered in more detail in the "Use" section.)

Remember that you don't FIND or SEEK anything in a sorted database. You can use the WHILE qualifier on a sorted database, however. In such a case, the LOCATE FOR...WHILE command is more useful than either a FIND or SEEK. You can't FIND or SEEK anything in a sorted database and must use the LOCATE command. (This situation is also covered in the "Use" section.)

LOCATE also introduces a new, undocumented qualifier, REST, as in "the REST of the database." Why REST? Perhaps you've done some searching on the database and now want to LOCATE something starting at the current record position and going on to the end of the database. You couldn't

LOCATE FOR condition

because III PLUS would start back at the beginning of the file. Likewise, you would need to know how many records are left in the file to

LOCATE NEXT n FOR condition

So how do you tell III PLUS to start LOCATEing from where you are to the end of the file?

LOCATE REST FOR condition

tells III PLUS to start at the current record location and search through the remaining records in the database. If you're at record 100 and there are 110 records in the file, you will LOCATE through 10 records. If you're at record 10 and there are 110 records in the file, you'll LOCATE through 100 records.

You can also mix and match LOCATE's qualifiers if you keep in mind that FOR isn't really a qualifier but a necessary part of the command.

Use   The two aspects of the LOCATE command discussed in this section have to do with the form

LOCATE FOR x WHILE y

and its use in both indexed and nonindexed databases. What exactly does it mean to say you have to FIND or SEEK something before you can LOCATE it in an indexed file? First, you don't have to FIND or SEEK something to use the LOCATE command in an indexed database. You can

LOCATE FOR condition

whether a database is indexed or not. However, if you

LOCATE FOR condition1 WHILE condition2

you may have some problems. The problem comes from the WHILE qualifier. The WHILE qualifier implies that the condition listed after it (condition2, in this example) exists in the current record in the current database. If you entered the preceding command and condition2 was not true you wouldn't LOCATE anything because III PLUS wouldn't go anywhere. You would have to set the record pointer to the first occurrence of condition2 with

```
FIND condition2
LOCATE FOR condition1 WHILE condition2
```

Note that this assumes the database is indexed on a field that contains condition2. Once you FIND condition2 in the indexed database, you can LOCATE FOR...WHILE condition2.

What about sorted files? You can't use FIND or SEEK on sorted files, so how do you handle those? Consider the following listing:

```
LOCATE FOR condition2
LOCATE FOR condition1 WHILE condition2
```

Here, you first LOCATE FOR condition2. Remember that condition2 is what you'll use as a WHILE condition. You have to LOCATE the first occurrence of condition2 before you can use it as a WHILE condition.

You should also know that the CONFIG.DB and SET EXACT ON/off commands affect how LOCATE works. You can tell III PLUS whether to LOCATE a close match or exactly what you want, as shown in the section on the FIND command earlier in this chapter. Note that EXACT affects the first characters in the LOCATE FOR condition. The exception to this rule occurs when you LOCATE a number. You must LOCATE the exact number when LOCATEing over numeric fields. An example would be

```
LOCATE FOR PAYAMOUNT = 100
```

n

n is included as a command because you can use a simple number at the dBASE prompt to move the record pointer. The n mentioned in this section is a straightforward number such as 1, 9, 83, 210, or 1069. It is not a numeric expression such as $100/10$, 2^4, or SQRT(9). You tell III PLUS to go to a particular record using a number, as shown in Figure 9-3.

SEEK

The SEEK command is one of two dBASE III PLUS commands that work exclusively with NDX files. The other command is FIND, covered earlier in this chapter.

Syntax   SEEK has only one form and no qualifiers.

```
-> DISP TITLE
Record#  TITLE
     10  Dictionary of Philosophy and Religion
-> 100
-> DISP TITLE
Record#  TITLE
    100  Fuzzies and other people
-> 575
-> DISP TITLE
Record#  TITLE
    575  Advanced Calculus
-> 1
-> DISP TITLE
Record#  TITLE
      1  Roget's University Thesaurus
-> 800
-> DISP TITLE
Record#  TITLE
    800  Medicine Show, The
-> 3
-> DISP TITLE
Record#  TITLE
      3  Words
->
```

Figure 9-3.   III PLUS will accept a number to position the record pointer in both the PROGRAM and INTERACTIVE modes

SEEK condition

Note that this condition is not delimited with quotes (" ") as was
the FIND condition. This is the most important difference between
SEEK and FIND, and is the major reason SEEK was included in
dBASE III and III PLUS when FIND was more than enough for
dBASE II. The examples used in this section parallel those used in
the FIND command section. Consider the following listing:

```
.> USE C:\LIBRARY\JDCBOOKS INDE C:\LIBRARY\JDCBATHR
.> SEEK "Kenneth Robeson"
.> DISP TITLE
Record#  TITLE
    156  Brand of the Werewolf
```

```
-> SEEK "Kenneth Robeson"
-> DISP TITLE
Record#   TITLE
    156   Brand of the Werewolf

-> SKIP
-> DISP TITLE
Record#   TITLE
    694   Man of Bronze

-> SKIP
-> DISP TITLE
Record#   TITLE
    154   Resurrection Day

-> SKIP
-> DISP TITLE
Record#   TITLE
    155   World's Fair Goblin

-> SKIP
-> DISP AUTHOR
Record#   AUTHOR
    590   Michel Bernanos
```

You want to SEEK "Kenneth Robeson" in the AUTHOR NDX file.
You use the command

SEEK "Kenneth Robeson"

because you're SEEKing the literal string "Kenneth Robeson". You
are not looking for a variable named Kenneth Robeson, but the literal
string "Kenneth Robeson". You tell III PLUS you want to SEEK a
literal string by enclosing that string in quotes (" "). III PLUS brings
you to the first occurrence of "Kenneth Robeson" in the database
(record 156) just as it did with FIND. Repeating the command
doesn't change anything, as it didn't change anything with FIND. III
PLUS sends you right back to record 156 each time you SEEK "Kenneth Robeson". You can SKIP and get to the next occurrence of
"Kenneth Robeson" in the NDX file (record 694). Note that the alphabetical ordering of titles is due to the NDX keyfields, as described in
the section on the FIND command. In any case, III PLUS will always
send you to the first occurrence of what you want to SEEK, no matter
how many times you try to SEEK it. You must then SKIP from
record to record, as you did in the FIND section. III PLUS automatically brings you to the next occurrence of what you want to

SEEK because the database is indexed on the field of interest. You can continue SKIPping until you come to a record that doesn't meet your SEEK condition (record 590, in this case).

The next thing to consider is what happens when you can't SEEK something. III PLUS will tell you it can't SEEK something if either the CONFIG.DB or SET TALK commands are ON.

Use   SEEK differs from FIND; here's where you learn about the differences. Unlike FIND, the SEEK command doesn't need the SEEK condition delimited before it can be used properly. This is most evident when using memory variables as the SEEK condition. For instance, here the memory variable NAME has been created and assigned the value "Paul Dickson".

```
-> NAME = "Paul Dickson"
Paul Dickson
-> SEEK NAME
-> DISP TITLE,AUTHOR
Record#  TITLE
     AUTHOR
     532  Official Rules
     Paul Dickson

-> SEEK &NAME
Variable not found
          ?
SEEK Paul Dickson
-> FIND NAME
No find
-> FIND &NAME
-> DISP TITLE,AUTHOR
Record#  TITLE
     AUTHOR
     532  Official Rules
     Paul Dickson

-> CLOSE ALTER
```

Can III PLUS SEEK that NAME? Most certainly. There you see the first evidence of major differences between FIND and SEEK. If you look further down in the listing, you'll see that you cannot

FIND NAME

The only way to use the NAME variable as defined in this example is with a macro substitution (FIND &NAME). But the listing tells us that SEEK doesn't like the macro version of NAME. It interprets the macro substitution literally. III PLUS assumes you want to SEEK what's inside NAME. You had to use the III PLUS macro (&) command with FIND to tell it there's a substitution going on. SEEK assumes a substitution is going on, so there's no need to tell it one is coming.

You can also tell III PLUS whether or not to look for a close match or for an exact match with the command

SET EXACT ON/off

as shown in Figure 9-4.

This example demonstrates the SET EXACT ON command being used with a memory variable and a literal string. You start with SET EXACT OFF, the dBASE III PLUS default. You want to SEEK "Hans". You know there are at least two books in the database that meet that criterion. III PLUS brings you to the first occurrence of Hans in the AUTHOR field. However, if EXACT is ON, there is no Hans in the database. You can ask for either of the EXACT names, Hans C. Ohanian or Hans Kung, and III PLUS will SEEK them, right?

Wrong! The SEEK command differs from FIND more than you

```
-> NAME = "Hans"
Hans
-> SEEK NAME
-> DISP TITLE,AUTHOR                                              AUTHOR
Record#  TITLE                                                    Hans C. Oh
     463  Gravitation and Spacetime
anian

-> SET EXACT ON
-> SEEK NAME
No find
-> SEEK "Hans"
No find
->
```

Figure 9-4.   The EXACT commands tell III PLUS whether to SEEK an EXACT match or reasonable facsimile of your request

thought. SEEK's idea of an EXACT match involves not only the characters but the length of the FIELD being SEEKed over. When you SET EXACT ON and try to SEEK, you won't find what you are seeking unless you match the SEEK condition length with the length of the field being SEEKed.

So far SEEK has been used with character strings exclusively. You can also use SEEK with numeric data. Here you encounter another major difference between SEEK and FIND. The SEEK command is

SEEK n

when used to SEEK a numeric value. Note that this isn't for alphanumeric numeric characters, but numeric data in numeric fields. The n in the above command is any valid dBASE III PLUS numeric expression, not just a plain number (shown in Figure 9-5). The FIND command didn't allow you to use evaluated expressions as its condition. SEEK does. Figure 9-5 shows that both .73 and 73/100 are allowed.

You can SEEK on the actual numeric value entered as a condition, provided that condition exists in the keyfield in the database. Further, the SEEK command allows you to use memory variables in any way, shape, or form when trying to SEEK a numeric expression. Each time you try to SEEK something using a memory variable or evaluated numeric expression, III PLUS evaluates the expression before using it as a condition. You cannot do this with the FIND command.

Advanced Use   There is a method of using the SEEK command that could be considered advanced. Like the GO/GOTO command, you can use the SEEK command to SEEK something in the current database based on the value of a field in another database. In other words, you can

SEEK A—>fieldname

where A is the alias for work area 1 and fieldname is the name of a field in the database in work area 1. This ability allows you to SEEK somewhere in your current work area based on expressions, fields, and evaluations located in other work areas.

```
-> USE EXPENSES INDE PAYAMOUNT
-> DISP NEXT 10 PAYAMOUNT
Record#    PAYAMOUNT
       5 *     0.00
      10 *     0.00
      13       0.00
      20 *     0.00
      33       0.00
      38       0.00
      32       0.73
      15       1.72
      30       4.50
       6       5.00
-> SEEK .73
-> DISP PAYAMOUNT
Record#    PAYAMOUNT
      32       0.73
-> SEEK 73/100
-> DISP PAYAMOUNT
Record#    PAYAMOUNT
      32       0.73
->
```

Figure 9-5.   The SEEK command allows you to SEEK numeric expressions, not just numbers

SKIP

The last command covered in this chapter is SKIP. The SKIP command does one thing. It moves the record pointer from where you are to where you say you want to be.

Syntax   The SKIP command's syntax is basically

SKIP n

where n is any valid dBASE III PLUS numeric expression. By default the SKIP command tells III PLUS to move forward one record. If you're on record 1 and SKIP, you'll be at record 2. If you're

```
Record#  PAYTO
      1  *Allstate
-> SKIP
Record No.      2
-> DISP PAYTO
Record#  PAYTO
      2  Allstate
-> GOTO 30
-> DISP PAYTO
Record#  PAYTO
     30  Camps Car Wash
-> SKIP
Record No.      31
-> DISP PAYTO
Record#  PAYTO
     31  Texaco
-> GO BOTT
-> SKIP
Record No.      40
-> SKIP
End of file encountered
       ?
SKIP
->
```

Figure 9-6.   The SKIP command won't let you SKIP past the end of the file

at record 200 and SKIP, you'll be at record 201. Note that you can't SKIP past the end of the database. This is shown in Figure 9-6. III PLUS will set the record pointer one record past the physical end of file and set the EOF( ) (End Of File) flag to TRUE. Further, if TALK is ON, III PLUS will tell you that you're at the end of the file.

SKIP shares GO/GOTO's ability to use both numbers and evaluated numeric expressions as part of the command, as shown in Figure 9-7. Note also that the SKIP command will move the integer value of the evaluated expression. This is shown in the lower part of Figure 9-7.

In the example, the user has SKIPped to record 26 and then entered

SKIP NUMBER/(2^4)

```
. USE EXPENSES
. DISP PAYTO
Record#  PAYTO
      1  *Allstate
. SKIP 10/2
. DISP PAYTO
Record#  PAYTO
      6  NH Turnpike
. SKIP 20
. DISP PAYTO
Record#  PAYTO
     26  J&D Video Inc.
. NUMBER = 100
. SKIP NUMBER/(2^4)
. DISP PAYTO
Record#  PAYTO
     32  Post Office
. ? NUMBER/(2^4)
       6.25
. ? 26 + 6.25        && WE WERE AT RECORD #26 AND SKIPped THE EXPRESSION VALUE
12.25
.                    && WHICH BROUGHT US TO RECORD #32
.
```

Figure 9-7.   You can use any valid dBASE III PLUS numeric expression
in a SKIP command

SKIP moves from where it is. It doesn't move from the beginning or
the end of the file. Thus, it evaluated NUMBER/(2^4) and got the integer value 6 (INT(6.25) = 6). It then SKIPped six records from
where it was, at record 26. In other words, III PLUS said "26 + 6 =
32, so I'll SKIP to record 32."

You can SKIP backwards as well as forwards by entering a negative value in the SKIP command, as in

SKIP —n

Again, n is any valid dBASE III PLUS numeric expression.

A last note is that, when TALK is ON, SKIP will tell you what
record you've SKIPped to. III PLUS won't tell you this when TALK is
OFF.

Use   The uses and advanced uses of SKIP tend to blend together.
Suppose you want to give the user the ability to SKIP any number of

records, forward or backward. All the user needs to do is enter a number. You don't allow the user to enter an expression for evaluation, although the code for that wouldn't be difficult to generate.

```
CASE ANSWER = 'S'
   @ 20,0 CLEA
   ACCE "SKIP how many ("-" to SKIP backwards) -> " TO SKIPNUM
   SKIP VAL(SKIPNUM)
   DO &GETTER
   CLEA GETS
   LOOP
```

The first thing you do is CLEAR part of the screen, making room for the prompt. You ask how many records the user would like to SKIP, convert that input to a value, and SKIP there. The GETTER and CLEAR GETS commands simply place the new records information on the screen. You LOOP back to the beginning when you're done.

Note that this code doesn't require any true error check. Even with TALK OFF, III PLUS won't let you SKIP somewhere you can't go. Repeatedly trying to SKIP to a nonexistent record doesn't interfere with the system in any way. You can include the code

```
*
IF EOF() .OR. BOF()
   WAIT "You can't SKIP there. Press any key to continue."
   LOOP
ENDI
*
```

directly after the SKIP command to let the user know he or she is once again attempting the impossible.

Memory Variable Commands

This chapter covers all the commands that can be used to manipulate memory variables. Some of the commands have been discussed in other sections and are only referenced here. Some may also affect database fields, but this chapter deals only with their memory-editing abilities.

=

The equal sign (=) is a memory-variable command in the sense that it tells III PLUS the value of a variable. The command has no actual form or syntax. You use the equal sign as you would use it in most programming languages:

variable = value

The equal sign is a recent implementation in dBASE; it was first documented in dBASE III. It makes the evaluation of variables much easier than the command

STORE value TO variable

although this older form does have some advantages (see the section on STORE later in this chapter).

You can use the equal sign to create new variables or assign values to existing variables. This usage is shown in Figure 10-1. The equal sign is used to create a new variable, ONE. The middle of Figure 10-1 shows the existing variable ONE getting a new value, 555. The bottom of Figure 10-1 shows ONE equaling an arithmetic expression. All are valid uses of the equal sign in III PLUS.

```
-> CLEAR MEMO
-> ONE = 1
-> DISP MEMO
ONE         pub   N          1  (          1.00000000)
    1 variables defined,        9 bytes used
  255 variables available,   5991 bytes available

-> ONE = 555
-> DISP MEMO
ONE         pub   N          555  (        555.00000000)
    1 variables defined,        9 bytes used
  255 variables available,   5991 bytes available

-> ONE = ONE/200
-> DISP MEMO
ONE         pub   N          2.77  (          2.77500000)
    1 variables defined,        9 bytes used
  255 variables available,   5991 bytes available

->
```

Figure 10-1.   You can use the equal sign to assign values to variables in III PLUS

The only shortcoming of the equal sign is that it can only operate on a single variable at a time. You can't

value = variable1, variable2,...

You can do that with the STORE command, as in

STORE value TO variable1, variable2,...

Note that value can be either an evaluated expression or a valid dBASE III PLUS data type in either STORE or =. It doesn't matter if you use character, logical, date, or numeric data in the command. You can't equate a MEMO field to a variable, however. Note that the equivalency function (=) can only be used with memory variables.

ACCEPT

The ACCEPT command has been used in most of the code shown in this book. This section will explain the syntax and use of ACCEPT.

Because the command has been used so much, the text won't give an advanced use.

The ACCEPT command is used to ACCEPT information from the user. It only ACCEPTS character data. Read the sections on the INPUT and WAIT commands later in this chapter if you're interested in noncharacter input. You can also use the GET and READ commands to get any data types (see Chapters 6 and 7 and the "LIST MEMORY" section in this chapter).

Syntax   The ACCEPT command has a simple syntax that can have one qualifier. The basic form is

ACCEPT TO variable

where variable is any memory variable. III PLUS will create a new memory variable if none exists with the listed name. This form of the command is shown in Figure 10-2. You should notice something strange in that figure.

Did you see that III PLUS only ACCEPTed text? Even when 12345 was entered, III PLUS decided that text was being entered. Note also that there were no other variables declared in the system prior to the entering of those two commands.

The second method of ACCEPTing information is with a prompt in front of the TO. This amounts to including a prompt as a qualifier.

```
-> ACCEPT TO CHARACTER
TEXTSTRING
-> ACCEPT TO NUMBER
12345
-> ? CHARACTER
TEXTSTRING
-> ? NUMBER
12345
-> ? TYPE("CHARACTER")
C
-> ? TYPE("NUMBER")
C
-> ? TYPE("CHARACTER") = TYPE("NUMBER")
.T.
->
```

Figure 10-2.   The standard form of the ACCEPT command

You can tell the user what you want to know with the command

ACCEPT "expression" TO variable

where variable is defined as previously and expression means anything you'd care to say. Consider Figure 10-3. Here you'll see that three different expressions, of increasing complexity, have been used in the ACCEPT command. The first prompt expression, "Look for what? —> ", is a simple prompt and is similar to many used throughout this text. Mary Poppins' favorite expression has been entered, to show there isn't any practical limit on what III PLUS will ACCEPT. The second prompt offers the user a bit more information on what is expected as a response. As before, there is no limit to what the user can answer. The last ACCEPT is a little different; a long prompt expression is used. III PLUS will use that prompt expression and send it to the screen as a best fit. As you can see, a best fit isn't always a good fit.

Use   The ACCEPT command is used to get information from the user into the system. This is almost always done programmatically, as few people will enter an ACCEPT command merely to have it come back at them a second later.

In the PROGRAM mode (and in the INTERACTIVE mode, if you wish) ACCEPT has some nice features. The first to explore is the use of the plus sign (+) in the prompt expression. Figure 10-4 shows the plus sign being used in the first prompt expression. You can use the plus sign to string text together. An example is

ACCEPT "PRESENT VALUE —>"+STR(number)+". NEW VALUE —>" TO var

---

```
-> ACCEPT "Look for what ? -> " TO LOOKER
Look for what ? -> supercalifragilisticexpealidotious
-> ACCEPT "Do you wish to go on (Y/N) ? -> " TO YORN
Do you wish to go on (Y/N) ? -> N
-> ACCEPT "I'M GOING TO KEEP ON TYPING UNTIL I RUN OUT OF SPACE ON THE SCREEN, J
UST TO SHOW YOU THAT 3+ WILL SCROLL IN AN ACCEPT COMMAND -> " TO LONGONE
I'M GOING TO KEEP ON TYPING UNTIL I RUN OUT OF SPACE ON THE SCREEN, JUST TO SHOW
  YOU THAT 3+ WILL SCROLL IN AN ACCEPT COMMAND -> hello
-> 
```

Figure 10-3.   These are all valid prompt expressions in the ACCEPT command

```
-> ACCE "THIS IS A TEST" + " OF THE '+' SYMBOL IN A PROMPT " TO PROMPT
THIS IS A TEST OF THE '+' SYMBOL IN A PROMPT
-> ACCE "DID YOU NOTICE I USED SINGLE QUOTES IN THE ABOVE ? " TO PROMPT
DID YOU NOTICE I USED SINGLE QUOTES IN THE ABOVE ? yes
-> ACCE "ONE THING YOU CAN'T DO IS USE THE " + ;
Syntax error
                                               ?
ACCE "ONE THING YOU CAN'T DO IS USE THE " + ;
->
```

Figure 10-4.   You can use the plus sign and single quotes in the prompt expression

where number is any valid dBASE III PLUS numeric expression or field and var is some memory variable. The preceding prompt can be seen in Figure 10-5. You may remember that the ACCEPT command won't take numeric data. You have to use the VAL function to convert the new character VAR back to a numeric VAR with

VAR = VAL(VAR)

This is also shown in Figure 10-5.

Figure 10-5 also shows the use of single quotes (' ') in the prompt expression. III PLUS doesn't care if you enclose the prompt expression in double quotes (" "), single quotes (' '), or square brackets ([ ]). All three delimiters are shown in Figure 10-6. The only thing to remember is to match the prompt expression delimiters on both ends of the expression. You can't

ACCEPT "UNBALANCED PROMPTS] TO ANSWER

```
-> ACCEPT "PRESENT VALUE -> "+STR(82.11,5,2)+". NEW VALUE -> " TO VAR
PRESENT VALUE -> 82.11. NEW VALUE -> 40.44
-> ? VAR
40.44
-> VAR = VAL(VAR)
-> ? VAR
       40.44
->
```

Figure 10-5.   The plus sign can be used with III PLUS functions to include noncharacter data in the prompt expression

```
-> ACCEPT "DOUBLE QUOTED PROMPT STRING" TO DQ
DOUBLE QUOTED PROMPT STRING
-> ACCEPT 'SINGLE QUOTED PROMPT STRING' TO SQ
SINGLE QUOTED PROMPT STRING
-> ACCEPT [SQUARE BRACKETED PROMPT STRING] TO SB
SQUARE BRACKETED PROMPT STRING
->
->
->
-> ACCEPT
Syntax error
        ?
ACCEPT
->
```

Figure 10-6. You can use single and double quotes and square brackets to delimit the prompt expression

because the left delimiter is a double quote and the right delimiter is a square bracket. The different delimiters do allow you to enclose expressions that are in the prompt. For example, you can

ACCE "Presently ' " + fieldname +" '. New data —> " to newfield

where fieldname is the name of a field in the current database and newfield is some memory variable. The preceding command would produce a prompt such as

Presently 'text from named field'. New data —>

There are some things you can't do with the ACCEPT command. First and foremost, you can't ACCEPT LOGICAL, NUMERIC, DATE, or MEMO fields. You'll also note that the bottom of Figure 10-4 has a syntax error on an ACCEPT prompt. The syntax error comes from using the semicolon (;) to tell III PLUS the prompt string is continued on the next line. But if you've looked closely at some of the code in this book, you'll realize that the semicolon has been used repeatedly to create long ACCEPT prompt expressions in some of the code. The solution to this juxtaposition in logic is straightforward: Consider continuing a prompt expression on more than one line. Figure 10-3 shows III PLUS's ability to scroll the prompt message during interactive input. Therefore, you don't have to continue it on a second line with a semicolon.

The second thing you can't do with the ACCEPT command has to do with interactive input. As mentioned, III PLUS scrolls during input when necessary. You can't scroll items when you're coding them; therefore, you have to be able to use the semicolon in a program listing.

The following listing shows a two-line program called ACCEPTOR. The first thing to notice about ACCEPTOR is that the single program line is an ACCEPT command broken into two lines. You can't make that break in INTERACTIVE mode, but there is no problem doing that in PROGRAM mode. Next, note that the line is perfectly executed when you DO ACCEPTOR.

```
-> TYPE ACCEPTOR.PRG
ACCEPT "WHICH DATABASE FIELD DO YOU WANT TO USE (1,2,3,...7)"
       +; " -> " TO FIELDNUM

-> DO ACCEPTOR
WHICH DATABASE FIELD DO YOU WANT TO USE (1,2,3,...7) -> 7
```

The III PLUS Text Editor, which you can use to write code with the MODIFY COMMAND command (see Chapters 3 and 4), will automatically word wrap and fix things so you don't need to use the semicolon. But remember that the semicolon isn't there for III PLUS's benefit, but for yours. It tells the person reading the code what goes where and why.

The last bit of information on the ACCEPT command has to do with fancy prompts. Earlier in this section, the text demonstrated III PLUS's ability to use character variables as part of the prompt expression. This implies you can use character variables by themselves as part of the prompt expression. Assuming there was a character variable

ACCPROMPT = "Yes, you can do this. Care to enter anything?"

```
-> ACCPROMPT = "Yes, you can do this. Care to enter anything?"
Yes, you can do this. Care to enter anything?
-> ACCEPT ACCPROMPT TO variable
Yes, you can do this. Care to enter anything?
```

Figure 10-7.   The ACCEPT command can use a character variable as the prompt expression

you could

ACCEPT ACCPROMPT TO variable

where variable is defined as just previously. The result is shown in
Figure 10-7.

AVERAGE

The AVERAGE command is covered thoroughly in Chapter 8. The
text mentioned there that the command is used primarily with database fields, but that it can also be used with memory variables when
you AVERAGE the sum of a database field with a memory variable.
Hence, the command is included in this chapter.

Briefly, the AVERAGE command is used to determine the
arithmetic mean of a database field over some selected portion of the
database. That can be done with any of the following AVERAGE
command forms:

```
AVERAGE
AVERAGE TO variable
AVERAGE fieldlist FOR condition
AVERAGE fieldlist WHILE condition
AVERAGE fieldlist NEXT n
AVERAGE fieldlist REST
AVERAGE fieldlist TO variable
AVERAGE fieldlist FOR condition1 WHILE condition2 TO variable
```

In all these cases, fieldlist can be one or several names of fields in
the current database. You can use the AVERAGE command to
determine the arithmetic mean of a memory variable added to a database field with the command form

AVERAGE field1+variable1, field2+variable2,...qualifiers

where field1 and field2 represent valid dBASE III PLUS database
field names from the current database, variable1 and variable2 represent valid dBASE III PLUS variable names, and qualifiers represents any mix of AVERAGE's qualifiers, as shown in Chapter 10.

There are several reasons for AVERAGEing database fields with
memory variables. Some of these uses include weighting averages,
adjusting curves, and modifying and distributing data.

The CLEAR ALL command was thoroughly discussed in Chapter 5. It is mentioned in this chapter because of its ability to remove every memory variable from the system. The command form is

CLEAR ALL

This command, entered either in the PROGRAM mode or inter-actively at the dBASE prompt, causes III PLUS to reset itself to its initial status. Whatever system defaults you've entered through DOS and the dBASE III PLUS CONFIG.DB file are active after the CLEAR ALL command is entered, but all files are closed, all work areas are empty, all III PLUS work-related information is forgotten, and, most important for this discussion, all memory variables are lost. A strong suggestion is that you use the SAVE command (see Chapter 3 and the section on the SAVE command later in this chap-

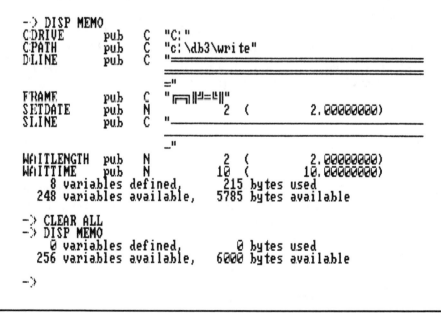

Figure 10-8. The CLEAR ALL command removes every memory variable from memory

ter) before you CLEAR ALL. This will prevent you from inadvertently losing needed memory variables. Figure 10-8 shows the effect of the CLEAR ALL command on memory.

CLEAR MEMORY

The CLEAR MEMORY command is a special case of the CLEAR ALL command. CLEAR ALL, described in the last section and in Chapter 5, resets the III PLUS system to the initial state. CLEAR MEMORY only erases existing memory variables from the system. The syntax of the command is identical to that of CLEAR ALL.

```
CLEAR MEMO
```

Note the use of the dBASE III PLUS four-letter-word convention in the preceding command. The action of the CLEAR MEMORY command is all-encompassing. No memory variables are sacred and all are removed from the system, just as was shown in Figure 10-8. The only difference is that CLEAR MEMORY only affects memory, not the entire III PLUS system.

There is no difference in what the CLEAR MEMORY command does in PROGRAM versus INTERACTIVE mode. You can selectively CLEAR memory variables in PROGRAM mode with the RELEASE command described later in this chapter.

COUNT

The COUNT command is covered thoroughly in Chapter 8. The command tells III PLUS to determine how many records in the current database meet some condition. The command forms are

```
COUNT
COUNT TO variable
COUNT FOR condition
COUNT WHILE condition
COUNT NEXT n FOR condition
COUNT REST FOR condition
COUNT REST TO variable
COUNT REST TO variable FOR condition
```

```
COUNT NEXT n WHILE condition
COUNT FOR condition1 WHILE condition2
COUNT NEXT n FOR condition1 WHILE condition2
COUNT NEXT n FOR condition1 WHILE condition2 TO variable
```

COUNT is included here because you can store the number of records COUNTed with any form of the COUNT command to a memory variable using the TO variable qualifier. Note that you can also use a memory variable as part of the condition in either the FOR or WHILE qualifiers. For example, the following code asks the user for a numeric value and then uses that variable as part of the FOR condition to COUNT the number of records in the EXPENSES database.

```
USE EXPENSES
SET DELI OFF
MAX = 100
CLEAR
a 1,0 SAY "WHAT IS THE MAXIMUM PAYAMOUNT VALUE? " ;
      GET MAX PICT "aR ->99999<-"
READ
COUNT FOR PAYAMOUNT <= MAX
```

One thing you should note in the code is that it SETs DELIMITERS OFF and then creates delimiters with the @...GET...PICTURE's @R function. The maximum PAYTO value is set to 100.

DO...WITH

The DO...WITH command is strictly a PROGRAM mode command that tells III PLUS what variables from the calling program will be used in the called routine in special ways. It is identical to parameter passing in most popular programming languages such as BASIC, FORTRAN, Pascal, and COBOL.

There is no distinction between advanced and normal use of this command because DO routine WITH variable list is a programming command. More information on other uses of the DO command can be found in Chapter 14. Note that this version of the DO command has nothing to do with the DO WHILE...ENDDO and DO CASE... ENDCASE commands. The DO command discussed here deals with passing memory variables between programs in a running III PLUS system.

Syntax   The DO...WITH command is the sending end of the command

PARAMETER variable list

discussed later in this chapter. The preceding command tells III PLUS that certain memory variables from the calling program are going to be used in the current routine, but those variables are going to be used with different names in this current routine. The sending command is

DO routine WITH variable list

There is one important thing to know about the sending command. The two lists must match in number of variables declared. For example, if you

DO aprg WITH x, y, z, t

the first executable command in aprg must be

PARAMETER ax, ay, az, at

The reason for this is that III PLUS will match variables with names. Remember that DO routine WITH variable list tells the called routine the number of variables it will be allowed to use in the receiving PARAMETER command. It acts like a telephone operator handling a person-to-person call. The calling program says, "I'm calling aprg, and I want to talk to x, y, z, and t." III PLUS takes over the telephone operator's job and makes contact with the called routine. The called routine answers the phone, and III PLUS says, "I have person-to-person calls for x, y, z, and t. Are they available?" The call won't go through if x, y, z, and t are not there to take the calls.

Note that the routine mentioned throughout this section can be either another PRG file or a PROCedure located in an open PRC file (remember that the text uses .PRC extensions to differentiate regular PRG files from PROC files).

Use   Many programming languages give the user the ability to pass variable values from one routine to another by using variable pseudonyms. You may call a variable XVAR in a calling routine and want to use XVAR's value in the called routine. Most times you would simply have the called routine perform the necessary arithmetic on

XVAR. There is a drawback to this procedure, however. The preceding scenario changes the value of XVAR that is returned to the calling routine.

What if you want to use the value of XVAR but don't want to use the name "XVAR" in the called routine? That is where the DO... WITH command comes in. It allows you to give variables different names in called programs, with each new name unique to the routine receiving the WITH variable list. (See the PARAMETER command later in this chapter for an example.)

You don't have to use the DO routine WITH variable list command to pass values to a called routine. III PLUS makes any values in the calling routine available to the called routine automatically. You may not want all changes in the called routine echoed in the calling routine, however. It is possible to send values with III PLUS's normal passing ability and with the DO...WITH command simultaneously. The only changes echoed in the calling routine are those passed through the DO...WITH command.

You can make use of a calling program's variable values in a called program in two ways. The first is to use the variable name as given in the calling program. The second is through the DO...WITH command. You can mix these two methods. This allows you to make use of the value of a calling program's variable in a called program, but be selective in what value is passed back for a given variable when RETURNing to the calling program. The listing presented in the PARAMETER command section later in this chapter gives examples of these uses.

DISPLAY MEMORY

The DISPLAY MEMORY command is normally used as a debugging tool. It is included in this chapter because of its ability to show the user the contents of memory at any given time on screen and in print. It is the close twin of LIST MEMORY.

Syntax   The DISPLAY MEMORY command is a special case of the DISPLAY command. You might consider the MEMORY part of the command as a qualifier. The command is

DISP MEMO

Note the use of the dBASE III PLUS four-letter-word convention in the preceding command form. The normal DISPLAY command is used to show the user information about a given database. The DISPLAY MEMORY command is used purely to show the user the current status of memory. An example is shown in Figure 10-9.

The DISPLAY MEMORY command (as well as the LIST MEMORY command, discussed later in this chapter) can be qualified to send memory information TO the PRINTer with

DISPLAY MEMORY TO PRINT

The following listing shows some interesting properties of the TO PRINT qualifiers.

```
·> DISP MEMO TO PRIN
Printer not ready.
              ?
DISP MEMO TO PRIN
·> DISP MEMO TO PRIN
MAX          pub   N      100   (          100.00000000)
CDRIVE       pub   C    "C:"
CPATH        pub   C    "c:\db3\write"
DLINE        pub   C    "MMMMMMMMMMMMMMMMMMMMMMMMMMMMMMMMMMM
                        MMMMMMMMMMMMMMMMMMMMMMMMMMMMMMMMMMMMMM
                        M"
FRAME        pub   C    "IM;:<MH:"
SETDATE      pub   N        2   (            2.00000000)
SLINE        pub   C    "DDDDDDDDDDDDDDDDDDDDDDDDDDDDDDDDDDDDDDD
                        DDDDDDDDDDDDDDDDDDDDDDDDDDDDDDDDDDDDDDD
                        D"
WAITLENGTH   pub   N        2   (            2.00000000)
WAITTIME     pub   N       10   (           10.00000000)
     9 variables defined,      224 bytes used
   247 variables available,   5776 bytes available

·> SET CONS OFF
·> DISP MEMO TO PRIN
MAX          pub   N      100   (          100.00000000)
CDRIVE       pub   C    "C:"
CPATH        pub   C    "c:\db3\write"
DLINE        pub   C    "MMMMMMMMMMMMMMMMMMMMMMMMMMMMMMMMMMM
                        MMMMMMMMMMMMMMMMMMMMMMMMMMMMMMMMMMMMMM
                        M"
FRAME        pub   C    "IM;:<MH:"
SETDATE      pub   N        2   (            2.00000000)
SLINE        pub   C    "DDDDDDDDDDDDDDDDDDDDDDDDDDDDDDDDDDDDDDD
                        DDDDDDDDDDDDDDDDDDDDDDDDDDDDDDDDDDDDDDD
                        D"
WAITLENGTH   pub   N        2   (            2.00000000)
WAITTIME     pub   N       10   (           10.00000000)
     9 variables defined,      224 bytes used
   247 variables available,   5776 bytes available
```

```
-> SET PRINT OFF
-> DISP MEMO TO PRIN
MAX           pub   N      100    (          100.00000000)
CDRIVE        pub   C    "C:"
CPATH         pub   C    "c:\db3\write"
DLINE         pub   C    "MMMMMMMMMMMMMMMMMMMMMMMMMMMMMMMMMMMM
                         MMMMMMMMMMMMMMMMMMMMMMMMMMMMMMMMMMMMMM
                         M"
FRAME         pub   C    "IM;:<MH:"
SETDATE       pub   N        2    (            2.00000000)
SLINE         pub   C    "DDDDDDDDDDDDDDDDDDDDDDDDDDDDDDDDDDDDD
                         DDDDDDDDDDDDDDDDDDDDDDDDDDDDDDDDDDDDDDD
                         D"
WAITLENGTH    pub   N        2    (            2.00000000)
WAITTIME      pub   N       10    (           10.00000000)
      9 variables defined,      224 bytes used
    247 variables available,    5776 bytes available
```

The first and most important property to remember is that III PLUS knows if the printer is available to accept information when you DISPLAY MEMORY TO PRINT. III PLUS isn't always so curious regarding the printer status when sending more mundane information to the printer. Note that you will not get the error message

Printer not ready.

Figure 10-9. An example of the DISPLAY MEMORY command showing the current status of memory

if your printer is off but you have an active print spooler or buffer somewhere between your printer and your computer. The spooler/buffer will accept the information and wait for the printer to come on line without sending III PLUS a not-ready message.

Also note that information is still sent to the screen even if you've told III PLUS to DISPLAY MEMORY only TO the PRINTer. This happens if you enter information in INTERACTIVE mode. You could include the code

```
SET CONS OFF
DISP MEMO TO PRIN
SET CONS ON
```

in a program. The result would be a DISPLAY only TO the PRINTer and not the screen, as here you SET the CONSOLE OFF before DISPLAYing MEMORY and back ON after you're finished DISPLAYing MEMORY.

Similarly, the SET PRINT OFF command has no effect on DISPLAY MEMORY TO PRINT regardless of whether the command is given in INTERACTIVE or PROGRAM mode. Not shown in the listing is the command

SET PRINTER TO device

and its effect on the DISPLAY MEMORY TO PRINT command. The SET PRINTER TO command is covered in Chapter 11 in detail, but its only effect is to tell III PLUS where to send output (printer1, printer2, and so on) and not how to send it. It doesn't affect what is printed, only where it is printed.

Use   The DISPLAY MEMORY command differs from the LIST MEMORY command in only one aspect, the difference between all DISPLAY and LIST commands: unlike the LIST MEMORY command, the DISPLAY MEMORY command knows when it's going to use more than one screen for information and provides a screen break with the prompt

Press any key to continue. . .

This prompt will also appear in printed output when you DISPLAY MEMORY TO PRINT.

GET

The GET command has been discussed in Chapter 7. It is primarily used to GET information into a database field. You can use GET to place information in an existing memory variable. This is a distinction between GET and any ACCEPT, INPUT, =, WAIT, or STORE command. You must have declared the variable in the GET command previously. In other words, you can't

@ x,y GET variable

unless sometime prior to that command you have entered something such as

STORE value TO variable

An example of this is shown in the following listing. There are no variables in memory and III PLUS won't let you GET SOMETHING. Once SOMETHING is declared, you are allowed to GET it.

```
-> CLEAR
-> DISP MEMO
     0 variables defined,          0 bytes used
   256 variables available,     6000 bytes available

-> a 10,0 GET SOMETHING
Variable not found
                        ?
a 10,0 GET SOMETHING
-> STORE 10 TO SOMETHING
-> a 10,0 GET SOMETHING
->
```

INPUT

The INPUT command has many of the abilities of the ACCEPT command plus a few more that make it somewhat more universal than the ACCEPT command. The ACCEPT command, used in most of the code shown in this book, was explained earlier in this chapter.

The INPUT command is used to take information from the user and make it usable to the system. Note that the INPUT command can INPUT a wide variety of data types, unlike ACCEPT, which only

ACCEPTS character data. You should read the sections on the ACCEPT and WAIT commands if you're interested in character input. You can also use the GET and READ commands to get any data types (see Chapters 6 and 7 and the section on the LIST MEMORY command later in this chapter).

Syntax   The INPUT command has a simple syntax that can have one qualifier. The basic form is

INPUT TO variable

where variable is any memory variable. III PLUS will create a new memory variable if none exists with the listed name. ACCEPT also creates variables if none existed in memory with the listed name; however, INPUT recognizes the listed variable's type if that variable exists. This is shown in Figure 10-10.

The INPUT and ACCEPT commands have been shown together to give you a better understanding of a basic difference and a similarity between them. The similarity is that both ACCEPT and INPUT can be used to get data from the user and put it into the system, and the command forms are identical. However, ACCEPT

```
-> ONE = 1
1
-> ? TYPE("ONE")
N
-> ACCEPT TO ONE
1
-> ? TYPE("ONE")
C
->
-> ONE = 1
1
-> ? TYPE("ONE")
N
-> INPUT TO ONE
1
-> ? TYPE("ONE")
N
->
```

Figure 10-10.   The INPUT command remembers an existing variable's type when INPUTting data

changes the numeric variable ONE to a character variable when you enter data. Note especially that even though the number 1 is entered as data, ACCEPT still reads the data as if it were character data. INPUT doesn't do that. It recognizes the existing variable's type as numeric before it gets any data from the user. The example in Figure 10-10 shows INPUT getting the NUMERIC value 1 from the user and sending the NUMERIC value 1 to the system. This is a principal difference between ACCEPT and INPUT. INPUT also goes a bit further by determining the type of new variables based on what you INPUT to them. If you use the command

INPUT TO NUMBER

and no variable NUMBER exists, III PLUS decides NUMBER's data type based on your response. INPUTting 3 will give NUMBER a numeric data type. INPUTting "3" will give NUMBER a character data type.

The preceding discussion also hints at how you get character data into the system with INPUT. Earlier the text mentioned the one sure way of telling III PLUS that something was character data was to enclose the character data in delimiters such as double quotes (""),

```
-> INPUT TO HELLO
"HELLO, HOW ARE YOU?"
-> ? HELLO
HELLO, HOW ARE YOU?
-> INPUT TO HELLO
'HELLO, HOW ARE YOU?'
-> ? HELLO
HELLO, HOW ARE YOU?
-> INPUT TO HELLO
[HELLO, HOW ARE YOU?]
-> ? HELLO
HELLO, HOW ARE YOU?
->
-> INPUT TO HELLO
"THIS SHOWS WHAT THE 'SINGLE QUOTE' CAN DO"
-> ? HELLO
THIS SHOWS WHAT THE 'SINGLE QUOTE' CAN DO
->
```

Figure 10-11. You tell INPUT that character data is coming by using delimiters

single quotes (''), and square brackets ([ ]). This is how you tell III PLUS that what you're INPUTting is character type data. An example of this is shown in Figure 10-11.

Naturally, you can add to anything that is delimited. Figure 10-12 shows how the user can make use of existing character and numeric variables to enter a response. Be aware that you can't include a numeric variable in character INPUT. You can get around that restriction by using the III PLUS STR( ) function to convert the NUMBER variable to character format.

The second method of INPUTting information is to put a prompt in front of the TO. This amounts to including a prompt as a qualifier. You can tell the user what you want to know with the command

INPUT "expression" TO variable

where variable is defined as just previously and "expression" means anything you'd care to say. There isn't any practical limit on what III PLUS will INPUT.

Use   The INPUT command is used to get information from the user into the system. This is almost always done programmatically,

```
-> CHAR = "AGAIN,"
AGAIN,
-> INPUT TO HELLO
[HELLO ] + CHAR + [ HOW ARE YOU?]
-> ? HELLO
HELLO AGAIN, HOW ARE YOU?
-> NUMBER = 33
33
-> INPUT TO AGE
[I UNDERSTAND YOU ARE ] + STR(NUMBER,2) + [ YEARS OLD.]
-> ? HELLO
HELLO AGAIN, HOW ARE YOU?
-> ? AGE
I UNDERSTAND YOU ARE 33 YEARS OLD.
->
->
```

Figure 10-12.   You can use the delimiters to add existing variable values to your INPUT and use the plus sign to create INPUT prompts

as few people will enter an INPUT command merely to have it come back at them a second later.

There are some things you can't do with the INPUT command. First and foremost, you can't INPUT DATE or MEMO fields. III PLUS will interpret any DATE format (xx/xx/xx) as numeric data if you're INPUTting to an existing character variable, an existing numeric variable, or a new variable. This is shown in Figure 10-13.

You'll also notice that the bottom of Figure 10-13 has the error message

Variable not found

The reason for that is III PLUS's inability to find the variable AUGUST. III PLUS thinks the user has INPUT a numeric expression that should be evaluated as

Divide 15 by AUGUST's value and divide the result by 86

```
-) CHAR = "TEXT STRING"
-) NUMBER = 12345
-) ? TYPE("CHAR")
C
-) ? TYPE("NUMBER")
N
-) INPUT TO CHAR
15/8/86
-) ? CHAR
        0.02
-) INPUT TO NUMBER
15/8/86
-) CHAR = "TEXT STRING"
-) INPUT TO CHAR
15 AUGUST 86
-) ? CHAR
        15
-) CHAR = "TEXT STRING"
-) INPUT TO CHAR
15/AUGUST/86
Variable not found
```

Figure 10-13. III PLUS needs you to tell it if INPUT data is character or numeric

This brings up an interesting feature of INPUT. It will accept existing variables as input data (shown in Figure 10-14). ACCEPT wouldn't do this. You can enter CHAR to an INPUT request, and III PLUS will INPUT the value of the variable CHAR. Entering CHAR to an ACCEPT request causes III PLUS to ACCEPT the text string "CHAR". The same restrictions apply to this as apply to regular data input. III PLUS will create new variables if the listed variable doesn't exist and will convert existing variables to the intended data type.

INPUT's ability to accept variable names brings us to error messages. Like ACCEPT, INPUT will give you a syntax error if you use the semicolon (;) to tell III PLUS the prompt string is continued on the next line in INTERACTIVE mode. You won't get a syntax error in PROGRAM mode. The III PLUS Text Editor, which you can use to

```
-> CHAR = [TEXT STRING]
-> GREETING = [HELLO]
-> INPUT TO CHAR
GREETING
-> ? CHAR
HELLO
-> NUMBER = 22
-> VALUE = 0
-> INPUT TO NUMBER
VALUE
-> ? NUMBER
        0
-> INPUT TO GREETING
NUMBER
-> ? GREETING
        0
-> TRUTH = .T.
-> INPUT TO TRUTH
T
Variable not found
.F.
-> ? TRUTH
.F.
->
```

Figure 10-14. You can use variable names as INPUT data and III PLUS will INPUT the value of the variable

write code with the MODIFY COMMAND command, will automatically word wrap so you don't need to use the semicolon.

The text has also mentioned the "Variable not found" error message. This message will occur on two occasions. One is when III PLUS can't find the variable you've named; that is the intended function of the command. The other time you'll get this error message is when you've forgotten to enclose the INPUT data in quotes. There is a lot of difference between entering the text string "NUMBER" and entering the variable name NUMBER. An example of this is also shown in Figure 10-14, this time using logical variables.

LIST MEMORY

The LIST MEMORY command is normally used as a debugging tool. It is included in this chapter because of its ability to show the user on screen and in print the contents of memory at any given time. It is the close twin of DISPLAY MEMORY.

Syntax   The LIST MEMORY command is a special case of the LIST command. You might consider the MEMORY part of the command as a qualifier. The command is

LIST MEMO

Note the use of the dBASE III PLUS four-letter-word convention in the preceding command. The normal LIST command is used to view information about a given database. The LIST MEMORY command is used purely to show the user the current status of memory. Like DISPLAY MEMORY, the LIST MEMORY command can be qualified to send memory information TO the PRINTer. (See the "DISPLAY MEMORY" section for details; LIST MEMORY works similarly in this respect.)

Use   Only one aspect of the LIST MEMORY command makes it different from the DISPLAY MEMORY command; that same difference applies to all LIST and DISPLAY commands. The LIST MEMORY command has no idea when it's going to use more than one screen for information and doesn't provide any screen breaks.

Memory Variable Commands   **375**

This factor can be particularly nettlesome when you call for printed output, when you LIST MEMORY TO PRINT, as long listings will go over page breaks and perforations.

M—>

Most users of III PLUS are familiar with work areas A through J and know you can SELECT A or SELECT B, and so on. They may not be aware that there is also a hidden work area, M; it cannot be SELECTed. This section discusses how to use that hidden work area in programming. The nature of this command mixes advanced and normal use.

Syntax   Work area M is a pseudonym for MEMORY. The M alias is used to distinguish a memory variable from a database field when they have similar names. For example, you could have a memory variable TODAY and a database field TODAY. Where will data be placed when you use the following command?

@ x,y GET TODAY

How do you tell III PLUS that the TODAY in the command is for the TODAY field in the database in work area A, as opposed to your memory variable TODAY? The simplest method is to use the work area alias A in the command as

@ x,y GET A—>TODAY

A brief note here about the precedence of databases over memory variables: III PLUS always assumes you want to GET information to the database first. Given the option of putting data into either a memory variable or a database field, III PLUS will always go for the database field. That means that including the work-area qualifier in the preceding command is a waste of time.

Figure 10-15 shows a database with one field, TODAY. The database is empty; therefore, TODAY has no value, as shown in the line

? TODAY

The next line appears to be getting the character value of the III

```
-> DISP STRUC
Structure for database: D:TODAY.dbf
Number of data records:        0
Date of last update   : 08/15/86
Field  Field Name  Type        Width    Dec
    1   TODAY       Date            8
** Total **                         9

-> ? TODAY
  /  /
-> TODAY = DTOC(DATE())
-> ? TODAY
  /  /
-> ? M->TODAY
08/15/86
->
```

Figure 10-15. Work area M allows you to use memory variables with the same names as database fields

PLUS DATE function into a variable called TODAY. Note that the equivalency function (=) can be used only with memory variables. You can't make a database field equal something.

Even though you may have told III PLUS that TODAY is equal to something, it doesn't agree. It tells you that TODAY is still empty when you use the ? TODAY query. You didn't lose information, nor did III PLUS misplace your data. The next line shows the command

? M—>TODAY

III PLUS responds with the character equivalent of the system date. This is an example of forcing III PLUS to use the memory variable (by using the = sign). What about an @...GET command where III PLUS must decide whether to use the memory variable or the database field? That instance is illustrated in Figure 10-16.

The M memory work-area designator solves the problem of getting data into memory. You can tell III PLUS to get data for a memory variable with

@ x,y GET M—>TODAY

The code that produced Figure 10-16 was entered interactively and is shown in the following listing.

Memory Variable Commands

```
-> CLEAR
-> a 20,0 SAY "INTO THE DATABASE -> " GET TODAY
-> READ
-> TODAY = SPACE(8)
-> CLEAR
-> TODAY = SPACE(8)
-> a 20,0 SAY "INTO THE DATABASE -> " GET TODAY
-> READ
-> ? TODAY
08/15/86
-> ? A->TODAY
08/15/86
-> ? M->TODAY

-> TODAY = "15 AUGUST 86"
-> ? M->TODAY
15 AUGUST 86
-> a 10,0 SAY "INTO MEMORY -> " GET M->TODAY
-> READ
-> ? M->TODAY
HELLO HOW RU
```

Use   The M work-area designator can be quite useful in situations in which you've intentionally given a memory variable the same name as a database field. Many applications do most of their work with memory variables. The result of all the memory arithmetic is a group of data, which is then saved to a database. Tax calculations involve these actions. Would someone actually use dBASE III PLUS for their tax work rather than use a spreadsheet package? Yes. Using III PLUS to handle tax work is an excellent choice. You can design databases that correspond to each of the IRS forms. Your clients will fall into two basic camps: personal and business. You can design the system to take care of batch work on personal and business tax forms. You can link individual tax forms and client records by social security number.

You want to keep historical records for your clients based on their yearly taxes. Many of the fields in each tax record will use names identical to the variable names in the database. Examples are TOTALINCOM, TOTALINTRST, STATETAX, CITYTAX, COUNTYTAX, and EXEMPTIONS. Note that each state will have differing tax codes as well. Most of these codes are in the form of numbers that individuals and businesses have to meet. You can place codes such as MAXIRADDCT (MAXimum IRA DeDuCTion), MAXDEDUCT, and MAXCHARITY into a database of state and federal laws. This allows for easier editing.

In any case, you can create and use a dBASE III PLUS tax sys-

```
INTO MEMORY  -)   : HELLO HOW RU:
INTO THE DATABASE -)   : 08/15/86:


-) TODAY = SPACE(8)
-) ? TODAY
08/15/86
-) ? A->TODAY
08/15/86
-) ? M->TODAY

-) TODAY = "15 AUGUST 86"
-) ? M->TODAY
15 AUGUST 86
-) ? M->TODAY
HELLO HOW RU
-) CLOSE ALTER
-)
```

Figure 10-16. Screen produced by @ . . . GET M —>TODAY

tem with more finesse by making use of the M work-area qualifier. All of your user prompts will be

@ x,y SAY "prompt" GET M —>variable

The system will get all the information it needs and then produce a tax form. This form can be either printed out or sent to the screen. Again, your commands will be

@ x,y SAY M —>variable

You can check over the screen or printed form for errors. If you accept the system's tax determination, your next block of commands would be

REPLACE field1 WITH M —>field1, field2 WITH M —>field2, . . .

Note that field1 and field2 are used as memory variable names in the preceding command because of the use of memory variables with the same names as fields in the database. The actual command might look like

REPL TOTALTAX WITH M —>TOTALTAX, IRADEDUCT WITH M —>IRADEDUCT, . . .

Memory Variable Commands   **379**

PARAMETER is strictly a PROGRAM mode command that tells III PLUS what variables from the calling program will be used in special ways in the called routine. It is identical to passed parameters in most popular programming languages, such as BASIC, FORTRAN, Pascal, and COBOL.

There is no distinction between advanced and normal use of this command, because PARAMETER is a programming command. Information on PARAMETER can also be found in Chapter 14. Note that the PARAMETER command has nothing to do with the parameter control commands discussed in Chapter 11. Most of those commands involve the use of the SET system. This PARAMETER command has to do with passing variables between programs in a running III PLUS system.

Syntax   The PARAMETER command is the receiving end of the command

DO routine WITH variable list

discussed in the DO...WITH command section earlier in this chapter. The preceding command tells III PLUS to start processing the named routine and use the listed variables as special cases in that routine. The receiving PARAMETER command is

PARAMETER variable list

There are two important things to know about the receiving PARAMETER command. First, it must be the first command in the called routine. The called routine can have no other commands (other than NOTE, *, and &&) before the PARAMETER command (not exactly true, as is shown in the "Use" section). Second, the two lists must match in number of variables declared. For example, if you

DO aprg WITH x, y, z, t

the first executable command in aprg must be

PARAMETER ax, ay, az, at

Use   Many programming languages give the user the ability to pass variable values from one routine to another using variable pseudonyms. You may call a variable XVAR in a calling routine and want to use XVAR's value in the called routine. Most times you would simply have the called routine perform the necessary arithmetic on XVAR. There is a drawback to this: the scenario changes the value of XVAR that is returned to the calling routine.

What if you want to use the value of XVAR but don't want to use the name XVAR in the called routine? That is where PARAMETERs come in. The III PLUS PARAMETER command allows you to give variables different names in different programs, with each new name unique to the routine receiving the PARAMETERs. The PARAMETER command is used in the following listing:

```
** MAIN MODULE
*
STORE 10 TO X, Y, Z, T
? "BEFORE CALLING APRG X, Y, Z AND T ARE "
? X, Y, Z, T
DO APRG WITH X, Y, Z
? "AFTER CALLING APRG X, Y, Z AND T ARE "
? X, Y, Z, T
*
** EOF

** APRG
*
PARAMETERS AX, AY, AZ, AT
AX = AX^2 + AY/(AZ + AT)
AY = AZ + AT
AZ = AT/AY
AT = AX/(AY + AZ)
? "IN APRG AX, AY, AZ AND AT ARE "
? AX, AY, AZ, AT
RETURN
*
** EOF

-> DO MAIN
BEFORE CALLING APRG X, Y, Z AND T ARE

        10          10          10          10
Wrong number of parameters.
                           ?
PARAMETERS AX, AY, AZ, AT
Called from - D:MAIN.prg
Cancel, Ignore, or Suspend? (C, I, or S) Cancel
Do cancelled

&& NUMBER OF PARAMETERS CORRECTED IN MAIN

** MAIN MODULE
*
STORE 10 TO X, Y, Z, T
? "BEFORE CALLING APRG X, Y, Z AND T ARE "
```

```
? X, Y, Z, T
DO APRG WITH X, Y, Z, T
? "AFTER CALLING APRG X, Y, Z AND T ARE "
? X, Y, Z, T
*
** EOF

&& NOTE COMMAND IN APRG PRIOR TO PARAMETER COMMAND

** APRG
*
X = X + 200
PARAMETERS AX, AY, AZ, AT
AX = AX^2 + AY/(AZ + AT)
AY = AZ + AT
AZ = AT/AY
AT = AX/(AY + AZ)
? "IN APRG AX, AY, AZ AND AT ARE "
? AX, AY, AZ, AT
RETURN
*
** EOF

-> DO MAIN
BEFORE CALLING APRG X, Y, Z AND T ARE
        10          10          10          10
IN APRG AX, AY, AZ AND AT ARE
        100.50       20          0.50        4.90
AFTER CALLING APRG X, Y, Z AND T ARE
        100.50       20          0.50        4.90
```

The top of the listing shows two programs, MAIN and APRG. APRG is called from MAIN. The first example shows MAIN and APRG with a different number of PARAMETERs being passed. MAIN passes three PARAMETERs, while APRG expects four PARAMETERs. The result is an error message.

The second half of the listing shows APRG with an executable command prior to the PARAMETER command. Note further that the executable command works on one of the variables in the calling program. Look at the result of running MAIN, and you'll see why you should or shouldn't have any executable code prior to the PARAMETER command.

Arithmetic is done on variable X before the PARAMETER command is entered. But what values are passed back to X when APRG RETURNs to MAIN? The value returned is the PARAMETER value, not the newly calculated X value.

This is useful information for the programmer/developer who is careful in coding. You can make use of a calling program's variable values in a called program in two ways. The first is to actually use the variable name as given in the calling program. The second is through the PARAMETER command. You can mix these two methods, as shown in the listing. This allows you to make use of the value of a calling program's variable in a called program, but be selective in which value is passed back for a given variable when RETURNing to the calling program.

PRIVATE

The PRIVATE command is one side of the PRIVATE PUBLIC command pair. Both are used in PROGRAM mode and tell III PLUS certain things about memory variables currently active in the system.

Syntax   PRIVATE has five basic forms. The forms all relate to hiding memory variables from various levels of calling and called programs and routines. The five forms are

```
PRIVATE variable list
PRIVATE ALL
PRIVATE ALL LIKE variable skeleton
PRIVATE ALL EXCEPT exception skeleton
PRIVATE ALL LIKE variable skeleton EXCEPT exception skeleton
```

The first listed command is the basic form and shows the minimum amount of information the user must give III PLUS to make anything PRIVATE in the system. In other words, you can't

PRIVATE

without giving III PLUS some idea of what variables you want PRIVATE. You must include the name of at least one currently active memory variable, as in

PRIVATE variable name

This tells III PLUS to hide the named variable from any called routines. The called routines can be other PRG files or open PROCedures. Figure 10-17 shows the status of memory before and after variables are made PRIVATE in a called routine. You can also make more than one variable PRIVATE by naming the variables

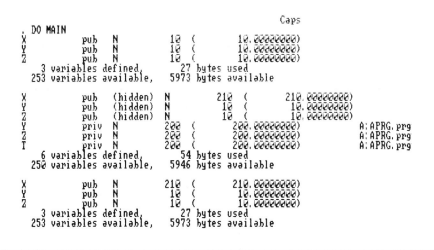

Figure 10-17. An example of the PRIVATE command

after the PRIVATE command. This is the

form of the command shown in the following listing:

```
** MAIN MODULE
*
PUBLIC X, Y, Z
STORE 10 TO X, Y, Z
DISP MEMO
DO APRG
DISP MEMO
*
** EOF

** APRG
*
X = X + 200
PRIVATE X, Y, Z, T
STORE 200 TO Y, Z, T
DISP MEMO
RETURN
*
** EOF
```

The programs in this listing were used to create Figure 10-17. Note that III PLUS hides only the named variables. The variables being hidden should be separated by commas (,). The next form of the command is

PRIVATE ALL

PRIVATE ALL tell III PLUS to hide every memory variable from the called routine or calling program. Note that PRIVATE ALL works both ways, depending on when it is entered. You can PRIVATE ALL before calling a routine, and III PLUS will hide all current memory variables from the called routine. Similarly, you can PRIVATE ALL once the called routine is running and hide all current memory variables from any other routines that will be called or have called the currently running routine. In other words, PRIVATE ALL only affects the current program's variables. The difference between PRIVATE and PUBLIC variables is covered in more detail in the "Use" section.

The next form to consider also makes use of a qualifier, but does so in a special way. The basic PRIVATE command will hide listed variables or ALL variables from memory. What if you want to hide a group of variables, but not ALL of them? You might

PRIVATE ALL LIKE variable skeleton

The preceding command tells III PLUS to hide only variables with names that fit a certain pattern. You could hide only variables with names that begin with C with

PRIVATE ALL LIKE C*

Similarly, you could hide all variables with names that begin with A with

PRIVATE ALL LIKE A*

You could be even more selective by narrowing the names of variables with the question mark wild card (?). You could hide all variables with names five characters long and have the last four characters be LINE with

PRIVATE ALL LIKE ?LINE

Valid III PLUS wild cards are the same as you'd use in DOS, the asterisk (*) and the question mark (?). You can use these symbols with other alphanumeric characters to constitute a variable skeleton, or the frame of a group of variable names. The concept is identical to that of asking DOS for a DIRectory of all files that begin with H by entering

DIR H*.*

The * tells III PLUS you don't care about the number of characters or what they are. Using wild cards tells III PLUS not to care about anything other than the listed character in the name. COY would become C??, CPATH would become C????, and both would be hidden with

PRIVATE ALL LIKE C*

If that is the case, what good are question marks as wild cards? You can use question marks to hide certain variables. You could tell III PLUS to hide only variables beginning with CO and containing up to eight additional characters with the command

PRIVATE ALL LIKE CO????????

This would hide COY and COELACANTH but not CONNECTICUT, as the last has nine letters, one more than was specified. Note that III PLUS will hide all variables with less than the specified number of characters in a name. You can mix and match the wild cards any way you wish. You can specify all variables with any first, second, third, and fourth letters of AIT, and any number of remaining letters with

PRIVATE ALL LIKE ?AIT*

The last form of the command is

PRIVATE ALL EXCEPT variable

where variable is any valid III PLUS variable name you want to use only in the currently running routine. This command can actually be used as either of the following:

```
PRIVATE ALL LIKE variable skeleton EXCEPT exception skeleton
PRIVATE ALL EXCEPT exception skeleton
```

There are two things to be aware of when using the preceding command. The exception skeleton works the same way a variable skeleton works. The LIKE form is the more restrictive of the two. You can hide ALL memory variables EXCEPT certain ones with

PRIVATE ALL EXCEPT exception skeleton

You would hide specific variables, with EXCEPTions, with

PRIV ALL LIKE variable skeleton EXCE exception skeleton.

Note the use of the dBASE III PLUS four-letter-word convention in the preceding command. Also be aware that III PLUS doesn't distinguish between UPPERCASE and lowercase letters in variable names. COY is the same as coy. Both would be hidden by the skeletons C* and C??.

Use   One of the first things to be aware of when working with memory variables is that some variables can be local (that is, specific to a certain routine) and some can be global and used by any routine. The concept of local and global variables is important in most programming languages, and III PLUS is no exception. III PLUS needs to know what variables are local to one program as opposed to being carried back and forth between programs.

PRIVATE is a programming command that tells III PLUS some variables are not to be used by any other routines, PROCedures, or programs called by the immediate program. This command is the equivalent of "It's my ball, so I'll decide who plays."

Assume you develop a system that has four levels of routines: MAIN, APRG, BPRG, and CPRG. The highest-level routine is MAIN. The second level is APRG, the third is BPRG, and the fourth is CPRG. The priority level is such that MAIN can call the other three, APRG can call BPRG and CPRG, BPRG can only call CPRG, and CPRG has no phone and can't call anybody. This hierarchical program structure is fairly common in III PLUS coding.

Say also that MAIN has variables A, B, and C. APRG has variables AA, AB, and AC. BPRG has variables BA, BB, and BC. CPRG has variables CA, CB, and CC. Each of the memory variables is declared in its respective program. You can pass any variables down the chute you care to with no special instructions to III PLUS. Whatever variables are changed at lower levels of the hierarchy are returned with their new values. But III PLUS will not allow you to pass variables up the chute that are created at lower levels of the hierarchy. In other words, A, B, and C are available to all levels of the system but CA, CB, and CC are only available to CPRG.

The last two sentences of the preceding paragraph imply AA,

AB, and AC are available to BPRG and CPRG, and BA, BB, and BC are available to CPRG. True. But what if you don't want AA, AB, and AC to be available to BPRG and CPRG? What if you don't want BA, BB, and BC to be available to CPRG? You use the PRIVATE command, of course. The first problem is solved by entering any of

```
PRIVATE AA, AB, AC
PRIVATE ALL LIKE A*
PRIVATE ALL LIKE A?
```

somewhere in APRG before it calls another routine. Note that the last two PRIVATE commands produce identical results even though two different wild card forms are used. A similar solution is executed for the second problem by replacing the preceding commands with

```
PRIVATE BA, BB, BC
PRIVATE ALL LIKE B*
PRIVATE ALL LIKE B?
```

at some point in BPRG before it calls another routine. Note also that variables are automatically RELEASEd when the routine that creates them RETURNs to its calling program. In other words, variables created in APRG do not remain active when APRG RETURNs to MAIN. This also means that you can't go from MAIN to APRG, back to MAIN, then to BPRG, and expect BPRG to have access to variables created in APRG.

PRIVATE forces a variable to stay beneath a certain level of control. Refer to Figure 10-17 and notice the middle listing. Note that III PLUS tells you which variables are PRIVATE and which are PUBLIC. Note further that III PLUS tells you where the PRIVATE variables are hidden (APRG, in this case). And, as a last note, recognize what happens to the variables in MAIN that have similar names to variables made PRIVATE in APRG—they are "hidden" from APRG even though they are PUBLIC variables. This is because III PLUS "hides" existing PUBLIC variables when similarly named variables are made PRIVATE in called routines.

PUBLIC

The PUBLIC command is one side of the PUBLIC PRIVATE command pair. Both are used in PROGRAM mode and tell III PLUS certain things about memory variables currently active in the system.

Syntax   PUBLIC has only one form,

PUBLIC variable list

where the variable list can be any one or several variables in the
system. Note that you must include some variable names with the
command. You can't just enter

PUBLIC

because III PLUS won't know what you want made available to the
entire system. You won't get an error message, but you won't get
much else, either.

The basic form tells III PLUS to show the named variable(s) to
any called routines. The called routines can be other PRG files or
open PROCedures. The variables being shown should be separated by
commas (,). Note that PUBLIC can't make use of the ALL qualifier.
The command

PUBLIC ALL

merely tells III PLUS to make a variable named ALL available to the
entire system. Similarly, you can't use ALL LIKE, ALL LIKE...
EXCEPT, or ALL...EXCEPT as qualifiers.

Use   One of the first things to be aware of when working with
memory variables is that some variables can be local (that is, specific)
to a routine, and some can be global and used by any routine. The
concept of local and global variables is important in most programming languages, and III PLUS is no exception. dBASE III PLUS
needs to know what variables are local to one program, as opposed to
being carried back and forth between programs.

The PUBLIC command tells III PLUS that some variables are to
be used by all other routines, PROCedures, or programs called by
any program. Assume you develop a system that has four levels of
routines, MAIN, APRG, BPRG, and CPRG. The highest level of the
routines is MAIN. The second level is APRG, the third is BPRG, and
the fourth is CPRG. The priority level is such that MAIN can call the
other three, APRG can call BPRG and CPRG, BPRG can only call
CPRG, and CPRG has no phone and can't call anybody. This hierarchical program structure is fairly common in III PLUS coding.

You can also say that MAIN has variables A, B, and C. APRG has variables AA, AB, and AC. BPRG has variables BA, BB, and BC. CPRG has variables CA, CB, and CC. The memory variables are declared in their respective programs. You can pass any variables down the chute with no special instructions to III PLUS. Whatever variables are changed at lower levels of the hierarchy are returned with their new values. But III PLUS will not allow you to pass variables up the chute that are created at lower levels of the hierarchy unless you use the PUBLIC command before you RETURN from those lower levels. In other words, A, B, and C are available to all levels of the system but CA, CB, and CC are only available to CPRG unless the command

PUBLIC CA, CB, CC

is entered from CPRG prior to RETURNing to the calling program. Further, once CA, CB, and CC are declared PUBLIC, any program, whether it calls CPRG or not, can use those three PUBLICed variables.

The preceding paragraph also implies that AA, AB, and AC are available to BPRG and CPRG, and BA, BB, and BC are available to

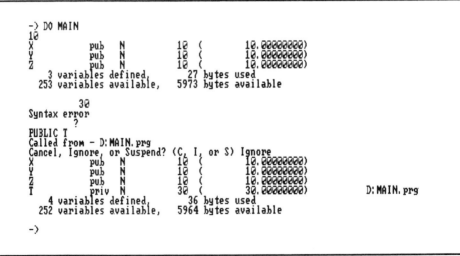

```
-> DO MAIN
10
X          pub  N       10 (       10.00000000)
Y          pub  N       10 (       10.00000000)
Z          pub  N       10 (       10.00000000)
     3 variables defined,     27 bytes used
   253 variables available,  5973 bytes available


          30
Syntax error
        ?
PUBLIC T
Called from - D:MAIN.prg
Cancel, Ignore, or Suspend? (C, I, or S) Ignore
X          pub  N       10 (       10.00000000)
Y          pub  N       10 (       10.00000000)
Z          pub  N       10 (       10.00000000)
T          priv N       30 (       30.00000000)              D:MAIN.prg
     4 variables defined,     36 bytes used
   252 variables available,  5964 bytes available

->
```

Figure 10-18. You must declare a variable PUBLIC before you use it in another command

CPRG without the use of the PUBLIC command. The PUBLIC command is most useful when you need to make variables available to the entire system from a program low in the hierarchy. In that situation, the PUBLICed variable is accessible to all levels of code and carries its value with it as it travels along. Note also that variables are automatically RELEASEd when the routine that creates them RETURNs to its calling program, unless those variables are declared PUBLIC. In other words, variables created in APRG do not remain active when APRG RETURNs to MAIN unless either APRG or MAIN declares those variables PUBLIC before the variables are created with some other command.

The preceding statement offers an important caveat to using PUBLIC. You can't declare a variable PUBLIC once it has been assigned a value by some other command. An example of this is shown in Figure 10-18. That screen was produced by the code shown in the following listing:

```
** MAIN MODULE
*
PUBLIC X, Y, Z
STORE 10 TO X, Y, Z
DISP MEMO
T = X+Y+Z
PUBLIC T
PUBLIC X, Y, Z
DISP MEMO
*
** EOF
```

III PLUS returns an error message for the command

PUBLIC T

because T was declared in the previous command

T = X+Y+Z

Note also that you can redeclare variables as PUBLIC at any time after they've been declared PUBLIC once. The second PUBLIC declaration doesn't affect the variables in any way.

A further difference between the use of PUBLIC and normal dBASE III PLUS memory management is that you couldn't go from MAIN to APRG, back to MAIN, then to BPRG and expect BPRG to have access to variables created in APRG. Declaring AA, AB, and AC PUBLIC, however, before using them would give BPRG access to them.

Also note that PUBLIC but nondeclared variables are assigned a logical value of .F. until they are given a value by some other command.

READ

The READ command has already been covered in detail in Chapters 6 and 7. It is mentioned in this chapter because you can use READ to change memory variables. Previously, READ has been used to alter database fields. All that was referenced for the use of READ with database fields is also true for its use with memory variables.

READ has one qualifier, SAVE. The command form is

READ SAVE

READ normally flushes the III PLUS input buffer of GETs, sending them into their respective memory variables or database fields. READ SAVE tells III PLUS not to flush the input buffer. All GETs in the buffer are sent to their respective memory variables or database fields, but are also kept in the input buffer to await the next set of GETs. The result of a READ SAVE used on memory variables would be identical to the result of using SET CARRY ON when APPENDing or INSERTing records to a database. Essentially, the last information entered is echoed on the current input screen.

RELEASE

RELEASE is a memory-management command that allows you to control what memory variables are kept in the system. You can selectively erase memory variables from memory to free space for other memory variables to use. Note that this doesn't affect the size of the memory buffer created with the CONFIG.DB MVARSIZ and MAXMEM commands.

Syntax   RELEASE has three basic forms. The forms all relate to making more memory available to the III PLUS system during a work session. One form of the command, RELEASE MODULE, is directly related to calling programs outside the III PLUS system and is discussed in Chapter 12. The two remaining forms can be broken into four versions of the basic RELEASE command. Those four versions are

```
RELEASE variable list
RELEASE ALL
RELEASE ALL LIKE variable skeleton
RELEASE ALL LIKE variable skeleton EXCEPT special variable(s)
```

The first listed command is the basic form and shows the minimum amount of information the user must give III PLUS to RELEASE anything in the system. In other words, you can't RELEASE without giving III PLUS some idea of what you want to RELEASE. You must include the name of at least one currently active memory variable, as in

RELEASE variable name

This tells III PLUS to erase the named variable from memory. Figure 10-19 shows the status of memory before and after the RELEASE

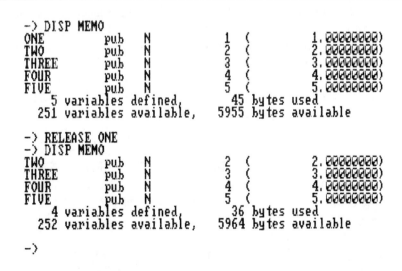

```
-> DISP MEMO
ONE          pub   N        1 (           1.00000000)
TWO          pub   N        2 (           2.00000000)
THREE        pub   N        3 (           3.00000000)
FOUR         pub   N        4 (           4.00000000)
FIVE         pub   N        5 (           5.00000000)
      5 variables defined,      45 bytes used
    251 variables available,  5955 bytes available

-> RELEASE ONE
-> DISP MEMO
TWO          pub   N        2 (           2.00000000)
THREE        pub   N        3 (           3.00000000)
FOUR         pub   N        4 (           4.00000000)
FIVE         pub   N        5 (           5.00000000)
      4 variables defined,      36 bytes used
    252 variables available,  5964 bytes available

->
```

Figure 10-19. MEMORY STATUS is changed after RELEASEing one variable

of one variable. You can also RELEASE more than one variable at a time by naming the variables after the RELEASE command. This is the

RELEASE variable list

form of the command and is shown in Figure 10-20. Note that III PLUS RELEASEs only the named variables. The variables being RELEASEd should be separated by commas (,). Note that III PLUS doesn't care if the variables actually exist when the RELEASE command is entered. The bottom of Figure 10-20 shows a second and third attempt to RELEASE TWO and THREE, and III PLUS apparently doing it. Even SETting TALK ON doesn't return an error message when you try to RELEASE nonexistent memory variables.

The next form of the command is

RELEASE ALL

RELEASE ALL works in several ways: its operational type depends on the mode it is used in. RELEASE ALL tells III PLUS to erase every memory variable from the system when it is used in INTERACTIVE mode; the command is then equivalent to CLEAR MEMORY. The command behaves differently in PROGRAM mode, however. RELEASE ALL only affects the current program's variables. PRIVATE and PUBLIC variables are discussed earlier in this chapter and are also mentioned in Chapter 14. To recap, a PUBLIC variable is one that can be used at any time by any routine, program, procedure, or other valid III PLUS program file when III PLUS is working in PROGRAM mode. PRIVATE variables are only used by the specific routines they are created in. In other words, if routine B is called from program A, and routine B creates a PRIVATE variable called BVAR, BVAR will not exist when III PLUS leaves B and returns to A.

You can also use qualifiers with RELEASE ALL, just as you can with PRIVATE ALL. See the PRIVATE ALL command earlier in this chapter for details. The commands work in identical ways in this respect.

Use RELEASE has many similarities to the CLEAR MEMORY command described earlier in this chapter. The major similarity is that both affect the status of the variables in memory. The CLEAR MEMORY command erases all active memory variables from the III

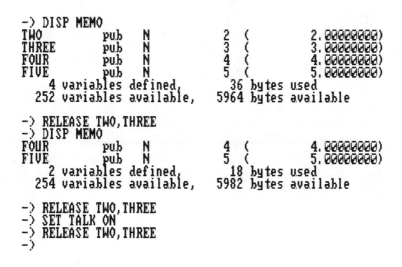

```
-> DISP MEMO
TWO          pub   N            2 (            2.00000000)
THREE        pub   N            3 (            3.00000000)
FOUR         pub   N            4 (            4.00000000)
FIVE         pub   N            5 (            5.00000000)
     4 variables defined,      36 bytes used
    252 variables available,   5964 bytes available

-> RELEASE TWO,THREE
-> DISP MEMO
FOUR         pub   N            4 (            4.00000000)
FIVE         pub   N            5 (            5.00000000)
     2 variables defined,      18 bytes used
    254 variables available,   5982 bytes available

-> RELEASE TWO,THREE
-> SET TALK ON
-> RELEASE TWO,THREE
->
```

Figure 10-20. RELEASE erases only the named variables from memory. However, it doesn't give any error messages when you try to RELEASE nonexistent variables

PLUS system, regardless of III PLUS's present mode. This book emphasized the two working modes of dBASE III PLUS, INTER-ACTIVE and PROGRAM. INTERACTIVE mode is what you enter directly at the dBASE dot prompt. PROGRAM mode occurs when III PLUS operates autonomically, directed by a series of commands either you or a programmer/designer has strung together in a PRG file.

These two modes directly affect the behaviors of many of III PLUS's commands; CLEAR MEMORY and RELEASE ALL are two such affected commands. The differences between INTERAC-TIVE and PROGRAM modes demonstrate the important distinction between the two commands. CLEAR MEMORY cannot be selective in any way. It is a one-shot command. If you CLEAR MEMORY, you lose all the variables you've been working with up to the point you entered the command. This is the case regardless of the mode you're in. The INTERACTIVE mode of RELEASE ALL is the equivalent of CLEAR MEMORY. Entering either command from the dBASE prompt will erase all memory variables from the system.

This is not the case in PROGRAM mode. The reason for the difference lies in the difference between INTERACTIVE and PRO-GRAM modes. PROGRAM mode causes III PLUS to focus on what's going on in the current work area. III PLUS is aware peripherally of what's going on in other work areas, but won't act on data in those other work areas unless specifically told to do so. INTERACTIVE mode causes III PLUS to be aware of what's going on everywhere in the system. The result is that RELEASE ALL has a limited effect in PROGRAM mode. PROGRAM mode RELEASE ALL only affects the memory variables that are created by the currently running routine. RELEASE ALL becomes a valuable tool in a system that runs several subroutines. Each subroutine has control over its part of variable memory without affecting any memory variables from the other subroutines or the main module. This was described briefly in the "Syntax" section and is covered in more detail here and in the "Advanced Use" section as it is an important programming concept in the III PLUS system. The "Advanced Use" section shows how RELEASE ALL works in code.

Likewise, the RELEASE ALL LIKE, RELEASE ALL LIKE... EXCEPT and RELEASE ALL EXCEPT each behave in one of several ways depending on the mode they're entered in. Each of the preceding commands only affects the immediate program/subroutine memory variables, when used in PROGRAM mode. The preceding commands affect all specified variables when used in INTERAC-TIVE mode.

Advanced Use   You should be comfortable with the concepts of global and local variables before reading this section. A global variable is a system-wide variable that can be accessed and used by any part of the system or any routines running in the system. A local variable is a variable that can be accessed only by the currently running routine or by the system while the current routine is running. You should read the sections on PUBLIC and PRIVATE variables and PARAMETER passing in this chapter if you still have questions about these subjects.

Say you have developed a system such as the one shown in the following listing:

```
** MAIN MODULE
*
CLEAR MEMORY
DO APRG
STORE 10 TO X, Y, Z
```

```
X = X^2 + Y/Z
? "FIRST LIST FROM MAIN, X = " + STR(X,10,2)
DO BPRG
? "SECOND LIST FROM MAIN, X = " + STR(X,10,2)
RELEASE ALL
DO CPRG
? "THIRD LIST FROM MAIN, X = " + STR(X,10,2)
*
** EOF


** APRG
*
STORE 20 TO A, M, N
A = A^2 + M/N
? "FROM APRG, A = " + STR(A,10,2)
RELEASE ALL
RETURN
*
** EOF


** BPRG
*
STORE 1 TO B, M, N
B = B^2 + M/N
X = B + X
? "FROM BPRG, B = " + STR(B,10,2)
? "FROM BPRG, X = " + STR(X,10,2)
 RELEASE ALL
 RETURN
*
** EOF


** CPRG
*
STORE .1 TO C, M, N
C = C^2 + M/N
X = X + C
? "FROM CPRG, C = " + STR(C,10,2)
? "FROM CPRG, X = " + STR(X,10,2)
CLEAR MEMORY
RETURN
*
** EOF
```

The display from this system is shown in Figure 10-21. The first part of the listing, MAIN MODULE, CLEARs MEMORY before doing anything else. This action is a good practice to get into, just so you can make sure there is nothing floating around in memory that will interfere with the smooth running of your application. Remember, the CLEAR MEMORY command affects all variable memory in the system, whether it's entered in INTERACTIVE or PROGRAM mode.

Next you DO the APRG subroutine, shown in the second block of the listing. Variables A, M, and N are created, some arithmetic is performed, and the results are posted. You RELEASE ALL the variables in APRG. So far, everything is behaving as you'd expect. You can assume no variables are carried from APRG back to MAIN, but you really don't know this for sure.

The next line of Figure 10-21 shows the value of X. X has just been created so, again, there is no problem. You DO the BPRG subroutine. This routine is similar to APRG except it performs some arithmetic on the local variables and the global variable X. You RELEASE ALL here as you did in APRG, but the result is what some might not expect. B, M, and N are RELEASEd, but X is returned to MAIN with the value calculated in BPRG. Therefore, the RELEASE ALL command entered in BPRG only affects the variables created in BPRG, not those created external to BPRG.

Immediately after you post the second list from MAIN, you

```
FROM APRG, A =      401.00
FIRST LIST FROM MAIN, X =      101.00
FROM BPRG, B =        2.00
FROM BPRG, X =      103.00
SECOND LIST FROM MAIN, X =      103.00
Variable not found
         ?
X = X + C
Called from - D:CPRG.prg
Called from - A:17-13.TXT
Cancel, Ignore, or Suspend? (C, I, or S) Ignore
FROM CPRG, C =        1.01
Variable not found
                        ?
? "FROM CPRG, X = " + STR(X,10,2)
Called from - D:CPRG.prg
Called from - A:17-13.TXT
Cancel, Ignore, or Suspend? (C, I, or S) Ignore
Variable not found
                              ?
? "THIRD LIST FROM MAIN, X = " + STR(X,10,2)
Called from - A:17-13.TXT
Cancel, Ignore, or Suspend? (C, I, or S) Ignore
->
```

Figure 10-21. Using RELEASE ALL with variables

RELEASE ALL. This causes all variables created in MAIN to be erased from memory. This is demonstrated by the error message

Variable not found

called from CPRG. III PLUS can work with the local variables created in CPRG, but X was RELEASEd before CPRG was called. Also, you CLEAR MEMORY in CPRG. This command, even though it is entered in CPRG, affects all memory variables in the system regardless of what routine created them. Using CLEAR MEMORY in a subroutine or PROCEDURE file erases all memory variables in the system. RELEASE ALL only affects those memory variables created by the currently running routine.

RESTORE

The RESTORE command is the counterpart of SAVE, discussed in the next section. The RESTORE command is used to bring memory variables stored in MEM files back into the current III PLUS system.

Syntax   The RESTORE command has two forms. The two forms affect memory differently. The basic command is

RESTORE FROM mem file

where mem file can be any valid dBASE III or III PLUS MEMory file created with the SAVE TO mem file command. The preceding command tells III PLUS to erase all existing memory variables and bring in all the variables in the named MEM file. The variables in the MEM file then become the current memory variables. Note that these MEM file variables will bring the values they had when they were SAVEd into the current system. The second form of the command is

RESTORE FROM mem file ADDITIVE

ADDITIVE is a qualifier for the RESTORE command. It tells III PLUS to keep all existing variables in the system and ADD(itive)

whatever variables are in the named MEM file to the system. A potential problem with this is having variables in the MEM file with the same name as those already declared in the system. III PLUS erases the existing variables and replaces them with the variables in the MEM file. This can cause some serious problems if you have declared something such as

NUMBER = 3

in the system and are RESTOREing something such as

NUMBER = "THREE"

Any operations on NUMBER are bound to go haywire, as it has changed data type.

Use   The RESTORE command is used to bring SAVEd memory variables back into the III PLUS system. This is useful when designing systems that have defaults set by the user.

Consider a system that sets defaults based on historical choices made by previous users. Such choices can be which printer port to use, whether or not to use a color monitor (if one is available), the width of memo fields, whether to run in an expert mode, and so on.

All of these things can be handled with some clever coding and a MEM file. Defaults can be set with code such as

```
* WRITUTIL.PRG < WRITE.PRG
* THIS PROGRAM IS THE UTILITY MODULE FOR THE WRITE.PRG
*
DO WHILE .T.
   CLEAR
   a 2, 0 TO 19,79 DOUBLE
   a 3,12 SAY [W R I T E    F O R    A    L I V I N G    ] +;
            [U T I L I T I E S]
   a 4,1 TO 4,78
   a  7,28 SAY [1. SET DATE TYPE]
   a  8,28 SAY [2. SET MESSAGE WAIT TIME]
   a  9,28 SAY [3. SET DEFAULT DRIVE]
   a 10,28 SAY [4. SET DEFAULT PATH]
   a 11,28 SAY [5. SELECT WORD PROCESSOR]
*    a 12,28 SAY [6. ]
*    a 13,28 SAY [7. ]
*    a 14,28 SAY [8. ]
*    a 15,28 SAY [9. ]
   a 17, 28 SAY '0. EXIT'
   STORE 0 TO selectnum
   a 19,33 SAY " select        "
   a 19,42 GET selectnum PICT "9" RANG 0,5
   READ
*
   DO CASE
```

```
        CASE selectnum = 0
          RETURN
        CASE selectnum = 1
          a 20,0 CLEA
          a 20,0 TO 23,79 DOUBLE
          a 21,28 SAY "1. SET DATE TO MM/DD/YY"
          a 22,28 SAY "2. SET DATE TO DD/MM/YY"
          a 23,33 SAY " select        "
          a 23,43 GET SELECTNUM PICT "9" RANG 1,2
          READ

          DATER = IIF(SELECTNUM = 1,"SET DATE AMER",;
                  "SET DATE BRIT")
          &DATER
        CASE selectnum = 2
          a 20,0 CLEA
          a 21,0 SAY "Current message wait time is " + ;
                  STR(WAITTIME)
          a 22,0 SAY "New message wait time -> " ;
                  GET WAITTIME PICT "99"
          READ
        CASE selectnum = 3
          a 20,0 CLEA
          a 21,0 SAY "Current default drive is " + CDRIVE
          a 22,0 SAY "New default drive is -> " ;
                  GET CDRIVE PICT "A"
          READ
          SET DEFA TO &CDRIVE
          CASE selectnum = 4
            a 20,0 CLEA
            a 21,0 SAY "Current default path is " + CPATH
            CPATH = CPATH + SPACE(30)
            a 22,0 SAY "New default path is -> " GET CPATH
            READ
            CPATH = TRIM(CPATH)
            SET PATH TO &CPATH
          CASE SELECTNUM = 5
            ACCE "What is the DOS command to start the " +;
                  "word processor? -> " TO WORDPROC
          OTIIE
            CLEA
            WAIT "SORRY, THAT ISN'T AN OPTION. " +;
                  "PRESS ANY KEY TO CONTINUE..."
      ENDCASE
   *
   ENDDO T
   *
   * EOF: WRITUTIL.PRG
```

This code handles drive, path, date, and message wait time for the
Personal Library System. There are several more options in the
actual system.

Note that this code doesn't have the RESTORE command. This
code is used to get system defaults from the user. These system
defaults are then SAVEd to a MEM file when the user quits the sys-

tem and returns to DOS. Then, when the user starts the system at some future time, these new defaults are RESTOREd. That code is shown below.

```
* SET SYSTEM DEFAULTS
REST FROM WRITE
SET PATH TO &CPATH
SET DEFA TO &CDRIVE
```

Here we only SET items from two RESTOREd memory variables, but the other memory variables are used later in the system.

SAVE

The SAVE command is the counterpart of the RESTORE command discussed in the last section. The SAVE command is used to store memory variables from the current system to MEM files.

Syntax   SAVE has six basic forms. The forms all relate to putting active memory variables into a MEM file. The six forms are

```
SAVE TO mem file
SAVE TO mem file variable list
SAVE TO mem file ALL
SAVE TO mem file ALL LIKE variable skeleton
SAVE TO mem file ALL EXCEPT exception skeleton
SAVE TO mem file ALL LIKE variable skeleton EXCEPT exception
skeleton
```

The first listed command is the basic form and shows the minimum amount of information the user must give III PLUS to SAVE anything in the system. In other words, you can't SAVE without giving III PLUS some idea of what variables you want SAVEd and where you want to SAVE them. You must include the name of at least one currently active memory variable, as in

SAVE TO mem file variable name

This tells III PLUS to place the named variable in the named MEM file. The MEM file can have any valid dBASE III PLUS file name. III PLUS will give the file a .MEM extension automatically. You can tell III PLUS to give the file a specific extension by including it in the SAVE command, as

SAVE TO SPECIAL.FLE

The preceding command would store all active memory variables to a MEM file called "SPECIAL.FLE". You would have to

RESTORE FROM SPECIAL.FLE

to access those variables, however. Note that no variables are listed in the preceding command but all active memory variables are SAVEd to the named file. The two command forms

```
SAVE TO mem file ALL
```

and

```
SAVE TO mem file
```

are identical in what they do. The SAVE command also allows you the option of SAVEing one or several active memory variables. You can SAVE more than one variable by naming the variables after the SAVE command with the command form

SAVE TO mem file variable list

The variables being SAVEd should be separated by commas (,).

The basic SAVE command will SAVE listed variables or ALL variables in memory. You can use qualifiers with SAVE TO ALL, just as you can with PRIVATE ALL. See the PRIVATE ALL command earlier in this chapter for details. The commands work in identical ways in this respect.

Use   SAVE is used to store memory variables from the current III PLUS system into a reusable MEM file. This is a useful ability when designing systems that have defaults set by the user.

As mentioned in the section on RESTORE, SAVE's best use is in setting defaults the user supplies to the system. A computer default is what the computer does when you fail to instruct it to do otherwise. The listing on page 400 shows code that gets a set of system defaults from the user. Normally, these system defaults are active only as long as the system is operating. A default is to be in the system and to be working during each work session. That would require the user to enter the defaults each time he or she started a work session.

A better alternative is to SAVE the defaults into a MEM file.

That file can be SAVEd at the end of each work session when the user returns the computer to DOS. Code to do that is simple.

```
SAVE TO WRITE
QUIT
```

Note that the code on page 400 does not SAVE new defaults. The user might change the defaults several times during a work session and so such disk work is unnecessary.

STORE

The STORE command provides III PLUS's principal means of getting values into memory variables. It has abilities similar to those of the equal sign (=) described earlier in this chapter, but can work on several variables at a time. The equal sign can only work on a single variable at a time. There is no advanced use of the STORE command.

Syntax   The STORE command has one form:

STORE value TO variable

This form is identical to the equal-sign form:

variable = value

The advantage of using STORE rather than the equal sign is the former's ability to STORE a single value to several variables simultaneously. This is done with

STORE value TO variable1, variable2, variable3,...

Note that the same value is STOREd to the listed variables. STORE doesn't limit you to what you can STORE to a variable. You can use other variables, as in

STORE variable1 TO variable list

You can use evaluated expressions, as in

STORE arithmetic expression TO variable list

You can even use database fields in the STORE command, as follows:

STORE field name TO variable list

STORE doesn't care if you use character, logical, date, or numeric data in the command. You can't STORE a MEMO field to a variable, however.

Use   The most important thing to remember about the STORE command is that III PLUS defaults to STOREing to memory variables instead of database fields. This is the opposite of the GET command described in Chapter 7 and earlier in this chapter. If you have a database with the field name RECEIVED and enter the command

STORE 1000 TO RECEIVED

III PLUS will not STORE 1000 TO the database field RECEIVED. It will create a new variable, RECEIVED, and STORE the 1000 TO that new variable. This can cause some programming problems and much confusion for those who are unaware of the M work area (see the M command section earlier in this chapter). They will use the STORE command as just described and believe they are STOREing information to the database. In reality, they are STOREing information to a single memory variable.

III PLUS does not use the STORE command for any database field work. You can use database fields as source values for memory variables, but you can't STORE something to a database field. Remember that you can use the work-area specifiers in front of a database field if you're getting data from a database not in the current work area:

STORE n —> field name TO variable

where n —> designates any of the ten III PLUS work area names (A through J), the name of the database in a work area, or the alias you assign a database when you USE it. For example, to STORE the value of the current RECEIVED field in work area 1 to a memory variable also called RECEIVED being used in work area 7, you'd enter

STORE A —> RECEIVED TO RECEIVED

SUM

The SUM command is covered thoroughly in Chapter 8. The text mentioned there that the command is used primarily with database fields. It can be used with memory variables when you SUM the sum of a database field with a memory variable; hence, it is included in this chapter. Briefly, the SUM command is used to determine the arithmetic sum of a database field over some selected portion of the database. That can be done with any of the SUM command forms shown here:

```
SUM
SUM TO variable
SUM field list TO variable list
SUM REST TO variable
SUM field list TO variable list REST
SUM field list TO variable list FOR condition
SUM field list TO variable list WHILE condition
SUM FOR condition
SUM field list FOR condition
SUM WHILE condition
SUM field list WHILE condition
SUM NEXT n field list
SUM field list TO variable list NEXT n
SUM field list TO variable list REST WHILE condition
SUM field list TO variable list REST FOR condition
```

In all these cases, fieldlist can be one or several names of fields in the current database. You can use the SUM command to determine the arithmetic sum of a memory variable added to a database field with the command form

SUM field1+variable1, field2+variable2,...qualifiers

where field1 and field2 represent valid dBASE III PLUS database field names from the current database, variable1 and variable2 represent valid dBASE III PLUS variable names, and qualifiers represents any mix of SUM's qualifiers, as shown in Chapter 8.

There are several reasons for SUMming database fields with memory variables. Some uses include weighting SUMs, determining statistical patterns and adjusting them, determining the best-fit factor for data, adjusting curves, and modifying and distributing data.

WAIT

The WAIT command has many of the abilities of the ACCEPT and

INPUT command. This section will explain the syntax and use of WAIT.

The WAIT command has two functions in III PLUS: to halt execution of the immediately running routine and to take information from the user and make it usable to the system. Note that the WAIT command is similar to the ACCEPT command in what it can WAIT for. ACCEPT and WAIT only take character data. You should read the section on INPUT if you're interested in getting noncharacter data. You can also use the GET and READ commands to get any data types (see Chapters 6 and 7 and the section on GET earlier in this chapter). The WAIT command is used primarily in programming applications.

Syntax   The WAIT command has a simple syntax that doesn't need any qualifiers. This is a distinction between WAIT and either INPUT or ACCEPT. The basic form is

WAIT

This tells III PLUS to halt whatever it's doing and display a standard prompt, "Press any key to continue...."

You can tell III PLUS to get whatever key is "pressed to continue" and store that key's value to a memory variable with

WAIT TO variable

```
-> WAIT
Press any key to continue...
-> WAIT TO VAR
Press any key to continue...3
-> ? TYPE("VAR")
C
-> WAIT TO VAR
Press any key to continue...T
-> ? TYPE("VAR")
C
-> GREETING = "AND FELICITATIONS! "
-> WAIT "GREETINGS " + GREETING TO VAR
GREETINGS AND FELICITATIONS! G
->
```

Figure 10-22.   WAIT prompts

III PLUS will create a new memory variable if none exists with the listed name. This is shown in Figure 10-22. ACCEPT and INPUT also create variables if none exist in memory with the listed name.

Both ACCEPT and WAIT can be used to get data from the user and put it into the system. The command forms are identical. However, WAIT only takes one character, while ACCEPT can take entire novels, should you wish to type them in. This is a principal difference between ACCEPT and WAIT.

The second method of WAITing for information is with a prompt in front of the TO. This method amounts to including a prompt as a qualifier. You can tell the user what you want to know with the command

WAIT "expression" TO variable

where variable is defined as just previously and expression is any delimited string. Naturally, anything that is delimited can be added to. You can include existing variables in your WAIT prompts as shown at the bottom of Figure 10-22. You can use numeric variables by converting them to text with the STR( ) function.

Use   The WAIT command is used to get information from the user into the system. This is almost always done programmatically, as few people will enter a WAIT command merely to have it come back at them a second later.

WAIT's stipulation that the user enter one character has some powerful uses. WAIT will take any character data as input, and it interprets a blank carriage return as a 0 value ASCII character. You can make use of this to develop a complex menu system that offers the user several options. The key to all that follows is

WAIT "Press the key for your selection —>" TO DOTHIS

All you need to know is that the user can select options as follows:

```
0 - EXIT PROGRAM
1 -> 9 - THESE CORRESPOND TO ASPECTS OF CLIENT RECORDS
A -> Z - THESE CORRESPOND TO SYSTEM PROGRAMS AND ANCILLARY .COM
FILES
a -> z - THESE CORRESPOND TO OPERATIONS ON CLIENT RECORDS
```

You need something that will take any of the information the preceding options can give. The solution is the WAIT command and the following code:

```
WAIT "Press the key for your selection -> " TO DOTHIS
*
DO CASE
   CASE ASC(DOTHIS) < 48
      DO ERRORMSS
   CASE ASC(DOTHIS) = 48
      SAVE TO SYSTEM
      QUIT
   CASE ASC(DOTHIS) < 58
      DO CLIRECMD
   CASE ASC(DOTHIS) < 65
      DO ERRORMSS
   CASE ASC(DOTHIS) < 91
      DO SYSPRGMD
   CASE ASC(DOTHIS) < 97
      DO ERRORMSS
   CASE ASC(DOTHIS) < 123
      DO CLIRECOP
   CASE ASC(DOTHIS) < 255
      DO ERRORMSS
ENDC
*
```

Note that it is assumed that nonprintable characters are going to get into WAIT. The first ones you WAIT for are the control codes. These have ASCII values less than 48. When you get them, you send out an error message. If you get 48, the ASCII value of 0, you SAVE your variables and QUIT to DOS. ASCII values less than 58 correspond to digits 1-9. Each of those is handled in the Client Record Modification routine. ASCII values from 58-64 represent :, ;, <, =, >, ?, and @. You don't do anything with these characters as far as this program is concerned, so send an error message when you get them. ASCII values less than 91—characters from A to Z—tell the program to do the SYSTEM and PROGRAM modules. ASCII values from 91-96 are other nonalphanumerics. ASCII values less than 122—characters from a to z—correspond to Client Record Operations. Lastly, any ASCII value over 122 gets an error message.

The code is straightforward and shows a powerful use of the WAIT command. You should note that the text uses an integer hierarchy for CASEs. First, there is a check for anything less than the ASCII value of 0 (48), then a check for 0, then a check for digits, then nonalphanumerics, UPPERCASE characters, more nonalphanumerics, lowercase characters, and graphics characters. This prevents the need for conditions such as

n <= ASC(DOTHIS) <= m

where n and m are the top and bottom of a range, such as 97-122 for lowercase letters.

ELEVEN

Parameter-Control Commands

The parameter-control commands are all the SET commands, CLEAR, EJECT, CLEAR FIELDS, CLEAR GETS, and CLEAR TYPEAHEAD. Parameter-control commands all share one trait: they affect how dBASE III PLUS sees the world, or how it shows you its world. Many of these commands are given here without "Advanced Use" and "Use" sections, as they are either on/off or transfer operations between devices.

The SET commands can be broken down into two types. The first are software switches, or "toggles." They turn something on or off in the III PLUS system. Such commands as SET CARRY ON and SET BELL ON are toggles, because both CARRY and BELL can be on or off depending on how you want III PLUS to do things. The second type of SET commands directs III PLUS's attention toward certain things. Examples of these commands are SET ALTERNATE TO, SET PRINTER TO, and SET CATALOG TO. They direct III PLUS's attention to creating an ALTERNATE file, sending output to a specific PRINTER, and using a specific CATALOG file, respectively.

This chapter covers three types of commands. The first are the non-SET parameter-control commands. The second are the SET toggles, and the third are the SET commands that direct III PLUS's attention elsewhere in the system. Note that many of the SET commands can be paralleled with CONFIG.DB commands (refer to Appendix C).

Following are the parameter-control commands that are not part of the SET parameter commands.

411

The CLEAR command has several qualifiers. This section covers the plain CLEAR command, unqualified. Information on the qualified CLEAR command can be found in Chapters 5, 7, and 10, as well as in this chapter (CLEAR FIELDS, CLEAR GETS, and CLEAR TYPEAHEAD).

Syntax   The CLEAR command is a single command that erases the screen. dBASE II programmers may remember that they had to use the ERASE command to blank the screen. This is not the case in dBASE III PLUS and has caused some problems for dBASE II programmers making the transition. The command is

CLEAR

without qualifiers.

Use   There isn't anything really to say about the unqualified CLEAR command. It is particularly useful with PRG files when menus are being generated. An example is shown in the following listing:

```
*
DO WHILE .T.
   CLEAR
   @ 2, 0 TO 14,79 DOUBLE
   @ 3,26 SAY "PERSONAL LIBRARY SYSTEM"
   @ 4,1 TO 4,78 DOUBLE
   @ 7,20 SAY [1. SELECT LIBRARY TO USE (CURRENT IS ] +;
NEWDRIVE + DBFILE + [)]
   @  8,20 SAY [2. EDITING MENU]
   @  9,20 SAY [3. REPORTS MENU]
   @ 10,20 SAY [4. LIBRARY PROGRAM UTILITIES]
   @ 12,20 SAY '0. EXIT'
   STORE 0 TO selectnum
   @ 14,33 SAY " select      "
   @ 14,41 GET selectnum PICTURE "9" RANGE 0,4
   READ
```

This listing is part of the main menu to the Personal Library System mentioned elsewhere in this book. The main menu comes up whenever the user is through working with other aspects of the program, such as database listings, I/O screens, and so on. Because you don't always know where other users have been before they get to the main menu, and because you don't always know what's been on the screen before they call up the main menu, you should CLEAR the screen. This ensures that you will have a blank page before you begin SAYing the menu options.

CLEAR FIELDS

The CLEAR FIELDS command is the counterpart to the SET FIELDS TO command discussed in the third section of this chapter. The SET FIELDS TO command tells III PLUS to show specific fields in the current database. This is equivalent to creating a filter that allows only certain fields to pass from the system to the user. The CLEAR FIELDS command eliminates the SET FIELDS filter from the current III PLUS system.

Syntax   The CLEAR FIELDS command is a qualified version of the CLEAR command. It directs III PLUS's attention to the fields set at some earlier time in a work session. The command is

CLEAR FIELDS

without qualifiers.

Use   The CLEAR FIELDS command eliminates all field filters created with all SET FIELDS TO commands. It operates in this way whether you are in INTERACTIVE or PROGRAM mode. Consider the following listing:

```
-> USE JDCBOOKS
-> SET FIELDS TO TITLE,AUTHOR
-> DISP
    500   Mysterious Island,
The                                      Jules
Verne

-> SELE 2
-> USE INCOME
-> SET FIELDS TO RECFOR,RECFROM
-> DISP
     1  DBASE III ADVANCED
PROGRAMMING                              Que
Corp
-> CLEA FIELDS
```

```
-> DISP
     1   DBASE III ADVANCED
PROGRAMMING                                            04/27/86 Que
Corp
2701.04 04/14/86
-> SELE 1
-> DISP
     500  Mysterious Island,
The                                                    Jules
Verne


Science
Fiction

JDC                        .F. .F.      0     0
.F.
```

Note the use of the dBASE III PLUS four-letter-word convention in the preceding listing. The listing shows two databases being opened in two different work areas. Each database has its fields set based on its own separate structure. Note that the SET FIELDS commands filter the databases so that only the fields listed in each SET FIELDS TO command are DISPLAYed.

In the previous example, you CLEARed FIELDS only in work area 2, but the effect of that action occurs throughout the system. Work area 1's and work area 2's SET FIELDS commands have been eliminated. Note that the CLEAR FIELDS command is not the same as

SET FIELDS TO

without any fields listed. That command only eliminates the current work area's SET FIELDS TO filter. In other words, SET FIELDS TO without a field list only affects the current database's field list. CLEAR FIELDS affects the field list in every work area.

CLEAR FIELDS also affects the SET FIELDS ON/off command. The SET FIELDS TO field-list command will remain active until you enter either

SET FIELDS TO

or

CLEAR FIELDS

The SET FIELDS TO field-list command will remain active but

will be ignored by III PLUS when you enter

SET FIELDS OFF

This tells III PLUS to keep the filter SET with SET FIELDS TO but
not to use it at present. The SET FIELDS on/OFF command is SET
ON automatically when you SET FIELDS TO field list. The CLEAR
FIELDS command automatically SETs FIELDS OFF.

CLEAR GETS

The CLEAR GETS command was discussed in Chapter 7. The command form is

CLEAR GETS

```
Record#  TITLE
      1  Roget's University Thesaurus
```

: Roget's University Thesaurus   :

: THIS IS A MEMORY VARIABLE:

->

Figure 11-1.   III PLUS will show information that exists at the GET
location

It is included in this chapter because CLEAR GETS determines the information kept in the input buffer. Information on setting the size of the input buffer and the CONFIG.DB GETS = n command can be found in Appendix C.

The CLEAR GETS command tells III PLUS to flush any information in the input buffer. The input buffer is used as an intermediate storage tank by III PLUS whenever it encounters an @...GET in either INTERACTIVE or PROGRAM mode. Two things happen when III PLUS encounters a GET command. If data exists in either the memory variable or database field that is being GETted, III PLUS will show that information at the GET location. This means that the code in the following listing will produce a screen like the one shown in Figure 11-1.

```
CLEAR
USE C:\LIBRARY\JDCBOOKS
DISP TITLE
MEMVAR = "THIS IS A MEMORY VARIABLE"
@ 10,0 GET TITLE
@ 12,0 GET MEMVAR
```

If no data exists in either the memory variable or the database field being GETted, III PLUS will show a blank space in the highlights in Figure 11-1.

Now, if you include a READ command at the end of the listing, you would be able to edit both database field and memory variable. (When you edit, you are changing the existing data or inputting new data.) The CLEAR GETS command is used when data exists and you don't want to change it.

The obvious way to prevent the user from making any changes is not to include a READ command at the end of some GET commands. That is a reasonable solution if you never intend to READ information at any point in your work session, but the assumption that you will not need to READ any information during a work session is unrealistic.

The solution is to flush the input buffer of any active GETS prior to READing the GETS you're interested in. If you had 20 GETS, all active and waiting to be edited, and you entered a CLEAR GETS followed by 20 more GETS and a READ, you'd only be able to EDIT the second 20 GETS. What use is that in the real world?

There are times you want to GET information from the database to the user but don't want to let the user do anything with that information. Such a time is when the system FINDs something in a database. You want the system to tell you what it found, and the most aesthetic way to so instruct the system is with @...SAY and @...GET commands. The @...SAY commands are grouped in a SAYER or SAY file. The @...GET commands are grouped in a GETTER or GET file. The function of GETTER files is to GET information from the user to the database and vice versa.

CLEAR GETS can tell III PLUS to flush the GET buffer of all information. Information that has already been GETted to the screen will stay there until it is either CLEARed or written over with some other data-display command.

CLEAR TYPEAHEAD

The CLEAR TYPEAHEAD command is similar to the CLEAR GETS command in that it flushes one of the memory buffers III PLUS sets up when you first start the dBASE III PLUS system. The CLEAR TYPEAHEAD command flushes the TYPEAHEAD buffer. Information on the CONFIG.DB TYPEAHEAD command can be found in Appendix C. Both use and advanced use of the command are discussed in the "Use" section.

Syntax   The command form is

CLEAR TYPEAHEAD

The command can be shortened, using the dBASE III PLUS four-letter-word convention, to

CLEA TYPE

Use   The CLEAR TYPEAHEAD command determines what information is kept in the III PLUS keyboard buffer. Don't confuse this buffer with the DOS keyboard buffer, nor should you liken the III PLUS keyboard buffer with any keyboard buffers created by keyboard-encoding programs such as SuperKey, Keyworks, and ProKey.

III PLUS creates its own keyboard buffer when you use either the CONFIG.DB TYPEAHEAD or SET TYPEAHEAD TO command. The TYPEAHEAD buffer can hold anywhere from 0-32,000 keystrokes. III PLUS's default value for the buffer is 20 keystrokes. Having the TYPEAHEAD buffer allows the user to continue inputting information while III PLUS works its way through complex manipulations.

That ability makes a keyboard buffer useful in a number of applications. With such a buffer, speed typists don't have to worry about losing information when the computer is working on something and they are already typing information into the system that will go on the next input screen. This same situation often presents a problem for people who have become so familiar with a system that they anticipate the system's prompts and answer before questions are asked. Between speed typing and anticipating prompts, the danger exists of putting the wrong information into the system without realizing it. The CLEAR TYPEAHEAD command provides the solution.

The CLEAR TYPEAHEAD command is used whenever the programmer/developer wants to be sure the user doesn't get the wrong information into the system at a particular time. One application in which it is particularly useful is when you are dealing with error messages. An example is shown in the following listing:

```
PROC ERRORMSS
CLEAR TYPEAHEAD
SET COLOR TO W+*
*
DO CASE
   CASE ERROR() = 1
      a 0,0 SAY "That file doesn't exist on drive "+;
      NEWDRIVE
      DO POOL
      SET COLOR TO
      RETU TO MASTER
   CASE ERROR() = 4
      a 24,50 say "Record Number -> END "
      a 0,0 SAY "You're at the end of the file now. "
   CASE ERROR() = 5
      a 24,50 say "Record Number -> END "
      a 0,0 SAY "You can't CONTINUE any further."+;
      "You're at the end."
   CASE ERROR() = 38
      a 24,50 say "Record Number -> 0 "
      a 0,0 SAY "You can't go any further."+;
      " You're at the beginning now. "
   CASE ERROR() = 42
      a 0,0 SAY "You must LOCATE before you can CONTINUE. "
```

```
            CASE ERROR() = 114
               CLEAR
               @ 10,10 TO 20,70 DOUBLE
               @ 15,15 SAY "The INDEX file is damaged, "+;
               "excuse me while I REINDEX"
               REIN
            CASE ERROR() = 125
               @ 0,0 SAY "Please turn the PRINTER ON."
            OTHE
               @ 0,0 SAY "I'VE ENCOUNTERED AN UNKNOWN ERROR. "+;
               "PLEASE TRY AGAIN"
      ENDC
      *
      DO POOL
      SET COLOR TO
      *
      ** EOP
      *
      PROC POOL
      LAPS = 0
      *
      DO WHILE LAPS < WAITTIME
         LAPS = LAPS + 1
      ENDD
      *
      ** EOP
```

The set of errors given in these CASE statements is not an exhaustive list of what can go wrong. What should be noted is that the CLEAR TYPEAHEAD command appears immediately at the start of the ERRORMSS procedure. Its presence makes sure there is no new information in III PLUS's keyboard buffer to interrupt the system. (You could also create a high-intensity blinking display with the SET COLOR TO command to get the user's attention.)

EJECT

The EJECT command affects the printer and print buffer, if these devices are attached to the system and are on when the system is running.

Syntax   The command can be entered in either INTERACTIVE or PROGRAM mode as

EJECT

Several commands and file types incorporate EJECT in their structure. Examples are LBL and FRM files and the REPORT and LABEL commands.

Use   The only function the EJECT command has is to force the printer to advance one page.

Most printers know how many lines are allowed on a page. The standard 11-inch-long page has 66 lines in 10 cpi (characters per inch) mode. This is also known as 6 lpi (lines per inch) mode. The same page can have 88 lines in either 12 or 15 cpi mode, also known as 8 lpi. No matter what lpi and cpi you're using, the printer will usually know ahead of time how many lines the system expects to fit on a page. This implies the printer knows where page breaks are and won't print over them unless told to do so. The printer knows where page breaks occur because it uses its own internal line counter. This counter tells the printer that it is currently on line 50 of a 66-line page, or line 30 of an 88-line page, and so on.

The EJECT command tells the printer two things. The first and most obvious is that it is to go to the top of the next page. Whatever page is currently under the printhead in the printer will be thrown clear of the printhead. A new page will be loaded in the printer and placed under the printhead. The second thing the EJECT command does is flush the printer buffer, if one exists. The reason EJECT flushes the printer buffer has to do with the difference between printing characters and moving the current page through the printer. Printing characters involves using the printhead and getting information on paper. Execution of the EJECT command involves moving the paper though the platen, rollers, tractor feed, cut-sheet feeder, and so on.

Printing priority is information first, paper movement second. The printer gets a command to EJECT a page and is therefore forced to first clear the print buffer of any information before throwing the page. This procedure is useful with commands like LIST TO PRINTER. This LIST command doesn't send a new page through the printer when III PLUS is done LISTing. The solution is something like

```
LIST TO PRINTER
EJECT
```

Following are the SET toggle commands—that is, those commands that can be SET either on or off. Examples of SET parameter on/off commands are SET EXACT on/OFF, SET ALTERNATE on/OFF, SET PRINT on/OFF, and SET CONSOLE ON/off. The defaults are given in UPPERCASE in each instance. Many of these commands have comparable CONFIG.DB commands and are discussed in Appendix C. Also note that some of these commands do not operate unless a SET parameter TO command has been entered first. Two of these are SET CATALOG on/OFF and SET ALTERNATE on/OFF.

SET

The SET command is an interactive, menu-driven command that is similar to the ASSIST menu system. The command is included in this chapter because it controls many of the SET toggle and SET parameter TO commands.

Syntax   The SET command can be used in either INTERAC-TIVE or PROGRAM mode. The menu system is activated with

SET

and opens with a screen similar to the one shown in Figure 11-2. There are 25 on/off toggles in the complete SET system. Not all of these toggles can be shown on one screen; pressing END will display the remaining SET toggles. (The toggles in the figure are the defaults set for the text's sample system. You may not have the same ones turned on and off.)

Note that the CATALOG option has neither an on nor an off after it. You must first SET CATALOG TO cat file before you can turn the CATALOG on or off. The system pictured here doesn't have any CAT files active, so III PLUS doesn't allow the option of turning one on or off.

Use   You move through the SET menu system with the cursor movement keys. The SET menu options are listed along the top row of the screen. You can select a menu option by moving the cursor to it and pressing RETURN or typing the first letter of the menu selection you want to activate. Through each menu option you can open a sub-menu similar to the ones shown in Figure 11-2.

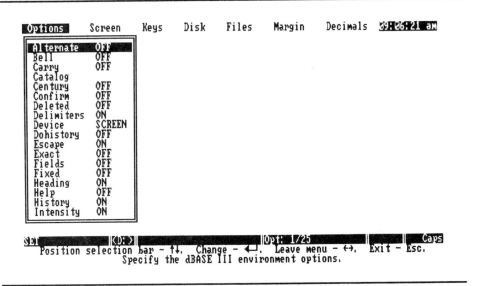

| Options | Screen | Keys | Disk | Files | Margin | Decimals | 09:06:21 am |

```
Alternate    OFF
Bell         OFF
Carry        OFF
Catalog
Century      OFF
Confirm      OFF
Deleted      OFF
Delimiters   ON
Device       SCREEN
Dohistory    OFF
Escape       ON
Exact        OFF
Fields       OFF
Fixed        OFF
Heading      ON
Help         OFF
History      ON
Intensity    ON
```

SET |(D:)| |Opt: 1/25| Caps
Position selection bar - ↑↓, Change - ↵, Leave menu - ↔, Exit - Esc.
Specify the dBASE III environment options.

Figure 11-2. The SET menu system's opening screen

This section will deal only with the SET OPTIONS submenu. This submenu corresponds to the SET parameter on/off commands covered in this part of the chapter. Figure 11-2 shows one option that is neither on nor off, DEVICE. The standard SET DEVICE TO command is actually a toggle that has SCREEN/printer in place of ON/off. The SET DEVICE TO command is also covered in Chapter 8. The remainder of the options are covered in this section of the chapter. You can find out about SET's Alternate option by reading the section on SET ALTERNATE on/OFF, and so on.

You can toggle each of the SET options on or off by highlighting it and pressing RETURN. Pressing RETURN once will turn an option off if it was on and on if it was off. For instance, highlighting ALTERNATE and pressing RETURN will toggle the ALTERNATE file ON or OFF, depending on its previous setting. You can move through the options list with the vertical-movement cursor keys (UP and DOWN ARROW, PGUP and PGDN, and HOME and END).

You tell III PLUS you've finished SETting things by pressing the ESCAPE key. III PLUS activates your SET commands and returns you to the dBASE prompt in INTERACTIVE mode or to the program in PROGRAM mode once you press the ESCAPE key.

The text mentioned earlier that you can use SET in the PROGRAM mode. You really shouldn't do that. Most programmers/developers spend a lot of time writing and creating their system. You don't want some user to have death-dealing power over your hard work. The majority of things you SET should stay as you SET them through the life of the program. You could create your own SET menu system. That would allow you control of what the user can SET.

SET ALTERNATE on/OFF

The SET ALTERNATE on/OFF command is used to echo/NOT ECHO screen information to the ALTERNATE file. The ALTERNATE file is created with the SET ALTERNATE TO txt file command. The SET ALTERNATE ON/off command was discussed in Chapter 4; refer to that chapter for details on its syntax and use.

SET BELL ON/off

The SET BELL command tells III PLUS to RING/not ring the buzzer/bell/noisemaker at different times during a work session.

Syntax   The command form is

SET BELL toggle

where toggle is either ON or off, depending on how much noise you like during a work session. The III PLUS system default is ON. You can find out how your system's BELL sounds by entering

? CHR(7)

at the dBASE prompt. CHR(7) is the ASCII CHaRacter code for the system bell. The number 7 comes from the days when computer terminals were actually teletypewriters, had no lowercase characters, and couldn't pass 20,000 volts at 400 amps through the keyboard and therefore had to go "DING!" to get your attention.

Use   The SET BELL toggle affects more than just your ears. III PLUS uses the bell when entering data in a GET command. Try entering the following code

```
HOLE = SPACE(5)
SET BELL ON
a 10,0 GET HOLE
READ
SET BELL OFF
a 10,0 GET HOLE
READ
```

in III PLUS. If you've typed in the code as it is listed, your cursor will be blinking in the GET field when you enter the first READ command. Just hold down the space bar until the cursor has moved through the field. You'll hear a ding when the cursor hits the last character position in the input field. You won't hear the ding when you repeat the exercise at the second READ command.

The purpose of this command use is to let users know when they are exiting from an input or edit field and are entering the next input or edit field. You can accompany the SET BELL toggle with the SET CONFIRM toggle (described later in this chapter) to force the user to press RETURN to exit from one input/edit field and go to the next one. III PLUS will keep on dinging at users until they've pressed RETURN, if you've SET BELL ON. This noise can do more than annoy users. It also might cause them to check their input visually for accuracy.

SET CARRY on/OFF

The SET CARRY toggle is designed for use with the data-addition commands APPEND and INSERT. The command is also one of the CONFIG.DB commands discussed in Appendix C.

Syntax   The command form is

SET CARRY toggle

where toggle can be on or OFF. The III PLUS default setting is OFF.

Use   The SET CARRY command's effect is felt when you add records with the APPEND, INSERT, and INSERT BEFORE commands. SET CARRY tells III PLUS to copy/NOT COPY the previous record's data to the new record. APPENDing with SET CARRY on tells III PLUS to get the data in the last record in the database and place it in the new, APPENDed record. Likewise, INSERTing with SET CARRY on tells III PLUS to get the data from the record at the present location and copy that data to the new, INSERTed record. INSERTing BEFORE with SET CARRY on tells III PLUS to get the data from the record directly before the present record location and copy that data to the new, INSERTed BEFORE record. This command is useful when entering repetitive data into a database. You can

SET CARRY ON

and have the last-entered record's information echoed in the record being entered. This can save you a lot of keystrokes. You should remember to SET CARRY OFF when you are through adding data, however. The SET CARRY toggle is not limited to a single work area, even in PROGRAM mode. You may SET CARRY ON in work area 1 and that same command will affect data being added to open DBFs in work areas 2-10.

Also note that the command doesn't affect either APPEND BLANK or INSERT BLANK. Those commands enter blank records into the database. Nothing is CARRYed into the new record when you APPEND BLANK or INSERT BLANK, even when SET CARRY is ON. You can CARRY into a new record regardless of any active FMT, NDX, CAT, VUE, or other dBASE III PLUS files. Lastly, any records created with SET CARRY on behave like regularly APPENDed and INSERTed records.

Those who read the sections in Chapter 6 on APPEND and INSERT may remember that you have to enter information into the APPENDed and INSERTed records for those records to remain in the database. The same is true for CARRYed, APPENDed, and INSERTed records. Unless you make some changes to the new record, it will not remain in the database. Note that the text is not discussing APPENDed BLANK or INSERTed BLANK records here.

Advanced Use   This section is going to differ slightly from the other "Advanced Use" sections in this book. It tells you why you don't want to use this specific command in a certain way.

If you've followed the code in this book, you may wonder why records in a database aren't duplicated with the SET CARRY ON and APPEND or INSERT commands. The preferred method here is to use the COPY NEXT 1 TO tank file command, followed by the APPENDing of the one record tank file to the desired database. The code that does that is shown in the following listing:

```
find desired record
*
COPY NEXT 1 TO TANK
APPEND FROM TANK
*
continue with work session
```

The reason is simple. You must make changes to the newly APPENDed or INSERTed record when SET CARRY is ON. If you don't make at least one change, the record will not stay in the database. So, even though the code used here causes III PLUS to do a bit more work than is necessary, it doesn't require a guarantee that the user will do some editing on the new record. That requirement is a fatal flaw with the SET CARRY ON command.

SET CATALOG on/OFF

The SET CATALOG toggle is directly related to the SET CATALOG TO command. Information on CAT files can be found in Chapter 2.

Syntax   The command form is

SET CATALOG toggle

where toggle tells III PLUS to select files/NOT TO SELECT FILES based on information stored in the currently active CAT file. CAT files are opened with the SET CATALOG TO cat file command.

Use   The SET CATALOG toggle tells III PLUS how to respond to the following queries:

```
MODIFY LABEL ?
MODIFY REPORT ?
MODIFY QUERY ?
MODIFY SCREEN ?
```

```
MODIFY VIEW ?
LABEL FORM ?
REPORT FORM ?
SET FILTER TO FILE ?
SET FORMAT TO ?
SET VIEW TO ?
USE ?
```

The III PLUS default is OFF because III PLUS is designed to start with no active CAT files. You can tell III PLUS to start working with an open CAT file with the CONFIG.DB CATALOG command (see Appendix C). You can also tell III PLUS to open a CAT file with the SET CATALOG TO cat file command. Both the SET and CONFIG.DB forms automatically SET CATALOG ON.

Note that this command is not the equivalent of the blank command

SET CATALOG TO

That command closes the open CAT file. The SET CATALOG toggle merely tells III PLUS whether or not to base file selections on information in the CAT file. Also note that the SET CATALOG toggle doesn't affect the query

SET CATALOG TO ?

The command makes a request to III PLUS directly, not to any user-based CAT files.

SET CENTURY on/OFF

The SET CENTURY toggle affects how III PLUS displays the last four digits of any date data type. The command has the same function as the CONFIG.DB CENTURY command discussed in Appendix C.

Syntax   The command form is

SET CENTURY toggle

where toggle is either on or OFF depending on whether you want/DO NOT WANT to see the first two digits of the year in your DATE fields. In other words, this command determines whether you see 1986 or 86. The default is OFF, which means you'd normally see the last two digits in the year field of a DATE field (86 for this year).

Use   The SET CENTURY toggle has the ability to fool III PLUS into making DATE fields appear bigger than they are. You can see this by creating a database with a DATE field. Such a database is shown in Figure 11-3. The top of the figure shows the RECDATE field eight characters long. Likewise, querying RECDATE for its data returns an eight-character date. You next SET CENTURY ON and repeat your query. This time, you're given a ten-digit date display, even though the database field is still only eight characters wide.

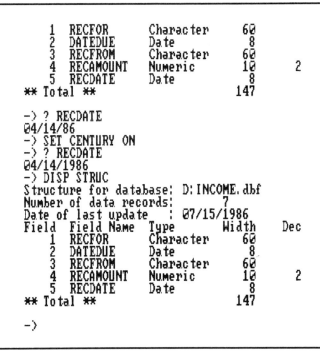

```
        1   RECFOR      Character    60
        2   DATEDUE     Date          8
        3   RECFROM     Character    60
        4   RECAMOUNT   Numeric      10        2
        5   RECDATE     Date          8
     ** Total **                    147

     -> ? RECDATE
     04/14/86
     -> SET CENTURY ON
     -> ? RECDATE
     04/14/1986
     -> DISP STRUC
     Structure for database: D:INCOME.dbf
     Number of data records:       7
     Date of last update   : 07/15/1986
     Field  Field Name  Type        Width   Dec
        1   RECFOR      Character    60
        2   DATEDUE     Date          8
        3   RECFROM     Character    60
        4   RECAMOUNT   Numeric      10        2
        5   RECDATE     Date          8
     ** Total **                    147

     ->
```

Figure 11-1.   The SET CENTURY toggle fools III PLUS into making DATE fields ten characters long even though the DBF file keeps the field eight characters wide

III PLUS defaults to dates in the twentieth century and requires you to enter the first two digits of the year if you're working with dates outside this century. Note that you cannot enter dates that are not twentieth-century dates with the CENTURY SET OFF, which is the system default. The SET CENTURY toggle works with any of the full-screen editing commands discussed in Chapter 7.

SET COLOR on/off

The SET COLOR toggle is an interesting feature of the III PLUS system in that it shows III PLUS's awareness of more than one monitor attached to the computer. The syntax is identical to that of the other on/off commands—it is

SET COLOR toggle

but toggle isn't as simple as on or off. The SET COLOR toggle is used to switch from a color monitor to a monochrome monitor, provided your system has both. A little more confusion is added because III PLUS takes its monitor cue from either the system or the CONFIG.DB file. The CONFIG.DB COLOR command tells III PLUS to use a color monitor if one is attached to the system. Assuming you have a color monitor attached to your system and the COLOR command in your CONFIG.DB file, entering

SET COLOR OFF

tells III PLUS to switch to the monochrome monitor. Again, this assumes you have a monochrome monitor attached to the system. If you don't have the COLOR command in your CONFIG.DB file, but the system is currently using the color monitor, and you enter

SET COLOR OFF

the computer will switch to the monochrome monitor. The following is a logic table for monitor states:

```
CONFIG.DB COLOR ON    ->    SYSTEM STARTS WITH COLOR MONITOR

      MONITOR STATUS -> MONOCHROME              COLOR
                            ACTIVE              ACTIVE
```

```
        SET COLOR           -NOTHING-           -SWITCH
          OFF                                 TO MONO-

        SET COLOR           -SWITCH             -NOTHING-
          ON                TO COLOR-
```

CONFIG.DB COLOR OFF OR NOT USED -> III PLUS STARTS WITH ACTIVE MONITOR

```
    MONITOR STATUS -> MONOCHROME             COLOR
                        ACTIVE               ACTIVE

        SET COLOR           -NOTHING-           -SWITCH
          OFF                                 TO MONO-

        SET COLOR           -SWITCH             -NOTHING-
          ON                TO COLOR-
```

Note that this command doesn't affect the SET COLOR TO options; it is merely a software switch that allows you to go from one monitor to

Figure 11-4.   The SET Screen menu option

another. If your system only has one monitor, the command

SET COLOR OFF

has no effect. However, the command

SET COLOR ON

is equivalent to CLEAR in that it CLEARs the screen.

Note that the COLOR option isn't on the SET Options menu. You can move the cursor to the SET Screen Menu (see Figure 11-4) and find out what monitor III PLUS thinks your system has by choosing the Display Type line. III PLUS assumes the monitor it starts with is the default monitor. This means it assumes the default is color if you start your III PLUS work session with a color monitor and defaults to monochrome if you start your work session with a monochrome monitor.

SET CONFIRM on/OFF

The SET CONFIRM toggle has one purpose: to tell III PLUS how to exit from a data-entry field. The command syntax is

SET CONFIRM toggle

where toggle has the conventional meaning of on or OFF. The following code demonstrates the SET CONFIRM toggle's properties:

```
HOLE = SPACE(5)
CLEAR
SET CONFIRM ON
a 10,0 GET HOLE
READ
SET CONFIRM OFF
a 10,0 GET HOLE
READ
```

Type something after you enter the first READ. III PLUS will not let you exit from the first @...GET...READ combination until you press RETURN. You will stay in the GET field forever or until you press RETURN when CONFIRM is ON. The second READ tells a different story. III PLUS exits from the GET field as soon as the field is filled. The SET CONFIRM toggle behaves identically to the CONFIG.DB CONFIRM command discussed in Appendix C.

SET CONSOLE ON/off

The SET CONSOLE toggle is unique among the SET parameter toggle commands, as SET CONSOLE only works in PROGRAM mode.

Syntax   The command's syntax is identical to those of all SET toggles:

SET CONSOLE toggle

where toggle is either ON or off. III PLUS defaults to ON.

Use   The SET CONSOLE toggle can only be used in the PROGRAM mode. III PLUS forces the CONSOLE ON in INTERACTIVE mode. The command is used to shut off the screen in PROGRAM mode.

Advanced Use   The "Use" section showed SET CONSOLE's ability to turn the screen off in PROGRAM mode. That code only showed SET CONSOLE's ability to hide screen output. SET CONSOLE can also be used to hide input. That ability lends itself to use of code designed for entering passwords. The following shows code that hides input from prying eyes.

```
USE password file
@ 10,10 SAY "ENTER YOUR PASSWORD -> " GET PSWD
SET CONS OFF
READ
SET CONS ON
```

Remember that this won't work in INTERACTIVE mode.

The SET DEBUG toggle is used as a debugging tool and is also referenced in Chapter 15.

Syntax   The command syntax is

SET DEBUG toggle

where toggle is either on or OFF. Note that III PLUS defaults to OFF unless the CONFIG.DB DEBUG command is ON.

Use   The command itself has no effect on III PLUS unless the SET ECHO command is also ON. You have to understand ECHO before you can understand DEBUG. ECHO tells III PLUS whether or not to list every interactive command or program line on the screen as it is executed. This procedure can cause confusion in a program that writes a menu to the screen. But what if you want to see the commands listed as they are being executed? Enter the SET DEBUG ON command. SET DEBUG tells III PLUS to send the ECHOed commands to the printer instead of to the screen. The result is a hard-copy list of the commands as they are being executed and a nice, clean screen that shows what the commands are doing. Note that the SET DEBUG toggle has no effect on III PLUS unless ECHO is turned ON, either with the SET toggle or the CONFIG.DB ECHO command.

Advanced Use   The SET DEBUG toggle will increase in effectiveness when used in conjunction with the SET STEP ON command. This combination tells III PLUS to query the user as to what to do next. SET DEBUG ON tells III PLUS to send that query to the printer. The result is the ability to see each program line as it is executed by III PLUS. Normally, III PLUS executes commands faster than the printer can list them. This might not prove satisfactory for debugging purposes; the following code is offered. (This code should be entered before you DO your PRG file.)

```
SET DEBUG ON
SET ECHO ON
SET STEP ON
```

The SET DELETED toggle tells III PLUS how to treat records marked with the DELETE command. Uses were given for the SET DELETED toggle in Chapter 7.

Syntax   The command syntax is

SET DELETED toggle

where toggle is either on or OFF. Note that III PLUS defaults to OFF unless the CONFIG.DB DELETED command is ON (see Appendix C).

Use   The SET DELETED toggle tells III PLUS whether or not to show records marked for DELETEion with the DELETE command. In that sense, it is a software filter, much like a filter used with a QRY file or the SET FILTER TO command. The filter used here is internal to III PLUS and doesn't show up in the database or in a DISPLAY STATUS command. An example of the SET DELETED toggle is shown in Figure 11-5. The top of Figure 11-5 shows a data-

```
-> USE INCOME
-> DELE NEXT 5
-> DISP ALL TRIM(RECFOR)
Record#  TRIM(RECFOR)
       1 *DBASE III ADVANCED PROGRAMMING
       2 *Reimbursement
       3 *Review
       4 *Article
       5 *DBASE III ADVANCED PROGRAMMING
       6  CONSULTING
       7  DBASE III ADVANCED PROGRAMMING
-> SET DELE ON
-> DISP ALL TRIM(RECFOR)
Record#  TRIM(RECFOR)
       6  CONSULTING
       7  DBASE III ADVANCED PROGRAMMING
-> 
```

Figure 11-5.   The SET DELETED ON command filters DELETED records from the system

base with some records marked for DELETEion. III PLUS shows which records are marked with an asterisk (*) immediately following the record number. After the execution of SET DELETED ON, the marked records are not DISPLAYed. Note that RECALL ALL, the command used to unmark ALL DELETED records, has no effect if SET DELETED is ON.

SET DELIMITERS on/OFF

The SET DELIMITERS toggle tells III PLUS to/NOT TO delimit data and memory-variable input fields. The command syntax is

SET DELIMITERS toggle

where toggle is either on or OFF. Note that III PLUS defaults to OFF unless the CONFIG.DB DELIMITERS command is ON.

This command doesn't create delimiters. You create delimiters with either the SET DELIMITERS TO or CONFIG.DB DELIMIT-ERS commands. The SET DELIMITERS toggle tells III PLUS to/NOT TO delimit input fields. III PLUS doesn't care if the input field is a memory-variable or a data field. Delimiters show the user the boundaries of the input field.

SET DOHISTORY on/OFF

The SET DOHISTORY toggle tells III PLUS to/NOT TO store pro-gram lines in a special memory buffer. The command syntax is

SET DOHISTORY toggle

where toggle is either on or OFF. Note that III PLUS defaults to OFF. There is no comparable CONFIG.DB command.

III PLUS normally creates a special memory buffer called HIS-TORY. This HISTORY buffer acts as a repository for command lines executed in PROGRAM mode. Note that the SET DOHISTORY tog-gle doesn't affect interactive commands entered at the dBASE prompt; it only affects program commands executed through a dBASE III PLUS PRG, PRC, or similar program file. This command doesn't create DOHISTORY. You create the HISTORY buffer with either the SET HISTORY TO or CONFIG.DB HISTORY commands.

The SET DOHISTORY command is useful during program development. The careful programmer can capture all the executed program lines into the HISTORY buffer. III PLUS will stop executing program lines when it encounters an error in the programming logic. The line that produced the error will be the last line in the HISTORY buffer if DOHISTORY is SET ON. You can also use the SET DOHISTORY command to capture lines that execute but don't produce the desired results. These are the worst kinds of bugs, as nothing tells you an error exists until after the damage has been done. The SET DOHISTORY toggle is also discussed in Chapter 15.

SET ECHO on/OFF

The SET ECHO toggle is used as a debugging tool and is also referenced in Chapter 15.

Syntax   The command syntax is

SET ECHO toggle

where toggle is either on or OFF. Note that III PLUS defaults to OFF unless the CONFIG.DB ECHO command is ON.

Use   The SET ECHO command was also referenced with the SET DEBUG toggle earlier in this chapter. Unlike SET DEBUG, SET ECHO affects III PLUS regardless of the status of SET DEBUG. ECHO tells III PLUS whether or not to list every interactive or program command on the screen as it is executed. This action can cause confusion in a program that writes a menu to the screen. The SET ECHO ON command is useful if you want to see program command lines listed as they are being executed. The SET ECHO toggle lists the command lines to the printer if SET DEBUG is ON.

Advanced Use   The SET ECHO toggle increases in effectiveness when used in conjunction with the SET STEP ON command. This combination tells III PLUS to query the user as to what to do next. SET ECHO ON tells III PLUS to list the command before it is executed. The result is the ability to see each program line on the screen before it is executed by III PLUS.

SET ESCAPE ON/off

The SET ESCAPE toggle is comparable to the DOS CONFIG.SYS BREAK ON command. The BREAK ON command tells DOS to stop whatever it's doing when the user presses the CTRL-BREAK key combination. The SET ESCAPE ON command tells III PLUS to stop whatever it's doing when the user presses the ESCAPE key.

Syntax   The command syntax is

SET ESCAPE toggle

where toggle is either on or OFF. Note that III PLUS defaults to ON unless the CONFIG.DB ESCAPE command is off.

Use   The SET ESCAPE toggle serves to ACTIVATE/deactivate the ESCAPE key, which will halt computation. Figure 11-6 shows III PLUS's reaction to the user pressing the ESCAPE key. Note that these messages come up because SET ESCAPE is ON—the III PLUS default.

```
-> DISP ALL                                                    DATEDUE  R
Record#  RECFOR                                      RECAMOUNT  RECDATE
ECFROM                                                         06/16/86 N
         6  CONSULTING                                  50.00 05/30/86
RPC
*** INTERRUPTED ***
-> DO BOXER
*** INTERRUPTED ***
Called from - D:BOXER.prg
Cancel, Ignore, or Suspend? (C, I, or S)
```

Figure 11-6.   The SET ESCAPE toggle tells III PLUS how to react to the ESCAPE key being pressed

The SET EXACT toggle tells III PLUS how specific to be when you FIND, SEEK, and LOCATE something in your database.

Syntax   The command syntax is

SET EXACT toggle

where toggle is either on or OFF. Note that III PLUS defaults to OFF unless the CONFIG.DB EXACT command is on.

Use   SET EXACT tells III PLUS how specific to be when looking for something. The syntax is given in the previous section. This section shows how the command operates.

If you have two text strings, "ABCDEF" and "ABC", III PLUS tells you that they aren't equal, as you'd expect. The actual evaluation would be

"ABC" = "ABCDEF"

Again, you'd expect III PLUS to say the two text strings aren't identical. What about the reverse equality?

"ABCDEF" = "ABC"

Do they match? III PLUS thinks they do. What's going on with the standard rules of equality? They're being abused by a computer, which doesn't think of equalities as we do. A computer looks at an expression such as

variable = value

and has no concept of equality. If you tell it

R1986 = "Receipts 1986"

the computer sets aside space in memory, places the text string "Receipts 1986" in the space, and gives the space the name R1986. Whenever the computer gets a request for R1986, it goes to that space in memory, looks for what is in the space, and uses whatever it finds, in this case, "Receipts 1986."

Now let's consider two separate text strings: "Receipts 1986" and

"Receipts". Is the text string "Receipts" also in the text string "Receipts 1986"? Yes. Is the reverse true? No. The text string "Receipts 1986" isn't part of the text string "Receipts". So how does III PLUS think of equivalencies? The first question, "Is 'Receipts' part of 'Receipts 1986'?" is read by III PLUS as, "Is the text string "Receipts" part of the text string 'Receipts 1986'?" III PLUS responds with Yes. The second question, "Is 'Receipts 1986' in 'Receipts'?" is read by III PLUS as, "Is the text string 'Receipts 1986' part of the text string 'Receipts'?" III PLUS says No.

Back to ABCDEF and ABC. ABC is one piece, a small part of ABCDEF. So, is "ABC" also in "ABCDEF"? Yes. Is "ABCDEF" also in "ABC"? No. Now, note how III PLUS determines the equivalency in Figure 11-7. The next-to-the-last query is

? "ABCDEF" = "BCD"

III PLUS returns No because of III PLUS's insistence on scanning for matches from left to right. You are actually asking III PLUS, "Is B the first character in ABCDEF?" The answer is No.

What happens when SET EXACT is ON? III PLUS begins thinking the way you would, as shown in the last line of the figure.

```
-> SET EXACT OFF
-> ? "ABC" = "ABCDEF"
.F.
-> ? "ABCDEF" = "ABC"
.T.
-> ? "ABCDEF" = "BCD"
.F.
-> SET EXACT ON
-> ? "ABCDEF" = "ABC"
.F.
->
```

Figure 11-7.   The SET EXACT command tells III PLUS how to answer questions of equivalency

The SET FIELDS toggle is the accompanying command to SET FIELDS TO. The command's syntax is

SET FIELDS toggle

where toggle has the conventional meaning of on or OFF. The SET FIELDS toggle tells III PLUS whether to pay attention to the fields list given in the SET FIELDS TO command. An example of this is shown in Figure 11-8. Figure 11-8 shows the INCOME database being USEd and then some fields being SET. The next command is DISPLAY. Note that only the fields listed in the SET FIELDS TO command are DISPLAYed. This happens because the SET FIELDS TO command automatically SETs FIELDS ON. III PLUS defaults to SET FIELDS OFF unless the CONFIG.DB FIELDS command is ON.

You next SET FIELDS OFF and DISPLAY again. III PLUS now DISPLAYs all the fields in the record. The last two lines SET FIELDS back ON and DISPLAY again. Note that the SET FIELDS toggle also affects fields SET with the SET VIEW TO command. A possible problem you might encounter with the SET FIELDS toggle

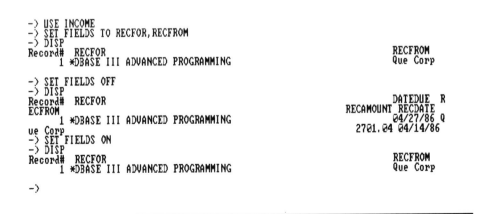

```
-> USE INCOME
-> SET FIELDS TO RECFOR,RECFROM
-> DISP
Record#  RECFOR                                              RECFROM
       1 *DBASE III ADVANCED PROGRAMMING                     Que Corp

-> SET FIELDS OFF
-> DISP
Record#  RECFOR                                                DATEDUE  R
ECFROM                                             RECAMOUNT RECDATE
       1 *DBASE III ADVANCED PROGRAMMING                      04/27/86 Q
ue Corp                                            2701.04 04/14/86
-> SET FIELDS ON
-> DISP
Record#  RECFOR                                              RECFROM
       1 *DBASE III ADVANCED PROGRAMMING                     Que Corp

->
```

Figure 11-8.   The SET FIELDS toggle affects III PLUS's reaction to the SET FIELDS TO command

is when you use it either before SETting FIELDS TO or after you've CLEARed FIELDS. SETting FIELDS ON when no fields have been SET will tell III PLUS that no fields are to be shown.

SET FIXED on/OFF

The SET FIXED toggle is the accompanying command to SET DECIMALS TO. The command's syntax is

SET FIXED toggle

where toggle has the conventional meaning of on or OFF. The SET FIXED toggle tells III PLUS whether to pay attention to the number of decimal places given in the SET DECIMALS TO command. An example of this is shown in Figure 11-9. Figure 11-9 shows the same RECAMOUNT field from the INCOME.DBF file with FIXED on and OFF. III PLUS defaults to OFF. SET FIXED ON tells III PLUS to show only the number of decimal places given in SET DECIMALS TO. SET FIXED OFF tells III PLUS to show two decimal places, which is the system default.

```
-> SET DECIMALS TO 5
-> SET FIXED OFF
-> ? RECAMOUNT
  2701.04
-> SET FIXED ON
-> ? RECAMOUNT
  2701.04000
-> SET DECIMALS TO 0
-> SET FIXED OFF
-> ? RECAMOUNT
  2701.04
-> SET FIXED ON
-> ? RECAMOUNT
  2701
->
```

Figure 11-9. The SET FIXED toggle affects the number of digits displayed after the decimal point

Parameter-Control Commands

The SET HEADING toggle affects how DISPLAY, LIST, SUM, and AVERAGE show the user their results.

Syntax   The command syntax is

SET HEADING toggle

where toggle is either on or OFF. Note that III PLUS defaults to ON unless the CONFIG.DB HEADING command is off.

Use   The SET HEADING toggle tells III PLUS TO/not to use column titles with DISPLAY, LIST, SUM, and AVERAGE commands. The column titles are the names you give the database fields when you create the database. An example is shown in Figure 11-10. Figure 11-10 shows HEADINGS ON and both a DISPLAY and SUM showing the names of the fields each command is working with. The next part of the figure shows HEADINGS OFF. Note that field names aren't included in the second DISPLAY and SUM responses, and that TALK has been SET ON so SUM will tell you what it has SUMmed.

```
-> SET TALK ON
-> SET HEADINGS ON
-> DISP RECFOR, RECFROM
Record#  RECFOR                                                          RECFROM
       1 DBASE III ADVANCED PROGRAMMING                                  Que Corp

-> SUM RECAMOUNT
       7 records summed
    RECAMOUNT
       6367
-> 1
-> SET HEADINGS OFF
-> DISP RECFOR, RECFROM
       1 DBASE III ADVANCED PROGRAMMING                                  Que Corp

-> SUM RECAMOUNT
       7 records summed
       6367
->
```

Figure 11-10.   The SET HEADINGS toggle affects what you're told about a DISPLAY, LIST, SUM, or AVERAGE

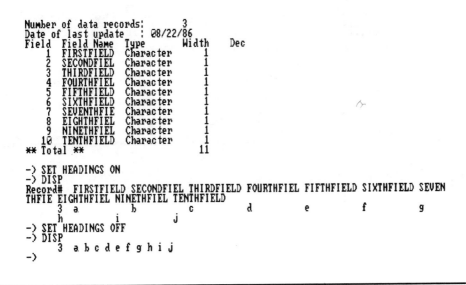

```
Number of data records:      3
Date of last update  : 08/22/86
Field  Field Name   Type      Width   Dec
    1   FIRSTFIELD   Character    1
    2   SECONDFIEL   Character    1
    3   THIRDFIELD   Character    1
    4   FOURTHFIEL   Character    1
    5   FIFTHFIELD   Character    1
    6   SIXTHFIELD   Character    1
    7   SEVENTHFIE   Character    1
    8   EIGHTHFIEL   Character    1
    9   NINETHFIEL   Character    1
   10   TENTHFIELD   Character    1
** Total **                     11

-> SET HEADINGS ON
-> DISP
Record#  FIRSTFIELD SECONDFIEL THIRDFIELD FOURTHFIEL FIFTHFIELD SIXTHFIELD SEVEN
THFIE EIGHTHFIEL NINETHFIEL TENTHFIELD
      3  a          b          c          d          e          f          g
         h                     i          j
-> SET HEADINGS OFF
-> DISP
      3  a b c d e f g h i j
-)
```

Figure 11-11.   The SET HEADINGS OFF command can be used to scrunch up output

Advanced Use   The SET HEADING toggle has the unique ability to bring order out of chaos on your screen. This is shown in Figure 11-11. Here you see a database, HEADBASE, that has ten fields that are each one character long. DISPLAYing a record from HEADBASE with HEADINGS SET ON makes a mess of the screen. SETting HEADINGS OFF and DISPLAYing creates a relatively civilized display. This sort of action can be useful when the names of database fields are too long to include in a DISPLAY command but you want the data to be shown. The designer can avoid confusion by including notes that tell the user the field precedence.

SET HELP ON/off

The SET HELP toggle affects one thing in III PLUS: it asks,

Do you want some help? (Y/N)

When you get into trouble, and if SET HELP is ON, III PLUS will tell you something is wrong and ask if you want some help. Answering **Y** to III PLUS's query drops you into the dBASE III PLUS Help system. You'll be dropped into the appropriate Help screen for the command that's giving you problems if III PLUS can figure out what's troubling you. You'll be dropped into the Help Main Menu if III PLUS doesn't know what you're doing wrong. III PLUS's HELP default is ON unless the CONFIG.DB HELP command is OFF.

SET HISTORY on/OFF

The SET HISTORY toggle tells III PLUS to/NOT TO store interactive command lines in a special memory buffer. The command syntax is

SET HISTORY toggle

where toggle is either on or OFF. Note that III PLUS defaults to ON. There is no comparable CONFIG.DB command.

III PLUS normally creates a special memory buffer called HISTORY. This HISTORY buffer acts as a repository for command lines both entered interactively and executed in PROGRAM mode. This command is the interactive equivalent of the SET DOHISTORY toggle. Note that the SET HISTORY toggle only affects interactive commands entered at the dBASE prompt. It doesn't affect program commands executed through a dBASE III PLUS PRG, PRC, or similar program file. This command doesn't create HISTORY. You create the HISTORY buffer with either the SET HISTORY TO or CONFIG.DB HISTORY commands. The SET HISTORY toggle is also discussed in Appendix C.

SET INTENSITY ON/off

The SET INTENSITY toggle is used with FULL-SCREEN EDITing mode only. SETting INTENSITY ON tells III PLUS to show data fields in reverse video. SETting INTENSITY OFF tells III PLUS to show data fields in the standard video mode. The command defaults to ON unless the CONFIG.DB INTENSITY command is OFF.

The two things to remember about the SET INTENSITY toggle are that it switches from standard video to reverse video and that it only affects full-screen operations. Full-screen operations are any that involve the SET FORMAT TO fmt file command, GETs, and their kin.

The concept of standard video to reverse video takes a bit of explaining. You tell III PLUS the difference between standard, reverse, and enhanced video with the SET COLOR TO command. The SET INTENSITY toggle switches between standard and reverse video on monochrome monitors, or standard and enhanced video on color monitors. A way to think of the difference between standard and enhanced video is to think of white versus blinding white. Standard video is white on black (or yellow on black, or green on black). Enhanced video is blinding white on black (or sun-bright yellow on black or verdant green on black).

SET MENU ON/off

The SET MENU toggle affects whether III PLUS SHOWS YOU/ does not show you the cursor-movement menu in full-screen editing commands. III PLUS's MENU default is ON unless the CONFIG.DB MENU command is OFF.

Syntax   The command syntax is

SET MENU toggle

where toggle can be either ON or off. Remember that this command only affects full-screen editing commands such as EDIT, APPEND, INSERT, anything done with the SET FORMAT TO fmt file, and CREATE and MODIFY file commands.

Use   The SET MENU toggle is interesting in that you can override the default setting with a function key. The F1 key, normally the

HELP key, serves to activate and deactivate the Menu system whenever you're in FULL-SCREEN EDITing mode. You can press F1 when you're in FULL-SCREEN EDITing mode and, if either SET MENU or CONFIG.DB MENU is ON, the menu is removed from the screen. Likewise, you can press F1 when you're in FULL-SCREEN EDITing mode and, if either SET MENU or CONFIG.DB MENU is OFF, the menu will be placed at the top of the screen.

Be aware that SET MENU takes precedence over the CONFIG.DB MENU command. If CONFIG.DB MENU is OFF, but you SET MENU ON, the system default becomes ON until you either SET MENU OFF or end the work session.

SET PRINT on/OFF

The SET PRINT toggle is a unique dBASE III PLUS command that mimics the effect of the CTRL-P system toggle. Both tell the computer to echo at the printer everything that is sent to the screen. The command syntax is

SET PRINT toggle

where toggle has the conventional meaning of on or OFF. The SET PRINT toggle tells III PLUS whether to send/NOT TO SEND whatever is on the screen to the printer. Following are examples of the workings of this command. The SET PRINT ON command can be used to replace

TYPE filename.ext TO PRINTER

with

```
SET PRINT ON
TYPE filename.ext
SET PRINT OFF
```

Another example would involve replacing LIST TO PRINT and DISPLAY TO PRINT commands. The comparable SET PRINT commands that mimic LIST TO PRINT are SET PRINT ON, LIST, and SET PRINT OFF. Note that the effects of the SET PRINT toggle are not the same with all commands. Both LABEL and REPORT com-

mands have a knowledge of page breaks, margins, and so on. You'll
get different results replacing

REPORT FORM frm file TO PRINT

with

```
SET PRINT ON
REPORT FORM frm file
SET PRINT OFF
```

SET SAFETY ON/off

The SET SAFETY toggle was mentioned in Chapter 7, in the "ZAP"
section, as providing a means of preventing the user from writing
over existing files. The SET SAFETY toggle actually affects all
commands that might write over existing files. The command syntax
is

SET SAFETY toggle

where toggle can be either ON or off depending on whether you want
TO WARN/not to warn the user when the user is about to write over
a file that already exists on the target disk. The III PLUS default is
ON unless the CONFIG.DB SAFETY command is OFF.

This command is useful when you work with systems that do a
great deal of writing to disk. Most times the programmer knows
when file writes are supposed to occur and codes them into the system. There are other times when you want to give the user the option
of saving a file to disk, but you, the programmer, aren't sure the user
knows what he or she is doing. That is where the SET SAFETY
toggle comes in handy. You can include the SET SAFETY ON command before any file-creation commands. When III PLUS encounters
the file-creation command and either the named file or a similarly
named file already exists on the target disk, III PLUS queries the
user if the user really wants to proceed. An example of this is shown
in Figure 11-12. Note that the SET SAFETY toggle only affects III
PLUS commands. You can write over existing files without being
queried if you use an external word processor to create PRG, PRC,
TXT, FMT, and like files, for example.

The SET SCOREBOARD toggle is provided as an aid to the users and is also covered in Appendix C. The command syntax is

SET SCOREBOARD toggle

Toggle doesn't have its normal on/off meaning with the SET SCOREBOARD command. The SET SCOREBOARD toggle is closely tied to the SET STATUS toggle, as mentioned in Appendix C. The SCOREBOARD toggle won't operate at all if the STATUS toggle is off. The III PLUS default for both STATUS and SCOREBOARD toggles is ON unless the CONFIG.DB STATUS and SCOREBOARD toggles are off. If the SET STATUS toggle is off, SET SCORE-BOARD can do one of two things. SET SCOREBOARD ON and the III PLUS system flags are shown at the top of the screen. SET SCOREBOARD off and no information is shown on the screen. SET STATUS ON and it doesn't matter if SCOREBOARD is ON or off; the system flags are shown in the STATUS line at the bottom of the screen.

```
-> SET SAFETY ON
-> USE BOOKS
-> COPY TO BOOKS2
BOOKS2.dbf already exists, overwrite it? (Y/N) No
-> SAVE TO 123.MEM
123.MEM already exists, overwrite it? (Y/N) No
-> ZAP
Zap D:BOOKS.dbf? (Y/N) No
-> CREATE BOOKS2
BOOKS2.dbf already exists, overwrite it? (Y/N)
```

Figure 11-12.   The SET SAFETY ON command tells III PLUS to query users when they're about to write over an existing file

SET STATUS ON/off

The SET STATUS toggle is used as an aid to the users and is also covered in Appendix C. The command syntax is

SET STATUS toggle

Toggle doesn't have its normal on/off meaning with the SET STATUS command. The SET STATUS toggle is closely tied to the SET SCOREBOARD toggle, as mentioned in the last section and Appendix C. The III PLUS default for both STATUS and SCOREBOARD toggles is ON unless the CONFIG.DB STATUS and SCOREBOARD toggles are off. The SET STATUS toggle tells III PLUS STATUS whether TO SHOW/not to show the STATUS line at the bottom of the screen. This is unlike the SCOREBOARD toggle, which determines if III PLUS STATUS shows system flags at the bottom/TOP of the screen. III PLUS STATUS always shows the STATUS line at the bottom of the screen. The SET STATUS toggle only tells III PLUS STATUS whether TO SHOW/not to show the STATUS line at all. SET STATUS ON and SCOREBOARD either ON or off and III PLUS system flags are shown in the STATUS line at the bottom of the screen. SET STATUS off, and no information is shown on the screen.

SET STEP on/OFF

The SET STEP toggle is used as a debugging tool and is also referenced in Chapter 15 and Appendix C.

Syntax   The command syntax is

SET STEP toggle

where toggle is either on or OFF. Note that III PLUS defaults to OFF unless the CONFIG.DB STEP command is ON.

Use   The command itself has no effect on III PLUS unless the system is running in PROGRAM mode. The command's purpose is to force a pause after each command line in the running program. Note that STEP doesn't normally ECHO the commands back at you as they are being executed. This is shown in Figure 11-13. The action of this command can cause a confusing display but does allow the programmer direct interactive control of a running program. Note that the STEP prompt

Press SPACE to step, S to suspend, or Esc to cancel...

allows you several options. You can continue to the next line in the code by pressing the space bar or stop the program completely by pressing the ESCAPE key. The S option allows the user great flexibility, however. SUSPENDing a program tells III PLUS to keep the program code active, but allows the user to enter commands directly from the keyboard. You could enter DISPLAY, DISPLAY STATUS, LIST, LIST STATUS, or DISPLAY MEMORY to determine the system state as each line is executed. This is a powerful debugging tool.

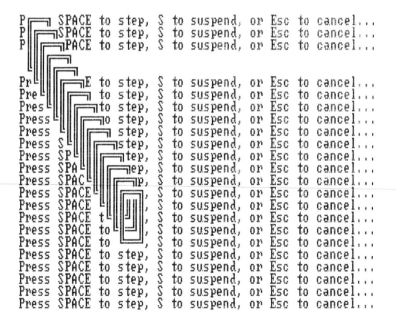

Figure 11-13.   The SET STEP toggle forces III PLUS to pause between each command line in a program file

After debugging you would enter

RESUME

to continue program execution at the last line. Note that STEP queries you before it executes a command.

Advanced Use   The SET STEP toggle increases in effectiveness when used in conjunction with the SET ECHO ON command. This tells III PLUS to show the user what's going on when it queries as to what to do next. The effect of SET STEP and ECHO ON can be further enhanced with the SET DEBUG ON command. This combination tells III PLUS to send that query to the printer. The result is the ability to see a hard copy of each program line as it is executed by III PLUS.

SET TALK ON/off

The SET TALK toggle tells III PLUS if it should let you know what it's doing.

Syntax   The command syntax is

SET TALK toggle

where toggle is either on or OFF. Note that III PLUS defaults to ON unless the CONFIG.DB TALK command is off.

Use   The SET TALK toggle tells III PLUS TO/not to inform you of its progress in certain operations. An example is shown in Figure 11-14 using the INDEX command. SET TALK ON, and III PLUS tells you how INDEXing is going. SET TALK OFF, and the only way you know the INDEXing is done is when the III PLUS prompt comes back. The SET TALK toggle also affects AVERAGE, COUNT, SUM, and similar commands, as shown in Chapter 8.

Advanced Use   The SET TALK toggle can be used in code to let the user know what's going on without making the programmer include status lines. Such an application is shown in the PACK

```
-> SET TALK ON
-> USE BOOKS
-> ? RECCOUNT()
        19
-> INDEX ON TITLE TO BOOKS
   100% indexed          19 Records indexed
-> USE JDCBOOKS
-> ? RECCOUNT()
        874
-> INDEX ON TITLE TO JDCBTTLE
   100% indexed          874 Records indexed
-> SET TALK OFF
-> USE BOOKS
-> INDEX ON TITLE TO BOOKS
-> USE JDCBOOKS
-> INDEX ON TITLE TO JDCBTTLE
->
```

Figure 11-14.   The SET TALK toggle tells III PLUS TO/not to let the
user know how certain operations are progressing

module in the following listing:

```
** ELEMENTARY PACKER.PRG
*
SET TALK ON
? "PACKING DATABASE TO REMOVE DELETED RECORDS"
PACK
SET TALK OFF
*
** EOF
```

The code in this listing is used in Figure 11-15. SETting TALK ON
tells III PLUS to let the user know how the PACK is progressing.
Similar logic can be used with the COPY, JOIN, APPEND, and similar commands.

SET TITLE ON/off

The SET TITLE toggle affects only one aspect of III PLUS: how III
PLUS works with CAT files. In particular, the SET TITLE toggle
tells III PLUS TO ASK/not to ask for file descriptions when adding

```
-> USE BOOKS
-> DELE RECO 3
-> 10
-> DELE NEXT 5
-> DO PACKER
PACKING DATABASE TO REMOVE DELETED RECORDS
       13 records copied
-> 
```

Figure 11-15. The PACKER.PRG code uses SET TALK ON and off to let the user know how things are proceeding

new files to the active CATALOG file. The command form is

SET TITLE toggle

where toggle corresponds to III PLUS ASKING/not asking for a description of the new file. The default is ON. There is no comparable CONFIG.DB command.

III PLUS calls the description a "title"; hence, the command is SET TITLE. The TITLE information is used when the user prompts

Select a DATABASE from the list.

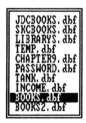

```
JDCBOOKS.dbf
SKCBOOKS.dbf
LIBRARYS.dbf
TEMP.dbf
CHAPTER9.dbf
PASSWORD.dbf
TANK.dbf
INCOME.dbf
BOOKS.dbf
BOOKS2.dbf
```

```
TITLES FROM SOME BOOKS IN JDCBOOKS
FILE
```

Figure 11-16. III PLUS uses the description TITLE information to tell the user the purpose of listed files

Parameter-Control Commands   **453**

III PLUS for a file and a CAT file is active. An example of the command's use is shown in Figure 11-16. This command is useful when the user, not the programmer, is creating files during a work session. If the user will be reusing the files and will be prompted to choose one, the programmer might SET TITLE ON. The user will then be prompted for a file description when the new file is created. Files that will become system files don't need TITLE information, as the user won't be allowed to USE them. Note that SET TITLE has no effect if SET CATALOG is OFF or no CAT file is active.

SET UNIQUE on/OFF

The SET UNIQUE toggle only affects NDX files, and only affects those at their creation. It tells III PLUS to create/NOT TO CREATE NDX files that act as road signs versus complete NDXes of their DBF files. The UNIQUE qualifier is discussed in Chapters 2 and 3.

Syntax   The command syntax is

SET UNIQUE toggle

where toggle is either on or OFF. Note that III PLUS defaults to OFF unless the CONFIG.DB UNIQUE command is on.

Use   To understand the SET UNIQUE toggle you have to understand the text's use of the term *road signs* in the III PLUS context. INDEXing a database creates III PLUS road signs and places them in an NDX file. Figures 11-17 and 11-18 show how III PLUS uses road signs and the effect SETting UNIQUE has on them. Figure 11-17 shows BOOKS.DBF being INDEXed with SET UNIQUE OFF. There aren't really any road signs in the NDX file. It's more like a phone book under the Smith or Jones listings. You have no idea where anything is in relation to anything else, but you do know there are at least fourteen computer-science titles in the BOOKS.DBF file. You also know that after the computer-sciences titles come the fairy tales.
Figure 11-18 shows BOOKS.DBF being INDEXed with SET

```
-> SET UNIQUE OFF
-> USE BOOKS
-> INDEX ON CATEGORY TO BOOKCTGY
-> DISP NEXT 15 CATEGORY
Record#  CATEGORY
     14  Computer Science
     91  Computer Science
     92  Computer Science
     93  Computer Science
     94  Computer Science
     95  Computer Science
     96  Computer Science
     97  Computer Science
    111  Computer Science
    112  Computer Science
    113  Computer Science
    114  Computer Science
    115  Computer Science
    116  Computer Science
    184  Fairy Tales
->
```

Figure 11-17.   The BOOKS database in INDEXed with SET UNIQUE
OFF here. Figure 11-18 shows the same situation but SETs
UNIQUE ON

UNIQUE ON. This NDX file does have road signs. The computer-
science titles begin their INDEX at record 14. Fairy tales begin at
184, fantasy at 23, fiction at 21, and so on. You also see there are
fifteen different types of entries in the CATEGORY field in the
BOOKS database.

The information given with UNIQUE on and with UNIQUE
OFF differs; both types of information are useful. Chapters 2 and
3 give applications of UNIQUE on and OFF. Note that the SET
UNIQUE toggle works identically to

INDEX ON field list TO ndx file UNIQUE

Comparable code using the SET UNIQUE toggle would be

```
SET UNIQUE ON
INDEX ON field list TO ndx file
SET UNIQUE OFF
```

```
-> SET UNIQUE ON
-> USE BOOKS
-> INDE ON CATEGORY TO BOOKSCTGY
-> DISP NEXT 15 CATEGORY
Record#  CATEGORY
     14  Computer Science
    184  Fairy Tales
     23  Fantasy
     21  Fiction
     17  History
     62  Horror
     22  Humor
     39  Liesure
    129  Martial Arts
    104  Mathematics
     61  Mystery
    191  Myth
     18  Philosophy
     15  Physics
     11  Science
->
```

Figure 11-18.   The BOOKs database is INDEXed with SET UNIQUE
ON here. Figure 11-17 shows the same situation but SETs
UNIQUE OFF

The SET commands in this section deal with how III PLUS should
affect parts of the system. These commands open and close files,
redirect output, modify the system's use of color, and so on.

SET

The SET command, also discussed earlier in this chapter, duplicates
several of the SET parameter TO commands. The SET command is
an interactive, menu-driven command that is similar to the ASSIST
menu system. The command is also included here because it controls
many of the SET toggle and SET parameter TO commands.

Syntax   The SET command can be used in either INTERAC-
TIVE or PROGRAM mode. The menu system is activated with

SET

There are 25 on/off toggles in the complete SET system, which were discussed in the SET section earlier in this chapter. The RIGHT and LEFT ARROW keys allow you to move from opening the Options menu to the SET Keys, SET Disk, SET Files, SET Margins, and SET Decimals menus.

Use   You move through the SET menu system with the cursor movement keys. Each of the SET menu options is listed along the top row of the screen. You can select a menu option either by moving the cursor to it and pressing RETURN or typing the first letter of the menu selection you want to activate. You can move through any menu with the vertical-movement cursor keys (UP and DOWN ARROW, PGUP and PGDN, and HOME and END). You tell III PLUS you've finished SETting by pressing the ESCAPE key. III PLUS activates your SET commands and returns you to the dBASE prompt in INTERACTIVE mode or to the program in PROGRAM mode once the ESCAPE key is pressed.

Figure 11-19.   The SET Screen menu gives you an example palette to judge your COLOR SETtings with

The first non-SET toggle menu is Screen. This menu duplicates the functions of the SET COLOR TO command. There are three COLOR SETtings available in III PLUS. The first color option is for the Standard Display. These are the colors that normally appear on the screen during a III PLUS work session. These are not the colors that appear in inverse video or enhanced display. An example of standard screen settings is shown in Figure 11-19. The second color option is Enhanced Display. The last color option is for Border settings, which can't be shown in any figure. You change any SETting by highlighting it and pressing RETURN. III PLUS changes the screen settings with each RETURN. The SET Screen menu even takes most of the guesswork out of SETting COLORs by giving you an example palette to the right of the Screen menu. More information on SETting COLORs can be found elsewhere in this chapter (SET COLOR ON, SET COLOR TO).

The next SET menu option is Keys. This menu is comparable to the SET FUNCTION TO and CONFIG.DB Fn commands. You edit the III PLUS default function key SETtings by highlighting the function key you wish to change and pressing RETURN. III PLUS

Figure 11-20. III PLUS marks the function key you're currently editing

responds by marking the highlighted key (see Figure 11-20). Note that the F1 key isn't available for editing. The F1 key is reserved by III PLUS as the HELP key. Also note that this menu only allows you to enter as much text as will fit in the window (33 characters). You can enter longer strings with the SET FUNCTION TO command.

The SET Disk menu is comparable to the SET DEFAULT TO, SET PATH TO, and CONFIG.DB DEFAULT and PATH commands. You change the first option, Default Disk Drive, by highlighting it and pressing RETURN. III PLUS changes the default drive SETting based on how many drives it thinks your system has. Note that available drives will differ on systems running DOS 3.xx, Network Operating Systems, and DOS 2.xx. The higher DOSes and network systems can use logical, virtual, and physical drives. The lower DOSes can only use physical drives. You change the Disk Drive Search Path by highlighting that option, pressing RETURN, and typing in the new Search Path (see Figure 11-21).

The SET Files menu is comparable to the SET ALTERNATE TO and CONFIG.DB ALTERNATE, SET FORMAT TO, and SET

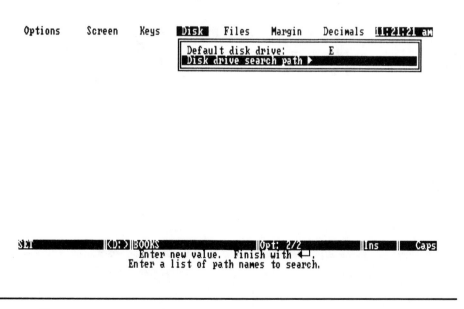

Figure 11-21. The SET Disk menu allows you to SET PATH and DEFAULT DRIVE information

Parameter-Control Commands

459

INDEX TO commands. You move through this menu and select options as you do with all the other SET menus, but III PLUS behaves differently with this menu. The first option, Alternate, causes III PLUS to prompt you for a proper filename (see Figure 11-22). The second option does two different things, based on the existence of an active CAT file. Figure 11-22 shows III PLUS displaying available FMT files based on no active CAT file. It displays FMT files on the default drive and path. An active CAT file tells III PLUS to display only the FMT files in the CATALOG. You can select an FMT file by highlighting your selection and pressing RETURN. III PLUS places your selection in the Format box of the SET Files menu. Similarly, III PLUS displays available NDX files based on the existence of an active CAT file. If no CAT file is active, III PLUS displays all NDX files on the default drive and path. If a CAT file is active, III PLUS only displays the NDX files in the CATALOG. You can tell III PLUS not to choose any FMT or NDX files by pressing the ESCAPE key once.

The SET Margins options are comparable to the SET MARGIN

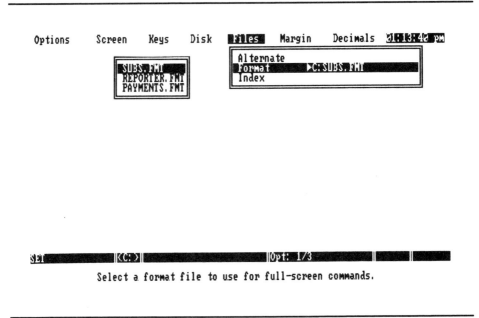

Figure 11-22.   The SET Files Format option lists available FMT files

TO, SET MEMOWIDTH TO, and CONFIG.DB MARGIN and MEMOWIDTH commands. You can enter new values by either entering the number manually or using the UP and DOWN ARROW keys. You use the cursor keys to tell III PLUS to increase or decrease the value by one for each keystroke. Note that III PLUS won't let you SET defaults greater than your system's page widths (see Figure 11-23).

The last SET menu option is Decimals. This operates similarly to the SET Margin options, but with limits of 0 and 15. You enter information by either typing in the value yourself or using the UP and DOWN ARROW keys to have III PLUS run through the numbers.

The text mentioned earlier that you can use SET in the PROGRAM mode—but it would be better if you didn't. Most programmers spend a lot of time writing and creating their system. You don't want some user to have death-dealing power over your hard work. The majority of things you SET should stay as you SET them through the life of the program. You could create your own SET Menu system. That allows you control of what the user can SET and allows you to sleep at night.

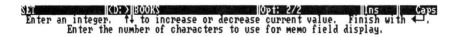

Options   Screen   Keys   Disk   Files   **Margin**   Decimals   **11:43:20 am**
Left report margin: 78
Memo field display width: ▶80

SET   KD: > BOOKS   Opt: 2/2   Ins   Caps
Enter an integer.   ↑↓ to increase or decrease current value.   Finish with ⏎.
Enter the number of characters to use for memo field display.

Figure 11-23.   The SET Margin menu lets you control REPORT MARGIN and database MEMO field with

SET ALTERNATE TO

The SET ALTERNATE TO command creates an ASCII text file that records all nonprogram commands and screen-displayed information. This command is identical to the CONFIG.DB ALTERNATE command. More information on the SET ALTERNATE TO command can be found in Chapter 3 and Appendix C. Note that this command is not the same as the SET ALTERNATE on/OFF command discussed in Chapter 4 and earlier in this chapter.

The SET ALTERNATE TO command has two forms. The first form is

SET ALTERNATE TO txt file

where txt file is any valid DOS filename. Note that III PLUS assumes a .TXT extension unless you specify a different extension with the command. This form of the command both opens a new ALTERNATE file and closes any open ALTERNATE file. In other words, the command string

```
SET ALTERNATE TO ALTER1
*
[III PLUS COMMANDS]
*
SET ALTERNATE TO ALTER2
```

tells III PLUS to first open an ALTERNATE file called ALTER1. Some III PLUS commands are executed and recorded to the ALTER1.TXT file. The second SET ALTERNATE TO command, SET ALTERNATE TO ALTER2, closes the ALTER1.TXT file and opens ALTER2.TXT as the new ALTERNATE file. The second form of SET ALTERNATE TO is

SET ALTERNATE TO

without listing any TXT file. This form is identical to the command

CLOSE ALTERNATE

discussed in Chapter 5, which closes an open ALTERNATE file.

SET CATALOG TO

The SET CATALOG TO command tells III PLUS to open in work area 10 the CAT file listed in the command. It is identical to the CONFIG.DB CATALOG command. More information on the SET CATALOG TO command can be found in Chapter 3 and Appendix C. Note that this command is not the same as the SET CATALOG on/OFF command discussed earlier in this chapter. The SET CATALOG TO command has two forms. The first form is

SET CATALOG TO cat file

where cat file is any valid dBASE III PLUS CATALOG file. Note that III PLUS assumes a .CAT extension unless you specify a different extension with the SET CATALOG TO cat file command. This form of the command both opens a new CATALOG file and closes any open CATALOG file. In other words, the command string

```
SET CATALOG TO CAT1
*
[III PLUS COMMANDS]
*
SET CATALOG TO CAT2
```

tells III PLUS to first open a CATALOG file called CAT1. Note that any files created while CAT1 is active are recorded in CAT1. Some III PLUS commands are executed. The second SET CATALOG TO command, SET CATALOG TO CAT2, closes the CAT1.CAT file and opens CAT2.CAT as the new CATALOG file. Both CAT files are opened in work area 10. This is true of any CAT file opened with the SET CATALOG TO cat file command. Remember that any CAT file is actually a specialized DBF file and can be USEd, EDITed, and APPENDed as a normal database file. The second form is

SET CATALOG TO

without listing any CAT file. This form closes any CAT file opened with the SET CATALOG TO cat file command. You can also close a CAT file opened with the SET CATALOG TO cat file command with

CLOSE ALL

Note that the command

CLOSE DATABASES

doesn't affect any CAT file opened with the SET CATALOG TO cat file command. More information on the CLOSE commands can be found in Chapter 5.

You can also use the SET CATALOG TO command as a query to III PLUS. The form

SET CATALOG TO ?

tells III PLUS to give the user a menu of available CAT files in the default directory and path.

SET COLOR TO

The SET COLOR TO command tells III PLUS what colors to use for standard and enhanced display and borders. It is comparable to the SET menu's Screen options. Note that this command is not the same as the SET COLOR on/OFF command discussed earlier in this chapter.

Syntax   The SET COLOR TO command syntax has three parts. Each part corresponds to a part of the screen's color patterns. The first part of the command controls standard video. The command form is

SET COLOR TO a

where a is some color indicated by one of the following letters:

BLACK	N
BLUE	B
GREEN	G
CYAN	BG
BLANK	X
RED	R
MAGENTA	RB
BROWN	GR
WHITE	W

Note that some of the colors are combinations of others. For example,

CYAN is BG (Blue/Green) and BROWN is GR (Green/Red). The preceding command tells III PLUS what color to use for characters in the standard display. You can tell III PLUS what to use for a standard background color with

SET COLOR TO a/b

where a and b are defined as a previously.

The second part of the command tells III PLUS what colors to use for enhanced displays. Enhanced displays are typically those used for GET commands and full-screen editing modes. That command form is

SET COLOR TO ,c

where c is defined as a and b previously. Note that there is a comma (,) before the c in the preceding command. This tells III PLUS that the user is interested in the enhanced-display colors and not in the standard-display colors. This is the only way to let III PLUS know you are listing enhanced-display colors. You can also tell III PLUS what background color to use for enhanced display as you did with standard display. The command is

SET COLOR TO ,c/d

where d is defined as a, b, and c above.

The third part of the command tells III PLUS what color to use for the border. The border is better shown than described, but it won't show up in a figure. The command form is

SET COLOR TO ,,e

where e is defined as a, b, c, and d previously. Note that there are two commas (,) before the e in the preceding command. This tells III PLUS that the user is interested in the border color and not in the standard- or enhanced-display colors. This is the only way to let III PLUS know you are listing a border color. You can't set a background border color.

You can mix these three forms to tell III PLUS you're SETting standard, enhanced, and border colors. The command form, including background colors, is

SET COLOR TO a/b,c/d,e

where a, b, c, d, and e are defined as previously. Some monitors aren't equipped to handle individual background colors and so the command is entered without background color indicators as

SET COLOR TO a,c,e

The text mentioned earlier that some of the colors are combinations of other colors. You can create your own palette by mixing colors as you wish. You can cause some startling effects by including some of the SET COLOR TO qualifiers, * and +. The asterisk (*) tells III PLUS to blink. The plus sign (+) tells III PLUS to show high intensity. The preceding command can become even more vivid by rewriting it as

SET COLOR TO GRB*/RB, RBG+/N, G+

This causes standard characters to blink, and both enhanced foreground characters and the border to be displayed in HIGH-INTENSITY mode.

People without color monitors can't have as much fun but can use U and I on monochrome monitors to add special effects. The U qualifier tells III PLUS to underline characters. The I tells III PLUS to display in HIGH-INTENSITY mode. Note that you can reSET the COLORs TO their default values with

SET COLOR TO

without a color list.

Use   There are several ways to make use of the SET COLOR TO command. You can hide input as it's being entered with

```
? "PLEASE ENTER YOUR PASSWORD -> "
SET COLOR TO X
ACCE TO PASSWORD
SET COLOR TO
```

Similarly, you can let users know how much of a screen they've edited by using one color combination for putting the data on the screen and another color combination for characters as they are entered.

One application of color that may prove useful is SETting different COLORS for different parts of the finished system. For example, you could use a red border for all AP menus, a blue border for all AR menus, and a green border for all PAYROLL menus. Each submenu has the same border color as the calling menu. This provides a visual cue for users should they exit from a menu system accidentally. You might also make it a point to use one color sequence for all data-entry screens, and another for all data-location screens. These visual cues can be useful for both programmer and user.

SET DATE

The SET DATE command is used to tell III PLUS what date format to use in all DATE fields and functions. The command syntax is

SET DATE format

The difference in DATE formats is shown in Figure 11-24. III PLUS defaults to AMERICAN.

```
-> SET DATE AMERI
-> ? DATE()
08/25/86
-> SET DATE ANSI
-> ? DATE()
86.08.25
-> SET DATE BRIT
-> ? DATE()
25/08/86
-> SET DATE ITAL
-> ? DATE()
25-08-86
-> SET DATE FREN
-> ? DATE()
25/08/86
-> SET DATE GERM
-> ? DATE()
25.08.86
->
```

Figure 11-24. The various SET DATE formats generated on 25 August 86

Parameter-Control Commands 467

The SET DECIMALS TO command tells III PLUS how many decimal places to show when division, SQRT, LOG, EXP, and VAL functions are performed. The SET DECIMALS TO command is often used with the SET FIXED toggle described earlier in this chapter.

Syntax   The command syntax is

SET DECIMALS TO n

where n can be any expression that evaluates to between 0 and 15. You can tell III PLUS to show decimal places based on an expression with

SET DECIMALS TO expression

as shown in Figure 11-25. Note that III PLUS always SETs the DECIMALS TO the integral value of the expression. Also note that III PLUS doesn't like to SET DECIMALS TO large numbers and will return an error message when you attempt to do so.

Use   The SET DECIMALS TO command has some interesting properties. First, it only affects certain types of calculations (mentioned in the "Syntax" section). Second, the number of decimals displayed from multiplications is the sum of the number of decimals of the multipliers. In other words, if you're multiplying numbers with two, four, and six places of accuracy, the result will have 12 places of accuracy. The limit to this is 15 places of accuracy. All other calculations base the resultant number of decimals on the precision of the numbers involved. If you're working with two numbers, one with 10 decimals and the other with 11, the result will have 11 decimal places of accuracy.

The SET FIXED toggle tells III PLUS whether to pay attention to the number of decimal places given in the SET DECIMALS TO command. SET FIXED ON tells III PLUS to show only the number of decimal places given in SET DECIMALS TO. SET FIXED OFF tells III PLUS to show two decimal places; two decimal places is the system default.

```
-> SET DECIMALS TO 10/3
-> ? 10/3
  3.333
-> SET DECIMALS TO 100/62
-> ? 100/62
  1.6
-> SET DECIMALS TO EXP(2)
-> ? EXP(2)
       7.3890561
-> SET DECIMALS TO LOG(10)
-> ? LOG(10)
  2.30
-> SET DECIMALS TO SQRT(1000)
Syntax error
                            ?
SET DECIMALS TO SQRT(1000)
-> ? SQRT(1000)
  31.62
->
```

Figure 11-25.   You can SET DECIMALS TO an expression, provided the
                 expression evaluates to something between 0 and 15

SET DEFAULT TO

The SET DEFAULT TO command tells III PLUS what disk drive to use as its own default. This command is comparable to the CONFIG.DB DEFAULT command discussed in Appendix C.

Syntax   The command form is

SET DEFAULT TO drive

where drive is any valid system drive. Note that DOS 3.xx and Network users can use logical, virtual, and physical drive designators. DOS 2.xx users are limited to physical and virtual drives.

Use   The SET DEFAULT command is used to have III PLUS switch between drives. It doesn't affect the system default; it only affects where III PLUS looks for files. This feature can be useful when designing systems that make use of several similar sets of files on different disks. You can write generic code that makes use of a variety of files without specifying the drives in the code. That same code can then be used on several different sets of similar files by preceding the generic code block with

SET DEFAULT TO drive

where drive is presumably a drive designator other than the current one.

SET DELIMITERS TO

The SET DELIMITERS TO command tells III PLUS what to use as delimiters for database and memory-variable input fields. This command is not the same as the SET DELIMITERS toggle described earlier in this chapter. More information on the SET DELIMITERS TO command can be found in Appendix C under the CONFIG.DB DELIMITER command. The command syntax is

SET DELIMITERS TO "c1,c2"

where c1 and c2 represent any screen-printable character. This command tells III PLUS to use c1 as the left delimiter and c2 as the right delimiter. Note that the quotation marks ("") must be included to tell III PLUS what the DELIMITERS are going to be. There are some variations on the preceding command. You can use

SET DELIMITERS TO "c"

where c is any screen-printable character. This form tells III PLUS to use the single character represented by c as both left and right delimiter. The last form of the command is

SET DELIMITERS TO DEFAULT

This form tells III PLUS to use the standard dBASE colon (:) DELIMITERS.

The text mentioned earlier that you had to include the quotation marks around the delimiters for III PLUS to know what the delimiters were. This isn't exactly so. You can use single quotes (''), double quotes (""), or square brackets ([ ]) to set off the delimiters. You must

```
-> SET DELIM TO ">("
-> SET DELIM TO "¢‖"
-> SET DELIM TO "*"
-> SET DELIM TO DEFAULT
-> SET DELIM TO
Syntax error
              ?
SET DELIM TO
->
```

Figure 11-26. The SET DELIMITERS TO command allows any print-
able character, including graphics characters, as field
delimiters

use one of these methods, however. III PLUS will give you an error
message if no delimiters are present or the delimiters aren't set off as
described. All of these conditions are shown in Figure 11-26. Note
that the delimiters will be shown unless the SET DELIMITERS
on/OFF command is OFF. III PLUS defaults to OFF unless the
CONFIG.DB DELIMITERS command is ON.

SET DEVICE TO

The SET DEVICE TO command is a parameter-control command
that allows you to tell III PLUS whether or not certain data will go to
the screen or printer. The information here is a capsule version of
that found in Chapter 8. The command form is

SET DEVICE TO device

where device can be either screen or printer. The SET DEVICE TO command tells III PLUS to send information to either the screen or printer. The specific information that is sent to either the screen or printer is whatever is SAYed in the @...SAY commands. Note that this command is not identical with the SET PRINT ON/off command discussed in Chapter 8 and earlier in this chapter. The SET DEVICE TO command tells III PLUS to send only @...SAY commands to the listed device. This can be useful in some applications. For example, you can make use of the ability to

SET DEVI TO PRIN

to create wide-carriage printed reports and display formats. Note the use of the dBASE III PLUS four-letter-word convention in the preceding command.

Two notes about the SET DEVICE TO command: First, this command only affects the output of @...SAY commands. It doesn't affect the output of ? and ?? commands. Second, your text or data may not print out immediately after this command is entered and an @...SAY is encountered if a print buffer is in operation.

SET FIELDS TO

The SET FIELDS TO command is used to create a special kind of filter in the III PLUS system. The SET FIELDS TO command is not the same as the SET FIELDS on/OFF command, covered earlier in this chapter.

Syntax   The command has three forms. The first is

SET FIELDS TO field list

where field list can be one or several fields in any active database. III PLUS defaults to showing all the fields in any active database. For example, a database file DBF1 may have ten fields named field1, field2, and so on to field10. You can tell III PLUS to show fields 1, 2, 6, and 10 with

SET FIELDS TO field1, field2, field6, field10

This tells III PLUS to view, add, or edit only those four fields, even though the database has ten fields. This is how the SET FIELDS TO command acts as a filter in the III PLUS system. You aren't using a QRY file or the SET FILTER TO command, but you are filtering fields from the user. You can tell III PLUS to SET the FIELDS from various work areas by using aliases in the command. SETting FIELDS in work areas 1, 2, and 3 would be done with

SET FIELDS TO A—>fielda, B—>fieldb, C—>fieldc

You could list as many fields from other work areas as you wished, provided you remembered to include a valid alias name before each field. These SET FIELDS would only show when you SELECTed their respective work areas. The second form of the command is

SET FIELDS TO ALL

This returns III PLUS to its default status and shows all fields in the active databases. The last form of the command is

SET FIELDS TO

with no field list given in the command. This tells III PLUS to show no fields from active files. An example of this is shown in Figure 11-27. The INCOME.DBF file is the same used elsewhere in this

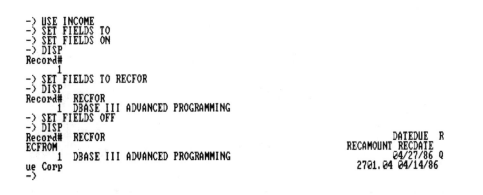

```
-> USE INCOME
-> SET FIELDS TO
-> SET FIELDS ON
-> DISP
Record#
        1
-> SET FIELDS TO RECFOR
-> DISP
Record#   RECFOR
        1 DBASE III ADVANCED PROGRAMMING
-> SET FIELDS OFF
-> DISP
Record#   RECFOR                                           DATEDUE  R
ECFROM                                            RECAMOUNT RECDATE
        1 DBASE III ADVANCED PROGRAMMING                   04/27/86 Q
ue Corp                                            2701.04 04/14/86
->
```

Figure 11-27.　　The SET FIELDS TO command doesn't affect III PLUS unless the SET FIELDS toggle is ON

book. Following the example, you could SET FIELDS TO without a field list. This tells III PLUS that there are no fields you want made available. You then SET FIELDS ON (the SET FIELDS toggle was discussed earlier in this chapter and is discussed later in the "Use" section under this command) to tell III PLUS to pay attention to the list given in the SET FIELDS TO command. The result is a blank DISPLAY. SETting FIELDS TO RECFOR, one of the INCOME.DBF fields, DISPLAYs the RECFOR field. SETting FIELDS OFF tells III PLUS to ignore the SET FIELDS TO field list command. The next DISPLAY command shows all the fields in the current record.

Use   The III PLUS documentation spends a great deal of time telling you what the SET FIELDS TO command will do. It is all summed up in the following two sentences:

```
If a command allows you to view, add or edit a database
field, the SET FIELDS TO command affects what you can view,
add or edit. Otherwise there is no effect.
```

The SET FIELDS TO command does have other interesting properties. It isn't like the FIELDS qualifier of several dBASE III PLUS commands. The FIELDS qualifier tells III PLUS what order to show or work with the fields being qualified. The SET FIELDS TO field

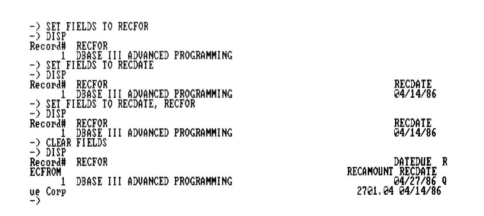

```
-> SET FIELDS TO RECFOR
-> DISP
Record#  RECFOR
      1  DBASE III ADVANCED PROGRAMMING
-> SET FIELDS TO RECDATE
-> DISP
Record#  RECFOR                                              RECDATE
      1  DBASE III ADVANCED PROGRAMMING                      04/14/86
-> SET FIELDS TO RECDATE, RECFOR
-> DISP
Record#  RECFOR                                              RECDATE
      1  DBASE III ADVANCED PROGRAMMING                      04/14/86
-> CLEAR FIELDS
-> DISP
Record#  RECFOR                                           DATEDUE  R
ECFROM                                           RECAMOUNT RECDATE
      1  DBASE III ADVANCED PROGRAMMING                       04/27/86 Q
ue Corp                                          2701.04 04/14/86
->
```

Figure 11-28.   The SET FIELDS TO command doesn't impose any order on the fields being listed. Also note that the SET FIELDS TO command is a cumulative operation

list doesn't impose any order on the fields being listed. This is shown in Figure 11-28.

You can SET FIELDS TO RECDATE, RECFOR, but III PLUS still DISPLAYs the fields in the order they appear in the database. Also note in Figure 11-28 that the SET FIELDS TO command is a cumulative operation. You first SET FIELDS TO RECFOR and then DISPLAY only that field. You next SET FIELDS TO RECDATE and then DISPLAY both RECFOR and RECDATE. You can continue adding one field to the active fields by naming the desired database field in consecutive SET FIELDS TO commands. All of this assumes the SET FIELDS toggle is ON.

You can also see the SET FIELDS TO command being used in Figure 11-8. That figure shows the INCOME database being used and then some fields being SET. The next command is DISPLAY. Note that only the fields listed in the SET FIELDS TO command are DISPLAYed. This happens because the SET FIELDS TO command automatically SETs FIELDS ON. III PLUS defaults to SET FIELDS OFF unless the CONFIG.DB FIELDS command is ON. You next SET FIELDS OFF and DISPLAY again. III PLUS now DISPLAYs all the fields in the record. The last two lines SET FIELDS back ON and DISPLAY again.

Note that the SET FIELDS TO command also affects FIELDS SET with the SET VIEW TO command. Note that SETting FIELDS ON when no FIELDS have been SET will tell III PLUS that no fields are to be shown. The SET FIELDS TO ALL command is identical to the CLEAR FIELDS command discussed earlier in this chapter.

SET FILTER TO

The SET FILTER TO command is used to create database field filters in the III PLUS system. These filters tell III PLUS to behave as if active database files only contain records that meet specific conditions. For more information on SETting FILTERs, see Chapter 2.

Syntax   The command has three forms. The first is

SET FILTER TO condition

where condition can be any valid III PLUS condition such as REC-FOR = "DBASE III PLUS: The Complete Reference" or RECDATE < DATE(). The condition can be based on a single field in the database or any combination of fields. For example, a database file DBF1 may have ten fields named field1, field2, and so on to field10. You can create a FILTER on several of the fields by stringing each field's condition with logical operators. You could filter fields 1, 2, 6, and 10 with

```
SET FILTER TO (field1=condition1 .AND.;
field2<condition2) .OR.;
(field6>condition6 .AND. field10#condition10)
```

This tells III PLUS to work with records that meet the preceding condition regardless of how many records the database actually has.

III PLUS defaults to no FILTER SET. This is the equivalent of the second form of the command:

```
SET FILTER TO
```

with no condition listed. The above form tells III PLUS to remove any active filter from the database. The last form of the command is

```
SET FILTER TO FILE qry file
```

This form of the command tells III PLUS to use the filter designed in the named QRY file. QRY files are discussed in Chapters 2, 3, and 4. A slight modification of this command can be used with active CAT files. The command

```
SET FILTER TO FILE ?
```

is a query to III PLUS. Any QRY files in the active CATALOG with codes that match the currently active database will be listed when the preceding command is entered.

Use   The SET FILTER TO command is a single-work-area command, unlike some other III PLUS SET commands. You can only SET a FILTER for the current work area. You can SET different FILTERs in different work areas, but this would be done on different databases. You can't open the same database in different work areas and apply different filters in each work area. It is also worth noting that FILTERs are automatically SET and are incorporated into all VUE files (see Chapters 2, 3, and 4).

The SET FORMAT TO command loads an FMT file into memory for full-screen operations. More information on SETting FORMATs can be found in Chapter 2.

Syntax   The command has three forms. The first is

SET FORMAT TO fmt file

This tells III PLUS to load the named FMT file into memory for full-screen operations. The FMT file loaded should be designed based on databases presently active in the system. You don't have to limit an FMT file to a database in the current work area, but the FMT file won't operate properly unless all the fields and variables SAYed and GETted are available to it. An example of this is shown in Figure 11-29. III PLUS defaults to no FORMAT SET. This is the equivalent of the second form of the command

SET FORMAT TO

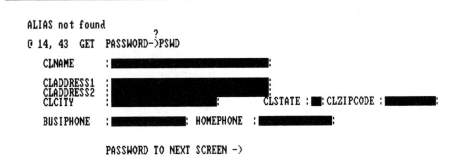

```
ALIAS not found
                      ?
@ 14, 43  GET  PASSWORD->PSWD

   CLNAME     :███████████████████:

   CLADDRESS1 :
   CLADDRESS2 :█████████████████████:
   CLCITY     :                    :      CLSTATE :██: CLZIPCODE :█████████:

   BUSIPHONE  :███████████: HOMEPHONE  :███████████:


      PASSWORD TO NEXT SCREEN ->




->
```

Figure 11-29.   The SET FORMAT TO fmt file assumes all necessary DBF files are active in the system

with no FMT file listed. The preceding form tells III PLUS to remove any active FORMAT from the database. This is identical to the CLOSE FORMAT command discussed in Chapter 5.

The last form of the command is

SET FORMAT TO ?

This is a query to III PLUS. Any FMT files in the active CATALOG with codes that match the currently active database will be listed when the preceding command is entered.

Use FMT files are specialized PRG files that only contain @...SAY and @...GET commands. They are covered in detail in Chapters 2, 3, and 4. Those sections cover all commands concerning creating, modifying, and using FMT files. Also note that FMT files are incorporated into all VUE files (see Chapters 2, 3, and 4). One thing to be aware of with FMT files is that any READ command automatically tries to READ the GETs in the FMT file. In other words, if you SET FORMAT TO fmt file and do some full-screen work, then create some memory variables or USE another DBF file and attempt to READ some GETs, III PLUS will assume you want to READ through the FMT file placed in memory with the SET FORMAT TO command. You must use either

SET FORMAT TO

or

CLOSE FORMAT

to make sure old FMT files don't infringe on new READ commands.

SET FUNCTION TO

The SET FUNCTION TO command allows the programmer to program the function keys. The SET FUNCTION TO command is comparable to the CONFIG.DB Fn command (see Appendix C).

All the function keys are programmable except F1, which dBASE III PLUS reserves for itself as the HELP key. The SET FUNCTION TO command allows you to assign strings up to 30 characters long to F2-F10, thus offering some programmability to these keys. III PLUS assigns the function keys defaults at startup. The defaults are

```
F1  -> HELP;                           &&unchangeable
F2  -> ASSIST;                         &&start ASSIST mode
F3  -> LIST;                           &&list database fields
F4  -> DIR;                            &&list databases
F5  -> DISPLAY STRUCTURE;              &&display database structure
F6  -> DISPLAY STATUS;                 &&display dBASE system status
F7  -> DISPLAY MEMORY;                 &&display memory variables
F8  -> DISPLAY;                        &&display database fields
F9  -> APPEND;                         &&add a record to the database
F10 -> EDIT;                           &&edit the current record
```

Only the F1 key is reserved by dBASE III PLUS. The remaining keys can be programmed by listing the keys and the desired program strings as follows:

SET FUNCTION n TO "string"

where n is any valid dBASE III PLUS expression that equates to a value between 2 and 10 and string is any 30-character string. The actual function key buffer is 9 keys * 30 characters large. You could program one function key with 198 characters and leave nine characters for each of the remaining eight function keys. You must delimit the string to tell III PLUS you are assigning commands and not variables to the function keys. Normally, you'd reprogram the function keys to perform certain tasks. An example of the reprogramming used while writing this book is

```
F2   - HELLO;
F3   - list;
F4   - dir;
F5   - display structure;
F6   - display status;
F7   - SET ALTER TO A:ALTER;SET ALTER ON;
F8   - CLOSE ALTER;
F9   - CLEAR;
F10  - EJECT;
```

The HELLO assigned to F2 is a memory program that is equivalent to rebooting III PLUS without leaving the III PLUS system. The only other reprogrammed keys are F7-F9. Note the use of the semicolon (;) in the commands. The semicolon tells III PLUS to act as if a carriage return exists in the string and enter the command. Hence, F7 is equivalent to the command lines

```
SET ALTER TO A:ALTER
SET ALTER ON
```

Note that the usual command form is

```
SET FUNCTION n TO "string"
```

Some computers don't use numbers as function-key designates. They use character symbols and system names to identify function keys. III PLUS can use those names and character symbols as

```
SET FUNCTION name or symbol TO "string"
```

SET HISTORY TO

The SET HISTORY TO command tells III PLUS how large a buffer to create for storing commands entered at the keyboard. This buffer is not the same as the TYPEAHEAD buffer. That one is used to store actual keystrokes. The HISTORY buffer stores command lines. The SET HISTORY TO command is comparable to the CONFIG.DB HISTORY command (see Appendix C). The SET HISTORY TO command tells III PLUS how many commands to remember in a special buffer. This buffer can then be used to replay commands entered either at the dBASE prompt or in a PRG file. The commands in the HISTORY buffer can be replayed by pressing the UP ARROW key from the dBASE prompt. The command is

```
SET HISTORY TO n
```

where n is any integer between 1 and 16000. The III PLUS default value is 20 command lines. Note that the SET HISTORY TO command only tells III PLUS what size HISTORY buffer to use. It doesn't tell III PLUS to begin recording interactive or program commands. You must use the SET HISTORY and SET DOHISTORY toggles to tell III PLUS to begin recording commands. Note that the dBASE III PLUS documentation says a value of 0 is valid for the CONFIG.DB and SET forms of the HISTORY command. THIS ISN'T CORRECT! Using a value of 0 causes some versions of dBASE III PLUS to trash out, especially when trying to RUN or ! an external program.

SET INDEX TO

The SET INDEX TO command tells III PLUS what NDX files to activate. More information on SETting INDEXes can be found in Chapter 2.

Syntax   The command has three forms. The first is

SET INDEX TO ndx file

This tells III PLUS to activate the named NDX file and use it to impose a logical order on the current database. Note that this form operates much as the second half of

USE dbf INDEX ndx

More information on opening NDX files with the USE command can be found in Chapter 5. The NDX file activated should be designed for the current database. III PLUS will give you an error message if the NDX file doesn't match the current database. III PLUS allows up to seven active NDX files for each in-USE database. You can open more than one NDX file with the SET INDEX TO command by separating the NDX files with commas (,) as in

SET INDEX TO ndx1, ndx2, ndx3, ndx4, ndx5, ndx6, ndx7

Note that this also sets precedence in how III PLUS FINDs and SEEKs. The preceding command tells III PLUS to update all seven NDX files as changes are made to the current DBF file, but you'd only be able to FIND and SEEK things based on the keyfields in ndx1. This is shown in Figure 11-30. Six NDX files have been opened with the SET INDEX TO command at the top of the figure. The listing of NDX files is identical to the order in which they were opened.

III PLUS defaults to no INDEX SET. This is the equivalent of the second form of the command,

SET INDEX TO

with no NDX file listed. The preceding form tells III PLUS to remove any active INDEX from the database. This is identical to the CLOSE INDEX command discussed in Chapter 5.

```
-> USE JDCBOOKS
-> SET INDE TO JDCBTITLE,JDCBATHR,JDCBEDTR,JDCBCTGY,JDCBSBJT,JDCBLIBR
-> DISP STAT

Currently Selected Database:
Select area:  1, Database in Use: D:JDCBOOKS.dbf   Alias: JDCBOOKS
    Index file: D:JDCBTITLE.ndx  Key: TITLE
    Index file: C:\LIBRARY\JDCBATHR.ndx  Key: trim(left(author,50))+upper(trim(l
eft(title,50)))
    Index file: C:\LIBRARY\JDCBEDTR.ndx  Key: TRIM(LEFT(EDITOR,50))+UPPER(TRIM(L
EFT(TITLE,50)))
    Index file: C:\LIBRARY\JDCBCTGY.ndx  Key: TRIM(CATEGORY)+UPPER(TRIM(LEFT(TII
LE,50)))
    Index file: C:\LIBRARY\JDCBSBJT.ndx  Key: TRIM(LEFT(SUBJECT,50))+UPPER(TRIM(
LEFT(TITLE,50)))
    Index file: C:\LIBRARY\JDCBLIBR.ndx  Key: TRIM(LIBRARY)+UPPER(TRIM(LEFT(TITL
E,50)))

File search path:   C:\LIBRARY
Default disk drive: D:
Print destination:  PRN:
Margin =      0
Current work area =    1   Delimiters are ':' and ':'

Press any key to continue...
```

Figure 11-30.   III PLUS orders the priority of the NDX files according
to the listing in the SET INDEX TO command

The last form of the command is

SET INDEX TO ?

This is a query to III PLUS. Any NDX files in the active catalog with
codes that match the currently active database will be listed when
the preceding command is entered.

Use   NDX files are created by III PLUS when you use the
INDEX command. This is covered in detail in Chapters 2 and 3.
Those sections cover all commands concerning creating and using
NDX files. Also note that NDXes are incorporated into all VUE files
(see Chapters 2, 3, and 4). One thing to be aware of with the SET
INDEX TO command is that it's not cumulative. The commands

```
SET INDEX TO ndx1
*
[COMMANDS]
*
SET INDEX TO ndx2
```

tell III PLUS to activate the ndx1 file with the first SET INDEX TO command. Some III PLUS commands are entered or executed, and a second SET INDEX TO command is encountered. This second SET INDEX TO command tells III PLUS to CLOSE ndx1 and open only ndx2. The second SET INDEX TO command is not the equivalent of

SET INDEX TO ndx1, ndx2

Nor does the SET INDEX TO command allow you to shift the precedence of NDX files without first closing them. The second SET INDEX TO command in

```
SET INDEX TO ndx1, ndx2, ndx3
*
[COMMANDS]
*
SET INDEX TO ndx3, ndx2, ndx1
```

is equivalent to

```
CLOSE INDEX
SET INDEX TO ndx3, ndx2, ndx1
```

It doesn't keep the NDX files active when it reorders their precedence in the III PLUS system. It fully CLOSEs them, then reactivates them. This is both time- and disk-intensive. You can use the SET ORDER TO command (discussed later in this chapter) to keep NDX files active while you change their precedence in the current scheme of things.

SET MARGIN TO

The SET MARGIN TO command tells III PLUS where to place the left-hand margin during printout. More information on SETting MARGINs can be found in Appendix C. This command affects all commands that have TO PRINT as a qualifier or otherwise send information to the printer. It has no effect on any screen-oriented commands. The MARGIN command adjusts the left-hand margin of printed output only. The command form is

SET MARGIN TO n

where n is any value between 0 and the right edge of your printer. You can achieve the same result with the CONFIG.DB MARGIN command. III PLUS assumes a value of 0 if none is given. Be aware that you can open yourself up for frustration by using this command. You might need to SET MARGIN TO something for some special printer forms but forget to SET MARGIN back TO 0 when you're through printing those special forms. The result will be that you'll see everything come out with some bizarre left-hand margin during the second print run. It is a good idea to use the SET MARGIN TO command in pairs. The first one SETs the MARGIN for a special print job, and the second one reSETs the MARGIN to its original value. This isn't necessary when you're setting a system default with the CONFIG.DB MARGIN command.

SET MEMOWIDTH TO

The SET MEMOWIDTH TO command specifies how wide database MEMO fields are to be displayed on the screen and during printout. More information on SETting MEMOWIDTHs can be found in Appendix C. The MEMOWIDTH command doesn't affect the left-hand margin of the MEMO field display. It only adjusts the width of the field as it appears on the screen and printout. The command form is

SET MEMOWIDTH TO n

where n is any integer between 0 and the upper limit of your system memory, in bytes. You can achieve the same result with the CON-FIG.DB MEMOWIDTH command. III PLUS assumes a width of 50, if none is given.

Note that the MEMO field is a special kind of data type that actually creates a new file when it is used. In a DBF file, a MEMO field only creates a field ten characters wide. Opening a MEMO field causes dBASE to create a separate DBT file. This file holds the actual memos that are then linked to the DBF MEMO fields. Normally, DBT files allow for memos 50 characters wide. Note that the MEMOWIDTH commands have no effect on the width of the MEMO fields if the WP command is used. Information on MEMO fields and DBT files can be found in Chapter 2.

SET MESSAGE TO

This command is useful for programmers who want to create custom prompts and Help messages for their systems. The SET MESSAGE TO command allows you to place a text string up to 79 characters wide at the bottom of the screen, in the area usually reserved for III PLUS's system messages. That is an important point. Any III PLUS system file that writes to the MESSAGE line will write over any messages created with the SET MESSAGE TO command. The line is otherwise free unless an @...GET, @...SAY, ACCEPT, INPUT, or WAIT places information there.

Also worth noting is that you won't see any message unless STATUS is ON. SETting STATUS off tells III PLUS to clear the bottom of the screen and keep it clear. That overrides any SET MESSAGE TO command (see Figure 11-31). The command form is

SET MESSAGE TO "string"

where string can be any valid 79-character text string. The key here is that III PLUS wants text strings (character expressions) as messages. Figure 11-32 shows that you can use numeric expressions, memory variables, and so on, as parts of the message. This also means you can include database fields and character variables in the message with commands such as

SET MESSAGE TO "text1" + character field or variable + "text2"

where text1 and text2 are valid character expressions, and the char-

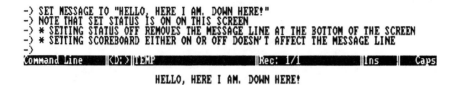

```
-> SET MESSAGE TO "HELLO, HERE I AM. DOWN HERE!"
-> NOTE THAT SET STATUS IS ON ON THIS SCREEN
-> * SETTING STATUS OFF REMOVES THE MESSAGE LINE AT THE BOTTOM OF THE SCREEN
-> * SETTING SCOREBOARD EITHER ON OR OFF DOESN'T AFFECT THE MESSAGE LINE
->
Command Line    |<D:>|TEMP                    ||Rec: 1/1              ||Ins  ||  Caps|

                      HELLO, HERE I AM. DOWN HERE!
```

Figure 11-31. STATUS must be ON for SET MESSAGES TO appear at the bottom of the screen

```
-> SET MESSAGE TO "HELLO, HERE I AM. DOWN HERE!"
-> NOTE THAT SET STATUS IS ON ON THIS SCREEN
-> * SETTING STATUS OFF REMOVES THE MESSAGE LINE AT THE BOTTOM OF THE SCREEN
-> * SETTING SCOREBOARD EITHER ON OR OFF DOESN'T AFFECT THE MESSAGE LINE
-> DISP MEMO
NUMBER      pub  N          3  (          3.00000000)
     1 variables defined,       9 bytes used
   255 variables available,  5991 bytes available

-> SET MESSAGE TO NUMBER
Not a Character expression
                         ?
SET MESSAGE TO NUMBER
-> SET MESSAGE TO STR(NUMBER)
->
Command Line     (D: )TEMP                  Rec: 1/1          Ins      Caps
```

3

Figure 11-32.   You can use memory variables and database fields as part
of the MESSAGE expression

acter sum of all three operands doesn't exceed 79 characters. III
PLUS will trim the total character expression to 79 characters if it
exceeds that width.

SET ORDER TO

The SET ORDER TO command tells III PLUS what precedence to
assign active NDX files.

Syntax   The command syntax is

SET ORDER TO expression

where expression evaluates to a number between 0 and 7. The
expression can evaluate to a noninteger value. III PLUS will assume
the highest integral value of the expression to SET the ORDER TO.
The command tells III PLUS what precedence to give open NDX
files. NDX files are opened with either

```
USE dbf INDEX ndx1, ndx2,...,ndx7
```

or

```
SET INDEX TO ndx1, ndx2,...,ndx7
```

Information on those commands can be found in Chapters 2 and 5 and earlier in this chapter.

Use   The text mentioned earlier that III PLUS allows up to seven active NDX files for each in-USE database. You can open more than one NDX file with either the SET INDEX TO or USE commands. This also sets a precedence in how III PLUS FINDs and SEEKs. The commands in the previous listing tell III PLUS to update all seven NDX files as changes are made to the current DBF file, but only to FIND or SEEK based on the keyfields in ndx1. The precedence of the NDX files will be identical to the ORDER in which they were opened.

There are several things you can do with the SET ORDER TO command that make it worth investigating. First, note that III PLUS creates an NDX file priority list based on the ORDER in which the NDX files are opened. In other words, the command

```
SET INDEX TO ndx1, ndx2, ndx3
```

tells III PLUS to FIND and SEEK based on the keyfields in ndx1. The ndx2 and ndx3 files are updated when changes are made to the current database, but you can't FIND or SEEK anything in them. You could change the ORDER of the NDX files by entering a second SET INDEX TO command such as

```
SET INDEX TO ndx3, ndx2, ndx1
```

but, as mentioned earlier, that first tells III PLUS to CLOSE all NDX files, then SET the INDEX priority to the new ORDER. That is both time- and disk-intensive and should be avoided. The solution is to use the SET ORDER TO command. You can tell III PLUS to behave as if the NDX files were opened with a different ORDER. For example, the last SET INDEX TO command above creates the ORDER

```
3, 2, 1
```

Parameter-Control Commands   487

This tells III PLUS to update all three NDX files but only SEEK and FIND based on ndx3. You can tell III PLUS to SEEK and FIND based on ndx2 with

SET ORDER TO 2

This tells III PLUS to act as if the *second* listed NDX file has top priority. The command

SET ORDER TO 3

tells III PLUS to act as if the *third* listed NDX file has top priority. The same holds for first and fourth through seventh listed NDX files. The power of the SET ORDER TO command is that it doesn't CLOSE and reSET INDEX TO, it merely shifts NDX file precedence in the III PLUS system. Note that III PLUS defaults to whatever ORDER the NDX files are opened in. You can tell III PLUS to act as if no NDX files are open or active with the second form of the command

SET ORDER TO

with no numeric expression listed. The preceding form tells III PLUS to remove any active ORDER from the database but to leave all NDX files open. The form is equivalent to

SET ORDER TO 0

This form of the command is particularly useful when you must LOCATE something in the database (see Chapter 9). Active NDX files tend to slow down LOCATEions. SETting ORDER TO 0 or blank allows you to speed up the LOCATEion process without CLOSEing any NDX files.

Advanced Use   Because the SET ORDER TO command allows the user such control over NDX file precedence, the text offers a report generator as an example of advanced use. The following listing shows a report writer using a database with five active NDX files:

```
** SAMPLE REPORT GENERATOR TO DISPLAY USE OF SET ORDER TO COMMAND
*
USE EXPENSES INDE CHECKNUM, PAYTO, PAYFOR, PAYDATE, PAYAMOUNT
TOPRINT = [PLAI]
*
```

```
DO WHIL .T.
   CLEA
   @ 2,0 TO 19,79 DOUB
   @ 3,28 SAY [E X P E N S E S    R E P O R T S    M E N U]
   @ 4,1 TO 4,78 DOUB
   @ 7,28 SAY [1. REPORT BY CHECK NUMBER]
   @ 8,28 SAY [2. REPORT BY TO]
   @ 9,28 SAY [3. REPORT BY FOR]
   @ 10,28 SAY [4. REPORT BY DATE]
   @ 11,28 SAY [5. REPORT BY AMOUNT]
   @ 12,28 SAY [6. REPORT TO ] + IIF(TOPRINT = [TO PRIN],;
             [screen/PRINTER], [SCREEN/printer])
   @ 17,28 SAY [0. EXIT]
   SELECTNUM = 0
   @ 19,33 SAY [ select > < ]
   @ 19,42 GET SELECTNUM PICT '9' RANG 0,6
   READ
*
   DO CASE
      CASE SELECTNUM = 0
         CLOS DATA
         RETU
      CASE SELECTNUM = 6
*
         IF TOPRINT = [TO PRIN]
            TOPRINT = [PLAI]
         ELSE
            TOPRINT = [TO PRIN]
         ENDI
*
         LOOP
      OTHE
         SET ORDE TO SELECTNUM
*
         IF TOPRINT = [TO PRIN]
            SET CONS OFF
         ENDI
*
   ENDC
*
   DO CASE
      CASE SELECTNUM = 1
         REPO FORM PAYCHKNM &TOPRINT
      CASE SELECTNUM = 2
         REPO FORM PAYTO &TOPRINT
      CASE SELECTNUM = 3
         REPO FORM PAYFOR &TOPRINT
      CASE SELECTNUM = 4
         REPO FORM PAYDATE &TOPRINT
      CASE SELECTNUM = 5
         REPO FORM PAYAMNT &TOPRINT
   ENDC
*
   SET CONS ON
ENDD
*
** EOF
```

Parameter-Control Commands   **489**

```
            IF TOPRINT = "PLAIN"
                TOPRINT = "TO PRINT"
            ELSE
                TOPRINT = "PLAIN"
            ENDI
*
        ENDCASE
*
        SET CONS ON
*
    ENDD
```

The problem is to get III PLUS to use certain NDX files for certain report forms. The solution can be seen in the case blocks in the second half of the code. You can SET the ORDER of the NDX files based on the report form about to be generated. This operation is particularly time-efficient. You never have to CLOSE or reSET INDEXes TO something, nor are you crowding memory with ancillary and useless commands. You SET the ORDER as you need to. Each separate case SETs the ORDER it needs, so you don't have to worry about having the wrong NDX file on top of the list for any one report form. As a final note, this code opens its own DBF and NDX files. If the DBF and NDX files were opened externally to this code, you would include

SET ORDER TO n

in the case selectnum = 0 block. The n would be based on the file priority originally SET when this block was accessed.

SET PATH TO

The SET PATH TO command tells III PLUS where to look for items on disks. It is not the same as the SET DEFAULT TO command covered earlier in this chapter. This command is comparable to the CONFIG.DB PATH command discussed in Appendix C. The SET PATH TO command tells dBASE where to look for files if they can't be found on the DEFAULT directory. The command is

SET PATH TO d1: \s11;d2: \s21 \s22;

where d1 and d2 are drive designations and s11, s21, and s22 are subdirectory designations. The other form of the command,

SET PATH TO

without a PATH list tells III PLUS to search only the current default
directory for files. You can add search paths with SET PATH TO
path list, but you can't limit III PLUS to looking only in a specific
directory with the SET PATH TO command. You would first have to
SET DEFAULT TO the specific drive containing the directory of
interest, then SET PATH TO that directory to limit searches to only
one directory in the system.

SET PRINTER TO

The SET PRINTER TO command is used to tell III PLUS which of
several devices to use for hard-copy output. Don't confuse the SET
PRINTER TO command with the SET PRINT toggle discussed in
Chapter 8 and earlier in this chapter.

Syntax   The command form is

SET PRINTER TO device

where device is any physical output device your computer is set up to
handle. III PLUS assumes the common DOS names for these devices,
as follows:

```
LPT1        PARALLEL PRINTER HOOKED TO PARALLEL PORT #1
LPT2        PARALLEL PRINTER HOOKED TO PARALLEL PORT #2
LPT3        PARALLEL PRINTER HOOKED TO PARALLEL PORT #3
COM1        SERIAL PRINTER HOOKED TO SERIAL PORT #1
COM2        SERIAL PRINTER HOOKED TO SERIAL PORT #2
```

Note that these are physical devices with DOS names. Your computer
must be designed to handle these devices, and the devices must be
active. III PLUS returns an error message when you attempt the
impossible. III PLUS starts with LPT1 as the default printer port.
You can return to LPT1 from any other device with

SET PRINTER ·TO

The blank tells III PLUS to return to the LPT1 default.

Use   Because III PLUS defaults to the LPT1 device as main printer when it starts, you would have to create an AUTOEXEC.PRG file that switched printer ports if your system uses some other device as the main printer. An example file would be

```
** AUTOEXEC.PRG TO SWITCH PRINTER PORTS ON START UP
*
SET PRINTER TO new device
*
** EOF
```

The preceding PRG file is insignificant. Unfortunately, it is the only way to force III PLUS to go automatically to another printer at startup. You would need to include the line

```
COMMAND = DO AUTOEXEC
```

in your CONFIG.DB file. Also note that you'd need to include

```
! MODE parameters
```

in AUTOEXEC.PRG if you were switching to a serial device. MODE is a DOS external command. Information on MODE can be found in your DOS manuals.

SET PROCEDURE TO

The SET PROCEDURE TO command tells III PLUS to load a PRC file into memory. Note that the .PRC extension is used to delineate PROCEDURE files from PROGRAM files. The command syntax is

```
SET PROCEDURE TO prc file
```

This tells III PLUS to load the named PRC file into memory. That is an important feature of this command. It loads the entire PRC file into memory, not just the parts of the file necessary for the immediate work. More information on PRC files can be found in Chapter 2. Because III PLUS loads the entire PRC file into memory, the PRC file should be designed based on maximum space and command efficiency. III PLUS can only load one PRC file into memory at a time, but that one file can contain up to 32 separate PROCEDURES. III PLUS defaults to no PROCEDURE SET. The command

SET PROCEDURE TO

with no PRC file listed tells III PLUS to CLOSE any open PRC file. This is identical to the CLOSE PROCEDURE command discussed in Chapter 5.

SET RELATION TO

The SET RELATION TO command is a powerful command that tells III PLUS how to link two databases. Information on SETting RELATIONs through VUE files can be found in Chapter 2.

Syntax   The SET RELATION TO command syntax is rich; it will be broken down into parts in this discussion. The first part of the command is

SET RELATION TO keyfield

This is an important point in the use of the SET RELATION TO command: This command tells III PLUS to link two databases. The linking is done based on a database field common to both DBF files. Both DBF files must be INDEXed on the same field for the SET RELATION TO command to work. Hence, the term *keyfield* is important.

The second part of the command involves naming the second file in the RELATION.

SET RELATION TO keyfield INTO dbf2

Note that dbf2 has an active NDX file associated with it. You would probably use the SET RELATION TO command in code that looked like

```
SELE A
USE adbf INDEX andx
SELE B
USE bdbf INDEX bndx
SET RELATION TO fielda INTO bdbf
```

There are alternative forms of the command. You can get around the need to use NDX files by SETting the RELATION based on record numbers in the primary database. The command form is

SET RELATION TO n INTO bdbf

This form of the command tells III PLUS to base the relation on the information in record n of the primary database. You can use any valid dBASE III PLUS numeric expression or evaluation for the value of n. III PLUS will tell you if the expression is beyond the record range of the primary database. RELATIONs can be removed from the III PLUS system with the command

SET RELATION TO

with no RELATIONs listed.

Use   The SET RELATION TO command is used to make two databases "track" each other. Tracking means that record movement in one database is reflected in the other database. This ability is useful in a number of applications. You can SET RELATIONs based on account numbers or client IDs between two databases. This saves you time moving between client-account and client-address information in two separate DBF files. Relations SET by client ID allow you to create FMT files that keep both DBF files properly ordered for EDITing and BROWSEing.

SET TYPEAHEAD TO

The SET TYPEAHEAD TO command tells III PLUS how large a buffer to create for storing keystrokes. This is not the same as the HISTORY buffer. That buffer is used to store commands entered interactively or throughout a program. The TYPEAHEAD buffer stores only keystrokes.

The SET TYPEAHEAD TO command is comparable to the CONFIG.DB TYPEAHEAD command. The SET TYPEAHEAD TO command determines the size of the TYPEAHEAD buffer. This buffer is similar to the PC's keyboard input buffer in that it captures what you type and saves it in memory until III PLUS is done doing something else and can read the keyboard again. Normally, the TYPEAHEAD buffer is set to 20 characters. This isn't much for a good typist and can be changed with the command

SET TYPEAHEAD TO n

where n can be any integer from 0 to 32000. Note that the SET TYPEAHEAD TO command is affected by the INKEY and related functions that monitor keyboard input. Note also that the TYPEAHEAD commands only work when ESCAPE is ON, either through the CONFIG.DB ESCAPE = ON or SET ESCAPE ON commands. You can remove any information in the TYPEAHEAD buffer with the CLEAR TYPEAHEAD command discussed earlier in this chapter.

SET VIEW TO

The SET VIEW TO command tells III PLUS to open the named VUE file. It is identical to the CONFIG.DB VIEW command. More information on the SET VIEW TO command can be found in Chapter 2. Information on VUE files is in Chapters 2, 3, and 4. The SET VIEW TO command has two forms. The first form is

SET VIEW TO vue file

where vue file is any valid dBASE III PLUS VIEW file. Note that III PLUS assumes a .VUE extension unless you specify a different extension with the SET VIEW TO vue file command. This form of the command both opens a new VIEW file and closes any currently open VIEW file. The second form is

SET VIEW TO ?

This form tells III PLUS to give the user a menu of available VUE files in the current CATALOG, if one is active.

The SET VIEW TO command is used to recall information about past III PLUS activity concerning DBF, NDX, SCR, and related files. This information is contained in the named VUE file. The VUE file contains the names of files that create screen images, formats, report forms, and so on.

TWELVE

Program Interfacing Commands

This chapter deals with commands that are normally used only by advanced programmers and system developers. The one possible exception is the RUN or ! command. That command tells III PLUS to use some program external to the dBASE III PLUS system, but not to exit from III PLUS to run it.

CALL

The CALL command is used after BIN files have been LOADed into memory. BIN files are BINary files. Much of the information regarding BIN file management is discussed with the LOAD command later in this chapter. If you are uncomfortable with the concept of BINary files and LOADing things into memory, you should remove your data and program disks from your machine before you experiment with the CALL and LOAD commands. If you must leave your disks in the machine during your experimentation, then at least write-protect them. If you're using a hard disk, borrow a friend's floppy drive machine.

The dBASE III PLUS CALL command is identical to CALL commands in most popular programming languages, including BASIC, FORTRAN, Pascal, and COBOL.

Syntax   The CALL command syntax is similar to the DO command syntax. Both commands share the ability to have III PLUS execute a routine not in the normal flow of the program. The DO command (see Chapters 10 and 14 for more information on the DO command) tells III PLUS to execute a PRG or PROCEDURE that isn't in the command file running currently. The CALL command tells III PLUS to execute a memory-resident BINary file. Such BIN files are placed in memory with the LOAD command (discussed later in this chapter). The primary form of the command is

CALL module

where module is the name of the LOADed BIN file. III PLUS will tell you if the routine CALLed isn't in memory. If that is the case, chances are you either didn't LOAD the routine or you misspelled the routine's name. Note that the CALL command only uses the filename part of the routine. It doesn't CALL routines based on their extension.

The CALL command is also similar to the DO command in its parameter-passing ability. That form of the command is

CALL module WITH variable list

where variable list can be any valid dBASE III PLUS variable name or value *that the called program can accept.* It is important that the CALLed program be able to accept whatever variables you pass it. The preceding command tells III PLUS that certain memory variables from the calling program are going to be used in the CALLed routine. Most BIN routines don't really care about variable names; they work directly with values. It isn't critical that the CALL command send the exact number of variables to the BIN routine. BIN routines are more concerned that they get at least as many variables as they're looking for. If the CALLed BIN routine expects three variables and you send it three, all is well. If you send it four, it will ignore the fourth variable. If you send it two, it will either assume the third variable has either a null or zero value, or it will crash. The severity of the consequences of not sending a BIN routine the correct number of variables depends on how important the missing variable is to the BIN routine. Note that the "routine" mentioned throughout this section must be a BINary file. You can translate some COM files directly to BIN files and LOAD and CALL them, but you must ensure that these COM-to-BIN files execute a RET FAR as their last instruction. (Much of this discussion refers to assembly programs. If you've used assemblers, compilers, and linkers, you won't be thrown by this information. If you haven't used them, the discussion may do you more harm than good.)

Use   The direct use of BIN modules is new in dBASE; that feature gives III PLUS some incredible abilities.

The III PLUS package comes with two BIN files on the Sample Programs & Utilities Disk. The two files, CURSOFF.BIN and CURSON.BIN, turn the cursor off and on, respectively. You can run the CBMENU2.PRG, also on the Sample Programs & Utilities Disk, to see how CALLing a BIN file can affect the system. You can design BIN files that forbid writing to a disk, forbid reading from a disk, lop off part of the screen, or forbid access to certain parts of your computer while the program is running.

A HELLO routine was mentioned in Chapter 11. This BIN file is used to flush the PC's memory and reload dBASE III PLUS without exiting from the III PLUS system. This use of a BIN file can be helpful for programmers in need of an ESCAPE key (see "SET ESCAPE ON/off" in Chapter 11 for more on ESCAPE keys).

LOAD

The LOAD command is the first half of the LOAD CALL command pair. CALL accesses BIN routines that first have been placed in memory with the LOAD command.

Syntax   The command syntax is

LOAD module

where module must be the name of an existing BINary file. III PLUS assumes a .BIN extension on the file unless you specify some other extension, such as

LOAD HELLO.FLS

Note that the preceding file, HELLO.FLS, is a BINary file. The extension on it just distinguishes it from other HELLO files on the same disk. Also note that you can use drive and directory information in the module name. An example is

LOAD C: \DB3 \BIN \HELLO.FLS

The preceding line tells III PLUS to LOAD the HELLO.FLS file located in the DB3 \BIN directory of drive C. III PLUS will tell you if it can't find the BIN file you're trying to LOAD.

Use   First and most important: you can only LOAD BINary files. The LOAD command doesn't care what extension you give the BIN file, but it must be a BIN file. If you try LOADing any other kind of file and then CALL that file, the results will be disastrous. The reason for disaster is that you're totally bypassing the III PLUS error-checking system when you LOAD and CALL a routine from memory. III PLUS doesn't check syntax, portability, and so on. It LOADs the file and assumes you know what you're doing. If you don't know what you're doing, don't LOAD anything.

III PLUS allows you to LOAD up to five routines. You LOAD each routine separately. Trying to

LOAD routine1, routine2,...

only LOADs the first listed routine. This is shown in Figure 12-1. In the example, III PLUS can't CALL the CURSOFF module because it wasn't LOADed.

You should also be aware of additional memory-management

```
-> LOAD A: CURSON,A: CURSOFF
-> CALL CURSOFF
File was not LOADed.
                ?
CALL CURSOFF
-> LOAD A: CURSOFF
-> CALL CURSOFF
-> CALL CURSON
-> CALL CURSOFF
->
```

Figure 12-1.   You can't LOAD more than one routine in a single LOAD command

problems that can occur when you LOAD BIN files. No BIN file can be larger than 32K. This includes any memory space needed by the BIN file for its own purposes. In other words, you can't LOAD a 30K BIN file that requires an additional 5K of memory for variable manipulations. The entire BIN file and its work space must fit in 32K. Because III PLUS allocates up to 32K for each LOADed BIN file, you must make sure the CONFIG.DB MAXMEM command is set to keep enough memory reserved for III PLUS should you RUN or ! some external program. Not reserving enough memory for III PLUS and RUNning an external program can cause everything to crash. The LOAD command doesn't check to see if you're LOADing a routine with a name similar to an already LOADed routine. The second routine will write over the first routine. This can also spell doom if you're not careful with what you're CALLing.

The III PLUS documentation gives several caveats that your BIN files must conform to if they are to execute properly in the III PLUS environment. These caveats are

```
ORG must have a 0 offset (no relocations upon entry).
The BIN routine must use variables as they are given in the
CALL...WITH command. No modifications or truncations are
allowed once the variables are active in DS:BX.
The BIN routine must restore CS and SS to their original,
CALLed values. This might mean some initial STACK work in
your BIN file.
```

The III PLUS documentation says that you can find out what BIN files are LOADed in memory with either

```
DISPLAY STATUS
```

or

```
LIST STATUS
```

The LOADed modules are listed after the function-key list. Note that some DOS versions won't LIST or DISPLAY the LOADed routines.

RELEASE MODULE

This section deals with the RELEASE command that only affects LOADed BIN files. Information on other forms of the RELEASE command can be found in Chapter 10.

Syntax   The command syntax is

RELEASE MODULE module

where module is the name of a previously LOADed BIN file. III PLUS will tell you if you try to RELEASE a nonexistent MODULE.

Use   The RELEASE MODULE command affects only LOADed BIN files. It indirectly affects system memory, however, in the act of clearing LOADed BIN files from memory. Each LOADed BIN file can be up to 32K long. LOADing any BIN file means system memory is being used for a specific purpose. Memory being used for a specific purpose is machine memory not available to the rest of the system for other work. The result is that five LOADed 32K BIN files are tying up just under 160K of machine memory. This is memory you could use for memory variables, file buffers, print buffers, and so on.

You can ease the strain on available memory with the RELEASE MODULE command. You RELEASE one MODULE at a time. III PLUS won't let you

RELEASE MODULE routine1, routine2,...

Note that you should RELEASE MODULEs whenever you finish with the routine that CALLs them. Don't tie up memory with unnecessary BIN files. A good housekeeping practice is to RELEASE MODULES LOADed in a PROC or PRG file before RETURNing, EXITing, or QUITting.

RUN or !

The RUN command tells III PLUS to execute an external COM, EXE, or DOS-resident command.

Syntax   The RUN command has two actual forms. The first is

RUN external

where external is some COM or EXE file or a DOS-resident command such as DIR, ERASE, DEL, or REN. The second form of the command is

```
! external
```

where external is defined as above and the exclamation point (!) takes the place of the RUN command. Either command tells III PLUS to look for the external outside of the III PLUS system. You can pass parameters to an external just as you pass parameters with DO... WITH (see Chapter 10) or variables with CALL (discussed earlier in this chapter). The command becomes either

```
RUN external parameters
```

or

```
! external parameters
```

Note that you can also use macro substitutions in the RUN command. The code

```
ACCEPT "WHAT FILE DO YOU WANT TO WORD PROCESS ? -> ",
TO FILENAME
! EDIT &FILENAME
```

prompts the user for a file to word process and then uses the named file in a macro substitution to pass the filename as a parameter to the word processor. You can even give your user the ability to choose the file to RUN externally by prompting for the external file's name with the code

```
ACCEPT "WHAT EXTERNAL FILE DO YOU WANT TO RUN? -> " TO DOIT
! &DOIT
```

Use   The RUN or ! command is useful in systems that use dBASE III PLUS as the shell and access externals for non-DBMS work. An example would be a system that runs III PLUS for most of the work, transfers information to some accounting package, transmits files over modems, handles word processing, and uses III PLUS as a shell for the whole system. A developer might want to design the system to auto-start in dBASE III PLUS and call the other packages from inside III PLUS. This is done with the ! or RUN command. Be aware that RUN looks for things on the system default, not the III PLUS default SET with either the DEFAULT or CONFIG.DB DEFAULT command. The system default will be the drive that booted dBASE III PLUS.

As always, when you do something that affects memory, there are caveats. First and most important is that III PLUS will go looking for the DOS COMMAND.COM file when you exit from the external package. In particular, III PLUS will go looking for COMMAND.COM wherever COMSPEC says COMMAND.COM is. You can find out where your system thinks COMMAND.COM is by entering

SET

at the DOS prompt. DOS will tell you various things about your system, one of which is the COMSPEC (see Figure 12-2).

Note that III PLUS reserves room for itself, open files, and active memory variables when you RUN an external file. You should make sure that the CONFIG.DB MAXMEM command reserves enough memory to hold all of III PLUS's necessaries before you RUN the external file. Even so, III PLUS might decide you don't have enough memory to RUN the external program and will—hopefully—tell you before it tries to load the external file into memory.

Another problem you might encounter concerns external files that stay in memory or set up their own buffers. Programs such as ProKey, Keyworks, Turbo Lightning, and others are memory resident. This means they stay in machine memory once you start them. III PLUS has no problems with these programs if they are loaded into memory before you boot III PLUS. The memory these programs take up is already set aside for them. But what if you're running III

```
C:\>SET
COMSPEC=C:\COMMAND.COM
PATH=C:\;C:\EDIT;C:\UTILITY;C:\NORTON;C:\DB3
PROMPT=$p$g

C:\>
```

Figure 12-2. The DOS SET command shows you where COMSPEC thinks COMMAND.COM is

PLUS and decide to RUN one of these memory-resident externals? III PLUS will give up machine memory not set aside with the CONFIG.DB MAXMEM command for whatever file you wish to RUN. However, III PLUS remembers how much memory it gave up and will want it back. If you RUN a memory-resident external file, that file takes memory for itself that it never returns to III PLUS. III PLUS goes looking for that memory or tries to write to it, and there goes your work.

Event Processing
Commands

Event processing involves the computer's ability to recognize a specified action by the user and take predefined action based on that action. A human equivalent might be ducking when you see someone walking up to you with a cream pie in his hand.

dBASE III PLUS has three event-processing commands. These commands all "watch" the user to see what the user will do. Two of them watch the user by monitoring the keyboard. The other watches to see whether the user attempts to do something that shouldn't be done. The three commands are

```
ON ERROR
ON ESCAPE
ON KEY
```

These three commands are covered in the dBASE III PLUS documentation in the "ON" section. Each of the three commands offers several abilities, so they are treated here in three different sections. Note that all three commands are shown when you either DISPLAY STATUS or LIST STATUS (see Figure 13-1).

ON ERROR

The first event-processing command is ON ERROR. This command watches the III PLUS system and "captures" any problems before they progress far enough to halt program execution.

507

```
-> DISP STAT

File search path:
Default disk drive: D:
Print destination:  PRN:
Margin =      0
Current work area =    1   Delimiters are ':' and ':'

On Keystroke:   DO OK2PASS
On Escape:      DO MELTORME
On Error:       DO ANYTHING
Press any key to continue...
```

Figure 13-1.   Both DISPLAY STATUS and LIST STATUS commands show the ON reroutes

Syntax   All ON commands share the same syntax. The first part of the command tells III PLUS ON what situation to take an action. The second part of the command tells III PLUS what to do if the situation does occur. The command syntax is

ON ERROR action

where the action can be any valid III PLUS command. A general error message can be given, as in Figure 13-2, or a more complex error-message system, based on III PLUS's error listings, may result from execution of this command.

Use   The ON ERROR command is a general purpose event-processing command. It doesn't really care what III PLUS error occurs; it will take the prescribed action based on any III PLUS error. Note that you must be active in the III PLUS environment for ON ERROR to act, and this command only works with III PLUS system errors. The dBASE III PLUS ON ERROR command does nothing for DOS system errors, errors with RUN and ! programs (see Chapter 12), and so on. If you were using III PLUS as the shell to a system that called an accounting or word-processing program, and those programs encountered an error, III PLUS would not act ON that error.

The ON ERROR command needs to be issued only once in a pro-

```
YOU DID IT NOW

YOU DID IT AGAIN




-> ON ERROR @ 10,0 SAY "YOU DID IT NOW"
-> ON ERROR @ 11,0 SAY "YOU DID IT AGAIN"
->
```

Figure 13-2.   The ON ERROR command can take any valid dBASE III PLUS command as its action

gram; it will then work throughout the entire session. Consider the following listing:

```
** LIBRARY.PRG MAIN MODULE FOR PERSONAL LIBRARIES
** COPYRIGHT JOSEPH-DAVID CARRABIS 1984,85,86
CLOS ALL
CLEA ALL
*
* THINGS TURNED ON
SET DELI ON
SET ESCA ON
SET INTE ON
*
* THINGS TURNED OFF
SET BELL OFF
SET CONF OFF
SET SAFE OFF
SET TALK OFF
*
REST FROM LIBRARY
SET PATH TO &CPATH
SET DEFA TO &CDRIVE
SET PROC TO LIBPROC.PRC
SET DELI TO '><'
*
ON ERROR DO ERRORMSS
```

This listing is the first part of the main module that handles the Personal Library System mentioned elsewhere in this book. The command to note for this section is the last command in the listing,

ON ERROR DO ERRORMSS

This command is entered only once in the entire system, here at the beginning. It need not be entered anywhere else during the work session to capture all ERRORs and direct III PLUS's attention to some file called ERRORMSS (mentioned in the "Advanced Use" section).

You can tell III PLUS to do several different things based ON ERRORs by putting different ON ERROR commands into your PRG file. Note that only the last entered ON ERROR action command will be activated by a III PLUS system error. The preceding command is used to capture all error conditions. You can tell III PLUS to take no action if an error occurs. Figure 13-3 and the following listing show the results of the ON ERROR action and ON ERROR commands.

```
-> CLEAR
-> ON ERROR @ 10,0 SAY "WRONG!!!!!!"
-> USE SDLFJA
-> ON ERROR
-> USER ASFJWR
*** Unrecognized command verb
          ?
USER ASFJWR
-> USE ALFDJIW
File does not exist
            ?
USE ALFDJIW
```

Figure 13-3 is the result of the code in the preceding listing. Note first that III PLUS doesn't give you its own error messages when ON ERROR is set to take some action. This is demonstrated in the first part of the listing and figure. The command

ON ERROR @ 10,0 SAY "WRONG!!!!!!"

tells III PLUS to use your error message and not its own. You next enter the command

ON ERROR

which tells III PLUS to shut off whatever ERROR path you've previously entered. Now III PLUS is set to use its own error messages when a problem occurs.

Advanced Use   Mentioned elsewhere in this book is the fact that errors will occur based on III PLUS's not knowing what you want to

```
WRONG!!!!!!




-) ON ERROR @ 10,0 SAY "WRONG!!!!!!"
-) ON ERROR
-) USER ASFJWR
*** Unrecognized command verb
          ?
USER ASFJWR
-) USE ALFDJIW
File does not exist
             ?
USE ALFDJIW
-)
```

Figure 13-3.   III PLUS uses its own error messages if there is no ON ERROR path set

do and your not knowing what you want to do. An example of the latter is when you try to FIND or SEEK something on an unINDEXed file. An example of the former is when you misspell a command. Both of these situations can occur when a vertical-market package or large system package is produced. The program developer can't hold the hand of the user forever and must rely on a complex error-trapping system that will take over in the developer's absence.

III PLUS allows you to set up this error-trapping system with the ON ERROR command. The following listing shows a typical error-management PROCedure file.

```
PROC ERRORMSS
*
DO CASE
   CASE ERROR() = 1
      @ 0,0 SAY "That file doesn't exist on drive "+NEWDRIVE
      DO POOL
      RETU TO MASTER
   CASE ERROR() = 4
      @ 24,50 say "Record Number ->   END   "
      @ 0,0 SAY "You're at the end of the file now. "
   CASE ERROR() = 5
      @ 24,50 say "Record Number ->   END   "
      @ 0,0 SAY "You can't CONTINUE any further."+;
      "You're at the end."
   CASE ERROR() = 38
```

```
             a 24,50 say "Record Number -> 0    "
             a 0,0 SAY "You can't go any further."+;
             "You're at the beginning now. "
        CASE ERROR() = 42
             a 0,0 SAY "You must LOCATE before you can CONTINUE. "
        CASE ERROR() = 114
             CLEAR
             a 10,10 TO 20,70 DOUBLE
             a 15,15 SAY "The INDEX file is damaged, "+;
             "excuse me while I REINDEX"
             REIN
        CASE ERROR() = 125
             a 0,0 SAY "Please turn the PRINTER ON."
        OTHE
             a 0,0 SAY "I'VE ENCOUNTERED AN UNKNOWN ERROR. "+;
             "PLEASE TRY AGAIN"
ENDC
*
DO POOL
*
PROC POOL
LAPS = 0
*
DO WHILE LAPS < WAITTIME
   LAPS = LAPS + 1
ENDD
*
RETU
```

Note that you don't have to make your error manager a PROCedure
file. You can use a PRG file or PRC file with the same command, ON
ERROR DO ERRORMSS. Note that the name, ERRORMSS, is this
text's term for ERROR MeSSages.

ON ESCAPE

ON ESCAPE is a special event-processing command. It monitors
only one thing the user might do: press the ESCAPE key. Chapter 11
discussed the ESCAPE key in dBASE III PLUS; it's much like the
DOS CTRL-BREAK and CTRL-ALT-DEL key combination. Pressing the
ESCAPE key tells III PLUS to stop whatever it's doing (see Figure
13-4). Note that the ON ESCAPE command is inactive in Figure
13-4. SET ESCAPE is ON, however, and each pressing of the ESCAPE
key causes the III PLUS message

*** INTERRUPTED ***

```
-> DIR
Database Files     # Records     Last Update      Size
7CSETANK.DBF            14       08/13/86           414
BOOKS.DBF             200        08/25/86         18297
BOOKS2.DBF             19        08/15/86          1225
BOOKS3.DBF             19        08/15/86          1225
BOOKS4.DBF             19        08/15/86          1225
COMMANDS.DBF          246        08/28/86         10042
*** INTERRUPTED ***
-> USE BOOKS
-> INDE ON TITLE TO BOOKS
    00% indexed
Index interrupted.  Index will be damaged if not completed.
Abort indexing? (Y/N) No
   100% indexed          200 Records indexed
-> COPY TO MBOOKS
No records copied
*** INTERRUPTED ***
->
```

Figure 13-4.   III PLUS tells you if pressing the ESCAPE key will harm a currently running operation

to come on the screen.

Syntax   All ON commands share the same syntax. The first part of the command tells III PLUS ON what situation to take an action. The second part of the command tells III PLUS what to do if the situation does occur. The ESCAPE command follows that convention. The ON ESCAPE command looks for one situation in particular: the user pressing the ESCAPE key. The command syntax is

ON ESCAPE action

where the action can be any valid III PLUS command. Note that III PLUS will produce an error message if pressing the ESCAPE key will do harm to the currently running operation, unless you specified some alternative ON ESCAPE action (see Figure 13-4).

Use   The ON ESCAPE command is a specialized event-processing command that works best in PROGRAM mode. This command works only when the ESCAPE key is pressed in the III PLUS system. The dBASE III PLUS ON ESCAPE command does nothing when you press ESCAPE while running DOS internal or external programs,

RUN and ! programs (see Chapter 12), and so on. If you were using III PLUS as the shell to a system that called an accounting or word-processing program, and those programs took some action based on the pressing of the ESCAPE key, III PLUS will not act ON it. You must be active in the III PLUS environment for ON ESCAPE to act. Like the ON ERROR command, ON ESCAPE only needs to be issued once in a program to work throughout the entire session.

You can tell III PLUS to do several different things based ON ESCAPEs by putting different ON ESCAPE commands into your PRG file. Note that only the last-entered ON ESCAPE action command will be activated when the user presses ESCAPE during a III PLUS work session. An example of using ON ESCAPE to do several different things, although the command is only entered into the system once, is shown in the "Advanced Use" section. You can tell III PLUS to revert to its own ESCAPE messages with

ON ESCAPE

This tells III PLUS to shut off whatever ESCAPE path you entered previously.

The combination of the ON ESCAPE command and the ESCAPE key will behave in different ways at different times, depending on what toggles and other commands are active in the current III PLUS system. First, the ON ESCAPE command won't do anything if ESCAPE is SET OFF at some point in the program. ON ESCAPE will operate perfectly until it encounters the SET ESCAPE OFF. It won't operate at all if the SET ESCAPE OFF is entered before the ON ESCAPE command.

The ON ESCAPE command won't capture III PLUS requests for the ESCAPE key. An example of this is provided by the prompt

Press SPACE to step, S to suspend, or Esc to cancel...

given by the SET STEP ON command (see Figure 13-5 and Chapter 11). The ON ESCAPE command also doesn't affect anything if the ESCAPE key is pressed before exiting from an @...GET READ database field or memory variable.

Unlike the ON KEY command, ON ESCAPE doesn't use the keyboard-input buffer to store information. The ESCAPE key is constantly polled by III PLUS. III PLUS can have a 400-character

```
-> SET STEP ON
-> SET ECHO ON
-> DO ONESCAPE
I = 0
Press SPACE to step, S to suspend, or Esc to cancel...
SET ESCAPE ON
Press SPACE to step, S to suspend, or Esc to cancel...
ON ESCAPE DO MESSAGES
Press SPACE to step, S to suspend, or Esc to cancel...
DO WHILE I < 1000
Press SPACE to step, S to suspend, or Esc to cancel...
   I = I + 1
Press SPACE to step, S to suspend, or Esc to cancel...
Do cancelled
->
```

Figure 13-5.   III PLUS won't obey the ON ESCAPE action command when it's using the ESCAPE key for its own purposes

TYPEAHEAD buffer but will still know when you've pressed the ESCAPE key, even if all the information in the TYPEAHEAD buffer hasn't been processed (see Chapter 11 for more information on the TYPEAHEAD buffer). Also note that if both ON KEY and ON ESCAPE are used in the same program, pressing the ESCAPE key will always route to the ON ESCAPE command, regardless of where the ON KEY command is placed in the code.

Advanced Use   You have seen how to use the ON ERROR command to utilize the III PLUS error messages. Now the text will demonstrate how to use ON ESCAPE to develop your own Help message system. Two pieces of code used to develop a sample Help message system are shown in the following listing:

```
** CUSTOM HELP MESSAGE SYSTEM KERNEL
** USED WITH CUSTOM HELPMSS.PRG FILE
*
** THE FOLLOWING COMMANDS SHOULD BE IN THE BEGINNING OF YOUR MAIN
*PROGRAM
*
SET MESSAGE TO "PRESS THE ESCAPE KEY FOR HELP"
SET STAT ON
PUBLIC FROMHERE
SET ESCAPE ON
```

```
ON ESCAPE DO HELPMSS WITH FROMHERE
FROMHERE = 0
*
** THE REMAINDER OF THIS CODE SERVES TO ILLUSTRATE THE KERNEL
*
CLEA
*
DO WHILE FROMHERE < 10
   ?
   a ROW(), 0 GET FROMHERE PICT "99"
   READ
   N = 1
*
   DO WHILE N < 100
      N = N + 1
   ENDD
*
ENDD
*
ON ESCAPE
SET MESSAGE TO
SET STATUS OFF
*
** EOF


** HELPMSS.PRG FILE
** USED AS CUSTOM HELP MESSAGE TANK
** DEMONSTRATES ON ESCAPE COMMAND
*
PARAMETER FROMHERE
*
DO CASE
   CASE FROMHERE = 1
      WAIT "YOU WERE ON SCREEN 1. PRESS ANY KEY TO CONTINUE"
   CASE FROMHERE = 2
      WAIT "YOU WERE ON SCREEN 2. PRESS ANY KEY TO CONTINUE"
   CASE FROMHERE = 3
      WAIT "YOU WERE ON SCREEN 3. PRESS ANY KEY TO CONTINUE"
   CASE FROMHERE = 4
      WAIT "YOU WERE ON SCREEN 4. PRESS ANY KEY TO CONTINUE"
   OTHE
      WAIT "I DIDN'T KNOW THAT COULD GO WRONG."+;
   "PRESS ANY KEY TO CONTINUE"
ENDC
*
N = 100
*
** EOF
```

The first part of the listing shows the actual kernel used to develop the custom Help message system. The last part of the listing shows a sample HELPMSS file that is filled as full systems are developed. The top file starts with six commands that drive the kernel. The first thing the developer does is let the user know where help is, with the SET MESSAGE TO. III PLUS won't display any MESSAGEs unless SET STATUS is also ON, so the developer must SET STATUS ON (see Chapter 11). Then, the developer creates a PUBLIC variable, FROMHERE, that gets pulled throughout the entire finished system. Wanting III PLUS to acknowledge the ESCAPE key, the developer SETs it ON. Next comes the all-important part of this kernel:

```
ON ESCAPE DO HELPMSS WITH FROMHERE
```

That one line paves the way for the custom Help and Help message system. The last line,

```
FROMHERE = 0
```

tells the HELPMSS routine what message to display. The rest of the code simply demonstrates the ON ESCAPE action command and isn't truly important.

The second block of code shows how the ON ESCAPE command can handle custom Help screens (see Figure 13-6). The FROMHERE variable is internal to the code written here. In particular, FROM-HERE is updated depending on where the user is in the system. The opening menu has a FROMHERE value of 0; the first submenu has a value of 1; the first submenu from that menu has a value of 11; the second submenu from the opening menu has a value of 2; the first submenu from that has a value of 21; and so on. The HELPMSS.PRG file can be extensive in a system with several menus and user options.

The preceding code blocks demonstrate the principles of designing an extensive Help system for any application. Note that III PLUS has been told to resort to its own ESCAPE system, SET STATUS OFF, and clear the MESSAGE area at the end of the custom Help kernel. Most important is the command

```
ON ESCAPE
```

Not entering that command tells III PLUS to keep the ON ESCAPE path open.

ON KEY

The last event-processing command to study is ON KEY. This command is a mixture of ON ERROR and ON ESCAPE. It is similar to ON ERROR because it is a general-purpose event processor. It is similar to ON ESCAPE in that the event that triggers ON KEY must be

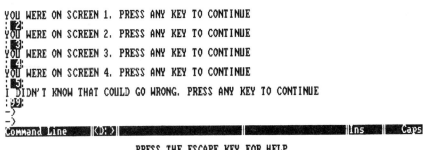

```
YOU WERE ON SCREEN 1. PRESS ANY KEY TO CONTINUE
:▊2!
YOU WERE ON SCREEN 2. PRESS ANY KEY TO CONTINUE
:▊3!
YOU WERE ON SCREEN 3. PRESS ANY KEY TO CONTINUE
:▊4!
YOU WERE ON SCREEN 4. PRESS ANY KEY TO CONTINUE
:▊5!
I DIDN'T KNOW THAT COULD GO WRONG. PRESS ANY KEY TO CONTINUE
:▊9!
-}
-}
```
Command Line ▐(D:)▌   ▐Ins▌ ▐Caps▌

PRESS THE ESCAPE KEY FOR HELP

Figure 13-6.   This is an example of ON ESCAPE tracking where the user is in a program

a keystroke entered by the user.

Syntax   All ON commands share the same syntax. The first part of the command tells III PLUS ON what situation to take an action. The second part of the command tells III PLUS what to do if the situation does occur. The command syntax is

ON KEY action

where the action can be any valid III PLUS command. ONKEY is often used in conjunction with the INKEY and READKEY functions.

Use   ON KEY is a specialized event-processing command that works best in PROGRAM mode. This command works when any key is pressed in the III PLUS system. The dBASE III PLUS ON KEY command does nothing when you press a key while running DOS internal or external programs, RUN and ! programs (see Chapter 12), and so on. If you were using III PLUS as the shell to a system that calls an accounting or word-processing program, keystrokes entered in those programs won't be affected by the III PLUS ON KEY command. You must be active in the III PLUS environment for ON KEY to act. Like the other ON commands, ON KEY only needs to be issued once in a program to work throughout the entire session.

You can tell III PLUS to do several different things based ON pressed keys by putting different ON KEY commands into your PRG file. Note that only the last-entered ON KEY action command will be activated when the user presses a key during a III PLUS work session. You can use the INKEY function with ON KEY in much the same way ON ESCAPE was used earlier in this chapter. An example of using the ON KEY command to do several different things, although the command is only entered into the system once, is shown in the "Advanced Use" section.

You must be sure to remove any ON KEY command path you've created when you're finished with the ON KEY command. You tell III PLUS to revert to its normal command-processing path with

ON KEY

This tells III PLUS to shut off whatever ON KEY path you've previously entered.

The ON KEY command behaves in different ways at different times, depending on what toggles and other commands are active in the current III PLUS system. First, the ON KEY command won't act upon an ESCAPE if an ON ESCAPE has been entered and SET ESCAPE is ON. SET ESCAPE OFF at some point in the program and ON KEY will operate perfectly. Also note that ON KEY will capture an ESCAPE if SET ESCAPE is OFF. ON KEY captures all keyboard input—with the exception of ESCAPE, as mentioned above—and stores it in the keyboard buffer.

All keys pressed in III PLUS are stored in the TYPEAHEAD buffer when ON KEY is being used without ON ESCAPE, with ON ESCAPE but with SET ESCAPE OFF, or without ON ESCAPE and SET ESCAPE OFF. This gives ON KEY some interesting properties. First, ON KEY looks ahead of what III PLUS is doing at present. III PLUS can be INDEXing a file. You can press any key. Normally, III PLUS would ignore your keyboard input. You can do something about it as shown in the following listing. This listing shows some whimsy as well as useful information.

```
** ON EXAMPLE FILE
*
I = 0
SET PROC TO DONTOUCH.PRC
ON KEY DO WARNING
ON ESCA DO NOWAYOUT
DO WAITER
*
** EOF
```

```
** DONTOUCH.PRC FOR ON KEY EXAMPLE FILE
*
PROC WARNING
CLEA
a 10,0 SAY "I TOLD YOU NOT TO TOUCH THE KEYBOARD"
*
PROC NOWAYOUT
SET COLOR TO W*+
CLEA
a 10,0 SAY "THERE'S NO WAY OUT!"
*
PROC WAITER
*
I = 0
DO WHIL I = 0
   I = INKEY()
ENDD
*
* EOF
```

The useful information is in the top block of code and can be summed up with the line

ON KEY DO WARNING

The warning that the user will get is seen in the second block of code. Note that after the ON KEY command appears the line

DO WAITER

The WAITER routine can also be seen in the DONTOUCH.PRC file. Note the use of the INKEY function to pass keystrokes from the buffer to the system. That is an important part of the ON KEY command. You must either READ, READKEY, INKEY, or WAIT TO to remove the keystroke from the buffer. If the keystroke isn't removed, you'll be caught in a software loop. III PLUS will repeatedly do whatever the ON KEY action is. The last suggestion, using the WAIT TO command to pass the keystroke to a variable, stores the keystroke to the named variable without WAITing for the user to press any other key.

Advanced Use   This section carries on the fight of making sure the user doesn't damage the system. Here you capture each key the user presses and examine it before sending it on to the heart of the system. The following listing shows two blocks of code. The first block is the kernel for an ON KEY action block. You can set up a DO WHILE ... ENDDO loop that traps all keystrokes until they can be examined by the second block, OK2PASS. OK2PASS would actually contain many more checks in an authentic system. Here you see how you would control such a system. Note that I is reset to 0 before you leave OK2PASS. This ensures that you'll stay in the loop until you're supposed to leave.

As a final note, make sure you reset

ON KEY

so that the routing doesn't stay in effect after your program has returned to the dBASE prompt.

```
** ON KEY KERNEL TO PASS VALID KEYSTROKES A PROGRAM
*
** THIS SECTION OF THE CODE CONTAINS SYSTEM SETS,
** RESTORES FROM MEM FILES,
** ETC
*
ON KEY DO OK2PASS WITH I
*
** THE REST OF THE CODE IS THE ACTUAL PROGRAM MODULE,
** INCLUDING MENUS
** AT SOME POINT YOU READ A MENU SELECTION
*
I = 0
*
DO WHILE I = 0
   a 19,35 SAY "SELECTION -> "
   a 19,50 SAY CHR(I)
ENDD
*
DO CASE
   CASE ....

ENDC
*
** EOF


** THIS MODULE MAKES SURE VALID KEYS ARE PRESSED BEFORE
** THE USER CAN DO DAMAGE
*
PARAMETER I
I = INKEY()
*
DO CASE
   CASE I < ASC("A")
      a 20,0
      WAIT "YOU MUST PRESS AN ALPHANUMERIC KEY. TRY AGAIN"
   CASE I > ASC("z")
      a 20,0
      WAIT "YOU MUST PRESS AN ALPHANUMERIC KEY. TRY AGAIN"
ENDC
```

```
*
I = 0
*
** EOF
```

dBASE III PLUS: The Complete Reference

Program Control Commands

Many of the commands in dBASE III PLUS can be used in either INTERACTIVE or PROGRAM mode. There is one group of commands that can be used only in PROGRAM mode, however. These commands tell III PLUS how to use the other commands, when to use them, and what to do if things go wrong. Many of these commands are actually separate parts of the same command. Two groups of four separate commands become the command streams

DO CASE...CASE...OTHERWISE...ENDCASE

and

DO WHILE...EXIT...LOOP...ENDDO

Similarly, three other commands become

IF...ELSE...ENDIF

and two other commands become

TEXT...ENDTEXT

Three of the commands—NOTE, *, and &&—perform the same function. All three allow the developer to document code.

Not mentioned in this chapter are commands that are normally used in PROGRAM mode but can be used interactively, such as ACCEPT, INPUT, and WAIT. These commands were covered in detail in Chapter 10. Many of the parameter-control commands, covered in Chapter 11, can be used in PROGRAM mode but are not covered here. Also not covered in this chapter are ways of creating PRG and PRC files. You can find out about the MODIFY COMMAND and MODIFY FILE commands in Chapters 2, 3, and 4.

Two methods for creating files that have not been described involve the CREATE command. Both methods make use of III PLUS's belief that COMMAND and FILE are reserved words. You can enter

CREATE COMMAND

and III PLUS will prompt you for a PRG filename. Any file created through this method will have a .PRG extension unless you specify otherwise. Likewise, you can create a TXT file by entering the command

CREATE FILE

III PLUS will prompt you for a .TXT filename. You can enter a different extension if you wish.

The majority of the commands in this chapter do not include "Advanced Use" and "Use" sections. Both use and advanced use of these commands can be seen in almost every other section of this book.

*

The command in this section has little to do with program control. It is used for documenting programs internally. All dBASEs use the asterisk (*) to tell the particular dBASE that the rest of the line is a comment. Use of the * command is similar to that of the semicolon (;) command used in assembler and the REM command used in the BATch and BASIC languages.

Syntax III PLUS uses the *, &&, and NOTE commands to separate comment lines from the rest of a program. You can use any of these commands interactively if you wish. This section concerns itself with the * command. The command form is

* text

where text is any single line of comment. Examples can be seen in many of the program segments listed in this book. You should specify that the text in the preceding command be a single line of comment.

This is true especially when using a word processor other than the III PLUS Text Editor. The III PLUS Text Editor knows how to wrap lines for the III PLUS command processor. Other text editors don't. WordStar, for example, will extend the line forever when used in PROGRAM EDITing mode (the Nondocument mode on the WordStar opening menu). The III PLUS Text Editor knows that the comment

```
·> TYPE 14-1.PRG

* THIS IS A SINGLE COMMENT LINE THAT I'M INTENTIONALLY MAKING SO
LONG (III PLUS
JUST WORD WRAPPED BETWEEN SO AND LONG) THAT III PLUS (ANOTHER
WORD WRAP BETWEEN
III AND PLUS) HAS TO WORD WRAP.

·> CLOSE ALTER
```

is actually one line of comment. Further, the III PLUS command processor treats the III PLUS Text Editor wrapped line as one line of comment, even though that line might extend over several hundred lines of code. Note that any other word processor, the DOS TYPE command, the DOS EDLIN.COM line editor, and similar text-displaying commands and programs will display the preceding comment as a single line instead of a word-wrapped line.

Use　　The text mentions elsewhere that the * is used to add comments and documentation to III PLUS programs.

A suggestion: Don't place comment lines in the final, working, installed code. They slow down the system.

You may remember that the III PLUS Text Editor doesn't like to work with listings of more than 5K. That is fine for short programs, but a 200-line listing that averages 25 characters per line is the upper limit of what you can do. Some command lines can go over 100 characters easily. So what do you do when you're using some other text editor to generate or edit programs and need to place comment lines in those programs? The III PLUS command processor won't acknowledge lines wrapped by other text processors; placing an * at the beginning of each line can get dull or, worse yet, be forgotten completely. The solution is to use some other commands to fool III PLUS into thinking that valid commands have been entered, but not to do anything with them. You can use another command pair, TEXT...ENDTEXT, as the core of your solution.

First, you have to understand what a comment line is as far as the computer is concerned. A comment line is something that takes up space, warrants no action, and shouldn't be seen or heard unless the user specifically asks to see or hear it. How do you get the computer to act that way when you don't use the normal commenting commands? Consider the following listing:

```
SET CONSOLE OFF &&
TEXT

THIS IS AN EXAMPLE OF USING COMMANDS OTHER THAN THE NORMAL
COMMENTING
COMMANDS TO FOOL III PLUS INTO PUTTING COMMENTS INTO THE MAIN
STREAM
OF THE PROGRAM.

NOTICE THAT I'M NOT USING *, && OR NOTE TO TELL III PLUS THAT
EVERYTHING
IN THE TEXT...ENDTEXT COMMAND IS COMMENTARY, BUT III PLUS BEHAVES
AS IF
THAT IS EXACTLY WHAT THESE LINES ARE.

AN IMPORTANT PART OF THIS COMMAND SEQUENCE IS THE SET CONSOLE
COMMANDS
AT THE START AND STOP OF THIS BLOCK. THEY PROVIDE THE ADDED
ABILITY OF
EDITING THEM OUT TO FORCE III PLUS TO DISPLAY THESE LINES WHEN
EXECUTING
THE PROGRAM.

ENDTEXT
SET CONSOLE ON &&
```

This command sequence is useful in more ways than just fooling III PLUS into thinking there's no internal documentation. Note that you can set the SET CONSOLE commands off with &&. III PLUS uses the && command to set off comments. The && has no effect on the code. They were placed here to set off the SET CONSOLE commands in this code from any other SET CONSOLE commands there might be in the rest of the code. Why? Sometime during the execution or debugging phase of developing or using the program that contains this code, it might be necessary to let the user/programmer know what's going to happen before it happens or read why the program was designed to do what it's doing. You can use a word processor to replace every occurrence of

SET CONSOLE OFF &&

with

* SET CONSOLE OFF &&

and every occurrence of

SET CONSOLE ON &&

with

WAIT

Provided the comments in the TEXT...ENDTEXT block aren't over 23 lines long, the user/programmer will be given information on why things are happening as they are.

The * can cause a problem when used in commands that contain the asterisk or ampersand as part of their argument. The asterisk is also used by III PLUS to indicate multiplication. Using the * after a multiplication throws III PLUS a curve, which in turn is handed back to you. (The solution to this problem is given in the section on && later in this chapter.)

As a final note, you can use the ";" to extend long comments over several lines. This is identical to extending long commercials over several lines with ";".

&

Throughout this book, the dBASE III PLUS documentation, and other dBASE books, you've seen the terms *macro* and *macro substitution*.

Take the second term and remove the first word. That is all the command is: a substitution.

Syntax   The macro command has a simple syntax:

&expression

Note that there is no space between the & and the expression that follows it. This is important. The preceding expression can be either a database character field or a memory variable.

Use   The & command tells III PLUS a substitution is about to occur. Consider Figure 14-1. Two memory variables, EXPRESSION and HELLO, have been created. III PLUS has been told that the value of EXPRESSION is the text string "HELLO", and the value of the variable HELLO is the text string "GREETINGS!". But when you ask III PLUS for the value of &EXPRESSION, the response is

```
-> EXPRESSION = "HELLO"
->
-> HELLO = "GREETINGS!"
->
-> ? EXPRESSION
HELLO
->
-> ? HELLO
GREETINGS!
->
-> ? &EXPRESSION
GREETINGS!
->
```

Figure 14-1.   The & command tells III PLUS a substitution is about to take place

"GREETINGS!". This happens because III PLUS interprets the command

```
? &EXPRESSION
```

as

```
FIND THE VARIABLE, EXPRESSION.
DETERMINE WHAT'S INSIDE EXPRESSION.
FIND THE VARIABLE NAMED INSIDE EXPRESSION.
DETERMINE THE VALUE OF THE VARIABLE NAMED INSIDE EXPRESSION.
```

This might seem like a complex, circuitous route to determining what goes where and why, but its uses are legion. The following code is a simple use of the macro command's substitution ability.

```
SELE 2
USE COMMANDS
COMMNUMBER = 0
CLEA
*
DO WHILE COMMNUMBER = 0 .AND. .NOT. EOF()
   TANK = SPACE(3)
   DISP NEXT 19
   ?
   ACCE "ENTER COMMAND NUMBER OR RETURN TO CONTINUE -> " TO TANK
   COMMNUMBER = IIF(LEN(TRIM(TANK)) = 0, 0, VAL(TANK))
ENDD
*
GOTO COMMNUMBER
DOTHIS = COMMAND
SELE 1
&DOTHIS
```

This short block of code uses a database that has one field, COM-MANDS, that is 30 characters long. Each field in COMMANDS is a valid III PLUS command. This block of code SELECTs work area 2, DISPLAYs COMMANDS' fields, and allows the user to select a command from a crude menu. The selection is then stored in a memory variable and executed when the code returns to work area 1. Note that you could use the database field directly in the macro substitution if you didn't SELECT a different work area. The "Advanced Use" section shows a more elegant use of the macro command for substitutions.

Advanced Use   How far can you go with macro substitutions before III PLUS argues with you? So long as the command is a valid III PLUS command, you can go as far as you want. An example of this is shown in the following listing, where the macro command is used to create an extensive DISPLAY command. This code segment is from the Personal Library System mentioned throughout this book, but the principles apply to any programming application.

```
        a 20,C CLEA
        STOR SPACE(10) TO DISPLAYWHAT, DISPLAYFOR
        a 21,0 SAY "Display What -> "
*
        DO WHIL .T.
           WHAT = SPACE(60)
           a 23,0 SAY "Display? " GET WHAT
           READ
*
           IF LEN(TRIM(WHAT)) = 0
              EXIT
           ENDI
*
           DISPLAYWHAT = IIF(DISPLAYWHAT = SPACE(1C), TRIM(WHAT),;
                            DISPLAYWHAT + ", " + TRIM(WHAT))
           a 21, 18 SAY DISPLAYWHAT
        ENDD
*
        a 22,0 SAY "Display For -> "
*
        DO WHIL .T.
           WHAT = SPACE(6C)
           a 23,0 SAY "For?      " GET WHAT
           READ
*
           IF LEN(TRIM(WHAT)) = 0
              EXIT
           ENDI
*
           DISPLAYFOR = IIF(DISPLAYFOR = SPACE(1C), TRIM(WHAT),;
                            DISPLAYFOR + ".AND. " + TRIM(WHAT))
```

```
          @ 22, 18 SAY DISPLAYFOR
      ENDD
*
      CLEA
*
      IF LEN(TRIM(DISPLAYFOR)) = 0
          DISP ALL &DISPLAYWHAT
          WAIT
      ELSE
          DISP ALL &DISPLAYWHAT FOR &DISPLAYFOR
          WAIT
      ENDI
*
```

You start by finding out what the user wants DISPLAYed. Some machinations occur, of which the final result is the building of DIS-PLAYWHAT. DISPLAYWHAT is a variable that literally holds WHAT the user wants DISPLAYed. Note that a III PLUS IIF function is used to build the DISPLAYWHAT variable from answers the user gives on screen line 23. This built DISPLAYWHAT is echoed to the user on screen line 21.

The second part of the DISPLAY command is the FOR qualifier. You do not look for WHILE qualifiers directly, although the ingenious user can include a WHILE qualifier and argument after a valid FOR argument has been entered without causing any problems. The FOR argument is built in the exact same way that the DIS-PLAYWHAT variable is built. The only thing left to do is tell III PLUS whether you're going to DISPLAY FOR something or not. A blank FOR argument will force III PLUS to give an error message. You test to see if there is any information in the DISPLAYFOR variable by determining how long it is. IF the LENgth of the TRIMmed DISPLAYFOR variable is 0, there is no information in it and you just

DISP ALL &DISPLAYWHAT

If there is information in the DISPLAYFOR variable, then you

DISP ALL &DISPLAYWHAT FOR &DISPLAYFOR

The only limit on how much information can go into these macro substitutions is the standard dBASE III PLUS 254-character limit.

&&

Like the * command discussed earlier, the command in this section has little to do with program control. It is actually used for documenting programs internally. III PLUS uses the double ampersand symbol (&&) to indicate that the rest of the line is a comment. The command is similar to the semicolon (;) command used in assemblers and the REM command used in the BATch and BASIC languages.

Syntax   III PLUS uses the (&&), *, and NOTE commands to separate comment lines from the rest of the program. You can use any of these commands interactively if you wish. This section concerns itself with the && command. The command syntax is

&& text

where text is any single line of comment. Note that this command is slightly different from the * command shown earlier. The && is most often found in code as

executable command && text

where executable command signifies any other III PLUS command that will result in some noncomment action. You specify that the text in the preceding command is any single line of comment. This is true especially for the && command, as this command is most often used on a line that already has some command, as shown in Figure 14-1. If you intend to enter long comment lines, you must use the III PLUS Text Editor. The III PLUS Text Editor knows how to wrap lines for the III PLUS command processor. Other text editors don't.

Note also that the command is a double ampersand, not a single ampersand. A single & throws III PLUS another curve, as shown in Figure 14-2. The single & is not a comment command but a macro instruction.

```
-> & THIS ISN'T A COMMENT LINE BECAUSE THERE IS ONLY ONE "&"
*** Unrecognized command verb
  ?
& THIS ISN'T A COMMENT LINE BECAUSE THERE IS ONLY ONE "&"
->
-> && THIS IS A COMMENT LINE BECAUSE THERE ARE TWO "&"
->
```

Figure 14-2.   The single & is a macro instruction, not a comment command

Use   This chapter mentioned earlier one difficulty with the *
command. III PLUS crashes when it encounters the * as a comment
while it's executing a command that uses the asterisk or ampersand
as part of its argument. An example of this is shown in Figure 14-3.
The * is also used by III PLUS to indicate multiplication. The
solution is shown in Figure 14-3. The && is used to let III PLUS
know the rest of the line is a comment, not part of the multiplication
stream.

CANCEL

The CANCEL command tells III PLUS to perform a special kind of
program halt. It is a single-line command, much like QUIT. Unlike
QUIT, CANCEL tells III PLUS to CLOSE all open program files.
Note that III PLUS differentiates PRG and PRC from FMT files,
even though the latter are only specialized program files. Although
the III PLUS Help screen states that the CANCEL command closes
open PRC (PROCedure) files, this is not true. The CANCEL command doesn't close open PRC files. The command form is

CANCEL

III PLUS closes only active PRG files. All DBF, NDX, FMT,
PRC, VUE, and similar files remain open and active when III PLUS
encounters a CANCEL command. This means that a main program
calling several subroutines, none of which are in a PRC file, will close
all open levels of PRG files when a CANCEL command is encoun-

---

```
-> * THIS IS A NOTE BECAUSE THE ASTERISK IS THE FIRST CHARACTER IN THE LINE
->
-> ? 5*7 THIS ISN'T A NOTE BECAUSE THE ASTERISK IS USED TO SHOW MULTIPLICATION
Unrecognized phrase/keyword in command
                    ?
? 5*7 THIS ISN'T A NOTE BECAUSE THE ASTERISK IS USED TO SHOW MULTIPLICATION
->
-> ? 5*7  * THE SAME PROBLEM OCCURS IN THIS LINE
Variable not found
                    ?
? 5*7  * THE SAME PROBLEM OCCURS IN THIS LINE
->
->
-> ? 5*7    && THIS HOW WE OVERCOME THE "*" PROBLEM
35
->
```

Figure 14-3.   The && takes up where * and NOTE leave off

```
-> DO CANCELER
Do cancelled
-> DISP STAT

Select area:  1, Database in Use: D:EXPENSES.dbf    Alias: EXPENSES

Select area:  2, Database in Use: D:COMMANDS.dbf    Alias: COMMANDS

Currently Selected Database:
Select area:  3, Database in Use: D:CHAPTER9.dbf    Alias: CHAPTER9
      Memo  file: D:CHAPTER9.dbt

Procedure file: D:BOXER.PRG
File search path:
Default disk drive: D:
Print destination:  PRN:
Margin =      0
Current work area =    3    Delimiters are ':' and ':'

Press any key to continue...
```

Figure 14-4. The CANCEL command affects only open and active PRG files

tered, even if the CANCEL command is encountered in the lowest PRG file on the totem pole. Also note that the last SELECTed work area will be the current work area when III PLUS executes the CANCEL command. Figure 14-4 is the result of the following code:

```
** CANCELER.PRG
*
SET PROC TO BOXER
USE EXPENSES
SELE 2
USE COMMANDS
SELE 3
USE CHAPTER9
CANCEL
*
** EOF
```

CASE

The CASE command is the second part of the four-part command

DO CASE...CASE...OTHERWISE...ENDCASE

The command syntax is

CASE condition

where condition is something that III PLUS can equate to either TRUE or FALSE. Also note that the CASE condition can't be a command itself, although you can use functions such as IIF and multiple logical statements. An example of this is shown in the following listing:

```
DO CASE
   CASE IIF(EXPRESSION = "HELLO", .T., .F.)
      ? "YES, IT'S TRUE"
   CASE EXPRESSION # "HELLO" .AND. NUMBER = 10
      ? "YOU CAN USE TWO OR MORE EXPRESSIONS FOR THE CONDITION"
   OTHE
      ? "NO, IT ISN'T"
ENDC
```

The two CASEs may look involved, but they're not. The first CASE makes use of the IIF function to determine if something is TRUE or FALSE. The use of CASE IIF instead of CASE condition is advantageous when something, such as tax rates or commissions, is calculated in steps. The CASE statement then takes the form

CASE variable > IIF(condition, step1, step2)

The second CASE in the listing determines its truth or falseness based on two separate conditions, each of which can be either TRUE or FALSE (Note: *Boolean algebra* applies.) Note that III PLUS executes only lines listed under the first TRUE CASE. In the preceding code, if EXPRESSION = "HELLO", only

? "YES, IT'S TRUE"

is executed. However, you could replace the preceding single line with as many program lines as you like, and each would be executed. If the second CASE were based on

EXPRESSION = "HELLO" .AND. NUMBER = 10

and EXPRESSION = "HELLO", the second CASE would never be executed, no matter what NUMBER equaled. The reason is that EXPRESSION = "HELLO" will be captured by the first CASE and that group of commands will be executed. Once a CASE is executed, III PLUS looks for the ENDCASE command and leaves the

DO CASE...CASE...OTHERWISE...ENDCASE

command stream. A last note: If no CASEs are TRUE, III PLUS will either execute whatever commands are listed under the OTHERWISE clause or, if there is no OTHERWISE clause, exit from the

DO CASE...ENDCASE command.

III PLUS's desire to find only the first TRUE CASE gives the programmer the option of making a do-nothing clause in a program. You can use CASE condition with absolutely no command lines under the CASE, and III PLUS will skip over the rest of the DO CASE ...CASE...OTHERWISE...ENDCASE command, find the END-CASE, and exit from the command stream.

DO

The DO command is a PROGRAM mode command that tells III PLUS what subroutine to call from the currently running module. It is also the interactive command that tells III PLUS what program to run. There is no distinction between advanced and normal use of DO because DO, regardless of interactive or program use, tells III PLUS to direct processing to some module other than the current one. Note that this section covers use of the DO command specifically. Information on the DO...WITH command, which is used to pass memory variables from the calling routine to the called subroutine, can be found in Chapter 10 and is summarized in the next section. This version of the DO command has nothing to do with the DO WHILE ...ENDDO or DO CASE...ENDCASE command. The command syntax is

DO command file

where command file can be any valid III PLUS program file. III PLUS assumes the named command file will have a .PRG extension unless you specify some other extension in the command. III PLUS will tell you if it can't find the listed file. In PROGRAM mode, this means everything will come to a crashing halt. It is important that the designer ensure the proper files are on the proper drives in the proper directories. A file-checking algorithm is given in Chapter 23.

DO...WITH

The DO...WITH command is strictly a PROGRAM mode command that tells III PLUS what variables from the calling program will be used in the called routine in special ways. It is covered in Chapter 10.

DO CASE

The DO CASE command is the first part of the four-part command

DO CASE...CASE...OTHERWISE...ENDCASE

The command syntax is

DO CASE

without any qualifiers or modifiers. Note that the DO CASE command tells III PLUS a series of options are going to be presented. These options take the form of CASE statements. III PLUS encounters the DO CASE statement and then determines which of the many CASE statements that follow is the single CASE statement it should act on. All other CASEs are ignored. III PLUS finds the first TRUE CASE and executes only those lines listed under it. It doesn't matter how many CASEs are in the command; processing will be transferred to the first TRUE CASE, and only the group of commands following that CASE will be executed. Once a CASE is executed, III PLUS looks for the ENDCASE command and leaves the command stream. A last note: If no CASEs are TRUE, III PLUS will either execute whatever commands are listed under the OTHERWISE clause or continue processing with the first command after the associated ENDCASE command.

DO WHILE

The DO WHILE command is the first part of the four-part command

DO WHILE...EXIT...LOOP...ENDDO

The command syntax is

DO WHILE condition

where condition is something that III PLUS can equate to either

TRUE or FALSE. Also note that the DO WHILE can't be a command itself, although functions such as IIF and multiple logical statements are allowed. The advantage to using IIF instead of a simple DO WHILE condition comes when mathematical step functions are involved. Step functions are found in tax preparation, commission rates, and feed-to-weight ratios. Boolean algebra applies in all cases.

Note that the DO WHILE command tells III PLUS to execute a block of code only WHILE a condition or conditions are met. You can EXIT from the DO WHILE command stream based on another condition, one external to the DO WHILE condition, with the EXIT command. Also, you can tell III PLUS that the rest of the commands aren't relevant to the current job with the LOOP command. All commands after the EXIT and LOOP commands are ignored. The EXIT command tells III PLUS to leave the DO WHILE stream. The LOOP command tells III PLUS to go back to the top of the DO WHILE stream. Note that if the initial condition in the DO WHILE command isn't TRUE, the entire DO WHILE...EXIT...LOOP... ENDDO command block is passed over and not touched by III PLUS.

ELSE

The ELSE command is the second part of the command

```
IF...ELSE...ENDIF
```

The normal condition sequence is

```
IF condition
   command series
ENDIF
```

where condition is any valid III PLUS expression that can be equated to either TRUE or FALSE, and command series represents any number of executable III PLUS commands, including comments. Note that the preceding command sequence takes action only if the IF condition is TRUE. What do you do about FALSE conditions? You make use of the logical IF TRUE...ELSE (IF FALSE). This can be expressed as

```
IF something is TRUE then do this thing
ELSE, IF something is NOT TRUE, then do this other thing
```

Note that the ELSE command is entered as

ELSE

without qualifiers or modifiers of any kind. In other words, III PLUS doesn't have to be told ELSE condition. III PLUS automatically acknowledges the countercondition to the IF condition. Also note that III PLUS will give the user an error message if it encounters an ELSE without a preceding IF. The ELSE command modifies the command sequence shown earlier to

```
IF condition
    command series
ELSE
    alternative command series
ENDIF
```

where alternative command series is defined as command series was defined previously. Note that the ELSE command isn't a necessary part of the IF...ENDIF command pair.

ENDCASE

The ENDCASE command is the last part of the four-part command

DO CASE...CASE...OTHERWISE...ENDCASE

The command syntax is

ENDCASE

without any qualifiers or modifiers. ENDCASE tells III PLUS it has encountered the end of the series of options initiated with the DO CASE command. These options take the form of CASE statements. III PLUS encounters the ENDCASE and stops looking for CASEs if neither TRUE CASEs nor an OTHERWISE command was encountered. It doesn't matter how many CASEs are in the command

DO CASE...CASE...OTHERWISE...ENDCASE

III PLUS stops looking for TRUE CASEs once the ENDCASE command is encountered. However, once a TRUE CASE is encountered, III PLUS looks for the ENDCASE command and leaves the command stream. A warning: Make sure all DO CASE commands in called routines have their ENDCASE commands in the same routines. You might find III PLUS searching endlessly for CASEs or not executing entire PRG files due to missing or misplaced ENDCASE commands.

ENDDO

The ENDDO command is the last part of the four-part command

DO WHILE...EXIT...LOOP...ENDDO

The command syntax is

ENDDO

without qualifiers or conditions of any kind. Note that the ENDDO command tells III PLUS it has reached the END of a DO WHILE command stream. This is an important flag in III PLUS, especially when you use the EXIT command. You can EXIT from the ENDDO command stream based on another condition, one external to the ENDDO condition, with the EXIT command. The EXIT command tells III PLUS to leave the DO WHILE command stream and continue processing with the command immediately following the DO WHILE command stream. If III PLUS can't find an ENDDO, it will return to INTERACTIVE mode. All commands after the EXIT in the DO WHILE stream are ignored.

A warning to the programmer: Make sure all DO WHILE commands in called routines have their ENDDO commands in the same routines. You might find III PLUS performing bizarre processing paths due to missing or misplaced ENDDO commands.

ENDIF

The ENDIF command is the last part of the command

IF...ELSE...ENDIF

The normal command sequence is shown in the listing on page 538, where condition is any valid III PLUS expression that can be equated to either TRUE or FALSE, and both command series and alternative command series represent any number of executable III PLUS commands, including comments. Note that III PLUS only acts upon the command series IF the condition is TRUE. FALSE conditions are handled by the alternative command series listed under the ELSE command. Note that the ENDIF command is entered as

ENDIF

without qualifiers or modifiers of any kind. Also note that III PLUS will give the user an error message if it encounters an ENDIF without a preceding IF. The ENDIF command tells III PLUS it has reached the end of the IF command stream; there are no more conditional commands left to execute.

ENDTEXT

The ENDTEXT command is the last part of the two-part command

TEXT...ENDTEXT

The two-part command is primarily used to include long text strings in a program.

Syntax   The command syntax is

ENDTEXT

without qualifiers or conditions. III PLUS isn't concerned with the lack of a preceding TEXT command and behaves neutrally when it encounters a lone ENDTEXT command.

Use   The TEXT...ENDTEXT command pair was demonstrated in the section on the * command earlier in this chapter. The command pair places character strings in the program without the use of @...SAY, ?, or ?? commands. Note that III PLUS places the text bracketed by TEXT...ENDTEXT on the line directly under the cursor and the following lines. If the cursor is on screen position

(21,58), III PLUS places the bracketed text from line 22 on down. The screen scrolls to accommodate all necessary text. This also means that bracketed text longer than 24 lines will be scrolled off the screen.

One use of the TEXT...ENDTEXT command pair is for copyright and opening messages. The following listing demonstrates a typical TEXT...ENDTEXT command pair used for that purpose. You CLEAR the screen before putting up any text and remove the text after 49 passes through the DO WHILE...ENDDO loop.

```
** START OF PROGRAM
**
CLEAR
*
TEXT
                            NAME OF PROGRAM

                         COPYRIGHT MESSAGES


                OPENING MESSAGES AND PRODUCT CAVEATS

ENDTEXT
*
N = 1
*
DO WHILE N < 50
   N = N + 1
ENDDO
*
CLEAR
**
** REST OF PROGRAM
```

EXIT

The EXIT command is the second part of the four-part command

DO WHILE...EXIT...LOOP...ENDDO

The EXIT command tells III PLUS to continue processing outside the DO WHILE stream. You can EXIT from the DO WHILE command stream based on another condition, one external to the DO WHILE condition. This command also tells III PLUS that the commands following the EXIT command in the DO WHILE stream aren't relevant to the current job. All commands in the DO WHILE stream after the EXIT command are ignored. The command syntax is

EXIT

without qualifiers or conditions of any kind. Note that the EXIT command tells III PLUS to continue processing with the command immediately following the ENDDO command at the end of the DO WHILE stream. The EXIT command tells III PLUS to leave the DO WHILE stream completely. Don't confuse the EXIT command with the LOOP command. The LOOP command tells III PLUS to go back to the top of the DO WHILE stream.

III PLUS will EXIT to INTERACTIVE mode only if there are no commands after the ENDDO command or EXITing from the immediate DO WHILE stream doesn't return control to a calling program. Finally, the EXIT command isn't a necessary part of the DO WHILE...ENDDO command.

IF

The IF command is the first part of the command

IF...ELSE...ENDIF

The normal command sequence is shown in the listing on page 538, where condition is any valid III PLUS expression that can be equated to either TRUE or FALSE, and both command series and alternative command series represent any number of executable III PLUS commands, including comments. Note that III PLUS acts upon the command series only IF the condition is TRUE. FALSE conditions are handled by the alternative command series listed under the ELSE command. Note that the IF command is entered as

IF condition

where condition is something that III PLUS can equate to either TRUE or FALSE. Also note that the IF condition can't be a command, although functions such as IIF and multiple logical statements are allowed. The advantage of using IIF instead of a simple IF condition comes when mathematical step functions are involved. Step functions are used in figuring such items as taxes, commission rates, and feed-to-weight ratios. Note that Boolean algebra applies in all cases. III PLUS will assume all commands after the IF command are part of the IF series until it encounters an ELSE or an ENDIF.

The IF command tells III PLUS to execute a block of code only IF a condition or conditions are met. This can be a one-way conditional statement if you remove the ELSE command from the IF stream. The stream becomes IF...ENDIF. III PLUS will totally pass by the IF...ENDIF block if the initial condition isn't TRUE. Normally, processing would go to ELSE's alternative command series, but with no ELSE, processing continues with the command immediately following the ENDIF command.

LOOP

The LOOP command is the third part of the four-part command

```
DO WHILE...EXIT...LOOP...ENDDO
```

The LOOP command tells III PLUS to continue processing with the first command following the initial DO WHILE condition command. This command also tells III PLUS the commands following the LOOP command in the DO WHILE stream aren't relevant to the current job. All commands in the DO WHILE stream after the LOOP command are ignored. The command syntax is

```
LOOP
```

without qualifiers or conditions of any kind. Don't confuse the EXIT command with the LOOP command. The LOOP command tells III PLUS to go back to the top of the DO WHILE stream. The EXIT command tells III PLUS to leave the DO WHILE stream completely.

This command finds many uses in DO WHILE streams that are several hundred lines long. The command is most often used as shown in the following listing.

```
DO WHILE condition
   command series
*
   IF another condition
```

```
        LOOP
    ENDI
 *
    remaining command series
ENDDO
```

Several commands can be in the first series. IF some condition is met, LOOP over the remaining commands in the series and start at the top of the DO WHILE stream again. Note that the LOOP command doesn't have to be in an IF...ENDIF command to function properly, nor is the LOOP command a necessary part of the DO WHILE...ENDDO command.

NOTE

The command in this section has little to do with program control. It is actually used for documenting programs internally. All dBASEs use the NOTE command to tell the particular dBASE that the rest of the line is a comment. This use is similar to using the semicolon (;) in assemblers and the REM command in the BATch and BASIC languages. III PLUS uses the NOTE, *, and && commands to separate comment lines from the rest of the program. You can use any of these commands interactively if you wish. This section concerns itself with the NOTE command. The command form is

NOTE text

where text is any single line of comment. You should specify that the text in the preceding command is any single line of comment. This is true especially when using a word processor other than the III PLUS Text Editor. The III PLUS Text Editor knows how to wrap lines for the III PLUS command processor. Other text editors don't.

OTHERWISE

The OTHERWISE command is the third part of the four-part command

DO CASE...CASE...OTHERWISE...ENDCASE

The command syntax is

OTHERWISE

without qualifiers or conditions. Note that III PLUS executes only
lines listed under the first TRUE CASE in the DO CASE stream. If
no CASEs are TRUE, III PLUS looks for an OTHERWISE command in the DO CASE stream and continues processing with the
first command after the OTHERWISE command. The OTHER-
WISE command isn't a necessary part of the DO CASE stream, but
note the flexibility of the command. It takes no conditions or qualifiers. If no CASEs are TRUE, III PLUS executes the OTHERWISE
command. This command is useful in designing immediate error
traps. You might want to have such a trap, for example, when the
user is supposed to press one of several keys and doesn't. A simple
code listing demonstrating this use of the command is

```
ACCE "WHAT IS YOUR CHOICE?   -> " TO ANSWER
*
DO CASE
   CASE ANSWER = first valid choice
      do something
   CASE ANSWER = second valid choice
      do something else
   .     .      . .      .       .
   .     .      . .      .       .
   OTHERWISE && NO VALID CHOICES WERE MADE
      WAIT "THAT ISN'T A VALID CHOICE."+;
      "PRESS ANY KEY TO CONTINUE."
ENDCASE
```

Here, the user is given a menu that shows several valid options. The
user presses an invalid key. The OTHERWISE command lets the
user know he or she has chosen the wrong key before it requests
another try.

PARAMETER

The PARAMETER command, also discussed in Chapter 10, is used
to tell a called routine what variables from the calling program it
will be working with. The PARAMETER command is the receiving
end of the DO...WITH command. The DO...WITH command sends

certain variables to the called routine. The standard form of the command is

DO something WITH variable list

The PARAMETER command should be the first executable command in the "something" the DO...WITH command calls. The PARAMETER variable list should match the DO...WITH variable list in both variable number and variable type. You can send more variables than you'll receive, but you must send at least as many variables as are listed in the PARAMETER command. More important to proper execution of called routines and calling programs than the number of variables sent is that the DO...WITH command and the PARAMETER command pass the same variable types back and forth. Any called routine can create its own, local variables or use the variables of the calling program. Local variables are RELEASEd when the called routine returns processing to the calling program. Variables used from the calling program are returned with their new values or variable types when the called routine returns processing to the calling program. The exception to the rule is variables passed with the DO...WITH and PARAMETER commands. III PLUS will either give you error messages or stop processing normally if you pass a character variable and return a date variable, and so on.

The PARAMETER command can be in a PROCedure or a called PRG file, but it must be in any file that is called with the DO...WITH command. Further, if a PROCedure or PRG file contains the PARAMETER command and isn't called with the DO... WITH command, III PLUS will give you an error message.

PRIVATE

The PRIVATE command is one side of the PRIVATE PUBLIC command pair. Both are used in PROGRAM mode and tell III PLUS certain things about memory variables currently active in the system. The PRIVATE command is discussed in Chapter 10.

PROCEDURE

The PROCEDURE command is a programming label, of sorts. It is used with SET PROCEDURE TO and DO in a special way. PROCEDUREs are special types of programs that the programmer decides are going to be used frequently. Frequently means almost always. Somewhere in the design and programming phases of development, someone decides that certain routines are going to be used so often that it would speed up the work process to place those routines in memory rather than have III PLUS go out to disk for them.

How do you tell III PLUS that some routines are so important they should be kept in memory? You can place up to 32 of the routines in a PROCedure file (see Chapter 2). PROCedure files normally have the .PRG extension and are similar to other PRG files. You tell III PLUS to load a PROCedure file into memory with the command

SET PROCEDURE TO prc file

III PLUS assumes the named file will have a .PRG extension. If you want to use the .PRC extension for housekeeping purposes, you must include the .PRC extension when you load a file with the preceding command. To load the A.PRC PROCedure file you would have to enter

SET PROCEDURE TO A.PRC

Note that the named PROCedure file stays in memory until III PLUS receives any of these commands:

```
CLOSE ALL
CLOSE PROCEDURE
SET PROCEDURE TO
SET PROCEDURE TO another prc file
```

III PLUS allows up to 32 separate PROCedures in a single PRC file. The PROCedure command is used at the start of each separate PROCedure in the PRC file. III PLUS places flags at each PROCedure command and considers the single PROCedure command as the PRC equivalent of end-of-file and beginning-of-file markers. It might be more proper to say end-of-procedure and beginning-of-procedure markers, in this case. The command syntax is

PROCEDURE procedure name

Each PROCedure command can have only one PROCedure name beside it. You shouldn't use two PROCedures with the same name, as III PLUS will always execute the first one in the list.

PUBLIC

The PUBLIC command is one side of the PUBLIC PRIVATE command pair. Both are used in PROGRAM mode and tell III PLUS certain things about memory variables currently active in the system. The PUBLIC command is discussed in Chapter 10.

QUIT

The QUIT command tells III PLUS to return to DOS. Returning to DOS forces III PLUS to CLOSE any open files, no matter what type they are. The QUIT command is a single-line command, much like CANCEL. Unlike CANCEL, QUIT tells III PLUS to CLOSE all open files, including program, database, format, view, query, and dbt files. The QUIT command also flushes any III PLUS memory buffers and releases all memory used by III PLUS during the work session. The III PLUS Help screen states that the QUIT command returns you to the operating system. Currently, that is DOS 2.xx and higher with either the Novell or IBM network. A future operating system may be UNIX. The command syntax is

QUIT

dBASE II programmers, note that dBASE III and III PLUS don't support the command

QUIT TO external file

found in dBASE II. The QUIT TO command has been replaced by RUN and ! in dBASE III and III PLUS. III PLUS doesn't care where it encounters the QUIT command. It will assume the program or user knows what's going on and will return to the operating system. This means that a main program that calls several subroutines, including PRC files, and all other open files will be closed and memory flushed when a QUIT command is encountered, even if the QUIT command is found in the lowest PRG file on the totem pole.

RESUME

The RESUME command is the second half of the SUSPEND RESUME command pair. The command syntax is

RESUME

without qualifiers or conditions. You have to understand SUSPEND to understand RESUME. SUSPEND tells III PLUS to halt a currently running program and return to INTERACTIVE mode. In that way, SUSPEND is similar to CANCEL. However, CANCEL closes all open PRG files and stops further program-file processing. SUSPEND tells III PLUS to halt a currently running program and return to INTERACTIVE mode, but keep all files, variables, and so on, opened by all valid active program files. Further, the SUSPEND command tells III PLUS to remember where it was in the currently running program file. So, you enter SUSPEND and you find yourself back at the dBASE prompt, but III PLUS has stopped processing only temporarily. It waits for you to give it the go-ahead to pick up exactly where it left off, with memory and files intact. You tell it to pick up where it left off with the RESUME command.

RESUME tells III PLUS to continue processing, with the command immediately following the SUSPEND command. Note that this command pair is valid only in a programming environment. III PLUS does nothing if no programs are running and RESUME is entered from the dBASE prompt.

The SUSPEND RESUME pair is especially useful in design work. The programmer can include the SUSPEND command at breakpoints in the code. III PLUS encounters the SUSPEND command and returns to the dBASE prompt, but all files are open, and programmatic memory is intact. The programmer can use the memory-viewing commands (Chapters 8 and 10) to investigate program status. After the programmer is satisfied, he or she can enter RESUME and III PLUS will pick up where it left off. Processing will continue until the next breakpoint is reached. Note that all SUSPENDs should be removed from the finished program unless the system is designed to allow the user interactive control of III PLUS.

The RETRY command is similar to the RETURN command. Both commands tell III PLUS to continue processing in the calling program. The RETURN command tells III PLUS to continue processing at the command immediately following the DO command that called the subroutine. The RETRY command tells III PLUS to continue processing at the DO command that called the subroutine. In that sense, the RETRY command can be thought of as a massive DO WHILE...ENDDO command around a called routine. The command syntax is

RETRY

without qualifiers or conditions. To understand the RETRY command, consider this example: Assume there is some routine, APRG, that is called from a main module, MAIN. You want to repeat the APRG routine until some condition is met. In particular, you don't want to perform any other commands in MAIN until some condition in APRG is met. MAIN processes the first set of commands and then shifts processing to the APRG routine. APRG processes its first set of commands and encounters the IF...ENDIF command. In particular, IF some condition is met, RETURN to the line in MAIN that called APRG. If the condition isn't met, continue processing until the end of APRG and return to the second command series in MAIN. The flow for this is shown in the following listing:

```
** MAIN.PRG
**
main command series 1
DO APRG
main command series 2
*
** EOF


** APRG.PRG
** CALLED FROM MAIN.PRG
**
aprg command series 1
*
IF condition
    RETRY
ENDIF
```

```
*
aprg command series 2
*
** EOF
```

The command sequence is identical to

```
** MAIN.PRG
**
main command series 1
*
DO WHILE condition
    aprg command series 1
ENDDO
*
aprg command series 2
main command series 2
*
** EOF
```

Given that the RETRY command can be mimicked by a DO WHILE...ENDDO construction, why use it? The RETRY command is useful in network applications. III PLUS can poll a file for availability. If the file isn't available, you can send a message to the user telling him or her to wait and then RETRY opening the file.

RETURN

The RETURN command can be thought of as a soft QUIT. RETURN tells III PLUS to flush PRIVATE memory associated with the currently running PRG file and continue processing with the command immediately following the command that called the routine. This is different from the RETRY command, which tells III PLUS to continue processing at the command that called the routine. The RETURN command is a single-line command, much like QUIT. Unlike QUIT, RETURN tells III PLUS to CLOSE only the currently running program file and flush only the currently running program's PRIVATE memory variables. This is not entirely true, however. The RETURN command doesn't close open PRC files, nor does a PROCedure need a RETURN command for III PLUS to know when it has reached the end of the PROCedure. The command form is

RETURN

III PLUS closes only the current PRG file. All DBF, NDX, FMT, PRC, VUE, and similar files opened by the current PRG file remain active when III PLUS encounters a RETURN command. Also note that the last SELECTed work area will be the current work area when III PLUS executes the RETURN command.

III PLUS will RETURN the user to the dBASE prompt if the user RETURNs from the highest level of the program system. Note that the highest level of a program system doesn't need a RETURN command to RETURN the user to the dBASE prompt.

RETURN TO MASTER

The RETURN TO MASTER command is a special form of the RETURN command described in the last section. It has all the properties of the RETURN command, but tells III PLUS to RETURN processing to the top-level PRG file. RETURN TO MASTER can also be thought of as a soft QUIT, but a harder QUIT than the normal RETURN. RETURN tells III PLUS to flush PRIVATE memory associated with the currently running PRG file and continue processing with the command immediately following the command that called the routine. RETURN TO MASTER tells III PLUS to flush non-PUBLIC variables and continue processing at the command in the top-level PRG file that called the first subroutine. Note that only variables declared PUBLIC or PRIVATE at the dBASE prompt and those declared in the top-level PRG are exempt from RETURN TO MASTER.

The RETURN TO MASTER command is a single-line command, much like RETURN. Unlike RETURN, RETURN TO MASTER tells III PLUS to CLOSE all program files, except the top-level PRG file, and flush all memory variables not declared either at the dBASE prompt or by the top-level program. The RETURN TO MASTER command doesn't close open PRC files, but a PROCedure does need a RETURN TO MASTER command if it is to RETURN processing to the highest-level PRG file instead of the PRG file that called it. The command syntax is

RETURN TO MASTER

All DBF, NDX, FMT, PRC, VUE, and similar files opened by the current PRG file remain active when III PLUS encounters a RETURN TO MASTER command. Also note that the last SELECTed work area will be the current work area when III PLUS executes the RETURN TO MASTER command. III PLUS will leave the user at the dBASE prompt if you RETURN TO MASTER from the highest level of the program system. Note that the highest level of a program system doesn't need a RETURN TO MASTER command to RETURN the user to the dBASE prompt.

SET PROCEDURE TO

The SET PROCEDURE TO command tells III PLUS to load a PRC file into memory. It is discussed in Chapter 11.

SUSPEND

The SUSPEND command is the first half of the SUSPEND RESUME command pair. More information on the SUSPEND command can be found in the section on RESUME earlier in this chapter. The command syntax is

SUSPEND

without qualifiers or conditions.

TEXT

The TEXT command is the first part of the two-part command

TEXT...ENDTEXT

The two-part command is primarily used to include long text strings in a program. The command syntax is

TEXT

without qualifiers or conditions. The TEXT...ENDTEXT command pair was demonstrated in the section on the * command earlier in this chapter. The command pair allows you to place character strings in the program without the use of @...SAY, ?, or ?? commands. Note that III PLUS places the text bracketed by TEXT...ENDTEXT on the line directly under the cursor and the following lines. If the cursor is on screen position (21,58), III PLUS places the bracketed text from line 22 on down. The screen scrolls to accommodate all necessary text. This also means that bracketed text longer than 24 lines will be scrolled off the screen.

One use of the TEXT...ENDTEXT command pair is to produce copyright and opening messages, as shown in the ENDTEXT section earlier in this chapter.

Debugging Commands
and Debugging Programs

This chapter covers the somewhat advanced topic of debugging commands. History buffs may want to know that the term *debugging* was actually coined because a moth got stuck in an old, tube-style computer in 1949. The legendary Rear Admiral Grace Hopper (retired) determined there was nothing wrong with the program and said the problem was in the hardware. They looked in the back of the machine and found a moth on the connectors to some tubes, the source of the electrical short in the computer. Admiral Hopper said the computer had to be "de-bugged." Debugging is a necessary part of system development.

Some of the commands in this chapter have been discussed in detail in other sections. When that is the case, references will be given to the other sections.

DIR

III PLUS supports a DIR command that is almost identical to the DOS DIRectory command. Both commands give the user a list of files available in the default drive and directory.

Syntax   III PLUS's DIR command syntax is identical with that of the DOS DIRectory commands. The only difference is that III PLUS's DIR command doesn't accept the DOS-level /P and /W switches. The command syntax is

DIR

III PLUS shows only the available DBF files when you enter the naked DIR command. dBASE II programmers may remember the comparable dBASE II DISPLAY FILES command. III PLUS also supports the DISPLAY FILES command but also supports the simpler DIR command.

You can tell III PLUS to list files other than DBF files by using wild cards and file skeletons in the DIR command. You can get a listing of NDX files with

DIR *.NDX

In addition, you can specify which files will be listed. For example, you can request a directory of all NDX files starting with B and having four-letter filenames with

DIR B???.NDX

III PLUS will show all files on the current drive and directory with

DIR *.*

This command is equivalent to the standard DOS DIR command. You can also tell III PLUS to list files not in the current drive and directory by including the drive and path designators, as in

DIR B:\DB3\STUFF

The preceding command looks for a disk in drive B, then looks for the DB3 subdirectory and, last, the STUFF subdirectory. It lists any DBF files in that directory.

Use   You can use DIR in PROGRAM or INTERACTIVE mode. The DIR command is similar to DISP FILES in that both stop the file listing when the screen is full and prompt the user with

Press any key to continue...

This feature is useful, as the user doesn't need fleet fingers to get things done. If you use the alternative LIST FILES command (also a holdover from dBASE II days) the command operation doesn't stop when the screen is filled.

The III PLUS DIR command shares a useful feature with all other III PLUS commands: You can use macros (see Chapter 14) to

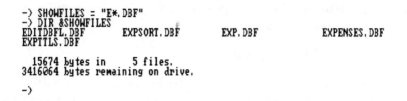

```
-> SHOWFILES = "E*.DBF"
-> DIR &SHOWFILES
EDITDBFL.DBF       EXPSORT.DBF        EXP.DBF        EXPENSES.DBF
EXPTTLS.DBF

  15674 bytes in     5 files.
3416064 bytes remaining on drive.

->
```

Figure 15-1.   You can use macros with the DIR command

get what you want. An example of this is shown in Figure 15-1. A variable, SHOWFILES, appears, with a value of "E*.DBF". III PLUS provides a list of all files that match that skeleton with the command

DIR &SHOWFILES

The DIR command is useful in debugging because it provides a listing of all file types to the screen. This comes in handy when III PLUS continually tells you that the file you're requesting isn't available in the current drive and directory.

DISPLAY FILES

As mentioned in the last section, III PLUS supports the DISPLAY FILES command. This command is a holdover from dBASE II and has all the properties of the III PLUS DIR command. Both commands give the user a list of available files in the default drive and directory. Much of what was said about the DIR command applies to the DISPLAY FILES command. This section will highlight the DISPLAY FILES command's unique features.

Like DIR, DISPLAY FILES defaults to showing available DBF files. Tell III PLUS to DISPLAY FILES other than DBF files with

DISPLAY FILES LIKE skeleton

where skeleton can be any mixture of wild cards (* to signify any number of characters and ? to signify a single character). Further, you can tell III PLUS to DISPLAY FILES on something other than the current drive and directory with

DISPLAY FILES LIKE drive: \path \skeleton

where drive: can be any valid drive for your system, path can be any valid path, and skeleton is defined as previously. You can DISPLAY DBF FILES in C: \DB3 \COMPLETE with

DISPLAY FILES LIKE C: \DB3 \COMPLETE *.DBF

as shown in Figure 15-2. Note that the upper portion of that figure shows the command entered without *.DBF and III PLUS saying there are no such files present. The lower portion of the figure shows the command with *.DBF and III PLUS returning a wide DISPLAY. This is an important aspect of the command. The LIKE qualifier needs to know LIKE what. You must specify some skeleton when using the LIKE qualifier to shift III PLUS's attention to another drive or directory.

```
-> DISPLAY FILES LIKE C:\DB3\COMPLETE
Database Files    # Records    Last Update    Size


3416064 bytes remaining on drive.

-> DISPLAY FILES LIKE C:\DB3\COMPLETE\*.DBF
7CSETANK.DBF      BOOKS.DBF         BOOKS2.DBF        BOOKS3.DBF
BOOKS4.DBF        C10CQRY.DBF       C10CT2.DBF        C10CTEST.DBF
7TANK.DBF         CHAPTER9.DBF      CLACCT.DBF        TED.DBF
EDITDBFL.DBF      LETTER.DBF        OTHER.DBF         PASS2.DBF
PASSWORD.DBF      PFSTEST.DBF       PROMPTS.DBF       SEFILE.DBF
TANK2.DBF         TEMP.DBF          EXPSORT.DBF       EXP.DBF
EXPENSES.DBF      RALPH.DBF         TED2.DBF          TED3.DBF
JOINFILE.DBF      BOOK.DBF          EXPTTLS.DBF       INCOME.DBF
MAGAZINE.DBF      MSSFILE.DBF       PACKTANK.DBF      TODAY.DBF
JDCBOOKS.DBF      TEST.DBF          HEADBASE.DBF      BOOK2.DBF
COMMANDS.DBF      MBOOKS.DBF

 786622 bytes in    42 files.
3416064 bytes remaining on drive.

->
```

Figure 15-2.   The DISPLAY FILES command needs a skeleton when you use the LIKE qualifier

The final form to consider is

DISP FILES LIKE skeleton TO PRIN

This tells III PLUS to send the DISPLAY TO the PRINTER as well as the screen. Note the four-letter-word convention in the preceding command. III PLUS will still prompt the user with "Press any key to continue..." even though the information is going to the printer. Note also that long listings will go over page breaks and not be formatted for printed output, and that you must use the LIKE qualifier with a skeleton if you're going TO PRINT.

DISPLAY HISTORY

The DISPLAY HISTORY command is a godsend to programmers. It provides a listing of all commands that are both entered at the dBASE prompt and executed in COMMAND mode. This section doesn't cover how to record those commands, only how to DISPLAY them. See Chapter 11 and the sections on RESUME and SET DO-HISTORY on/OFF later in this chapter for more on recording information into the HISTORY buffer.

Syntax   You can enter the DISPLAY HISTORY command directly, as

DISPLAY HISTORY

or with one or two modifiers. The preceding command tells III PLUS to list all commands entered into the HISTORY buffer in chronological order. III PLUS starts the listing with the first command entered and goes down the line to the last command entered (which is, of course, DISPLAY HISTORY). Note that this is a DISPLAY command; III PLUS will list a certain number of commands, and then prompt the user with

Press any key to continue...

as shown in Figure 15-3. III PLUS will DISPLAY all the commands in the HISTORY buffer with the execution of the preceding command. The HISTORY buffer defaults to 20 commands, but that

```
-> DISP HIST
DIR &SHOWFILES
CLEAR
SHOWFILES = "E*.DBF"
DIR &SHOWFILES
DIR TO PRINT
DISP FILES TO FILE
DISP FILES TO PRINT
DISP FILES
DISP FILES LIKE *.DBF TO PRINT
CLEAR
EJECT
SET HISTO TO 100
DIR /W
DIR /P
DIR
DIR *.*
Press any key to continue...
```

Figure 15-3.   III PLUS DISPLAYs the command HISTORY in chronological order

default can be modified with the SET HISTORY TO command (see Chapter 11 and SET DOHISTORY on/OFF later in this chapter). You can tell III PLUS to list a specific number of commands with

DISP HIST LAST n

where n is any valid III PLUS numeric expression. Note the dBASE III PLUS four-letter-word convention in the preceding command. For example, the command

DISP HIST LAST 10

tells III PLUS to DISPLAY only the LAST 10 commands in the HISTORY buffer.

The final form to consider is

DISP HIST TO PRINT

This tells III PLUS to send the DISPLAY TO the PRINTER as well as the screen. Note the four-letter-word convention in the preceding command. III PLUS will still prompt the user with "Press any key to continue...," even though the information is going to the printer.

Note also that long listings will go over page breaks and not be formatted for printed output. You can mix the LAST n and TO PRINT qualifiers without causing any problems.

Use   The DISPLAY HISTORY command is a powerful debugging tool when used to record program lines as they are executed. You must tell III PLUS to record program lines with the SET DOHISTORY command (see Chapter 11 and later in this chapter).

III PLUS will record all program lines up to the point where the HISTORY buffer becomes full. Once the HISTORY buffer is full, III PLUS begins throwing out stored command lines, starting with the oldest information. In Figure 15-3, the lines at the top of the DISPLAY would be removed from the HISTORY buffer first. For debugging purposes, the last command stored in the HISTORY buffer would be the one that caused your program to fail. This assumes you're recording program lines because you want to debug your system. You can use the HISTORY buffer to record lines of a totally debugged program if you want, but that slows execution by as much as 25%. III PLUS must record each command as it is executed. This requires more memory management on its part than straight execution and slows down the system.

DISPLAY MEMORY

The DISPLAY MEMORY command is covered in Chapters 8 and 10.

DISPLAY STATUS

The DISPLAY STATUS command is similar to the DISPLAY MEMORY command in that it gives the user or programmer specific information about the system when the command is entered. Like all DISPLAY commands, DISPLAY STATUS prompts the user with

Press any key to continue...

when the screen is full of information. The command syntax is

DISPLAY STATUS

This form of the command tells III PLUS to send the following information to the screen:

```
ACTIVE WORK AREAS
OPEN DATABASES IN THOSE WORK AREAS
NDX FILES ASSOCIATED WITH THE DATABASES
FMT FILES ASSOCIATED WITH THE DATABASES
QRY FILES OR FILTERS ACTIVE ON THE DATABASES
RELATIONS BETWEEN DATABASES
VUE FILES ACTIVE AND IN WHAT WORK AREAS
FILE SEARCH PATH
DEFAULT DISK DRIVE
PRINT DESTINATION
LEFT MARGIN ON PRINTED REPORTS
CURRENTLY ACTIVE WORK AREA
DELIMITERS
EXISTENCE OF ANY EVENT PROCESSING COMMANDS
STATUS OF SET TOGGLES, INCLUDING DEVICE
FUNCTION KEY COMMANDS
LOADED BIN FILES
```

A sample DISPLAY STATUS is shown in the following listing:

```
-> DISP STAT

Select area:  1, Database in Use: D:jdcbooks.dbf   Alias:
JDCBOOKS
    Index file: c:\library\jdcbttle.ndx  Key: title
    Index file: c:\library\jdcbathr.ndx  Key:
trim(left(author,50))+upper(trim(left(title,50)))

Select area:  2, Database in Use: D:EXPENSES.dbf   Alias:
EXPENSES
    Index file: D:EXPENSES.ndx  Key: payto
    Format file: D:EXPENSES.fmt

Select area:  3, Database in Use: D:COMMANDS.dbf   Alias:
COMMANDS
Press any key to continue...


Currently Selected Database:
Select area:  4, Database in Use: D:BOOKS.dbf  Alias: BOOKS

Alternate file: A:ALTER.txt
File search path:
Default disk drive: D:
Print destination:  PRN:
Margin =      0
Current work area =    4    Delimiters are ':' and ':'

On Escape:      DISP MEMO
Press any key to continue...

ALTERNATE   - ON   DELETED   - OFF  FIXED      - OFF  SAFETY
    - OFF
```

```
BELL         - OFF  DELIMITERS - ON    HEADING    - ON
SCOREBOARD   - OFF
CARRY        - OFF  DEVICE     - SCRN  HELP       - OFF  STATUS
   - OFF
CATALOG      - OFF  DOHISTORY  - OFF   HISTORY    - ON   STEP
   - OFF
CENTURY      - OFF  ECHO       - OFF   INTENSITY  - ON   TALK
   - OFF
CONFIRM      - OFF  ESCAPE     - ON    MENU       - OFF  TITLE
   - ON
CONSOLE      - ON   EXACT      - OFF   PRINT      - OFF  UNIQUE
   - OFF
DEBUG        - OFF  FIELDS     - OFF

Programmable function keys:
F2  - assist;
F3  - list;
F4  - dir;
F5  - display structure;
F6  - display status;
F7  - SET ALTER TO A:ALTER;SET ALTER ON;
F8  - CLOSE ALTER;
F9  - CLEAR;
F10 - EJECT;
```

The only variation on the command is the TO PRINT qualifier. The command is

DISPLAY STATUS TO PRINT

This tells III PLUS to dump the information TO the PRINTer. Note that III PLUS knows if the printer is available to accept information when you DISPLAY STATUS TO PRINT, and that information is still sent to the screen even when you've told III PLUS to DISPLAY STATUS only TO the PRINTer. The DISPLAY STATUS command is used purely to show the user the current STATUS of the III PLUS system, but note how complete the STATUS report is. DISPLAY STATUS can be useful to the system developer during the debugging phase of programming. The developer can make use of both the DISPLAY STATUS and the DISPLAY MEMORY commands in the following code:

```
WAIT TO DISPWHAT
DISPWHAT = UPPER(DISPWHAT)
*
DO CASE
   CASE DISPWHAT = "M"
       DISPLAY MEMORY
   CASE DISPWHAT = "S"
       DISPLAY STATUS
ENDC
*
```

This short piece of code will not affect anything else in a program but provides an excellent window into the status of the system. This block of code is placed wherever the user wants a breakpoint. A variable, DISPWHAT, is created with a WAIT command. The WAIT command prompts the user with

Press any key to continue...

and places the value of the pressed key into the DISPWHAT variable. Here DISPWHAT is replaced with the UPPERCASE value just in case the user or programmer enters a lowercase letter. If the user or programmer types **M** or **m**, the system then DISPLAYs MEMORY. If the user or programmer types **S** or **s**, the system then DISPLAYs STATUS. Pressing any other key causes III PLUS to ignore the DO CASE...ENDCASE block. Another method of achieving the same goal is to place the command

ON ESCAPE DO DISPLAYER

in a program. The DISPLAYER.PRG file in the preceding command is an extended list of DISPLAY commands similar to the DO CASE...ENDCASE block shown in the listing on page 565 but including several more options. Note that this disables the ESCAPE key's normal III PLUS program halt function.

DISPLAY STRUCTURE

The DISPLAY STRUCTURE command generates a listing of the data fields, their data type, their length, and decimal places (for numeric data types). Like all DISPLAY commands, DISPLAY STRUCTURE prompts the user with

Press any key to continue...

when the screen is full of information. The command syntax is

DISPLAY STRUCTURE

This form of the command tells III PLUS to list the current database's file structure to the screen. Note that this command lists only the structure of the current database. You can't use this command to

DISPLAY the STRUCTURE of a database in work area 9 when you're in work area 1. The only variation on the command is with the use of the TO PRINT qualifier. The command syntax is

DISPLAY STRUCTURE TO PRINT

This tells III PLUS to dump the information to the PRINTer. Note that III PLUS knows whether the printer is available to accept information when you DISPLAY STRUCTURE TO PRINT and that information is still sent to the screen even when you've told III PLUS to DISPLAY STRUCTURE only TO the PRINTer. DISPLAY STRUCTURE can be useful to the system developer during the debugging phase of programming.

```
** DISPLAYER DEBUGGING TOOL
*
WAIT "S(TATUS), M(EMORY) OR D(ATABASE STRUCTURE) -> ";
TO DISPWHAT
DISPWHAT = UPPER(DISPWHAT)
*
DO CASE
    CASE DISPWHAT = "D"

        DISP STRUC
    CASE DISPWHAT = "S"
        DISP STAT
    CASE DISPWHAT = "M"
        DISP MEMO
    OTHER
        CANCEL
ENDC
*
** EOF
```

This listing shows the short file, DISPLAYER.PRG, mentioned in the last section. The PRG file can have several more CASEs, if the programmer needs them. DISPLAYER is activated when you press the ESCAPE key (remember that

ON ESCAPE DO DISPLAYER

is used earlier in the code). The logic of the previous examples holds here, with the addition of the CANCEL command, if the user or programmer actually wants to INTERRUPT III PLUS's processing. This doesn't provide the immediate response that the ESCAPE key usually affords the user, but one must make do with what one has.

LIST FILES

As mentioned earlier in this chapter, III PLUS supports the DIS-PLAY FILES command. Naturally, anything that can be DIS-PLAYed can be LISTed. This command is a holdover from dBASE II and has all the properties of the III PLUS DISPLAY FILES command. Both commands give the user a list of available files in the default drive and directory. Much of what was said about the DIS-PLAY FILES command applies to the LIST FILES command (refer to the "DISPLAY FILES" section earlier in this chapter). There is only one difference between the two commands. DISPLAY FILES pauses once a screen is full and prompts the user with

Press any key to continue...

LIST FILES doesn't pause for anything and never prompts the user.

LIST HISTORY

The LIST HISTORY command is identical to the DISPLAY HIS-TORY command (see the "DISPLAY HISTORY" section earlier in this chapter) in all aspects save one. DISPLAY IIISTORY pauses after filling a screen with information and prompts the user with

Press any key to continue...

LIST HISTORY doesn't stop for anything and continues sending information to the screen until it is done.

LIST STATUS

The LIST STATUS command is similar to the DISPLAY STATUS command (see that section earlier in this chapter) in all ways save one. Like all DISPLAY commands, DISPLAY STATUS prompts the user with

Press any key to continue...

when the screen is full of information. LIST STATUS doesn't prompt the user or stop for anything.

LIST STRUCTURE

The LIST STRUCTURE command generates a list of the data fields, their data type, their length, and decimal places (for numeric data types) and is identical to the DISPLAY STRUCTURE command in all ways except the DISPLAY command's standard pause and prompt features. See the DISPLAY STRUCTURE command earlier in this chapter for information on its syntax and use.

LIST STRUCTURE can be useful during debugging. The developer can use the trick mentioned in the "DISPLAY STRUCTURE" section and shown here, especially with systems that have large LISTings. This may be particularly advantageous with systems that employ several hundred memory variables and large file structures. It makes use of the TO PRINT qualifier, but behaves identically to the DISPLAYER module discussed in the "DISPLAY STRUCTURE" section. The next listing shows the LISTER.PRG file.

```
** LISTER DEBUGGING TOOL
*
WAIT "S(TATUS), M(EMORY) OR D(DATABASE STRUCTURE) -> ";
TO LISTWHAT
LISTWHAT = UPPER(LISTWHAT)
SET CONS OFF
*
DO CASE
   CASE LISTWHAT =  "D"
      LIST STRUC TO PRIN
   CASE LISTWHAT =  "S"
      LIST STAT TO PRIN
   CASE LISTWHAT =  "M"
      LIST MEMO TO PRIN
   OTHER
      CANCEL
ENDC
*
SET CONS ON
*
** EOF
```

It is assumed that

ON ESCAPE DO LISTER

has been placed somewhere earlier in the code. The logic of the listing just previous to this one holds here. Note that this only sends information TO the PRINTER, thus preserving screen integrity if the need arises.

RESUME

The RESUME command is covered in Chapter 14. It is the second half of the SUSPEND RESUME command pair. The command syntax is

RESUME

without qualifiers or conditions. SUSPEND tells III PLUS to halt a currently running program and return to INTERACTIVE mode but keep active all files, variables, and so on, opened by all valid program files. Further, the SUSPEND command tells III PLUS to remember where it was in the currently running program file. You tell III PLUS to pick up where it left off with the RESUME command.

RESUME tells III PLUS to continue processing with the command immediately following the SUSPEND command. Note that this command pair is valid only in a programming environment. III PLUS does nothing if no programs are running and RESUME is entered from the dBASE prompt.

The power of the SUSPEND RESUME pair comes from its ability to let the programmer make changes to databases, memory variables, NDX files, and so on, in the middle of running a program and is especially useful in design work. The programmer can include the SUSPEND command at breakpoints in the code. III PLUS encounters the SUSPEND command and returns to the dBASE prompt, but all files are open and programmatic memory is intact. The programmer can use the memory-viewing commands (Chapters 8 and 10) to investigate program status. After the programmer is satisfied, the programmer can enter RESUME, and III PLUS will pick up where it left off. Processing will continue until the next breakpoint is reached. Note that all SUSPENDs should be removed from the finished program unless the system is designed to allow the user interactive control of III PLUS.

SET DEBUG on/OFF

The SET DEBUG toggle is discussed in Chapter 11 and Appendix C. This section provides an overview of the command as it applies to debugging programs. The command syntax is

SET DEBUG toggle

where toggle is either on or OFF. Note that III PLUS defaults to OFF unless the CONFIG.DB DEBUG command is ON. The command itself has no effect on III PLUS unless the SET ECHO command is also ON. SET DEBUG tells III PLUS to send ECHOed commands to the printer. III PLUS normally directs ECHOed output to the screen. The result of these actions is a hard-copy list of the commands as they are executed and a nice, clean screen of what the commands are doing.

SET DOHISTORY on/OFF

The SET DOHISTORY toggle is also referenced in Chapter 11 and Appendix C. This section only highlights the toggle's one function. The SET DOHISTORY toggle tells III PLUS whether or not to record program lines as they are executed. Note that this command has nothing to do with commands entered at the keyboard. Keyboard commands are records with the SET HISTORY toggle. The SET DOHISTORY command records only commands that are executed in PROGRAM mode. The best way to remember the difference between the commands is to use the name as a mnemonic. The DOHISTORY toggle is active only when you DO something.

SET ECHO on/OFF

The SET ECHO toggle is discussed in Chapter 11 and Appendix C. This section deals only with the ECHO toggle's use in the debugging environment. The command syntax is

SET ECHO toggle

where toggle is either on or OFF. Note that III PLUS defaults to OFF unless the CONFIG.DB ECHO command is ON. The SET ECHO ON command is useful if you want to see program command lines listed as they are executed. The SET ECHO toggle lists the command lines to the printer if SET DEBUG is ON.

SET HISTORY TO

The SET HISTORY TO toggle is also referenced in Chapter 11 and Appendix C. Note that this command tells III PLUS how large to make the HISTORY buffer. It doesn't tell III PLUS to record commands entered at the dBASE prompt. The latter action is performed by the SET HISTORY ON/off command. The command syntax is

SET HISTORY TO n

where n can be any value between 0 and 16,000. Note that some systems will cause memory errors if you SET HISTORY TO 0.

The SET HISTORY TO command is a useful debugging command in the sense that it tells III PLUS how many lines of a program to record. You can have an extensive listing, as III PLUS allows up to 16,000 commands to be stored. Note that this large a number of stored commands—actually, anything over 500 lines—can affect machine memory. The HISTORY buffer that is SET with this command affects how much room III PLUS reserves for itself should you use the RUN or ! command. If you plan on SETting HISTORY TO something over 500, you should change the MAXMEM command in your CONFIG.DB file accordingly (see Appendix C).

SET STEP on/OFF

The SET STEP toggle is discussed in Chapter 11 and Appendix C. This section provides an overview of the toggle's use in debugging situations. The command syntax is

SET STEP toggle

where toggle is either on or OFF. Note that III PLUS defaults to OFF unless the CONFIG.DB STEP command is ON. The command itself has no effect on III PLUS unless you're in PROGRAM mode. The command forces a pause between command lines in the running program and prompts the user or programmer for the next action. Note that the STEP prompt

Press SPACE to step, S to suspend, or Esc to cancel...

allows you several options. You can continue to the next line in the code by pressing the space bar or stop the program completely by pressing the ESCAPE key. Note that this Escape option isn't affected by the status of the ON ESCAPE command. The S option allows the user great flexibility, however. SUSPENDing a program tells III PLUS to keep the program code active but to allow the user to enter commands directly from the keyboard. This is a powerful debugging tool. After debugging, you would enter

RESUME

to continue program execution at the last line. Note that STEP queries you before it executes a command.

The SET STEP toggle can be made particularly effective when you use it in conjunction with the SET ECHO ON command. This tells III PLUS to show the user what's going on when it asks what to do next. You can enhance the effects of SET STEP and ECHO ON further by using the SET DEBUG ON command. This combination tells III PLUS to send STEP's query to the printer. The result of that procedure is the ability to see a hard copy of each program line as it is executed. Your screen doesn't get cluttered and confused, but you still have direct interactive control for debugging purposes.

SET TALK ON/off

The SET TALK toggle is discussed in Chapter 11 and Appendix C. This section provides an overview of the command as it applies to debugging situations. The command syntax is

where toggle is either on or OFF. Note that III PLUS defaults to ON unless the CONFIG.DB TALK command is off.

The SET TALK toggle tells III PLUS TO/not to inform you of its progress in certain operations such as AVERAGEing, INDEXing, SORTing, SUMming, COUNTing, and so on. SET TALK ON, and III PLUS tells you how these and similar operations are progressing and what their results are in the case of execution of commands such as AVERAGE and SUM. SET TALK OFF, and the only way you'll know III PLUS has completed your request is seeing the prompt come back.

The SET TALK ON/off command is useful in debugging because it tells the programmer exactly how III PLUS is progressing or what values are going to be assigned to variables and database fields. This information provides the programmer with a report on database field and memory variable values, sizes of files, and more. Unless such information is useful to the user, the programmer should remove or SET OFF the SET TALK commands when the system is installed. You might want to use a word processor to SET all the TALK toggles OFF. Eventually something may go wrong, and you will be called back to debug the system. All you need do at that time is SET TALK back ON and see what's happening where.

SUSPEND

The SUSPEND command is discussed in Chapter 14. This section provides an overview of the SUSPEND command in debugging situations. The SUSPEND command is the first half of the SUSPEND RESUME command pair. The command syntax is

SUSPEND

without qualifiers or conditions. SUSPEND tells III PLUS to halt a currently running program and return to INTERACTIVE mode but keep active all files, variables, and so on, opened by all valid program files. Further, the SUSPEND command tells III PLUS to remember where it was in the currently running program file. You tell it to pick up where it left off with the RESUME command. Note that this command pair is valid only in a programming environment. III PLUS does nothing if no programs are running and SUSPEND is entered from the dBASE prompt.

The SUSPEND command allows putting the finishing touch on the DISPLAYER and LISTER programs shown in the sections on DISPLAY STATUS and LIST STRUCTURE. Neither of those programs lets the programmer or user do anything once they've DISPLAYed or LISTed information. Further, the information goes right off the screen in either case—not a satisfactory arrangement. The solution is to include the following code at the end of either of those programs:

```
WAIT "I(NTERACTIVE) -> " TO INTERACTIVE
*
IF INTERACTIVE = "I" .OR. INTERACTIVE = "i"
   SUSPEND
   SET STATUS ON
   SET MESSAGE TO "TYPE 'RESUME' AND PRESS RETURN TO CONTINUE"
ENDI
*
```

This short block allows the programmer to take action and modify the program environment based on the results of the DISPLAYed or LISTed information.

User Assistance
Commands

This chapter covers the first commands that users generally encounter—the ones they look for as soon as they've opened the package. None of these commands have advanced uses. They include ASSIST, the CATALOG commands, and HELP.

The CATALOG commands are actually a summary of the help modes III PLUS offers when you open a CAT file with the SET CATALOG TO command (see Chapters 2, 3, and 11 and Appendix C).

Some commands that you might expect to find in this section are not included. You might consider directory commands such as DIR, DISPLAY FILES, and LIST FILES as user-assistance commands. Information on those commands can be found in Chapter 15.

ASSIST

The ASSIST command has been mentioned throughout this book, but you've seen it as the ASSIST mode and the ASSIST menu system. Ashton-Tate is so concerned that the ASSIST menu system be accessible to users that it has assigned F2 the value "assist;". This makes F1 the reserved HELP key and F2 a programmable ASSIST key.

This section covers the different aspects of the ASSIST menu system. You access the menu system by entering

ASSIST

or pressing the F2 key—that is, if no one has assigned it some other function.

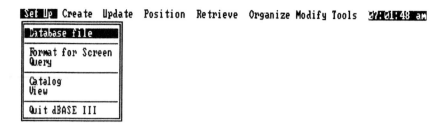

Database file

Format for Screen
Query

Catalog
View

Quit dBASE III

ASSIST |<D:>| |Opt: 1/6
Move selection bar - ↑↓. Select - ↵. Leave menu - ↔, Help - F1. Exit - Esc.
Select a database file.

Figure 16-1. The ASSIST Set Up screen

Figure 16-1 shows the opening ASSIST screen, which is also the Set Up menu. You can move through the ASSIST menu options with the cursor keys. The LEFT and RIGHT ARROW keys and HOME and END keys move you through the top row of menu selections (Set Up, Create, Update, Position, Retrieve, Organize, Modify, and Tools). Note that you can also move to a particular ASSIST menu selection by pressing the first letter of that menu option. For example, you can select the Tools submenu by pressing T. The UP and DOWN ARROW keys and PGUP and PGDN keys move you through the submenus. The LEFT and RIGHT ARROW keys also serve to confirm your choices in the submenus. You make actual selections by pressing RETURN.

If you're using a color monitor or a screen that can show shading or background highlighting, you'll notice that some of the menu selections aren't as bright as others or that the selections differ from one another in color. You'll only be able to select highlighted options as you move through the ASSIST system.

Note that the ASSIST system automatically SELECTs the current work area. All ASSIST work is done in work area 9 if you start the ASSIST session in work area 9.

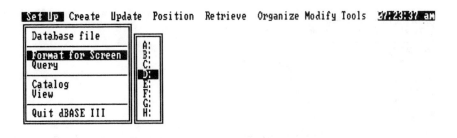

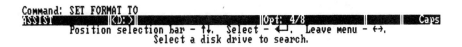
```
Command: SET FORMAT TO
```

Figure 16-2.   III PLUS answers with a drive list one a Set Up function is selected

Set Up

The ASSIST Set Up screen is shown in Figure 16-1. This is the opening ASSIST screen. It shows six options, divided into four sections: Database file; Format for Screen, Query; Catalog, View, and Quit dBASE III. You use the Set Up screen to load existing files into the III PLUS system. Note that if you move the cursor to any of the Set Up menu selections and press RETURN, III PLUS answers with a drive list (Figure 16-2). III PLUS works with logical and physical drives; this means your system might show drives that differ from someone else's. Also note that DOS 2.xx users won't have the drive selections of either Network or DOS 3.xx users. Once you have chosen a drive, III PLUS lists the available files that meet the request type (see Figure 16-3). This is the key to your understanding of the Set Up submenu: You can only choose files that exist on the selected drive. Note that in Figures 16-2 and 16-3 FMT files have been selected on drive D and that the only files listed are FMT files on drive D. You'll meet the same circumstance if you choose any one of the five file types available through the Set Up menu.

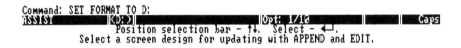

Figure 16-3.   III Plus shows the requested file types once a drive is chosen

The Set Up menu also acknowledges the way in which certain files are ordered in the III PLUS system. For example, if you request a DBF file, III PLUS will ask if the DBF file is INDEXed. III PLUS marks the NDX files you choose in the order you choose them (see Figure 16-4), and the prompt line directly above the STATUS line builds your command line as you select NDX files. The problem with this system is that III PLUS doesn't check the validity of NDX files until after you've built the command line. You could have chosen NDX files that weren't related to the selected DBF file—which happened in this example—and not know you've caused a problem until you've made your selections (see Figure 16-5). The good news is that III PLUS doesn't punish you or damage files when you commit this error. It simply returns you to the Set Up menu. III PLUS will only show you files in the CATALOG if you've told III PLUS to use a CAT filter, through either the Set Up Catalog option or the SET CATALOG TO commands.

Note that the Quit dBASE III option drops directly to the operating system. It offers no ancillary messages that tell you that files need to be closed or that work has to be saved.

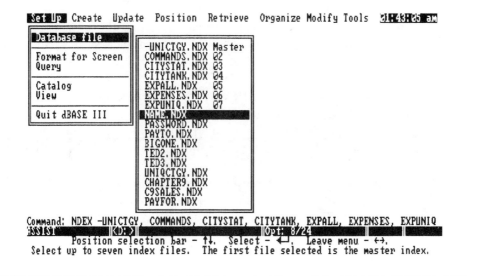

```
Set Up  Create  Update  Position  Retrieve  Organize Modify Tools  11:43:05 am
┌─────────────────┐  ┌──────────────────────────┐
│ Database file   │  │ -UNICTGY.NDX  Master     │
├─────────────────┤  │ COMMANDS.NDX  02         │
│ Format for Screen│ │ CITYSTAT.NDX  03         │
│ Query            │  │ CITYTANK.NDX  04         │
├─────────────────┤  │ EXPALL.NDX    05         │
│ Catalog         │  │ EXPENSES.NDX  06         │
│ View            │  │ EXPUNIQ.NDX   07         │
├─────────────────┤  │ NAME.NDX                 │
│ Quit dBASE III  │  │ PASSWORD.NDX             │
└─────────────────┘  │ PAYTO.NDX                │
                     │ BIGONE.NDX               │
                     │ TED2.NDX                 │
                     │ TED3.NDX                 │
                     │ UNIQCTGY.NDX             │
                     │ CHAPTER9.NDX             │
                     │ C9SALES.NDX              │
                     │ PAYFOR.NDX               │
                     └──────────────────────────┘
Command: NDEX -UNICTGY, COMMANDS, CITYSTAT, CITYTANK, EXPALL, EXPENSES, EXPUNIQ
ASSIST              KD: >                        Opt: 8/24
            Position selection bar - ↑↓.  Select - ↵.  Leave menu - ←→.
Select up to seven index files.  The first file selected is the master index.
```

Figure 16-4. III PLUS builds the command line as you make selections

```
Set Up  Create  Update  Position  Retrieve  Organize Modify Tools  9:36:53 am




Index file does not match database
ASSIST              KD: >BOOKS                   Rec: 1/200              Caps
                    Press any key to continue work in ASSIST.
```

Figure 16-5. III PLUS doesn't tell you you've made an error until you've
built the command

Create

The Create menu, shown in Figure 16-6, lets the user create III PLUS work files. The key word in the last sentence is *work*. Note that DBT, SCR, TXT, and like files are not included. Such files are ancillary to work files (a DBT file is actually part of a DBF file, an NDX file is an addendum to a DBF file, an SCR file is only used during design and never during work, and so on).

The Create menu works similarly to the Set Up menu. You select the file you want to create and are then prompted to name a drive on which to create the file. You are then asked to give the file a name. Note that this prompting pattern is slightly different if you have activated a CAT file through either the SET CATALOG TO command or the ASSIST Set Up menu. Activating a CATALOG tells III PLUS where files are going to be created. When you have done so, you will not be asked for a drive but you will be asked for a filename.

Update

The Update options, shown in Figure 16-7, deal with commands that modify or alter DBF files. Only DBF files are affected by these com-

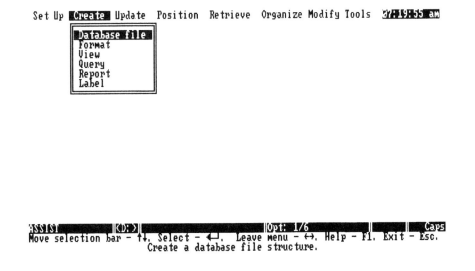

Figure 16-6. The ASSIST Create screen

mands. You can select any of the Update options by moving the cursor to the option and pressing RETURN. Note that this menu option has nothing to do with the UPDATE command. The ASSIST Update menu option deals with APPENDing, EDITing, DISPLAYing, BROWSEing, REPLACEing, DELETEing, RECALLing, and PACKing a database. You can find information on the separate Update menu options in the following chapters of this book:

Update Menu Options	Chapter(s)
Append	6
Edit	7
Display	8
Browse	6, 7, 8
Replace	7
Delete	7
Recall	7
Pack	7

None of these options is available if you have not selected a database file.

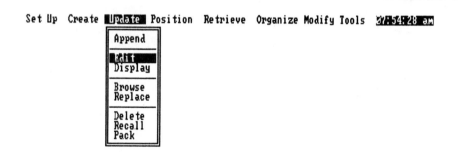

Figure 16-7. The ASSIST Update screen

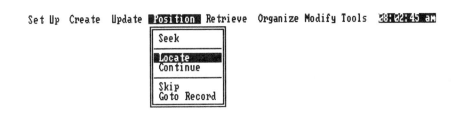

Figure 16-8.   The ASSIST Position screen

Position

The Position menu options help you get from where you are to where
you want to be. Figure 16-8 is the ASSIST Position submenu. Note
that there is no Find option. You may remember from earlier discussions on the FIND and SEEK commands (see Chapter 9) that SEEK
is the more general command of the two. Also note that you will not
be allowed to SEEK something if no NDX file is active. If you select
Seek when an NDX file is active, however, III PLUS will prompt you
for the SEEK expression. You can enter any valid expression for the
active DBF-NDX combination. III PLUS will tell you it can't find the
entered expression or if you type in an invalid expression.

The Locate option is a bit more involved than the Seek option,
but no more complex. Chapter 9 describes how the LOCATE command operates. All of III PLUS's abilities are available through the
ASSIST Position Locate options (see Figure 16-9). You tell III PLUS
what to LOCATE, as you would with the interactive LOCATE command. You start by building a search condition (as shown in Figure
16-9). III PLUS offers you all the help it can by listing available

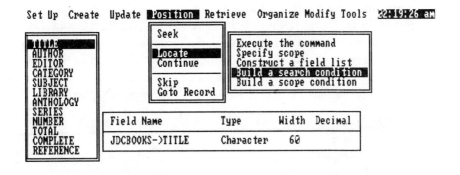

Figure 16-9. You tell III PLUS what to LOCATE by building a search condition

fields, the type of data, and the size of the field. Once you have chosen a field, you must tell III PLUS what to do with it (see Figure 16-10). This process can be repeated for a field list and scope condition. You can't choose the Continue option until something has been LOCATEd.

The Skip and Goto options behave exactly as do their interactive counterparts. Skip prompts for the number of records to SKIP; positive and negative values are valid input (see Figure 16-11). If you choose Goto, it prompts you to select one of three options—Top, Bottom, or Record. If you choose the Top or Bottom option, you'll move automatically to the top or bottom record. The Record option prompts you for the record number to GOTO. You can find more information on the separate commands in this menu in Chapter 9 in the sections on SEEK, LOCATE, CONTINUE, SKIP, and GOTO.

Retrieve

The options listed in the Retrieve menu deal with getting information from the database to the user (see Figure 16-12). The List, Display,

Sum, Average, and Count options all share the selection screens pictured in Figures 16-9 and 16-10, as shown in Figure 16-13. The Report and Label options behave as do the REPORT and LABEL commands in INTERACTIVE mode. Neither Report nor Label options are available if you don't specify any FRM or LBL files with the Set Up menu (see Figure 16-14). You can find more information on the commands in this menu in the following chapters:

Retrieve Menu Options	Chapter(s)
List	8
Display	8
Report	2, 8
Label	2, 8
Sum	8, 10
Average	8, 10
Count	8, 10

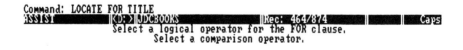

Figure 16-10. Once a field is selected, you must tell III PLUS what to do with that field

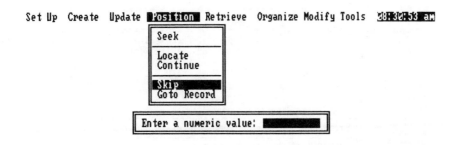

Set Up Create Update **Position** Retrieve Organize Modify Tools `08:30:53 am`

```
            ┌──────────────┐
            │ Seek         │
            ├──────────────┤
            │ Locate       │
            │ Continue     │
            ├──────────────┤
            │ Skip         │
            │ Goto Record  │
            └──────────────┘

        ┌────────────────────────────┐
        │ Enter a numeric value:     │
        └────────────────────────────┘
```

Command: SKIP
ASSIST |<D:>|JDCBOOKS |Rec: 464/874
           Enter new value. Finish with ⏎.
      Position the file pointer by skipping records.

Figure 16-11.   You must tell III PLUS where to SKIP to

Set Up Create Update Position **Retrieve** Organize Modify Tools `08:42:10 am`

```
            ┌──────────────┐
            │ List         │
            │ Display      │
            │ Report       │
            │ Label        │
            ├──────────────┤
            │ Sum          │
            │ Average      │
            │ Count        │
            └──────────────┘
```

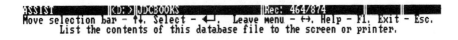

ASSIST |<D:>|JDCBOOKS |Rec: 464/874
Move selection bar - ↑↓. Select - ⏎. Leave menu - ↔. Help - F1. Exit - Esc.
     List the contents of this database file to the screen or printer.

Figure 16-12.   The ASSIST Retrieve screen

User Assistance Commands   **585**

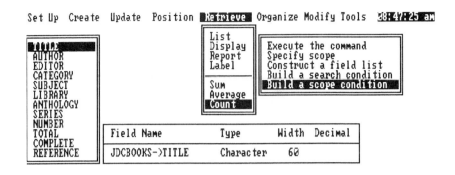

Figure 16-13. The List, Display, Sum, Average, and Count Retrieve options all share the same information screen

Figure 16-14. III PLUS won't access the Report or Label options if no FRM or LBL files are specified with the Set Up menu

Organize

The Organize menu, shown in Figure 16-15, has three options: Index, Sort, and Copy. III PLUS offers you a great deal of help in using each option properly. Figure 16-16 shows the prompt for the Index option, Figure 16-17 shows the prompt for the Sort option, and Figure 16-18 is the Copy prompt. Note that after you've created the field list for the Sort option, you are prompted for a valid dBASE III PLUS filename. The Copy option prompts you for information after you've entered a filename to which you want to COPY information. You can find more information on the Organize menu options in the following chapters:

Organize Menu Options	Chapter(s)
Index	2, 3
Sort	3
Copy	3

Set Up Create Update Position Retrieve ▮Organize▮Modify Tools ▮8:54:02 am▮

```
┌───────┐
│▮Index▮│
│ Sort  │
├───────┤
│ Copy  │
└───────┘
```

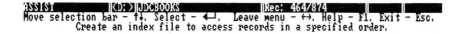

ASSIST▮   ▮ D: ▮ JDCBOOKS▮   ▮Rec: 464/874▮   ▮   ▮
Move selection bar - ↑↓. Select - ↵. Leave menu - ↔. Help - F1. Exit - Esc.
Create an index file to access records in a specified order.

Figure 16-15.   The ASSIST Organize screen

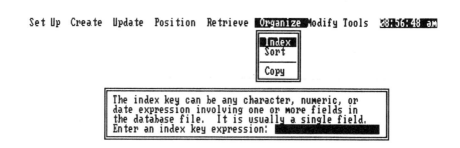

Figure 16-16.   The Index option prompt

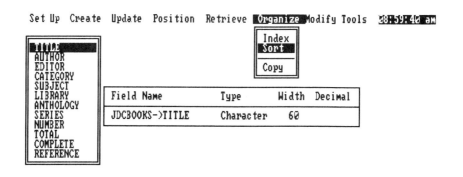

Figure 16-17.   The Sort option prompt

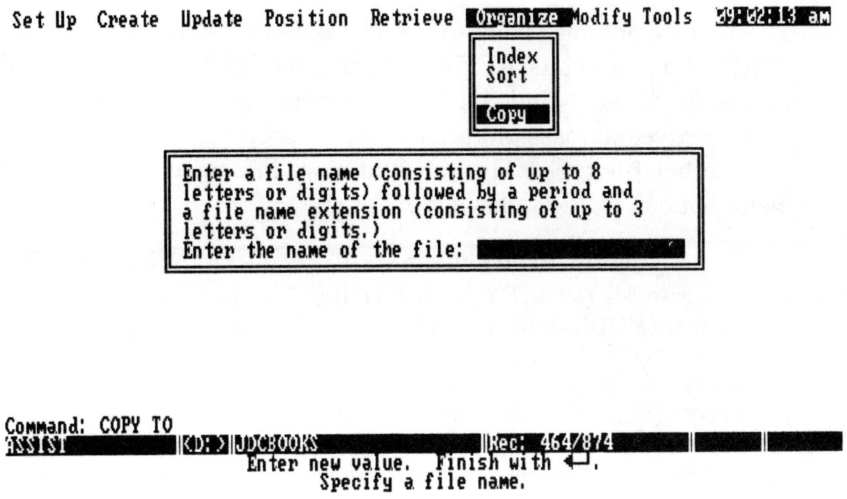

Set Up Create Update Position Retrieve `Organize`Modify Tools `09:02:13 am`

```
          Index
          Sort
          Copy
```

```
Enter a file name (consisting of up to 8
letters or digits) followed by a period and
a file name extension (consisting of up to 3
letters or digits.)
Enter the name of the file: ████████████████
```

Command: COPY TO
`ASSIST`   `KD: > JDCBOOKS`   `Rec: 464/874`
                    Enter new value. Finish with ←.
                      Specify a file name.

Figure 16-18.   The Copy option prompt

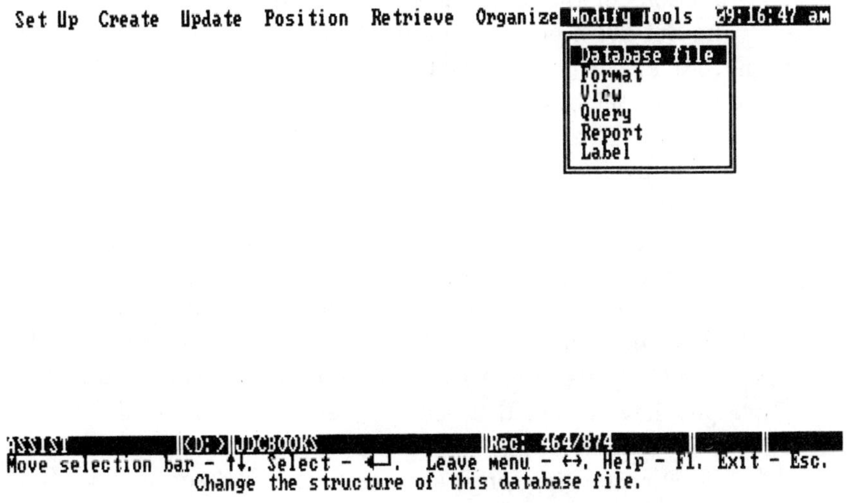

Set Up Create Update Position Retrieve Organize`Modify`Tools `09:16:47 am`

```
               Database file
               Format
               View
               Query
               Report
               Label
```

`ASSIST`   `KD: > JDCBOOKS`   `Rec: 464/874`
Move selection bar - ↑↓. Select - ←. Leave menu - ↔. Help - F1. Exit - Esc.
                Change the structure of this database file.

Figure 16-19.   The ASSIST Modify screen

User Assistance Commands   589

Modify

The Modify options, shown in Figure 16-19, follow the logic of the dBASE III PLUS MODIFY commands. III PLUS won't let you MODIFY a file it can't find. III PLUS defaults to MODIFYing the currently active database but allows you to specify an existing file of any of the other file types. You can find more information on the Modify menu options in the following chapters:

Modify Menu Options	Chapter(s)
Database file (MODIFY STRUCTURE)	4
Format (MODIFY SCREEN)	2, 4
View (MODIFY VIEW)	4
Query (MODIFY QUERY)	2, 4
Report (MODIFY REPORT)	2, 4
Label (MODIFY LABEL)	2, 4

Tools

The Tools menu, shown in Figure 16-20, has two parts. The first is a potpourri of options that perform rudimentary housekeeping tasks (Rename, Erase, Set Drive, and so on). The second part has the special functions of IMPORTing and EXPORTing files.

The Set drive option is equivalent to the SET DRIVE TO command. III PLUS prompts you with a list of available drives for your system. You select one of the listed drives, and that becomes the default drive. This option isn't available if you have SET a CATALOG.

The Copy file option behaves in one of two ways, depending on whether an active CAT file exists. Having an active CAT file causes III PLUS to prompt you with DBF files listed in the CAT file. The lack of an active CAT file causes III PLUS to prompt for a source drive and then list all files on that drive. Note that having an active CAT file limits your selection to DBF and associated files. Not having an active CAT file allows you to COPY any file on the source drive. Once you have selected a source file, III PLUS asks for a target filename.

The Directory option is similar to the DIR command. III PLUS prompts you for the type of file you want listed when you select this option.

The Rename option is identical to the RENAME command. III

```
Set drive
Copy file
Directory
Rename
Erase
List structure

Import
Export
```

ASSIST   (D: >)JDCBOOKS   Rec: 464/874
Move selection bar - ↑↓. Select - ↵. Leave menu - ↔. Help - F1. Exit - Esc.
      Duplicate the contents of an existing file to create a new file.

Figure 16-20. The ASSIST Tools screen

PLUS prompts you for a file to RENAME and then for a new name. Note that it tells you when you're using the name of an existing file.

The Erase option is identical to the interactive ERASE command. III PLUS prompts you in the same way it prompts you if you select the Rename option.

The List structure option is identical to the interactive LIST STRUCTURE command. It assumes a DBF file is currently active and only prompts you regarding LISTing TO the PRINTER.

The second part of the Tools menu is Import and Export. III PLUS prompts you for a filename to IMPORT from or EXPORT to. It recognizes foreign file types and builds the command accordingly.

You can find more information on the Tools options in the following chapters:

Tools Menu Options	Chapter(s)
Set drive (SET DEFAULT TO)	11, App. C
Copy file	3
Directory (DIR, DISPLAY FILES)	15
Rename	4

Erase (ERASE, DELETE FILE)	4
List structure	15
Import (IMPORT, APPEND FROM type)	3, 6
Export (EXPORT, COPY TO type)	3

The CATALOG commands have been listed elsewhere in this book but have not been listed together. These commands let the user select specific files that appear in an active CAT file. These commands fall under the category of "user assistance" commands because of their prompting action, and they include

```
LABEL FORM ?
REPORT FORM ?
SET CATA TO ?
SET FILTER TO FILE ?
SET FORMAT TO ?
SET INDEX TO ?
SET VIEW TO ?
USE ?
```

Note that these commands function properly only when you have opened a CAT file with some form of the SET CATALOG TO command. You can activate any file type, regardless of whether it appears in the current CATALOG, simply by selecting it with the proper command. Note that III PLUS will add the file to the CATALOG and prompt for information on the file if the SET TITLE toggle is ON (see Chapter 11).

The HELP system is extensive. The III PLUS HELP system even offers help on using the HELP system. The Help menu is shown in Figure 16-21. The options are self-explanatory. You can find out how to get started in dBASE III PLUS by selecting option 1. Option 2 offers a glossary of III PLUS terms. Option 3 guides you through basic DBMS operations. Option 4 shows you how to CREATE a DBF file after assessing your needs and intended uses of that file. Option 5 shows you how to use the DBF file you created in option 4, and Option 6 presents help in using the commands and functions of the program.

Each menu option leads to a Help screen. You move through these Help screens with the PGUP and PGDN keys. Pressing PGDN takes you to the next Help screen associated with the given topic. You press PGUP to move to the previous menu or the previous Help screen for a given topic. You can always get back to the previous menu by pressing F10.

```
Help Main Menu

1 - Getting Started
2 - What Is a ...
3 - How Do I ...
4 - Creating a Database File
5 - Using an Existing Database File
6 - Commands and Functions




HELP        |<D: >|JDCBOOKS              ||Rec: 1/874
    Position selection bar - ↑↓. Select - ←┘. Exit with Esc or enter a command.
              ENTER >
```

Figure 16-21.   The Help Main menu

LABEL FORM ?
and REPORT FORM ?

These commands tell III PLUS to list all LBL (or FRM) files that were created with the current DBF file. Note that only LBL (or FRM) files created with a specific DBF file will be listed. Chapter 3 mentioned that you could CREATE an LBL or REPORT file with one database and then use that file with another database of identical structure. If you CREATE an LBL or REPORT file with an open CAT file, however, III PLUS will associate the LBL (or FRM) file only with that one DBF file, regardless of how many databases it could be used with. You can select a listed LBL (or FRM) file by moving the cursor to it and pressing RETURN. III PLUS will immediately begin listing the LBL or FRM files, basing that listing on the parameters set in the LBL file during its CREATEion or MODIFY-cation (see Chapters 2, 3, and 4).

SET CATALOG TO ?

The SET CATALOG TO ? command is the one command in this section that doesn't have to be preceded by the command

SET CATALOG TO cat file

This command is transferred directly to the III PLUS command processor when executed and tells III PLUS to list all available CATALOGs. III PLUS knows which CATALOGs are available because it keeps a master list, called CATALOG.CAT, of all the CAT files created by the user or programmer. You can find more information on CAT files and their creation in Chapters 2, 3, and 11 and Appendix C.

SET FILTER TO FILE ?
and SET FORMAT TO ?

These commands tell III PLUS to list all QRY or FMT files that were created with the current DBF file. Note that only QRY files created with a specific DBF file will be listed. You can create a QRY or FMT file that is usable with several different DBF files, but if you CREATE a QUERY or FORMAT file with an open CAT file, III PLUS will associate the QRY or FMT file only with that one DBF file, regardless of how many databases it could be used with. You can select a listed QRY or FMT file by moving the cursor to it and pressing RETURN. The FILTER SET by the QRY or FMT file will affect all relative III PLUS operations immediately and will continue that effect until you enter

SET FILTER TO

or

SET FORMAT TO

See Chapters 2, 3, 4, and 11 for more information on QRY and FMT files and SETting FILTERs and FORMATs. See Chapters 7, 10, and 11 for more information on FMT files and SETting FORMATs.

SET INDEX TO ?

This command tells III PLUS to list all NDX files that were created with the current DBF file. Note that only NDX files created with a specific DBF file will be listed. You can create an NDX file that is usable with several different DBF files, but if you CREATE an INDEX file when you have an open CAT file, III PLUS will associate the NDX file only with that one DBF file, regardless of how many databases it could be used with. You can select a listed NDX file by moving the cursor to it and pressing RETURN. Note that III PLUS allows up to seven open NDX files for each active DBF file and lets you select up to seven NDX files with the SET INDEX TO ? command. The first selected NDX file is the master INDEX. The order in which the NDX files are opened will affect all relative III PLUS operations immediately and continue that effect until you enter

```
SET INDEX TO
SET ORDER TO 0
```

See Chapters 2, 3, and 11 for more information on NDX files and SETting INDEXes.

SET VIEW TO ?

This command tells III PLUS to list all VUE files that are in the active CATALOG. Note that selection of the VUE file is not based on the existence of any other active files. It is only based on what VUE files are in the CATALOG. The reason for this is that VUE files hold information on DBF, DBT, NDX, FMT, and QRY files themselves. You can select a listed VUE file by moving the cursor to it and pressing RETURN. The VUE file's settings will affect all relative III PLUS operations immediately and continue that effect until you enter

```
SET VIEW TO
```

See Chapters 2, 3, and 11 and Appendix C for more information on VUE files and SETting VIEWs.

USE ?

This command tells III PLUS to list all DBF files created while the current CAT file was active. Only DBF files created with the current CAT file will be listed. If you created a certain DBF file when the current CAT file wasn't active, that DBF file will not be listed when you use the USE ? command. You can select DBF files listed through the USE ? file by moving the cursor to the desired file and pressing RETURN. See Chapters 2 and 5 for more information on DBF files and their use.

Networking Commands

The one big difference between dBASE III PLUS and all the other dBASEs is that it has a built-in networking ability. That ability means new features and commands. The individual user can access many of these new features and commands, provided the user follows the dBASE III PLUS network-installation procedure. All single-user III PLUS commands are available to the III PLUS network user. This chapter covers only those commands that are new or are modified with networking.

Modified commands are discussed in the first part of the chapter, and new commands are discussed in the second. Note that the chapter doesn't provide any information on installing the networked version of dBASE III PLUS (see Appendix B).

This section covers commands that are slightly modified to work in the NETWORK mode. This also means the commands work in new ways when they are used by a single user operating the networked dBASE III PLUS, even when no network is present.

All of these commands have to do with preserving data integrity. All DBMSs make preserving data integrity a priority, regardless of whether they have networking ability. But the network situation puts a demand on the software to make sure no two people can make changes to the same part of a file at the same time. Imagine a situation in which you and a coworker both need to alter the contents of file A's 24th record. Imagine further that you both access that record at the same time. Whose work gets a higher priority? Part of that priority is determined by the level the system manager has assigned each job. You and your coworker might also have passwords that tell

III PLUS who has higher priority. In any case, only one of you can make changes at any one time. Somewhere along the line, either the programmer or III PLUS has to decide who gets in and who gets out of the file. Certain commands handle this access priority automatically. The commands that lock out other users automatically are

```
APPEND
APPEND BLANK
APPEND FROM
AVERAGE
BROWSE
COPY
COPY STRUCTURE
COUNT
DELETE ALL
INDEX
JOIN
RECALL ALL
REPLACE ALL
SORT
SUM
TOTAL
UPDATE
```

What Networking Does

The whole point of networking is to share information. Networking lets several people use the same database. This can cause problems. For example, two or more people may want to use the same database at the same time and shouldn't. III PLUS automatically stops others from accessing a database when any one person is working on it. On the other hand, your work may involve only one record in the entire database. It's foolish to tie up an entire database because of one person's record needs, so you can specifically tell III PLUS to lock only one record.

These situations place a burden on the programmer. It is possible to lock a record or file and forget to unlock it. The result of this neglect is either an error message or an infinite loop. The error message tells the user there is a problem. The infinite loop ties up the computer until someone unplugs the system. The programmer should consider including code similar to that shown in the following listing:

```
** start of program file
ON ERROR DO ERRORMSS WITH N,M
```

```
**
** code
**
N = 1
CLEA
*
DO WHILE .NOT. FLOCK()
   USE database
*
   IF FLOCK() .OR. N > 200
      EXIT
   ELSE
      ? "THAT DATABASE IS IN USE. I'M GOING TO TRY AGAIN."
      N = N + 1
   ENDIF
*
ENDD
*
IF N > 200
   WAIT "I THINK SOMETHING IS WRONG AT (program position). " +;
   "CALL FOR HELP."
   CLOSE ALL
   LOGOUT && (or QUIT)
ENDI
*
N = 0
**
** rest of code
**


** ERRORMSS.PRG
**
PARAMETER N,M
CLEA
*
DO CASE
   CASE N > 200
      WAIT "THERE IS A PROBLEM AT (M). CALL FOR HELP."
      CLOSE ALL
      LOGOUT (or QUIT)
   CASE ERROR() = 108
      ? "THAT FILE IS IN USE. I'LL TRY AGAIN."
      N = N + 1
      RETRY
   CASE ERROR() = 109
      ? "THAT RECORD IS IN USE. I'LL TRY AGAIN."
      N = N + 1
      RETRY
   CASE ERROR() = 130
      SET MESSAGE TO "PRESS CTL-O TO LOCK THE RECORD FOR EDITING"
      RETRY
   CASE ....
   ...
ENDC
*
** EOF
```

Two variable parameters in this listing bear investigation. N is used as a programmed time-out error. A time-out error is something that occurs when the computer or software has made several attempts to do something and hasn't succeeded. Rather than continue, the system tells the user that something is wrong. A common example of such a situation is when the system attempts to read from a nonexistent disk. III PLUS or DOS will tell you the drive isn't ready. This message comes on the screen only after the system has made several attempts to read from or write to the nonexistent disk.

The N parameter is a time-out variable that counts the number of attempts made to do something—in this case, access a file or record. If some number of attempts are unsuccessful—this example arbitrarily specifies 200—the user is told that something is wrong. Using N to count unsuccessful attempts at accessing files forces the developer to ensure that N = 0 when going into each block that accesses a file.

The M parameter can be anything the programmer desires. Most times it is the name of the last working PRG file, the working PROCedure, or the program line that was last executed. This last requires extensive housekeeping on the developer's part. An easy way to number lines of code is to pass the code through the EDLIN.COM DOS line editor.

The Record Lock Toggle

There is a major difference between viewing a database and changing a database. Note that any file or record can be read. It is the other operation, writing to a file or record, in which locking and protection become issues. This section deals with situations in which a user needs to change one record in a network setup. III PLUS includes a feature that allows a user to view records in a file without locking the file or the records. Most operations are done at the record level, so there is no need to lock an entire file when you are going to use only one record. The useful feature is selected with the key combination

CTRL-O

(you press the CTRL and O keys simultaneously). This operation directly affects the CHANGE and EDIT commands. Both of these commands allow you to perform full-screen operations on existing records in a database. Full-screen viewing of data requires no locking, but full-screen editing does.

III PLUS doesn't allow you to EDIT or CHANGE data unless the record is locked. The programmer can give the user some control over the situation with the following code:

```
EDITING = .T.
*
DO WHILE EDITING
    EDIT && (or CHANGE)
    SET MESSAGE TO "PRESS CTL-O TO UNLOCK THE RECORD."
    a x,y SAY "EDIT/CHANGE ANOTHER? -> " GET EDITING PICT "Y"
*
    DO CASE
        CASE LOCK()
            a x,y SAY "RECORD IS STILL LOCKED. CTL-O UNLOCKS IT."
            LOOP
        CASE .NOT. EDITING
            EXIT
    ENDC
*
```

Note that the user must unlock the record before that user is allowed to move to another record for EDITing and/or CHANGEing.

The text mentioned previously that all single-user commands can be used in network applications. There are five commands that act identically with their single-user counterparts, with the exception that they give more information in NETWORK mode than they do in SINGLE USER mode. The commands are

```
CHANGE
DISPLAY STATUS
EDIT
LIST STATUS
SET
```

The CHANGE and EDIT commands were described in the last section. DISPLAY STATUS and LIST STATUS also give the user the file status (locked or unlocked). The SET command has all the properties mentioned in Chapter 11, but it also includes the ability to ENCRYPT files and make their use EXCLUSIVE to one user.

This section covers new commands that become available in NETWORK mode.

DISPLAY USERS

This command is similar to all the DISPLAY function commands. DISPLAY USERS is most often used by system operators to find out who is doing what where. It provides a list of which stations are active and currently logged into the III PLUS system. The command syntax is

DISPLAY USERS

without qualifiers or conditions.

You can send this information to the printer with

DISPLAY USERS TO PRINT

LOGOUT

The LOGOUT command is exclusive to network applications that actually use the network. This command has no effect on single system users making use of network features. The command syntax is

LOGOUT

This command specifically looks for the DBSYSTEM.DB file. The system operator creates the file by using the PROTECT utility included with the dBASE III PLUS package. If no DBSYSTEM.DB file exists, LOGOUT returns you to the dBASE prompt. LOGOUT clears the display and returns you to the LOGIN screen if PROTECT has been used to create a DBSYSTEM.DB file.

System developers, note that much of your protection work can be undone by someone erasing or otherwise damaging the DBSYSTEM.DB file. You should take steps to guarantee this file's existence and integrity. A method you might find useful is to use the DOS ATTRIB.COM file to both hide the file and make it read only.

SET ENCRYPTION ON/off

The SET ENCRYPTION toggle is normally ON in NETWORK mode and provides an interesting form of security. The command syntax is

SET ENCRYPTION toggle

III PLUS defaults to ENCRYPTION ON. This means that any DBF files created in NETWORK mode are ciphered. This ciphering provides additional file security for network users, but remember that not all III PLUS users are going to be using a network. There may be times that a central office uses a network but remote offices don't. You can't send those remote offices an ENCRYPTed file and expect them to do any work on it, as III PLUS will post an error that the remote office is powerless to resolve. Note also that ENCRYPTION is automatic when you access files through a PROTECTed session. A PROTECTed session is one initiated through LOGIN/LOGOUT routines designed by the system operator and the PROTECT utility.

SET EXCLUSIVE ON/off

The SET EXCLUSIVE toggle tells III PLUS that any DBF or NDX file opened by one station cannot be accessed by any other station until that DBF or NDX file is closed. This is a networking version of the "File is already open" message single users get when they try to open a file in more than one work area. The command syntax is

SET EXCLUSIVE toggle

Many of SET EXCLUSIVE's abilities can be mimicked by the DOS ATTRIB.COM file.

UNLOCK

The UNLOCK command is the second half of a command pair. The funny thing about the command pair is that the user can't access the first part of the pair. III PLUS automatically performs file and record locks based on access level and user identification. It is up to the user or programmer to ensure that each file or record is UNLOCKed, however.

Consider a situation in which someone uses the CTRL-O command to lock a record for EDITing but forgets to UNLOCK the record. The programmer can ensure that the record is available to other users by including the UNLOCK command in the code close to the point where the user stopped EDITing the record. Similarly, the programmer can ensure a file's accessibility by including an UNLOCK command in the code directly after a user stops performing a file operation (such as APPEND, RECALL ALL, or DELETE ALL). The command syntax is

UNLOCK

which removes the last issued locking command, whether the lock was file- or record-oriented. You can modify the UNLOCK command to release all file and record locks with

UNLOCK ALL

The basic UNLOCK command only affects the last lock activated in the current work area. If you request a file lock in work area 5, following that request with

UNLOCK

tells III PLUS to make that file available to other users regardless of the current work area at their station. If you lock a file in work areas 1, 2, and 5, however, and lock records in work areas 7, 8, and 9, following that with the command

UNLOCK ALL

frees ALL the locked records and files in all work areas at the given station.

There is a particular hazard in UNLOCKing ALL for any one station. You might UNLOCK something before a user is through with a given file. This will not interrupt the system, but it can cause frustration for users. The command is useful in the development stage, where it is necessary to determine access paths. A strong recommendation is that the UNLOCK ALL command be reserved for development use in any application.

USE EXCLUSIVE

This command is actually a combination of two commands:

```
USE files
```

and

```
SET EXCLUSIVE ON
```

In all ways previously discussed in this book, USE EXCLUSIVE is identical to the non-networked USE command. The EXCLUSIVE qualifier tells III PLUS that the file put in USE is to be restricted to the current user in the current work area. The command syntax is

```
USE files EXCLUSIVE
```

where files represents any combination of DBF and NDX files. The EXCLUSIVE qualifier can be used before or after the file list, as follows:

```
USE EXCLUSIVE dbf INDEX ndx1, ndx2,...
USE dbf INDEX ndx1, ndx2,... EXCLUSIVE
```

Note that the EXCLUSIVE qualifier affects all files listed, regardless of where the qualifier is placed in the command. Also note that this can cause a problem if you have designed a system that uses one NDX file to order several DBF files. You must take steps to ensure that the single NDX file is not requested by other users while it is being USEd EXCLUSIVEly.

As a last point, the USE EXCLUSIVE command can lock one file in a system in which all files are designed to be open. Assume one of the first commands III PLUS interprets is SET EXCLUSIVE OFF. This command will affect all future processing. What happens when one file must be locked? You USE the one file EXCLUSIVEly. When you then CLOSE the file, either with CLOSE DATA or the naked USE command, all users can use that file without restrictions.

dBASE III PLUS
Operators

There are certain concepts that hold in all types of work; they are the basics of mathematics and logic. You can communicate with III PLUS using these concepts because of a shared knowledge. III PLUS knows about these things because Ashton-Tate's programmers spent a lot of time coding it that way.

The mathematical and logical concepts, called *operators* in III PLUS, are

```
+  (ADDITION)
-  (SUBTRACTION)
*  (MULTIPLICATION)
/  (DIVISION)
** (EXPONENTIATION)
.AND.
.OR.
.NOT.
```

The mathematical operators are easily understood. They always return a numeric value. (Experienced dBASE programmers may now protest that the situation is not that simple because the plus (+) and minus (−) signs can also be used for string concatenations. A string concatenation is the manipulation of two text strings to produce a third text string.)

The logical operators are used to evaluate expressions that contain one of two conditions: true or false. You use these operators to determine test conditions, such as DO something WHILE something else is true (or false).

Mathematical Operators and Numbers

The mathematical operators are reserved for operations that return a numeric result. These operators behave as you'd expect. You add two numbers or variables with a command such as

```
ANSWER = N + M
```

where N and M are two numbers and ANSWER is their sum. N and M can also be two numeric variables, or one can be a number and the other a numeric variable. Figure 18-1 shows how you can use various combinations of numbers and numeric expressions with III PLUS's mathematical operators.

There is something interesting in Figure 18-1 that might have escaped your attention. Multiplying (or adding or subtracting or dividing) numbers is called a direct operation. In other words, III PLUS doesn't have to go looking in memory for a variable's value when it computes the answer. As a result, standard laws of precision hold. In Figure 18-1, this means that

```
5*10
```

```
-> ? 5*10
  50
-> FIVE = 5
-> TEN = 10
-> ? FIVE * TEN
                    50
-> ? TEN ** FIVE

              100000.00
-> TWENTY = 20
-> ? TWENTY - 10
        10
-> ? "TWENTY" + "FIVE"
TWENTYFIVE
->
```

Figure 18-1. III PLUS's mathematical operators can be used with either numeric variables or numbers

returns 50 with standard accuracy. You can tell III PLUS has returned the answer with standard accuracy because the 50 is placed close to the left-hand side of the screen. III PLUS didn't go looking in memory for any values and, hence, returned the simplest form of what was asked. Also in Figure 18-1 two variables, FIVE and TEN, are assigned the values of 5 and 10, respectively. Asking III PLUS

FIVE * TEN

forces III PLUS to go looking in memory for values. All numeric values have 15.9 places of accuracy in memory. The result? III PLUS returns the correct answer for the multiplication, but note where III PLUS places the answer on the screen. III PLUS has used the full 15.9 places of accuracy to perform the calculation. All arithmetic operators will do this. More places of accuracy mean more chance for error. III PLUS tells us that 5*10 is 50 with two places of accuracy. That's good, because that's what it was told to do. But it also tells us that FIVE * TEN is 50.000000000. You can't see all those digits normally, and even if you could, it wouldn't matter. What does matter is that repeated calculations could turn the least significant digits into 1's instead of leaving them as 0's. Over time, those changes can affect computations.

Mathematical Operators and Text Strings

There are two mathematical operators that you can use with text strings. A text string is anything delimited with double quotes (" "), single quotes (' '), or square brackets ([ ]). The two mathematical operators are the plus (+) and minus (−) signs.

The plus sign is straightforward in what it does and how it operates. Adding two text strings together produces a longer, third text string, which is the character concatenation of the two original text strings. The plus sign allows you to add two or more complete text strings to create a third text string. An example is shown at the bottom of Figure 18-1. The two text strings "TWENTY" and "FIVE" are added together to produce "TWENTYFIVE". You could add any number of text strings together to produce any combination you wish.

This has been demonstrated implicitly elsewhere in this book. (See the sections on the ACCEPT, INPUT, and WAIT commands.)

The minus operator behaves a little differently from the plus operator. It performs the concatenation as the plus operator does, but it has the added benefit of truncating trailing blank spaces from the first argument of the operation. Consider the text strings

```
"HELLO     "
```

and

```
"HOW ARE YOU?"
```

The first text string includes five trailing blank spaces. Subtracting the second string from the first produces

```
"HELLOHOW ARE YOU?     "
```

The five blank spaces have been repositioned to the end of the combined text string. Of course, the preceding is not an aesthetic combination of the two text strings. That is because of the choice of text strings, however, not the minus operation.

Logical Operators

III PLUS uses three logical operators to perform all true/false evaluations. These three operators allow III PLUS to perform all Boolean tests. Don't worry if the term *Boolean* is new to you. Simply put, all Boolean operations answer the question, "Is this true?"

The first part of a two-part expression "10=10 .AND. 5=5" is true. You can represent that part with .T. Representing the expression with .T. is basically no different from performing any algebraic substitution, such as YEAR = 1986 or BALANCE = $2000. The only slight difference is that you've directly substituted the expression with its value, which is .T(rue). You have ".T. .AND. 5=5".

You can replace the second part of the expression with its Boolean value as well. It is true so the expression becomes

```
.T. .AND. .T.
```

What if you change the expression so that part two is no longer true? For example, 5=3. The first part of the expression retains its original value, .T. The second part of the expression has a new value, .F(alse). The replaced expression then becomes

.T. .AND. .F.

Remember that Boolean operations answer the question, "Is this true?" and not "Is part of this true?" The entire expression must be true for an .AND. Boolean operation to be true. One false expression, no matter how many true ones surround it, makes the entire expression false when you consider .ANDs.

The next Boolean operator is .OR. .OR. says, "Is anything here true?" If the answer is yes, the .OR. operation is true. The above two-part expression can be replaced with

.T. .OR. .F.

Either part of the expression can be true. Both can be true, but all you need is one part or the other to be true for the Boolean .OR. to return true.

The last Boolean operator to discuss is .NOT. If something is true, and you're more interested in the times it is false, you're interested in .NOT. Suppose the first part of the above expression is still .T. The second part is also .T., but it is .T. because .NOT. (5=3) and

.NOT. (.F.) = .T.

The entire expression can be replaced with

.T. .OR. .NOT. .F.

Obviously, .NOT. .F. is .T., so the preceding can be simplified to

.T. .OR. .T.

The .NOT. operator is useful when you want to do something until a condition is met, such as scan records until you reach the end of a file. An example is

DO WHILE .NOT. EOF( )

You can mix and match the Boolean operators, but remember to evaluate their logic before you combine them and use those combinations in code.

Database Functions

This chapter covers the functions that act on databases at the field, record, or file level.

BOF( )—Beginning of File

The BOF( ) function determines whether the record pointer comes before the first logical record in the database. Whenever you open a DBF with the naked USE command, the record pointer goes to record 1. Entering GOTO 135 puts the record pointer on record 135 (if such a record exists). APPENDing creates a new record and places the record pointer on that new record. The naked USE command tells III PLUS that the logical and physical order of the database is going to be the same. Record 1 is the first physical record in the database, and because there is no special ordering scheme, it is also the first logical record in the database. What happens when you tell III PLUS to USE a database with an NDX file?

For one thing, you've told III PLUS to impose a different order on the DBF. In particular, you want the DBF to be ordered according to the key in the NDX file. This means that the first physical record in the database may no longer be the first logical record in the database. Record 1 will still be the first physical record in the database, but the identity of the first logical record depends on the particular INDEX key. An example of this is shown in the following listing:

```
-> USE JDCBOOKS
-> GOTO TOP
-> DISP NEXT 10 TITLE
Record#   TITLE
        1   Roget's University Thesaurus

        2   Oxford American Dictionary

        3   Words

        4   American Heritage Dictionary

        5   Webster's New World Dictionary

        6   Book of Jargon, The

        7   bartlett's Familiar Quotations

        8   Handbook of Good English, The

        9   Roget's International Thesaurus

       10   Dictionary of Philosophy and Religion

-> SET INDEX TO JDCBTTLE
-> GOTO TOP
-> DISP NEXT 10 TITLE
Record#   TITLE
      464   "...and then we'll get him"

      226   'Salem's Lot

      859   1-2-3 Business Formula Handbook

      860   1-2-3 Financial Macros

      862   1-2-3 For Business

      863   1-2-3 Macro Library

      864   1-2-3 Tips, Tricks, and Traps

      869   101 Science Fiction Stories

      390   13 Clues for Miss Marple

      164   13 Crimes of Science Fiction, The
```

The top of the listing shows the physical order of the DBF file, starting at record 1 and continuing to the end of the file. This is also the logical order because, by not specifying an NDX file, you told III PLUS to impose its own logic on the order of the DBF. III PLUS's logical order is FIFO (First In First Out); hence, physical and logical orders are the same.

The bottom of the listing shows that a logical order has been imposed when you tell III PLUS to SET the INDEX file to JDCBTTLE, which uses TITLE as the keyfield. You GOTO the TOP of the file as you did before, but now there is a new listing. III PLUS DISPLAYs information based on your logic, not on its own. There is a difference between the file's logical and physical order.

How does BOF( ) play into all this? Consider the following listing:

```
-> USE JDCBOOKS
-> GOTO TOP
-> DISP TITLE
Record#  TITLE
      1  Roget's University Thesaurus

-> ? BOF()
.F.
-> SKIP -1
-> ? BOF()
.T.
-> SET INDEX TO JDCBTTLE
-> GOTO TOP
-> DISP TITLE
Record#  TITLE
    464  "...and then we'll get him"

-> ? BOF()
.F.
-> SKIP -1
-> ? BOF()
.T.
-> GOTO 1
-> DISP TITLE
Record#  TITLE
      1  Roget's University Thesaurus

-> SKIP -1
-> ? BOF()
.F.
-> SET INDE TO
-> GOTO 464
-> DISP TITLE
Record#  TITLE
    464  "...and then we'll get him"

-> SKIP -1
-> ? BOF()
.F.
```

You open the JDCBOOKS file without an NDX file. The TOP (first) record in the database is 1, and SKIPping −1 places you before the first logical record in the database (remember that logical and physical orders are the same without an NDX file). So, are you at the beginning of the file (BOF( ))? Yes, .T.

Next, you open the JDCBTTLE.NDX file. Remember that this file imposes your logic on the database. The first record is 464. SKIPping −1 again places you at BOF( ). Why? Because the BOF( ) function concerns itself with only the logical beginning of file, not the physical beginning of file. You can GOTO 1 while the NDX file is active and SKIP −1, but that doesn't place you at the logical beginning of file. Likewise, when there is no active NDX file, you can GOTO 464 and SKIP −1; this also doesn't place you at the logical beginning of file. You must remember there is a difference between physical and logical order; that is the key to this function. You can use the BOF( ) function interactively, as shown in the previous listing. The syntax is

```
BOF( )
```

with no arguments in the parentheses. You can also use it in programs. The BOF( ) function will return one of two values, .T. or .F. This makes it invaluable in testing situations such as the one following:

```
IF BOF()
DO WHILE BOF()
DO WHILE .NOT. BOF()
CASE BOF()
```

Remember that in each of the preceding examples action is taken based on whether or not the record pointer is at the logical beginning of file.

DBF( )—Database Filename

You use the DBF( ) function to determine the name of the active database file. You can use the command interactively or in PROGRAM mode. The syntax is

```
DBF( )
```

with nothing in the parentheses. DBF( ) returns the name of the active database file; or it returns nothing if one isn't open in the current work area. This action is useful in several ways. The particular use shown here is handy during system development and debugging. Start with

```
SET FUNC 4 TO "DO WHERE;"
```

You don't have to use F4, but the WHERE.PRG code is useful when attached to one of the function keys. The code itself is shown in the following listing. This short piece of code provides the programmer with a quick list of which DBFs are in USE where. This information is identical to what you would receive if you used the DISPLAY STATUS command, without all the ancillary information you would receive with the latter that you might not have use for.

```
** WHERE (IS IT?).PRG
**
N = 65
*
DO WHIL N < 75
    WORKAREA = CHR(N)
    SELECT &WORKAREA
    ? "WORK AREA " + WORKAREA + " IS USING " + DBF()
    N = N + 1
ENDD
*
** EOF
```

DELETED( )—Deleted Record

The DELETED( ) function was discussed in detail in the sections on the DELETE, PACK, ZAP, and SET DELETED OFF/on commands. The function returns either .T. or .F., depending on whether the current record has been DELETEd. This function returns the logical .T. or .F. for the current record regardless of whether SET DELETED is on or OFF.

EOF( )—End of File

The EOF( ) function determines whether the record pointer appears after the last logical record in the database. Record pointers and logical records were discussed in the section on the BOF( ) function. In all ways, those discussions are valid for the EOF( ) function. Like BOF( ), EOF( ) is only concerned with the logical record order. Consider the following listing:

```
-> USE JDCBOOKS
-> GOTO BOTTOM
-> DISP TITLE
Record#   TITLE
    874   Literary Agents: How to Get & Work with the right one for you

-> ? EOF()
 .F.
-> SKIP
-> ? EOF()
 .T.
-> SET INDEX TO JDCBTTLE
-> GOTO BOTTOM
-> DISP TITLE
Record#   TITLE
    617   Zorba the Greek

-> ? EOF()
 .F.
-> SKIP
-> ? EOF()
 .T.
-> GOTO 874
-> SKIP
-> ? EOF()
 .F.
-> SET INDEX TO
-> GOTO 617
-> SKIP
-> ? EOF()
 .F.
```

You open the JDCBOOKS file without an NDX file. The BOTTOM (last) record in the database is 874, and SKIPping places you after the last logical record (remember that logical and physical orders are the same without an NDX file) in the database. So, are you at the end of the file (EOF( ))? Yes, .T.

Next, you open the JDCBTTLE.NDX file. Remember that this file imposes your logic on the database, not III PLUS's logic. The last record is 617. SKIPping again places you at EOF( ). Why? Because the EOF( ) function concerns itself only with the logical end of file, not the physical end of file. You can GOTO 874 while the NDX file is active and SKIP, but that won't place you at the logical end of file. Likewise, when there is no active NDX file, you can GOTO 617 and SKIP; this also doesn't place you at the logical end of file. You must remember there is a difference between physical and logical order; that is the key to this function.

You can use the EOF( ) function interactively as shown in the previous listing. You can also use it in programs. The EOF( ) function will return one of two values — .T. or .F. This makes it invaluable in testing situations. Most often the EOF( ) function is used to tell III PLUS to continue some action on a record-by-record basis until the end of file is reached.

FIELD( )—Database Field Name

The FIELD( ) function is a powerful tool that was demonstrated in Chapter 3. It returns the name of the listed field, provided one exists that matches the expression in the parentheses. The syntax is

FIELD(numeric expression or variable)

You could place a value between 1 and 128 in the parentheses, and III PLUS would return the name of the corresponding database field in the current work area. You can ask only for fields between 1 and 128 because III PLUS allows only 128 fields in a database. You can ask for a nonexistent field, and III PLUS will return a blank.

The FIELD( ) function has some idiosyncrasies that can be frustrating for the uninitiated. First, you can't use macros with the FIELD( ) function. In other words, you can't use an expression like

&FIELD(n)

where n is a valid numeric expression. FIELD( ) returns a character expression, but you can't always operate on the character expression as you'd like. You can't enter a command such as

EDIT FIELDS FIELD(n)

because III PLUS will return with the "Syntax error" message. You can pass the FIELD( ) function through other functions without problems, but it returns either errors or strange results when you use it with commands (see Figure 19-1). You should test your FIELD( ) application before including it in any code.

```
-> EDIT FIELDS FIELD(4)
Syntax error.
                      ?
EDIT FIELDS FIELD(4)
-> ? FIELD(4)
CATEGORY
-> ? LEFT(FIELD(4),5)
CATEG
-> ? RIGHT(FIELD(4),5)
EGORY
-> ? SUBSTR(FIELD(4),3,2)
TE
-> ? "ATE"$FIELD(4)
.T.
-> ? AT("ATE",FIELD(4))
          2
-> DISPLAY FIELD(4)
Record#   (4)
    618     4

->
```

Figure 19-1.   The FIELD( ) function has some idiosyncrasies that can
get in the way of code development

FOUND( )—Data Found

The FOUND( ) function was discussed in the sections on the LOCATE,
FIND, SEEK, and CONTINUE commands. The syntax is

FOUND( )

with nothing in the parentheses. FOUND( ) is a logical function that
is .T. if III PLUS finds whatever you are looking for and .F. if it
doesn't. This function has several applications, including adding
passwords to entry systems (assuming you don't have enough memory
or don't care to use the dBASE III PLUS PROTECT utility). The
following method makes use of FOUND( ) when searching large databases on non-INDEXed fields. The next listing shows two modules.
You can include the first module, FOUNDER.PRG, in code where it
is needed. You can place the second module, ESCAOFF.PRG, in a
PRC file or leave it external to the code. The purpose of FOUNDER
is to LOCATE desired records in either un-INDEXed files or in non-

keyfields. It also assumes some action is going to be taken based on the information FOUND( ). The action taken is entirely up to the programmer. The text uses the ON ESCAPE command to provide an EXIT or RETURN from an otherwise infinite loop in the DO WHILE...ENDDO command.

```
** FOUNDER.PRG
**
ACCE "WHAT DO YOU WANT TO FIND? -> " TO FINDTHIS
ACCE "WHERE DO YOU WANT TO FIND IT? -> "TO FINDWHERE
LOCA FOR "&FINDTHIS"$&FINDWHERE
ON ESCA DO ESCAOFF
*
DO WHIL FOUND()
    CLEA
    ? "I FOUND IT!" + CHR(7)
ENDD
*
not FOUND messages
&& need RETURN here if FOUNDER is called
*
** EOF

** ESCAOFF.PRG
**
ON ESCA
EXIT && could be a RETURN command if FOUNDER is called
*
** EOF
```

LUPDATE( )—Last Update Function

The LUPDATE( ) function returns a DATE data type. In particular, it returns the L(ast recorded) UPDATE to the currently active DBF. This command doesn't tell you when the file was last viewed. The LUPDATE( ) function returns the date the file was last EDITed, CHANGEd, MODIFYed, APPENDed, or PACKed. Any of the database viewing commands, when used only to view a file, do not affect the last recorded update of the file. The syntax is

LUPDATE( )

with nothing in the parentheses. Figure 19-2 shows the LUPDATE( ) function in INTERACTIVE mode. LUPDATE( ) returns a blank date when no database is in USE.

```
-> USE
-> ? LUPDATE()
  /  /
-> USE JDCBOOKS
-> ? LUPDATE()
26/08/86
-> USE 7TANK
-> ? LUPDATE()
15/08/86
-> USE CHAPTER9
-> ? LUPDATE()
26/08/86
-> USE BOOKS
-> ? LUPDATE()
25/08/86
-> ? DBF() + " WAS LAST UPDATED ON " + DTOC(LUPDATE())
D:BOOKS.dbf WAS LAST UPDATED ON 25/08/86
->
```

Figure 19-2.   The LUPDATE( ) function returns a DATE data type corresponding to the last recorded update of the currently active DBF

The last part of the figure also shows how you can use LUPDATE( ) in a creative manner. It also makes use of the DBF( ) function mentioned earlier in this chapter. That being the case, LUPDATE( ) can be put to use in several applications in the business environment. What is offered here is something that tells the user the differences between the current database and any existing backup of that database.

```
** LUPDATER.PRG
**
CLEA
ACCE "WHERE IS THE BACKUP DISK? -> " TO TARGETDRIVE
SOURCE = DBF()
TARGET=TARGETDRIVE+":"+RIGHT(LEFT(DBF(),AT(".",DBF())-1),;
       LEN(LEFT(DBF(),AT(".",DBF())-1))-2)
USE
SELE 2
USE &TARGET
? "LAST BACKUP WAS " + CDOW(LUPDATE()) + ", " + DTOC(LUPDATE())
OLDRECS = RECCOUNT()
? "THAT FILE HAS " + STR(OLDRECS,6) + " RECORDS"
USE
SELE 1
USE &SOURCE
?
```

```
? "THE CURRENT FILE HAS " + STR(RECCOUNT() - OLDRECS,6) +;
  " MORE RECORDS"
DOIT = .T.
@ 10,0 SAY "OKAY TO MAKE A BACKUP? (Y/N) ->" GET DOIT PICT "Y"
READ
*
IF DOIT
   COPY TO &TARGET
ENDI
*
** EOF
```

There is nothing especially fancy about the LUPDATER file. New users might be thrown by the apparently involved function statement when the TARGET file is named. It may look involved, but it isn't. The long string of functions does nothing more than take the current DBF( ), "D:BOOKS.dbf", and strip off the ".dbf" part of the name, and then the "D:" part of the name. This leaves "BOOKS", which is added to TARGETDRIVE and ":" to create the TARGET filename. The showpiece here is the LUPDATE( ) function, as that function tells the user when the last recorded update of the file was made.

NDX( )—Index Filename

The NDX( ) function is a powerful tool that returns the name of the listed NDX, provided one exists that matches the expression in the parentheses. The syntax is

NDX(numeric expression or variable)

You could place any value between 1 and 7 in the parentheses, and III PLUS would return the name of the corresponding NDX file in the current work area. You can ask only for NDXes between 1 and 7 because III PLUS allows only seven active NDXes per database. Note that you can ask for a nonexistent NDX, and III PLUS will return a blank. The following listing shows examples. (III PLUS returns an error message if you ask for the name of an invalid NDX file.)

```
-> USE JDCBOOKS INDE JDCBTTLE
-> ? NDX(1)
D:JDCBTTLE.ndx
-> ? NDX(2)

-> ? NDX(0)

***Execution error on NDX(): Invalid index number.
```

One method of using this function is in modifying the WHERE.PRG file shown earlier. You can add code to the DO WHILE...ENDDO loop to have WHERE also show active NDX files.

```
** WHERE (IS IT?).PRG
**
N = 65
*
DO WHIL N < 75
   WORKAREA = CHR(N)
   SELECT &WORKAREA
   ? "WORK AREA " + WORKAREA + " IS USING " + DBF()
   M = 1
*
   DO WHIL M < 8
*
      IF LEN(NDX(M)) = 0
         ? "NO NDX FILES"
         EXIT
      ELSE
         ? "NDX FILE " STR(M,1) + " -> " + NDX(M)
      ENDI
*
      M = M + 1
   ENDD
*
   N = N + 1
ENDD
*
** EOF
```

A warning: Ten active DBFs each with seven NDXes will produce a 70-line display. This will scroll off the screen. You may want to include a WAIT command before SELECTing new work areas.

RECCOUNT( )—Total Number of Database Records

The RECCOUNT( ) function was demonstrated in Chapter 3. The function returns the total number of records in the currently active database. The syntax is

RECCOUNT( )

with nothing in the parentheses. This function is the equivalent of

COUNT

without qualifiers. The only difference between the two operations is in how they arrive at their identical conclusions (see Chapter 8). The COUNT command does a sequential counting of each record in the file. The RECCOUNT( ) function merely reads the information from the file header. This difference makes RECCOUNT( ) valuable when you want to determine differences between files, as shown in the LUPDATE( ) section earlier in this chapter. The function returns only the total number of records in the currently active database. You have to SELECT a different work area to determine the RECCOUNT( ) of the database there.

RECNO( )—Database Record Number

The RECNO( ) function returns the position of the record pointer in the currently active database. The syntax is

RECNO( )

with no argument in the parentheses. Several applications demonstrated in this book make use of the RECNO( ) function. The first has to do with letting the user know where that user is in the database. Consider the following listing:

```
PROC LIBSAY
CLEA
ə   2, PLACE SAY DBFILE
ɑ   4,  3   3AY "Title"
ə   6,  3   SAY "Author"
ə   7,  3   SAY "Editor"
ə   9,  3   SAY "Category"
ə  10,  3   SAY "Subject"
ə  12,  3   SAY "Library"
ə  14,  3   SAY "Anthology"
ə  14, 16   SAY "Series"
ə  14, 26   SAY "Number"
ə  14, 39   SAY "Total"
ə  14, 51   SAY "Complete"
ə  16,  3   SAY "Reference"
ə   3,  1  TO  3, 78     DOUBLE
ə   1,  0  TO 18, 79     DOUBLE
ə  24, 50 SAY "Record Number -> " + STR(RECNO(),4,0)
```

This is a SAY PROCedure for the Personal Library System. The last item in the list is

@ 24, 50 SAY "Record Number —> " + STR(RECNO( ),4,0)

This lets the user know what record is being looked at. This information is useful when the user wants to GOTO a specific record. The user doesn't have to FIND, SEEK, or LOCATE the desired information, because the RECNO( ) is given.

Another use of RECNO comes from how III PLUS reacts to SETting INDEX files TO something. The following listing shows how SETting an INDEX file TO something changes the record pointer, even though no "movement" was performed by the user.

```
-> USE JDCBOOKS
-> GOTO 200
-> ? RECNO()
       200
-> DISP TITLE
Record#  TITLE
    200  Black Water: The Book of Fantastic Literature


-> OLDPLACE = RECNO()
-> ? OLDPLACE
       200
-> SET INDE TO JDCBTTLE
-> DISP TITLE
Record#  TITLE
    464  "...and then we'll get him"


-> GOTO OLDPLACE
-> DISP TITLE
Record#  TITLE
    200  Black Water: The Book of Fantastic Literature
```

You could find yourself merrily EDITing a record, SETting an INDEX, and then lost in the database, with no idea where the EDITed record is in the file. This can happen easily especially when you have to LOCATE information in an un-INDEXed file or non-keyfield and then SET an INDEX TO something. You lose what you LOCATEd. What can you do? The next listing shows how you can solve that problem.

```
USE dbf
LOCATE FOR something somewhere
RIGHTHERE = RECNO()
SET INDEX TO ndx1, ndx2,...
GOTO RIGHTHERE
```

There is also a method of avoiding this problem. That involves the SET ORDER TO command and makes use of the fact that SET

ORDER TO doesn't affect the record pointer:

```
USE dbf INDEX ndx1, ndx2,...
SET ORDE TO
LOCATE FOR something somewhere
SET ORDER TO 1
```

Readers wondering why you would shut off NDX files when you LOCATE should read the section on LOCATE (it takes longer to LOCATE over an NDX file).

RECSIZE( )—Database Record Size

RECSIZE( ) is another function demonstrated elsewhere in the book (see the sections on the COPY command). The syntax is

RECSIZE( )

without arguments of any kind. The function returns the size of any

```
-> ? RECSIZE()
     676
-> ? RECSIZE() * RECCOUNT()
           590824
-> DIR JDCBOOKS.DBF
JDCBOOKS.DBF

 591360 bytes in     1 files.
3362816 bytes remaining on drive.

-> ? 591360 - 590824
      536
-> 200
-> ?RECSIZE()
     676
-> ? DISK()
   3362816
-> ? DISK()/RECS()
      4974.58
->
```

Figure 19-3.   Some uses of the RECSIZE( ) function

one record in the database. It doesn't matter where the record pointer is in the database; all the records in any one database will be the same size. This is because each record is designed in the same way and allows the same amount of information into each field in each record. An empty record and a full record take the same space in memory and on disk. Figure 19-3 shows some interesting uses of the RECSIZE( ) function.

The top of the figure shows a randomly selected record being RECSIZEd. You can use the RECSIZE and RECCOUNT functions to determine the size, in bytes, of all the records in the file. (This result isn't the same as the size of the DBF file. The DBF file also contains file-header information.) You can use RECSIZE and RECCOUNT to learn that the JDCBOOKS.DBF file has a file header of 536 bytes. You can also use the RECSIZE and DISKSPACE functions (shortened with the dBASE III PLUS four-letter-word convention to RECS and DISK) to determine how many more of this database's records will fit on your disk. (This isn't exactly true. The file-header size increases slightly as the number of records increases.)

Numeric Functions

The numeric functions provide III PLUS with power. They allow III PLUS to do things normally reserved for languages such as Pascal, BASIC, and C. The individual functions are ABS, EXP, IIF, INT, LOG, MAX, MIN, MOD, ROUND, SQRT, STR, TRANSFORM, and VAL. Many of these functions have been used in the code elsewhere in this book.

ABS( )—Absolute Value

The ABS( ) function returns the ABSolute value of the value in the parentheses. The syntax is

ABS(n)

where n can be a numeric expression or a number. For those unfamiliar with mathematics, the ABSolute value of any number is the positive value of that number. The ABSolute value of 22 is 22. The ABSolute value of −22 is also 22, because 22 is the positive value of −22. Often the ABSolute value of a number is shown graphically as a "V" type function:

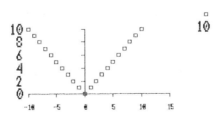

The spreadsheet data that created that graph is shown in the following listing:

```
VALUE      ABS VALUE
-10          10
 -9           9
 -8           8
 -7           7
 -6           6
 -5           5
 -4           4
 -3           3
 -2           2
 -1           1
  0           0
  1           1
  2           2
  3           3
  4           4
  5           5
  6           6
  7           7
  8           8
  9           9
 10          10
```

The ABS( ) function is used a great deal in mathematical manipulations. It is unfortunate that many engineers don't know of III PLUS's various functions. III PLUS could make their work much easier. One such application involves mechanical engineering and the construction business. This application has some extension to other trades, so it is described here.

Construction and many other trades bill by quantity of product, with rates differing depending on the amount of product sold. Construction blueprints are often modified several times during the design and building phase, and sometimes results can be negative. Nobody likes to bill negative values. Further, these changes often affect a great many other variables in the construction process. The solution is to recognize that some changes are going to be acceptable and within the original specifications and some are not. You would design a database such that each record holds the construction variables for a specific set of changes. When changes are made, regardless of whether the changes to the design result in negative values, you can

GOTO ABS(change)

and pull up a listing of the variables that correspond to that change.

III PLUS will tell you if you try to GOTO a nonexistent record, and that in turn tells you you've exceeded the limits of the original design, blueprint, or specification.

EXP( )—Napierian Exponential

The EXP( ) function is another function that finds more use in mathematics and engineering than in most other applications. The syntax is

EXP(n)

where n is either a numeric expression or a number. EXP( ) returns the Napierian, or natural, exponent of whatever value is in the parentheses. This is sometimes confused with base 2 arithmetic (the binary system). It shouldn't be. All values in the natural system are keyed off the value of e, which is approximately 2.72. The binary system is keyed off the value of 2. Remember that the EXP( ) function is equivalent to

e^n

The differences between the two systems are shown here:

```
-> DO EXPER
EXP(  0) = e^  0 =        1.00, 2^ 0 =        1.00
EXP(  1) = e^  1 =        2.72, 2^ 1 =        2.00
EXP(  2) = e^  2 =        7.39, 2^ 2 =        4.00
EXP(  3) = e^  3 =       20.09, 2^ 3 =        8.00
EXP(  4) = e^  4 =       54.60, 2^ 4 =       16.00
EXP(  5) = e^  5 =      148.41, 2^ 5 =       32.00
EXP(  6) = e^  6 =      403.43, 2^ 6 =       64.00
EXP(  7) = e^  7 =     1096.63, 2^ 7 =      128.00
EXP(  8) = e^  8 =     2980.96, 2^ 8 =      256.00
EXP(  9) = e^  9 =     8103.08, 2^ 9 =      512.00
EXP(10) = e^10 =    22026.47, 2^10 =     1024.00
```

IIF( )—Immediate IF

IIF( ) is one of the additions to III PLUS that make the program a joy to use. It is included as a numeric function, but you can use IIF( ) for anything you'd use an IF...ELSE...ENDIF command for. Here, you'll see first how the function works, and then see the actual function syntax. The form (not the actual syntax) is

IIF(something is true, this, or this if it is false)

The "something is true" statement can be anything III PLUS can evaluate to either .T. or .F. Examples are

```
DTOC(DATE()) = "17/09/86"
BALANCE > CREDITLIMT
MYNAME = "Joseph-David Carrabis"
```

Immediately following the "something is true" is "this". In other words, if the first expression in IIF( ) is true, this is what III PLUS will use. If the first expression in IIF( ) is false, however, it will use the third expression in IIF( ).

You can use IIF( ) interactively, but its power is best shown in programs. The syntax is

variable = IIF(something is true, this, or this if it is false)

This follows the syntax of all the other functions, but notice the difference with IIF( ). All the other functions result in a single possible value for the answer. IIF( ) can put one of two values in the variable, depending on the truth or falsehood of the "something is true" expression. An equivalent IF...ELSE...ENDIF would be

```
IF something is true
   variable = this
ELSE
   variable = this
ENDIF
```

IIF( ) takes the five lines and transforms them into a single line of code; hence the name "Immediate IF function." Examples of IIF( ) were shown in the DISPLAY command section. To highlight that example, the next listing shows IIF( ) being used to build a DISPLAY command. This listing also demonstrates that you can use IIF( ) in nonnumeric situations. IIF( ) is used to create two macro substitutions in this example. You can find more information on the exact reason for these macros in the DISPLAY command section.

```
DISPLAYWHAT = IIF(DISPLAYWHAT = SPACE(10), TRIM(WHAT), ;
              DISPLAYWHAT + ", " + TRIM(WHAT))
```

```
DISPLAYFOR = IIF(DISPLAYFOR = SPACE(10), TRIM(WHAT), ;
                 DISPLAYFOR + ".AND. " + TRIM(WHAT))
DISPLAY &DISPLAYWHAT FOR &DISPLAYFOR
```

A powerful use of IIF( ) is with CASE statements. The Immediate IF property of IIF( ) lets you use

CASE IIF(something is true, this, or this if it is false)

The CASE command evaluates the IIF( ) and will be used based on if the "something is true". This effectively lets you double the number of possibilities with the same number of CASE statements. Ten CASEs will give you 20 possibilities, five CASEs will give you 10 possibilities, and so on. Note that IIF( ) is an Immediate IF function, not an If and only IF function.

INT( )—Integer

The INT( ) function is sometimes called the Step function because it returns the INTeger value of any number. Here III PLUS breaks away from the standard rules of mathematics slightly. Normally, the INTeger value of a number is the highest integer contained in that number. The integer value of 8.5 is 8, as 8 is the highest whole number (integer) in 8.5. In standard math the integer value of -8.5 would be -9. Why? The highest whole-number value in -8.5 is -9, not -8 as you might think. The mathematical value of -8 is greater than -9 (remember the standard number line?). So, in the real world, INT(-8.5) would be -9. III PLUS doesn't think along the lines of standard math. It thinks INT(-8.5) is -8.

Examples of dBASE's integer values for a series of numbers from -10 to 10 are shown in the following listing:

VALUE	INTEGRAL VALUE
-10	-10
-8.67	-8
-7.34	-7
-6.01	-6
-4.68	-4
-3.35	-3
-2.02	-2
-.69	0
.64	0

```
1.97        1
3.30        3
4.63        4
5.96        5
7.29        7
8.62        8
9.95        9
```

The syntax is

INT(n)

where n is any valid dBASE III PLUS numeric expression or value.

There are several uses for INT( ). One has to do with the GOTO command and is similar to the use shown with the ABS( ) function. You can create a database such that the record numbers correspond to a set of variables or values that are used according to calculated results. INT( ) lets you use

GOTO ABS(INT(n))

This tells III PLUS to GOTO the sixth record if $6<=n<7$, the seventh record if $7<=n<8$, and so on. INT( ) also has the normal mathematical uses.

LOG( )—Napierian Logarithm

The LOG( ) function is another function that finds more use in mathematics and engineering than in most other applications. The syntax is

LOG(n)

where n is either a numeric expression or a number. LOG( ) returns the Napierian, or natural, LOGarithm of whatever value is in the parentheses. This function is sometimes confused with base 10 logarithms. It shouldn't be. All values in the natural system are keyed off the value of e, which is approximately 2.72. Base 10 logs are obviously keyed off the value 10.

Often you need to use base 10 logarithms and not base e logs. There is a handy method of conversion. One of the laws of logarithms is that the log of any number in any base equals the log of the number divided by the log of the base when the last two share the same base. That can be simplified to

$$Log_n M \quad D \quad \frac{Log_e M}{Log_e n}$$

or, for our purposes,

$$Log_{10} M \quad = \quad \frac{Log_e M}{Log_e 10}$$

So, to find the LOG base 10 of any number, you'd use

LOG(any number)/LOG(10)

MAX( )—Maximum Value

MAX( ) determines which of two and only two values is the greater. The syntax is

MAX(n,m)

where n and m can be any valid dBASE III PLUS numeric expression or value.

Often, MAXimizing functions find use in yield determinations. A situation in which someone gets the greater yield of two possible values, for example, makes use of MAXimizing functions. Consider the line

PAY = MAX(SALARY, IIF(SALES>YEARLYSALARY, SALES/10, COMMISSION))

This makes use of IIF( ) as well as MAX( ) but demonstrates how you can compare three or more variables in a single MAX( ) function. Here, you can determine someone's pay based on how that person's sales were for some period. If the sales were greater than yearly salary, there is the chance the salesperson will qualify for 10% of total sales as pay for that period. Good salespeople love this. If they didn't sell more in one period than their yearly salary, they will get a commission based on their sales. This is also good. But what about the trainee? It would be nice to give that person something to live on while learning the trade, so if the trainee didn't do too well on commissions, she or he can still make a straight salary.

MAX( ) deals only with immediate values. You can't include database field names and expect MAX( ) to return the MAXimum value of the fields throughout the entire database. It will return the MAXimum value for the fields in the current record only.

MIN( )—Minimum Value

MIN( ) determines which of two and only two values is the lesser. The syntax is

MIN(n,m)

where n and m can be any valid dBASE III PLUS numeric expression or value.

Often, MINimizing functions find use in yield determinations. An example of a common sales yield determination was shown in the last section. Like MAX( ), the MIN( ) function deals only with immediate values. You can't include database field names and expect it to return the MINimum value of the fields throughout the entire database. It will return the minimum value for the fields in the current record only.

MOD( )—Modulo Arithmetic

The MOD( ) function is another advanced math function that has several uses. The syntax is

MOD(n,m)

The following explanation is offered for those not familiar with MODulo arithmetic. Back in grade school, when you were first learning how to divide one number by another number, you learned about remainders. You were taught to say

10/3 = 3 r. 1

which meant that 3 goes into 10 three times, and there is a 1 left over.

In the next grade you were told

10/3 = 3 1/3

which meant that 3 goes into 10 three and one-third times. Sometime after that they tried to confuse you one more time by telling you the real answer was 3.33.

Now, as a businessperson, you have an interest in using dBASE III PLUS in general and MOD( ) in particular. Go back to the first lesson in arithmetic:

10/3 = 3 r. 1

You are also more interested in what is left over after the division than in the division itself. In other words, the remainder of 1 is more important than 10/3. The remainder is so important that you need know only its value, not the result of the actual division. This remainder has a special name: it is a MODulo. An example of MODulo arithmetic is shown in the following listing:

```
In all cases, the equation is


MOD(-10,value_in) = value_out


        -10             0
         -9            -1
         -8            -2
          7             3
         -6            -4
         -5             0
         -4            -2
         -3            -1
         -2             0
         -1             0
          0             0
          1             0
          2             0
          3            -1
          4            -2
          5             0
          6            -4
          7            -3
          8            -2
          9            -1
         10             0
```

MODulo arithmetic is particularly interesting when results are graphed. An example is shown in the next illustration, the "Wolf

Spider" function. The values are taken from the previous listing.

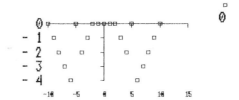

ROUND( )—Roundoff

The ROUND( ) function tells III PLUS how many decimal places are valid in a calculation. This is different from the SET DECIMALS TO and SET FIXED toggle commands discussed in Chapter 11. Some people also confuse ROUND( ) with INT( ). INT( ) tells III PLUS to use the highest integer value contained in an expression as that expression. INT(8.5) is 8, INT(−8.5) is −8 (this isn't true mathematically, but it's true in dBASE). ROUND( ) tells III PLUS how many decimal places to use. The number returned won't necessarily be an INTeger value, but it will be accurate to some predefined number of decimal places.

Similarly, the SET DECIMALS TO command tells III PLUS how many decimal places to display. It says nothing about the relative accuracy of those decimals. The SET FIXED toggle merely tells III PLUS whether to show all the decimal places allowed with the SET DECIMALS TO command. How ROUND( ) works is shown in the next listing.

```
** ROUNDER.PRG
**
HERE = EXP(20)
N = 9
*
DO WHILE N > -10
   ? "EXP(20) = " + STR(EXP(20),19,10) + ", ROUND(EXP(20)," +;
   STR(N,2) + ") = " + STR(ROUND(HERE,N),19,10)
   N = N - 3
ENDD
*
** EOF


-> DO ROUNDER
EXP(20) = 485165195.409790277, ROUND(EXP(20), 9) =
```

```
485165195.409790277
EXP(20) = 485165195.409790277, ROUND(EXP(20), 6) =
485165195.409789979
EXP(20) = 485165195.409790277, ROUND(EXP(20), 3) =
485165195.410000086
EXP(20) = 485165195.409790277, ROUND(EXP(20), 0) =
485165195.000000000
EXP(20) = 485165195.409790277, ROUND(EXP(20),-3) =
485164999.999999881
EXP(20) = 485165195.409790277, ROUND(EXP(20),-6) =
484999999.999999821
EXP(20) = 485165195.409790277, ROUND(EXP(20),-9) =
0.0000000000
```

ROUND( ) rounds things off to a specific number of decimal places. The syntax is

ROUND(n,m)

where n and m are numeric expressions or numbers.

SQRT( )—Square Root

SQRT( ) returns the square root of whatever is in the parentheses. The syntax is

SQRT(n)

where n can be any valid dBASE III PLUS numeric expression or number. You can determine the square root of 36 with

SQRT(36)

Similarly, you can determine the square root of a variable with

SQRT(variable)

The typical square root example involves determining the hypotenuse of a right triangle. The formula is

$a^2 + b^2 = c^2$

Therefore,

$c = +SQRT(a^2 + b^2)$

The plus sign (+) is included in the preceding line to ensure you get a positive result. It isn't necessary with III PLUS, as it won't do polar work or use imaginary numbers. It is also worth knowing that III PLUS has no knowledge of trig functions.

STR( )—Value to Text String

The STR( ) function is another function used widely in this book. It was demonstrated in the previous listing. The syntax is

STR(numeric expression, total digits, total decimal places)

The numeric expression can be any valid III PLUS number or numeric expression. The previous listing showed STR( ) using numeric expressions, ROUND( ) and EXP( ), and a variable, HERE. You can also use a direct number, such as

STR(200.46,6,2)

The preceding tells III PLUS to convert the number 200.46 to a six-character string. Two of the characters will be from the decimal places in 200.46. The problem involves six characters because the decimal point counts as a character when converting. You can enter the function without the last value, as in

STR(200.46,6)

This is the same as entering

STR(200.46)

Both return 200. The reason for this oddity is that III PLUS doesn't know how many decimal places to use, so it opts for none.

TRANSFORM( )—Transform Expression

This function is new with III PLUS; it can be called a "prettifier." The concept of prettifiers was introduced in the sections on @...GET and @...SAY. There III PLUS's use of PICTURE and FUNCTION qualifiers in the @...SAY and @...GET statements was mentioned. TRANSFORM( ) also makes use of the PICTUREs and FUNCTIONs originally described there. You can find exact information on the PICTURE and FUNCTION qualifiers in those sections. Here, their use in the TRANSFORM function is discussed.

Think of TRANSFORM( ) as a method of taking something and placing a different structure on it. You can take a pointillist painting and TRANSFORM it into the same painting in the rococo style.

The TRANSFORM( ) function takes something from a database or memory and places a new structure on it. Consider the next listing:

```
-> ? HERE
   485165195.409790277
-> ? MYNAME
Joseph-David Carrabis
-> ? TRAN(HERE,"999,999,999.999999999")
485,165,195.409790277
-> ? TRAN(MYNAME, "@R X X X X X X X X X X X X X X X X X X X X X
X X X")
J o s e p h - D a v i d   C a r r a b i s
```

Valid PICTURE and FUNCTION arguments have been used in the TRANSFORM( ) function, and the III PLUS four-letter-word con-

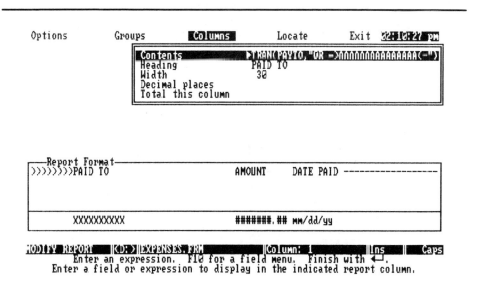

Figure 20-1.   You can use TRANSFORM( ) in FRM files

vention has been used. You can use TRANSFORM( ) in FRM files (see Figure 20-1), LISTs, DISPLAYs, and so on. The following listing shows how Figure 20-1's FRM file changes the REPORT.

```
-> REPORT FORM EXPENSES PLAIN

                                        EXPENSES REPORT FORM

            PAID TO                         AMOUNT DATE PAID


        ** PAID FOR Rental Insurance

          ->Allstate        <-             57.00 07/12/86
        ** Subtotal **
                                           57.00

        ** PAID FOR Auto Expense

          ->Allstate        <-            246.00 07/12/86
        ** Subtotal **
                                          246.00

        ** PAID FOR Rent, Utilities

          ->Susan Carrabis <-            332.89 07/12/86
        ** Subtotal **
                                          332.89

        ** PAID FOR Office Supplies

          ->Susan Carrabis <-            298.00 07/12/86
        ** Subtotal **
                                          298.00

        ** PAID FOR Toll

          ->NH Turnpike     <-              5.00 07/12/86
        ** Subtotal **
                                            5.00

        ** PAID FOR Office Supplies

          ->Computer Town   <-             14.50 07/08/86
        ** Subtotal **
                                           14.50

        ** PAID FOR Motel

          ->Am Ex           <-             39.27 07/09/86
        ** Subtotal **
                                           39.27

        ** PAID FOR Delphi
```

```
 ->Am Ex            <-            27.95 07/09/86
** Subtotal **
                                 27.95

** PAID FOR

 ->Gas             <-             6.50 07/03/86
 ->Gas             <-            10.50 07/05/86
** Subtotal **
                                 17.00
** PAID FOR Auto Expense

 ->Ford Motor Cred<-            305.33 07/10/86
** Subtotal **
                                305.33

** PAID FOR Postage

 ->Post Office     <-             1.72 07/12/86
** Subtotal **
                                  1.72

** PAID FOR Magazine

 ->Science Fiction<-             22.00 07/29/86
** Subtotal **
                                 22.00
*** Total ***
                               1366.66
```

VAL( )—Numeric Text String to Numeric Value

The VAL( ) function is used widely in this book. It can be thought of as the mirror function of STR( ). STR( ) takes a numeric expression or value and converts it to a text string. VAL( ) takes a numeric text expression or variable and converts it to numeric data. The syntax is

VAL(numeric text expression or variable)

The numeric text expression or variable can be any valid III PLUS character list. The expression doesn't even have to be numeric characters, as shown in the next listing:

```
-> DISP MEMO
NUMBER       pub   C   "633"
MYNAME       pub   C   "Joseph-David Carrabis"
    2 variables defined,       28 bytes used
  254 variables available,   5972 bytes available
```

```
-> ? VAL(NUMBER)
633.0000000000
-> ? VAL(MYNAME)
                        0.0000000000
```

The two variables are both character-type data. NUMBER is numeric text, however, and VAL( ) returns the numeric equivalent of the character string. MYNAME is not numeric text. As a result, MYNAME has no value.

In any case, you can use VAL( ) to convert data from character to numeric expressions. As an example, say that you are to develop a system for a catalog order house. The firm wants to price its catalog items based on the last seven characters in the item's stock number. You enter all the stock numbers in the database. When that is done, you enter

REPL ALL PRICE WITH VAL(RIGHT(STOCKNUM,7))

The preceding statement tells III PLUS to REPLACE ALL the PRICE fields in the database WITH the VALue of the RIGHT-most 7 characters in the STOCKNUM field.

String Functions

This chapter deals with III PLUS's string functions. All the string functions share the ability to manipulate text or character strings in various ways. Many of these functions have been used in code elsewhere in the book, and they will be merely referenced here.

$—Can I Find It Here?

The dollar sign ($) string function is not the best-documented function in III PLUS, but it is a useful tool and worth learning. The $ function is a logical function in that it returns .T. or .F. The power comes from what the .T. and .F. reveal.

Syntax   The syntax is

(text to find)$(place to find it)

The text to find can be a character string delimited with double quotes (""), single quotes (''), or square brackets ([ ]), or a character-type variable. The place to find it can be another delimited character string, a character-type variable, or a database field. Note that you can't use $ with MEMO fields. You use variables as

variable1$variable2

and database fields as

variable$field

You can use any mixture of database fields, variables, and literals with the $ function.

Use   Perhaps sometime when you are coding you want to know whether something can be found somewhere—in particular, whether one text string is part of another text string. Say you are putting together a car-pool directory, and want to know every rider who works on Memorial Drive in Cambridge. Some people have entered their work address as 32 Memorial Drive, others as Orion Bldg., Memorial Drive, and so on. All you are concerned with is a listing of the people who work on Memorial Drive. How do you ask III PLUS if people have "Memorial Drive" as part of their address?

"Memorial Drive"$WORKADDRESS

If someone's WORKADDRESS contains the text string "Memorial Drive", the $ function returns .T. If not, $ returns .F. You can get a LIST of who works on Memorial Drive with

LIST NAME,HOMEPHONE FOR "Memorial Drive"$WORKADDRESS

The preceding command line assumes the car-pool database has fields NAME, HOMEPHONE, and WORKADDRESS.

Advanced Use   Following are two examples of advanced use of the $ function. One is fairly common among dBASE programmers; the other appeared earlier in this book. The first example comes from menu systems. Typically, you offer the user a number of menu selections. Assume that, no matter what characters indicate what selections, they will be entered as characters and not as numbers. In other words, even if your menu system determines selections with 1, 2, 3, . . ., you will design your code to read those selections as characters and not as numbers.

You read in the selection and have a DO CASE . . . ENDCASE command to direct III PLUS's attention to the desired task. But what if the user failed to enter a valid response to the menu? Most programmers check for menu-entry errors with an OTHERWISE command in the DO CASE . . . ENDCASE command. If all the CASEs are false, you pick the OTHERWISE option. The OTHERWISE option holds some message such as, "That isn't a valid choice. Please try again." But what if your DO CASE . . . ENDCASE command holds several CASE statements (several is more than 20)?

That's a lot of CASEs to evaluate before getting to OTHERWISE. Can you use $ to save some time? Yes. The solution looks like this:

ANSWER$"123456789ABCDEFGHIJQ"

The following listing shows how this appears in code. Note that the "!" PICTURE template is used in the @...GET command to ensure that you have to test only UPPERCASE input. The code checks for a valid response immediately upon entering the DO CASE... ENDCASE command. This saves the computer valuable processing time.

```
** MENU SYSTEM USING $ AS ERROR CHECK
**
DO WHIL .T.
   ANSWER = " "
   &&
   && PLACE MENU ON SCREEN
   && MENU OPTIONS ARE 1, 2, 3, 4, 5, 6, 7, 8, 9,
   &&                  A, B, C, D, E, F, G, H, I,
   &&                  J and Q
   &&
   && GET ANSWER PICT "!"
*
   DO CASE
      CASE .NOT. ANSWER$"123456789ABCDEFGHIJQ"
         && ERROR MESSAGE
         LOOP
      CASE ...
      ...
      ...
   ENDC
*
ENDD
*
** EOF
```

The second advanced use for the $ function is a slick trick that will impress your friends. Say you create a large database field (or variable) and need to read the record based on information in that one large field. Further, assume the information you need is buried deep within the field. Such a case was shown in the LOCATE command section, when the task was to find one editor in a single field that contained the names of several editors. The following listing shows how the command that performs such a search looks. This example uses LIST. You could code for LOCATE, EDIT, CHANGE, or whatever. The uses of $ are endless.

```
-> USE JDCBOOKS
-> LIST EDITOR FOR "Greenberg"$EDITOR
Record#   EDITOR
     61   Bill Pronzini, Barry N. Malzberg, Martin H. Greenberg ,
Barry N. Malzberg, Martin H. Greenberg
     63   Isaac Asimov, Martin H. Greenberg, Charles G. Waugh ,
Martin H. Greenberg, Charles G. Waugh
     65   Robert Silverberg, Martin H. Greenberg

     66   Bill Pronzini, Barry M. Malzberg, Martin H. Greenberg

     68   Frank D. McSherry, Jr., Charles G. Waugh, Martin H.
Greenberg
    120   Bill Pronzini, Barry N. Malzberg, Martin H. Greenberg

    164   Isaac Asimov, Martin H. Greenberg, Charles G. Waugh

    165   Isaac Asimov, Martin H. Greenberg, Charles G. Waugh

    177   Frederik Pohl, Martin H. Greenberg, Joseph D. Olander

    194   Terry Carr, Martin H. Greenberg

    209   Francis M. Nevins, Jr., Martin H. Greenberg

    210   Martin H. Greenberg, Richard Matheson, Charles G. Waugh

    822   Bill Pronzini, Barry Malzberg, Martin H. Greenberg

    869   Martin H. Greenberg, Charles G. Waugh, Jenny-Lynn Waugh
```

ASC( )—The ASCII value

The ASC( ) function returns the ASCII value of the left-most character in its argument. The syntax is

ASC(string)

where string can be a delimited text string, a character-type variable, or a single delimited character. This function works only on the
left-most character for its argument. Consider the following listing.
ASC( ) works only on the left-most character of the text string, "J", in
all cases. In all cases, it returns the ASCII value of "J", 74.

```
->  ? ASC("Joseph-David Carrabis")
  74
-> ? ASC("J")
  74
-> MYNAME = "Joseph-David Carrabis"
-> ? ASC(MYNAME)
  74
```

A use of ASC( ) was shown involving DO CASE...ENDCASE commands and menu systems. Again, assume the user has several menu options to choose from. The difference is that the menu selections fall into distinct groups. The first group includes the characters "1" to "9," the second group includes the UPPERCASE characters "A" to "Z," and the third group includes the lowercase characters "a" to "z."

The system can take one of three distinct paths, depending on the menu selection. Each of these paths then acts on the actual menu response. The code looks like this:

```
DO CASE
    CASE .NOT. ANSWER$;
"123456789ABCDEFGHIJKLMNOPQRSTUVWXYZabcdefghijklmopqrstuvwxyz"
        && ERROR MESSAGE
        && LOOP TO TOP OF MENU
    CASE ASC(ANSWER) < 58
        && DO NUMBER PROGRAMS
    CASE ASC(ANSWER) < 91
        && DO UPPERCASE PROGRAMS
    CASE ASC(ANSWER) < 123
        && DO LOWERCASE PROGRAMS
ENDC
```

This block of code essentially replaces the DO CASE...ENDCASE block in the "Advanced Use" example listing for the $ function. The ASCII value of "9" is 57; therefore, this routine will branch to the number-based programs if the ASCII value of the ANSWER is less than 58. Similarly, the ASCII values for "Z" and "z" are 90 and 122, respectively. $, described in the last section, is used in the first CASE as an error check. You must list the CASEs in ascending ASCII order if this block of code is to work properly.

AT( )—Starting location of string

AT( ) has similar properties to those of $. You can use either to determine whether one string is located in another string. The $ function returns .T. or .F., depending on whether the first text string is located in the second text string. The AT( ) function returns where the first text string starts in the second text string. The syntax is

AT("text string to find","text string to find it in")

Both the text string to find and the text string to find it in can be delimited text strings, character-database fields, or character variables. The following listing shows AT( ) returning the starting location of various text strings. MYNAME can be found starting at character position 1 in the text string "Joseph-David Carrabis". Likewise, "David" starts at character position 8 in MYNAME. Note that AT( ) returns 0 if it can't find the first text string in the second.

```
-> ? MYNAME
Joseph-David Carrabis
-> ? AT(MYNAME,"Joseph-David Carrabis")
        1
-> ? AT("David",MYNAME)
        8
-> SOURCE = DBF()
D:JDCBOOKS.dbf
-> TARGET =
"A:"+SUBSTR(LEFT(SOURCE,AT(".",SOURCE)-1),AT(":",SOURCE)+1)+".O
LD"
A:JDCBOOKS.OLD
```

Many programmers use AT( ) to create a logical test such as

IF AT("this",that) # 0

This translates into

"this"$that

This listing also shows another use of AT( ). It is the method used repeatedly in this book. The AT( ) function allows you to perform selective truncations. Here the SUBSTR( ), LEFT( ), and AT( ) functions are used to cut off "D:" and ".dbf" from the SOURCE. The first AT( ) function tells III PLUS where to start performing a LEFT( ) character truncation. The last AT( ) tells III PLUS where to start performing a SUBSTR( ) character truncation. The DBF( ) function could be used, as in

TARGET="A:"+SUBS(LEFT(DBF( ),AT(".",DBF( ))−1,AT(":",DBF( ))+1)+".OLD"

to produce the same result. SOURCE = DBF( ) was entered only to help the reader follow along. Lastly, note the four-letter-word convention in the preceding line.

The CHR( ) function can be thought of as the mirror function to ASC( ). ASC( ) returns the ASCII value of the left-most character in its argument. CHR( ) takes the ASCII value as its argument and returns the corresponding character. The syntax is

CHR(n)

where n can be any valid dBASE III PLUS numeric expression or number. CHR( ) gives the programmer a great deal of control over such things as screen images. The following listing is a small program that lists on the screen the various CHR( )s. One of the more interesting ones is CHR(7), which rings the system bell.

```
** CHRER.PRG TO SHOW CHARACTER EQUIVALENTS OF ASCII CODES
**
N = 0
*
DO WHIL N < 256
    ? "Character " + STR(N,3) + " IS -> " + CHR(N)
    N = N + 1
ENDD
*
** EOF
```

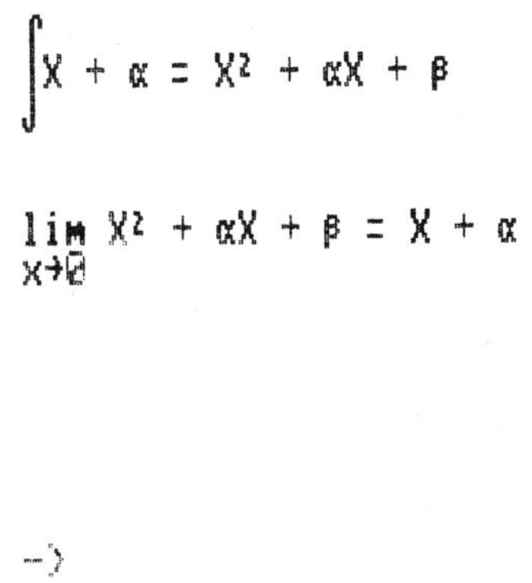

$$\int X + \alpha = X^2 + \alpha X + \beta$$

$$\lim_{X \to 0} X^2 + \alpha X + \beta = X + \alpha$$

-)

Figure 21-1. An example of the fancy features available with the CHR( ) function

You can use CHR( ) in any number of FRMs, FMTs, or LBLs. Some of the possible uses are shown in Figure 21-1. The code that created that figure is given in the following listing:

```
CLEAR
@ 5,0 SAY CHR(244)
@ 6,0 SAY CHR(179)+"X + "+CHR(224)+" = X"+CHR(253)+" +
"+CHR(224)+"X + "+CHR(225)
@ 7,0 SAY CHR(245)
@ 10,0 SAY "Lim X"+CHR(253)+" + "+CHR(224)+"X + "+CHR(225)+" = X
+ "+CHR(224)
@ 11,0 say "x"+CHR(26)+"0"
```

ISALPHA( )—Is the First Character an Alpha Type?

ISALPHA( ) is another function that works on only the first character in a text expression. The syntax is

ISAL(string)

where string can be any valid III PLUS delimited text string, a memory variable, or a database field. Note the four-letter-word convention in the preceding example.

ISALPHA( ) returns .T. or .F., based on whether the first character in the string is an ALPHA character. ISALPHA( ) tests for ALPHA characters in an alphanumeric string. It doesn't test for numeric input to a character data type. An example of this is shown in the following listing. Asking III PLUS to evaluate ISAL (NUMBER) causes an error message, because NUMBER is not alphanumeric data.

```
-> ? NUMBER
        32
-> ? ISAL(NUMBER)
Invalid function argument.
            ?
? ISAL(NUMBER)
-> ? THIS
32 FOXMOOR
-> ? ISAL(THIS)
 .F.
-> ? MYNAME
Joseph-David Carrabis
-> ? ISAL(MYNAME)
 .T.
-> ? ISAL("JOSEPH")
 .T.
```

You can ask ISAL(THIS) because THIS is the alphanumeric string "32 FOXMOOR". It evaluates "32 FOXMOOR" and returns .F., because the first alphanumeric character in "32 FOXMOOR" is not an ALPHAbetic character; it is a numeric character.

ISLOWER( )—Is the First Character Lowercase?

ISLOWER( ) is a modified version of ISALPHA( ). Like ISALPHA( ), it works only on the first character in a text expression. Unlike ISALPHA( ), it determines whether the first character in the text expression is lowercase or not. The syntax is

ISLO(string)

where string can be any valid III PLUS delimited text string, a memory variable, or a database field. Note the four-letter-word convention in the preceding example.

ISLOWER( ) returns .T. or .F., based on whether the first character in the string is a lowercase alphabetic character. ISLOWER( ) tests for lowercase letters. It doesn't test for numeric input to a character data type. ISLOWER( ) returns .F. if the first character in an alphanumeric expression is a numeric character.

ISUPPER( )—Is the First Character UPPERCASE?

ISUPPER( ) is a modified version of ISALPHA( ) and is the mirror function to ISLOWER( ). Like ISALPHA( ) and ISLOWER( ), ISUPPER( ) works only on the first character in a text expression. Unlike ISALPHA( ), it determines whether the first character in the text expression is UPPERCASE or not. The syntax is

ISUP(string)

where string can be any valid III PLUS delimited text string, a memory variable, or a database field. Note the four-letter-word convention in the preceding example.

ISUPPER( ) returns .T. or .F., based on whether the first character in the string is an UPPERCASE alphabetic character. ISUPPER( ) tests for UPPERCASE letters. It doesn't test for numeric input to a character data type. ISUPPER( ) returns .F. if the first character in an alphanumeric expression is a numeric character.

LEFT( )—Left-most Characters

The LEFT( ) function performs a special type of character truncation. Normally, characters are truncated from the right side of a text string. Occasionally, you may need to truncate character strings from the left of the text string. That is what LEFT( ) does. The syntax is

LEFT(string, number of characters from left to truncate)

A demonstration of LEFT( ) is given in the following listing. This little program takes any input (a name, in this case) and uses the LEFT( ) and RIGHT( ) functions to perform truncations, as shown in Figure 21-2.

```
** LEFTRITE.PRG TO DEMONSTRATE LEFT() AND RIGHT()
**
N = 0
ACCE "YOUR NAME? -> " TO NAME
CLIPPED = NAME
CLEA
*
DO WHIL LEN(CLIPPED) > 0
   ? SPACE(N) + LEFT(CLIPPED,1)
   CLIPPED = RIGHT(CLIPPED, LEN(CLIPPED) - 1)
   N = N + 1
ENDD
*
** EOF
```

If nothing else, you should be getting an appreciation of how versatile all of III PLUS's functions are. In this short piece of code, four different string functions have been used.

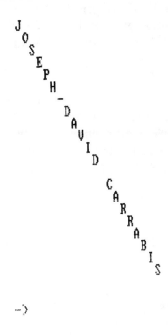

Figure 21-2.   A demonstration of the LEFT( ) and RIGHT( ) functions

LEN( )—String Length

The LEN( ) function returns the number of characters in a text string. The syntax is

LEN(string)

where string can be any delimited character string or variable. III PLUS returns an error message if you try to find the LENgth of numeric data. LEN( ) was demonstrated in the previous listing. The first instance is in the line

DO WHIL LEN(CLIPPED) > 0

where CLIPPED is a text variable. As long as there are characters in CLIPPED (as long as the LENgth of CLIPPED is greater than 0),

execute the DO WHILE...ENDDO loop. The second instance of
LEN( ) is inside the DO WHILE...ENDDO loop. You use LEN( ) to
evaluate the variable CLIPPED each time through the loop with

```
CLIPPED = RIGHT(CLIPPED, LEN(CLIPPED) - 1)
```

The preceding line tells III PLUS to give CLIPPED a new value
based on the RIGHT-most characters currently in CLIPPED. How
many of the RIGHT-most characters will go into CLIPPED's new
value? One less than it has now. You find that number by getting the
LENgth of CLIPPED and subtracting 1 from it.

LOWER( ) — Lowercase from UPPERCASE Conversion

LOWER( ) is used to convert UPPERCASE text to lowercase text.
The syntax is

```
LOWER(string)
```

where string can be a delimited text string or character variable.
LOWER( ) doesn't care where the UPPERCASE characters are in a
text string; it will find them and convert them to lowercase. This is
shown in the following listing. Note that LOWER( ) doesn't affect
numeric characters.

```
-> ? MYNAME
Joseph-David Carrabis
-> ? LOWER(MYNAME)
joseph-david carrabis
-> ? THIS
32 FOXMOOR
-> ? LOWER(THIS)
32 foxmoor
```

A useful piece of code using LOWER( ) is shown in the next listing.
Sometimes people place UPPERCASE and lowercase letters where
they don't belong. The program in this listing makes sure that
"JOSEPH-DAVID CARRABIS" is really "Joseph-David Carrabis".
Note that the hyphen test is included.

```
** LOWUP.PRG TO DEMONSTRATE LOWER() AND UPPER() FUNCTIONS
*
ACCE [YOUR NAME -> ] TO CLIPPED
NAME = UPPE(LEFT(CLIPPED,1))
*
DO WHIL LEN(CLIPPED) > 0
    CLIPPED = RIGHT(CLIPPED, LEN(CLIPPED) - 1)
*
    IF LEFT(CLIPPED, 1) = ' ' .OR. LEFT(CLIPPED, 1) = '-'
        NAME = NAME + LEFT(CLIPPED, 1) + UPPE(SUBS(CLIPPED,2,1))
        CLIPPED = RIGH(CLIPPED, LEN(CLIPPED) - 1)
    ELSE
        NAME = NAME + LOWE(LEFT(CLIPPED, 1))
    ENDI
*
ENDD
*
? NAME
*
** EOF
```

LTRIM( )—Trim Leading Blanks

The LTRIM( ) function is new, making its first appearance in III
PLUS. dBASE programmers have always had the TRIM( ) function.
TRIM( ) removes trailing blanks from a character string. LTRIM( )
removes leading blanks from a character string. The syntax is

LTRIM(string)

where string is any delimited character string, character variable, or
database field. An example of LTRIM( ) is shown in the following
listing:

```
-> ? STRING
                          text string
-> ? LTRIM(STRING)
text string
```

LTRIM( ) isn't selective in how many blanks it truncates from the
text string. It takes all that it can find. A method for keeping one
leading blank (for aesthetic purposes) on character strings is

string = " " + LTRIM(string)

The REPLICATE( ) function is new, but it has already found use with some programmers. REPLICATE( ) tells III PLUS to repeat the first listed character a specified number of times. The syntax is

REPLICATE(character to repeat, number of repetitions)

The character to repeat can be any of the 255 characters available to the IBM PC and its clones. The number of repetitions can be any valid numeric expression or number you like, depending on your purpose. A sample program that shows how REPLICATE( ) works is given in the following listing. This example uses the CHR( ) function to convert a numeric argument into a character argument. REPLICATE( ) works with only characters as its first argument.

```
** REPLER.PRG TO DEMONSTRATE REPLICATE() FUNCTION
**
STORE 0 TO N,M,X,Y,Z,T
CLEA
@ 1,0 SAY "WHAT CHARACTER FOR LEFT MARGIN (ASCII CODE)? -> " ;
      GET N PICT "999" RANG 1,255
@ 2,0 SAY "WHAT CHARACTER FOR RIGHT MARGIN (ASCII CODE)? -> " ;
      GET M PICT "999" RANG 1,255
@ 3,0 SAY "WHAT CHARACTER FOR THE TOP MARGIN (ASCII CODE)? -> " ;
      GET X PICT "999" RANG 1,255
@ 4,0 SAY "WHAT CHARACTER FOR THE BOTTOM MARGIN "+;
      "(ASCII CODE)? -> " GET Y PICT "999" RANG 1,255
@ 5,0 SAY "WHAT CHARACTER FOR THE MIDDLE LINE (ASCII CODE)? -> ";
      GET Z PICT "999" RANG 1,255
@ 6,0 SAY "WHAT CHARACTER FOR FILLING SPACE (ASCII CODE)? -> " ;
      GET T PICT "999" RANG 1,255
READ
MIDDLELINE = REPL(CHR(Z),79)
LEFTCHAR = CHR(N)
RIGHTCHAR = CHR(M)
BLANKMIDDLE = LEFTCHAR + REPL(CHR(T),77) + RIGHTCHAR
TOPPART = REPL(CHR(X),79)
BOTPART = REPL(CHR(Y),79)
N = 1
CLEA
@ 0,0 SAY TOPPART
*
DO WHIL ROW() < 20
   ? IIF(ROW()/3 = INT(ROW()/3),MIDDLELINE,BLANKMIDDLE)
ENDD
*
? BOTPART
*
** EOF
```

On that note, you should know that you can enter characters directly with the ALT-keypad functions. It does simplify the code considerably, but can also cause more confusion than it's worth.

REPLER.PRG should demonstrate some potentially useful things to designers and developers. You are not limited to commands such as

```
@ x,y TO z,t DOUBLE
```

and variations on that theme. You can create your own pretty pictures by selecting characters with the CHRER.PRG shown in the CHR( ) section earlier in this chapter and then modifying REPLER.PRG, just shown, to make some beautiful menus.

RIGHT( ) — Right-most Characters

The RIGHT( ) function performs the opposite character truncation of the LEFT( ) function and is its mirror equivalent. Normally, characters are truncated from the right of a text string. This is the function you use to do that. RIGHT( ) truncates characters from the right edge of a text string. The syntax is

```
RIGHT(string, number of characters from right to truncate)
```

RIGHT( ) has been used throughout this book in code, most recently in the LEFT( ) function action. There the line was entered as

```
CLIPPED = RIGHT(CLIPPED, LEN(CLIPPED) - 1)
```

The purpose of RIGHT( ) in the preceding line is to remove the first character from the text variable CLIPPED. Another demonstration of RIGHT( ) is given in the LOWUP program in the LOWER( ) function section earlier in this chapter. Essentially, the same process is going on in both listings. Both demonstrate how you can use RIGHT( ) to perform a special kind of truncation.

RTRIM( )—Trim Right Blanks

The RTRIM( ) function is new and is really the TRIM( ) function in disguise. dBASE programmers have always had the TRIM( ) function. TRIM( ) removes trailing blanks from a character string. RTRIM( ) performs this same function, but it is included in III PLUS as a balance to the LTRIM( ) function. RTRIM( ) removes right blanks from a text string. The syntax is

RTRIM(string)

where string is any delimited character string, a character variable, or a database field. RTRIM( ) isn't selective in how many blanks it truncates from the text string. It takes all that it can find. In the following listing, both TRIM( ) and RTRIM( ) return the same result on FINFRONT.

```
-> FINFRONT = "SPACE, THE FINAL FRONTIER" + SPACE(30)
SPACE, THE FINAL FRONTIER
-> ? LEN(FINFRONT)
        55
-> RTRIMMED = RTRIM(FINFRONT)
SPACE, THE FINAL FRONTIER
-> TRIMMED = TRIM(FINFRONT)
SPACE, THE FINAL FRONTIER
-> ? RTRIMMED = TRIMMED
.T.
-> ? LEN(RTRIMMED)
        25
-> ? LEN(TRIMMED)
        25
```

SPACE( )—Create Blank Text Strings

SPACE( ) is a function that primarily saves the programmer room in coding. It has a numeric argument but produces a character result. At first, the result of SPACE( ) might appear a blank. That is, you use SPACE( ) to create blank text strings—character strings where every character is a blank. SPACE( ) has been used in many listings in this book. The syntax is

SPACE(n)

where n can be any valid III PLUS numeric expression or number. Entering

NOTHING = SPACE(10)

tells III PLUS to create a new variable, NOTHING, or use it if it already exists, and give it a value of

"_____"

The underlining has been included to emphasize the blank spaces.

STUFF( )—Stuff String with Character

STUFF( ) is another new function. STUFF( ) lets you "superimpose" a character or characters on an existing text string. It lets you STUFF new information into an old character variable or database field. The syntax is

STUFF (existing string, starting position, number of characters in the existing string to replace with STUFFing, character or text to STUFF the existing string with)

Here is a breakdown of that listing: The first argument to STUFF( ) is the existing text string. This can be a delimited expression, a character database field, or a variable. It can be any number of characters long, within III PLUS's limits.

The second argument is the position in the existing string where you want to start STUFFing something. This can be any valid III PLUS numeric expression or number, but it must equate with a number that corresponds to a character within the length of the existing expression. In other words, if the existing expression is only 20 characters long, you can't have a starting position of 21 or greater.

The third argument is the number of characters in the existing string to replace with STUFFing. The number of characters in the existing string to replace with STUFFing has the same caveats on it as the starting position argument. You can STUFF more characters than exist in the existing string. III PLUS merely removes the remaining part of the existing expression and replaces it with the STUFFing.

The last argument can be either a single character or a text expression itself. It is what you're going to use to STUFF the existing string.

You can even STUFF the existing string with itself (see the following listing):

```
-> ? MYNAME
Joseph-David Carrabis

-> ? STUFF(MYNAME,5,10,MYNAME)
JoseJoseph-David Carrabisarrabis

-> ? STUFF(MYNAME,5,5,MYNAME)
JoseJoseph-David Carrabisvid Carrabis

-> ? STUFF(MYNAME,5,1,MYNAME)
JoseJoseph-David Carrabish-David Carrabis

-> ? STUFF(MYNAME,5,50,MYNAME)
JoseJoseph-David Carrabis

-> ? STUFF(MYNAME,5,50,REPL(CHR(219),50))
Jose[[[[[[[[[[[[[[[[[[[[[[[[[[[[[[[[[[[[[[[[[[[[[[[[[[
```

Note how STUFF( ) is affected by its arguments. The first STUFF( ) function places MYNAME in MYNAME beginning at the fifth character. Once it has finished STUFFing MYNAME, it completes the listing beginning at the fifteenth character. Why? It was asked to start at the fifth character and STUFF the next ten characters. A similar example is shown in the second STUFF( ) line. STUFFing starts at the fifth character, as it did earlier. But now only five characters are STUFFed. Hence, the final display is longer than the previous STUFF( ) line. This logic follows for the third STUFF( ) line.

The fourth STUFF( ) line shows what happens when the third argument specifies more characters than exist in the existing string. Finally, the last STUFF( ) line shows continuous STUFFing.

SUBSTR( )—Get Substring from Text

The SUBSTR( ) function was demonstrated in the sections on the AT( ) and LOWER( ) functions earlier in this chapter, as well as elsewhere in this book. SUBSTR( ) stands for SUBSTRing. The function is used to pull one text string from another. The syntax is

SUBSTR(text expression, starting position, number of characters of the text expression to use in the SUBSTRing)

The first argument, text expression, can be any delimited character string, a character database field, or a memory variable. The starting position is the position in the text expression of the first character you want in the SUBSTRing. The third argument is the number of characters of the text expression to use in the SUBSTRing. Both starting position and number of characters of the text expression to use in the SUBSTRing can be any valid III PLUS numeric expression or number. You can enter the function without the third argument (see the following listing). Note that SUBSTR( ) counts from left to right when a third argument is given.

```
•> ? MYNAME
Joseph-David Carrabis
•> ? SUBSTR(MYNAME,8,5)
David
•> ? SUBSTR(MYNAME,8)
David Carrabis
```

TRIM( )—Trim Right Blanks

The TRIM( ) function is one of the oldest dBASE functions. It shares the workload of TRIMming right-hand blank spaces with the new III PLUS RTRIM( ) function. TRIM( ) removes trailing blanks from a character string. TRIM( ) can be thought of as removing right blanks from a text string. The syntax is

TRIM(string)

where string is any delimited character string, a character variable, or a database field. TRIM( ) isn't selective about how many blanks it truncates from the text string. It takes all that it can find. The listing in the RTRIM( ) function section earlier in this chapter shows that both TRIM( ) and RTRIM( ) return the same result on FINFRONT.

UPPER( ) is used to convert lowercase text to UPPERCASE text. The syntax is

UPPER(string)

where string can be a delimited text string or character variable. UPPER( ) doesn't care where the lowercase characters are in a text string; it will find them and convert them to UPPERCASE. UPPER( ) doesn't affect numeric characters.

A useful piece of code using UPPER( ) is shown in the LOWUP program listing in the section on the LOWER( ) function earlier in this chapter. The code was designed because sometimes people place lowercase letters where they don't belong.

Date Functions

This chapter covers all the date functions in III PLUS: CDOW, CMONTH, CTOD, DATE, DAY, DOW, DTOC, MONTH, and YEAR.

Something a little different will happen in this chapter. Instead of seeing some small piece of code for each function, you'll see a program that is useful and makes use of all III PLUS date functions. The following listing shows this code, CALENDAR.PRG, and Figure 22-1 is a sample of CALENDAR's screen.

```
** CALENDAR.PRG
** COPYRIGHT 1986 JOSEPH-DAVID CARRABIS
*
SET ESCA ON
SET CENT ON
SET SCOR OFF
SET STAT OFF
SET TALK OFF
SET DELI OFF
SET CONF OFF
PRINTIT = .F.
ANSWER = "A"
SET DATE BRIT
DATEBRIT = .T.
DATETYPE = "BRIT"
INDENT = 5
DOMENU = .T.
*
DO WHILE .T.
*
   DO WHILE DOMENU
      CLEA
      @ 0,0  TO 22, 79    DOUBLE
      @ 2,1  TO  2, 78    DOUBLE
      @ 1,4  SAY "C A L E N D A R    G E N E R A T O R" +;
      "          TODAY IS -> " + DTOC(DATE())
      WEEKFILL = REPL(CHR(176),25)
      MONTHFILL = REPL(CHR(177),25)
```

```
            YEARFILL = REPL(CHR(178),26)
            BOTTFILL = REPL(CHR(219),78)
            N = 3
   *
            DO WHILE N < 22
   *
               IF N < 13
                  @ N,1 SAY WEEKFILL
                  @ N,27 SAY MONTHFILL
                  @ N,53 SAY YEARFILL
               ELSE
                  @ N,1 SAY BOTTFILL
               ENDI
   *
            N = N + 1
            ENDD * FILLS
   *
            @ 3,8   SAY "  WEEKLY   "
            @ 3,35  SAY " MONTHLY   "
            @ 3,61  SAY "  YEARLY   "
            @ 4,8   SAY " CALENDAR "
            @ 4,35  SAY " CALENDAR "
            @ 4,61  SAY " CALENDAR "
            @ 7,3   SAY "A. THIS WEEK           "
            @ 8,3   SAY "B. REST OF THIS WEEK "
            @ 9,3   SAY "C. ANY WEEK, ANY YEAR"
            @ 7,28  SAY "D. THIS MONTH          "
            @ 8,28  SAY "E. REST OF THIS MONTH "
            @ 9,28  SAY "F. ANY MONTH, ANY YEAR"
            @ 7,56  SAY "G. THIS YEAR          "
            @ 8,56  SAY "H. REST OF THIS YEAR"
            @ 9,56  SAY "I. ANY YEAR           "
            @ 14,16 CLEA TO 18,62
            @ 15, 25  SAY "L. PRINT CALENDAR -> NO   "
            @ 16, 25  SAY "M. DATE FORMAT    -> DD/MM/YY"
            @ 17, 25  SAY "N. PRINT INDENT   ->  5 CHARS"
            @ 3, 26   TO 13, 26
            @ 3, 52   TO 13, 52
            @ 14, 16  TO 18, 62
            @ 20,33 SAY " Q -> QUIT "
            @ 22,31 SAY "SELECT ->    <- "
            DOMENU = .F.
   *
        ENDD *DOMENU
   *
        @ 22,41 GET ANSWER PICT "!"
        READ
   *
        DO CASE
           CASE .NOT. ANSWER$[ABCDEFGHILMN]
              SET CENT OFF
              SET CONF OFF
              CLEA
              RETURN
           CASE ANSWER = "L"
              @ 15,46 SAY IIF(PRINTIT,"NO ","YES")
              PRINTIT = .NOT. PRINTIT
```

```
         LOOP
      CASE ANSWER = "M"
         @ 16,46 SAY IIF(DATEBRIT,"MM/DD/YY","DD/MM/YY")
         DATETYPE = IIF(DATEBRIT,"AMER","BRIT")
         SET DATE &DATETYPE
         DATEBRIT = .NOT. DATEBRIT
         @ 1,64 SAY DATE()
        LOOP
      CASE ANSWER = "N"
         @ 17,46 GET INDENT PICT "99" RANG 0,20
         READ
         LOOP
      CASE ANSWER = "A"
         START = DATE() - DOW(DATE())
         STOP = START + 7
      CASE ANSWER = "B"
         START = DATE()
         STOP = DATE() + 7 - DOW(DATE())
      CASE ANSWER = "C"
         START = DATE()
         @ 22,24 SAY "ENTER START DATE ->   /  /      <- "
         @ 22,44 GET START
         READ
         STOP = START + 7
         @ 22,0 SAY CHR(200) + REPL(CHR(205),78) + CHR(188)
         @ 22,31 SAY "SELECT ->   <- "
      CASE ANSWER = "D"
         START = DATE() - DAY(DATE()) + 1
         SET DATE BRIT
         STOP = CTOD(STR(DAY(START),2) + "/" +;
         STR(MONTH(DATE()) + 1,2) + "/" + STR(YEAR(START),4))
         SET DATE &DATETYPE
      CASE ANSWER = "E"
         START = DATE()
         SET DATE BRIT
         STOP = CTOD("1/" + STR(MONTH(DATE()) + 1,2) + "/" +;
         STR(YEAR(START),4))
         SET DATE &DATETYPE
      CASE ANSWER = "F"
         START = DATE()
         @ 22,24 SAY "ENTER START DATE ->   /  /      <- "
         @ 22,44 GET START
         READ
         SET DATE BRIT
         STOP = CTOD(STR(DAY(START),2) + "/" +;
         STR(MONTH(START) + 1,2) + "/" + STR(YEAR(START),4))
         SET DATE &DATETYPE
         @ 22,0 SAY CHR(200) + REPL(CHR(205),78) + CHR(188)
         @ 22,31 SAY "SELECT ->   <- "
      CASE ANSWER = "G"
         START = CTOD("1/1/" + STR(YEAR(DATE()),4))
         STOP = CTOD("1/1/" + STR(YEAR(DATE()) + 1,4))
      CASE ANSWER = "H"
         START = DATE()
         STOP = CTOD("1/1/" + STR(YEAR(DATE()) + 1,4))
      CASE ANSWER = "I"
         START = DATE()
```

```
                    a 22,24 SAY "ENTER START DATE ->   /  /     <- "
                    a 22,44 GET START
                    READ
                    SET DATE BRIT
                    STOP = CTOD(STR(DAY(START),2) + "/" +;
                    STR(MONTH(START),2) + "/" + STR(YEAR(START) + 1,4))
                    SET DATE &DATETYPE
                    a 22,0 SAY CHR(200) + REPL(CHR(205),78) + CHR(188)
                    a 22,31 SAY "SELECT ->    <- "
            ENDC
     *
            DOIT = .F.
            SAYTHIS="STARTING "+CDOW(START)+", "+;
            LTRIM(STR(DAY(START)))+" "+LEFT(CMONTH(START),4)+" "+;
            STR(YEAR(START),4)+". ENDING "+CDOW(STOP) +;
            " "+LTRIM(STR(DAY(STOP)))+" "+LEFT(CMONTH(STOP),4)+" "+;
            STR(YEAR(STOP),4)+". OK? (Y/N) -> "
            a 24,1 CLEA
            a 24,1 SAY SAYTHIS GET DOIT PICT "Y"
            READ
     *
            IF DOIT
                LINE = REPL("=",79 - INDENT)
                SP = SPACE(INDENT)
     *
                IF PRINTIT
                    SET DEVI TO PRIN
                    SET CONS OFF
                    SET PRIN ON
                ELSE
                    CLEA
                ENDI
     *
                a 3,(40 - (LEN(CMONTH(START)) +;
                LEN(STR(YEAR(START),4,0)))/2) SAY UPPER(CMONTH(START)) +;
                " " + STR(YEAR(START),4,0)
                a 6,0 SAY SP
     *
                DO WHIL START # STOP
                    ? SP + CDOW(START)
                    ? SP + STR(DAY(START),2,0) + " " + CMONTH(START) +;
                    " " + STR(YEAR(START),4,0)
                    ? SP + DTOC(START)
                    ? SP + LINE
                    START = START + 1
     *
                    IF PROW() > 55 .AND. PRINTIT
                        EJECT
                        a 3,(40 - (LEN(CMONTH(START)) +;
                        LEN(STR(YEAR(START),4,0)))/2) SAY UPPER(CMONTH(START)) +;
                        " " + STR(YEAR(START),4,0)
                        a 6,0 SAY SP
                    ENDI
     *
                ENDD
     *
                IF PRINTIT
                    SET CONS ON
```

```
            SET PRIN OFF
            SET DEVI TO SCREEN
            EJECT
        ELSE
            WAIT
            DOMENU = .T.
        ENDI
    *
    ENDI * DOIT
*
ENDD
*
** EOF
```

Enter this code and you'll be able to generate calendars for any
week, month, or year. The calendars can go to screen or printer but
not to both simultaneously. You can improve the program in two
ways. First, you can have it pause during screen listings. There is
probably no need for that, however, unless you use the second
improvement, which is tying CALENDAR.PRG to a database. This
combination would essentially give you a DAYTIMER utility. All
date functions are affected by the SET DATE command, and some
are affected by the SET CENTURY toggle.

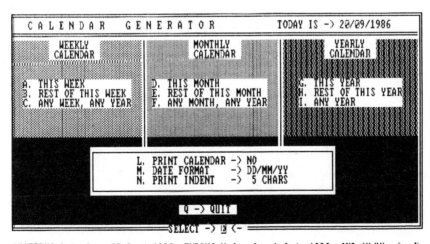

STARTING Saturday, 20 Sept 1986. ENDING Wednesday 1 Octo 1986. OK? (Y/N) -> N

Figure 22-1.   CALENDAR.PRG's screen

Date Functions

CDOW( )—Character Name
of the Day of the Week

CDOW( ) returns the name of the day of the week. The syntax is

CDOW(date argument)

where date argument can be any date-type variable or database field. CDOW( ) is used three times in CALENDAR.PRG. The first occurrence is when the user's date selections are echoed back in the SAY-THIS variable. You create the SAYTHIS variable—in part—with the CDOW( ) function. Note that a date-type variable is used as each CDOW( )'s argument. CDOW( ) is also used to put the day name in CALENDAR's listings (see Figure 22-2).

CMONTH( )—Character
Name of the Month

CMONTH( ) returns the name of the month. The syntax is

CMONTH(date argument)

where date argument can be any date-type variable or database field. CMONTH( ) is used seven times in CALENDAR.PRG. The first occurrence is when the user's date selections are echoed back in the SAYTHIS variable. You create the SAYTHIS variable—in part—with the CMONTH( ) function. A date-type variable is used as each CMONTH( )'s argument. CMONTH( ) is also used to put the header on the output and the month name in CALENDAR's listings (see Figure 22-2).

CTOD( )—Character String to Date

CTOD( ) returns a date-type variable from a character-type argument. The syntax is

CTOD(text string in a date format)

SEPTEMBER 1986

```
Saturday
13 September 1986
13/09/1986
======================================================================
Sunday
14 September 1986
14/09/1986
======================================================================
Monday
15 September 1986
15/09/1986
======================================================================
Tuesday
16 September 1986
16/09/1986
======================================================================
```

Figure 22-2.   A sample of CALENDAR's output

where text string in a date format can be any character-type variable
or database field, provided it looks like DD/MM/YY or MM/DD/YY
or some other variation on that theme (see the SET DATE command
section for more on this).

CTOD( ) is used seven times in CALENDAR.PRG. The first
occurrence is when the STOP variable is created in CASE ANSWER
– "D". STOP is created—in part—with the CTOD( ) function. Three
separate functions must be used to get a usable result. You get the
DAY( ) of a date-type variable, and then convert the number to a
STRing, and finally convert that result and the rest of the text to a
date variable with CTOD( ). This same procedure follows for each use
of the CTOD( ) function.

DATE( )—System Date

The DATE( ) function is used a total of 19 times in CALEN-
DAR.PRG. It's a popular function. The DATE( ) function returns the
system date in whatever form SET DATE dictates. You can find

more information on the SET DATE command in Chapter 11. The syntax is

DATE( )

without any arguments. The function reads the system date from a clock if one is installed. The reason DATE( ) is used so much in CALENDAR.PRG has to do with the need to create a basis for the START and STOP variables.

DAY( )—Numeric Day of the Month

DAY( ) returns the numeric day of the month. III PLUS takes leap year into account. The syntax is

DAY(date argument)

where date argument can be any date-type variable or database field. DAY( ) is used seven times in CALENDAR.PRG. The first occurrence is in CASE ANSWER = "D". The calendar is started on the system DATE( ) minus one less than the number of days gone in the month. DAY( ) is also used when the user's date selections are echoed back in the SAYTHIS variable. You create the SAYTHIS variable—in part—with the DAY( ) function. A date-type variable is used as each DAY( )'s argument.

DOW( )—Numeric Day of the Week

DOW( ) returns the numeric day of the week. The syntax is

DOW(date argument)

where date argument can be any date-type variable or database field. DOW( ) is used three times in CALENDAR.PRG. The first occurrence is in CASE ANSWER = "A". DOW( ) is used to determine the START and STOP dates for the weekly calendars. A date-type variable is used as each DOW( )'s argument.

DTOC( )—Date to Character String

DTOC( ) returns a character-type variable from a date-type argument. It is CTOD( ) in reverse and is the mirror to that function. The syntax is

DTOC(date argument)

where date argument can be any date-type variable or database field. III PLUS returns a character expression in the SET DATE format (DD/MM/YY, MM/DD/YY, or some other variation on that theme. See the SET DATE command section for more on this).

DTOC( ) is used twice in CALENDAR.PRG. The first occurrence is when the screen header with "TODAY IS" is created. The second occurrence is during output. The SET DATE format of the counter is listed as the last line of each date's line.

MONTH( )—Numeric Month of the Year

MONTH( ) returns the numeric month of the year. The syntax is

MONTH(date argument)

where date argument can be any date-type variable or database field. MONTH( ) is used four times in CALENDAR.PRG. The first occurrence is in CASE ANSWER = "D", where the STOP date is determined using MONTH( ) to create a CTOD( ) string. A date-type variable is used as each MONTH( )'s argument.

YEAR( )—Numeric Year

YEAR( ) returns a numeric value corresponding to the year part of a date argument. This command is affected by the SET CENTURY toggle (see Chapter 11). SET CENTURY OFF and YEAR( ) only return the last two digits of the year. In other words, everything takes place in this century. SET CENTURY on, and years are returned as 1986, 1987, and so on. The syntax is

YEAR(date argument)

where date argument can be any date-type variable or database field. YEAR( ) is used 14 times in CALENDAR.PRG. The first occurrence is in CASE ANSWER = "D", where the STOP date is determined using YEAR( ) to create a CTOD( ) string. A date-type variable is used as each YEAR( )'s argument. Other small uses for YEAR are to create SAYTHIS, and during output for headers and to put the year in each date's listing.

Environmental Functions

This chapter covers all the environmental functions in III PLUS. These functions cover such things as system evaluation, file existence, and disk space.

Many of these functions have been used in other listings throughout this book and will be referenced as such. Also, you can shorten each of the function names, when the function name is longer than four characters, with the dBASE III PLUS four-letter-word convention. DISKSPACE( ), for example, can be entered as DISK( ).

COL( )—Screen Column

The COL( ) function returns an integer representing the current cursor COLumn position. This refers to screen coordinates, not printer coordinates (see PCOL( ) and PROW( ) for printer addressing). This function defaults to the current monitor if more than one monitor is available to the system.

Syntax   The syntax is

COL( )

without an argument. III PLUS returns a numeric value corresponding to the current screen COLumn position. The standard cursor-position format

@ x,y

corresponds to

```
@ ROW( ), COL( )
```

which can produce some interesting results.

Use   The following code covers the screen with whatever text you place in the @...SAY command. This isn't tremendously useful, but it gives you an idea of how ROW( ) and COL( ) work.

```
@ 0,0
*
DO WHIL ROW() < 24
   @ ROW(),COL() SAY "HELLO"
ENDD
```

The preceding code uses ROW( ) as a means of evaluating a DO WHILE...ENDDO loop. This hints at III PLUS's ability to perform absolute cursor positioning based on tests made with ROW( ) and COL( ). Absolute cursor positioning takes the form of either

```
@ $,Y
```

or

```
@ X,$
```

The first coordinate pair, ($,Y), tells III PLUS to place information at the current ROW position but at COLumn position Y. The preceding Y value is entered by the programmer. The second coordinate pair, (X,$), tells III PLUS to place information at ROW position X but at the current COLumn position. The X value is entered in this example. Absolute cursor positioning can use any valid III PLUS arithmetic operation as part of the argument. For example, you could ensure that information is placed five ROWs down and ten COLumns to the right of the current position with

```
@ $+5,$+10 SAY text
```

You can ensure that information is placed five ROWs above and ten COLumns to the left of the current cursor position with

```
@ $-5,$-10 SAY text
```

III PLUS knows that the first $ represents the ROW position and that the second $, after the comma (,) in the command, represents the

COLumn position. You can use the dollar sign ($) in cursor-placement commands (@ commands) in which you might otherwise use the ROW( ) and COL( ) functions, as shown in the following listing. This code produces identical output to the listing shown earlier.

```
@ 0,0
*
DO WHIL ROW() + 1 < 24
   @ $,$ SAY "HELLO"
ENDD
```

COL( )'s companion is ROW( ). ROW( ) returns the current cursor ROW position. ROWs run from 0 to 24 and represent the vertical axis. COLumns run from 0 to 79 and represent the horizontal axis.

DISKSPACE( )—Free Disk Space

DISKSPACE( ) returns the free disk space of the default disk in bytes. The syntax is

DISK( )

without an argument. Note the use of the dBASE III PLUS four-letter-word convention in the preceding line. This function was used in Chapter 3, in the section on the JOIN command. You can find an explanation of its use in code there.

ERROR( )—Error Number

ERROR( ) returns a numeric value that corresponds to the particular error III PLUS encountered while processing. A complete list of possible errors is included in the III PLUS documentation. The syntax is

ERROR( )

without an argument. This function has been used repeatedly in this book, and you can find explanations of its use in code in Chapter 13, "Event Processing Commands."

FILE( )—File Existence

The FILE( ) function returns either .T. or .F., based on whether the named file exists. This function has been mentioned elsewhere in this book; a suggested use of the function has been to determine whether certain files existed before making copies or backups of existing files. This section will show the basis for that operation.

Syntax   FILE( )'s syntax is

FILE("drive: \path \[path \. . .]filename.ext")

where drive and path are necessary only if you want III PLUS to search for a file on a drive and path other than the defaults. You must include the filename and the extension in the command. If there is no extension, you must include a period to let III PLUS know there isn't an extension. The entire filename, including drive, path, and extension, should be enclosed in double or single quotes. For example, if the current defaults are drive A and no path and you enter

FILE("ROWCOL.PRG")

III PLUS will look on drive A for the ROWCOL.PRG file and return either .T. or .F., depending on whether the file is there. You could enter

FILE("C: \DB3 \COMPLETE \filename.ext")

to specify that III PLUS look on drive C in directory path DB3 \COMPLETE for the named file, as well. Again, III PLUS would return either .T. or .F., depending on whether the file exists on the specified drive and path.

Use   You may need to ensure all the files you've created for a system are available to that system each time someone starts it up. III PLUS makes this kind of check quite easy with the use of CAT files. The section on CAT files showed that III PLUS will modify the CATALOG if it can't find all the files listed in that CATALOG. This isn't much good when you are using the CAT file to tell you what should be available. The solution is to use the CAT file structure for your own purposes. The following listing shows the PATH field from a typical CAT file. This information uses the drive and path data as well as the filename.

```
-> USE COMPLETE.CAT
-> DISP ALL PATH
Record#  PATH
       1  D:JDCBOOKS.dbf

       2  C:\LIBRARY\SKCBOOKS.dbf

       3  C:\LIBRARY\LIBRARYS.dbf

       4  D:TEMP.dbf

       5  D:CHAPTER9.dbf

       6  names.qry

       7  CHAPTER7.fmt

       8  CHAPTER7.vue

       9  D:PASSWORD.dbf

      10  D:tank.dbf

      11  D:INCOME.dbf

      12  D:BOOKS.dbf

      13  D:BOOKS2.dbf

      14  BOOKS.dbf

      15  JDCBTTLE.ndx

      16  BOOKS.ndx

      17  D:ted.dbf

      18  D:TED2.dbf

      19  ted.lbl

      20  tank.lbl

      21  D:MAGAZINE.dbf

      22  MAUDS.ndx

      23  D:MSSFILE.dbf

      24  MSSAUDS.ndx

      25  MAGMSS.scr

      26  MAGMSS.fmt

      27  SKCTTLE.ndx
```

You make use of that information in the following code:

```
** FINDFILE.PRG TO DEMONSTRATE FILE() FUNCTION
**
*
NOFILE = .F.
USE COMPLETE.CAT && can be any CAT file
*
DO WHILE .NOT. EOF()
*
   FINDTHIS = PATH
*
   IF .NOT. FILE("&FINDTHIS")
      ? "I CAN'T FIND " + FINDTHIS
      NOFILE = .T.
   ENDI
*
   SKIP
ENDD
*
IF NOFILE
   DO GETFILES
ENDI
*
** EOF
```

The PRG file is self-explanatory. The only part of the code not given is the GETFILE.PRG program that actually replaces files not found. You can include PRG and PRC files in the CAT files simply by APPENDing records as you would to any other DBF file.

FKLABEL()—Function Key Label

This function won't make much sense to anyone not involved in system development. The syntax is

FKLABEL(n)

where n can be any valid numeric expression or number. The function returns the name of the function key corresponding to the value n. Most PCs have function-key names such as F2, F3, and so on up to F10. III PLUS, however, runs on machines other than PCs. Some of these other machines don't recognize function keys as F2, F3, and so on. Their function keys bear more exotic names such as SETUP, PAGE, NEXT, HELP, and JUMP. Further, some systems have more than ten function keys. You use this function to determine what the present system's function-key names are on the keyboard. The standard IBM PC, PC XT, and PC AT allow nine function keys, F2-F10. F1 is reserved by III PLUS for its own Help system.

FKMAX( )—Maximum Number of Function Keys

This function won't make much sense to anyone not involved in system development. The syntax is

FKMAX( )

without an argument. The function returns the number of function keys allowed on the current system. IBM PC, PC XT, and PC AT computers allow nine function keys, F2-F10 (F1 is reserved by III PLUS for its Help system). III PLUS, however, runs on machines other than PCs, some of which have more than ten function keys. You can use this function to determine how many function keys are available and, when used with FKLABEL( ) (shown in the previous section), what their names are on the keyboard.

GETENV( )—Get Environment

This function won't make much sense to anyone not involved in system development. The syntax is

GETENV("DOS SET environment parameter name")

where the DOS SET environment parameter can be any entry made through the DOS internal SET command. You can use this command to test III PLUS interaction with the system. If you are not familiar with the DOS SET parameters, consider the following listing:

```
-> ! SET
COMSPEC=C:\COMMAND.COM
PATH=C:\;C:\EDIT;C:\UTILITY;C:\NORTON;C:\DB3
PROMPT=$p$g
```

```
-> ? GETENV("COMSPEC")
C:\COMMAND.COM
-> ? GETENV("PATH")
C:\;C:\EDIT;C:\UTILITY;C:\NORTON;C:\DB3
-> ? GETENV("PROMPT")
$p$g
-> ? GETENV("RALPH")

-> ? GETENV(NORTON)
Variable not found.
                    ?
? GETENV(NORTON)

->
```

The beginning of the listing is a request to execute the DOS SET command. The SET command returns the current DOS SET environmental parameters if no SET strings are entered. You will probably have DOS SET environmental parameters that differ from those in the listing, but you should have something telling you and the computer where COMSPEC is. Some of the DOS SET parameters are entered automatically by the computer when it boots. Some are entered through the CONFIG.SYS and AUTOEXEC.BAT files, if any exist.

This example shows three DOS SET parameters. You can then query the system through III PLUS with the GETENV( ) function. Each DOS SET parameter's name is enclosed in double (or single) quotes. III PLUS returns an error message if no quotes are used and a blank if no corresponding DOS SET parameter exists.

You can also use variables in GETENV( ). You could create a variable, THISRIGHT, with the value "C:\COMMAND.COM", and perform tests such as

```
? THISRIGHT = GETENV("COMSPEC")
```

or do evaluations such as

```
THISRIGHT = GETENV("COMSPEC")
```

Macro substitutions are allowed. For example:

```
THISRIGHT = "COMSPEC"
? GETENV("&THISRIGHT")
```

INKEY( )—ASCII Value of Last Input Key

This function was demonstrated in Chapter 13 in the section on the

ON KEY command. The syntax is

```
INKEY( )
```

without an argument. INKEY( ) returns the ASCII value of the last key pressed by the user. This function is often used in conjunction with the ON KEY command, as discussed in Chapter 13. The function is affected by the contents of the TYPEAHEAD buffer and returns the values of keys in that buffer in a First In, First Out (FIFO) manner. This means that INKEY( ) reads keys already in the buffer rather than keys just entered into the buffer. This can pose a problem if immediate branching is necessary based on entered keys. In such cases, you should remove the TYPEAHEAD buffer completely with SET TYPEAHEAD TO 0. Also note that this function removes an entered key from the TYPEAHEAD buffer without letting any other command or function act on the key's value or meaning. You can see the INKEY() values for various keys with the following code

```
** INKEYTST.PRG FOR DEMONSTRATING INKEY() VALUES
** USE THE ESCAPE KEY TO EXIT THIS ROUTINE
*
I = 0
*
DO WHIL .T.
   I = INKEY()
   ? I
ENDD
*
** EOF
```

ISCOLOR( )—Is a
Color Monitor Active?

This function returns either .T. or .F., based on whether the active monitor is a COLOR monitor. The syntax is

```
ISCOLOR( )
```

without an argument. It returns .T. if the system has a COLOR monitor and that monitor is the active monitor, and an .F. if the system doesn't have a COLOR monitor or the COLOR monitor isn't active. Some systems use the 16-shades-of-green monitors that are fed screen data through color cards. These monitors will test .T. with ISCOLOR( ), even though they aren't true COLOR monitors.

MESSAGE( )—Error Message

MESSAGE( ) returns the text string that corresponds to the particular ERROR III PLUS encountered while processing. A complete list of possible MESSAGEs and ERRORs is included in the III PLUS documentation. The syntax is

MESSAGE( )

without an argument. This function isn't the same as the ERROR( ) function, although the two functions share some aspects of the III PLUS system. ERROR( ) returns the numeric value of the ERROR encountered while executing an instruction. Each ERROR also has a corresponding MESSAGE. These MESSAGEs include things such as

```
Invalid Function Argument
File not found
File already in use
Alias already in use
Variable not found
```

The MESSAGE( ) function determines which MESSAGE to return based on the last ERROR encountered by III PLUS during processing.

OS( )—Operating System

This function won't make much sense to anyone not involved in system development. The syntax is

OS( )

without an argument. OS( ) returns the name of the current operating system. This can be DOS 2.xx, DOS 3.xx, Novell, IBM Network, UNIX, and so on. The function is quite useful, as different operating systems allow you to do different things. Experienced programmers can use OS() to include several features in their systems, thus making them more transportable. You can, for example, start up your system with a DO CASE...ENDCASE block such as

```
DO CASE
   CASE LEFT(OS(),5) = "DOS 3"
      && load in function key overlays, seek out peripherals,
      && determine memory availability and load in memory
      && resident
      && BIN files
   CASE LEFT(OS(),5) = "DOS 2"
      && set up system to RUN externals as you can't LOAD them as
      && BIN files
   CASE LEFT(OS(),4) = "MOVE"
      && seek out other terminals
      && determine availability of system files on disk farm
   ...
   ...
ENDCASE
```

PCOL( )—Printer Column

The PCOL( ) function returns an integer representing the current Printer COLumn position. This refers to PRINTER coordinates, not screen coordinates (see COL( ) and ROW( ) for information on screen addressing). This function defaults to the current printer if more than one printer is available to the system.

Syntax   PCOL( )'s compatriot function is PROW( ). PROW( ) returns the current Printer ROW position. ROWs can be of any value and represent the vertical axis. COLumns can be of any value for which the printer is set and represent the horizontal axis. The syntax is

PCOL( )

without an argument. III PLUS returns a numeric value corresponding to the current Printer COLumn position. The standard position format

@ x,y

corresponds to

@ PROW( ), PCOL( )

Use   One of the advantages to printer addressing versus screen addressing is that the former allows you to create two custom output formats, one for the screen and the other for the printer. Many of the listings in this book make use of a logical variable, PRINTIT. PRINTIT is .T. if you want to print something and .F. if you want only a screen listing. You can use this same logic to develop code such as

```
IF PRINTIT
   a PROW() + 5, PCOL() SAY text1
   a PROW() + 1, PCOL() + 1 SAY text2
   ...
   ...
ELSE
   a 0,0 CLEA
   a $+1,$ SAY text1
   ...
   ...
ENDI
```

You can use relative addressing with the PCOL( ) function but not with the PROW( ) function. You can also backspace with PCOL( ), but you can't feed paper in reverse with PROW( ).

PROW( ) — Printer Row

The PROW( ) function returns an integer representing the current Printer ROW position. This refers to PRINTER coordinates, not screen coordinates (see COL( ) and ROW( ) for information on screen addressing). This function defaults to the current printer if more than one printer is available to the system.

Syntax   PROW( )'s compatriot function is PCOL( ). PCOL( ) returns the current Printer COLumn position. ROWs can be of any value and represent the vertical axis. COLumns can be of any value for which the printer is set up and represent the horizontal axis. The syntax is

PROW( )

without an argument. III PLUS returns a numeric value corresponding to the current Printer ROW position. The standard position format

@ x,y

corresponds to

@ PROW( ), PCOL( )

Use   Many of the listings in this book make use of a logical variable, PRINTIT. PRINTIT is .T. if you want to print something and .F. if you want only a screen listing. An example of PRINTIT's use was shown in the previous section.

READKEY( )—Read Value of Key Used to Exit from Full-Screen Editing

READKEY( ) is a useful tool for the system developer or programmer who is designing a system that branches to different routines based on the user's activities. Basically, the READKEY( ) function tells III PLUS how someone has exited from the APPEND, BROWSE, CHANGE, CREATE, EDIT, INSERT, MODIFY, or READ operations. Each of these commands is a full-screen editing command. READKEY( ) doesn't act on any other commands.

Syntax   READKEY( )'s syntax is

READKEY( )

with no arguments. The function returns a numeric argument that is based on the key that is pressed to exit from one of the full-screen editing commands listed in the introduction to this section. READKEY( ) returns values based on two separate events. First, READKEY( ) returns values between 0 and 36 if no changes are made to the database fields or memory variables in FULL-SCREEN EDIT mode. Values between 256 and 292 are returned if changes are made to database fields or memory variables in FULL-SCREEN EDIT mode. The actual values are

KEY NAME	RETURNED VALUE WITHOUT UPDATE	RETURNED VALUE WITH UPDATE
BKSPC	0	256
CTL-A	2	258
CTL-B	9	265
CTL-C	7	263
CTL-D	1	257
CTL-E	4	260
CTL-END	14	270
CTL-F	3	259
CTL-H	0	256
CTL-HOME	33	289
CTL-J	5	261
CTL-K	4	260
CTL-L	1	257
CTL-LEFT ARROW	8	263
CTL-M	15	271
CTL-N	11	267
CTL-PgDn	35	291
CTL-PgUp	34	290
CTL-Q	12	268
CTL-R	6	262
CTL-RIGHT ARROW	9	264
CTL-S	0	256
CTL-U	10	266
CTL-W	14	270
CTL-X	5	261
CTL-Z	8	264
DOWN ARROW	5	261
END	3	259
ESC	12	268
F1	36	292
HOME	2	258
LEFT ARROW	0	256
PgDn	7	263
PgUp	6	262
RETURN (PAST END)	13	N/A
RETURN (START)	16	272
RIGHT ARROW	1	257
UP ARROW	4	260

Use   READKEY( ) offers the programmer some highly sophisticated skills for use in code development. It gives the programmer
control over any editing the user performs. READKEY( ) doesn't
care what is being done during FULL-SCREEN EDIT mode, just
how you exit from that mode. This function gives you the ability to
test how the user exited from a record update and query whether the
changes are permanent and should be the basis for an update to the
entire file, should be ignored, should not be ignored even though the

user exited by using ESC, and so on. This is pressed one step further in the "Advanced Use" section. You should recognize that not all updates and exits from databases are intentional. You can now query the user for verification when editing is occurring.

Advanced Use   You can edit a group of memory variables just as easily as you can edit a database record. Take a CREATE SCREEN- or MODIFY SCREEN-generated FMT file and note that the Screen generator automatically includes the alias name of the source file in the FMT file. Use any word processor or the III PLUS Text Editor to change each occurrence of the alias name to "M —>", the MEMORY field designator. Initialize the variables somewhere in the code before the FMT file is accessed and use READKEY( )'s ability to determine how the user ended the EDITing/APPENDing/INSERTing session. Is everything all right? Then proceed. Is something wrong? Query the user before doing anything else. Were changes made? Does the user want to try working on the same record again? These are the questions you will want to ask.

ROW( )—Screen Row Position

The ROW( ) function returns an integer representing the current cursor-ROW position. This refers to screen coordinates, not printer coordinates (see PCOL( ) and PROW( ) for information on printer addressing). This function defaults to the current monitor if more than one monitor is available to the system.

ROW( )'s companion function is COL( ). ROW( ) returns the current cursor ROW position. ROWs can be numbered from 0 to 24 and represent the vertical axis. COLumns can be numbered from 0 to 79 and represent the horizontal axis. The syntax is

ROW( )

without an argument. III PLUS returns a numeric value corresponding to the current screen ROW position. The standard cursor position format

@ x,y

corresponds to

@ ROW( ), COL( )

This can produce some interesting results, which are discussed in the COL( ) section of this chapter.

TIME( )—System Time

The TIME( ) function returns the current system TIME. This information is read from the clock, if a clock is present. The syntax is

TIME( )

without any arguments.

TYPE( )—Data or Variable Type

The TYPE( ) function allows the programmer a unique type of error-trapping ability. Often a system is designed that allows the user to create queries on the fly. Such queries as LOCATEs, DISPLAYs, FINDs, and SEEKs all bring your system to a halt when you enter an improper query item. You can often rectify this situation with the ON ERROR command and ERROR( ) function. That is one worthy avenue. Another avenue involves determining the viability of the query string. This section explains how you might use such an avenue in system development.

Syntax   The TYPE( ) function is used to determine the data type of its argument. The syntax is

TYPE("argument")

where argument can be a memory variable, a database field, or an expression. Following are some examples.

```
-> NUMBER = 17
-> WORD = "HELLO"
-> TRUTH = .T.
-> ? TYPE("TRUTH")
L
-> ? TYPE("WORD")
C
-> ? TYPE("NUMBER")
N
-> ? TYPE("NOTDECLARED")
U
-> ? TYPE("NUMBER+WORD")
U
```

These examples demonstrate the use of TYPE( ) to determine the data type of various memory variables. The variable name in quotes is included in each case.

The standard data types that you can evaluate are CHARACTER, NUMERIC, LOGICAL, and MEMO. There is no DATE data type. III PLUS returns the letter C, N, L, or M, depending on the data type of its argument. III PLUS can also return a U, corresponding to an UNKNOWN data type. This is also demonstrated in the preceding listing.

Use   The "Syntax" section showed how to use TYPE( ) in its standard form. You can also use TYPE( ) to determine the validity of strings. You can evaluate such things as

"HELLO"S"ABCDHELLOEFGHI"

by entering

TYPE('"HELLO"S"ABCDHELLOEFGHI"')

III PLUS returns L for LOGICAL. In other words, the argument to the above TYPE( ) function is a logical possibility. An illogical possibility would be something such as

TYPE('"HELLO" = NUMBER')

III PLUS tells you that is an illogical TYPE by returning U for UNKNOWN. How is this useful in the real world? Say you want to give the user the ability to LOCATE things. In particular, you want the user to be able to enter what they want to LOCATE from the keyboard, not from a menu. That gives the user power. You need a good error-checking system to make sure the user doesn't damage things beyond repair. Use TYPE( ) as follows:

```
-> USE JDCBOOKS
-> FINDTHIS = "AUTHOR = 'Isaac Asimov'"
-> ? TYPE("&FINDTHIS")
L
-> USE
-> ? TYPE("&FINDTHIS")
U
-> USE JDCBOOKS
-> LOCATE FOR &FINDTHIS
-> DISP TITLE,AUTHOR
Record#   TITLE
    AUTHOR
    703   Fantastic Voyage
    Isaac Asimov
```

The JDCBOOKS.DBF file includes the database field AUTHOR. It is therefore LOGICAL for a user to have an expression such as

"AUTHOR = 'Isaac Asimov'"

Taking JDCBOOKS.DBF out of USE makes the expression UNKNOWN. But you can also use the preceding expression with LOCATE to find the desired record. You can use the expression in code, as follows:

```
-> ** LOCATER.PRG TO DEMONSTRATE TYPE() FUNCTION
**
*
DO WHIL .T.
   ACCE "ENTER LOCATE STRING -> " TO FINDTHIS
*
   IF TYPE("&FINDTHIS") = "U"
      WAIT "I CAN'T LOCATE THAT. "+;
      PRESS RETURN TO TRY AGAIN OR ANY OTHER KEY TO EXIT." ;
      TO AGAIN
      AGAIN = IIF(LEN(AGAIN) = 0, "LOOP", "RETURN")
      &AGAIN
   ELSE
      LOCATE FOR &FINDTHIS
      RETURN
   ENDI
*
ENDD
*
** EOF
```

The key to LOCATER.PRG's success is the TYPE( ) function in the IF...ENDIF block. TYPE( ) evaluates the expression entered.

VERSION( )—Version of
dBASE III PLUS in Use

This function won't make much sense to anyone not involved in system development. The syntax is

VERSION( )

without an argument. VERSION( ) returns the name of the current III PLUS program version. The function is quite useful, as different versions of III PLUS behave differently with different operating systems and will no doubt have greater abilities as time goes on. Experienced programmers can use VERSION( ) to include several features in their systems, thus increasing their transportability. A similar example to the one just described was demonstrated in the OS( ) function section earlier in this chapter.

Network Functions

This chapter is strictly for people working with III PLUS in network setups. It doesn't matter which network you use, as the functions are transparent to the network. What is important is your understanding of how priorities are set in networks. You should read through your network documentation and, if you've not had much experience with networking systems, plan a day of experimenting before you apply any network commands or functions to a working environment.

This chapter covers four functions—ACCESS( ), FLOCK( ), LOCK( ), and RLOCK( ). The four functions are really only three. The last two, LOCK( ) and RLOCK( ), perform the same task.

ACCESS( )—The Access-Level Function

ACCESS( ) allows the programmer to add an extra level of protection to a system. The syntax is

ACCESS( )

with no argument. ACCESS( ) returns the access level of the last logged-in user. ACCESS levels are set with the PROTECT utility in the III PLUS package. The last logged-in user is always the last person to access the system. The programmer can make use of that fact in many ways. The obvious way is with a command sequence such as

```
IF ACCESS() < n
    ? "SORRY, YOU CAN'T DO THAT HERE."
    RETURN && OR QUIT, WHATEVER
ENDI
```

where n is some predetermined value that designates what levels of ACCESS gain entrance to the system. This is fine if system access is of a closed-door type. Often it is not. There are users who will have some access, users who will have somewhat more access, and so on. These differences can be handled with a start-up code such as

```
DO CASE
   CASE ACCESS() <= 1
         && ACCESS LEVEL 0 IS A SINGLE USER MODE
         && ACCESS LEVEL 1 IS FOR BASIC LEVEL USERS
         && YOU CAN INCLUDE CODE HERE THAT SETS FLAGS FOR THE PARTS
         && OF THE SYSTEM THESE USERS CAN ACCESS
   CASE ACCESS() = 2
         && THE NEXT LEVEL OF ACCESS
         && THIS CODE SHOULD SET OTHER FLAGS TO TELL III PLUS WHAT
            && PARTS OF THE SYSTEM THESE USERS CAN ACCESS
      ...
      ...
   CASE ACCESS() = 8
         && THE HIGHEST LEVEL OF ACCESS
         && THESE PEOPLE ARE HOLDING THE THIRD TABLET AND SHOULD
         && HAVE ACCESS TO THE ENTIRE SYSTEM.
         && ***** SYSOPS! YOU MAY WANT TO RESERVE THIS LEVEL OF
         && ***** ACCESS FOR YOURSELF!
ENDCASE
```

The preceding code makes use of the programmer's ability to lock up parts of the system with flags. These flags are specific software switches that the programmer includes in the code. Here flags are used to stop people from going where they shouldn't go. Each of the preceding CASEs includes code that builds the flag based on the user's ACCESS level and name. Each program that follows starts off with code similar to the IF...ENDIF block shown at the beginning of this chapter. The big difference between the codes is that here flags are polled, whereas the earlier code polls the ACCESS level. That level changes when new users come onto the system (remember that ACCESS( ) returns the ACCESS level of the last logged-in user). Each requested program, routine, or subroutine starts with a line such as

```
IF KEYIN = "flag1" .OR. KEYIN = "flag2"...
```

if you build your flags as character strings. You may find it easier to build your flags as numeric values. This allows you to use the simpler code

```
IF KEYIN < n
```

FLOCK( )—The Locked-File Function

FLOCK( ) determines whether a file is LOCKed on the network. It returns a .T. if the file is locked or an .F. if the file isn't locked. The syntax is

FLOCK( )

without an argument. The purpose of this function is to prevent more than one user from making major updates to a file at a given time. Having more than one user access and modify an entire file at a given point in time causes a collision. FLOCK( ) appears in code in situations such as

```
USE dbf
SET MESSAGE TO "PRESS ESCAPE TO EXIT AND DO SOMETHING ELSE"
ON ESCA EXIT
*
DO WHIL FLOCK()
   ? "FILE BUSY"
ENDD
*
ON ESCA
SET MESSAGE TO
```

A means of exiting from the loop that polls the availability of the database is included. This avenue is important when several people need to access a file during a work session.

LOCK( ) and RLOCK( )—The Locked-Record Functions

LOCK( ) and RLOCK( ) are identical functions. Each determines whether a specific record in the open database is LOCKed on the network. Each function returns a .T. if the record is locked and an .F. if the record isn't locked. Their syntaxes are

LOCK( )

and

RLOCK( )

without an argument. The purpose of these functions is to prevent more than one user from making changes to a record at a given time. Having more than one user access and modify a specific record at a given point in time causes a collision. LOCK( ) or RLOCK( ) appears in code in situations identical to that shown in the previous listing. The only difference is that FLOCK( ) is replaced by LOCK( ) or RLOCK( ) and the message in the DO WHILE...ENDDO loop says the record, not the file, is busy. A means of getting out of polling the availability of the record is included.

DBC and DBL

This appendix covers two programs included on the Sample Programs & Utilities Disk in the dBASE III PLUS package. These programs perform many functions, but their key features are code compression and encryption.

DBC is the dBASE Coder. It takes programs and applications you've written and translates them into a special code format that can be read and executed by III PLUS. DBL is the dBASE Linker. The separate pieces of an application must be brought together in one file. This consolidation takes place through a process called linking. DBL performs that linking.

If you take any application or individual program that works in dBASE III PLUS and run it through DBC and DBL, you'll see some impressive results. First, the code will be shortened. It has been translated from ASCII text to the compressed form. Typically, after compression the code will have decreased in length from 30%-50%. That change can be significant. Code 100K long in ASCII format can be compressed to 50K-70K. You'll also notice that the code runs faster in the compressed form. Lastly, the compressed code offers the programmer some extra security. The code is rewritten in a pseudo-compiled form. This makes tampering difficult and is useful should you opt to market your application. Ashton-Tate sells a condensed version of III PLUS, dBRUN+, which you can use with compressed code, thereby bypassing some of the cost of a full dBASE III PLUS package for either yourself or a client.

DBC handles the first step in two-part code compression. Figure A-1 shows the separate commands that DBC can use. You can start the program (DBC is not a III PLUS command or function) by typing

```
DBC
```

at the DOS prompt. This tells DBC to prompt the user for filenames with

```
Enter a source filename (.src) or press ENTER to end:
```

You can enter the name of a single file or press ENTER at this time. Entering a filename causes DBC to work on the code. When it's finished with that, it prompts for another filename or an end of session. The files that can go through DBC include any valid, working dBASE III PLUS PRG and PRC files. You need do nothing to the code you've written to have it go through DBC for compilation. You should write any code blocks (DO CASE...ENDCASE, IF...END-IF, DO WHILE...ENDDO) more than 32K long as separate PRG files, and then access them with the DO command in the original file. In other words, you should rewrite long code blocks as subroutines. Also note that separate files passed through DBC are compiled as separate files. You can link all the parts of an application into one file with DBL; this procedure is discussed in the next section.

DBC works most smoothly with files having extensions of .SRC (SouRCe). You can use any extension but you must enter the extension if you're not using .SRC. Any file run through DBC will be compiled with the same filename and a .PRG extension. This means DBC cannot use a file with a .PRG extension as a source file.

An alternative method for starting DBC involves use of the switches shown in Figure A-1. The command form is

```
DBC -Cheader -Idebug -Ooutput -Rinput -Ssource
```

where the switches have the following meanings:

-C It is nice to let people know who wrote the code and how to get in touch with the developers when something goes wrong. You can include this information directly in your source code, but that isn't

```
C:\>dbc ?

dBCODE (2.06) MS-DOS/PC-DOS ***
COPYRIGHT (c) ASHTON-TATE 1985, 1986
AS AN UNPUBLISHED LICENSED PROPRIETARY WORK.
ALL RIGHTS RESERVED.
dBASE III RunTime+ Pseudo-Compiler

Usage: dbc [ -cfile -i[prefix] -oprefix -rfile -sprefix file...]

     FLAGS (order arbitrarily, don't concatenate!)

     -c   ASCII copyright header file
     -i   generate information file(s) (.dbg)
     -o   destination directory
     -r   response file
     -s   source directory

     file...   dBASE III source code file(s) (.src)

  *** END RUN   dBCODE

C:\>
```

Figure A-1.   Commands and switches that DBC uses

always the ideal solution. A better idea is to write an ASCII text file that lists all important information separately. You can write this file with any word or text processor in ASCII mode. You can then tell DBC to include this ASCII text information file, also called a header file, in your compiled code during the operation of DBC. You do all this with the -C switch. You include the header filename and extension after -C in the same line that you call DBC, as shown in the preceding command form.

-I   Even though you have debugged the original III PLUS PRG and PRC files, problems may crop up during compilation. You tell DBC to create a file showing the hexadecimal location of each input line in the source file. Consider the following listing:

```
Input file: boxer.sav

Output file: boxer.prg                    Format: 1.1


   BYTE    LINE

     8      1
```

18	5
2C	6
2E	7
76	8
BE	9
C0	10
C2	11
D6	13
EA	15
FE	16
108	17
139	20
14A	21
15B	22
15F	23

The original BOXER.PRG program is shown in the following listing:

```
** BOXER PRG FOR MAKING PRETTY BOXES
*
*
STOR 0 TO WIDE,LONG
STOR 1 TO STARTX,STARTY
CLEA
@ 10,0 SAY "HOW LONG DO YOU WANT THE BOX (1-20)? -> " GET
LONG RANG 1,20
@ 11,0 SAY "HOW WIDE DO YOU WANT THE BOX (1-10)? -> " GET
WIDE RANG 1,10
READ
CLEA
*
DO WHIL STARTY+WIDE < 79
*
   IF STARTX+LONG > 23
      STARTY = STARTY+WIDE
      STARTX = 1
   ENDI
*
   @ STARTX,STARTY TO STARTX+LONG,STARTY+WIDE DOUBLE
   STARTX = STARTX+1
   STARTY = STARTY+1
ENDD
*
** EOF
```

The file has been renamed as BOXER.SAV to prevent any filename conflicts between DBC's input and output files. The original BOXER file is 25 lines long, of which only the first 23 lines are compilable. DBC doesn't bother with comment lines and passes over them. There are comment lines in the first 23 lines of code, but these are ignored during compilation as well. The first listing shows the location in the compiled file, by byte, of each line in the input file. Line 1 of BOXER.SAV starts at byte 8 in the output BOXER.PRG file. Line 1 is actually read as the first four lines in BOXER.SAV because lines 1 through 3 are comment lines. Line 4 is where the real code begins. The next line to be compiled is line 5, which starts at byte 18 in the output file. The rest of the input file follows.

-O   The preceding paragraph mentioned the renaming of BOXER.PRG as BOXER.SAV to prevent filename conflicts between input and output files. This is necessary because most people name their dBASE III PLUS PRG files with the .PRG extension. DBC wants to generate output files with the .PRG extension. This means DBC will try to read a file and write to it simultaneously. Not a good idea. You can leave your input files as PRG files if you specify a different output directory. For example, your input files are in the C:\DB3\PROGRAM directory. You want to run DBC from there, but doing so would produce an error message. You can enter either of the following commands:

```
DBC -OC:\DB3\COMPILED
DBC -OC:\DB3\COMPILED -Rinput
```

The first command tells DBC to place all output files in the C:\DB3\COMPILED directory and prompts you for each input file. The second form is identical to the first, but it tells DBC to get its input from another file.

-R   This switch tells III PLUS to look in a special file for the names of files to compile. An input file for the Personal Library System would be

```
LIBRARY
LIBEDIT
LIBREPT
LIBPROC
LIBUTILL
LIBUTILM
LIBUTILS
```

This file is an ASCII text file, and each line in the file has a hard carriage return. No extensions are included on the filenames, but the files have been renamed from PRGs to SRCs. You enter this input file, called LIB.SRC, into DBC with the command

```
DBC -RLIB.SRC -other switches
```

DBC and DBL   **703**

-S This switch is the other side of -O. -O told DBC where to put the output. -S tells DBC where to look for input files. It behaves identically to the -O option, except that DBC will limit its input file search to the listed directory.

DBL — The dBASE Linker

DBL provides the second step in two-part code compression. This operation isn't always necessary. You should use it only when an application contains more than one file. Figure A-2 shows the separate commands that DBL can use. You can start the program (DBL is not a III PLUS command or function) by typing

```
DBL
```

at the DOS prompt. This tells DBL to prompt the user for filenames with

```
Enter an output filename (.prg) or press ENTER to end:

Enter a source filename (.prg) or press ENTER to end:
```

You enter the name for the output file or press ENTER. Entering a filename causes DBL to put up the second prompt, which asks for a source file or an end of session. You now can enter filenames one at a time. All named files will be linked into the single, named output file. You must enter the master program in an application as the first file to link.

Any files passed through DBC can go through DBL. You need do nothing to the DBCed code to have it go through DBL for linking. DBL works best with files with extensions of .PRG. You can use any extension but you must enter the extension if you're not using .PRG. Any file run through DBL will be compiled with the same filename and a .PRG extension.

An alternative method for starting DBL involves the switches shown in Figure A-1. The command form is

```
DBL -Cheader -Idebug -Foutput -Rinput -Ssource -P filename
```

where the switches have the following meanings:

```
C:\>dbl ?

dBLINKER (2.06)  MS-DOS/PC-DOS ***
COPYRIGHT (c) ASHTON-TATE 1985, 1986.
AS AN UNPUBLISHED LICENSED PROPRIETARY WORK.
ALL RIGHTS RESERVED.
dBASE III RunTime+ Linker

Usage: dbl [ -cfile -foutfile -i[prefix] -p -rfile -sprefix file...]

        FLAGS (order arbitrarily, don't concatenate!)

        -c    ASCII copyright header file
        -f    output filename (.prg)
        -i    generate information file (.map)
        -p    prefix significant in filename compare
        -r    response file
        -s    source directory

        file...    dBCODE code file(s) (.prg)

C:\>
```

Figure A-2.   Commands and switches that DBL uses

-C   This switch has the exact same meaning here as it did in the DBC section.

-I   You've debugged both the dBASE III PLUS and DBC files, but there are still some problems. You tell DBL to create a file showing the relative file sizes and hook locations. Consider the following listing:

```
Output File: MEL.PRG


Files Defined & Referenced:

*** Count:    0



Files Defined & NOT Referenced:

    Input File      Vs. Offset   Size     Input File     Vs.
Offset      Size
```

DBC and DBL   **705**

```
     CHRER.PRG          1.1      7      47    BOXER.PRG           1.1
     4F      159
```

```
*** Count:      2
```

```
Files Referenced & NOT Defined:
```

```
*** Count:      0
```

Two entirely separate files, CHRER.PRG and BOXER.PRG, were linked in this operation. The debugging (MAP) file tells you that no defined files were referenced (CHRER and BOXER didn't call each other). Two defined files were not referenced, however. The last section, defined but not referenced, has to do with external programs such as word processors that are called into the code. Compare the previous listing with the following, a MAP file created from linking the Personal Library System.

```
Output File: LIB.PRG
```

```
Files Defined & Referenced:
```

Input File	Vs.	Offset	Size	Input File	Vs.
Offset	Size				
LIBUTILM.PRG	1.1	356	1CF	LIBUTILS.PRG	1.1
526	404				
LIBUTILL.PRG	1.1	92B	156E	LIBEDIT.PRG	1.1
1E9A	9BC				
LIBREPT.PRG	1.1	2857	D05		

```
*** Count:      5
```

```
Files Defined & NOT Referenced:
```

Input File	Vs.	Offset	Size	Input File	Vs.
Offset	Size				
LIBRARY.PRG	1.1	7	34E	LIBPROC.PRG	1.1
355D	992				

```
*** Count:      2
```

Files Referenced & NOT Defined:

Reference Offset	Offset	Reference
ERRORMSS.PRG 29D	82	POOL.PRG
GETLIBR.PRG 2F9	2DB	LIBSAY.PRG
LIBFILL.PRG 51A	301	POOL.PRG
GETLIBR.PRG 91F	8C5	POOL.PRG
POOL.PRG 1AD0	1203	POOL.PRG
POOL.PRG 1E9B	1E8E	EDITMENU.PRG
LIBFILL.PRG 1FDD	1FB2	ERRORMSS.PRG
LIBFILL.PRG 205C	1FE7	LIBGETS.PRG
EDITMENU.PRG 20B0	2065	LIBGETS.PRG
LIBFILL.PRG 213B	20DA	LIBFILL.PRG
LIBSAY.PRG 2381	2379	LIBFILL.PRG
EDITMENU.PRG 2519	238A	POOL.PRG
EDITMENU.PRG 25C6	2523	POOL.PRG
LIBFILL.PRG 25D5	25CC	EDITMENU.PRG
LIBFILL.PRG 2687	267E	EDITMENU.PRG
LIBGETS.PRG 2800	275E	LIBFILL.PRG
EDITMENU.PRG 284B	2809	POOL.PRG
LIBSAY.PRG 2B5C	2B54	LIBFILL.PRG
POOL.PRG 3EB6	3C2A	POOL.PRG

*** Count: 38

All the referenced and undefined files are in the PRC file.

-F   This switch allows you to enter an output filename in the command line. DBL assumes the filename has a .PRG extension unless you specify otherwise.

-R   This switch tells III PLUS to look in a special file for the names of files to compile. It is identical to the -R switch described in the DBC section.

-S   This switch tells DBL where to look for input files. It is identical to the -S option described in the DBC section.

-P   Normally, DBL doesn't require much information about path, directory, and drive during compilation. It produces linked files that assume all necessary files will be in the same directory as the linked file. This isn't always the case. Sometimes you'll include a line such as

USE D: \STORAGE \MARCH \BACKUP

and mean exactly that: USE the BACKUP.DBF file on drive D in subdirectory STORAGE \MARCH. DBL would normally ignore the drive and path information and interpret the preceding as

USE BACKUP

The -P option tells DBL to pay attention to your directory and path listings.

filename   You can include the name of an input file, other than the -R input option, simply by including the filename in the command line. If you go this route, you must list this file before you specify an -R file.

Using III PLUS
on a Network

The main difference between III PLUS and previous versions of dBASE III is the networking ability of III PLUS. You cannot install the networked version of III PLUS on any computer that already has either dBASE III or III PLUS on the hard disk.

Before you attempt to use network applications, you should be familiar with certain terms. Most important are *file server* and *remote station*.

File Server The computer and hard disk combination that will be used as the center of the network. It stores all the files used by the entire system. One way to conceptualize the file server is to think of a starfish. The heart of the starfish, where all the arms join, is actually the file server.

Remote Station Any computer tied to the system that is not the file server. To continue with the previous illustration, any arm of the starfish is a remote station. Individual users not working at the file-server computer are working at remote stations. The term *remote* can be misleading. It doesn't necessarily mean you are in the next room, next building, or next town. A remote station can be on the other side of the desk from the file server. You will also hear a remote station called a work station.

APPENDIX B

At the time this book was written, you must have either the IBM PC Network or the Novell Advanced Netware/86 LANs on your system to use the III PLUS networking ability. You must have DOS 3.0 or higher to make use of the III PLUS networking commands and functions, even if you're not using dBASE III PLUS on a network system. Each station running DOS 3.x needs a minimum of 384K of main memory. Each remote station will get a separate copy of dBASE ACCESS. The dBASE III PLUS package comes with one copy of dBASE ACCESS. You can get other copies of dBASE ACCESS in the dBASE III PLUS LAN Pack, available through your dealer or directly from Ashton-Tate. If you're interested in using the networking features in a single-user mode, your PC will need a minimum of 640K main memory and a hard disk. A hard disk and 640K RAM are required for the file server. Each workstation should have disk drives available, either through the network or as physical components of the individual station.

Networked applications require more information in the CONFIG.SYS file than do single-user applications. The CONFIG.SYS file contains a group of instructions that tell DOS how certain things are going to be done. The first networked CONFIG.SYS command is

FCBS = 16,8

This command is an acronym for File Control BlockS and tells DOS how many files can be opened through file-control blocks. A file-control block is a software algorithm that takes control of file reads and writes, which are normally handled by DOS. The above FCBS command tells DOS that up to 16 files can have file-control blocks at any one time and that DOS must leave at least 8 files opened by file-control blocks open at all times. In particular, the first 8 files opened cannot be closed. The command

FCBS = 12,9

tells DOS that up to 12 files can be opened using file-control blocks at any one time, but DOS must leave the first 9 files that were opened with file control blocks constantly active.

This command is important to networking applications because it tells DOS how many files can be shared and is the network analog of the single-user CONFIG.SYS FILES command. Should you get errors because a file has been closed in a network situation, you can try increasing the first value in the FCBS command. You must not have the first and second values of the FCBS command set equal.

DOS closes the least-used FCBS file when a new file is needed in a network situation. You may get an error message such as

```
FCB unavailable
Abort, Retry, Ignore?
```

This is a DOS-level error message, although you may experience it in a dBASE III PLUS networked work session. The safest thing to do is type A for ABORT, bring the system down, and modify the CONFIG.SYS file to increase the FCBS. You don't have to do this immediately, but the problem will definitely return if you take no action. The FCBS command has no effect on the system when the network is not running.

The second new command,

```
LASTDRIVE = x
```

is actually a DOS 3.x command. DOS 3.0 and higher can make use of the SUBST command. This command tells DOS to make believe the system has more disk drives than are physically present. The command that tells DOS how many disks the system will have is the LASTDRIVE command. Literally, it tells DOS the last drive allowed on the system. DOS 3.x assumes that E is the last acceptable drive letter unless you tell it otherwise and ignores the LASTDRIVE command completely if you specify fewer physical drives than the computer has active. This command is necessary in a network situation, as it tells DOS what drive call letters (A through Z) are valid and can be accessed by remote users.

Configuring Your Equipment

This appendix details how to use the CONFIG files to get the most out of III PLUS on your equipment.

The CONFIG.SYS File

The first file to consider is CONFIG.SYS. This file tells your computer how to configure memory, whether there are special physical and virtual devices (a mouse, ANSI, VDISK, and so on) attached to your computer, and how to handle some of the commands to the disk drives.

The CONFIG.SYS file is located in the root directory of a hard disk system or on the boot disk of a floppy disk system. You may already have a CONFIG.SYS file on your computer's boot disk. If so, for both floppy and hard disk systems, make sure the file contains the two lines

```
FILES = 20
BUFFERS = 15
```

Floppy disk users need only have these two lines in a CONFIG.SYS file on the disk they'll use to boot dBASE III PLUS. It is not necessary to delete any other lines from the CONFIG.SYS file unless they are also commands for files and buffers. Having more than 15 buffers allows dBASE to keep more items in memory, but the size of each item is smaller than it would be if only 15 buffers existed. Similarly, having fewer than 15 buffers means fewer items are kept in memory, but each item is larger than if 15 buffers existed. Fewer than 10 files available won't allow dBASE to boot properly. Fewer than 15 files allows dBASE to boot, but using a few NDX files along with your database might result in the message

TOO MANY FILES OPEN

Twenty files is about the optimum number for dBASE III PLUS, but you may want to experiment.

The CONFIG.DB File

Perhaps the most important file for using dBASE III PLUS is the CONFIG.DB file. This file tells dBASE III PLUS exactly how to behave during the work session. The rest of this section goes into detail about the use of each CONFIG.DB command. Not all CONFIG.DB commands have to be used. Usually, they will be used to override system defaults. System defaults are shown in UPPERCASE letters.

The CONFIG.DB file can contain three types of commands to override system defaults. The first type tells III PLUS to turn certain features on or off. The second type of CONFIG.DB file gives III PLUS physical considerations for the system, such as files to open, programs to run, screen color, and which peripheral to activate. The third type of command tells III PLUS how to use and set up memory. Remember that only the first two groups of commands listed in the CONFIG.DB file can be overridden by commands in any running dBASE III PLUS PRG file.

The following is an alphabetic list of all CONFIG.DB commands. Remember that some of the CONFIG.DB commands are actually dBASE III PLUS defaults—you don't have to enter them. Using an improper CONFIG.DB command will produce an error message but will not stop III PLUS from operating. III PLUS will assume the default value for a command it cannot read properly.

ALTERNATE   This echoes screen information to a file for later analysis. You might use this, for example, when you need to track errors during the beta phase of product testing. You activate the ALTERNATE file with

ALTERNATE = filename

in the CONFIG.DB file. dBASE III PLUS automatically gives the ALTERNATE file a .TXT extension. You can also access the ALTERNATE command inside III PLUS with the SET ALTERNATE TO command. When accessing the ALTERNATE file from inside III PLUS, however, you must also use the SET ALTERNATE ON command to ensure that screen information is captured to the ALTERNATE file.

BELL dBASE is designed to ring the PC's bell (actually, CHR(7)) when a data entry field has been filled. The bell will not ring if you only type 5 characters into a 10-character field, but it will ring if you attempt to type 11 or more characters into a 10-character field. The default BELL setting is ON. You can turn the BELL ON or OFF from the CONFIG.DB file with the command

BELL = ON/off

You can access the BELL command inside III PLUS with the SET BELL OFF/on command.

BUCKET Data is often entered in a specific format, or with specific limits on what is valid input. A specific input format is handled by the dBASE III PLUS PICTURE qualifier. For instance, you may want specific data to be entered only as a six-character alpha code. The PICTURE format for that is

@ x,y GET data PICT "AAAAAA"

A code for a six-character alphanumeric code, where the first two characters are alpha and the last four are numeric, is

@ x,y GET data PICT "AA9999"

The result in the first example is that dBASE III PLUS only allows you to enter alpha characters. The result in the second example is that you could only enter data such as AB1234, CZ5555, mQ2323, Op0987, and so on. You could not enter something such as 300-ZX in either situation.

What about the limiting of input data? III PLUS handles that with the RANGE qualifier. The RANGE qualifier tells dBASE the least and greatest values that are allowed during input. These limiting values can be other data, memory variables, database fields, computing values, or any other valid dBASE III PLUS argument. Each time you use a PICTURE or RANGE qualifier with a GET command, you use some memory to hold the format and limits. The CONFIG.DB BUCKET command tells III PLUS how much memory to reserve for these PICTURE and RANGE qualifiers. The BUCKET command has a range of 1K to 31K. If you ask for a 35K BUCKET, you will receive a CONFIG.DB error message. The command is used in the CONFIG.DB file as

BUCKET = n

where n is any value between 1 and 31. You cannot access the BUCKET command outside the CONFIG.DB file.

CARRY   There will be times when you'll want to use the same data in several records. This command is most often used in conjunction with FMT files and the APPEND and INSERT commands. Basically, you use the CARRY command to fill in a new record's fields with information from the preceding record (you CARRY information from the last record to the new record). You can then edit the new record's fields and make the limited number of corrections necessary. APPENDing causes information from the last record in the database to be used in the new record. INSERTing causes information from the immediately preceding record to be used in the INSERTed record. The default CARRY setting is OFF. The CARRY command is used in the CONFIG.DB file as

CARRY = ON/off

You can access the CARRY command outside the CONFIG.DB file with the SET CARRY ON/off command.

CATALOG   III PLUS can use a special type of database, called a CATALOG, to keep track of associated files. The CAT file acts as a special filter for the III PLUS system. Activating a CAT file tells III PLUS to ignore all files not listed in the CATALOG. For instance, you may want to use only the NDX, VUE, SCR, and other files associated with a Receivables database. These might be filed in a CATALOG file called RECEIVAB.CAT. You can activate any valid CATALOG file from the CONFIG.DB file using the command

CATALOG = filename

III PLUS assumes the file has a .CAT extension and will give an error message if no filename.CAT exists. You can activate the CATALOG command inside III PLUS with the SET CATALOG TO filename and SET CATALOG ON/off commands. An open CAT file uses work area 10; this can limit your use of other files. You can find more information on the CAT file in Chapter 2.

CENTURY   The CENTURY command allows you to control how III PLUS displays dates. For instance, this text section was written 23 June 86. If CENTURY were ON, dBASE III PLUS would write the same information as 23 June 1986. The difference is subtle, but useful when you are designing a system that references historical data. The CENTURY command is issued from the CONFIG.DB file as

CENTURY = on/OFF

You can access the CENTURY command outside the CONFIG.DB file with the SET CENTURY on/OFF command.

COLOR   III PLUS makes use of color monitors when it is told they are available. You can give this information to III PLUS in the CONFIG.DB file with the COLOR command. You can use the COLOR command to control the screen-border color, foreground color, background color, and similar screen attributes. This command is used in the CONFIG.DB file as

COLOR = foreground/background, enhanced (foreground/background), border

The first group of colors represents the foreground and background of the standard display. The second group represents the colors of an enhanced foreground and background. The last parameter tells III PLUS what color to use as the border. You can access the COLOR command outside the CONFIG.DB file with the SET COLOR TO and SET COLOR OFF/on commands. You can find more information on the COLOR command in Chapter 11.

COMMAND   This CONFIG.DB command instructs III PLUS to begin executing a specified PRG file automatically, immediately after displaying the copyright message. Its use is similar to including the line

dBASE

in an AUTOEXEC.BAT file to have the PC start running the dBASE package automatically. The COMMAND command cannot be executed outside of the CONFIG.DB file and has the form

COMMAND = DO programfile

where filename is the name of an executable dBASE III PLUS PRG file. To have III PLUS begin running the MAIN.PRG file automatically, for example, you would use

COMMAND = DO MAIN

The COMMAND doesn't have to be DO filename. You can use any III PLUS command, including QUIT.

CONFIRM   You use the CONFIRM command to force dBASE III PLUS to stay in a data-entry field until a RETURN is entered. In other words, you will not be allowed to move from one data-entry field to another simply because you've filled the field with data. You'll have to type RETURN before III PLUS will let you move to the next data-entry field when CONFIRM is ON. You use the command in the CONFIG.DB file as

CONFIRM = on/OFF

You can access the CONFIRM command outside the CONFIG.DB file with the SET CONFIRM on/OFF command.

CONSOLE   The CONSOLE command stops all output to the screen except the @ x,y SAY...GET commands. You will not be able to use the ?, ??, ACCEPT, INPUT, and similar screen-interaction commands when CONSOLE is OFF. You will still be able to use the @ x,y SAY...GET commands, however, to paint the screen and transfer information from the user to the system and vice versa. This command has no effect on output directed to the printer. You use the CONSOLE command in the CONFIG.DB file as

CONSOLE = ON/off

This command is also somewhat interesting in that you can't use it in INTERACTIVE mode—that is, from the dBASE prompt. You can use it in a program as SET CONSOLE ON/off.

DEBUG   The DEBUG command tells dBASE to send ECHOed output to the printer instead of to the screen. You use this command in the CONFIG.DB file as

DEBUG = on/OFF

You can use the DEBUG command either in a program or interactively. The latter form of the command is SET DEBUG on/OFF. To have the DEBUG command send ECHOed output to the printer in either INTERACTIVE or PROGRAM mode, you must have it accompanied by either the SET ECHO ON command or the CONFIG.DB ECHO = ON command.

DECIMALS   The DECIMALS command tells III PLUS how many decimal places to display during division, square root, log, and exponential math operations, and as a result of the VAL( ) function. The default is two decimal places. You use it in the CONFIG.DB file as

DECIMALS = n

where n is an integer value between 0 and 14. You can issue the DECIMALS command outside the CONFIG.DB file with the SET DECIMALS TO n command.

DEFAULT   You use this command to tell III PLUS which drive (not directory) to use for reading and writing all files. These files include PRG, NDX, FMT, FROM, CAT, and so on. You use the command in the CONFIG.DB file as

DEFAULT = d

where d indicates a specific logical or physical drive. You don't have to specify a physical device as the DEFAULT. This command is especially useful for DOS 3.xx users, who can make use of the DOS SET and ASSIGN commands, or users with RAMdisks and Vdisks. dBASE will assume the currently logged drive is the DEFAULT. You can use this command outside the CONFIG.DB file with the SET DEFAULT TO d command.

DELETED   The DELETED command tells III PLUS to act as if a filter exists that hides all DELETEd records from the rest of the system. You use this command in a CONFIG.DB file as

DELETED = on/OFF

Outside the CONFIG.DB file, you can use this command as SET DELETED on/OFF. The DISPLAY and GOTO commands and RECORD and NEXT qualifiers do not behave normally when either the CONFIG.DB command or the SET DELETED on/OFF command is ON. If either form of the DELETED command is ON, for example, you'll be able to DISPLAY only non-DELETEd records and the current record (the one immediately under the record pointer). Likewise, you can GOTO any record, regardless of whether it is DELETEd. To DISPLAY a specific DELETEd record that is not the current record, you use the command

DISPLAY RECORD n

where n is the specific, DELETEd record. To DISPLAY the NEXT n records, you use the command

DISPLAY NEXT n

Here, n signifies the number of records to DISPLAY. But, if you DELETE some of the n records, only the record that is currently pointed to by the record pointer will be DISPLAYed. The other DELETEd records will be ignored.

DELIMITER   You use the first version of this command to determine the appearance of data-entry fields. It lets you decide whether you want something to bracket the fields. You use it in a CONFIG.DB file as

DELIMITER = "><"

The characters to use in bracketing the data-entry fields are enclosed in quotes (" "). You can use this command outside the CONFIG.DB file as SET DELIMITER TO. There are several options for delimiting characters. dBASE III PLUS uses the colon (:) as the default right and left DELIMITER. You summon the colon prompt in the CONFIG.DB file by not issuing the DELIMITER command. You can use any valid ASCII characters between 0 and 255 as the delimiting characters. This command is most often used side by side with the second version of the DELIMITER command, as follows:

DELIMITER   You use this second version of the DELIMITER command to tell dBASE whether to use the delimiters listed in the first version of the command, as shown previously. You use this version of the command to shut off any bracketing that might have been gained with the commands SET DELIMITER TO and DELIMITER = CONFIG.DB. You use it in the CONFIG.DB file as

DELIMITER = on/OFF

You can use it outside the CONFIG.DB file with the SET DELIMITER on/OFF command.

DEVICE   DEVICE determines whether any @ x,y SAY commands are sent to the screen or printer. You use it in the CONFIG.DB file as

DEVICE = SCREEN/printer

You can also use the command in the SET DEVICE TO SCREEN/printer form outside the CONFIG.DB file. Only @...SAY commands are affected by the DEVICE command. All other screen-oriented commands are sent to the screen, no matter what the DEVICE status is.

ECHO   The ECHO command tells dBASE III PLUS to repeat all commands, regardless of whether you entered them at the dBASE prompt or from a PRG file, at the screen. This command can be useful when you are trying to debug your PRG files. You use the ECHO command in the CONFIG.DB file as

ECHO = on/OFF

You can also use the command outside the CONFIG.DB file as SET ECHO on/OFF. When both the ECHO and DEBUG commands are ON, III PLUS repeats all commands at the printer.

ESCAPE   The ESCAPE command lets III PLUS know whether it should stop all activity whenever you press the ESCAPE key. This feature can be both good and bad. It is good because it gives you the chance to stop PRG files during execution. It is bad because III PLUS will stop everything and anything that it is doing when you execute the command. This includes INDEXing, SORTing,

UPDATEing, and similar activities. You use the ESCAPE command as

ESCAPE = ON/off

Outside the CONFIG.DB file, you use it as SET ESCAPE ON/off.

EXACT   The EXACT command affects how dBASE III PLUS searches for information with the LOCATE, FIND, and SEEK commands. When EXACT is OFF, III PLUS will only match as many characters as are available in the search key. In other words, a search key of "Ed" will result in FOUND( ) = .T. for database fields of "Edward," "Edit," and "Edify" when EXACT is OFF. When EXACT is ON, however, a search key of "Ed" will only return FOUND( ) = .T. if it can find the value "Ed" in the index field. You use the EXACT command in the CONFIG.DB file as

EXACT = OFF/on

You use it outside the CONFIG.DB file in the SET EXACT on/OFF command.

Fn   This CONFIG.DB Fn command actually covers the use of all the function keys except F1, which dBASE III PLUS reserves for itself as the HELP key. The Fn command allows you to assign strings up to 30 characters long to each of the function keys 1-9, thus offering some programmability to these keys. The function keys come configured with the following defaults:

```
F1 -> HELP;                        &&unchangeable
F2 -> ASSIST;                      &&start ASSIST mode
F3 -> LIST;                        &&list database fields
F4 -> DIR;                         &&list databases
F5 -> DISPLAY STRUCTURE;           &&display database structure
F6 -> DISPLAY STATUS;              &&display dBASE system status
F7 -> DISPLAY MEMORY;              &&display memory variables
F8 -> DISPLAY;                     &&display database fields
F9 -> APPEND;                      &&add a record to the database
F10 -> EDIT;                       &&edit the current record
```

Only the F1 key is reserved by dBASE III PLUS. You can program these keys in the CONFIG.DB file by listing the keys and the desired program strings as follows:

```
F2 = "DO SETUP;"
F3 = "DIR;ACCE "Which file? " TO DBF;USE &DBF;"
F4 = "SET FIELDS TO AMOUNT,RECDATE,RECFROM;"
F5 = "DIR *.PRG;ACCE "Which program? " TO PRG;DO &PRG;"
F6 = "DO GENACCT;"
```

```
F7 = "SET COLOR TO B/G+,R/W,N;"
F8 = "SET COLOR TO ;"
F9 = "DO WRAPUP;"
F10 = "QUIT;"
```

Going from top to bottom, these Fn commands in the CONFIG.DB file have been set to tell III PLUS to:

- Begin running the SETUP.PRG file when the F2 key is pressed

- When F3 is pressed, give DIRectory listing of all the databases, ask which one to USE, then USE the database entered

- Only show information on the AMOUNT, RECDATE, and REC-FROM fields when F4 is pressed

- When F5 is pressed, give a DIRectory listing of all PRG files, ask which one to run, and then DO that PRG file

- Run the GENACCT.PRG file when F6 is pressed

- Set the screen colors to blue on bright green in the foreground, red on white in ENHANCED mode, and black border when F7 is pressed

- Set the screen colors to their defaults when F8 is pressed

- Run the WRAPUP.PRG file when F9 is pressed

- QUIT to DOS when F10 is pressed

You can use the Fn command outside the CONFIG.DB file as SET FUNCTION n TO string, where n is any number between 2 and 10, inclusive, and string is any character string of 30 or fewer characters. Each string is terminated with a semicolon (;). The semicolon tells III PLUS to perform a RETURN at the end of the string. The ; thus enters the string into III PLUS as a command.

GETS   This command tells III PLUS how many GET commands to leave open before it flushes the input buffer. One of the ways dBASE transfers information from the user to the system is through the GETS command, as in @ x,y SAY prompt GET data. The data that dBASE GETs is placed in an area of memory called an input buffer. This buffer normally empties after each READ statement. (You GET some data by READing it. As soon as you're through READing the data, dBASE sends the data into the database, into the memory variables, or wherever it was supposed to go.) Sometimes you may want to ensure that several GETs can be open before the information is sent elsewhere in the system. This situation may occur when you use an FMT input file that is several screen pages long. That's where the CONFIG.DB GETS command comes in. You use the GETS command to tell III PLUS how much memory to keep open as an input buffer. This buffer is still flushed after each READ, but dBASE defaults to only 128 GETs. The command allows you to reserve enough memory to keep anywhere from 35 to 1023 GETs active in memory before flushing the input buffer. You use the command as

GETS = n

where n is any integer from 35 to 1023. You cannot access this command outside the CONFIG.DB file.

HEADINGS   You use this command to suppress the column listings on DISPLAY, LIST, SUM, and AVERAGE commands. You use it as

HEADINGS = ON/off

You can use the command outside the CONFIG.DB file as SET HEADINGS ON/off. This command doesn't affect the REPORT FORM headings.

HELP   This command does not activate and deactivate the HELP screens or the F1 key. You use it to stop III PLUS from asking whether you want some help when you've entered a command improperly. You use it in the CONFIG.DB file as

HELP = ON/off

and outside the CONFIG.DB file as SET HELP ON/off.

HISTORY   The HISTORY command tells III PLUS how many commands to remember in a special buffer. You then can use this buffer to replay commands that you entered either at the dBASE prompt or in a PRG file. You can replay the commands in the history buffer by pressing the UP ARROW key at the dBASE prompt. You use the command as

HISTORY = n

where n is any integer between 1 and 16000. You can use the HISTORY command outside the CONFIG.DB file as SET HISTORY TO n. It has a default value of 20. The HISTORY command normally only records commands you entered at the dBASE prompt. You must use this command in conjunction with the SET DOHISTORY OFF/on command to record commands issued from a PRG file. The dBASE III PLUS documentation says a value of 0 is valid for the CONFIG.DB form of the HISTORY command. This isn't correct. Using a value of 0 causes some versions of dBASE III to crash, especially when you are trying to RUN or ! an external program.

INTENSITY   This command activates dBASE's ENHANCED VIDEO mode when in FULL SCREEN EDIT mode. You enter it as

INTENSITY = ON/off

You can also use it as SET INTENSITY ON/off outside the CONFIG.DB file.

MARGIN   This command only affects printed output. It has no effect on any screen-oriented commands. The MARGIN command adjusts the left margin of printed output. You use it as

MARGIN = n

where n is any value between 0 and the right edge of your printer. You can achieve the same result with the SET MARGIN TO n command. III PLUS assumes an n value of 0 if none is given.

MAXMEM   You cannot access the MAXMEM command outside the CONFIG.DB file. It tells dBASE how much memory to reserve for itself when running an external program, such as a word processor or accounting package. Normally, III PLUS reserves 256K of main memory for itself and all open variables and files when a ! or RUN command is executed. The command form is

MAXMEM = n

where n is any integer value between and including 256 and 720. The more memory you reserve for dBASE III PLUS the less memory you'll have to run external packages under dBASE.

MEMOWIDTH   This command determines the width of MEMO fields in a database. A MEMO field is a special kind of data type that actually creates a new file when you use it. This special file is called a DBT file (see Chapter 2 for more information). Normally, DBT files allow memos 50 characters wide. You can change this in the CONFIG.DB file with

MEMOWIDTH = n

where n is any integer between 0 and the upper limit of your system memory, in bytes. You can also change memo width with the SET MEMOWIDTH TO n command. The MEMOWIDTH commands have no effect on the width of the MEMO fields if you use the WP command.

MENU   You use this command to turn the cursor movement menus on and off when you are in FULL SCREEN EDIT mode. The command is

MENU = ON/off

and is SET MENU ON/off outside the CONFIG.DB file. In FULL SCREEN EDIT mode, with MENUs ON, the F1 key acts as a toggle to turn the menus on and off.

MVARSIZ   You cannot access this command outside the CONFIG.DB file. It tells dBASE how much memory to set aside for memory variables. There is a 256-character limit on the number of memory variables dBASE III PLUS will allow. What you can alter about the memory variables is how much precision they will keep. MVARSIZ doesn't change the number of variables, but it does alter the amount of memory space each variable can occupy. An example of its use would be in placing long strings into memory variables. These strings might get clipped unless enough room existed in memory to hold the entire string. You use the command as

MVARSIZ = n

where n can be any integer between 1 and 31, representing 1K to 31K.

PATH   The PATH command tells dBASE where to look for files if they can't be found on the DEFAULT directory. The CONFIG.DB version of the command is identical to the DOS PATH command

PATH = dl: \sll;d2: \s2l \s22;

where d1 and d2 are drive designations and s11, s21, and s22 are subdirectory designations. You can use the command outside the CONFIG.DB file as SET PATH TO.

PRINT This command tells dBASE to direct everything except @...SAY commands to the printer. All ?, ??, DISPLAY, LIST, and similar screen commands will be sent to the printer and not listed at the screen when you use PRINT. The command is

PRINT = on/OFF

You can also use it as SET PRINT on/OFF outside the CONFIG.DB file.

PROMPT You cannot access the PROMPT command outside the CONFIG.DB file. You use it to create a special prompt. The default dBASE prompt is a period (.). You can change this with

PROMPT = string

where string can be any character string, including any of the 255 ASCII characters.

SAFETY This command tells dBASE either to warn you or not to warn you when you're about to perform a potentially destructive database operation, such as PACK, ZAP, or ERASE. This command is useful for the novice but not for the experienced user. The command form is

SAFETY = ON/off

SAFETY ON will stop PRG file execution to warn the user even if the programmer doesn't want execution stopped. You can achieve the same result with SET SAFETY ON/off.

SCOREBOARD III PLUS uses a special prompt and message system that involves both the SCOREBOARD and the STATUS lines. An ON SCOREBOARD tells III PLUS to tell you if data entry is outside a specified range, if a record is deleted, and if you're in INS or OVERWRITE mode. You use it as

SCOREBOARD = ON/off

and as SET SCOREBOARD ON/off outside the CONFIG.DB file.

STATUS   You use the STATUS command in conjunction with the SCOREBOARD command to determine what information III PLUS gives the user during a work session and where that information is displayed on the screen. The command form is

STATUS = ON/off

and is SET STATUS ON/off outside the CONFIG.DB file.

STEP   The STEP command tells dBASE to execute all PRG files one line at a time. After each line is executed, III PLUS prompts you to stop the PRG file, do the next line, or enter your own line for processing. The command form is

STEP = on/OFF

and is SET STEP on/OFF outside CONFIG.DB.

TALK   This command tells dBASE to let the user know the results of intermediate operations in such commands as INDEX, REINDEX, and PACK. The command form is

TALK = ON/off

and is SET TALK ON/off outside CONFIG.DB.

TEDIT   You cannot access TEDIT outside CONFIG.DB. It tells III PLUS what word processor to use for the MODI COMM, MODI FILE, MODI SCREEN, and similar commands. The command form is

TEDIT = word processor

where word processor is any executable word processor (such as WordStar or WordPerfect). Normally, dBASE uses its own line-oriented word processor to edit these files. You must have enough memory available to the system to save dBASE in memory and then load in the word processor for this option to work.

TYPEAHEAD   The TYPEAHEAD command determines the size of the TYPEAHEAD buffer. This buffer is similar to the PC's keyboard input buffer in that it captures what you type and saves it in memory until III PLUS is done doing something else and can read the keyboard again. Normally, the TYPEAHEAD buffer is set to 20 characters. This is too limiting for a good typist. You can change the setting in the CONFIG.DB file with

TYPEAHEAD = n

where n can be any integer from 0 to 32000. You can alter the TYPEAHEAD buffer outside the CONFIG.DB file with SET TYPE-AHEAD TO n. Both forms of the TYPEAHEAD command are affected by the INKEY and related functions that monitor keyboard input. The TYPEAHEAD commands only work when ESCAPE is ON, either through the CONFIG.DB ESCAPE = ON or SET ESCAPE ON commands.

UNIQUE   You use the UNIQUE command to create NDX files that only list the first occurrence of a repeated index key. This feature can be useful when you create NDX files that act as signposts for large databases. The command form is

UNIQUE = on/OFF

You can access the command soutside CONFIG.DB with SET UNIQUE on/OFF.

VIEW   You use this command to recall information about past III PLUS activity concerning DBF, NDX, SCR, and related files. This information is contained in a VUE file. The VUE file is similar to a CAT file in that it contains the names of a group of related files. The CAT file, however, contains the names of active DBF, NDX, and similar files. The VUE file contains the names of files that create screen images, formats, report forms, and so on. The command form is

VIEW = filename

where filename is the name of any valid dBASE III PLUS VUE file. The alternate form of the command is SET VIEW TO filename.

WP   The WP command, like the TEDIT command, tells III PLUS what word processor to use for file modification. The WP command only affects the word processor you are using in the MEMO fields. The command form is

WP = filename

where filename can be any word-processing program. The word processor will not be loaded for use on the MEMO field unless there is enough memory to do so. The dBASE III PLUS Text Editor will be used in MEMO fields if this command is omitted. You can't access this command outside the CONFIG.DB file.

CompuServe®	CompuServe, Inc.
dBASE II®	Ashton-Tate
dBASE III®	Ashton-Tate
dBASE III PLUS™	Ashton-Tate
Framework®	Ashton-Tate
IBM®	International Business Machines Corporation
Keyworks™	Alpha Software Corporation
Lotus®	Lotus Development Corporation
Multiplan™	Microsoft Corp.
Netware®	Novell, Inc.
Novell®	Novell, Inc.
1-2-3®	Lotus Development Corporation
PFS®	Software Publishing Corp.
ProKey™	Rosesoft, Inc.
Rolodex™	Zephyr American Corporation
SideKick®	Borland International, Inc.
The Source™	Telecomputing Corporation
SuperKey®	Borland International, Inc.
Turbo Lightning™	Borland International, Inc.
UNIX™	AT&T Bell Laboratories
VisiCalc®	VisiCorp
WordPerfect™	Satellite Software International
WordStar®	MicroPro International Corp.

TRADEMARKS

731

G

GET, 234, 245-251, 369
Get environment function, 681
GETENV( ), 681
GETS (CONFIG.DB), 234, 723
GETTER files, 416
GO/GOTO, 40, 334-338
Group totals, 28

H

Hardware and software
  requirements, 1-4
HEADER qualifier, 312
HEADINGS (CONFIG.DB),
  724
HELP (CONFIG.DB), 724
Help messages, designing, 485
HELP system, 596
HELPMSS.PRG, 515
HISTORY (CONFIG.DB), 724
HISTORY memory buffer, 435,
  444, 480, 559, 570

I

IF, 537, 542
IIF( ), 216, 631
Immediate IF, 631
IMPORT, 125
INDEX, 126-131, 194
    compared with SORT, 149
    Filename, 623
    files, setting precedence
      for, 486
Indexes, setting, 481
INKEY( ), 683
INPUT, 278, 369-375
INSERT, 224, 424
    BEFORE, 424
Installing dBASE III
  PLUS, 1
INT( ), 633
Integer function, 633

INTENSITY (CONFIG.DB),
  725
Internal flag, 239
ISALPHA( ), 652
ISCOLOR( ), 683
ISLOWER( ), 653
ISUPPER( ), 653

J

JOIN, 131-140

K

Key expression, index, 128
Keyboard buffer, 418
Keys, 40

L

L template, 249
LABEL files, 31, 102
LABEL FORM, 177, 306
LABEL FORM ?, 592
Labels
    designing, 32
    outputting to a file, 307
    printing, 34, 306
Last Update Function, 621
LASTDRIVE, 711
LBL files, 31, 103, 177
Leading blank trim function,
  657
LEFT( ), 654
Left-most character function,
  654
LEN( ), 655
LIBRARY.PRG, 188, 509
Linker, dBASE, 699-708
LIST, 20, 308
    FILES, 566
    HISTORY, 566
    MEMORY, 375
    STATUS, 566, 601
    STRUCTURE, 567

MVARSIZ (CONFIG.DB), 726

N

O

P

TEXT...ENDTEXT, 553
TIME( ), 680
TO, 271. *See also* @
TOP qualifier, 335
TOTAL, 156
Total Number of Database
  Records, 624
Trailing blanks, 660, 663
Transfer kernel, 293
TRANSFORM( ), 640
Transform expression function,
  640
TRIM( ), 663
Two-level condition, 53
TXT files, 22, 59, 80
TYPE, 320
TYPE( ), 690
TYPE qualifier, 77
TYPEAHEAD (CONFIG.DB),
TYPEAHEAD buffer, 480, 494

U

UNIQUE (CONFIG.DB), 729
UNIQUE NDX file, 131
UNIQUE qualifier, 454
UNLOCK, 603
UPDATE, 262-268
UPPER( ), 664
Uppercase
  and lowercase, 151
  from lowercase conversion,
    664
  function, 653
USE, 42, 71, 200, 202-205
USE ?, 86, 595
USE EXCLUSIVE, 605
User assistance commands,
  575-596

V

VAL( ), 279, 288, 325, 643

Value to text string function,
  640
VAR, 325
Variables
  calling, 498
  calling from a program,
    365
  controlling memory, 392
  displaying, 305
  erasing, 395
  evaluating, 353
  global and local, 396
  hiding memory, 383
  input of existing, 374
  PRIVATE and PUBLIC,
    383-392
  restoring, 399
  saving, 402
  storing defined, 36
VERSION( ), 693
Video modes, 445
VIEW (CONFIG.DB), 729
VIEW files, 62, 495
VisiCalc, 70
VUE files, 62, 90, 115, 181, 495

W

WAIT, 278, 406-410
WHILE condition, 537
WHILE qualifier, 73
  using, with AVERAGE,
    285
  using, with CHANGE, 231
  using, with COUNT, 292
  using, with DELETE, 238
  using, with DISPLAY, 299
  using, with LOCATE, 341
  using, with SORT, 153
  using, with TOTAL, 158
WKS format, 70, 82

Work areas, 105, 148, 262, 302,
    473
    hidden, 376
    selecting, 198
WP (CONFIG.DB), 729
WRITUTIL.PRG, 400

X

X function, 273
X template, 249

Y

YEAR( ), 673

Z

Z function, 250
ZAP, 20, 242, 268-270
    example program using,
    270

The manuscript for this book was prepared and submitted to Osborne/McGraw-Hill in electronic form. The acquisitions editor for this project was Jean Stein, the associate editor was Elizabeth Fisher, and the project editor was Fran Haselsteiner. The technical reviewer was Patricia Hampson of Applied Computer Consulting, Oakland, California.

Cover art by Bay Graphics Design Associates; cover supplier is Phoenix Color Corp.

Book printed and bound by R.R. Donnelley & Sons Company, Crawfordsville, Indiana.

DISKETTE
ORDER FORM

Use this form to order companion diskettes containing all the macros and command sequences in "dBASE III Plus: The Complete Reference". Make check or money order payable to "Northern Lights" (No cash, please). MasterCard or Visa orders are welcome but must be accompanied by a signature.

NAME: _____ COMPANY: _____

ADDRESS: _____

CITY: _____ STATE: _____ ZIP CODE: _____

COUNTRY: _____ Phone: (____) _____

PLACE BOOK PURCHASED: _____

5¼″ Disks (DOS 2.0 or higher)

Quantity: _____ @ $25 U.S.   Total: $ _____

@ $30 Foreign

3½″ Disks

Quantity: _____ @ $30 U.S.   Total: $ _____

@ $35 Foreign

METHOD OF PAYMENT (check one)

☐ Money Order # _____ ☐ Check # _____

☐ Visa Card # _____ ☐ M/S Card # _____

SIGNATURE: _____ EXP DATE: _____
          (signature required for all charge card users)

Send this form to: NORTHERN LIGHTS, INC.
                     P.O. BOX 3861
                     NASHUA, NH
                     03061

Northern Lights ships all orders by first class mail. Please allow six weeks for delivery. Orders will be shipped Federal Express at the purchaser's expense.

Osborne/McGraw-Hill assumes NO responsibility for this offer. This is solely an offer of the author and not of Osborne/McGraw-Hill.

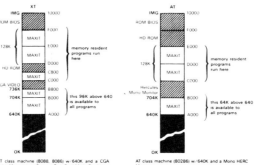